The Politics of the
Middle East

The Politics of the

Middle East

Monte Palmer

Emeritus, Florida State University

THOMSON
™
WADSWORTH

Australia • Canada • Mexico • Singapore • Spain
United Kingdom • United States

Edited by Janet Tilden
Production supervision by Kim Vander Steen
Cover design by Jeanne Calabrese Design
Composition by Point West, Inc.
Printed and bound by P.A. Hutchison

ISBN: 0-87581-442-5

Library of Congress Catalog Card No. 2001135279

Wadsworth/Thomson Learning
10 Davis Drive
Belmont CA 94002-3098
USA

For information about our products, contact us:
Thomson Learning Academic Resource Center
1-800-423-0563
http://www.wadsworth.com

For permission to use material from this text, contact us by
Web: http://www.thomsonrights.com
Fax: 1-800-730-2215
Phone: 1-800-730-2214

Printed in the United States of America
10 9 8 7 6 5 4 3

Contents

Preface

Most books on the politics of the Middle East take one of two basic approaches. The first traces the evolution of the region over time and aims to provide the reader with an evolving picture of the region and its complexities. The second includes case studies of a broad range of countries in order to provide the reader with snapshots of the region's diverse societies and political systems. The disadvantage of the first approach is that readers learn little about any one country and find it difficult to analyze events occurring in a single country. The disadvantage of the second approach is that snapshots of a multitude of countries tend to be formalistic and neglect the broader dynamic of regional politics.

The objective of the present text is to walk a fine line between the two approaches described above. Case studies provide a detailed analysis of the political process in the six countries that dominate the politics of the region: Egypt, Israel, Syria, Saudi Arabia, Iraq, and Iran. Particular emphasis is placed on the evolution of each country and the complex array of forces that guide its politics. Foremost among these forces are the elites that formulate policy, the institutions charged with executing policy, the group dynamic of each country (civil society), and mass political behavior. Also stressed are the environmental contexts that shape the politics of each country, including political culture, political economy, and interaction with the regional and international communities. The book endeavors to provide the reader with tools for analyzing both the dominant countries in the Middle East and the dynamics of the region as a whole.

The list of individuals who deserve my sincerest thanks for making this book possible must invariably include both my current colleagues at the American University of Beirut and the countless individuals who have guided my career over the past 35 years. Most are residents of the region, and many would probably prefer not to be mentioned by name. As I cannot thank all who deserve my appreciation by name, I will thank them collectively and beg their understanding. This also spares them guilt by association for my errors of fact and judgment. I do, however, wish to acknowledge that the book was reviewed in part or in whole by my colleagues Nazar Hamzeh and Hilal Khashan. They did their best to keep me on track but share none of the responsibility for the final product. I also wish to express my appreciation to Ted Peacock and Dick Welna of F. E. Peacock Publishers, Inc., for encouraging me to embark upon this project. While both claim to be my editor-in-chief, that role is reserved for my wife, Princess A. Palmer.

1

Introduction

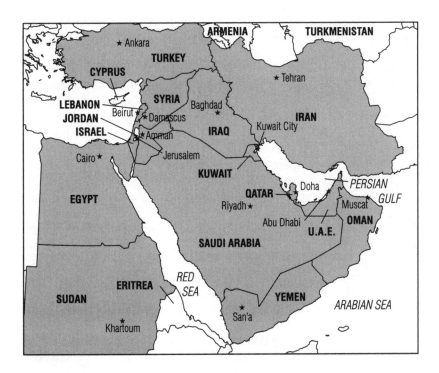

Few regions of the world approach the richness of the Middle East's past, the turmoil of its present, or the uncertainty of its future. While the world stands in awe of the religious and historical shrines of the Middle East, the political tumult of the region has made it the focal point of world attention for more than half a century. Nor is there any indication that this attention will diminish in the years to come.

In the pages that follow, we will trace the evolution of Middle Eastern politics over the course of the modern era and suggest the likely direction of the region's politics during the early years of the twenty-first

1

century. Particular emphasis will be placed on the politics of Egypt, Israel, Syria, Saudi Arabia, Iraq, and Iran, the six countries most likely to shape the character of the Middle East during the next decade. These six countries also hold the key to resolving the region's most enduring conflicts, including the Arab-Israeli conflict and the continuing crisis in the Persian Gulf.

WHAT IS THE MIDDLE EAST?

Before beginning this endeavor, a few comments are in order regarding the geography, culture, demography and economy of the Middle East, as well as the nature of politics, our central theme. The Middle East is generally defined as the vast geographic area that embraces North Africa and much of Western Asia. As indicated on the adjacent map, it is bordered on the south by the countries of sub-Saharan Africa, on the north by Greece and Eastern Europe, and on the northeast by Afghanistan, Russia, and the newly independent states of Central Asia (Cressey 1960). The latter could reasonably be considered part of the Middle East, for most are Islamic in character and many have strong cultural and ethnic links to Turkey and Iran (Winrow 1995; Herzig 1995). Much of the same could be said of Afghanistan, although this is a matter of interpretation. Eritrea, Djibouti, and Somalia, three partially Arabized countries in the Horn of Africa, are considered by the Arab League to be part of the Middle East, but this, too, is a matter of interpretation.

Three geographic features, in particular, have had much to say about the character of the Middle East and its people. Of these, the first is the region's location as a crossroads between the continents of Europe, Asia, and Africa. Rare, indeed, was an empire on one of the three continents that did not add its stamp to the region. Most recently, the Middle East was the primary battleground in the Cold War between the United States and the former Soviet Union, the legacy of which continues to influence Middle Eastern politics today.

The second geographic factor of note is the Middle East's abundance of oil, the magnitude of which is outlined in Table 1.1. Oil has brought the region incredible wealth, but it has also made it the focal point of conflict and international intrigue (Gillespie and Henry 1995), a topic that will be elaborated upon throughout the book.

The final geographic factor that has shaped the Middle East's unique character is the scarcity of its water. The Middle East contains 5 percent of the world's population, yet possesses less than 1 percent of its fresh water. Inevitably, access to fresh water has been a primary source of conflict in the region, a process that can only accelerate as

Table 1.1
Arab Oil Producers—Proved Reserves (in billions of barrels)

Country	End of 1998	Share of World Reserves (%)
Algeria	9.2	0.9
Egypt	3.5	0.3
Iran	89.7	8.5
Iraq	112.5	10.7
Kuwait	96.5	9.2
Libya	29.5	2.8
Oman	5.3	0.5
Qatar	3.7	0.4
Saudi Arabia	261.5	24.8
Syria	2.5	0.2
Tunisia	0.3	<0.05
United Arab Emirates	97.8	9.3
Yemen	4.0	0.4
Other Middle East	0.2	<0.05
Total Middle East	716.2	68.1

Source: www.bp.com/worldenergy/oil/index.htm.

Figure 1.1
Water Resources in the Middle East and North Africa

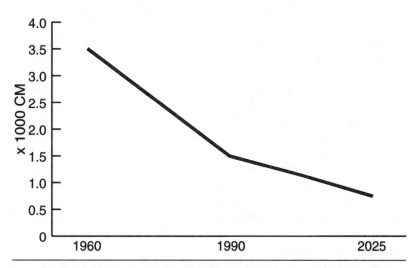

Projected Renewable Water Resources Per Capita in the Middle East & North Africa

Source: From Scarcity to Sercurity: Averting a Water Crisis in the Middle East and North Africa, World Bank Report (1996); www.israeleconomy.org/strategic/water.htm.

Table 1.2
Water-Scarce Countries of the Middle East and North Africa

1955	1990	2025
Bahrain	Bahrain	Bahrain
Jordan	Jordan	Jordan
Kuwait	Kuwait	Kuwait
	Algeria	Algeria
	Israel	Israel
	Occupied Territories	Occupied Territories
	Qatar	Qatar
	Saudi Arabia	Saudi Arabia
	Somalia	Somalia
	Tunisia	Tunisia
	United Arab Emirates	United Arab Emirates
	Yemen	Yemen
		Egypt
		Ethiopia
		Iran
		Libya
		Morocco
		Oman
		Syria

Source: Adel Darwish, "Water Wars," Lecture given at the Geneva Conference on Environment and Quality of Life, June 1994; www.israeleconomy.org/strategic/water.htm.

water reserves continue to deteriorate (World Bank 1996) (see Figure 1.1 and Table 1.2.) Although only three Middle Eastern countries were classified as "water-scarce" in 1955, that category encompassed 14 countries in 1990 (Darwish 1994). It is expected to include virtually all of the Middle East by 2025 (Darwish 1994). The region must rationalize its use of fresh water if this very real potential for conflict is to be avoided (Allan 1997, 1999). It must also find more reasonable mechanisms for sharing the water resources that do exist (Allan 2001).

In addition to being a geographic region, the Middle East also constitutes a cultural region, the citizens of which share a broad array of social and cultural patterns that differ markedly from those of the inhabitants of sub-Saharan Africa, Eastern Europe, and South Asia. Many of these cultural values reflect the pervasiveness of the Islamic religion and the region's tribal past, topics to be discussed shortly. They also reflect the influence of common historical trends and, for the Arabs, a common language. Cultural and social similarities have made the political boundaries of the Middle East extremely porous, and rare is an event in one area of the Middle East that does not have ramifications throughout the region as a whole.

Although most people in the Middle East share a common culture, the region is also marked by profound ethnic, religious, and linguistic

Table 1.3
Demographic Characteristics of the Middle East[1]

Country	Population[2] July 2000 est. (Non-nationals in Parentheses)	Population 14 and Under[2] (%)	Total Literacy[2]* (%)	Female Literacy[2] (1995 est.) (%)	Urban Population[3] (%)	Number of Children per Woman[2] (2000 est.)
Algeria	31,193,917	35	62	49	59.6	2.8
Bahrain	634,137 (228,424)	30	85	74	92	2.8
Egypt	68,359,979	35	51	39	45	3.2
Iran	65,619,636	34	72	66	61	2.2
Iraq	22,675,617	42	58	45	NA	4.9
Israel	5,842,454 [4]	28	95	93	NA	2.6
Jordan	4,998,564	38	87	79	73	3.4
Kuwait	1,973,572 (1,159,914)	30	79	75	96	3.3
Lebanon	3,578,036	28	86	82	89	2.1
Libya	5,115,450 (162,669)	36	76	63	NA	3.7
Mauritania	2,667,859	46	38	26	56	6.3
Morocco	30,122,350	35	44	31	55	3.1
Oman	2,533,389 (527,078)	41	80	NA	82	6.1
West Bank/Gaza	2,842,000	NA	16	NA	70	NA
Qatar	744,483	26	79	80	92	3.3
Saudi Arabia	22,023,506 (5,360,526)	43	63	50	85	6.3
Sudan	35,079,814	45	46	35	35	5.5
Syria	16,305,659	41	71	56	54	4.1
Tunisia	9,593,402	30	67	55	65	2.0
Turkey	65,666,677	29	82	72	74	2.2
U.A.E.	2,369,153 (1,576,472)	30	79	80	86	3.3
Yemen	17,479,206	47	38	26	25	7.1
The Middle East	291,000,000	NA	65	54	58	3.5

[1]Statistics related to the Middle East vary dramatically from source to source.

[2]Information from CIA *Factbook*, Internet (http://www.odci.gov/cia/publications/factbook/indexgeo.html).

[3]Information from The World Bank, Internet (http://wbln0018.worldbank.org/mna/mena.nsf).

[4]Includes Israelis in West Bank, Golan Heights, Gaza, E. Jerusalem.

*Literacy CIA *Factbook* Definition: age 15 and over can read and write.

diversity (Barakat 1993). From an ethnic perspective, the Middle East might usefully be viewed as a large circle with the Arabs at its core and the non-Arabs at the periphery (Flory and Agate 1989). Prominent among the latter would be the Turks, Iranians, Israelis, Kurds, and Berbers.

Both the Arabs and the non-Arabs, in turn, are divided by religious and sectarian conflicts. The Muslims are divided between Sunni and Shi'a sects, the Jews range from reformist to ultra-conservative, and the Christians are divided into a seemingly infinite variety of congregations, many of which trace their origins to the days of the Messiah. Interspersed between the region's three major religions are an endless array of smaller religious minorities including the Alawites, Druze, Yazidies, and Zoroastrians, to name but a few.

The basic economic and demographic features of the Middle East are summarized in Tables 1.2 and 1.3 and portray a region of profound extremes. Kuwait and the United Arab Emirates rank among the wealthiest countries in the world; Egypt and the Sudan among the poorest. The countries of the Middle East also vary dramatically in the size of their populations, with Bahrain having less than a million citizens, while Egypt and Iran have more than 70 times that figure. As we shall see throughout the book, both factors—wealth and demography—have played a major role in shaping the destiny of the region (Kerr and Yassin 1982).

SOME COMMENTS ON POLITICS

Turning to issues of politics, we accept Harold Laswell's dictum that politics is "who gets what, when and how" (Laswell 1958). A particular virtue of Laswell's definition is that it is the same the world over. As such, it places Middle Eastern studies in a global framework. Politics is politics, wherever it occurs.

A second virtue of Laswell's definition is that it places Middle Eastern politics within the broader constellation of social science disciplines. Indeed, Laswell's definition of politics could serve equally well as a definition of economics, sociology, or culture. This broad applicability is important, for as we shall see shortly, the lines between politics, society, economics, and culture are often difficult to disentangle in the Middle East. Laswell's definition is also broad enough to incorporate international influences on the politics of the Middle East. This aspect is a matter of utmost importance, for few areas of the globe have been subject to greater international pressures than the Middle East.

A third virtue of Laswell's definition is that it encompasses both conflict and cooperation. The struggle for control of scarce resources is conflictive by nature, but victory in that struggle depends upon the marshaling of collective forces, be they families, tribes, religious groups, ethnic associations, political parties, or nation-states. One cannot understand the politics of the Middle East without understanding how the citizens of the region coalesce in the struggle to determine who gets what, when and how.

And finally, Laswell's definition of politics is dynamic. This is an important consideration, for the Middle East is an ever-changing region in which new complexities are constantly being added to the old. One must appreciate the influence of the past without being lulled into believing that the history must necessarily repeat itself. Rather, a constant and pervasive tension exists between the ways of the past and the demands of the present.

SOME ORGANIZATIONAL COMMENTS

In the present chapter we will examine three cultural-historical factors that have helped to provide Middle Eastern politics with its unique character: tribalism, Islam, and colonialism. Each of these three factors has imprinted the inhabitants of this region with a view of society and politics that is uniquely Middle Eastern in nature. Tribalism organized society on the basis of kinship ties and in the process fragmented the Middle East into a multitude of tribal communities, each representing a world unto itself and each in conflict with its neighbors. Islam brought to this tribal world a message of unity and faith and attempted to reorganize the region into a grand religious state (Umma) organized according to the precepts of the Koran (Khadduri 1955). Islam became the faith of the vast majority of the region's citizens, yet tribalism and kinship remained its primary form of social organization. Western colonization of the Middle East began in the nineteenth century, challenging the ways of the East with Western visions of secularism and of societies organized as nation-states rather than tribes or religious communities (Emerson 1960). The West viewed itself as "modern" and condemned the region's kinship and religious values as archaic. If the Middle East were to attain the power and prosperity of the West, according to the "modernists," the Middle East would have to reinvent itself along Western lines (Palmer 1997).

This emphasis on modernization was epitomized by Mustafa Kemal (Ataturk), the Turkish general who forged the Turkish Republic following

Table 1.4
Dates of Independence for Countries of the Middle East

Country	Date of Independence
Algeria	1962
Bahrain	1971
Egypt	1922
Iran	1979*
Iraq	1932
Israel	1948
Jordan	1946
Kuwait	1961
Lebanon	1943
Libya	1951
Mauritania	1960
Morocco	1956
Oman	1650
Qatar	1971
Saudi Arabia	1932†
Sudan	1956
Syria	1946
Tunisia	1956
Turkey	1923*
United Arab Emirates	1971
Yemen (South)‡	1967

*Year that the current political system came into force, not date of independence (Iran and Turkey were not colonized).

†Saudi Arabia was not colonized by the West.

‡N. Yemen not colonized by the West; S. Yemen colonized by UK and received independence in 1967.

the collapse of the Ottoman Empire in World War I. Turkey, Ataturk reasoned, had been humiliated by the West because it remained locked in the ways of the past. Its salvation, accordingly, would be to discard the past and embrace the ways of the industrialized West. The quasi-religious monarchy that had guided the Ottoman Empire was replaced in 1924 by a republic. Islamic law gave way to a Swiss legal code. Family names, a rarity during the Ottoman Empire, became mandatory. The fez and other forms of traditional dress were forbidden, the Latin script replaced Arabic script as the medium for writing the Turkish language, and industrialization was pursued with a vengeance (Brockelmann 1960).

The countries of the Middle East and their dates of independence are listed in Table 1.4. Turkey and Iran were not colonized but were introduced to Western values via a multitude of commercial and military contacts. Both attempted to resist the West by becoming Western. Saudi Arabia and Yemen (North) also escaped Western colonization but had little contact with the West in the years prior to World War II. They remain among the most traditional areas in the Middle East today.

The modern values instilled by Western imperialism left an indelible mark on the Middle East, yet the region did not become modern in the Western sense of the word. Rather, vestiges of modernity have co-existed in an uneasy tension with the values of Islam and tribalism, each attempting to assert its dominance.

This mix of kinship, religion, and Westernization, then, has produced a culture that differs substantially from that of the surrounding areas. It has also produced a cultural region of infinite complexity. Although most residents of the Middle East share at least some of the region's cultural characteristics, the influence of those characteristics varies dramatically from country to country and even from individual to individual. All Middle Easterners do not behave alike any more than all Americans or all Europeans behave alike, but as we shall see throughout the ensuing analysis, the existence of a shared culture does influence the politics of the region.

THE IMPORTANCE OF KINSHIP

The study of Middle Eastern politics logically begins with a discussion of kinship, for the most enduring social relationships in the Middle East have traditionally been those of blood (Barakat 1993). Small nuclear families were virtually indivisible from larger extended families consisting of grandparents and several layers of aunts, uncles, cousins, and grandchildren. Networks of extended families merged into clans (encompassing second, third, and sometimes fourth cousins) and eventually into tribes, the members of which were presumed to have a common ancestor, although this was not necessarily the case. Tribes reached their zenith in nomadic societies, while extended families and clans tended to remain the dominant form of social organization in settled areas (Barakat 1993; Wittfogel 1957; Gellner 1987; Hart 1998).

Tribes in fertile areas tended to become sedentary cultivators, while those of the Middle East's vast deserts adopted a nomadic lifestyle, moving from place to place in search of water and pasture. Even the most fertile areas of the Middle East, however, were limited in the number of people they could support, and the weaker of the sedentary tribes were forced into a nomadic existence (Cressey 1960). Most of the tribes in the Arab East, including the tribes of Israel, had their origins in the Arabian Peninsula. It is this common origin that explains the similarities in the Arabic and Hebrew languages, both of which are of Semitic origin. Iranians, by contrast, are believed to be descendants of the Aryan tribes that invaded the area in approximately 900 BC, with the name Iran being a reflection of their Aryan ancestry. They would later adopt the Arabic script, but the Iranian (Farsi) language shares little in common with its Semitic counterparts. Much the same is true of the Turks and Kurds, both of whom represent distinct ethnic configurations (Coon 1961).

The extended family, along with the clan and the tribe, nurtured individuals into adulthood, teaching them what to believe and how to behave. Paramount in this regard was the demand for total and unquestioned loyalty to the family. Individual survival was indivisible from the survival of the family, and individuals lacking the support of a strong family possessed neither status nor power. Loyalty to the family was followed by loyalty to the clan and in turn by loyalty to the tribe. There was little basis for loyalty beyond the tribe, for nation-states did not exist. Invariably, extended families competed for control of the clan, and clans competed for control of the tribe (Gluckman 1965; Gellner 1987). Tribes, for the most part, existed in a state of uneasy conflict as they competed for pride, power, and pasture.

The emphasis on kinship solidarity is easy to understand, for kinship provided the best hope for security in a very uncertain world (El-Aref 1944). Some idea of the pervasive insecurity of life in traditional kinship societies is provided by Ayrout's description of governmental efforts to modernize an Egyptian village during the 1930s.

> The customs, life and manners of the peasant should be looked at attentively, patiently and sympathetically. Then we can account for the failure of many attempts to improve village housing.
>
> At (village) B, the windows are spacious and large, and thus exposed to cold, heat and burglars. The inhabitants therefore stop them up with bricks.
>
> At (village) D, the stairs are outside the house. Security has been overlooked. The result is that the fellahin (peasants) destroy the stairs and build up steps of mud from inside the house.
>
> At (village) E, the builders have decided, for the sake of health, to permit no mixing of people and animals; there is an outer cattle pen. But this does not offer enough security against robbery and disease. Therefore the peasants rebel and drive them into the bedroom (Ayrout 1962, 129).

The need for kinship solidarity encouraged marriages within the clan, i.e., among first and second cousins. In some instances, marriage alliances were arranged shortly after birth. In others, a male son was given the option of marrying his cousin before other alliances were considered. Endogamous marriages strengthened family cohesiveness and reduced tensions arising from conflict over mate selection and the payment of dowries. Endogamous marriages continue to be common in many areas of the Middle East:

According to universally accepted definitions, blood relatives include first, second and third cousins. The countries which are setting these new records, as reported recently in *Al Hayat* newspaper, are led by Iraq, where 58 percent of the citizens marry their cousins. Saudi Arabia follows closely with 55 percent of its people choosing to wed relatives. Next are the Kuwaitis and Jordanians with 54 percent and 50 percent respectively. As far as marriages strictly between first cousins, Jordan is the world leader, reaching 32 percent, followed by the Saudis at 31 percent, and then the Iraqis and the Kuwaitis, each at 30 percent (Zein 1996, 9).

When marriage occurred outside of the family, it was between members of parallel social strata.

Most other tribal customs were also designed to promote kinship solidarity, not the least of which was a profound respect for age. Seniority, more than any other factor, determined one's position within the family. Such respect for age finds expression in the following Arabic proverb: one day older, one year wiser. By and large, it was the eldest male who ruled the family, and the eldest female who supervised the affairs of the women. Allocating authority on the basis of age and gender had the virtue of minimizing conflict within the family. Unfortunately, it also added rigidity to the structure of Middle Eastern society by rewarding age and gender at the expense of merit.

Family solidarity was further strengthened by cultural and religious beliefs that glorified the virtues of resignation, acceptance, and fatalism. Such beliefs were vital to the survival of the family and the tribe, for the more individuals accepted their fate as the natural order of things, the less likely they were to rebel against the rigidities of patriarchal authority. The socialization process, moreover, was simple and direct. Daughters emulated their mothers; sons their fathers. Prevailing norms were sanctified by the religions of the day and reinforced by social pressures. One got along by going along. The acceptance of traditional customs was also facilitated by the physical and intellectual isolation of the traditional environment. Most individuals lived in isolated tribes and scattered villages. Even the residents of the pre-industrial cities of the pre-Islamic era found communications hampered by status divisions and a pervasive sense of interpersonal distrust born of kinship antagonisms. What was to be gained by sharing information with potential enemies? Because the early residents of the Middle East seldom came in contact with new information, they had little cause to question the credibility of their social beliefs. It was the way of their world.

Interviews conducted by Daniel Lerner in rural Turkey during the 1950s illustrate both the profound respect for age and the fatalistic outlook of early Middle Eastern societies.

(In your community who is the one whose thoughts are most highly respected?) My uncle the Sheikh. He is tall, old and respectable. He sits on his pillow all day long in his own tent and people of the tribe come around for advice. (Why is he a leader?) He is the eldest in the family and the people in the tribe go for the advice of the eldest. (Why?)… Our respect is according to age, for experience counts a lot with us.

We like to rest our heads from such responsibilities (as government). We eat our daily bread, thank our God and are satisfied and happy. Our Sheikh alone may worry about that because that is his business (Lerner 1958, 323).

What remained of individual freedom was constricted by the all-compelling need to protect the family's honor. Families of the Middle East operated on the principle of collective responsibility, and errant behavior by one member of the family brought shame—and danger—to the family as a whole. As in the American legend of the feuding Hatfields and McCoys, incidents of theft, murder, and sexual license were avenged against the family rather than the individual. The burden of maintaining family honor fell disproportionately on females, for the slightest sexual indiscretion by a female cast shame on the family as a whole and often resulted in her death at the hands of a father or brother. In societies in which everyone was watching everyone, it was far better to seclude women than to have the family's honor fall prey to the prying eyes of neighbors. In Egypt, the Sudan, and much of Africa, the female genitalia were mutilated before puberty to reduce the potential for infidelity, a practice that continues among the poorer classes today.

Finally, the kinship cultures of the Middle East placed immense value on large families. The honored woman was the woman who produced an endless number of children; the good man was the man who could sire such a brood. Families of 15 or more children were commonplace, with the numbers being even higher in polygamous relationships. Again, the need for large families was inherent in the logic of the kinship system. The power of a family was often a function of its size, and male children were a vital economic asset. The need for children was made all the more urgent by the prevalence of tribal warfare and by unsanitary living conditions that found a majority of children dying before the age of ten.

Beyond shaping the values and behavior of their members, the family and tribe determined their occupations, selected their spouses, defined their recreational groups (mainly relatives), protected them from their enemies, cared for their welfare in time of illness and old age, and policed their behavior to minimize inter-family conflict. In so doing, the kinship unit provided the individual with his or her identity. One's station in life was essentially that of the family or tribe. Some early authors went so far as to suggest that tribal individuals lacked an ego independent of the family. Such assertions are difficult to document, but they illustrate the profound importance of the family and tribe within an individual's life.

The same principles can be applied in the social and economic spheres, with all members of the same age and gender category performing nearly identical or readily interchangeable tasks (Nash 1966). If one family herded sheep, most families herded sheep. With little in the way of specialization, production was low and most tribes eked out a meager existence with little margin of error. Droughts and other external disasters were devastating and further accentuated the uncertain nature of traditional life, described by Thomas Hobbes as being "solitary, poor, nasty, brutish and short" (Hobbes 1651). Power and authority within the Middle Eastern family were patriarchal in nature, with the dominant male, usually the eldest, exercising near-absolute authority over the members of the family. Decisions flowed from top to bottom and were seldom subject to dispute. The same pattern was followed within the clan and tribe, with the eldest male of the dominant family or clan serving as its sheikh. Other clan leaders formed a tribal council, with their influence corresponding to the power of their family or clan. In theory, tribal leadership was based upon merit and constituted a form of tribal democracy. In reality, power was often hereditary.

Once in power, tribal leaders consolidated their authority by assuring that much of the tribe's wealth found its way to supporters and allies. Favors were granted as an act of generosity by the tribal leader, thereby creating a bond of obligation between the chief and the supplicant. Even today, the King of Saudi Arabia holds a weekly session in which any citizen of the kingdom can petition the king for a special favor, be it an operation, scholarship, or forgiveness for a transgression.

Beyond force and the distribution of economic rewards, the power of the chief was rooted in a tribal culture that stressed loyalty, passivity, respect for age, and conformity. The chief was the patriarch or father of his family, and his power, while often compassionate, was absolute.

As tribes grew larger and dominated their neighbors, patriarchal authority was transformed into patrimonial authority, the major difference being that the chief could no longer claim kinship to all members of his realm (Bill and Springborg 1997). Unable to count on the kinship loyalties of conquered tribes, patrimonial leaders often aligned themselves with a charismatic religious leader in the hope of substituting religious ties for those of kinship (De Corancez 1995; Vassiliev 1998). It was also common for victorious leaders to take wives from conquered tribes, thereby creating a new basis for kinship alliances. By and large, however, patrimonial rule was imposed by force and maintained by force. When the power of the dominant tribe waned, usually with the passing of the dominant chief, the kingdom would splinter and the process of conquest and decay would repeat itself.

THE CONSEQUENCES OF TRIBALISM

The Middle East has undergone profound changes in the course of the past century, but the tribalism has left an indelible stamp on the political process of the region (Khoury and Kostiner 1990). Although rarely nomadic and bearing little resemblance to the swashbuckling bedouins of the romantic era, tribes remain the dominant form of social organization in the more traditional areas of the Middle East, including most of the Arabian Peninsula. Saudi Arabia and the sheikhdoms of the Persian Gulf, however modern they may appear, remain tribal monarchies, a topic to be explored at some length in Chapter 5. Northern Iraq and the surrounding territories remain in the throes of a civil war between Kurdish tribes, albeit a civil war colored with the slogans of socialism and nationalism. During the 1980s, a civil war between competing factions of South Yemen's Marxist government was transformed into a tribal war as each side turned to its tribal allies for support. Despite its Marxist appearance, South Yemen's government was tribal in content. It is important, accordingly, not to be swayed by labels or official ideologies, the superficial nature of which may be profoundly misleading.

Families and clans, moreover, persist as the dominant form of social organization in regions long removed from their tribal past. Saddam Hussein's closest associates are drawn largely from his family, as were those of Hafez al-Asad, the former president of Syria. Politics in Lebanon, perhaps the most modern of the Arab states, continues to be dominated by big families, a circumstance that is pervasive throughout the region.

Other influences of tribalism are more subtle, but no less important. Many observers find the patriarchal values of the Middle East to be inherently authoritarian, inegalitarian, and anti-democratic (Khashan 2000b). Condemnations of the region's disregard for human rights have been vehement, directed particularly at the subjugation of women.

Family loyalties continue to compete with loyalty to the state and it is probably safe to assume that most residents of the Middle East place the interests of the extended family far above the interests of the state.

This in turn, has made politics in the Middle East inherently dependent upon family connections or "wasta." Little gets done in most countries of the region without a kinship contact of one form or another.

The emphasis on large families has also resulted in the Middle East having one of the highest rates of population growth in the world. The population of Egypt, for example, has increased from approximately 20 million in 1960 to more than 70 million in 2000 with the percentages for Iran being parallel to those of Egypt. While both countries have made progress in the areas of economic and social development, their populations have increased more rapidly than the capacity of the state to meet the basic needs of its subjects. Unemployment is high, education lagging, housing scarce, and services dismal, problems that can only get worse as approximately half of the population of the Middle East is under 20 years of age (World Almanac 2000, www).

The influence of kinship is waning, but family ties continue to provide a critical support network for individuals in a region marked by inefficient governments (Barakat 1993). As discussed by Sharabi, this fact will not change until the states of the region are able to provide for the needs of their citizens in a more effective manner.

> In neopatriarchal society, a person is lost when cut off from the family, the clan, or the religious group. The state cannot replace these protective primary structures. Indeed, the state is an alien force that oppresses one, as is equally civil society, a jungle where only the rich and powerful are respected and recognized. In one's actual practice one conducts oneself morally only within the primary structures (family-clan-sect); for the most part, one lives amorally 'in the jungle,' in the society at large (Sharabi 1988, 35).

While it is easy to condemn the negative influence of kinship loyalties on the politics of the Middle East, Westerners are likely to view with envy the sense of belonging, caring, and family solidarity that permeates Middle Eastern culture. It is also profoundly ethnocentric of the West to assume that it alone has found a key to social paradise. The depersonalization and psychological pressures of Western society suggest otherwise.

RELIGION AND POLITICS IN THE MIDDLE EAST

Religion and politics are so intertwined in the affairs of the Middle East that it is often difficult to disentangle one from the other. Israel proclaims itself to be a Jewish state, yet lacks a formal constitution because of the inherent difficulty involved in defining precisely what constitutes a Jew. Iran is a theocracy, the senior leaders of which are

Islamic clerics. Saudi Arabia, Pakistan, Iran, and the Sudan proclaim the Koran to be their constitution, and an even larger number of countries have made Islam the official religion of the state and the Koran the ultimate source of law.

Many of the dominant political groups within the region are also overtly religious in character. Turkey was ruled by the leader of an Islamic political party for a brief period during the 1990s, and Israel's religious parties have a profound influence on policy making in the Jewish state. The Islamic Fundamentalists pose a continuing challenge to the secular governments of the Middle East and in 1990 launched a civil war in Algeria that had claimed some 70,000 lives by the turn of the century. Egypt has been spared a civil war to date, but the potential of an Islamic uprising remains present, a topic discussed at length in Chapter 2.

The mingling of religious and political values is equally pervasive among the citizens of the Middle East. A recent survey in Cairo, for example, found that some 71 percent of the respondents favored religious censorship of the mass media. More than 90 percent supported religious instruction in Cairo's schools (Palmer, Sullivan, and Safty 1996). The percentages in a parallel survey of Lebanese Muslims was similar (Khashan and Palmer 1998).

The Middle East's position as home of three major religions has also subjected the region to far greater intervention by the major powers than would otherwise have been the case. Britain declared Palestine to be a national home for the Jews in 1917, just as the emergence of Israel as an independent state in 1948 owed much to the support of the United States and the Soviet Union. As we shall see in Chapter 3, the support of the world Jewry continues to provide Israel with far greater influence on the international stage than its small population and minuscule size would justify.

Of the three major religions to emerge from the Middle East, Christianity and Judaism are well known in the West and require little elaboration. This is far less the case with Islam, the chosen faith of some 90 percent of the Middle East's population. According to UN figures, Islam claims nearly 1.9 billion adherents worldwide, the distribution of which is estimated in Table 1.5. One simply cannot understand the politics of the Middle East without at least a rudimentary knowledge of Islam.

Islamic History

Islam shares much in common with both Judaism and Christianity, and a clear line of progression exists between the three religions (Busse

Table 1.5
Islam Today

Region	Muslims as Percentage of Population
The Arab World	90–100
Non-Arab Areas of the Middle East, including Central Asia (excluding Israel and Armenia)	90–100
South Asia (India: 5–20%)	90–100
Remainder of Asia (Indonesia: 90–100%)	0–50
Sub-Saharan Africa adjacent–the Arab World	50–100
Remainder of Africa	0–50
Europe (Russia: 5–20%)	0–5
North America	0–5
Latin America	0–5
Oceania	0–5

Source: These figures represent composites gleaned from multiple sources, including country figures from the *CIA Factbook*. Figures vary from source to source, and many are dated and unreliable.

1997). The Torah, the holy book of Judaism, glorifies an all-powerful God—the one God—who created the universe and stands in judgment of its inhabitants. Jews, according to the Torah, are the "chosen people." They enjoy a special relationship with their God, but are minimally concerned with garnering new converts to the Jewish faith. The Christian Bible consists of two testaments. The Old Testament is the Jewish Torah, and the New Testament transforms Judaism into a mass religion centering on the figure of Christ, the Son of God. In contrast to the Jews, Christians are evangelical and are enjoined by God to convert all humankind to his glory. Christians, too, view themselves as a chosen people possessed of a special relationship with God.

The God of the Jews and the Christians is also the God of the Muslims. Indeed, "Islam" means submission to the will of God. Members of the Islamic faith are referred to as Muslims, or "those who submit." Islam acknowledges the major prophets of the Jews, including Adam, Noah, Moses, and Abraham, and Christ is recognized as a major prophet, but not as the Son of God. (Islam does, however, accept the virgin birth of Christ.) The Koran, the law of God as revealed to the Prophet Mohammed, refers to Christians and Jews as "people of the book." Christians and Jews, from the Islamic perspective, had been converted to a belief in the one God by earlier prophets, but have refused to accept the teachings of the Prophet Mohammed, God's final prophet. As believers in one God, they are to live in peace among Muslims. Muslims also view themselves as God's chosen people and, like the Christians, believe that it is their religious duty to convert all non-Muslims to the glory of God.

Much like the Torah and the Bible, the Koran provides Muslims with a guide to salvation. The Koran, however, far exceeds either the Torah or the Bible in instructing Muslims on the ordering of their political, economic, and social lives, a topic to be addressed shortly. The Prophet Mohammed (AD 570–632) proclaimed the birth of the Islamic faith in AD 610, following his summons as the final prophet of God. Muslims refer to the period before this date as the Jahaliya or time of ignorance. The Prophet Mohammed was born in Mecca as a member of the Hashemite clan of the tribe of Quaraysh. Mecca, at that time, was the center of a multitude of idolatrous religions, most of which focused on the Kaaba, an ancient temple believed to embody the divine presence (Peters 1994). Awed by the Kaaba and its pantheon of gods, the tribes of the region began making annual pilgrimages to Mecca, declaring the month of pilgrimage to be free of raiding and bloodshed (Armajani 1970). Mecca's holy status, as well as its location on the main caravan routes to Syria, Egypt, Palestine, and Iraq, had transformed the city into a cosmopolitan trading center familiar with the basic tenets of both Judaism and Christianity. Elements of both would be incorporated into Islam.

Like most prophets, Mohammed was condemned as a heretic, and in 622, he and his followers were forced to flee to the neighboring city of Yathrib, now called Medina. The Hijrah, the flight of the Prophet Mohammed and his followers, marks the beginning of the Islamic calendar. Political economists might note that much of the opposition to the Prophet Mohammed was based upon the fear that his monotheistic message would destroy the pilgrimage so important to the prosperity of Mecca (Brockelmann 1960). Yathrib, at the time, was in a state of near civil war, and the Prophet Mohammed was welcomed as both its political and spiritual leader. His political role added a practical dimension to his spiritual views and, unlike either Judaism or Christianity, Islam addressed political issues in great detail.

In 630 the Prophet Mohammed returned victorious to Mecca, the inhabitants of which were duly converted to Islam. The new religion also incorporated the pilgrimage, thereby allaying the major economic concerns of Mecca's merchants. The remainder of the Arabian Peninsula would soon fall under the Prophet Mohammed's sway as his legions, fired by religious zeal and the lure of booty, offered the vanquished a choice between salvation or death. As people of the book, Jews and Christians were allowed to live in peace with their Muslim hosts.

Subsequent expansion by the Prophet Mohammed's successors would see the Islamic empire spread throughout the Middle East and incorporate large areas of Spain, most of Eastern Europe, and the northern regions of the Indian sub-continent including the current countries of Afghanistan, Pakistan, and Bangladesh. Muslims also constitute approximately 11 percent of India's one billion citizens. While much of the early empire was forged by the sword, merchants and missionaries would later extend the sway of Islam to regions as distant as Indonesia and Malaysia, most inhabitants of which are practicing Muslims. China and Thailand also have large Muslim minorities.

The Basic Principles of Islam

Mohammed, it is important to note, is revered as a prophet of God rather than as an extension of God. He was a mortal being chosen by God to receive his message and, as such, possessed no supernatural powers. Islam acknowledges both angels and the devil, the latter being a fallen angel. God also created the jinn, creatures who occupy a position akin to angels. As described by Nasr in Tabatabai:

> Having been endowed with a spirit, the jinn, like men, possess responsibility before God. Some are "religious" and "Muslim." These are intermediate angels, the psychic forces that can lead man from the physical to the spiritual world through the labyrinth of the intermediate world or barzakh. Others are malefic forces that have rebelled against God, in the same way that some men rebel against the Divinity. Such jinn are identified with "the armies of Satan" (*junud al-Shaytan*) and are the evil forces which by inducing the power of apprehension (*wahm*) and imagination (*khayal*) in its negative aspect lead man away from the Truth which his intelligence perceives by virtue of the innate light that dwells within him (Tabatabai, n.d., 236).

Muslims are expected to execute five obligations, often referred to as the pillars of Islam. First, they must witness that "There is no God but God and Mohammed is his Prophet." This, as Armajani writes, "is the most oft-repeated sentence in the world of Islam. It is whispered in the ear of the newborn child, it is repeated throughout his life, and it is the last sentence uttered when he is laid in the grave. It is used to call the faithful to prayer and it has served as the battle cry of Muslim soldiers in all the wars of Islam" (Armajani 1970, 45). Second, Muslims are required to pray five times a day at specified intervals. Prayers begin at dawn and end late in the evening. Most Islamic countries interrupt radio and television programming during the periods specified for prayer. Third, Muslims are expected to give generously of their wealth. This includes both Zakat, a religious tax equal to 2.5 percent of an individual's income, and the broader practice of giving alms to the poor. Fourth, Muslims are expected to fast during the holy month of Ramadan. The fast is not obligatory for travelers or the ill, but must be executed when their circumstances have normalized. Finally, every Muslim is required to make at least one pilgrimage or "Hajj" to Mecca if their circumstances allow. Most Muslim countries assist their poor in making the Hajj. Although not a formal "pillar" of Islam, Muslims are also expected to serve their faith by fighting in "jihads" or holy wars. One of the clearest admonitions in this regard is the Koranic passage stating that "Warfare is ordained for you, though it is hateful to you; but it may happen that ye hate what is good for you" (Koran 2:216). Many Fundamentalist groups, it should be noted, do consider the jihad to be an obligatory pillar of Islam. Muslims are also obliged to obey Koranic injunctions against drinking alcohol, gambling, eating pork, and committing usury, and are generally encouraged to be honest and decent citizens who serve the Islamic community by engaging in good works.

The Law of Islam

The foundation of Islamic law is the Koran, the word of God as revealed to the Prophet Mohammed. As the word of God, the Koran is absolute, unassailable, and cannot be changed. Heated debates, however, continue to exist over the precise meaning of many passages. When early Muslims were faced with circumstances not fully addressed by the Koran, they sought guidance from both the sayings and behavior of the Prophet Mohammed, a body of tradition collectively referred to as the Sunna (Dekmejian 1995). Islamic scholars have recorded the existence of some 600,000 Hadiths (sayings of the Prophet) and, while many scholars distinguish between the behavior of the Prophet (Sunna) and the sayings of the Prophet (Hadiths), most information on the Prophet Mohammed's behavior is, in fact, provided by the Hadiths. The line between the Sunna and the Hadiths, then, is fine, indeed. Only those Hadiths dating from the early years of Islam are considered to be authentic or "orthodox." The others, some originating centuries after the passing of the Prophet, are categorized as being either fair or weak in authenticity. In this regard, each Hadith begins with an acknowledgment of its source, i.e., "So-and-so said to so-and-so that the Prophet handled this matter in a particular way." Only about 2500 Hadiths fall into the orthodox category, although there is no consensus on this figure.

As the realm of Islam expanded and the memory of the Prophet became more distant, Islamic law had recourse to "ijtihad," a consensual interpretation reached by leading Islamic scholars or "ulema" (Schacht 1964). This practice continues today in the Shi'a branch of Islam, but was restricted several centuries ago by the Sunnis. As will be discussed at a later point, this provides Shi'a theologians with greater flexibility than their Sunni counterparts (Tabatabai, n.d.).

Collectively, the Koran, the Sunna, the authentic Hadiths, and to a lesser extent, the ijtihads, constitute the body of Islamic law referred to as the "Sharia." It is this law which guides the lives of Muslims. As the demands of the modern world present an endless array of circumstances unanticipated by the Sharia, Islamic scholars also have recourse to the use of analogy (Schacht 1964; Levy 1962). A leading religious scholar, for example, was recently asked if artificial hearts were allowed by the Sharia. His response was to cite the Prophet's acceptance of artificial limbs for those wounded in battle, a process designed to assist the proper functioning of the body. This was clearly distinguished from cosmetic operations designed to beautify the body, a process, by implication, to be avoided. In this regard, the Sharia divides acts into five categories: obligatory, meritorious, permissible, reprehensible, and forbidden (haram) (Schacht 1964, 107).

Formal Islam Versus Informal Islam

Islamic law, as described above, provided the foundation of "establishment Islam" (a term used to describe the official Islamic leadership) but tended to be formalistic and impersonal. Many Muslims, accordingly, began to form religious groups of a less legalistic and austere nature that would enable them to pursue the mystical search for truth and achieve a personalized union with God (Gilsenan 1978; Al-Shaibi 1991; Hamzeh and Dekmejian 1996). While early theologians resisted the establishment of such groups, referred to as Sufis, they gradually gained acceptance and now constitute an important part of the Islamic community (Johansen 1996). Historically, the most famous of the Sufi were the Whirling Dervishes, a group renowned for incorporating whirling dances into their rituals.

Sufism, however, was only one form of popular or informal Islam. The advent of the colonial era had found the Islamic way of life challenged by the superior military and economic power of Europe as well as by its heady ideal of a society ordered on the principles of secularism and reason (Dekmejian 1985). The ways of the past were disparaged by Europeans, and Western styles of dress and social behavior, most of which were offensive to Islamic sensibilities, became commonplace among the more Westernized segments of the Middle Eastern community. Particularly offensive to devout Muslims were the Western use of alcohol and a lack of prudence in the dress of women.

The Islamic reaction to the challenge of Westernization was twofold. On one side, Muslim intellectuals such as Jamal al-Din Afghani (1838–1897) and Mohammed Abduh (1849–1905) attempted to strengthen Islam by interpreting Islamic doctrine in a manner that would accommodate the technological advances of the West (Dekmejian 1995). On the other, a wave of preachers lashed out at the growing influence of Western values and called for a return to a society based on the fundamental principles of the Koran and Sunna (way of the Prophet), hence the term *Fundamentalism*. In 1928, the popular reaction to Westernization took organizational form as Hasan Al-Bana, an Arabic teacher in Egypt, founded the Muslim Brotherhood under the rallying cry, "God is the answer" (Mitchell 1969). The goal of the Brotherhood, as will be discussed at length in Chapter 2, was to restore Egypt to an Islamic form of government similar to that practiced by the Prophet Mohammed.

Since the founding of the Muslim Brotherhood in 1928, so many varieties of Islamic Fundamentalism have emerged that they have become difficult to classify. Indeed, Dekmejian documents the emergence of some 174 Fundamentalist groups between 1970 and 1990 (Dekmejian 1995, 1998; Eickelman and Piscatori 1996). Some advise their followers to flee from the present era of corruption and ignorance by forming religious colonies in the mountains or deserts; other advocate reforming society from within. Of the latter, some Fundamentalist groups focus on political action; others minister to the faithful by providing social services and guidance. Of those focusing on politics, some seek to destroy secular governments by force, others to capture them by legitimate means (Hamzeh 2000). Some groups focus on a single strategy; others combine a multitude of strategies. Some groups are very narrow (strict constructionist) in their interpretation of an Islamic state; others, and especially the Shi'a, are more flexible. Some want to combine Islamic theology with the benefits of Western technology; others reject all vestiges of Westernization. Regardless of the vast differences within the Fundamentalist movement, the ultimate goal remains the same: returning to a political and social order founded on basic Islamic principles.

Much of the world associates Islamic Fundamentalism with the violent activities of Fundamentalist groups in Algeria, Egypt, Iran, and Palestine. The focus on Fundamentalist violence has diverted attention from a broader Islamic revival that has occurred throughout the Muslim world since the 1970s. The revival is reflected in increased attendance at mosques, electoral victories for Islamic parties, sporadic outbreaks of violence, and a growing support for Islamic issues in public opinion surveys (Bill 1984). The most visible evidence of the Islamic revival has been the resurgence of Islamic dress among the women of the Middle East, although a considerable debate exists over the exact meaning of the veiling phenomenon (Saleh 1990).

Scholars have attempted to explain the Islamic revival in a variety of ways. For some, it is part of a clash of religions that has ebbed and flowed since the crusades and beyond (Davis 1987; Shepard 1987). As Westernization has become more prevalent in the region, so has the Islamic reaction. Others see the Islamic revival as a defensive reaction to a flawed process of modernization. Westernization attempted to replace the traditional political institutions of the Middle East with those of Europe but succeeded only in creating political systems that were tyrannical, corrupt, and exploitative. Rather than solving the problems of the region, Westernization merely added to its despair. As the coherence of Middle Eastern societies weakened, a growing number of individuals turned to popular religious groups to meet their material and psychological needs (Hinnebusch 1985; Mustafa 1995).

Expanding on this theme, several scholars link the Islamic revival to the Arab defeat in the June War of 1967 (Ajami 1992). More than any other event, the collapse of the Arab armies in six days signaled the failure of secular Arab nationalism to either protect its people or meet their basic needs. Whatever its forms or causes, Islamic Fundamentalism is probably the single most dominant political movement in the Middle East today.

The Political Consequences of Islam

The influence of Islam on the history and political evolution of the Middle East has been profound. Most fundamentally, the conversion of much of the Middle East to Islam created a political community that transcended the bonds of kinship. By so doing, it paved the way for a dazzling Islamic civilization that could not have been achieved by the region's inward-looking tribes, each a world unto itself. It also transformed the Middle East into a cultural configuration, most members of which shared a common religious identity, value structure, and history. As a result of this shared identity, political linkages in the Middle East tend to be far stronger and more prevalent than they are in other geographic regions such as Latin America, Africa, or Asia. Little happens in one area of the Middle East that does not have repercussions throughout the region as a whole, the spread of Islamic Fundamentalism being a case in point. The Arabs form an even tighter cultural configuration, blending a common language and ethnic identity with intense pride in being the founders of Islam. Arab history was also Islamic history, and the glories of the Arab world were essentially those of the Prophet Mohammed and his Arab successors or *Caliphs*, the Arabic name for the successors of the Prophet.

The highly political character of Islam also provided the Middle East with a philosophical orientation that found the unity of church and state to be both logical and desirable. If one believed in an all-powerful God, what was to be achieved by separating religion and politics? This is a very important consideration, for it helps to explain why many people in the Middle East do not share the Western aversion to religious rule.

The Islamic experience, moreover, provided the peoples of the Middle East with a profound sense of historical pride. As the next section will illustrate, the Islamic empires of the Middle Ages achieved a level of civilization unknown in Europe at that time. Unfortunately, the glories of the past stand in stark contrast to the impotence of the Islamic world today, and many Muslims find themselves pondering the reasons for their fall from grace.

Perhaps because of this strong sense of historical presence, the most potent political symbols in the Middle East today tend to be Islamic symbols. King Abdullah II of Jordan is a direct descendent of the Prophet, while the official title of the King of Saudi Arabia is "His Majesty, the protector of the two holy shrines (Mecca and Medina)." Iran, of course, is an Islamic theocracy. Even Saddam Hussein, once an avowed secularist, has instituted Islamic law and vowed to transform Iraq into an Islamic state.

Political opposition in most countries of the Middle East has also taken religious form, with Islamic Fundamentalism having become the dominant avenue of resistance to the region's authoritarian regimes. Algeria has been reduced nearly to civil war, while Egypt has become the focus of protracted violence. It is the Fundamentalists, moreover, who now provide the main opposition to peace with Israel.

Islamic Influence on Economic Development

The Islamic states generally rank lower on World Bank indices of economic development than most other areas of the Third World, with the exception of Africa.[1] As economic and technological development require a high level of innovation and creativity, some scholars have suggested that the region's slow pace of development can be attributed to the rigidity of Islamic law and Islam's emphasis on fatalism and passivity. The Koran and the Hadiths, for example, stress God's control over all dimensions of human life, leaving little scope for human volition. Indeed, no phrase is more common in the Muslim

[1]The oil states enjoy a higher standard of living than most states of the world, but that wealth is based almost entirely on royalties from oil deposits that were developed by the West. Should the oil disappear, there would be little to sustain their economies.

world than *in sha Allah*, "if God wills." Other observers, however, note that great civilizations did flourish under Islamic rule. They also point out that the Prophet Mohammed was an innovator par excellence and cite the many passages in the Koran that inspire innovation and creativity. The slow pace of development in the Middle East, in their view, is attributable to the divisive legacy of tribal culture, an adverse colonial history, and the emergence of an international system that has found it expedient to fragment the Muslim world into a myriad of mini-states, none of which is strong enough to challenge the interests of the West.

Islam and Democracy

In much the same manner, a debate has emerged over the compatibility of Islam with democratic political systems. As with most complex religions, Islam contains both democratic and anti-democratic traditions. Those who argue that Islam is inherently democratic stress its emphasis on equality. Everyone is equal in the eyes of God, and all Muslims share the same rights and obligations. The emphasis on equality is reinforced by the fact that orthodox Islam (Sunni) does not have a priesthood or hierarchical authority structure. Rather, questions of import, including succession and religious leadership, have traditionally been decided by consultation. The Prophet Mohammed, it will be recalled, refused to name a successor, leaving that choice to his followers. Islam, moreover, stressed tolerance toward Christian and Jewish minorities ("people of the book") living within the Islamic world. A wide variety of diverse groups could and did prosper under Islamic rule. The recent experience of Iran also suggests that democracy is compatible with Islam, a topic to be discussed at length in Chapter 7.

The Middle East's addiction to authoritarianism, in the view of those stressing Islam's democratic underpinnings, is a manifestation of its tribal past, the selfish nature of its elites, and the meddling influence of foreign powers, not its Islamic heritage. Much the same argument may be made in regard to the subjugation of women. Islam embraced limited polygamy, but it also eliminated many of the worst abuses of gender discrimination common in the pre-Islamic era.

The arguments of those contending that Islam is inherently anti-democratic, however, are also strong. Armajani, for example, argues that consultation over succession and other issues of key importance have been limited to a very few individuals, and have had more to do with smoke-filled rooms than with current notions of popular sovereignty (1970). He goes on to note that Greek law, the foundation of Western concepts of democracy, is based upon the reasoning power of man. Being relative rather than absolute, human law can keep pace with changing circumstances and lends itself to the art of compromise so critical to democratic practice. Islamic law, by contrast, is the revealed law of God and is not subject to change by human beings. Constituting a moral imperative, it does not lend itself to compromise or change (Armajani 1970, 108).

THE TRIBE VERSUS ISLAM: CONFLICT AND ACCOMMODATION

Islam created a political community that transcended the bonds of kinship, but clans and tribes remained the basic units of social organization for the vast majority of the region's people. An inherent tension thus developed between a religion that accorded absolute loyalty to the vicars of God and a tribal lifestyle that made kinship loyalty a matter of personal survival. During periods of civilization and refinement such as those characterized by Abbasid Baghdad or Fatimid Cairo, the Islamic state extended its dominance over the tribes, curbing internal warfare and stimulating commerce and agriculture. With the weakening of centralized authority, the tribes reasserted their authority, pillaging caravans and attacking the agrarian villages on the fringe of the desert. Political relationships between the sacred and the profane, then, were much like the persistent tension between desert and sown: the fellah or peasants extended their realms during times of plenty, and the desert reclaimed its own during periods of drought and famine.

The same tension between Islam and the tribe existed in the social sphere. Islam, like other religions, could only find acceptance for its major principles by accommodating the dominant customs of the day, however repugnant they may have been to its founder (Rubin 1995). The dominant principle in Islam was submission to the one God and the creation of an Islamic state or Umma. To achieve this principle, Islam accommodated customs such as polygamy that were deeply entrenched in the local culture, although the Prophet Mohammed himself remained monogamous throughout his marriage to his first wife, to whom he was devoted. With the passing of his first wife, Mohammed took wives from diverse tribes in order to consolidate the core of the Islamic movement with ties of blood as well as faith. The founder of modern Saudi Arabia would follow the same practice during the early decades of the twentieth century. Polygamy also served an important social function by facilitating the large families so important to the survival of the tribe and offering a support system for women and children left destitute by the ravages of tribal warfare. Having said this, we note that Islam greatly restricted the practice of polygamy by limiting a man to four wives and requiring that all wives be treated with total equality.

In the end, the most powerful movements in the pre-colonial history of the Middle East were those that combined religious and tribal authority. The Islamic invasions relied heavily on tribal armies, and the Prophet Mohammed himself decreed that four-fifths of the spoils of war against the infidels should go to the armies, and one-fifth to the Islamic state. Tribal warfare thus continued to be a way of life, its focus merely being transformed into a religious cause. This pattern continued well into the twentieth century, with the fusion of religious and tribal authority providing the foundation of both the Saudi and Libyan kingdoms.

THE ISLAMIC CONQUEST

Orthodox Caliphs

The Prophet Mohammed died on June 8, 632, having extended Islam throughout most of the Arabian Peninsula. His passing created a crisis of succession, for Mohammed, in keeping with his role as prophet, had failed to name a successor. Some of his followers believed that the successor to Mohammed should be a member of the Prophet's family, while others thought the Caliph should be drawn from the broader reaches of the Quraysh tribe or selected on the basis of piety and good works. Space limitations preclude recounting the succession process, but suffice it to say that the first four Caliphs were both early supporters and relatives of the Prophet Mohammed. Abu Bakr, the first Caliph, was a close friend and father-in-law of the Prophet Mohammed, as was Umar, the second Caliph. Uthman, the third Caliph, was a son-in-law of the Prophet Mohammed and a member of the powerful Umayyad clan of the Quraysh tribe. Ali, the fourth Caliph, was both a cousin and son-in-law of the Prophet Mohammed, making him the logical candidate for the Caliphate in the eyes of those who believed that the Caliph should be a direct descendant of the Prophet (Tabatabai, n.d.).

Abu Bakr maintained Islam's domination of the Arabian peninsula in the unsettled circumstances following the Prophet Mohammed's death. This was not an easy task, for many of the tribes, having been converted by force, rebelled against the Islamic government. Some even tried to extend their power by discovering their own prophets (Armajani 1970). Umar, fueled by Islamic zeal and the need to occupy the energies of his tribal warriors, extended the Islamic conquest to

Egypt, the Fertile Crescent (Syria, Palestine, Lebanon, Iraq) and much of Iran. Expansion brought the Islamic empire much-needed wealth, for Muslims were not required to pay taxes other than the Zakat. Conquests continued under Uthman, but the leadership of the Islamic state was losing much of its religious zeal as Uthman, now in his seventies, allowed his relatives to usurp most of the senior positions in his administration. Corruption was rampant, with Uthman reportedly selling governorships for cash or slave girls (Armajani 1970). His most lasting contribution to Islam was the formal canonization of the Koran.

Sunni Versus Shi'a

Ali succeeded Uthman in 656, removing most of the latter's appointees and moving the seat of government to Kufa, an ancient city not far from the present city of Baghdad. Mu'awiya, the governor of Syria and a relative of Uthman, refused to recognize Ali as Caliph, thereby precipitating a civil war between a Syrian branch of Islam heavily influenced by Byzantine culture and an Iraqi-Iranian branch of Islam heavily influenced by Persian culture. Ali prevailed, but Mu'awiya consolidated his position in Syria and, in AD 660, had himself proclaimed Caliph. Islam now had two Caliphs, giving rise to a theological schism as fundamental as that separating Protestants and Catholics in post-reformation Europe. As the cousin and son-in-law of the Prophet Mohammed, Ali was the only acceptable candidate for Muslims who believed that the Caliphate should remain in the family of the Prophet. He was also a pious man who earned the support of those who believed that the Caliphate should be awarded on the basis of merit. Beyond being a question of doctrine, the conflict between Mu'awiya and Ali was also one of geo-politics. The center of Mu'awiya's support was Damascus and Jerusalem, while Ali found strong support among the Persian officials who increasingly dominated the eastern regions of the empire. Was Islam to be ruled from the West or from the East?

After Ali's assassination in Kusah in 661, his supporters—referred to as Shi'a or partisans of Ali—rallied around his two sons, Hassan and Husein, both of whom were subsequently assassinated. The Shi'a believe that Hassan was murdered by Mu'awiya in 673, while Husein was murdered in 680 by Yazid, Mu'awiya's successor, in order to prevent him from establishing a rival Caliphate in Iraq. Both would subsequently become holy martyrs of Shi'a Islam.

With the death of Hassan and Husein, the Shi'a, believing that the Caliphate must remain in the line of Ali through his wife Fatima, the daughter of the Prophet Mohammed, rejected the legitimacy of the

Umayyad Caliphs and created a branch of Islam that differed profoundly from that of the Sunni Islam. As described by Yahya Armajani:

> Failing to establish their claim by politics or by war, the Shi'is separated
> permanently from the majority and founded a religion of their own,
> complete with theology, philosophy, government, and ethics. Religious-
> ly, Shi'ism has Zoroastrian, Nestorian, and other overtones, and has sup-
> plied Islam with mysteries, saints, intercessors, belief in atonement, and
> a spirit of high cult, all of which are repugnant to the majority of Sunnis.
> The Sunnis consider the Koran infallible, while the Shi'is place infalli-
> bility in a man, the Imam who is sinless and has been considered as a
> man-God. The Shi'is believe in the doctrine of the Return. This has many
> things in common with the return of the deliverer in Zoroastrianism,
> the coming of the Messiah in Judaism, and the "second coming" of Jesus
> in Christianity. The majority of the Shi'is believe that there were twelve
> imams and that the twelfth, the Mahdi ("messiah") has disappeared and
> shall return at the end of time when he will bring the whole world under
> the jurisdiction of Shi'i Islam (Armajani 1970, 101).

The Shi'a belief that the hidden Imam would reappear and lead the
Muslim community to salvation led to the evolution of religious leaders empowered to rule the Shi'a community until the time of the
Imam's return. Such individuals, often referred to as ayatollahs, were
imbued with mystical powers that transcend those of the temporal
world, mystical powers that enabled them to control their followers
far more effectively than the Sunni ulema who possessed no such mystical powers. One was not dealing with mere mortals, but with agents
of the divine, a process that reached its apex with the writings of the
Ayatollah Khomeini.

In sharp contrast to the mysticism of the Shi'a, the Sunnis follow a
more literal interpretation of the Sunna, or way of the Prophet. There
are no hidden Imams, nor are Sunni spiritual leaders imbued with supernatural powers. Aside from the Caliphate, now vacant, the religious elites of Sunni Islam consist of learned scholars or ulema, the
most senior of which are the Mufti (senior religious judges), the directors of Waqfs or religious endowments (charitable works), and the rec-
tors of Islamic universities such as Al-Azhar University in Cairo. Aside
from these positions, Sunni Islam lacks an overarching organizational
structure, and each congregation more or less selects its own preachers
(muazin) and prayer leaders. In many instances, the selection is made
by the Government.

The differences in organizational structure of the Sunni and the Shi'a
branches of Islam are significant, for the more complex organizational
structure of the Shi'a enables their leaders to mobilize their followers
far more effectively than their Sunni counterparts (Halm 1997). As we

shall see in Chapter 7, the organizational advantages of the Shi'a played a crucial role in sustaining the Islamic revolution in Iran. Such differences also raise questions about the ability of Fundamentalist leaders in Egypt and Algeria, countries currently threatened by the prospect of Islamic revolutions, to sustain those revolutions should they occur. This topic will be discussed at length in our analysis of Egyptian politics. The profound differences between Shi'a and Sunni Islam also casts doubt on the prospects for a unified Islamic world should an increasing number of Middle Eastern countries fall under the sway of Islamic regimes. Revolutions are fueled by emotion, but they are sustained by discipline and organization. Perhaps responding to these problems, many Sunni Fundamentalist groups have embraced Shi'a concepts such as Imam (renewer of the faith) and Emir (prince of the faithful), concepts that provide a profound emotional link between the Fundamentalist leaders and their followers.

The Glories of the Empire

Following the death of Ali, the last of the four orthodox Caliphs, power shifted from the Arabian Peninsula to the Umayyads in Damascus, and from there to the Abbasids in Baghdad, the Fatimids in Cairo, Andalusians in Spain, and the Ottoman Turks in Istanbul, incorporating at one time or another large portions of Spain, Eastern Europe, and India. The Ottoman Empire in the West was paralleled by the empire of Safavid Turks in Tehran (1500–1779). The Umayyads and the Ottomans were Sunnis, while the Abbasids, Fatimids, Egyptians, Spaniards, and Safavids were Shi'a.

The era of empire and expansion saw the Middle East emerge as the center of world civilization (Hourani 1997). The Islam that emerged from the era of empire and expansion, however, was a far more complex religion than that of the Prophet Mohammed and his immediate successors. The invasion of Syria and Palestine had brought the desert warriors of Arabia into contact with the splendors of Byzantium, while their conquests in Mesopotamia had introduced them to the rich civilization of Persia (Hitti 1956). The demands of empire also proved too taxing for the informal style of rule that had characterized the early years of the Islamic era and forced an ever greater reliance on professional administrators. The Bedouin warriors who had spearheaded the Islamic invasion were poorly suited to the task of administration, and the job fell naturally to the more cultured Syrians and Persians, depending upon the location in question. In the process, the center of political power in the Islamic world shifted from the Arabian Peninsula to the new centers of imperial power. Indeed, with Mu'awiya's establishment of the Umayyad Caliphate in Damascus, the Arabian Peninsula had ceased to be the political center of Islam (Brockelmann 1960).

Great empires brought commerce, culture, and science to the region, but the empires inevitably succumbed to fragmentation born of social and economic jealousies, a process portrayed by Lewis in reference to the decline of the Abbasid Caliphs of Iraq:

> The rapid economic development of the Near and Middle East in the centuries that followed the accession of the Abbasid Caliphs subjected the social fabric of the Empire to a series of dangerous stresses and strains, gathering numerous movements of discontent and open rebellion against the established order. These movements were mainly economic and social in origin, some with a national colouring. Diverse in their causes and circumstances and in the composition of their following, they had this much in common, that they were almost all religiously expressed. Whenever a grievance or a conflict of interests created a faction in Islam, its doctrines were a theology, its instrument a sect, its agent a missionary, its leader usually a Messiah or his representative (Lewis 1958, 99).

The final thrust of empire was provided by the Ottoman Turks in the West and the Safavid Turks in the East. At its zenith, the Ottoman empire stretched from North Africa to Vienna. Had Vienna fallen, the history of Europe might be far different than it is today. As it is, the Turkish occupation of Eastern Europe established a strong Islamic presence in the region, and particularly in Bosnia and Albania.

Unlike their predecessors who had relied largely on tribal armies fired by the zeal of Islam and the lure of booty, the Ottoman sultans created a professional army of Christian slaves who had been converted to Islam. The members of this slave army, referred to as Janissaries, or "new army," were not allowed to marry, thereby eliminating the kinship loyalties that had proven so destructive to earlier empires. Their sole loyalty, at least in theory, was to the sultan. Being slaves, moreover, the Janissaries were the private property of the sultan, thereby removing them from the control of the Sheikh al Islam, the dominant religious figure in the Empire (Armajani 1970). This was not a minor consideration, for the power of the Sheikh al Islam often rivaled that of the weaker sultans, many of whom had become preoccupied by the affairs of the harem. Indeed, at least eleven sultans were deposed by religious order (Armajani 1970). As the empire declined, the power, arrogance, and corruption of the Janissaries grew proportionally, their leaders often becoming the power behind the throne. They also began to marry, thereby diluting their loyalty to the Sultan. A Janissary rebellion against the sultan in 1826 led to their slaughter by a parallel army created by a sultan fearful of the growing power of his protectors (Armajani 1970).

The Safavids, also of Turkish origin, invaded Iran in 1500 and, under the leadership of Shah Abbas, extended their empire to include Afghanistan, Pakistan, northern India, and most of the Muslim areas of Central Asia. Although they were of Turkish origin, the Safavids soon embraced Persian language and culture and made Iran the center of their empire. In the process they also became zealous Shi'as, putting them at odds with the Sunni Ottomans and condemning both empires, the Ottoman and the Safavid, to centuries of conflict. In the final analysis, neither empire was able to overcome the other, with the schism between the two Islamic powers serving only to weaken the Muslim world in the face of a resurgent West.

The Empire in Decline

In spite of its earlier glories, the final centuries of the Islamic empire were ones of stagnation and decline as local leaders asserted their independence from central authority and the European powers began a relentless colonization of Muslim territories (Antonius 1965; Zeine 1958). This decline was as true of the Ottomans in the West as it was of the Safavids in the East. Indeed, it was only jealousy among the European powers that kept the collapse of the Ottoman Empire, the "sick man of Europe," from being more rapid than it was (Marriott 1956).

Some authors have attributed the empire's decline to the fragmentation of Islam into diverse sects, while others blame the continuing influence of tribalism and kinship. Gifted leaders forged glorious empires, only to see their efforts squandered by squabbles among less-gifted heirs.

There were, however, more practical reasons for the decline of the empire as well. Except for brief periods of enlightened leadership, the rulers of the empire were corrupt and despotic. During the latter centuries of the Ottoman Empire, for example, the Turkish sultans auctioned the right to collect taxes within the empire to the highest bidder, a process often referred to as tax farming (Warriner 1957). While this practice assured a stable income for the sultan's profligate lifestyle, the methods of the tax farmers were brutal and shattered any bond of support that may have existed between the sultan and his subjects. Indeed, the Prophet Mohammed's efforts to forge an Islamic nation based upon trust between the rulers had long ago given way to fear and alienation. The more brutal governments became, the more individuals sought protection within the confines of their tribal, religious, and ethnic communities.

The Islamic empire, moreover, had little in common with the modern nation-state in which the citizens of a particular geographic region form a political community based upon common interests and shared identity. Rather, the Islamic empire had become a grand mosaic of tribal, religious, and ethnic groups, each with interests unto itself. The Turks gave explicit acknowledgment to this situation by making the leader of each religious sect responsible for the well-being of its members. Thus, the patriarch of the Greek Orthodox Christians was responsible for his flock, and so forth. Each group was considered a "millet" and was more or less self-governing as long as it remained quiescent and paid its allotted tribute to the sultan. By its very nature, the millet system fragmented the people of the Middle East and militated against the process of nation building.

In combination, the above factors kept the Islamic empire from keeping pace with social, economic, political and technological changes occurring in Europe. While the Islamic empire languished, the colonial powers had evolved into industrial nation-states. Nationalism replaced kinship as the basis for social integration, while religious doctrine was challenged by philosophies based on science, reason, and individualism. Industrialism created wealth and commerce, and it stimulated advances in education and medicine. It also created advances in bureaucratic technology that enabled the state to control the affairs of its citizens in a manner unknown in the East.

Predictably, an industrialized Europe found the Middle East easy prey for its imperialist ambitions. Indeed, the life of the average individual in the Middle East at the dawn of the colonial era was not markedly different from that of the average individual during the era of the Prophet Mohammed. Most lived in tribes or other kinship groups, and education was largely restricted to memorization of the Koran. Disease and famine remained commonplace.

Although the Islamic empire collapsed in the face of pressure from an industrialized West, the era of the empire transformed Islam from an obscure desert religion into a global religion that now claims approximately one-fifth of the world's population as adherents. It also provided the Middle East with a cultural cohesion and identity that continues to define the region's character. What happens in one area of the region invariably has repercussions throughout the region as a whole, the ongoing Islamic revolution being a case in point. This said, the era of the empire was not able to eliminate the scourge of tribalism. This task was made even more difficult by a political culture of distrust and alienation born of centuries of despotic rule.

THE ERA OF COLONIALISM

Although space limitations preclude a full accounting of the collapse of the Islamic empire, suffice it to say that the years between 1900 and World War I saw a steady erosion of Ottoman power in Europe as one after another of the Balkan regions either proclaimed its independence or was reclaimed by the Austro-Hungarian Empire (Marriott 1956). Turkey was also forced to allow Russia to intervene in Turkish affairs on behalf of the Orthodox Christians and France to serve as the protector of the Empire's Roman Catholics. The picture was much the same in Iran, with the Safavids losing ever-larger swaths of land to the Russians.

Prior to the nineteenth century, Western penetration of the Middle East had been indirect, taking the form of commercial concessions and demands for extraterritorial rights. Sustained colonization of the region began with the French occupation of Algeria in 1830, and the establishment of a British protectorate in Egypt in 1882. The same era would see the sheikhdoms of the Persian Gulf place their foreign affairs in the hands of the British in exchange for an annual stipend and guaranteed territorial rights. With the dismemberment of the Ottoman Empire at the end of World War I, Syria and Lebanon became mandates[2] of France, while Iraq and Palestine fell to the British. The French had already colonized much of North Africa, and the British were well ensconced in Egypt and the Persian Gulf. Under the mandate system, the European powers were expected to prepare the territories under their control for their eventual independence and self-government. This responsibility, however, did not weigh heavily on the minds of either the French or the British.

Political and Economic Consequences of the Colonial Experience

European motivations for colonization of the Middle East were both economic and strategic. From the economic perspective, the lands of the Middle East represented a rich market for European goods. It was also hoped that they would provide a cheap and reliable source of raw materials such as oil for the industries of Europe. From a strategic perspective, the European powers viewed the Middle East as a region of key geo-political importance, control of which could tip the European balance of power in their favor. British interest in the region was particularly strong, for the Middle East provided the most direct route to

[2]Mandates were devised by the League of Nations to placate American resistance to the further colonization of the Third World. At least in theory, mandatory powers were expected to prepare the territories under their control for eventual independence.

India, the crown jewel of the British Empire. In the case of Italy's occupation of Libya, the ostensible motivation for colonization was national pride, Mussolini rallying his followers with promises of a new
Roman Empire.

The most immediate result of Western colonialism was fragmentation of the Middle East into a multitude of small dependencies, each of
which would eventually become an independent state. A few areas,
mainly Turkey, Iran, North Yemen, and the central parts of the Arabian Peninsula, were spared colonization: Turkey and Iran for political
reasons involving the European balance of power, the Arabian Peninsula because of its inhospitable terrain.

The nature of countries created, moreover, had more to do with the
global interests of the colonial powers than it did with the background
and interests of the peoples affected. Thus, Kuwait, a sparsely populated region smaller than the state of Rhode Island, was made an
independent country while the homeland of the Kurds, which encompassed much of northern Iraq and adjacent areas in Turkey, Syria, and
Iran, was not. As the Kurdish example illustrates, boundaries were
also drawn with little concern for the ethnic and religious composition of their inhabitants, paving the way for the ethnic and religious
conflict that has become endemic to the region. Colonial administrators, moreover, did little to ameliorate communal tensions in the
colonies. Rather, most found it expedient to consolidate their control
over the colonies by playing one group against another, thereby exacerbating tensions that were already well developed.

Having staked their claim to the region, the colonial powers now set
about restructuring Middle Eastern society to make it compatible with
their economic and strategic interests. This meant that the economies of
the colonial territories were integrated into the economy of the European power. Rather than developing their own industrial and technological base, the territories supplied the economies of Europe with raw
materials and absorbed their excess industrial production. Upon
achieving independence, accordingly, most states in the region were
predominantly agricultural in character and continued to depend upon
the mother country for financial and technological assistance. This relationship was particularly strong in France's North African colonies
(Morocco, Algeria, and Tunisia) and continues to be so today. Indeed,
so many North Africans migrated to France in search of work that they
now constitute some 6 percent of the French population (*Economist*,
June 12, 1993).

Effective economic exploitation also required that the legal systems
of the colonies be brought in line with those of the colonial power. This
posed problems in two areas. First, most laws pertaining to individual

behavior were based on Koranic law and were often at odds with the secular legal codes of Britain and France. Confused legal systems thus emerged that were a mixture of both. In some cases, different laws applied to different groups, with Europeans abiding by one set of rules and natives by another. Laws in the rural areas also tended to remain more traditional than those in the city. Such confusion continues in the legal systems of the Middle East today, with the current revival of Islamic values resulting in a re-Islamization of many of the region's legal systems.

Particularly problematic were laws pertaining to property. Much land in the Middle East was the collective property of the clan or tribe, and land rights were based upon custom rather than written deeds. In other cases, land was technically owned by the state but was controlled by a particular family or clan. Again, there were no written deeds. Colonial economic policies, however, required stringent definitions of ownership, and collective lands were subsequently deeded to their presumed owners, more often than not the tribal chief or other dignitaries who spoke in the name of the clan or tribe (Warriner 1957). Collective land thus became private land, with the prominent families becoming landlords and the less prominent becoming peasants or landless sharecroppers. Such feudal distinctions, minimal at first, became pronounced as later generations of the landed gentry moved to the urban areas, leaving the management of their farms to exploitative foremen with little interest in the welfare of the masses. This process was particularly pronounced in Iraq but occurred in other areas of the region as well.

The absence of deeds continues to be a serious problem in the Israeli-occupied West Bank, for the Jordanian government was in the process of issuing deeds when the territory was seized by Israel in the June War of 1967. As land without formal deeds was presumed to be the property of the Jordanian government, the Israelis claimed it as their own and began to distribute it to Jewish settlers. Even as the Israelis and the Palestinians seek to work out a lasting peace in the occupied territories, the Israeli government is removing the few remaining bedouin tribes from areas that it wants to settle prior to the final peace (*Newsworld International*, Feb. 11, 1997).

The economic and strategic exploitation of the colonies also required an infrastructure of roads, railroads, canals, and telecommunications, few of which existed during pre-colonial times. Although designed to serve the Europeans, the new infrastructure stimulated communications among the peoples of the Middle East in a manner that had not been possible in the past. In so doing, it facilitated the spread of the nationalist and religious movements that would eventually spell the end of colonialism (Cole 1993).

Colonial exploitation also meant that the Middle East had to be made safe for Europeans. Key to this process was the institution of modern health practices and the control of diseases that had long been the scourge of the region. However laudable the revolution in health practices may have been from a humanitarian perspective, it had the unintended effect of triggering an explosion in the region's population. As noted above, Middle Eastern culture had traditionally placed a strong emphasis on large families, for a majority of children (the backbone of kinship societies) failed to reach adulthood. With the introduction of modern health techniques, more children survived the rigors of childhood and more adults lived longer. Culture, however, changes slowly, often over the course of several generations. High birth rates, accordingly, continued to be the norm, producing far more people than the meager agrarian economies of the region could sustain. Although population growth is easing, populous countries such as Egypt, Iran and Algeria face crushing financial problems as they attempt to feed, clothe, care for, educate, house, and employ populations that have tripled or quadrupled in the five decades since the end of World War II.

The population crisis, in turn, created a crisis in urbanization as rural migrants flocked to the cities in search of work. Urbanization brought an ever-larger share of the population into contact with Western lifestyles. Among some migrants, closer contact with the West led to the adoption of Western values. This was particularly the case for those who worked for foreigners or who were fortunate enough to receive a Western education. Urbanization, however, also brought slums, grinding poverty, and a sense of hopelessness as the poor came to realize the extent of their misery. For many recent migrants, moreover, direct contact with foreigners served only to heighten their sense of resentment against the foreign powers who had both humiliated them and desecrated their religious values. As will be elaborated shortly, it was this sense of outrage that fueled the nationalist movements of the colonial era. It continues to fuel Islamic Fundamentalism today.

Finally, the efficient exploitation of a colonial territory required a class of cooperative natives to assist in controlling the indigenous population. This class generally consisted of police, soldiers, minor administrative assistants, teachers, and commercial clerks. British administrators built on their experience in India, where they had sought "to form a class who may be interpreters between us and the millions whom we govern; a class of persons, Indian in blood and color, but English in taste, in opinions, in morals, and in intellect" (Mansingh 1986, 40). The French did much the same. The emerging Westernized elite was also augmented by the sons of tribal leaders, old aristocrats from the former regime, and native merchants, many of whom had also received a Western education. While the Westernized elite reaped the material advantages to be gained from association with the colonial power, the poor sank ever deeper into despair.

In the case of Turkey and Iran, former seats of the empire that were spared the burden of colonization, a Westernized elite emerged as a result of growing contact with the West and the slow but inevitable introduction of Western technology. Both Turkey and Iran, for example, had increasingly relied upon Western advisors to upgrade their respective armies. As will be discussed shortly, it was this Westernized elite (generally consisting of army officers, bureaucrats, and intellectuals) who attempted to save the Islamic empire by modernizing it.

The role of the Westernized elite as an agent of social change was profound. The Western elite served as role models or style setters for the youth of the colonies. They were living proof of the advantages that accompanied Westernization and the superiority of Western lifestyles. The Westernized elite would also become the vanguard in the Middle East's struggle for independence.

The "civilizing" activities of the colonial powers often resulted in the establishment of rudimentary school systems and the adoption of a European language as a second and frequently official language. The French, for example, "discouraged" the teaching of Arabic in its North African colonies, hoping to supplant it with the French language and culture. Algeria, an Arabic country, would thus attain independence with most of its citizens illiterate in their native language. The same was true to a lesser extent in Morocco and Tunisia. Be this as it may, education provided access to the mass media and, eventually, the emergence of indigenous newspapers, radio, and cinema.

Finally, the "civilizing" activities of the colonial powers also included limited experimentation with consultative assemblies. Such experiments were limited in scope and usually occurred during the latter stages of colonial rule.

The cultural and intellectual turmoil unleashed by Western domination of the Middle East gave rise to a variety of political movements ranging from mild calls for reform to armed confrontation with the West. As a general principle, the political response to the Western domination was in direct proportion to the scope of the Western presence. The more intrusive the presence of the West, the more violent the Middle Eastern response.

The impact of colonialism on the Middle East, then, was profound. It fragmented the area into a multitude of mini-states, each with its own set of elites and vested interests (Owen 1992). It was these elites who would eventually lead the drive to independence. Colonialism brought about a revolution in health care, but it also ignited a population explosion that has condemned much of the region to poverty. Colonialism enhanced the economic and communication infrastructure of the region, but only to the degree that it served the economic and strategic interests of the mother country. Upon receiving their independence, accordingly, most states in the region remained economic dependencies of the West. Colonialism introduced Western education to the Middle East, albeit to a narrow class designed to serve the interests of the colonial powers. In so doing, it spread the heady philosophies of nationalism and socialism that became the hallmark of the era of revolution that characterized the region during the 1950s and 1960s. Colonialism, however, also shook the confidence of a population profoundly confident of the superiority of its culture and forced that population to reassess its prospects for the future (Smith 1957). While some in the region advocated increased Westernization, others argued that the solution to their problems lay in a return to Islam as it was practiced during the era of the Prophet and his immediate successors. Still others looked for ways to bridge the gap between the material superiority of the West and the moral superiority of Islamic culture.

For all of its impact, however, colonialism did not succeed in reshaping the region. Rather, it merely added one more layer of complexity to an already complex region. The Middle East, as Sharabi writes, has become "modernized" without becoming modern, a situation he refers to as "neopatriarchy":

> Neopatriarchal society, as 'modernized,' is essentially schizophrenic, for beneath the immediately encountered modern appearance there exists another latent reality. Between these two there is opposition, tension, contradiction. Analysis of this phenomenon will provide the key to understanding the dynamics and patterns of behavior characteristic of neopatriarchy, and will enable us to grasp a fundamental insight: *Patriarchal societies, regardless of their variety on the manifest level, all share in the same deep structures.*
>
> From this perspective we can immediately grasp the curious aspect shared by all types of neopatriarchy, *the absence equally of genuine traditionalism and of authentic modernity.* In *'modernized'* patriarchy it is just as hard to find a truly modern individual or institution as it is to locate genuinely traditional ones. Indeed, both types are anomalous, whether in the conservative or in 'progressive' countries of the Arab world. In neopatriarchal society (whether in its conservative or progressive seg-

ments or variants), the dominant type of individual is the 'modernized.' This is even more true today than a generation or two ago; for the most remote countries and countryside in the Arab world have in the last two or three decades been drawn into 'modernity' (Sharabi 1988, 23–24).

POLITICS OF THE MIDDLE EAST SINCE WORLD WAR II

It was in this environment, then, that the Middle East embarked upon the post–World War II era. Not only had the region been divided into a multitude of mini-countries, but each country found itself fragmented by concerns of kinship, class, ethnicity, religion, ideology, and levels of modernity. Few countries in the region had stable governments, and all were struggling to build political institutions that could meet the needs of their people. To make matters worse, the world itself was being divided into US and Soviet power blocs. States in revolution against their colonial rulers inclined naturally toward the Soviet Union. Most had little interest in communism, but their immediate concerns were shaped by fears of an imperialist revival and a desire for rapid economic growth whatever its immediate costs in terms of freedom or economic sacrifice. Regimes still clinging to tradition, by contrast, inclined toward the United States and looked to the former colonial powers for protection against the revolutionaries. It was not long, accordingly, before the region was divided into competing blocs: a progressive, socialist bloc headed by Egypt and Syria, and a pro-American conservative bloc centering on Saudi Arabia, Iran, Iraq, and Jordan. Iraq would fall from the ranks of the conservatives in 1958, igniting Western fears that the region's massive oil resources would soon fall into the hands of the Soviets. Washington spared no efforts to stem the "Red Menace."

The tortured history of the Middle East during the post–World War II era reflects this lethal blend of domestic fragmentation, institutional weakness, and international manipulation. In many instances, events happened with such rapidity that it is difficult to establish clear lines of cause and effect. Everything seemed to be happening at once. In other cases, events moved slowly, only to explode into cataclysmic events such as the June War of 1967, the stunning 1979 victory of the Islamic Fundamentalists in Iran, or the Palestinian uprising of 2000.

By and large, the events of the post–WWII era fall into four historical periods, each with its own characteristics, constraints, and opportunities. The years between the end of World War II and the defeat of the Arab forces in the June War of 1967 are referred to as the era of revolution and optimism, for it was during this era that the countries of the region shook off the remaining vestiges of colonialism and became fully independent. It was also a period of profound optimism in the Arab world as a new generation of modernizing leaders led by Gamal Abdul Nasser struggled to unite the Arab World under the banners of nationalism, socialism, and modernity. Industrialization and education were pursued with a vengeance, and the peoples of the region increasingly migrated from the rural areas to massive urban conglomerates such as Cairo and Baghdad. In addition to accelerating the process of social change, the populist revolutions added yet another layer of complexity to the political mosaic of the Middle East. Also adding to the region's complexity was the birth of Israel in 1948 and the as yet unending struggle to forge a lasting peace between the Jewish state and its regional neighbors.

Israel's devastating defeat of the Arab armies in the June War of 1967 shattered Nasser's vision of socialist modernity and led to an era of disillusionment and reassessment. The June War was far more than just another scrimmage between the Arabs and the Israelis. Rather, it represented an historical benchmark that reshaped the politics of a region. From a geo-political perspective, Israel now controlled all of Palestine, including more than one million Palestinians living in the Gaza Strip and the West Bank. From a psychological perspective, the June War humiliated the Arabs and created an atmosphere of profound self-doubt. This sense of despair can only be understood in the context of the equally profound optimism that had preceded the war and the very real belief that more than two decades of military and industrial modernization had leveled the playing field between Israel and the Arabs.

The defeat also shattered faith in the secular promises of Arab nationalism. Prosperity would come, Nasser had promised, when Israel had been defeated and a unified Arab nation had claimed its rightful place in the world community. It was the Arabs, however, who had been defeated, and an Arab world that had waited in vain for the promises of Arab nationalism to lift them from a life of poverty was now overwhelmed by an abiding sense of despair.

By shattering the myth of secular nationalism, moreover, the June War had created a psychological vacuum. Faith and hope are essential elements of the human experience, and many people in the Arab world now sought salvation in a return to Islam and particularly the idealized vision of Islam preached by the Muslim Brotherhood. Once again, another layer of complexity was added to the Middle Eastern equation.

By 1979, Islamic Fundamentalism had emerged as the dominant political force in most areas of the Middle East, launching what we refer to as the era of resurgent Islam. The era began with the Islamic victory in Iran and soon threatened to spawn Islamic revolutions within many countries that had formerly championed secularism, including Egypt and Algeria. The Fundamentalists also turned on the tribal monarchies of the Gulf, accusing them of hypocrisy, immorality, and subservience to the United States, a topic discussed at length in Chapter 5. The peace treaty signed between Egypt and Israel in 1979 also contributed to the restructuring of politics in the Middle East and ended the myth of Arab solidarity.

Finally, the collapse of the Soviet Union in 1990 ushered in an era of American dominance that President Bush would proclaim to be the era of the new world order. The Middle East would now have to adjust to US control of the world economic and political systems, its staunch support of Israel, its advocacy of capitalism, and its unbridled hostility to Islamic Fundamentalism (do Ceu Pinto 1999; Tibi 1997).

In the chapters that follow, we will examine the political process in six of the dominant countries in the Middle East and review the major factors that have shaped that process. The discussion in each chapter is organized along the historical periods reviewed above with the greatest degree of emphasis being placed on the post-colonial eras. As we shall see throughout the ensuing chapters, Middle Eastern politics is the product of a wide variety of factors. The elites of the Middle East attempt to orchestrate who gets what, when and how in the region, but often find their best-laid plans go for naught because of the weakness of their political institutions. The leaders of the Middle East tend to be strong, but their political institutions are not. Elites and institutions, in turn, are constrained by the attitudes and behaviors of their citizens as well as the group, cultural, economic, and international milieus in which they exist. Finally, the behavior of both states and elites is profoundly influenced by their regional and international environment. Most Western scholars stress domestic factors such as elites and groups in their analysis of Middle Eastern politics. Scholars from the Arabic and Islamic worlds, by contrast, attribute most of what happens in the region to the machinations of the major powers, particularly the United States. It is the major powers, in their view, that determine who gets what, when and how. Each of the above perspectives is vital to understanding how the people of the Middle East do politics, as each adds important insights into what has become a very complex puzzle.

2

The Politics of Egypt

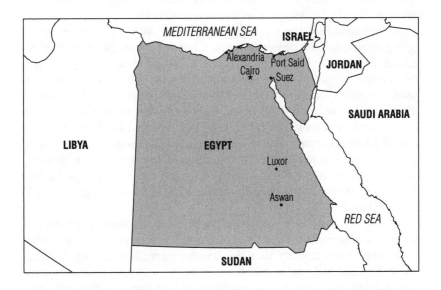

Egypt is the core state of the Arab world. Egypt possesses the largest population in the Arab world, its dominant army, its most vibrant mass media, and its strongest industrial base. Egypt is also host to the Arab League, a regional organization designed to increase political, military, and economic cooperation among the Arab states. No other Arab state approaches Egypt in terms of its regional and international influence.

Egypt's dominant position within the Arab world is summed up by the Arabic expression "um Al Arab"—mother of the Arabs. Little happens in Egypt that does not have a direct impact on neighboring countries. During the 1950s and 1960s, Egypt was the focal point of an Arab resurgence that ignited anti-Western revolutions in Lebanon, Jordan, Iraq, Syria, Yemen, and Libya. Not all were successful, but the tide of Arab nationalism appeared irresistible. American interests in Saudi Arabia and other oil-producing states were placed in jeopardy, as was the security of Israel, a state that most Arabs believed to be a creation of Western imperialism.

Politics in the Middle East, however, are subject to abrupt and startling changes. The 1980s and 1990s found Egypt to be the champion of regional cooperation. Peace was made with Israel, and Egypt became the ally of the United States. Egyptian cooperation was vital to the United Nations' victory over Iraq's Saddam Hussein in the Gulf War of 1991, and it remains vital to maintaining order in what is probably the most politically volatile region in the world today.

Understandably, the United States and its Western allies are struggling to assure that Egypt remains a bastion of moderation and regional cooperation. Toward this end, the United States provides Egypt with some $2 billion in foreign assistance each year. The World Bank, International Monetary Fund, and various other donors also provide Egypt with foreign aid. All in all, Egypt receives more foreign assistance than any other country of the Third World.[1] In return for their aid, the United States and other international donors have pressured Egypt to increase the pace of its transition from a socialist dictatorship into a capitalist democracy. A democratic and capitalist Egypt, in their view, is essential to the stability of the Middle Eastern region (World Bank 1992).

Progress toward democracy and political moderation, unfortunately, is undermined by Egypt's grinding poverty and by a population that grows more rapidly than the country's fragile economy can support. Foreign aid and rising oil revenues have helped to keep the Egyptian economy afloat, as has the increased but tentative privatization of Egypt's industries. Egypt's economic problems, however, remain far from solution as the gap between rich and poor widens. The Egyptian population is losing patience with its government, and radical Islamic (Muslim)[2] Fundamentalist groups are vowing to transform Egypt into an Islamic government somewhat similar to that of Iran. The mood of the masses was recently summed up by an Egyptian friend: "We have tried socialism and we have tried capitalism. Both have failed. Why not try Islam?" The Algerian elections of 1992 did result in a presumed victory for the Islamic Fundamentalists, and only military intervention prevented the transformation of Algeria into an Islamic state. The suppression of the 1992 elections resulted in a near

---

[1]Russia is rapidly overtaking Egypt as the major recipient of foreign assistance from the world community.
[2]Adherents of the Islamic faith are referred to as Muslims.

civil war that claimed the lives of more than 70,000 Algerian citizens. An Islamic victory in Egypt would almost certainly trigger Fundamentalist revolutions throughout the Arab world.

In this chapter, we will trace Egypt's tortuous path toward democracy and capitalism. Egypt's success in these endeavors will have much to say about the future of democracy and capitalism in the region.

HISTORY AND CULTURE

The glories of pharaonic Egypt require little recounting. Egypt was the cradle of Western civilization, its pyramids and monuments standing in testimony to a people of dazzling creativity. The pharaonic period, however, came to an end several thousand years ago as Egypt succumbed to a seemingly endless succession of foreign invaders including the Babylonians, Persians, Greeks, Romans, Arabs, Crusaders, Turks, French, and British. Indeed, Egypt would not reclaim full control of its own destiny until 1952. Be this as it may, modern Egyptians remain intensely proud of their pharaonic heritage. Egyptians are Arabs in language and culture, but they are also profoundly aware of their uniqueness as Egyptians.

Of the long procession of foreign invasions, none would have a more lasting influence on Egyptian society than the Arab invasions of the seventh century. Fired by the zeal of the new Islamic (Muslim) religion, tribal armies from the Arabian Peninsula[3] would impose their language, culture, and religion on a vast territory that ranged from Spain in the West to India in the East. Arabic would become the language of Egypt, and Islam the religion of more than 90 percent of its population. Of the non-Muslims, most would be Coptic Christians[4] (Carter 1986).

By the tenth century, Egypt had become the political center of the Islamic world, a position that it maintained for some two hundred years. The splendors of Cairo dazzled visitors of this era.

> I saw a series of buildings, terraces, and rooms. There were twelve adjoining pavilions, all of them square in shape.... There was a throne in one of them that took up the entire width of the room. Three of its sides were made of gold on which were hunting scenes depicting riders racing their horses and other subjects; there were also inscriptions written in beautiful characters. The rugs and hangings were Greek satin and moiré

[3]Modern Saudi Arabia.
[4]The Coptic Church centers on the Patriarchate of Alexandria, one of the four major centers of early Christianity, the others being Rome, Constantinople, and Antioch. Egypt also possessed a substantial Jewish minority.

woven precisely to fit the spot where they were to be placed. A balustrade of golden latticework surrounded the throne, whose beauty defies all description. Behind the throne were steps of silver. I saw a tree that looked like an orange tree, whose branches, leaves, and fruits were made of sugar. A thousand statuettes and figurines also made of sugar were also placed there (Khusraw in Behrens-Abouseif 1990, 7).

It was during this era that the Al-Azhar mosque, the world's oldest and most famous center of Islamic learning, was established. Al-Azhar is both a mosque and a university, and its sheikh (rector) is one of the most influential political figures in modern Egypt.

The history of modern Egypt begins with the reign of Mohammed Ali, an Albanian adventurer sent to Egypt in 1789 as part of a joint Turko-British military operation designed to end the French occupation of Egypt.[5] The French were evicted, and Mohammed Ali surfaced as the head of an Egyptian government nominally loyal to the Sultan of Turkey. Mohammed Ali, however, felt little loyalty to the Sultan of Turkey or to any other power (Marsot 1984; Fahmy 1997). His dreams were of empire, and Egypt was to be the base of that empire. Egyptian fellahin (peasants) were welded into the strongest army in the Middle East and were soon to conquer much of the land area that now constitutes the Sudan, Israel, Jordan, and Saudi Arabia (Goldschmidt 1988; Cuno 1992; Dowell 1931). On two occasions, they threatened to conquer Turkey itself, but both efforts were stymied by the British army (Lawson 1992). Turkey had become a pawn in Britain's efforts to establish a balance of power in Eastern Europe, and the British would not allow those efforts to be upset by an Albanian adventurer (Marriott 1956). Mohammed Ali was forced to abandon his dreams of an empire but was recognized by the British as the hereditary monarch of Egypt. Egypt's royal family was born.

By and large, the political and economic structure of Egypt during this period was remarkably similar to the feudalism of medieval Europe, with an aristocracy of large landowners providing financial support to the monarchy in exchange for the right to rule their fiefdoms as they saw fit. How they achieved these objectives was of little concern to the royal family (Lane 1954; Toledano 1990). As described by Bonne:

> Nobody knew how much was extorted from the fellahin or how much of the receipts from taxation was stolen on the way to the Treasury.... Justice was a matter of bribes, property a matter of favour, life a matter of luck.

---

[5]Napoleon I had invaded Egypt shortly after the French Revolution in 1789, hoping to add the North African state, a possession of Turkey, to the French Empire. Ever fearful of French power, the British joined with the Turks to frustrate the venture.

> Public opinion regarded the dishonesty of officials as a matter of course. What it regarded as ideal was the maintenance of a single tyrant, in order to prevent the rise of many. If the Sheikhs of the villages were left to themselves, they made use of every opportunity to exploit the peasants under their control. Those appointed over them repeated the same process within their domains. Corruption was not their only defect; they were also ignorant. Experience was the official's sole equipment, and it usually taught him how to rob wisely and shrewdly (Bonne 1955).

The profligate lifestyle of the royal family exhausted Egypt's meager financial resources and led to increasingly desperate measures to extract revenue from Egypt's fellahin (Cole 1993). The construction of the Suez Canal in 1869 provided the Egyptian government with royalties from canal traffic, but even this new source of revenue could not satisfy the appetites of the monarch. Short of cash, the Khedive (king) sold Egypt's 40-percent share in the Suez Canal to British and French investors[6] (Longgood 1957). Once the Canal funds had been squandered, the heirs of Mohammed Ali turned to deficit financing. With little in the way of new resources, it was only a matter of time until Egypt defaulted on its loans. England and France responded by seizing the Egyptian custom houses. Henceforth, customs revenues, Egypt's most reliable form of taxation, would reach the king only after Egypt's creditors had been paid (Henry 1996). The seizing of the custom houses sparked a brief rebellion in 1881, with the rebellion's leader, Ahmed Urabi, proclaiming that "By the name of Allah, beside whom there is no God, we shall no longer be inheritable and from this day on we shall not be enslaved" (Scholch 1981). The Urabi revolution led to the British occupation of Egypt, but it also marked the first outpouring of Egyptian nationalism. It would not be the last (Meyer 1988).

Egypt, however, did not become a British colony (Berque 1967). Rather, a protectorate was established in which the heirs of Mohammed Ali ruled with the active guidance of the British High Commissioner. This arrangement provided Britain with a strong military presence in Egypt that would continue in one form or another until after the Second World War.

The British protectorate was unpopular from its inception. The palace chafed under the fiscal rules imposed by the British High Commissioner, and much of Egypt's predominantly Muslim population was offended by the British disregard for Islamic culture. The British use of alcohol, prohibited by the Koran, was particularly offensive to Muslims, as were British attitudes towards women. Westernized Egyptians, moreover, smarted from racist policies that excluded them from

---

[6]The result was that Britain and France controlled 100 percent of the shares in the Suez Canal.

British-owned hotels and restaurants (Goldschmidt 1988, 42–44) and were deeply offended by the "capitulations," a legal system that allowed foreigners to be tried in special councilor courts staffed by non-Egyptians (Berque 1967, 235–250). Prosperous Egyptians exempted themselves from the vagaries of Egyptian law by purchasing a foreign passport, as did members of Egypt's large Greek and Jewish communities, the dominant forces in Egyptian commerce (Beinin 1998). Egyptians had become second-class citizens in their own country.

By the early 1920s, hostility to British occupation would find expression in two political movements. The first was the Wafd Party, a broad coalition of nationalist groups dedicated to liberating Egypt from British rule (Berque 1967, 284). The second organization was the Muslim Brotherhood, a secret religious organization dedicated to the creation of an Islamic state in Egypt (Husaini 1956). There was considerable overlap between the two movements, as the Muslim Brotherhood was also violently opposed to the British presence in Egypt.

The British granted Egypt quasi-independent status in 1922 but retained the right to station troops on Egyptian soil. Egyptian politics throughout the inter-war period would remain a three-way struggle between the British Embassy, the king, and the Wafd (Youssef 1983; Gershoni and Jankowski 1995). King Fu'ad, the monarch of the era, had little love for either democracy or the British and was deposed by the British shortly before World War II in response to his pro-German leanings. Fu'ad was succeeded in office by his son, Farouk, a particularly corrupt and inept leader who shared the despotic inclinations of his father (Al-Fatah 1990).

The advent of World War II saw a reassertion of British control as Egypt was transformed into a staging camp for British forces in the Middle East. The end of the war ushered in a period of profound political instability, as the British sought to remain a key force in Egyptian politics while the king, more corrupt than ever, struggled to rule as an absolute monarch. The Wafd continued to press for greater democracy, but the party had lost much of its nationalist zeal and become the party of the wealthy (Berque 1967). The influence of the Muslim Brotherhood had also been weakened by the assassination of its founder.

The turmoil of Egyptian politics was paralleled by growing violence between Jews and Arabs in the British mandate of Palestine, Egypt's neighbor to the northeast. Britain withdrew from Palestine in 1947, and the United Nations partitioned the area into Arab and Jewish sections as a prelude to establishing separate Jewish and Arab countries. War between the Palestinian Arabs and the Jews erupted immediately upon the British withdrawal, with most Arab states, including Egypt, entering the war on the side of the Palestinians.

King Farouk sent his army to Palestine in the misguided belief that the Jews couldn't fight. Victory assured, Jerusalem would be ruled from Cairo (Interviews with Hassan Pasha Youssef, Head of the Royal Diwan, 1983). Poorly led and poorly armed, the Egyptian forces succeeded in liberating only the Gaza strip, a sparse coastal area adjacent to the Egyptian border.

Smarting from their defeat at the hands of the Jews and frustrated by the ineptness of their political leaders, a small group of junior army officers headed by Gamal Abdul Nasser formed the Free Officers, a secret military organization dedicated to the modernization of Egyptian society (Baker 1978). Most of the Free Officers were from lower-middle-class backgrounds and had been profoundly influenced by the rhetoric of the Wafd and the Muslim Brotherhood. By and large, their ideology was a blend of populism and nationalism. Egypt, according to the slogans of the young revolutionaries, was to be liberated from the British, from its parasitic aristocracy, and from the exploitative class of Greeks and Jews that dominated the Egyptian economy. The Free Officers were also motivated by a desire to avenge the humiliation of Egypt's colonial past. Servility to foreigners could no longer be tolerated.

Arab defeat in the Arab-Israeli War of 1948 had also undermined whatever domestic support the king may have enjoyed. Rioters swept through Cairo in January of 1952, torching many of the "foreign-only" hotels and clubs so offensive to nationalist sentiments. The king made little effort to quell the turmoil. Approximately six months later, on July 22, 1952, the Free Officers ousted Farouk in a bloodless coup. The king sailed for Italy on his royal yacht while Nasser and the Free Officers set about the task of ruling Egypt.

Their task would not be an easy one. The Egyptian population was mired in poverty and disease and was growing at an alarming rate that outpaced Egypt's meager resources. More people meant more starvation. Land remained concentrated in the hands of a narrow aristocracy hostile to the revolution, and British troops were stationed throughout Egyptian territory. Fears of a Western counter-coup were pervasive, for the Western powers were unlikely to accept a challenge to their dominance of the region. Centuries of foreign domination and misgovernment, moreover, had created a chasm of distrust between the government and the people. Recoiling from oppressive rulers, Egyptians sought security in the solidarity of their families rather than in the protection of the state. In the case of the Coptic minority, security was also to be found in religious solidarity. Egyptians, accordingly, were slow to develop the sense of political community or civic culture that had played such a crucial role in the political development of the West. Rather, Egypt became a society of families and clans, each competing with the other for scarce resources. Egyptians distrusted the government and they distrusted each other. Abdul Nasser described this painful situation shortly after the Free Officers seized power in 1952:

> Every leader we came to wanted to assassinate his rival. Every idea we found aimed at the destruction of another. If we were to carry out all that we heard, then there would not be one leader left alive. Not one idea would remain intact. We would cease to have a mission save to remain among the smashed bodies and the broken debris lamenting our misfortune and reproaching our ill-fate.
>
> Complaints and petitions poured upon us in thousands. If these did refer to cases worthy of justice, or mentioned oppression that might be redressed, they would be understandable and logical. The majority of these were but persistent demands for revenge as if the revolution were meant to be a weapon for revenge and hatred.
>
> If I were asked then what I required most my instant answer would be, "To hear but one Egyptian uttering one word of justice about another, to see but one Egyptian not devoting his time to criticize willfully the ideas of another, to feel that there was but one Egyptian ready to open his heart for forgiveness, indulgence and loving his brother Egyptian." Personal and persistent selfishness was the rule of the day. The word "I" was on every tongue. It was the magic solution of every difficulty and the effective cure for every malady (Nasser 1955).

The Era of Revolution and Optimism

The Revolution of 1952 ushered in a new era of optimism. The quasi-parliamentary institutions that had evolved under the monarchy were abolished and replaced by a Revolutionary Command Council (RCC) composed of Nasser and his most trusted associates among the Free Officers (Gordon 1992; El-Din 1992). Abolished too, were the Wafd and other political parties of the era. Efforts had been made to work with the Wafd and other political groups in order to place Egypt on the path to democracy, but to no avail. The military demanded unity and sacrifice while Egypt's civilian politicians sought little more than a continuation of the corrupt and divisive policies of the old regime. Egypt needed sacrifice and discipline, not chaos (Dekmejian 1975). Following a 1954 assassination attempt, the Muslim Brotherhood was also driven underground and remained dormant throughout much of the Nasser era.

Changes in the economic and social arena were equally dramatic (Beattie 1994; Wahba 1994). Egypt's largest farms were expropriated by the government and their lands redistributed among the peasants. This redistribution deprived the landed aristocracy of much of their power and provided the regime with a Robin Hood image among the poor. Schools and health clinics also mushroomed as the government sought to eliminate the scourges of illiteracy and poverty. Graduates of the new schools and universities were guaranteed a job with the government.

For the most part, however, Nasser and the Free Officers remained in the background, allowing formal power to be exercised by General Neguib, a respected military leader of moderate political views. The appointment of a figurehead president was designed to reassure both the West and Egypt's established elite that the new regime did not pose a threat to their interests. Nasser and the Free Officers, moreover, needed time to figure out how best to modernize Egypt and its population. None of Egypt's new leaders possessed broad experience in either government or economics. They would have to learn by trial and error (Ginat 1997; El-Gamasy 1993).

General Neguib chafed under the figurehead role assigned to him and challenged Nasser for leadership of the revolution (Neguib 1955). He was removed from office in 1954, some two years after the July revolution, and Nasser ascended to the presidency (Woodward 1992).

The Nasser who replaced General Neguib possessed a far clearer picture of Egypt and its future than had the young officer who deposed the hapless Farouk some two years earlier. Egypt's future prosperity, in Nasser's view, would be secured through a program of rapid industrialization that would bring the country and its population on par with the nations of the West. The West was invited to cooperate in Egypt's modernization, but only on the condition that Egypt be treated as a sovereign and independent nation. Foreign troops would no longer be welcome on Egyptian soil. Nasser's attitude toward Israel was ambivalent. He had little love for the Jewish state but placed the economic development of Egypt above foreign policy concerns. Israel could exist as long as it did not threaten the security of Egypt.

The centerpiece of Nasser's modernization plan was to be the Aswan Dam, a towering structure that would span the narrows of the Nile River in a sparsely populated region not far from the Sudanese border. Electric power generated by the dam would fuel an economic miracle, providing jobs for Egypt's masses and transforming Egypt into a modern industrial state. The dam would also control the Nile's floods, providing a dramatic expansion of Egyptian agriculture. The Aswan Dam, moreover, was to be a symbol of hope and progress: a symbol designed to legitimize the revolutionary regime and to generate popular support for its programs. Nasser also attempted to build a bond of trust between the government and the masses by forging a "social contract" in which a benevolent dictatorship would use the resources of the state to provide all of its citizens with an acceptable quality of life (Amin 1995). Economic democracy would take precedence over political democracy (Nasser, n.d.).

The West applauded Nasser's goal of economic development and his moderate stance toward Israel. Nasser, or so it seemed at the time, promised to emerge as a stabilizing force in this tumultuous region, and aid was promised for the construction of the Aswan Dam. The honeymoon between Nasser and the West, however, was to be short-lived. The United States pressured Nasser to join a proposed military alliance designed to encircle the Soviet Union, but he refused, claiming that the new alliance, the Central Treaty Organization (Baghdad Pact) was merely colonialism in a new guise. The purpose of his revolution had been to liberate Egypt from foreign domination, not encourage it.

Giving deed to his words, Nasser demanded the evacuation of British troops from Egyptian soil, a demand reluctantly accepted by a Britain still clinging to dreams of empire. Clashes between Palestinian fighters seeking shelter on Egyptian soil and Israeli forces further complicated matters and soon escalated into clashes between Israeli forces and the Egyptian army, with the latter suffering heavy loses. Nasser demanded Western arms in order to resist Israeli incursions, but the West refused, citing a desire to avoid an arms race in the region. Nasser responded by purchasing arms from the Soviet Bloc, thereby shattering the West's monopoly of power in the Middle East. In one fell swoop, the Soviet Union had gained entree into the Middle East and the Mediterranean basin, and the Western Alliance (NATO) had been placed at risk. The United States demanded that Nasser rescind the communist arms deal. He refused, and in 1956 the United States canceled its aid for the Aswan Dam (Kunz 1991; Kingseed 1995; Gorst and Johnman 1997). Nasser responded by nationalizing the Suez Canal, vowing to use its revenues to finance the Aswan Dam. It was Egypt's sovereign right to do so, as the canal was wholly within Egyptian territory.

Israel, fearful of Nasser's escalating popularity in the Arab world, conspired with Britain and France to occupy the Suez Canal and thereby to bring down the Nasser regime. Israeli forces stormed the canal in October of 1956, while Britain and France, acting according to script, demanded the right to occupy the Suez Canal under the pretext of protecting international shipping. The second Arab-Israeli war had begun. When Egypt refused to cede the canal, it was occupied by British and French forces. The three conspirators, however, had failed to consult with an American administration that was attempting to counter Soviet influence in the Third World by stressing America's history as a revolutionary, anti-colonial power (Brands 1993; Holland 1996). Eisenhower sided with Egypt, forcing the French, British, and Israeli forces to withdraw from Egyptian territory. Nasser reigned victorious.

In a brief period of two years, then, Nasser had evicted British troops from Egyptian soil, shattered the Western arms monopoly in the Middle East, nationalized the Suez Canal, and defeated, albeit politically, the combined forces of Israel, France, and Britain. In the eyes of Egypt and the entire Arab world, Nasser had become a hero of towering proportions, a leader who more than met Weber's description of a charismatic leader "endowed with supernatural, superhuman...powers" (Weber 1947).

The experience of the 1956 War changed the direction of Egyptian policy in three key ways. First, Nasser began to transform Egypt into a socialist economy, a process that began with the nationalization of British and French property shortly after the 1956 War. This process was extended over the next few years until virtually all non-agrarian enterprises employing more than a handful of workers had been nationalized and placed under government control. Nasser, however, was not a communist. Rather, he went out of his way to base Egyptian socialism on Koranic principles (Al-Sharbasi, no date). His goal was the creation of an Egypt that was as equitable as it was prosperous. Socialism and military rule were merely the means to that end (Hosseinzedeh 1989, 71–72). Capitalism and party politics, in the view of Nasser and his colleagues, had brought Egypt little more than poverty, inequality, and conflict. Egypt's military leaders would use their authority to assure that Egypt's scarce resources were allocated in a just and productive manner. Once economic and social development had been achieved, Egypt would become a true democracy in which educated and prosperous Egyptians could make wise and judicious choices. Such, at least, was the theory.

Second, having abolished Egypt's traditional political parties, Nasser was finding it difficult to rule without a political organization of some type. An Egyptian population drugged by centuries of oppression and foreign domination had to be energized if the revolution were to achieve its goals. This task could be carried out only by a political party.

While Nasser needed a political organization to mobilize the Egyptian masses, he remained deeply opposed to the revival of a multi-party system. Party conflict, from Nasser's perspective, would merely reinforce the divisiveness of an Egyptian society already fragmented by conflict and distrust. He also feared that a strong political party would challenge the authority of the military regime. Nasser wanted a political organization capable of defending the revolution and mobilizing the masses, but he did not want an independent political organization that would constrain his own authority.

Nasser, accordingly, began to experiment with the creation of a government-sponsored political organization that would perform the role of political parties without the tension and conflict created by excessive competition. Egyptians would learn democracy and civic responsibility within the confines of a single political party. With time and economic development, guided democracy would give way to pluralistic democracy.

The result of this experimentation was the Arab Socialist Union. The Arab Socialist Union (ASU) would be open to all Egyptians other than the enemies of the revolution, a category that included large landowners, communists, and the Muslim Brotherhood. The new party would penetrate all echelons of Egyptian society, from the remotest villages to the slums of Cairo (Baker 1978, 109–114). Its members would be the revolution's cadres. It was they who would mobilize the Egyptian masses and guide their energies toward the achievement of revolutionary goals. It was also they who would be the eyes and ears of the revolution, constantly vigilant to the machinations of its enemies. The new party was to perform other functions as well. It would serve as a forum for debate, a channel of communication, an agent of political socialization, and a conduit for recruiting the "best and the brightest" into the service of the revolution.

Finally, Nasser's near defeat in the Arab/Israeli War of 1956 convinced him that Egypt would never be free from external threat as long as his Arab neighbors remained subservient to the West. His resentment of foreign domination, moreover, was shared by thousands of students, military officers, and intellectuals throughout the Arab World. Indeed, Arab nationalism was rapidly becoming the dominant political ideology of the region (Doran 1999). The message of Arab nationalism was both simple and powerful. The Arabs are one people united by a common history, a common culture, a common language and, for the most part, a common religion. Once powerful, the Arabs now found themselves fragmented into a multitude of petty countries manipulated by the Western imperialists and Israel. All that was required for a resurgence of Arab power was the reunification of the Arab people into a single state.

However potent its message, the Arab Nationalist movement had historically lacked a dominant leader capable of marshaling its diverse and conflicting wings. Nasser provided that leadership. A union of Egypt and Syria was forged in 1958, being followed in a few months by the overthrow of the pro-Western monarch of Iraq. Saudi Arabia,

Lebanon, and Jordan all teetered on the brink of collapse and their fall seemed imminent. When the Arab World had been united, Nasser vowed, the humiliation of 1948 would be redressed. Israel would be returned to the Palestinians and Egypt would become the core of a reunified Arab state.

The dreams of Arab unity and socialist prosperity, however, were to prove elusive. The union with Syria was short-lived, and pro-Western regimes in Lebanon, Saudi Arabia, and Jordan were stabilized by the US and Britain. The 1960s also found Egypt embroiled in the Yemeni Civil War, a disastrous involvement that paralleled the US experience in Vietnam. Egyptian forces controlled the major cities but could not subdue the tribes that dominated Yemen's impenetrable countryside (Al-Hadidi 1984). The morale of the Egyptian forces flagged as defeat became inevitable. The collapse of the Yemeni venture was followed in short order by the outbreak of the June War of 1967. This conflict, the third of the Arab-Israeli wars, would see Israel rout Egyptian forces in less than six days.

Results on the socialist front were equally depressing. Having abolished the private sector, the Egyptian government found itself saddled with the full burden of development. It was the government that would build Egypt's factories, educate its children, and feed its population. Who else could do it? Reflecting its new and diverse responsibilities, the Egyptian bureaucracy would swell from 250,000 employees in 1952 to approximately 1,200,000 by 1970 (Ayubi 1982). The number of ministries would increase from 15 to 28 during the same period. Public corporations would jump from 1 in 1957 to 38 in 1963. By 1970 their number would reach 46 (Palmer, Leila, and Yassin 1988).

Bureaucratic expansion, however, was not motivated solely by Nasser's desire to transform Egypt into an industrial power. Government service was also to provide jobs for the thousands of graduates emerging from the revolution's expanded educational system. Under the "graduates policy," university students were guaranteed a bureaucratic position upon graduation.

Superficially, at least, the graduates policy appeared to be compatible with the rapid expansion of the bureaucracy. Talent was in short supply within the bureaucracy; the graduates, presumably the cream of Egyptian society, needed jobs. Things, however, were not as they seemed. The urgency of the moment precluded the rational allocation of personnel on the basis of need or qualifications. Jobs had to be done and programs had to be put into operation. If existing organizations faltered, new units were created, producing a morass of overlapping jurisdictions and contradictory regulations. The new graduates, moreover, were poorly trained and their skills ill-suited to the demands of technological modernization. Most had specialized in the arts, law, or the humanities, and practical skills were rare. As years passed, the number of graduates demanding government employment would far exceed the needs of the bureaucracy, further exacerbating problems of administrative confusion and mismanagement. Wages were low, but job security was high. As it was virtually impossible to be fired from government employment, Egyptians began to look upon a government job as a right rather than as an obligation. Low wages and the absence of merit-based work incentives also led to a pervasive sense of lethargy. Egypt, then, would succumb to the same socialist work ethic that undermined the economy of the Soviet Union. A society increasingly dependent upon the state was unwilling to work hard enough to make the state effective.

Nasser had set two goals for the bureaucracy. The first goal was to develop an efficient mechanism for the economic and social development of Egypt. The second goal was to use the bureaucracy as a dumping ground for the surplus of poorly trained graduates pouring out of Egypt's newly created high schools and universities. The developmental goal required a lean and professional bureaucracy dedicated to the goals of national development. The welfare goal required that bureaucratic units accept all graduates regardless of their qualifications. The welfare goal became the order of the day. Applicants were assigned to units with little concern for skills or aptitude. Many offices became so over-staffed that individuals had to fight for desk space.

The developmental and welfare functions of the bureaucracy were soon to be joined by a third function, a patronage function. Loyal supporters of the Nasser regime were rewarded with government jobs. Political appointees had even less incentive to work hard than did officials appointed under the graduates policy, inasmuch as they had connections.

The political front was equally problematic as Nasser's state-sponsored political party, the ASU, failed to become the revolutionary instrument that he had hoped for (Baker 1978). Fearing any independent source of political authority, Nasser and his supporters kept the ASU under tight rein. The ASU also suffered from a shortage of cadres willing to dedicate their lives to the revolution and its objectives. While some Egyptians joined the ASU out of revolutionary fervor, most were motivated by expediency and opportunism. Membership in the ASU increased one's chances of securing a good position in the bureaucracy and provided connections, or "wasta." It was also the avenue to power at local and regional levels. Opportunists, unfortunately, make poor cadres. Their dedication was to themselves, not to the goals of the revolution. The ASU would thus become a large self-serving political bureaucracy not unlike the Communist Party bureaucracy of the Soviet Union.

In sum, the young revolutionaries who had seized power in the summer of 1952 had vowed to transform a backward and subservient monarchy into a modern industrial republic. After a lapse of 5000 years, Egypt would again be independent, prosperous, and proud. Theirs was to be more than a coup d'état; it was to be a revolution that would shake the very roots of Egyptian society.

In retrospect, there can be little doubt that the revolution of 1952 did shake Egyptian society to its roots. Monarchy gave way to a republic, capitalism to socialism, and the exploitation of the masses to social reform. Dramatic advances were made in education, social welfare, and industrialization. The Nasser years also did much to transform Egypt's political culture. The dazzling foreign policy successes of the early Nasser years created a sense of pride and national identity among a population long subject to foreign domination. Indeed, Egypt had become the vanguard of Arab nationalism. And yet, the aftermath of the June War of 1967 would find Egyptians neither proud, nor prosperous, nor fully independent. The war had destroyed the myth of nationalism, the Egyptian economy was stagnant, and Egyptian independence had become compromised by subservience to the Soviet Union.

The Nasser era was also to unleash a revolution of rising expectations with which it was ill prepared to cope. The masses had expected little from the monarchy. Nasser, by contrast, had promised to transform Egypt into a socialist paradise. Egypt was to become a land of plenty. The more difficult things became, the more grandiose the government's promises. The revolution in rising expectations was also fueled by the explosion in mass education. Educated people demand more of the government than illiterate citizens do.

It is also important to note that the Nasser revolution was not a proletarian revolution but a revolution by lower middle-class officers against a privileged aristocracy (Imam 1987). The masses benefited from the revolution, but were not part of the revolt. Nasser expropriated the largest of Egypt's land holdings but did not crush the capitalists as a class. Rather, Egypt's capitalist class was merely incorporated into the bureaucracy, a position it used to undermine the socialist regime from within (Ansari 1986).

The Era of Reassessment

Egypt's disastrous defeat in the June War led to a need for reassessment. Egyptian forces faced the Israelis across the Suez Canal, the economy was depressed, and the Egyptian population was demoralized. The military, once viewed as the saviors of Egypt, was disgraced, its officers scorned (Hamid 1992). Arab nationalism and socialism were equally victims of the war. Both had proven to be false gods. Abdul Hakim, the commander of the Egyptian forces and long-time friend of Nasser, committed suicide under somewhat clouded circumstances. Nasser resigned, but his resignation was rejected in the face of a mass outpouring of popular support. Nasser was a tarnished hero, but a hero nonetheless.

Surveying the wreckage of the 1967 war, Nasser launched a scathing critique of his own regime and called for the establishment of a democratic political system. His proposal was rejected by the members of the RCC, and prospects of implementing his reforms were overwhelmed by subsequent events. As Abdel Magid Farid recounts Nasser's comments at the meetings of the RCC:

> What is important is that the leaders do not criticize and carp at each other because it is we, the high-ranking officials in the system, who have caused the system to crack. Each one of us is destroying what another one is doing whereas all of us, at every level, should be aware of our united destiny.
>
> Moreover, sensitivity among us has reached the point where we are afraid to criticize each other at meetings. I believe that the only solution is for us to create a real "challenge" in the true sense of the word, to hasten to correct the mistakes that have been committed....
>
> When it was first formed there was a healthy political atmosphere within the Revolutionary Command Council: discussions among the members were at their most intense, and final decisions were taken by the majority. But matters progressed and later the state broke down into several undeclared parties: Abdel Hakim's party, Zakariya's party, al-Sadat's party, Ali Sabri's party, and so on. Abdel Hakim wanted to build himself up by using the army. Zakariya wanted to build himself up using the police. Al-Sadat wanted to build himself using the National Assembly, and Ali Sabri wanted to build himself up using the Arab Socialist Union. The system thus fell apart. Every group of us wanted to get rid of the other groups (Farid 1994, 87–88).

The War of Attrition   In 1969, his army having been rebuilt by the Soviet Union, Nasser launched what he referred to as the War of Attrition. The Egyptians could not force the Israelis from the Suez Canal, but artillery bombardments and lightning raids could make them pay dearly for their occupation. Nasser well understood that Israel was reluctant to accept heavy casualties and viewed this as the major chink in the Israeli armor.

The Egyptian attacks achieved their goal, but rather than forcing an Israeli withdrawal from the Canal Zone, they prompted an Israeli effort to bomb Egypt into submission, a bombing campaign that included not only military bases and industrial plants, but also the very environs of Cairo itself. Nasser was again rescued from devastation by the Soviets who, for all intents and purposes, took over Egypt's air defenses, including the piloting of Egyptian aircraft. A truce was declared in 1970, and Nasser died shortly thereafter. The dominant figure of modern Arab history had passed from the scene.

Nasser was succeeded in office by Anwar Sadat, his vice president and a charter member of the Free Officers. The situation facing Sadat was bleak. The devastation of the June War had been compounded by the devastation of the war of attrition. The Soviets had quelled the Israeli attack, but not without extending their control over the Nile republic. Two decades after the revolution, Egypt remained dependent on a foreign power. Indeed, at the time that Sadat assumed power there were some 21,000 Soviet "advisors" in Egypt (Zahran 1987).

Anwar Sadat, moreover, possessed none of Nasser's charisma. Many Egyptians viewed him as a weak individual who had been placed in office as a figurehead president until more powerful forces could sort out the course of the revolution (Heikal 1983). The Soviet Union distrusted Sadat, preferring that the Egyptian presidency go to an Egyptian military leader with communist leanings. American officials also had little faith in Sadat, assuming that his tenure in office would be brief (Heikal 1983).

Sadat's goals upon assuming office were economic development, freeing Egypt (and himself) from Soviet domination, and building a personal base of support among both the military and the public. The key to earning this support would be his ability to secure the return of the Sinai Peninsula, which had been occupied by Israel since the Six-Day War.

How this goal was to be accomplished was not clear. Israel showed little inclination to negotiate, the United States seemed disinclined to force an Israeli withdrawal, and the USSR was reluctant to see Egypt embark on another military misadventure.

Egypt's political institutions, moreover, were in disarray. The facade of guided democracy established by Nasser remained a farce, and the Egyptian bureaucracy became more lethargic than ever. If the ASU had served Nasser poorly, it served Sadat not at all. The leaders of the ASU opposed Sadat's presidency in 1970 and subsequently used the ASU apparatus to undermine his authority.

Sadat, however, proved to be a remarkably resilient individual. He crushed an attempted coup by leftist elements in the ASU in 1971 and moved rapidly to create a counterweight to the left by reviving the Muslim Brotherhood. The fundamentalist organization was not granted legal status, but it was allowed to establish branches in schools and universities and to perform welfare services for the poor of Egypt's teeming slums. From this base, the fundamentalists gained control of the "street" and were soon engaged in pitched battles with the Egyptian left. The situation, however, remained dicey.

Simultaneously, Sadat attempted to open negotiations with both Israel and the United States, but received encouragement from neither. In 1971, accordingly, Sadat signed a new 15-year treaty of cooperation and friendship with the USSR. The formal opening of the Aswan Dam was celebrated by the two countries the same year. While dramatic in scope, the new treaty was little more than a stopgap measure by both sides. The USSR was reluctant to weaken its access to the Mediterranean and assumed that Sadat's reign would be temporary. Sadat, by contrast, viewed the USSR with profound distrust and doubted that the USSR would allow an armed crossing of the Canal. This armed crossing was paramount, for unless Sadat could cross the Canal, neither he nor Egypt would be able to emerge from the shadow of the past. Much was promised by both sides, but little was delivered. Indeed, it was barely a year later that Sadat expelled the Soviets for "excessive caution" in regard to a future conflict with Israel. Rather than facilitating a new war with Israel, the Soviets had become an obstacle to Sadat's efforts to reclaim the Sinai Peninsula.

Sadat's eviction of the Soviets paved the way for a rapprochement with the United States, yet seemed to preclude any serious effort to force an Israeli withdrawal from the Canal Zone. How could Egypt attack without Soviet support? It was the Soviets, after all, who had built, trained, and armed the Egyptian military. Without a credible show of force, Israel had little cause to take the Egyptian leader seriously. Much the same was true of an Egyptian population who had watched Sadat's much-heralded "year of decision" pass without action. The domestic situation had continued to deteriorate, as had Sadat's grip on power.

In retrospect, the unknown element in the equation appears to have been King Faisal of Saudi Arabia. Relieved at the passing of Nasser, the Saudi monarch found the moderation of Sadat much to his liking. He certainly had little desire to see the rebirth of a radical regime in Egypt. He also understood that the Arabs could not normalize relations with Israel from a position of weakness. A successful crossing of the Canal by Egyptian forces, in Faisal's logic, would shore up Sadat's tottering regime and establish the Arabs as a credible fighting force. It was for these reasons, then, that Saudi Arabia largely financed preparations for a limited Arab attack on Israeli positions along the Suez

Canal and the Golan Heights (Syria). One could also speculate that the Saudis were also behind the expulsion of the Soviets. Israeli intelligence monitored the Arab buildup but found it difficult to give credence to an Egyptian army that it had humiliated so easily in the past. The Israelis also found it difficult to envision an Egyptian attack without Soviet support.

When the joint Egyptian-Syrian attack occurred on October 6, 1973, the Jewish holy day of Yom Kippur, Israel was caught unprepared. The Egyptian army displayed consummate skill in crossing the Canal, and Israeli forces were forced to retreat with heavy losses. Egyptian forces had also benefited from Soviet support despite the strained relations between the two countries (Hermann, Hermann, and Anderson 1992). Without massive US aid to Israel and profound confusion in the relations between Egypt and Syria, the situation could have been far worse. Israeli forces eventually regrouped, and by the time the hostilities ceased, they had occupied yet more Egyptian territory. The damage, however, had been done. The Egyptians had demonstrated their capacity to fight, and the myth of Israeli invincibility had been shattered. Saudi Arabia, Libya, and other oil-producing countries, while not engaging in the hostilities, slashed oil exports to the United States and its European allies. At long last, the Arabs had used their oil weapon. The economic structure of the industrial world was shaken, and world attention was focused on Sadat.

The United States arranged for a withdrawal of Israeli forces from the Canal Zone in January of 1974, and in June of the same year the United States and Egypt reestablished diplomatic relations. Egypt had begun its slide into the American orbit. Over the next five years the process would accelerate dramatically.

Egypt's victory in the October War also freed Sadat from Nasser's shadow and transformed him into the "hero of Suez." His popularity soaring, Sadat crushed his opponents and proclaimed sweeping economic reforms designed to revive Egypt's moribund economy.

Launched in 1974, the goal of Sadat's infitah, or new economic opening, was to revive the Egyptian economy by lifting Nasser's ban on capitalism (Gillespie 1984). Henceforth, Egypt would possess a mixed economy in which private-sector firms would be free to compete with the public sector. American aid and Western investment, Sadat promised, would make Egypt the economic hub of the Middle East. Egypt, moreover, had traded guns for butter (Waterbury 1978). The "peace dividend" would allow Egypt to scale back its military expenditures and concentrate on economic development. Prosperity was assured. Also assured was a revival of Egypt's capitalist class as a further counterweight to Sadat's leftist opponents (Imam 1987).

While Sadat was going from victory to victory on the international front, the domestic scene had started to unravel. Having assisted Sadat in crushing the left, the Muslim Brotherhood and its offshoots now represented the best-organized political force in Egypt other than the army. There was also growing evidence of fundamentalist influence in the latter. By the mid-1970s, the Islamic groups had sensed their growing power and had begun to press Sadat, who had been a member of the Muslim Brotherhood during the pre-revolutionary era, to Islamize the Egyptian political system.

Sadat attempted to counter the growing pressure from the Muslim Brotherhood by reviving the Arab Socialist Union, albeit with a leadership loyal to himself rather than to his opponents. Sadat, like Nasser, hoped that the reformulated ASU would provide broad-based mass support for his regime. It did not. Much as before, the revived ASU served as little more than a machine for distributing patronage to Sadat's supporters. The public remained apathetic.

Sadat also sought to block the growing influence of the Fundamentalists by strengthening his infitah. Beyond an attempt to rejuvenate the Egyptian economy, Sadat now looked to the infitah as a means of reestablishing Egypt's capitalist class as a political force in Egypt. Well educated, well organized, well financed, and very Westernized, the revived bourgeoisie or capitalist class would serve as a counterweight to the Fundamentalists.

The infitah stimulated limited economic growth but severely aggravated social tensions in Egypt. The new capitalist class acquired extraordinary wealth that it displayed with unabashed ostentation. The lifestyle of the ordinary Egyptian, by contrast, continued to deteriorate. The gap between rich and poor was widening and becoming ever more visible. Class tensions came to a peak in 1977 when, upon the strong urging of the US and the International Monetary Fund, Sadat cut government subsidies on bread and other vital substances. Riots erupted throughout the length and breadth of Egypt and were quelled only by the cancellation of the economic reforms (Gillespie 1984). Sadat had violated the social contract forged between Nasser and the Egyptian people.

Shaken by the riots, Sadat promised the Egyptian population a return to democracy. Egypt, Sadat declared, would have three independent political parties: a party of the left, a party of the capitalist right, and a party of the center. Sadat disavowed membership in any of the three parties, claiming to stand above politics. Virtually all government officials, however, became members of the centrist party, it being well understood that this was the party of Sadat. The Wafd Party also resurfaced in 1977, calling itself the New Wafd Party. Egypt had thus evolved into a qualified multi-party state, although the communists and Nasserites were still proscribed from forming an independent political party, as was the Muslim Brotherhood.

In July of 1978, Sadat made yet another about-face on the domestic front, announcing the creation of the National Democratic Party (NDP), of which he would be president. Members of the centrist party, barely a year old, resigned to become members of Sadat's National Democratic Party. The NDP took over the buildings and organizational network of the now-defunct ASU, providing a remarkable continuity in membership and party organization between Sadat's ASU and the NDP. The more things changed, the more they stayed the same. Egypt had become a multi-party state, but only one party mattered.

It was at this moment that Sadat stunned the Egyptian public by proclaiming his willingness to go "even unto" the Israeli parliament in his unrelenting search for peace. Menachem Begin, the Israeli prime minister, provided the requisite invitation and Sadat duly addressed the Israeli Knesset in November of 1977. Some observers accused Sadat of attempting to quell the domestic storm by creating an international circus. Others suggested that Sadat was on a massive ego trip fueled by the international media and the blandishments of US presidents (Interviews, Cairo, 1977–84). Still others viewed him as a realist who saw peace as a requirement for the development of Egypt and the Arab World (Ibrahim, Saad E. 1996).

Sadat's address to the Israeli Knesset led to the Camp David Peace Accords sponsored by President Carter. Entitled "A Framework for Peace in the Middle East," the accords would lead to the signing of a formal peace treaty between Israel and Egypt on March 26, 1979. Much of the Sinai had already been returned to Egypt, and the rest would be forthcoming in stages.

While the world applauded Sadat's dramatic peace initiatives—both he and Begin would receive Nobel Peace Prizes—conditions on the domestic front continued to deteriorate. Fundamentalist agitation bordered on open warfare and by 1980 had led to the cancellation of all party activity. In September of 1981 Sadat ordered the arrest of more than 1500 political activists, many of them Muslim Fundamentalists. He was assassinated a month later. The Egypt of Sadat had now become the Egypt of Mubarak.

Egypt Under Mubarak: The Eras of Islamic Resurgence and the New World Order

The passing of Sadat found Egypt in a quandary. Dependence on the Soviet Union had given way to dependence on the United States. Peace had been made with Israel, but Egypt had been ostracized from the Arab world, its natural constituency. Islamic Fundamentalists, flushed with victory in Iran, now viewed Egypt as their next target. The assassination of Sadat had merely been the opening salvo in what promised to be an enduring conflict.

Egypt's political institutions, moreover, were in disarray and offered little support to the new president. As Mubarak summarized the situation a few years after taking office:

> We had before us (upon assuming office) the prospect of crumbling public services and utilities. The situation was the result of years of accumulated paralysis and neglect. Citizens complained of the situation from the moment they opened their eyes in the morning until they returned from work. The flow of water was inadequate and irregular. Electric current fluctuated, and extended blackouts were common. Communications moved at a snail's pace. Roads were impassable. Television was limited. The decay of the sewer system turned some streets and quarters into swamps....
>
> Medical equipment in public hospitals is old and in short supply. Public services (bureaucracy) oppress the citizens with routine and delay. Free education has lost much of its effectiveness and the expense of college education is oppressive to Egyptian families. Then there are the problems of housing shortages, rising prices, vanishing goods, and of houses collapsing on their inhabitants. The list of problems our people complain of is endless, yet they are forced to put up with them (Mubarak 1985).

If the Mubarak regime were to survive, accordingly, it would have to strengthen both Egypt's political system and its economy. The two processes were intertwined, for the Egyptian population had wearied of slogans and symbolic gestures. Either the government would meet the needs of its population or its survival would be in question.

Neither political nor economic reform, however, would be easy. Movement toward greater democracy threatened to empower the Fundamentalists. Mubarak, moreover, had little faith in the Egyptian masses. As he would explain to the US Congress:

> This country was under pressure for years and years, and when you open the gate for freedom, you will find many terrible things taking place. If you have a dam and keep the water until it begins to overflow, and then you open the gates, it will drown many people. We have to give a gradual dose so people can swallow it and understand it. The Egyptians are not Americans (*NYT*[7], Oct. 12, 1993, A3).

The economic situation was equally dicey (Harik 1997). The social contract introduced by Nasser had provided Egyptians with jobs and

[7]The *New York Times.*

subsidies in return for their patience. In spite of the infitah, things had remained much the same under Sadat. Nothing short of drastic economic reform was likely to revive Egypt's moribund economy. Serious economic reform, however, required a cutback in the subsidies that now consumed some 30 percent of the Egyptian budget. It also required trimming the Egyptian bureaucracy and transforming Egypt's state-owned industries into viable enterprises. This latter transformation, in turn, could be achieved only by closing the most inefficient operations and trimming the work force of the others. Such measures, however, would swell the ranks of Egypt's unemployed, already hovering in the 25-percent range. Reducing subsidies, moreover, was fraught with danger, a fact that had been amply demonstrated by the bread riots of 1977. A repeat performance could well throw the country into chaos.

It was within this environment, then, that Hosni Mubarak assumed the presidency of Egypt in October of 1981. The transition was orderly, but the underlying tensions could not be disguised. Mubarak, like Sadat before him, continued to rule under the "emergency" provisions of the Egyptian constitution, but promised progress toward democracy as soon as the country had returned to normal. He also called upon Egyptians "to work harder and do more." The economic situation was grave, he said, adding that "Egypt's problems cannot be solved by the government alone." These were sobering words for an Egyptian population long accustomed to flamboyant promises and inflammatory rhetoric. In the meantime, Mubarak attempted to split the ranks of the Fundamentalists by distinguishing between the Muslim Brotherhood from the more radical groups that had emerged during the 1970s. While the latter were prosecuted as the assassins of Sadat, the Muslim Brotherhood was allowed to organize on a quasi-legal basis.

Parliamentary elections were held in 1984, and the Muslim Brotherhood, although proscribed from becoming a formal political party, forged an electoral alliance with the Wafd, a recently rehabilitated remnant of the Wafd of the pre-Nasser era. While the nature of the Egyptian electoral system assured victory for the ruling National Democratic Party, the joint Wafd/Muslim Brotherhood ticket displayed unexpected strength and threatened to make Egyptian elections something more than a charade (Makram-Ebeid 1996).

Despite Government efforts to split the Fundamentalists, the ensuing years would witness a gradual upsurge in political violence, much of it centering on Islamic issues. Particularly serious was the 1986 riot by Egyptian security guards, a special low-level military unit used by the Ministry of the Interior to guard public buildings. Staffed by young recruits, the security guards went on a four-day rampage in which bars, tourist hotels, and other symbols of Westernization offensive to the Fundamentalists were burned. Order was restored by the army, but the regime's authority was clearly shaken.

The 1987 Parliamentary elections saw the Muslim Brotherhood switch its support to the Labor Party, once a party of the left, now brandishing the Brotherhood's slogan "Islam is the Solution." Even a sham democracy was becoming problematic for the Mubarak regime.

Also problematic was growing pressure from the United States and the international community to end Egypt's economic chaos by privatizing its economy. With the 1986 riots still fresh in his mind, however, Mubarak was reluctant to further inflame mass emotions by threatening the social safety net of an Egyptian population already living on the brink of disaster. In Mubarak's words:

> I wonder about those who advocate selling the public sector, because this would be a dangerous step taken at the cost of the simple citizen, because the private sector operates according to the needs of the market, and its prices are high. So what is the simple citizen to do? Frankly, he will starve. From here social envy starts and crime flourishes. This envy has serious effects on the social structure. The public sector regulates the private one, thus offering goods to the public at reasonable prices, because state control is a must. Selling the public sector would create a socio-economic problem. I am careful to maintain social peace and balance. These are the fundamentals for me. So I reiterate that the public sector is an essential foundation of the Egyptian social and economic structure. As for tourism, we have opened the door for investments and handed over several hotels to the private sector. But as for national industries essential for further production, they must remain in public ownership (Mubarak 1987, 28–33).

Another parliamentary election was held in 1990, but it was boycotted by the major opposition parties, who condemned it as a farce. Mubarak lamented the boycott but made no concessions on election procedures.

Although election procedures precluded the Brotherhood from gaining more than symbolic representation in the Parliament, it had fared much better in organizational elections held to determine the leadership of Egypt's major professional associations. As described by Joel Campagna:

> Since the early 1980s, the group made important inroads within the governing councils of the nation's professional associations in a trend that has continued to the present day. By 1990 it had won electoral victories that resulted in political control of most major professional associations for doctors, engineers, dentists, merchants and pharmacists. In September 1992, it gained a majority of seats (14 out of 25) on the ruling council of the prestigious bar association—an event which, according to one

journalist, sent "shock waves through liberal and secular circles in Egypt and elsewhere in the Arab world" (Hubbel 1992). The Brotherhood's bar association victory was particularly significant, for it marked the end of a close relationship between the ruling National Democratic Party (NDP) and the lawyers' association, which in the past had served to legitimize government legislation and other policies (ibid). Moreover, through its new position of power in the association, the Brotherhood hoped to use its influence with judges and legislators in order to further its aim of implementing Islamic law into the Egyptian constitution (Campagna 1996, 289–290).

Egypt's participation in the 1991 Gulf War as an ally of the United States also played poorly with Egyptian citizens and might have led to widespread rioting had the war not ended so quickly (Interviews, Cairo, 1991). The Fundamentalists capitalized on this sentiment to press their attack on the government. As described by Aoude:

> Until July 1992, Islamic forces controlled many villages and small towns in several governorates in Egypt. In some cases they had political power that paralleled the Egyptian state (Interviews, 1992). They fomented religious conflict through armed attacks against Christians, primarily in Upper Egypt. They assassinated their critics, as for an example in June 1992 when they assassinated a major liberal thinker, Dr. Farag Fudah. A few days later they assassinated several people in the town of Dayrut, most of whom were Christians.
>
> Until the current crackdown against the fundamentalists, security forces were known to turn the other way when Islamists broke the law and threatened members of local communities. Some members of the security forces and the police even encouraged the increasing influence of the Islamists (Aoude 1994, 19).

By 1993, the Egyptian Minister of Interior would openly declare "We are at war. People will have to die on both sides" (*NYT*, Nov. 28, 1993, A8). Mubarak's response to the escalation in Fundamentalist violence was brutal, but less than effective. Each claim of government victory was followed with a new round of assassinations and attacks on foreign tourists. The latter devastated the Egyptian economy as tourist revenues dropped by some 40 percent.

The same period saw the Mubarak regime change its views on economic reform and become the champion of privatization (Harik 1997). Large public-sector enterprises were put on the auction block, and the Egyptian currency became freely convertible. These and other reforms, however, were not applied with enthusiasm, and Western hopes for a wholesale restructuring of the Egyptian economy were disappointed. Nevertheless, the transition from socialism to capitalism was building steam (Lofgren 1993).

Mubarak ran for a third term as president in 1993, a process the *New York Times* described as "a strange, ungainly ballet where choreographed admirers are herded in from the wings to pay homage to a leading man with no rival" (*NYT*, Oct. 4, 1993). *The Middle East Times* also reported that the heads of Egypt's public-sector enterprises were ordered to get out the vote "or else," and that the Higher Council of Youth and Sport, a government agency, offered a "T-shirt for LE 10"— about three US dollars—to youths attending a pro-Mubarak rally in the Cairo Stadium (Apiku 1999).

It was within this environment that the Mubarak regime entered the 1995 parliamentary elections. Egyptians were accustomed to electoral fraud, but its magnitude in the 1995 elections shocked even supporters of the regime. *The Middle East Times* reported that in some areas of Cairo, "The police ejected the opposition, shut the polling stations, and filled the ballot boxes to the brim" (Dec. 10–16, 1995). Other observers reported some 620 injuries and 45 deaths, not to mention the incarceration of some 100 members of the Muslim Brotherhood running as independents (Makram-Ebeid 1996; Campagna 1996). Not surprisingly, the ruling NDP emerged with 96 percent of the seats in the Majlis as-Saab, the lower house of the Egyptian Parliament.

Mubarak was elected to a fourth term of office in 1999, with procedures not markedly different from those of 1993. Mubarak's fourth term in office has been characterized by two major themes: the destruction of the Fundamentalists and the pursuit of capitalism at the expense of democracy. The attack on Fundamentalist terrorism was particularly vicious, but by 1998 the level of violence had abated and Mubarak claimed victory over his adversaries. The Fundamentalist threat had not vanished, but Fundamentalist leaders had been forced to change tactics, a topic that will be elaborated upon shortly. Even in this regard, however, all was not well. September of 1999 would witness another attempt on Mubarak's life, albeit by a lone knife-wielding assailant. Mubarak survived with a small cut on his hand, and the event was written off as the work of a lunatic (Reuters, *DS*, Sept. 9, 1999). Be this as it may, the assassination attempt raised serious questions about the ability of the Egyptian security services to protect the president, and heads rolled (Apiku 1999). The emergency laws that had been in place since the assassination of Sadat were also extended, prompting an opposition parliamentarian to comment, "You are sending a message to the outside world that you have not smashed the terrorists like you claimed and that the country is not stable" (cited in Apiku, 2000, 9, www).

The assassination attempt also raised serious questions about the fate of Egyptian politics after Mubarak. The Egyptian president had yet to name a vice president, and no heir apparent was in sight, although Mubarak's son was appointed to the governing board of the NDP in the spring of 2000. Satirical comments on the elevation of Mubarak's son led to the arrest of Saad Eddin Ibrahim in the summer of 2000. Chiding Mubarak, it must be noted in fairness, was not Ibrahim's only crime. He had also produced a video instructing Egyptians on their voting rights (*NYT*, July 10, 2000, A10).

The apparent tranquility of Egyptian politics was shattered in the fall of 2000 by two events that threatened the stability of the Mubarak regime. The first of these events was the eruption of violence in the Israeli-occupied West Bank and Gaza Strip, portions of which were nominally under the control of the Palestinian Authority. The Israelis responded with an overwhelming display of force that left more than 504 Palestinians dead during the first eight months of the uprising, approximately one-third of them under the age of 18. Israelis suffered some 88 deaths during the same period, a topic discussed at length in the next chapter (*NYT*, May 24, www). Riots protesting the Israeli action flared in Egyptian universities and were mirrored by massive protests following Friday prayers at Al-Azhar mosque, Egypt's leading Islamic shrine. Mubarak, the strongest supporter of peace with Israel in the Arab world, withdrew the Egyptian ambassador from Tel Aviv in protest, a move taken over the strong objections of the United States. Diplomatic relations with Israel were not severed, but a key pillar of regional stability had threatened to collapse. In reality, Mubarak had little choice in the matter, well understanding that protests of any variety could soon turn against the government.

The second event that threatened to alter the course of Egyptian politics was the 2000 parliamentary elections, a ponderous event that stretched over the better part of a month as the regime struggled to avoid the violence of the 1995 elections, which had resulted in 45 deaths and severe criticism of the security forces. Stung by the farcical nature of the 1995 elections—the ruling National Democratic Party received 95 percent of the seats in the People's Assembly—Mubarak decreed that it would be the judiciary and not the security forces of the Ministry of Interior that monitored the polling booths. This action was a major step toward greater democracy, and it stimulated unaccustomed interest in an electoral process normally viewed with apathy and cynicism.

The elections were contested by the National Democratic Party, a broad range of ineffectual opposition parties, and a staggering array of independent candidates, many of whom represented the banned Muslim Brotherhood. The first round of elections resulted in a crushing defeat for the NDP, with the ruling party capturing only 27 percent of the available seats and many of its senior leaders losing their seats in the Assembly. The independents, including seven Muslim Brothers, swept a majority of the seats, facing the NDP with the prospect of minority status in the parliament if the same trend continued in the second and third stages of the elections.

The situation, however, was not as dire as it appeared at first blush. No sooner had the results of the first stage of the election been announced than the vast majority of the independents elected to the Assembly "joined" the NDP. Some were true independents who shifted to the NDP for opportunistic reasons, but most were long-time members of the NDP whose flawed backgrounds were an embarrassment to a party suffering from accusations of corruption and influence peddling. In a much-publicized effort to clean up its image prior to the elections, the NDP purged many of its less savory candidates from the party's lists and encouraged them to run as independents. This strategy had the added advantage of confusing the voters and thereby assuring that the party would win its fair share of the seats.

The same process repeated itself during the second and third stages of the elections, with the Muslim Brotherhood picking up more than enough seats to make it the leading opposition group in the People's Assembly. It would undoubtedly have received more seats if the security forces had not forcibly kept Brotherhood supporters away from the polling booths. As a member of the British House of Lords who observed the elections would note, the Ministry of Justice supervised the inside of the polling booth but not the outside (Khan 2000). When the votes were finally tallied, the NDP had won 388 seats in the People's Assembly, a sharp drop from the 410 that it had won in the 1995 election. The critical point to be made, however, was that a majority of the Egyptian electorate had voted against the NDP and that it was only the treachery of the pseudo-independents that had allowed the party to retain its dominance of the Assembly (Sal'eh 2000).

The 2000 elections had also seen Jamal Mubarak, the president's son, stake his claim for leadership of the Party and the country once his father had stepped down. Proclaiming himself the spokesman of Egypt's youth, he had conducted a series of youth conferences for younger political leaders throughout the length and breadth of Egypt in the four months leading up to the election, the last of which was entitled "Returning Hope to the National Democratic Party" (Jabar 2000a).

As the magnitude of the NDP's debacle became known, Jamal Mubarak seized the moment to condemn the NDP for having totally lost contact with the Egyptian population and called for the immediate replacement of a discredited leadership with younger cadres of whom he was the obvious spokesman (Jabar 2000a). He also complained that people were fed up with a party they viewed as corrupt and self-serving, further noting that the extension of the emergency laws did little to help its image. Given the nature of Egyptian politics, such a statement would have been unthinkable without the approval of his father.

Other observers would also note that the senior Mubarak's tepid response to Israeli actions against the Palestinians had resulted in votes for the Muslim Brotherhood and that the withdrawal of the Egyptian ambassador had come only after the outbreak of riots.

EGYPTIAN POLITICS TODAY AND BEYOND

The eras of Nasser and Sadat were punctuated by dramatic events, each of which threatened to alter the course of Egyptian history. Mubarak's 20-year reign, by contrast, has seen few such events. Rather, it has been a cautious regime that has found it difficult to take decisive action. Progress has been made in Egypt's transition from socialism to capitalism, but it has been slow and halting. Progress toward democracy, once substantial, has ground to a halt. Even the Government's war on the Fundamentalists has been marked by caution and apprehension. In many ways the regime appears to be immobilized, bending to pressures when they become insurmountable but lacking a clear vision of Egypt's future. Incrementalism and "muddling thorough" may be acceptable strategies for the rich countries of the First World, but Egypt does not enjoy that luxury.

In the remainder of this chapter, we will explore possible explanations for the profound caution of the Mubarak presidency. In the process we will have the opportunity to examine Egypt's political institutions, the actors that give life to those institutions, and the broader cultural, economic, and international pressures that shape Egyptian politics.

Elites and Institutions

As all roads in Egypt lead to Mubarak, the logical place to seek clues to the plodding nature of the Mubarak regime is within the personality of Mubarak himself. Rather than being a visionary on the scale of Nasser or Sadat, Mubarak seems to view himself as a senior bureaucrat assigned the responsibility of guiding the ship of state through troubled waters. Far more cautious than his predecessors, he proceeds slowly, making narrow, step-by-step decisions based upon consultations with a wide variety of groups. He also tends to read reports in great detail and does not like surprises. For better or for worse, Mubarak's personality style lends itself to incrementalism. It is not clear, however, that his incremental mode of decision making is conducive to solving Egypt's massive social and economic problems. Massive problems often require radical solutions.

Many observers also believe that the broader elite surrounding Mubarak has lost its zeal (Jabar 2000a). While the regime continues to rule in the name of Nasser's revolution, little of that revolution remains. Indeed, one gets the impression that Mubarak's supporters are more concerned with clinging to their privileged positions than they are with finding solutions to Egypt's massive social and economic problems (Maisa 1993). This point is critical to understanding the immobility of Egyptian politics, for the secondary elite under Mubarak plays a greater role in the decision-making process than it did under either Nasser or Sadat. This is partly a function of Mubarak's personality, but it also reflects the greater complexity of Egyptian politics in the present era.

This secondary elite during the Mubarak regime includes senior military officials, the inner circle of the ruling National Democratic Party, the Presidential Office, heads of key bureaucratic agencies, and senior members of the Islamic religious establishment. Collectively, they represent the pillars of the Mubarak regime.

The Presidential Office, for example, is a special bureaucracy of several thousand members who assist the president in political and security matters (Gomaa 1991). It also includes a special intelligence service and a special presidential army, the Republican Guards. Its leaders serve as "gatekeepers," regulating access to the president and controlling the information the president receives on key issues.

The heads of Egypt's major bureaucratic agencies, in turn, advise the president on key policy issues. Collectively they form a cabinet headed by a prime minister whose major responsibility is guiding the president's program through a subservient parliament dominated by the semi-official National Democratic Party.[8] Prime ministers are changed at will, and the formation of a new "Government" is often used to signal a change in policy. If the new policies are successful, the president takes the credit. If the policies fail, the prime minister and cabinet take the blame and give way to a new "team."

The details of most economic policies, for example, are crafted by the prime minister in association with those ministers charged with

---

[8]There has yet to be a female prime minister in Egypt.

regulating diverse aspects of the Egyptian economy. This group constitutes the core of what is referred to as the "economic club" (Bahgat 1991). The president sets the tone, while the prime minister and cabinet work out the details (Bahgat 1991). Much also depends on the ability of the ministers to force the president's policies through a moribund bureaucracy, a challenging task at best.

The National Democratic Party   The National Democratic Party, for its part, is Mubarak's link to the civilian power structure at the national and local levels. Much like the Arab Socialist Union of the Nasser and Sadat eras, the National Democratic Party is a massive political bureaucracy. Village and neighborhood organizations form the base of the NDP's organizational pyramid, followed in turn by organizations at the district (markaz) and provincial (governorate) levels. This elaborate organization structure is capped by a national secretariat headed ultimately by President Mubarak, the president of the Party.

The role of the NDP leadership is to provide Egypt's quasi-military regime with resounding majorities in the parliament. Possessing little in the way of a concrete ideology, Egyptians are attracted to the NDP by the lavish use of "wasta." The members of the NDP enjoy greater access to government jobs and receive preferential treatment in their dealings with Egypt's all-pervasive bureaucracy. Both concerns are of vital importance in a country in which little can be accomplished without "connections" of one form or another. The NDP also assures its dominance by providing landowners, businessmen, and other notables with privileged positions in the Party apparatus. Mubarak's son even complained that he had heard a provincial leader brag that he had brought a drug dealer into the Party because he had a large following (Jabar 2000a). The notables reciprocate by using their considerable influence to "encourage" voting for the NDP. Election laws have also been manipulated in favor of the NDP. Until recently, for example, election laws required that a party receive 8 percent of the vote to be represented in the parliament. The votes of parties receiving less than 8 percent automatically went to the majority party, i.e., the NDP. It is difficult to summarize Egyptian electoral laws, for each new election brings a new set of electoral procedures designed to serve the interests of the NDP. Many are eventually declared unconstitutional, but by that time a new election is on the horizon and the process repeats itself.

The NDP's domination of the People's Assembly has enabled Mubarak to rule under the guise of parliamentary democracy without fear of serious opposition to his policies. Much like the other pillars of the Mubarak regime, however, the NDP is also experiencing deep internal divisions. Personality conflicts abound, younger leaders are frustrated by the dominance of the Party's old guard, liberal and conservative wings of the party spar over economic and social policy, and local leaders chafe under the centralized control of national leadership. Recent efforts to increase the membership base of the party have only increased these conflicts (*Al-Ahram*, Oct. 21, 1992). Whether recent shakeups in the Party's politburo—including the addition of more Copts and women—can alleviate the tension remains to be seen (*Cairo Times*, Feb. 10, 2000, www). Finally, the party has suffered from the same lethargy and opportunism that beset the ASU. It is a party motivated by patronage rather than ideology. Indeed, it is difficult to pin down precisely what the party stands for, other than perpetuation of a status quo that is becoming increasingly untenable.

This fact was made patently clear by the Party's defeat in the 2000 legislative elections, with the NDP receiving only 38 percent of the seats in the People's Assembly. The independents were the big winners with 58 percent of the seats in the Assembly. The fact that 218 independents joined the NDP after the election did not alter the reality that an overwhelming majority of Egypt's electorate had voted against the ruling party (*Al-Ahram Weekly*, Nov. 2000, 23–29). The results would have been worse if the security forces had not harassed opposition voters, particularly those suspected of being sympathetic to the Muslim Brotherhood. This task was not inordinately difficult, for male supporters of the Muslim Brotherhood generally wear beards to symbolize their attachment to the Islamic faith.

In the final analysis, the NDP emerged with 388 seats (85 percent) in the Assembly, but it was a much chastised NDP that could no longer pretend to have a popular mandate for its policies. The opposition parties won a combined total of 16 seats, the Muslim Brotherhood 17, and the true independents 17.[9]

Jamal Mubarak, the president's son, immediately called for sweeping reforms, accusing the NDP of lethargy, stagnation, insensitivity, venality, and incompetence. In particular, he complained that the Party had been deluded by its "paper membership" into believing that it had the support of the masses. In reality, he noted, the Party was dominated by a class of discredited leaders who had lost touch with Egypt's changing circumstances. He went on to say that the Party had failed to exercise care in the selection of its candidates and that the Party had lost its cadre of dedicated party workers. The NDP, he said, could not sustain its dominant position in Egyptian politics without a gigantic ef-

---

[9]Ten additional members of the Assembly were appointed by the president, a prerogative specified by the Egyptian constitution. Two additional seats were contested and not included in the total.

fort to build a new generation of younger cadres who were in touch with Egypt and its problems (Jabar 2000a, paraphrased by the author). Other reports had accused provincial leaders of selling places on the Party's list, that being a near guarantee of election to the People's Assembly, at least until the debacle of the 2000 elections (El Ebraash 2000).

The Islamic Establishment   The Islamic establishment consists of the senior Islamic religious figures in Egypt, the foremost of whom are the Minister of Religious Endowments, the Grand Mufti or Judge, and the Rector of Al-Azhar, Cairo's renowned Islamic university. These leaders, in turn, are surrounded by a variety of senior religious scholars collectively referred to as the ulema. The government plays a dominant role in the appointment of senior religious officials, thereby assuring that the religious establishment is headed by individuals whose views are compatible with those of the president. Under Nasser, the Islamic establishment was headed by religious scholars who shared the regime's reformist views. Under Sadat and Mubarak, it has become more conservative. Whatever the case, all Egyptian governments have sought the blessing of the ulema for their policies.

Egypt's religious elite has long enjoyed considerable influence under the Mubarak regime, and the regime goes out of its way to stress its religious credentials (Bianchi 1989). Mosques are built and maintained by the Ministry of Waqfs (religious endowments), Al-Azhar University has been expanded and glorified, Islamic programs abound on Egyptian television, and Egypt maintains a separate Koranic radio station. The Egyptian media also breaks for prayers five times a day, in line with Islamic traditions. The role of the religious establishment, for its part, is to persuade devout Muslims that working within their traditional Islamic institutions is a more effective strategy for achieving Islamic goals than the violence of the extremists. Senior Islamic leaders have free access to Mubarak, and their influence has increased in response to the Fundamentalist threat. The very closeness of the Islamic establishment to the Mubarak regime, however, has diminished its moral authority. As Mullaney writes:

> The Egyptian "ulama" are faced with a number of serious problems, e.g., role conflict, morale, ideological land class cleavages, deprofessionalization. In the opinion of this writer, the most debilitating problem, however, is that of leadership. Current leadership, embodied particularly in the persons of the rector of al-Azhar and the mufti, is deemed weak and ineffective. The harshest critics within the Islamic opposition characterize the existing leadership as politically subservient, unprincipled, morally bankrupt, even hypocritical and opportunistic (Mullaney 1995, 233–234).

The Military   Of the five pillars of the Mubarak regime, the military is by far the most important. Egypt continues to be a predominantly military regime, some progress toward democracy notwithstanding. Most of Mubarak's senior advisors are drawn from the military, as are key figures in the Presidential Office, the bureaucracy, the NDP, and the local government apparatus. This is particularly true of governors and district officials. Military officers enjoy subsidized housing and every other perk that a poor society can bestow upon them.

In spite of its privileged position in Egyptian society, the Egyptian military is not necessarily of one mind. Many officers are loyal to Mubarak, but others incline toward the Nasserites, the New Wafd, or the Islamic Fundamentalists. Indeed, the military leadership has long been restrained in its criticism of the Fundamentalist movement, and most operations against the Fundamentalists have been carried out by special security forces under the control of the Minister of Interior rather than by the army. Information concerning this and most other military questions, unfortunately, remains limited. Suffice it to say that the Mubarak regime works hard to assure the officer corps that its privileged and influential role in Egyptian politics will remain intact.

Conflicts within the secondary elite, then, have more than contributed to the immobility and confusion of the Mubarak regime. To make matters worse, the presidential office, the military, the NDP, the religious establishment, and the bureaucracy have all attempted to "capture" Mubarak as a means of increasing their own power. Mubarak, like his predecessors, has attempted to avoid manipulation or "capture" by pitting one agency against another (Gomaa 1993, personal communication with the author). This grand balancing act provides the president with multiple sources of information, but it also creates confusion within the ranks of the government.

Political Institutions

The incremental nature of Mubarak's decision making is also dictated by the weakness of his political institutions, particularly the parliament, the courts, and the bureaucracy. The bureaucracy, which was discussed earlier, remains moribund. Nevertheless, it continues to absorb massive resources and generally serves as a brake on Egypt's social and economic development. It is difficult to reform the bureaucracy, as many of its key members were appointed for political reasons and their removal would threaten the regime (Gomaa 1991). The regime is also reluctant to exacerbate already severe problems of unemployment for fear of stimulating popular unrest.

The Parliament On paper, the Egyptian parliament differs little from the parliaments of Europe on which it has been patterned. A People's Assembly (Majlis as-Saab), or lower house, is popularly elected, while the Consultative Assembly (Majlis as-Shoura), or upper house, is largely appointed. The Egyptian Constitution stipulates that the People's Assembly (Majlis as-Saab) must approve all legislation including the annual budget (Republic of Egypt: parliament.gov.eg., www). As in the US, a presidential veto can be overridden by a vote of two-thirds of its members. This, however, has yet to happen. Laws enacted by the president during periods of emergency rule must be submitted to the People's Assembly for ratification once the emergency period has ended. Both the prime minister and the members of his cabinet are responsible before the People's Assembly. Confidence may be withdrawn from the Government as a whole (prime minister and cabinet) or from an individual minister. In the latter instance, the minister in question is forced to resign but the Government remains in place. Members of the People's Assembly also possess the right to interrogate ministers and the senior members of ministerial staffs. Finally, the People's Assembly plays an important role in the nomination of the president. If a president dies, resigns, or is incapable of fulfilling presidential responsibilities, the president of the People's Assembly serves as the head of government while the members of the Assembly nominate a new candidate for the presidency. Only one person is nominated for the presidency, and that person is presented to the public by means of a plebiscite, in which the public may vote for acceptance or rejection. If the public rejects the nomination (this has never happened), the People's Assembly will nominate a second candidate who will again be presented to the public in a plebiscite.

The constitutional powers of the People's Assembly, unfortunately, are largely theoretical. It is the leader of the National Democratic Party—President Mubarak—who has the final say on what legislation the Assembly will pass. Somewhat fair legislative elections, moreover, have only become a feature of Egyptian politics in the last few years, and even these elections have been structured to assure overwhelming victories by the semi-official NDP. The Muslim Brotherhood, Egypt's dominant opposition movement, is banned from direct political participation. Voter turnout has traditionally been low, and opposition parties often choose to boycott elections as a means of protesting questionable electoral procedures. Needless to say, the 2000 elections have brought new life to Egypt's electoral process (*Al-Ahram Weekly*, Nov. 9–15, 2000, www).

In addition to its weakness and general ineffectiveness, the People's Assembly has also been wracked by corruption scandals ranging from narcotics trafficking to the securing of huge loans from government-owned banks without collateral, few of which were repaid.

The Consultative Assembly (Majlis as-Shoura), or upper house of the parliament, is a less democratic body, one half of its members being selected by the president. The Consultative Assembly, as its name suggests, is an honorific debating society designed to air issues of public importance (Bianchi 1989). Its sessions are often broadcast on Egyptian television, but the body has little legislative authority. Cynics refer to it as a rest home for "burned out" officials (Springborg 1989).

Does this mean that the Egyptian parliament is totally irrelevant? Not at all. The existence of a functioning parliament and the holding of parliamentary elections, however flawed, are important steps in the democratic process. The NDP always wins, but opposition parties have the opportunity to present their case. This, too, has contributed to the immobility of a Mubarak regime desirous of moving toward greater democracy but fearful of the results. The opposition parties, although poorly represented, have also benefited from the considerable disarray that exists within the ruling establishment. Egypt's social and economic problems are so massive that no one is quite sure how to solve them. While some of Mubarak's advisors advocate more capitalism, others demand a return to socialism. By and large, the regime appears to be stalled somewhere between the two extremes (Ansari 1985). The same is true in virtually every area of debate. To some extent, the parliament serves as an important lightning rod in Egyptian politics (Nyrop 1983). Egypt's social and economic problems are not being effectively addressed by the Egyptian government, and the Egyptian population is extremely frustrated. The parliament provides at least a partial airing of those frustrations.

The Courts   The Egyptian Constitution provides for an independent judiciary as well as for a Constitutional Court. The Constitutional Court supervises the judicial system and possesses the right to declare laws and other acts of government unconstitutional. It also interprets the meaning of laws judged to be ambiguous. The broader structure of the Egyptian legal system is based upon French (Napoleonic) canon law, with adjustments being made for the predominantly Islamic character of Egyptian society. Islamic law takes precedence in marriage, divorce, and other areas referred to as personal statutes. The Islamic Fundamentalists would like to see the Koranic role in Egyptian law greatly expanded, and the Mubarak regime seems to be moving, however grudgingly, in this direction.

The Egyptian courts operate with reasonable efficiency in dealing with routine matters and are generally free of political influence. Politically sensitive issues are more problematic. The Constitutional Court's power to review government decisions can be overridden by the president's emergency powers, and the president also has the option of sending issues of state security to military courts rather than to civilian courts. Islamic Fundamentalists are generally tried by military courts, thereby depriving them of procedural rights guaranteed by the Constitution. The military has its own legal system and is not subject to civilian law.

These limitations aside, the Constitutional Court has played a vigorous role in strengthening Egyptian democracy. Unfair election laws have twice been declared unconstitutional by the Court, and the Court has nullified some 180 pieces of legislation since 1979 (Hibra 2000). The Court has also played a vigorous role in blocking government attempts to restrict the activities of political parties and has been accused of attempting to subvert the parliament by bringing its members to trial for grand fraud and trafficking in narcotics (Rizk 1999b). Most recently, the judiciary supervised Egypt's legislative elections, a precedent that may or may not be repeated, given the skittishness of the NDP.

The Constitutional Court cannot rival the presidency as a source of political power, but it has developed at least some precedents for independent action (Maisa 1993). The president has also allowed unpopular policies to be overridden by the Constitutional Court as a means of saving face. Rather than backtracking in the face of popular opposition, he can claim to be strengthening Egyptian democracy. Recently, for example, the Court invalidated a controversial law prohibiting female students from wearing Islamic dress to schools. The government capitulated in the name of democracy, thereby freeing itself from a policy that would have been difficult, if not dangerous, to enforce.

Taken collectively, the institutional pattern outlined above contributes to the immobility of Egyptian politics in several ways. First, as all initiatives for action rest with President Mubarak, his personal tendency toward caution serves as a brake on the system as a whole. Second, the quasi-democratic nature of Egypt's political institutions have made it increasingly difficult for the regime to silence the opposition. Elections, although "shaped," are held and opposition candidates do speak out. This, too, has led to increased caution. Third, the system continues to find policy implementation difficult. For all of its talk of bureaucratic reform, the Mubarak regime continues to depend upon a bureaucracy widely described as self-serving, lazy, corrupt, rigid, lacking in creativity, insensitive to the public, and fearful of taking responsibility (Palmer et al. 1988). Indeed, the Egyptian bureaucracy is now viewed as a major obstacle to the economic and social development of Egyptian society (Allam 2000).

THE GROUP BASIS OF EGYPTIAN POLITICS

The concept of civil society centers on the belief that progress toward a more democratic society requires a strong framework of non-governmental associations to stimulate public debate and to serve as a buffer between the rulers and the ruled (Kornhauser 1959; Norton 1994). The components of civil society in Egypt fall roughly into five categories: (1) political parties, (2) pressure groups, (3) private voluntary organizations (PVOs and NGOs), (4) sectoral interest groups that, while lacking a clear organizational structure, command the attention of the government, and (5) public opinion.

Egypt has witnessed the rapid growth of non-governmental groups and associations and now possesses far more non-governmental entities than any other Arab country. Most play a role in focusing public attention on the Mubarak regime and, as such, help to explain its caution. An interesting question, however, arises concerning the role of Egyptian parties, groups, and associations in the democratic process. Two points are of particular interest in this regard. First, many of Egypt's most active non-governmental agencies incline toward religious Fundamentalism. As such, their role in creating a more open society is open to question, at least as the term is understood in the West. Second, many of Egypt's non-governmental associations were created by the government for the purpose of better controlling the Egyptian population. This applies to political parties, labor and professional unions, and benevolent associations. The heavy hand of the government became even heavier with the passing of a new associations law in 1999.

Although it is convenient to break Egypt's civil society into its component parts for the purpose of discussion, it is vital to understand that each part builds upon the others. Nowhere is this overlapping more evident than in regard to the Islamic movement, the only serious opposition to the Mubarak regime. The Fundamentalists operate at all levels of Egypt's civil society, and each has become a battleground in the struggle to determine Egypt's future.

This being the case, it may be useful to first provide a survey of the main components of Egypt's civil society, such as it is, and then focus specifically on the continuing struggle between the Mubarak regime and the Fundamentalists for control of Egypt.

Political Parties

The Mubarak era has witnessed a proliferation of political parties unthinkable during the reigns of his predecessors (Kassem 2000). Some have deep roots in Egyptian society, while others are little more than empty shells left over from the Sadat era. The picture is made more complicated by the fluidity of Egyptian parties. Parties emerge only to merge with their competitors or to splinter as a result of personality conflicts or ideological differences. No matter how many other parties emerge, however, the ruling National Democratic Party (NDP) always wins.

For all of its complexity, the Egyptian party system is dominated by four distinct tendencies: the socialist left, the center, the capitalist right, and the Islamic groups. The parties of the left, now dominated by the Nasserites and the Tagammu (communist, far left), advocate a return to socialism. For many Egyptians, the dynamism of the Nasser era also stands in sharp contrast to the rudderless drift of the present regime. Leftist promises of full employment and free services also possess a strong appeal for the millions of Egyptians facing unemployment, escalating health and educational costs, and inadequate housing. The capitalist right, in turn, is dominated by the New Wafd, a party that advocates a complete break with Egypt's socialist past. Public-sector enterprises continue to control most of Egypt's larger industries. The religious right has largely taken over the Socialist Labor Party and would transform Egypt into an Islamic theocracy. By and large, the Socialist Labor Party is little more than a front for the Muslim Brotherhood. Spanning the middle of these disparate and seemingly irreconcilable tendencies is the ruling National Democratic Party. Its ideological position, such as it is, calls for a mix of socialism, capitalism, and religion. Of the above parties, only the NDP and the religious right possess more than a skeletal organizational structure. The Wafd finds its major support within the business community, while the Nasserites and other leftists find much of their support among students and intellectuals. The support of the religious right is fairly broad-based but, as will be discussed shortly, it is centered in the lower and middle classes. All Egyptian parties are beset by deep internal divisions.

A recent survey conducted by the semi-official Al-Ahram Center for Political and Strategic Studies indicates that 8.4 percent of the Egyptian population are associated with a formal political party. Figures for individual parties were not available, but it is safe to assume that the overwhelming majority of party members are affiliated with the National Democratic Party (Center for Political and Strategic Studies, 1998, Public Opinion Survey: Preliminary Results, 1998).

A leading Egyptian intellectual and former director of the Center for Political and Strategic Studies attributes the weakness of opposition parties to the negative image of the opposition presented by the government media. This stigma, he suggests, "has made many citizens reluctant to stand behind the banners of the opposition parties for fear of being branded as an opponent of the regime (Sha'ib 1999, translated by M. Palmer). The head of the opposition parties' coordination committee, in turn, attributed the dismal showing of the legal opposition parties to the cozy relationship between the opposition and the powers that be. "The fact that the electorate chose to vote for individuals and not parties reflects a lack of trust in all political parties" (Salah Eissa, in Abdel-Latif 2000, 1).

The influence of Egypt's quasi-democratic parties is threefold. First, the existence of a broad range of political parties creates the facade of democracy, a matter of great importance to a Mubarak regime attempting to convey a democratic image. Second, the existence of multiple legal political parties has fragmented the opposition into so many diverse groups that coordinated opposition to the Mubarak regime has become virtually impossible. Third, the weakness of the legal party system has forced an emphasis on alternative forms of political expression. In this regard, the same intellectual mentioned above suggests that the absence of true political activity—openness—has forced people to rely on basic religion, family, and clan affiliations to compensate for a lack of true political access. This emphasis on non-political affiliations, in turn, has further contributed to the stagnation of the government (Sha'ib 1999). One might add that it has also led to support for the Fundamentalists.

Sha'ib elaborates upon the above themes, suggesting that the weakness of Egypt's political parties forced the politicization of professional associations, labor unions, and other pressure groups. The opposition could not win national elections, but it has been able to gain control of many of Egypt's most powerful professional associations, a topic to which we turn next (Sha'ib 1999).

Pressure Groups

The latter years of the monarchy had witnessed the emergence of a wide variety of labor unions, business organizations, professional associations, and other Western-type pressure groups in Egypt. With the advent of revolutionary socialism in the 1950s, the business groups disbanded, while the labor, peasant, and professional associations were brought under government control (Bianchi 1989, 126–144; Posusney 1997). Egypt's professionals were also organized into a variety of government-sponsored syndicates in order to better control their activities and ensure their subservience to the regime. Of these, the most prominent were the syndicates of the journalist, lawyers, teachers, and engineers (Bianchi 1989). Each elected its own leaders, but the victory of government candidates was never in doubt.

Sadat's 1974 infitah, or new economic opening, witnessed a revival of business associations. The influence of these associations, however, has been weakened by their inability to agree on a common strategy for dealing with the Mubarak regime. Labor, peasant, and most professional associations remain under government supervision today, but that supervision has lessened as syndicate elections have become increasingly dominated by opposition parties, including the Fundamentalists. Indeed, by the mid-1900s, the Muslim Brotherhood dominated the largest of Egypt's 22 main professional organizations including medical, legal, and engineering associations, demonstrating that the appeal of Fundamentalism was not limited to the lower classes (*NYT*, June 12, 1994, 3).

Stunned by growing Fundamentalist influence within Egypt's professional associations, recent legislation has tightened governmental control of all groups and associations, leading to renewed charges of dictatorship and oppression. Human Rights Watch has openly condemned the 1999 Associations Law, claiming that it unreasonably restricts freedoms of association and assembly. These restrictions, of course, were intentional (Associated Press, May 28, 1999). Be this as it may, the Muslim Brotherhood saw its foothold in the professional associations curtailed.

Private Voluntary Organizations and Non-Governmental Organizations

Political parties and pressure groups are manifestly political in orientation, but private voluntary organizations (PVOs) and nongovernmental organizations (NGOs) (the terms are often used interchangeably) ostensibly exist to provide material and spiritual services to the population. By the mid-1990s, Egypt could boast some 15,000 registered PVOs, more than any other Arab country. The actual number is larger, for many have avoided registering with the government.

The development of PVOs was encouraged by the government as a means of providing basic services to the poor, a task that had long exceeded the capacity of the Egyptian bureaucracy. The government participates in the selection of the leadership councils and some, but not all, receive government stipends (Sullivan 1994; Singerman 1995). Be this as it may, the Fundamentalists have found the Islamic benevolent associations to be a fertile ground for recruitment, with some being controlled by the Fundamentalists on an "informal" basis (Mustafa 1995). This is not a minor consideration, for some Islamic benevolent societies have more than a million members.

Informal Sectors

In addition to the parties and pressure groups surveyed above, Egyptian politics is also influenced by a variety of social sectors including the residents of Greater Cairo, students, the Copts, social classes, and women.

Cairo as a Pressure Group   The citizens of Cairo, although seldom thought of as a pressure group, represent a critical sector whose interests must be addressed (Weede 1986). Cairo is the seat of Egypt's government, industry, commerce, banking, communications, mass media, education, religion, culture, health care, and tourism. Little of significance occurs in Egypt that is not controlled in one way or another by Cairo. The more than 13,000,000 Cairo residents constitute more than a fourth of Egypt's population, and a strike in Cairo can cripple the entire country. When one speaks of controlling the "streets," it is the Cairo streets of which they are speaking. To lose control of Cairo is to lose the capacity to rule.

Not surprisingly, the citizens of Cairo receive favored treatment in terms of food distribution, services, education, and housing. Life in many areas of Cairo is difficult, but it is far less difficult in Cairo than in the countryside. In a cruel irony, unfortunately, the favored position of Cairo has led to the city's inordinate growth. A city of 3,000,000 in 1960 will soon become a city of 20,000,000 in a few years. Cairo is where the action is.

Students   Egyptian university students constitute a vibrant political force. They are the most idealistic, the most intellectually aware, and the most articulate segment of Egyptian society. Their awareness of injustice is unfailing. The politicization of Egyptian students also finds its origins in a profound sense of insecurity and frustration. Many Egyptian students (some place the figure at 25 percent or higher) face the prospect of unemployment after graduation. Of those who do find jobs, many will find them in the lower rungs of the bureaucracy—a marginal existence at best.

Civic disturbances are generally initiated by university students, and if promising, are joined by disgruntled workers, high school students, and other dissidents. Some student disturbances are spontaneous; most have been inspired by external political groups such as the Nasserites or the Muslim Brotherhood.

Mubarak is attempting to strengthen the student wing of the ruling National Democratic Party, but it is the Fundamentalists who are now the dominant force in student politics. The government's response has been to clamp down on student organizations and, failing that, to keep demonstrations bottled up within university compounds. Fundamentalist students are also arrested on a regular basis as a means of intimidation (Schemm 1999). Most recently, popular anger over Israeli attempts to suppress the new Palestinian intifada erupted in demonstrations at Egypt's major universities as well as in the environs of Cairo's Al-Azhar mosque. Scores of students were arrested, as were a variety of opposition figures (Hassan-Gorden 2000; Khalil 2000).

The Copts   Coptic Christians represent approximately 8 percent of the Egyptian population and constitute a far higher percentage of the population in the politically sensitive area of greater Cairo.[10] Historically, as Nadia Farah points out, Copts have been well integrated into the fabric of Egyptian society and therefore have not constituted a cohesive political group.

> In the Egyptian case, while religion is an important descriptive criterion, it does not play a major role in social stratification. The Coptic minority is not isolated either economically, politically, or geographically. The Copts are found in elites, the middle class, the working class and the peasantry. While Copts are not fully represented in the political system...they are not excluded from the political or bureaucratic systems. Moreover, the Copts do not form a political group; they vary in their political ideology and allegiance. Culturally, the Copts are non-distinctive from Muslims.... Both groups share the same Egyptian culture. In this sense, the Copts do not form an ethnic group (Farah 1987, 57).

This picture, however, is rapidly changing. The dramatic rise of the Islamic Fundamentalists and their demands for an Islamic state now threaten to destroy Egypt's long tradition of tolerance and religious harmony. Religious conflicts have become commonplace since the latter days of the Sadat regime. Should present trends toward the Islamization of Egypt continue, yet another key element of Egypt's political stability will come unraveled.

Social Classes   Many Egyptian scholars find social classes to be a key element of Egyptian politics. As described by Saad Eddin Ibrahim:

> The reality or perception of these multiple crises is affecting Egypt's various socioeconomic groups differently, at least in degree if not in kind. The new middle class (professionals, technocrats, and bureaucrats) is becoming impoverished and feels a loss of its century-old role as the leading political force in society. The 'lumpenproletariat' is the fastest

---

[10]Estimates of the size of Egypt's Coptic population vary from 5 to 10 percent.

growing of Egypt's socioeconomic formations. No longer confined to small pockets in big urban centers, the lumpenproletariat now forms about one-third to one-fourth of Egypt's total population, and has spread to rural areas and rural–urban fringes of middle-size towns. It is the most flammable and manipulable socioeconomic formation. Out of its ranks, lower-middle-class Islamic activists can easily recruit, indoctrinate, and deploy followers. The third significant socioeconomic formation is the upper class, which in the last two decades has grown much richer, thanks to Sadat's Open-Door Economic Policy, and less socially and civically responsible (Ibrahim, S.E., 1996, 76–77).

Women as a Political Force   The political role of women in Egypt is difficult to assess. By Middle Eastern standards, Egyptian women have made dramatic progress toward economic and political equality. By Western standards, they remain an exploited underclass in a male-dominated society (Rugh 1986). Women possess the right to vote, and they are represented in the People's Assembly, and to a lesser extent, in the cabinet. The legal status of women, although restricted, has also witnessed improvement in recent years. A 1979 personal statutes law now requires a man to notify his wife in writing that he has divorced her. The law also states that the wife has the right to divorce her husband if he chooses to take a second wife, a practice limited largely to the rural areas. In such an instance, the woman retains a legal right to the family's lodging until remarriage or until the children are no longer in her custody, i.e., 12 years for girls and 10 years for boys. The polygamy provision remains controversial, as it could be interpreted as a contravention of Islamic law. These issues, however, continue to be a matter of heated debate within the Egyptian Parliament, with a 2000 version of the Personal Statutes Law enhancing the ability of women to file for divorce. This is not a minor consideration, for it is estimated that some seven million people are currently seeking legal separation (Hammond 2000; Sachs 2000).

In the economic sphere, the changing role of women has been dramatic (Sullivan 1986). Females now constitute approximately 30 percent of the urban labor force. The picture is much the same in the field of education, with females now accounting for approximately one third of the students attending Egyptian universities—a dramatic increase over the 7 percent of the pre-revolutionary era. Progress in the areas of education and employment has been far greater in the urban areas than in the countryside, with illiteracy rates among rural females being in the 70-percent range. It is probable that Egyptian women will continue to gain equality in the economic sphere, inasmuch as the realities of Egyptian economic life increasingly require two incomes. Indeed, a good job contributes markedly to the marriageability of Egyptian females.

Despite significant progress in the economic sphere, women do not constitute an organized force in Egyptian politics. The surge of Islamic Fundamentalism has produced a greater conservatism in Egyptian society, and even the economic gains of Egyptian women are being called into question.

Survival Networks   Underpinning the above groups and interests are a vast array of patron-client and self-help networks that enable average Egyptians to survive in a society that excludes them politically and that is slowly dismantling the social contract on which they have come to depend for their survival (Singerman 1995). As Diane Singerman writes, such networks are the people's way of fighting back:

> The boundaries of this particular community are not localized, isolated or insular because the *sha'b* intentionally incorporate more powerful, resourceful, and skilled individuals and institutions into their networks to strengthen them. Networks connect individuals and households with communal and national institutions, thus transcending the supposedly strict boundary between public and private spheres. Informal networks are effective precisely because they are designed to function within a formal system pervaded by informal structures and processes. Although the membership and configuration of each network varies, there is a common reflex in these communities to establish networks to solve problems, arbitrate disputes, and fulfill specific objectives: thus networks are very responsive to changing internal and external forces (Singerman 1995, 269).

Public Opinion   Public opinion in Egypt finds expression in a variety of outlets ranging from the ubiquitous political joke to periodic riots. Other indicators of public opinion include commentary in the press, results of elections (such as they may be), and even the dress code adopted by Egyptian citizens. Islamic dress is prominent among females, but commentators are not sure whether such dress is a political statement or merely a convenience. As Rugh writes:

> Increasingly since 1967, a new Islamic style of dress has appeared on the streets of major cities in Egypt. In some cases the dress indicates the wearer's more fundamentalist view of religion; in others it is worn more as the latest fashion, akhir moda. In this second group, the same girls who several years ago might have worn a mini-skirt as the latest fashion adopt more modest styles now because they have become popular. A study carried out by the National Centre for Social and Criminological Studies found that more than sixty percent of their sample of educated

Egyptian women wear Islamic dress. Of these, forty percent claim they wear it for reasons of modesty and cost, twenty-five percent because it's fashionable, ten percent to avoid going to a hairdresser, and five percent because they feel that men are less likely to molest a modestly dressed woman (Rugh 1986, 149; for survey data see Radwan 1982).

As in so many other instances, Mubarak is attempting to strike a balance between freedom of expression on one hand and the maintenance of regime security on the other. As the above example illustrates, assessing public opinion in Egypt remains difficult. The government does not allow the free use of opinion polls, for adverse results could well serve as an invitation to revolution if they showed majority support for the Fundamentalists. A unique exception to this rule was a 1997–1998 public opinion poll conducted by the Al-Ahram Center for Strategic and Political Studies. Among other things, the results indicated that the citizens of Cairo vote at a lower rate than citizens in the rural areas and are less inclined to join political parties than their rural counterparts. Much the same is true of Egyptian youth. Reading between the lines, these figures suggest that the NDP is losing its grip in Cairo and must rely on the influence of local notables allied with the NDP to score large majorities in the rural areas. It is also interesting to note that the public sector is more involved in electoral politics than the private sector, the former being under the direct control of the NDP. The higher and better-educated classes are more politically aware than the lower classes but choose to work through pressure groups rather than political parties (*Al-Ahram Survey* 1998).

The survey also found that the citizens of Cairo were cynical, while those of the countryside were more willing to give the government the benefit of the doubt. The sincerity of rural responses to the questionnaire, however, remains open to doubt, for the rural areas have little familiarity with such things and many respondents may have been inclined to disguise their views (Palmer, Sullivan, and Safty 1996).

The Egyptian press, for the first time since 1952, is now playing an important if guarded role in criticizing government policies. Mubarak's policies are openly criticized by the opposition press, something that would not have happened during the reigns of Nasser and Sadat. Mubarak prides himself on not having confiscated a single publication during his tenure in office. Egypt's leading literary figures were asked to testify to this fact during the tenth anniversary of Mubarak's rule, with Neguib Mahfuz, Egypt's Nobel Prize–winning author, acknowledging that Egypt enjoyed extensive freedom of the press "within the limits of our traditions" (*Al-Ahram*, Oct. 10, 1991).

The hard core of Egyptian public opinion has traditionally found expression in the sarcastic political humor that fuels conversation in Cairo's ubiquitous coffee shops. While much of Egypt's political humor loses its bite in translation, suffice it to say that Nasser, himself, found mass humor to be a subversive force and attempted to suppress it (Hamouda 1990). Much of the current Egyptian humor portrays Mubarak as a plodding and indecisive bureaucrat.

While difficult to assess, public opinion is taken very seriously by the Mubarak regime. The "information" section of the President's Office is charged with both monitoring and shaping public opinion, as are the Ministry of Information and the National Democratic Party. The results of the 2000 parliamentary elections, needless to say, caught the attention of all of the above agencies. The opinions of Cairo's residents, as might be expected, are of far more importance to Egypt's leaders than the opinions of Egypt's provincial citizens. Cairo is the pulse of Egypt.

Islam and Civil Society in Egypt

Egyptian intellectuals point to Egypt's burgeoning civil society as a dramatic force in Egypt's evolution toward a more democratic political system. As suggested earlier, however, the dominant force in Egypt's civil society consists of Islamic activists of diverse persuasions. They are less concerned with creating a democratic Egypt than with the establishment of an Islamic Egypt.

Viewed in this light, Egypt's parties, associations, and other components of civil society have become the arena for a three-way struggle between a government attempting to perpetuate the status quo, political reformers attempting to push Egypt toward greater democracy, and Islamic activists attempting to create a more Islamic society. The two main forces in this struggle are the government and the Islamic activists. The conflict between these two opposing forces has become the stuff of Egyptian politics.

The term "Islamic activists" encompasses a broad spectrum of citizens who support a more Islamic society, if not the creation of an Islamic state (Shukri 1990). Islamic activists range from individuals who support a greater role for religion in Egypt's political life to the Fundamentalist extremists who have attempted to seize power by force. The latter, as we shall see shortly, are a small and fragmented group. The number of people preferring an Islamic state, by contrast, is large indeed. An informal survey of American University of Cairo students, for example, found that almost 55 percent of the respondents were sympathetic to the Islamic revival while 45 percent were not. Need-less to say, the Copts predominated in the latter category (Palmer, Sullivan and Safty 1996). The same survey also indicated the profound influence of religion on Egyptian society, with more than 90 percent of the population supporting religion in schools, and 70 percent supporting religious censorship. These figures find support in Egypt's overflowing mosques and leave little doubt that Islam provides the moral underpinning of Egyptian society.

Islamic activists of one form or another have penetrated all levels of Egyptian civil society outlined above (Mustafa 1992, 1995). While united in the goal of achieving an Islamic state, members of the Islamic community do not agree on how an Islamic state is to be achieved or how it is to be governed. Indeed, the main weakness of the Islamic revival has been the dissension within its ranks.

The most high-profile Islamic groups have been those leading the charge for the creation of an Islamic state. Of these, the Muslim Brotherhood is the oldest and most visible element of the Islamic right. It is also the motherlode from which the dominant extremist groups have splintered.

Created in the 1920s by Hassan al-Banna, the Brotherhood preached a message that was both simple and poignant. Egypt's plight, in the view of the Brotherhood, was caused by the decadence of the ruling elite and by the foreign influences that sustained that elite. God's word, as revealed by the Prophet Mohammed, was both clear and unequivocal. To follow the word of God was to achieve eternal salvation; to ignore it was to court damnation. It was the duty of Muslims to crush foreign decadence and forge a government based on Islamic principles. The strategy of the Brotherhood was threefold: teaching and preaching, providing welfare services for the poor, and political activism (Husaini 1956, 103–105). Given the restrictive nature of Egypt's regimes, that activism inclined toward violence. Be this as it may, the Brotherhood's strategy was based upon the belief that it was possible to reform Egyptian society from within.

Not all Muslim Brothers, however, accepted al-Banna's assumption that it was possible to reform Egyptian society from within. Shocked by Nasser's rush to modernity, Sayyid Qutb, one of the Brotherhood's leading intellectuals, argued that the secular society being forged by Nasser differed little from the era of ignorance, the Jahiliya, that prevailed in pre-Islamic Arabia. Mohammed had created an Islamic society by destroying the heathen society of his day. It was now the obligation of modern Muslims to do the same. There was no room for compromise between the sacred and the profane (Moussalli 1999).

Sayyid Qutb was put to death by Nasser, but his writings would provide the philosophical foundation for the Fundamental extremists of the 1970s. They, like he, rejected the concept that Egyptian society could be reformed from within. The new extremists gained notoriety in 1974 when an organization known as the "military group" provoked a direct confrontation with the Sadat regime by occupying a military barracks. Either naive, idealistic, or both, the attempted coup (if such it was) was crushed by Sadat, and many of its leaders paid with their lives. The movement later resurfaced as Jihad, the group that assassinated Sadat on October 6, 1981.

Nasser drove the Brotherhood into remission following a failed assassination attempt in 1954, but its organizational roots remained intact. When it was revived by Sadat in 1971, accordingly, it soon gained control of the street and became a critical element in Sadat's effort to crush the left. Sadat's reliance upon the Brotherhood provided the organization with quasi-legal status, and it was officially viewed as a "reformist" organization seeking to fulfill its religious objectives within the framework of Egypt's "constitutional" political system (Hinnebusch 1988). The Brotherhood's leadership had also aged, the firebrands of the prewar era becoming the elder statesmen of the 1970s.

The tacit acceptance of the Brotherhood as a quasi-legitimate political organization provided it with increased scope for political activity. Election alliances were forged with the New Wafd and other parties of the capitalist right. More recently, the Brotherhood has simply incorporated the Socialist Labor Party and the much smaller Liberal Party. The Brotherhood also dominates Egypt's most important student and professional unions, and has deepened its mass base by opening a vast network of Islamic schools and clinics. As Saad Ibrahim writes:

> The MB and its sympathizers have not confined themselves to profit-making enterprises, politics, or professional associations. A broad range of health and social services are rendered under the catch-word "Islamic." Many of these were started by original Muslim Brotherhooders in the 1970s. Among the widespread facilities are the medical services to be found in more than twenty thousand non-governmental mosques. Many have operating facilities for minor surgeries, and quite a few are full-fledged medical complexes. The Islamic clinics charge their clients a nominal or modest fee for a generally better and more compassionate service than their state-run counterparts. Similar educational and other social services are rendered by nonviolent Islamic activists. Often these are located on the premises of non-governmental mosques. They are run on a low-cost overhead basis, and generally provide good-quality services given the donated time and expertise of their volunteer workers (Ibrahim, S.E. 1996, 60–61).

Indeed, some estimates suggest that as much as 10 percent of the Egyptian population uses the services provided by the Brotherhood and its related organizations (*Chicago Tribune*, Nov. 24, 1994). In many ways, the Islamic elements are creating a social infrastructure parallel to that of the state.

Assessing the strength of the radical Islamic groups today is a difficult task. Some estimates count as many as ninety different Fundamentalist groups, the size and policies of which vary dramatically (Mustafa 1992, 1995; Shukri 1990). Some have attempted to destabilize the government by assassinating government officials or foreign visitors, including a 1995 attack on the life of Mubarak and the 1997 slaughter of some 67 tourists at Luxor. Others, by contrast, have sought to isolate themselves from Egypt's corrupting environment by building religious communities in the desert. Biding their time, they wait for the moment of return.

Fundamentalist leaders during the 1970s and 1980s tended to be young and well-educated individuals from rural origins who found themselves frustrated by the decadence and inequities of Egyptian society (Ibrahim 1980; Ansari 1986; Ayubi 1980). More recently, there is evidence that the extremist leadership is being drawn from the lower classes (Ibrahim, S. E. 1996, 74). The Fundamentalists are well funded and have a broad base of support throughout all areas of Egyptian society, including the military, the police, and the educational system. In the fall of 1994, for example, the government was forced to begin a purge of pro-Islamic teachers from Egypt's 25,000 schools, a venture that would seem doomed to failure before it began (*NYT*, Oct. 4, 1994, A4).

Both the Muslim Brotherhood and its offshoots have experienced considerable success in penetrating all elements of Egypt's civil society. As noted earlier, the Muslim Brotherhood has all but taken over the Socialist Labor Party. Election victories continue to be scored in Egypt's student and professional associations, although the results are subject to annulment by the government. Egypt's massive benevolent associations continue to provide a recruitment ground for the broad range of Fundamentalist organizations. The Fundamentalists also control many of Egypt's private mosques, government efforts to the contrary notwithstanding.

The Fundamentalists, moreover, control the street. In Egypt, as in most other countries of the Third World, street demonstrations often turn violent, testing the government's resolve and threatening to trigger broader religious and class violence. More often than not, such demonstrations begin in the universities and spread to labor unions and other groups.

Faced with a challenge that bordered on open revolution, Mubarak intensified his anti-terrorist campaign on all fronts. First and foremost, known Fundamentalist groups were attacked with a new savagery and their leaders forced to flee. Suspects were arrested and tried by military courts, thereby avoiding the niceties of civilian law. Some were put to death; others received long prison terms. The security of tourist sites was increased, and border patrols were strengthened. The government also abandoned earlier efforts to splinter the Fundamentalist movement by allowing the Muslim Brotherhood quasi-legal status while hunting the extremists as criminals (Rizk 1999a). Even here, however, the government has shown signs of indecision.

In a further change of tactics, the Mubarak regime attempted to reduce its anti-terrorist assaults on innocent citizens, a widespread practice that had stimulated support for the Fundamentalists. In 1999, a carrot was added to the stick as the Mubarak regime released 1000 prisoners (Saadeq 1999a). In addition to portraying the regime in a compassionate light, this move reduced the role of Egypt's prisons in building solidarity among the Fundamentalists.

The above moves were matched by efforts to reassert government control over domestic mosques and Islamic benevolent associations. As the policy was described by the Minister of Waqfs: "We do not order preachers to discuss specific subjects and we do not send them written sermons…. Individuals who undertake to give sermons or religious lessons in a mosque must obtain prior permission…from one of the 27 regional offices of the Ministry" (Zaqzuq 1999). He further noted that the target date for nationalizing Egypt's 27,000 private mosques was 2002. Past efforts to rein in the domestic (non-governmental) mosques have failed for lack of certified preachers, but the government has redoubled its efforts in this area.

More subtly, the Mubarak regime has attempted to deny the terrorists the glory of martyrdom by referring to them as common criminals. Constant reference is also made to the virtual civil war launched by the Fundamentalists in Algeria, a civil war that has claimed some 70,000 lives over the course of the past decade. Few Egyptians welcome the prospect of similar carnage on the Nile.

The government has also attempted to shore up its Islamic credentials. Censorship of books judged inappropriate by Al-Azhar has increased, as has funding for mosques and other overtly Islamic projects. In regard to the former, the American University of Cairo was forced to remove two books from its curriculum: Maxime Rodinson's *Muhammat*, and Alifa Rifaat's *Distant View of a Minaret*. The latter had been part of the university's core curriculum for the previous five years (Shoreh 1998).

Parallel efforts have been made to strengthen the role of "state Islam." State Islam, according to Mullaney, presents Islam as a "private" faith designed to guide the moral values of the individual believer. Islam is also portrayed as a spiritual faith that focuses on good works rather than politics. Above all, state Islam is a non-violent faith that uses its moral authority to promote social cohesiveness (Mullaney 1995). As portrayed in this light, Islam is fully compatible with a modern nation-state.

This view is the diametric opposite of that of the Fundamentalists, who recognize only the sovereignty of God and reject the subservience of Islam to a secular government. The Koran speaks of an Islamic state and, in the view of the Fundamentalists, it is the obligation of Muslims to replace secular states with an Islamic state ruled by Koranic principles (Mullaney 1995).

On the international front, pressure was put on Kuwait and other Gulf states to curtail the donations of their citizens to Fundamentalist organizations working in Egypt. Kuwaiti Fundamentalists, in particular, were accused of supporting their Egyptian brethren (Saadeq 1999b). More often than not, this meant suspending contributions to Islamic NGOs with suspected links to the Fundamentalists. Mutual agreements for the exchange of convicted terrorists were signed between Egypt and a variety of states and led to the handing over of some 68 terrorists in the 1994–1995 period (Saadeq 1999b). Pressure was also placed on the United States and the countries of Western Europe to stop sheltering known Fundamentalists, an effort marked by Egypt's hosting of an anti-terrorist summit in 1996. US cooperation increased precipitously in the wake of the 1997 bombings of the US embassies in Nairobi and Dar Issalam.

By the end of 1998, Mubarak seemed to claim victory over the extremists, noting that Egypt had witnessed only 14 terrorist-related deaths to police and civilians during 1998, as opposed to 160 terrorist-related deaths during the preceding year.

The extremists were far from admitting defeat, but 1997 had seen several of the imprisoned Fundamentalist leaders call for an end to "military operations" (Barakat and Sadiq 1998). The new initiative was duly announced by the "Islamic Lawyers," a shadowy group who serve as intermediaries between the imprisoned members of Jihad and the Jamiat (the Islamic groups) and the outside world. The Muslim Brotherhood has a separate legal staff (Rizk 1999a).

Why, then, had some 16 years of violent confrontation with the government come to an end? Interviews with various intellectuals, extremist and otherwise, by Barakat and Sadiq offered several answers to this question, all of which have much to say about the nature of Egyptian politics.

1. Government attacks had weakened the ability of extremist groups to sustain a "military" campaign against the government. Casualties, arrests, and the flight of leaders abroad had all increased, depriving the extremists of a critical core of activists. Tightened security measures had also made terrorist attacks more costly, as had increased police penetration of the areas in which the extremists had found their strongest support, including urban slums, the densely populated agricultural regions, and the villages of Upper Egypt.

2. International support for the extremists had decreased as a result of pressure from the United States and Europe. This included curtailment of the money, arms, and training grounds that the extremists required to sustain their operations. Particularly hard hit were training grounds in Pakistan and Afghanistan. Support networks in the US and Europe were also crippled by domestic anti-terrorist agencies.

3. Domestic support for the extremists decreased as a result of increased government control of mosques and Islamic benevolent associations. This diminished support led to reduced financial contributions and impaired efforts to recruit new cadres. Attracting manpower as well as money was becoming problematic.

4. The intensity of Fundamentalist violence had proven repulsive to many Egyptians who were otherwise supportive of the Islamic Revival. This was all the more the case because violence seemed to have become an end in itself. The extremists had lost touch with the values of the broader Islamic community and may have inadvertently pushed people toward the government's position.

5. In much the same manner, violence against tourists, while depleting government resources, also burdened the vast number of Egyptians who depended upon the tourist industry for their survival. The tactics of the extremists thus ran counter to the economic interests of many of their potential supporters.

6. The leadership of the extremist movement was becoming increasingly divided. Diverse groups found it difficult to coordinate their activities, and growing tension existed between the leadership in prison, a group now in its fifties, and the younger activists who were managing the day-to-day operations of the

movement. Tension also existed between the leadership within Egypt and the leadership in exile, the former of whom were bearing the brunt of the "new realities."

7. The Fundamentalist leadership had traditionally lacked a realistic assessment of the government's anti-terrorist capacity. Government pressures forced that reassessment, leading to a change of strategy.

8. The Fundamentalists lacked concrete solutions to the problems confronting Egyptian society. The slogan "God is the Solution" was not enough for an increasingly sophisticated population searching for tangible solutions to practical problems.

9. Finally, the critiques of the Fundamentalist movement focused on its parochialism and its failure to learn from the experience of Fundamentalist movements in Iran, Turkey, Malaysia, Algeria, Pakistan, and Afghanistan, countries in which the Fundamentalists have scored major successes.

If the strategies of the Mubarak regime have been successful in stemming the tide of violence, they have neither crushed the Fundamentalist movement nor altered its goals. Rather, they have forced the extremists to adjust their strategies to reflect the "new realities."

These new strategies center on a renewed emphasis on teaching, preaching, and the provision of vital services to Egypt's poor. New efforts are also being made to join the mainstream of Egyptian politics. Toward this end, 1998 saw Fundamentalist lawyers applying for permission to create an Islamic Party that would operate within Egypt's democratic framework. The government's response was cool.

This new strategy, while still a matter of debate, attempts to bring the Fundamentalist movement back in line with its support base and to portray the Fundamentalists in a positive rather than a negative light. The more the Fundamentalists can capture the high ground, the more the Mubarak regime will be forced to bear the burden of its ineptitude, secularism, repression, and corruption. In the meantime, the Fundamentalists will have time to rebuild and train new cadres and to improve their organizational effectiveness.

There is no clear indication that the Fundamentalists have foresworn the use of violence. Fundamentalist violence abated after the assassination of Sadat in 1981, only to reassert itself with a vengeance a few years later (Ibrahim, S. E. 1996). Those Fundamentalist leaders forced to flee abroad have likened their flight to the Prophet's flight from Mecca to Medina (Saadeq 1999b). Once the heat is off, they will return. Indeed, one author speculates that periods of flight may actually strengthen Fundamentalist movements. Contacts are made with a broader range of Fundamentalist movements, organizational methods are improved, and new sources or arms and money may be forthcoming. Exiled leaders have also found fertile ground for proselytization among Muslim minorities in Europe (Saadeq 1999b).

Although Mubarak's anti-Fundamentalist strategy was successful in forcing at least a temporary reorientation in anti-government terrorism during the final years of the twentieth century, it did little to allay many of the basic causes of the Fundamentalist movement. The economic position of the poor continues to be desperate and stands in sharp contrast to the brash ostentation of the rich. One also sees few signs that the government has enhanced its capacity to meet the needs of the poor. Opportunities for non-Islamic expression, moreover, have decreased. By emasculating the legitimate political parties, the government has left its opponents little choice but to incline toward the Fundamentalists. This fact was made patently evident by the Muslim Brotherhood's success in Egypt's 2000 parliamentary elections, a success that saw the Brotherhood emerge as the dominant opposition bloc in the People's Assembly (Jabar 2000b). Indeed, the 2000 elections appear to have revived the spirit of the Muslim Brotherhood and their allies (Saleh 2000).

THE CONTEXT OF EGYPTIAN POLITICS

In addition to its institutions and actors, Egypt's politics are profoundly influenced by its cultural, economic, and international environments. All have contributed to the immobility of the Mubarak regime, some by impeding change and others by forcing a more rapid pace of change than the system can bear.

Political Culture

Three dimensions of Egypt's political culture are particularly important to understanding the dynamic of Egyptian politics and, in particular, the immobility of the Mubarak regime. First, the most obvious of these is Islam, a topic that has already been discussed at length. Suffice it to say that Islamic values must be weighed in all policy decisions.

Second, occasional riots notwithstanding, Egyptian political culture is seemingly docile. Islamic militancy continues to cast a shadow over Egypt's uncertain march toward democracy, if such it is, but the much-feared Fundamentalist uprising has yet to materialize. By Middle Eastern standards, the Egyptian political system has been remarkably stable. Egyptian political culture, from this perspective, is the product of centuries of foreign domination that taught the Egyptian people that revolt was futile. Over time, this sense of hopelessness became part of the Egyptian cultural map that was passed on from generation to generation. Whether or not this explanation is valid, the apparent docility of the Egyptian population has been a clear plus for the Mubarak regime (Al-Manoufi 1979).

Third, centuries of foreign domination created a chasm of distrust between the government and the people. Recoiling from oppressive rulers, Egyptians sought security in the solidarity of their families rather than in the protection of the state. In the case of the Coptic minority, security was also to be found in religious solidarity. Egyptians, accordingly, were slow to develop the sense of political community or civil society that loomed so large in the political development of the West. Rather, Egypt became a society of families and clans, each competing with the others for scarce resources. Egyptians distrusted the government, and they distrusted each other. This sense of distrust and political alienation continues to haunt a Mubarak regime trying desperately to mobilize the Egyptian masses behind his programs. Rare is a Mubarak speech that does not call upon Egyptians to work harder for the good of their country.

Political Economy

While there can be little doubt about the influence of culture on Egyptian politics, the influence of economics is equally pervasive (Waterbury 1983; Richards and Waterbury 1990; Richards 1991). Nasser's revolution, in the view of many political economists, was a revolt of the middle classes against an exploitative aristocratic class. Nasser's "social contract" with the Egyptian public, moreover, was in reality an economic contract that traded political acquiescence for economic security. The quality of services was rudimentary, but few Egyptians starved.

The socialism of the Nasser era had been unequal to the task of economic development, and Sadat inherited a country that was falling ever deeper in debt as it attempted to maintain a welfare system that promised Egypt's citizens jobs, housing, education, medical care, and subsidized food. Viewed from the political economic perspective, the economic realities of the 1970s left Sadat little option but to experiment with capitalism and scale back the costs of Nasser's welfare society.

The economic dislocations created by Sadat's infitah, in turn, helped to fuel the Islamic revival that was to become the dominant political force in Egypt. Most of the leaders of the Fundamentalist movement evolved from economic classes that had been excluded from power by the Sadat regime (Habib 1989).

As one might expect, Mubarak's rush to capitalism during the past decade has not been without its problems (Sullivan 1990). Egypt's social contract has become increasingly tattered, and the gap between rich and poor is ever more glaring. While Egypt's per capita income in 1998 was $1294, its minimum wage was "$20 a month for a six-day, 48-hour work week" (US Government 1998). Egyptian unemployment figures continue to hover between 10 and 13 percent, although informal estimates place the number at closer to 20 percent. As a leading Egyptian economist noted in a recent interview, moreover, no one is quite sure of the government's standard of employment (interviews 1999). Is it a steady, full-time job, or does it include part-time or seasonal employment? All seem to be included in the government figures, thereby disguising severe problems of underemployment. Accusations of corruption are frequent, although Mubarak has maintained a reputation for honesty. It is those around him that are the problem. Particularly worrisome, from the government's perspective, are mass fears that future privatization, including those of Egypt's unprofitable heavy industries, will result in layoffs, increased support for the Fundamentalists, and reduced benefits.

Problems aside, Egypt's private-sector growth has been impressive by any standards, and the international financial community is pushing Mubarak to complete the reform process, now mid-stream, with all due haste. Growing disparities in wealth, they argue, invariably accompany the transition from socialism to capitalism. Such is the nature of capitalism. If investors are to create jobs and wealth, they must be rewarded for their risks. Over time, the industries that they create will provide the jobs and skills necessary to lift Egypt from its poverty. In the meantime, the US and the IMF are urging Mubarak to bite the bullet and to stay the course.

Out of realism or caution, the Mubarak regime has been disinclined to rush the pace of economic reform (*Al-Ahram Weekly*, Nov. 23–29, 2000). Rather, the regime has attempted to walk a fine line between providing enough reform to stimulate the Egyptian economy and simultaneously keeping mass tensions in check by maintaining what is left of the social contract. Economic reforms may be essential for the sake of future development, but they cannot be allowed to threaten the stability of the regime. Rarely does a day go by in which *Al-Ahram*, Egypt's semi-official newspaper, does not reassure Egypt's masses that the poor will not be forgotten. Mubarak has also promised not to privatize either the utilities or strategic military industries, both of which employ a high percentage of the Egyptian work force. Government subsidies remain on key consumer goods, and reform of an obstructionist bureaucracy has remained as elusive as ever.

Vacillation perpetuates the Mubarak regime from year to year, but it does not solve Egypt's underlying social and economic problems. Indeed, the longer the regime delays taking decisive action, the more severe its economic problems have become. Each year a million new Egyptians require education, housing, and health care. Each year a new wave of graduates compete for jobs that do not exist. For the present, the gap between what Egyptian society produces and what it spends is being covered by oil revenues and foreign assistance from the United States and other donor agencies, but neither oil revenues nor foreign aid have placed Egypt on the path to self-sufficiency. Foreign aid must inevitably end, and dependency on oil revenues leaves Egypt vulnerable to sharp fluctuations in the world oil market. Prosperity one year can become despair the next.

Egypt and the West: Dependence or Interdependence?

International and regional pressures have also contributed to the immobility of the Mubarak regime. The United States provides Egypt with $2 billion in foreign assistance on an annual basis. The price of that aid has been quite explicit. First, the United States and other members of the donor community are placing enormous pressure on Egypt to complete its transition from socialism to capitalism, a transition that is currently in mid-course with the most difficult stages of privatization yet to be implemented. The United States has also made tepid efforts to promote Egyptian democracy (computers have been bought for the members of the legislature) but is reluctant to push for political reforms that might strengthen the Fundamentalists. Second, the US expects Egypt to honor its peace treaty with Israel, to protect Saudi Arabia and the Gulf Sheikhdoms, and to stand as a US ally against Iraq and Iran.

All of these demands appear to be unpopular with a large segment of the Egyptian population. Rapid economic reform, as noted above, threatens the subsidies and welfare services to which Egyptians have long been accustomed. Egyptian support for the 1991 UN invasion of Iraq was opposed by many Egyptians, and Mubarak, being sensitive to the public mood, refused a subsequent US request to participate in a proposed 1998 strike against Iraq. Egyptians do not like to serve the US by killing other Arabs and Muslims. Egypt has honored its peace treaty with Israel, but the Mubarak regime has repeatedly been stung by Israel's hard-line tactics toward the Palestinians and other Arab countries. Mubarak complains, but words do not lead to action. While relations between Egypt and Israel could hardly be described as warm, Egypt does not want renewed hostilities with Israel (Cohen 1990).

Bold headlines in Egypt's semi-official *Al-Ahram* newspaper proclaim that Egypt is an "equal partner" of the United States, but the US presence in Egypt is so massive that it is difficult to ignore. To make matters worse, the $3 billion in US aid to Israel is simply transferred to the Israeli treasury, while the $2 billion granted to Egypt is minutely controlled by a massive USAID bureaucracy resident in Cairo, the organizational chart for which requires ten pages. The Egyptians find this differential treatment to be demeaning and drag their feet on projects of primary interest to the United States. Indeed, virtually all of the projects and sub-projects funded by the United States Agency for International Development (USAID) have to be approved by both the United States and Egypt, a laborious process that pits one bureaucracy against another. Over the course of the past decade, for example, the United States has earmarked more than $500,000,000 to improve local government in Egypt. USAID wanted the money to be used to improve skills, facilities, and democratic procedures, but the Egyptians placed the project under the control of a senior cabinet minister charged with strengthening the base of the ruling National Democratic Party. As a result, little progress was made in strengthening grassroots democracy, while a great deal of money found its way into the hands of party supporters (Palmer 1992). Protest from the United States was muted, for strengthening a compliant Mubarak regime was more important to the United States than strengthening local governments.

Again, the result has been vacillation and indecision as the Mubarak regime struggles to convince the United States that it is a valuable ally while simultaneously trying to convince its own people that it is not an American puppet (Mubarak 1999).

LOOKING TOWARD THE FUTURE

The Egypt of today bears little resemblance to that of the Nasser era. Revolutionary Councils have given way to a constitutional structure not dissimilar to that of France. Executive power is divided between a strong president and a weak prime minister selected by the president. Legislative authority resides in a parliament elected in somewhat fair elections, and a Constitutional Court possesses the power to declare acts of the government unconstitutional. It has done so on several occasions. The single party apparatus of the Nasser era has been replaced by a multi-party system, albeit a multi-party system in which the government's party always wins. The Egyptian press is freer than at any time since the Nasser Revolution of 1952, and the rigid socialism of the earlier era has been challenged by a growing private sector.

Nevertheless, the Egypt of today is very much the product of the Nasser era. The president of the Egyptian Republic is still a military officer, as are his major advisors. The parliament and the courts, while vigorous in the execution of their responsibilities, pose little challenge to the presidency. In spite of some progress toward privatization and economic reform, the Egyptian economy continues to be hamstrung by a massive bureaucracy. Decentralization has been much discussed by government leaders, but few effective measures have been taken in that direction. Egypt continues to be an intensely centralized state.

The Egypt of today has also inherited the problems of the past (McDermott 1988). The population explosion continues. The 20 million Egyptians of the revolutionary era have now become 70 million. That figure is expected to reach 125 million by the year 2020. Poverty continues, although few Egyptians are threatened with starvation. Housing shortages are critical, as are unemployment and underemployment. Official estimates place the unemployment figure in the 20 percent range, but unofficial estimates are much higher. From one-third to one-half of all working Egyptians, moreover, are underemployed, a euphemistic term for disguised unemployment (US Embassy 1994).

The capitalist reforms of the Sadat and Mubarak eras have also created new problems. Much of the new wealth that has been produced by the infitah has gone to a relatively narrow stratum of Egyptian society. While a minority of the Egyptian population enjoys unparalleled prosperity, most Egyptians find life increasingly difficult. Many Egyptian intellectuals also feel that Egypt is in danger of becoming dependent upon the United States. While this may or may not be the case, the two billion dollars in foreign aid that the US provides to Egypt annually does assure that American views will receive a careful hearing in Cairo. The growing strength of the Islamic Fundamentalists, moreover, threatens to undermine the viability of Egypt's quasi-democratic political institutions. It is in this environment, then, that Egypt confronts the challenges of the twenty-first century.

3

The Politics of Israel

*Occupied by Israel—status to be determined.

Note: Most countries of the world do not recognize Jerusalem as the capital of Israel and have their embassies in Tel Aviv.

Israel is a nation of paradoxes. Its roots are anchored in the ancient kingdoms of David and Solomon, yet its history as a modern state began in 1948. Israel proudly proclaims itself to be a Jewish state, yet many of its citizens—perhaps a majority—are secular in orientation. Israel is a minuscule country, hardly bigger than the state of New Jersey, yet its symbolic importance to the world Jewish community has made it a major actor on the world stage. Israelis are united in their commitment to Israel's survival, yet they seem to agree on little else, including the nature of a Jew (Orr 1994). Israel is one of the world's most enduring democracies, yet it is routinely condemned by the United Nations and Amnesty International for violating the human rights of its Palestinian subjects (Israel and the UN, Ministry of Foreign Affairs, www).

In this chapter, we will examine these paradoxes and other complexities of Israeli political life. Particular emphasis will be placed on the tension that exists between the need for solidarity in the face of external danger and the compelling need to give expression to the many divisions that fragment Israeli society. In this regard, it is important to note that Israel's citizens come from a broad variety of social and ideological backgrounds. Many of Israel's earliest settlers came from Eastern and Central Europe and were very Western in outlook. It was they, often referred to as the Ashkenazi or Western Jews, who fought the war for independence and who established Israel's political institutions. The war for independence—the Arab-Israeli War of 1948—also brought a massive influx of Middle Eastern or Sephardic Jews to Israel. The Sephardic or Eastern Jews knew little of Western ways, possessed few technical skills, and generally reflected the traditional attitudes of the countries from which they had migrated. By and large, they formed a lower class in Israeli society, the vestiges of which still remain (Smooha 1998). To these two groups of immigrants would be added a growing class of *Sabras*, or native-born Israelis, who had never known life in the diaspora. With the collapse of the Soviet Union in 1990, new waves of Soviet Jews would find their way to Israel, as would a small cluster of Jews from Ethiopia. The Soviet Jews, now approaching 25 percent of the Israeli population, have tended to be highly skilled professionals, while those from Ethiopia brought little to Israel but their labor. Differing class and geographic backgrounds have also brought differing ideological views. Many of the early immigrants from eastern Europe were ardent socialists and sought an egalitarian society. Many of the Sephardim, by contrast, inclined toward capitalism, as did the growing number of native-born Israelis. Much the same was true in the religious realm, with the Western Jews tending to be far more secular than their Eastern counterparts. As Arian notes, "In Israeli politics one of the dominant criteria is ethnicity, not the Jewish and non-Jewish distinction, but intra-Jewish ethnicity" (Arian 1997, 32).

In addition to the diversity of its population, several other factors have had a profound impact upon the evolution of Israeli politics. Of particular importance is Israel's position as the focal point of three of the world's great religions: Judaism, Christianity, and Islam. Because of its religious significance, events in Israel generate a tremendous amount of world attention, and Israel probably garners more press coverage per square inch of territory than any other country on earth. While Israeli leaders have generally used the limelight to their advantage, they inevitably find themselves playing to a foreign audience. This does have an impact on decision making in both the foreign and domestic arenas.

Beyond being the focal point of three major religions, Israel is a Jewish state. All Jews have the right to Israeli citizenship, regardless of their country of origin. Jewishness, however, is a culture as well as a religion, and many of Israel's citizens, as noted above, are non-religious (Liebman and Susser 1998). Others are reform Jews or conservative Jews, both of whom subscribe to a more flexible interpretation of Jewish religious law than the orthodox and ultra-orthodox Jews. This divide is described by Liebman and Susser:

> While Israeli Jews would appear to be divided into a secular and religious sector, a more appropriate division would be into three population groups. First is the majority of religiously observant Jews, who subscribe to a religio-political culture and who represent roughly 20 percent of the population. Second, there is a radical secular public, representing about 10 percent of the Jewish population, who define themselves as totally nonobservant religiously and who favor not only separation of religion and state but the dejudization of the state. They are sometimes referred to as post-Zionists. Finally, there is the vast majority of the Jewish population, who are somewhat observant of religious custom and who continue to favor a Zionist—that is, a Jewish—state (Liebman and Susser 1998, 15).

One of the major fault lines of Israeli politics, as we shall see throughout the chapter, has been the struggle to define the proper role of religion in the political life of a religious state.

Israeli politics has also been shaped by the fact that it has spent its entire history as a modern country in conflict with its Arab neighbors, not the least of which is the Palestinian population forced into exile by the creation of Israel. In effect, a new diaspora has merely replaced the old. Approximately 1.1 million Palestinians live within the boundaries of Israel proper, while some 1.5 million live in the Palestinian territories occupied by Israel during the 1967 War (*Ha'aretz*, May 9, 2000). A larger number reside in Jordan, where they constitute some 70 percent of the population, while still others live in refugee camps in Lebanon and Syria or have migrated to the Gulf or the West. All Palestinians, however, are adamant in their desire for a return to Palestine, however limited its boundaries. This seemingly irreconcilable conflict between two claimants to the same land has found expression in an unrelenting pageant of terrorism and counter-terrorism (Trapp 1994). Ironically, Israeli scientists now suggest that Israelis and Palestinians share common genes, a finding they interpret as indicating a common ancestry (*Ha'aretz*, May 9, 2000, www).

Security considerations crowd the Israeli political agenda and have forced Israel to allocate an exceptionally large portion of its budget to military expenditures. These financial outlays, in turn, have forced Israel into debt and ipso facto increased its dependence upon the United States. Life in a perpetual state of war has also created a "fortress mentality," the worst aspects of which have found expression in the often brutal suppression of the Palestinians living on the West Bank or Gaza Strip, territories occupied by Israel in the June War of 1967 (Ezrahi 1998).

Much will be said of the Palestinian experience throughout this chapter, for it is doubtful that Israel will ever find a lasting peace until the Palestinian issue is settled. This is true today more than ever, for Israel's leaders must now choose between trading land for peace— returning the Palestinian lands occupied by Israel during the 1967 War, or incorporating those lands, part of historical Israel, into the Israeli nation. The former option offers the promise of peace, the latter the restoration of the promised lands of ancient Israel.

Finally, Israeli politics has been influenced by both the small size of the country and the sparseness of its natural resources, not the least of which is water. The small size of Israel makes the country vulnerable to attack and has been used to justify the creation of buffer zones in Lebanon and the Occupied Territories. A war fought within Israel, its military strategists point out, would destroy the country regardless of who claimed victory. Israel's minuscule size also places an upper limit on the size of the population that it can sustain within its present borders. Even without the vast divide of distrust that separates the Jews and the Palestinians, it is doubtful that the country could support both communities. Today, both communities are approaching the six million mark.

In this chapter we begin by examining Israel's history and culture and then trace the events that have shaped its politics. After exploring Israel's history, we will examine the operation of its political system today. We will follow the same format in each of the remaining chapters of the text.

HISTORY AND CULTURE

The lands of geographic Palestine, like most of the Middle East, stretch deep into the reaches of history (Sharkansky 1991). Semitic tribes from the Syrian and Arabian deserts began to settle in the region around 5000 BC, with the Hebrews arriving in approximately 1300 BC. The term "Semitic" refers to a linguistic grouping that includes both the Hebrew and Arabic languages (Orlinsky 1961, 145).

The history of Israel, from the Israeli perspective, begins when Moses, the leader of a nomadic Hebrew tribe, was guided by God to lead his people into Palestine (or Canaan, as it was then known). As recounted by the Old Testament:

> And the Lord said unto Moses in the plains of Moab by the Jordan at Jericho, "Say to the people of Israel, when you pass over the Jordan into the land of Canaan, then you shall drive out all the inhabitants of the land before you, and destroy all their figured stones, and destroy all their molten images, and demolish all their high places, and you shall take possession of the land and settle in it, for I have given the land to you to possess it" (Numbers XXXIII: 50–55).

> And I will give to you and to your descendants after you, the land of your sojournings, all the land of Canaan, for an everlasting possession (Genesis XVII: 8).

The Israelites were successful in conquering much of Canaan—the term *Israel* was first used during this period—but would subsequently succumb to invasions by the Philistines, Egyptians, Babylonians, Persians, Greeks, and Romans (Orlinsky 1961). The invasion of the Philistines forced the Hebrew tribes to unite under Saul in 1020 BC, a date that marks the creation of the first Israeli kingdom (Orlinsky 1961). The kingdoms of David and Solomon, which soon followed, represented the "golden age" of ancient Israel. It was during David's reign that Jerusalem was conquered and made the capital of the Hebrew state. David would also design the temple that was to become a focal point of the Jewish faith. As described by Orlinsky:

> The centralization of political authority in the abode of the king called for a corresponding focus for religious jurisdiction, and David's ministers began to plan the erection of a royal chapel, a magnificent edifice which would represent the earthly dwelling of Israel's invisible God. To provide fitting service for the Temple, a priesthood was established and musical guilds were organized...(Orlinsky 1961, 64).

While space does not allow a recounting of the history of ancient Israel, suffice it to say that the internal divisions led to the fragmentation of the Jewish state and its subsequent subjugation by a variety of foreign invaders, including the Assyrians, Babylonians, and Romans. It was the Romans who expelled the Jews from the Holy Lands in 135 BC, giving rise to the diaspora—the dispersion of Jews throughout Europe and the Middle East.

Aside from serving as a source of national pride, the ancient history of most countries has little relevance to their modern politics. This is not the case in Israel, for it is the Jewish kingdoms of ancient Israel that justify the Israeli claim to Palestine. Indeed, some Israelis argue that the present state of Israel should incorporate all of the lands of ancient Israel, an area that would include portions of Lebanon, Jordan, and Syria (Gilbert 1979, 1). For many Jews, moreover, the lands of Israel are more than an artifact of history; they are the "Promised Land." The Temple of David is a holy site of profound political and religious significance, as is Hebron, the capital of the Jewish state prior to the conquest of Jerusalem (Sharkansky 1997b).

Israelis often talk of "collapsed time," as if the period of some two thousand years that passed between the expulsion of the Jews from Jerusalem and the creation of the Jewish state of Israel in 1948 was little more than a momentary interruption in the course of Jewish history. The Jews had merely returned to their promised land.

Expelled from the lands of Israel, the Jews migrated throughout Europe and the Middle East where they either assimilated with the dominant Christian or Muslim populations or lived in minority enclaves. There was little choice in the matter, for both European and Middle Eastern societies at the time were organized along religious lines. One either joined the majority population or lived in exclusion. Persecution was frequent, but less so among the Muslims than among Christians, who blamed Jews for the death of Christ. (Indeed, it was only recently that the Vatican absolved the Jews of the murder of Christ.) Majority populations, moreover, often viewed the minorities in their midst with suspicion and all too frequently used them as scapegoats for their own deficiencies, a process that continues today (Allport 1954). Political leaders, in turn, found it expedient to divert mass hostility from their own regimes by focusing it on the Jews. This trend became particularly noticeable in the nineteenth century as the European monarchs of that era found their power threatened by the liberalism engendered by the French and American revolutions. As described by Rodinson:

> In 1879 a fateful event took place. Bismarck, personally devoid of any prejudice against the Jews, found it expedient for his internal policy to launch a campaign of "anti-Semitism," to use the term which had recently become popular in Germany, where certain writers of small influence had been developing this theme as a stick with which to beat liberalism. The weapon proved effective, and it was taken up to meet similar political circumstances in Austria, France, and Russia in the years which followed.
>
> But in Russia, where Jewish communities of the medieval type still survived in large numbers, the reactionary Tsar Alexander III decided to avenge the death of his father on the Jews (Alexander II was killed by revolutionaries in 1881). The Tsarist administration likewise deliberate-

ly developed anti-Semitism as a political weapon against liberal ideas, and used it with great success among the more backward classes of the population, who were unleashed on the defenseless Jewish communities. The Russian pogroms filled the civilized world with horror (Rodinson 1969, 12).

The link between liberalism and the Jews was easy to establish, for many European Jews had viewed political liberalism as an opportunity to escape the cruel choice between assimilation and seclusion. Jewish intellectuals, in particular, found the restrictions of their ancient faith to be at odds with the spirit of reason ushered in by the French Revolution and were active participants in the effort to create national societies in which individuals were judged by their merits rather than their ancestry (Sharkansky 1991). Karl Marx was of Jewish origin, and Jews played a prominent and visible role in virtually all of the leftist movements that swept Europe during the eighteenth and nineteenth centuries.

Zionism

As the situation in Eastern Europe became increasingly untenable, a growing number of Jews looked to the lands of their ancestry as a potential refuge, a process stimulated by the publication of Theodor Herzl's *A Jewish State* in 1886. Herzl's book gave birth to the Zionist movement, the first congress of which was held in 1887. Herzl argued that Jews would never be fully assimilated in Europe and inevitably would continue to be persecuted. The only solution, he argued, was the creation of a Jewish state in which Jews would be able to live without persecution and practice their religion as they wished. Argentina and Uganda were both suggested as possible sites for the new state, but the suggestions were rejected because of their lack of emotional appeal. Only a promised return to the ancient lands of Zion (Israel) would suffice to rally the entire Jewish community behind the Zionist project (Rodinson 1969, 13). The first Zionist Congress was followed by the establishment of a World Zionist Organization charged with creating a Jewish state in Palestine.

Zionism, as preached by Herzl, was preeminently an expression of Jewish nationalism. The Jews would have their own country, much as the French and British had theirs. Religious Jews could practice their faith as they saw fit, but Israel would be a home for all Jews, secular as well as religious. Judaism is a culture as well as a religion, and even fully assimilated Jews such as Herzl possessed a strong emotional attachment to Jewish traditions (Orr 1994). The wave of anti-Semitism sweeping Europe, moreover, did not distinguish between religious and non-religious Jews. The persecution of both groups was equal.

Ironically, the emergence of the Zionist movement was paralleled by embryonic stirrings of Arab nationalism. The stage was thus set for an inevitable clash between two rival ideologies: Judaism and Zionism on one side, Islam and Arab nationalism on the other. Zionism and Arab nationalism were secular ideologies, but both drew heavily upon religious symbolism. The Islamic invasion had incorporated the lands of geographic Palestine into the Arab/Islamic world in AD 637, and for the next 1300-plus years, it would be the Arabs who toiled in the lands of Palestine. This history, in the view of the Arab nationalists, gave them a far greater claim to Palestine than events that had transpired in antiquity.

The Ottoman authorities had eased the ban on Jewish immigration to Palestine in 1880, and a steady trickle of Jews began to join the approximately 24,000 Jews who resided in Palestine at the time. These new settlers, between 20,000 and 30,000 in number, are referred to as the first *aliyah* or wave of immigration, a Hebrew word suggesting the "going up" (Arian 1997, 403). Jews, however, represented only about 10 percent of the population, and thoughts of a Jewish state were remote, at best (Rodinson 1969, 14). A second aliyah arrived in the years between 1905 and the outbreak of the World War I, most of whom were Russian socialists fleeing from the failed Russian revolution of 1905. It was this group that would subsequently set the ideological tenor for the Israeli state and provide much of its early leadership. Nevertheless, numbers remained small, and by the end of World War I, Jews constituted no more than 12 percent of the Palestinian population, or 85,000 out of a total population of 739,000 (Rodinson 1969, 20).

While immigration to Palestine had been slow in the years prior to World War I—most Jews preferred to immigrate to the United States rather than the harsh environs of Palestine—the World Zionist Organization had actively sought the support of Western governments for its project. Their efforts came to fruition during the course of World War I as a British Government anxious to gain the support of American and Russian Jews for the war effort assented to their demands. The issue was contentious, but shortly before the end of the war Lord Balfour issued a vaguely worded statement declaring Britain's support for the Zionist cause. A parallel statement would later be issued by the League of Nations.

> His Majesty's Government views with favour the establishment in Palestine of a national home for the Jewish people, and will use its best endeavours to facilitate the achievement of this object, it being clearly understood that nothing shall be done which may prejudice the civil

and religious rights of existing non-Jewish communities in Palestine, or the rights and political status enjoyed by Jews in any other country (Fraser 1980, 18).

Upon the defeat of Ottoman Turkey in World War I, Britain was allocated the mandate for Palestine, and the Jewish Agency, the executive body of the World Zionist Organization, accelerated its settlement of Jews in Palestine. The Balfour Declaration, however, was shrouded in conflict from the date of its inception. The British had earlier implied that control of Palestine would go to the Arab leader of Mecca in return for his willingness to lead a revolt against the Turks, although this matter, too, remained ambiguous (see Chapter 5). Also problematic was the vague wording of the Balfour Declaration itself. What precisely was meant by the phrase "national home for the Jews"? Did this mean that Jews were free to settle in Palestine or, as interpreted by the Zionists, did it call for the establishment of a Jewish state? If one accepted the latter interpretation, how was this state to be established without prejudicing the "civil and religious rights of existing non-Jewish communities"? Matters were not made easier by the nature of the mandate system established by the League of Nations. Mandates were not colonies. Rather, the mandatory powers were entrusted with leading the former axis colonies toward self-government. At least on the surface, this implied a government that represented all of the residents of the territory.

The Zionists, however, suffered from no ambiguity. The Jewish Agency, the executive body of the World Zionist Organization, began to buy land in Palestine and to provide financial assistance for Jewish immigrants. Initial waves of migration were disappointing, but increased rapidly with the onslaught of Hitler and his threatened extermination of the Jewish people. By 1936, Jews constituted 30 percent of the Palestinian population, as compared to less than 12 percent in 1922.

As immigration increased, the Jewish community began to develop its own political institutions, or Yishuv. These included an elected Assembly with the power to levy taxes and an all-encompassing labor union called the Histadrut. In addition to its role as a labor union, the Histadrut also served as an investment company, landowner, insurance company, and social security agency. Eventually, the Yishuv would also add a military wing, the Haganah. The Yishuv thus represented a state within a state and was far better organized than a Palestinian community fragmented by family and personality conflicts.

Invariably, the rapid increase in Jewish immigrants threatened the Arab population in Palestine, many of whom found themselves marginalized by the growing economic dominance of the Jews. Much of the land purchased by the Jewish Agency had been sold by absentee

Arab landlords, many resident in Beirut. As land purchases increased, the number of displaced Palestinians increased proportionally. The purpose of the land purchases had been to settle Jews, not Arabs.

Fearing that they would soon become a minority in their own land, the Palestinians revolted against the British authorities in 1936. The British responded with force, but the rebellion raged for three years before being fully suppressed. The intensity of the Palestinian revolt, together with mounting anti-British sentiment throughout the region, forced the British to rethink their Palestinian strategy. World War II was rapidly approaching, and the British had become increasingly apprehensive over pro-Axis sentiments among the Arabs. The Middle East lay astride the route to India, the Jewel of the British Empire, and by the mid-1930s Britain's military and industrial establishments were becoming increasingly dependent upon Middle Eastern oil. German domination of the Middle East would jeopardize Britain's access to both India and oil.

Faced with these new realities, the British began to vacillate in their support for the Zionists. In 1939, the British Government issued a White Paper that sharply reduced the level of Jewish immigration to Palestine and severely restricted the sale of Arab land to Jews. Palestine was also promised eventual independence as a bi-religious state in which the Arabs would constitute a two-thirds majority. The timing of the White Paper, from the Zionist perspective, could hardly have been worse. Anti-Semitism in Germany—and many other areas of Europe—was now approaching its zenith, and Palestine was viewed as the main refuge for Europe's beleaguered Jews.

It was now the Jews who revolted against the British, with terrorist organizations such as the Irgun and the Stern Gang launching violent attacks against British targets (Bauer 1970; Rodinson 1973). A truce was called during World War II, but the Jewish revolt resumed in 1944 and in 1945 with the Haganah, the military wing of the Yishuv, joining the fray. Two future Israeli prime ministers, Menachem Begin and Yitzhak Shamir, played leading roles in the terrorist struggle against the British (Begin 1951).

The Jewish revolt raged until 1947, when the British Government announced that it would withdraw from Palestine within a few months. The issue was turned over to the United Nations, which subsequently announced that Palestine would be divided into two independent entities, one Jewish and the other Arab. The arrangement satisfied neither side, and upon the withdrawal of the British forces on May 14, 1948, David Ben-Gurion proclaimed the rebirth of the Israeli state. War flared as Arab armies surged into Palestine to reclaim Palestine for the Arab world. They succeeded only in retaining two patches of the original Palestinian mandate: the Gaza Strip, a narrow coastal plain adjacent to Egypt, and a far larger segment of land adjoining the West Bank of the Jordan River. A majority of the Palestinians fled the country under circumstances that continue to be a source of debate. The Israelis claim that the Palestinians were urged to flee by Arab leaders, while the Palestinians point to the systematic terror employed by Israeli forces against Arab villagers. The most vicious incident in this regard was the systematic massacre of all 254 inhabitants of the Palestinian village of Deir Yassin, the news of which was used to set the residents of neighboring villages to flight (Polk, Stamler, and Asfour 1957).

Arab bitterness against Israel was intense. Arab nationalists viewed the Jewish state as an extension of Western imperialism in the heart of the Arab world. In point of fact, Herzl, the founder of the World Zionist Organization, had earlier proclaimed that, "We should there form a portion of the rampart of Europe against Asia, an outpost of civilization as opposed to barbarism" (Herzl 1896, 29). Muslim leaders similarly railed at the fall of Muslim lands to the Jews, and Egypt's Muslim Brotherhood sent volunteers to fight in Palestine. Underlying the hostility toward Israel was a profound sense of Arab humiliation. Even today, Arabs refer to the 1948 War as the *nakba*, or "catastrophe."

The Era of Revolution and Optimism

Israel entered the era of independence with profound optimism. The revolt against the British had been successful, the Arabs had been defeated, and the new state of Israel had been created. The regional environment was hostile, but the new state enjoyed strong support from Western powers as well as world Jewry. Even the Soviet Union had hastened to recognize the new state.

Problems, however, abounded. Israel was desperately poor and depended upon foreign support for its survival. Defense expenditures were enormous, and the influx of new settlers strained the meager resources of the new state to the breaking point. Of these settlers, many were survivors of the Holocaust who had earlier been denied entry to Palestine by the British. Even more problematic were the Jewish refugees from the Arab world who now flooded into Israel to escape retribution for the Arab defeat in the 1948 War. The culture of the eastern Jews, as noted earlier, was far more conservative than that of their European counterparts in both their social and religious views.

Few problems, however, were greater than that posed by the Palestinians. While the birth of Israel had brought an end to one diaspora, it had created another. It was now the Palestinians rather than the Jews who were homeless. It was now they, many of whom were condemned to squalid refugee camps and exploited by rival Arab leaders, who sought salvation in a return to the lands of their ancestors. If the Jews viewed the future with optimism, the Palestinians viewed it with despair and engaged in a relentless pursuit of a Palestinian homeland. Israel could make peace with its neighboring countries, but how was it to make peace with a parallel population that held claim to the same land? This was all the more problematic because Israel was to be a Jewish state. By definition, the incorporation of a Palestinian population of parallel size would destroy the Jewish character of the state and pose inordinate security problems. Indeed, the some 160,000 Palestinians remaining in Israel at the time of independence, although formally Israeli citizens, were considered security risks and placed under military control. Travels of any distance required a military permit and, because it was often difficult to tell a Jew from a Palestinian, the latter were required to carry special identity cards. Palestinians were also precluded from serving in the military (Rodinson 1969, 51). The Israelis did not want to integrate the Palestinians into the new Jewish state. They had conquered Palestinian land but were unsure what to do about the Palestinians.

Equally pressing for the new state was the problem of land. Approximately 80 percent of Palestinian land had been vacated during the war and was now used by the Israeli government to settle Jews. How could it be returned to its Palestinian owners? (Rodinson 1969, 51). If anything, the need to settle Jews required more land.

The political institutions designed to confront these problems were essentially those inherited from the Yishuv of the colonial era. The Assembly became the Knesset, a unicameral parliament of 120 members elected on the basis of proportional representation. If a political party gained 5 percent of the popular vote, it received 5 percent of the seats in the Knesset. The members of the Knesset, in turn, elected the prime minister by a simple majority vote. Once elected, the prime minister pieced together a Government consisting of the cabinet as well as a variety of junior positions. A Government remained in office for a five-year term or until it was forced to resign by a vote of no confidence in the Knesset.

In actual practice, of course, the formation of a Government would be a very complex process. Israeli opinion was divided into three major tendencies or party clusters: a leftist (socialist) bloc, a right-wing bloc that inclined toward capitalism and ultra-nationalism, and a religious bloc whose primary concern was assuring that Israel retained its religious character. These three clusters, in turn, were fragmented into even smaller factions. Rather than a single religious party, for example, Israel possessed three or four religious parties, each with its own religious and social orientation. The same three blocs form the cornerstone of Israeli politics today.

The first Israeli elections were contested by 21 political parties. The Mapai, the forerunner to the Labor Coalition of today, gained some 35 percent of the vote but could only govern in coalition with a number of smaller parties, including the religious parties. The formation of a stable coalition, accordingly, involved considerable horse trading as each party vied for choice positions in the Government. This pattern would remain throughout the era, with the swing role of the religious parties giving them far greater influence than their support among the electorate would warrant (Rodinson 1969, 48).

Other political institutions included a symbolic presidency and an elaborate court system that distinguished between secular and religious law. Secular law was uniform across the country, but personal statutes such as marriage and divorce varied according to faith and were administered by religious courts. These and other issues were addressed in a series of basic laws passed during the early sessions of the Knesset. Israel does not possess a formal constitution because of the complexity of drawing a clear line between secular authority and religious authority. A special committee to prepare a constitution was established in 2000, but the outlook is not promising (*JP*[1], Jan. 18, 2000).

Israel's first Government was headed by David Ben-Gurion, the leader of the Mapai (Labor) Party. Ben-Gurion was a committed Zionist and an equally committed socialist. Not only was Israel to be a Jewish state, but it was to be a state that stressed social equality. Ben-Gurion was to become the towering figure of modern Israeli history and it was his hand, more than any other, that would set the course of Israel's history.

Despite Ben-Gurion's stature, he lacked a majority in the Knesset and was forced to piece together a coalition government from among Israel's multitude of ideological currents, a tortuous process at best. Achieving a coalition proved to be impossible without the support of the religious parties, and Ben-Gurion, a secularist, was forced to give extraordinary power to the Orthodox rabbis. To make matters worse, Ben-Gurion's own party was rife with conflict. Relations between Ben-Gurion and Moshe Sharett, his foreign minister, would become particularly strained over Israel's Arab policy, a topic to be discussed shortly (Sharett 1978, reprinted in Rabinovich and Reinharz 1984). The

[1]*Jerusalem Post.*

leaders of the Histadrut (labor federation) also wielded great influence, as did the leaders of the military, upon whose survival Israel depended.

By and large, political debate in Israel would revolve around five pre-eminent concerns: security, Jewishness, land, peace, and nation building. Security was of foremost importance, for unless the survival of the state could be assured, everything else was moot. Security issues focused on defense, but they also involved the economic viability of the new state. Israel was a small state with few natural resources, and its survival depended on its capacity to provide for the needs of its population. Israel was also to be a Jewish state. It was to be a place where Jews could live without prejudice, and it was to be a haven for a world Jewry still reeling from the horrors of the Holocaust. Israel's survival, moreover, required the support of the world Jewish community, and its foreign policy would have to reflect the concerns of that community. The issue of land was equally problematic. In addition to historic considerations, additional land would be required to settle more Jews. Land, moreover, was vital to the defense of Israel. Israel was only ten miles wide at its narrowest point, and its communications could easily be severed by an enemy attack. The small size of the state also dictated the need for buffers. Israel could defend itself, but little would be gained if the country were to be destroyed in the process.

The ultimate security of Israel, of course, required a lasting peace with its Arab neighbors. At what price, however, was peace to be achieved? Acceptance of the prevailing UN peace plan would require a return to Israel's pre-1948 boundaries and force the repatriation of a large Palestinian population within Israel's body politic. This prospect was anathema to a large segment of the Israeli population and posed a security nightmare. A return of the Palestinians also threatened the Jewish character of the state and limited the possibility for increased Jewish immigration. Israelis wanted peace, but it would have to be a peace that addressed Israel's overriding concerns for security, the Jewish character of the state, and the role of land as it pertained to the issues of defense and Jewishness.

Adding to the political debate was Israel's need to galvanize itself into an effective nation. Israel's political institutions, while largely inherited from the Yishuv, had to be strengthened and extended. Masses of new immigrants, many from Middle Eastern backgrounds, also had to be integrated into the social, economic, and political life of the nation. The new immigrants had to become something more than Jews; they had to become "modern" Israelis. Little, moreover, could be achieved without the rapid development of the Israeli economy. Aid from the world Jewish community was generous, but the ongoing economic survival of the Jewish state required more than handouts. The Israeli state had to become economically viable in its own right.

Virtually all segments of Israeli society accepted the importance of security, Jewishness, land, peace, and nation building as the cornerstones of Israeli policy. Bitter debates, however, raged over questions of priority and strategy. Debates over the handling of the Arabs were particularly intense. While Ben-Gurion advocated an iron fist toward the Arabs, Sharett pushed for accommodation, arguing that Israel's ultimate survival depended upon peace with its neighbors (Sheffer 1996). The use of excessive force, according to Sharett, would create more problems than it would solve (Brecher 1974). So vital was foreign policy to Israel's security that virtually all cabinet meetings began with a debate on that topic.

The question of religion was equally contentious and, as noted above, had precluded the establishment of a formal constitution. The price for the participation of the religious parties in the ruling coalition, moreover, had been control of the rabbinical courts by the Orthodox rabbis as well as large subsidies to synagogues and religious schools and the suspension of public transport on the Sabbath. Many of these blue laws were supported by American Jews, leading one secular Israeli Jew to note with bitterness, "The salvation of the American Jews is conveniently assured by the strict religious observance imposed on Israeli Jews, while their consciences are assuaged and their supposed duty as Zionists fulfilled at the price of certain financial sacrifices" (Rodinson 1969, 49).

Unable to agree on a constitution, Israeli leaders established guidelines for the country's ongoing institutional development through a variety of Basic Laws passed by the Knesset during the ensuing years. Ironically, the first of these, the Basic Law defining the procedures of the Knesset itself, was not passed until 1958. Others included laws referring to land under Israeli control (1960); the president (1964); the Government (Cabinet) (1968); the state economy (i.e., taxes and the budget) (1975); the army (1976); and the Jerusalem Law (formally establishing Jerusalem as the capital (1980) (Rabinovich and Reinharz 1984, 41). The Law of Return was passed in 1950 and is generally treated as a Basic Law. The Law of Return states that every Jew has the right to come to Israel as an immigrant. A 1952 law extended the Law of Return by allowing all Jews the right to Israeli nationality even if they chose to retain their original nationality.

Israel's political situation was far less chaotic than the circumstances might suggest, for the Israelis, much like the British, possessed an unwritten constitution. The basic rules of Israeli politics were developed during the colonial era and were broadly accepted by the Israeli population. Stability was also provided by the dominant position of the Mapai Party and the profound respect enjoyed by Ben-Gurion. The regional environment also left little scope for internal dissension. Israelis could either work together or perish. Ben-Gurion's policies sometimes stretched the limits of Israeli democracy, but the tensions of the period offered little time for debate.

In 1952, Ben-Gurion strained his popularity by proposing that Israel accept war reparations from West Germany. The thought that the Germans would be able to atone for the Holocaust was repugnant to a broad spectrum of Jews and sparked severe rioting in Jerusalem. Money, however, was of the essence. Defense expenditures consumed between 30 and 40 percent of the budget, and the costs of settling Jewish immigrants was enormous (Rodinson 1969, 45).

In 1953, a second crisis would erupt over Ben-Gurion's hard-line policy toward the Arabs. In October of that year, a Palestinian raid on an Israeli village killed a woman and two children. The Israeli army responded with a particularly brutal attack against a Jordanian village, blowing up some forty houses and killing 53 villagers (Rodinson 1969, 69). The raid symbolized Israel's iron fist policy toward terrorism, and served notice to Arab leaders that they would be held responsible for Palestinian attacks emanating from their territory. A strong show of force, in Ben-Gurion's view, was also needed to calm an Israeli population increasingly anxious over the capacity of the Jewish state to defend itself. There had been a net outflow of Jews from Israel in 1953.[2] Security had become far more than the defense of Israel's boundaries. If the Jewish state were to survive, it had to provide a secure domestic environment for its citizens. The Palestinian raids could not defeat the Israeli army, but they could raise the price of living in Israel to unacceptable levels. Ben-Gurion accepted responsibility for ordering the raid, and resigned a few months later. He was replaced in office by Moshe Sharett.

Sharett accepted the need to maintain Israel's expanded boundaries, but as suggested above, felt that Arab states shared a mutual interest in peace. The important objective, in his view, was to penetrate the wall of hysteria that separated the two parties and search for common ground. This objective, according to Sharett, could be achieved more effectively by subtle negotiations than by continued affronts to a much-battered Arab pride. The Arab world was also changing. Syria had been rocked by several coups d'état and Nasser, having seized

---

[2]At one point, an anonymous emigrant posted a note at the airport suggesting that the last Israeli to leave should turn out the lights.

power in Egypt, had secured the evacuation of British troops from Egyptian territory. The long-term interests of Israel, Sharett argued, were better served by negotiating with Nasser than by forcing him into a radical position.

Crisis followed crisis, and in 1955 Ben-Gurion returned to the Government as Minister of Defense. The Israeli Government was now at odds with itself. Sharett was the prime minister, but Ben-Gurion remained the effective leader of the country. Barely eleven days after returning to the Government as Minister of Defense, Ben-Gurion ordered a raid on Egyptian troops in the Gaza Strip, reportedly to punish the Egyptian authorities for allowing Palestinians to launch raids into Israel from the Gaza region. Forty Egyptian troops were killed, and many more were wounded. In reality, there had been little Palestinian "infiltration" into Israel during this period, and the Israeli press speculated that the Israeli attack had been designed as a pre-emptive measure to teach the Egyptians a lesson and to reassure a nervous Israeli public (Yaari in Rabinovich and Reinharz, 1984).

Furious with the Israeli assault, Nasser had demanded increased arms from the United States. Washington equivocated, indicating that it would provide arms only if Egypt joined the newly formed Baghdad Pact. As discussed in the preceding chapter, Nasser chose instead to purchase arms from the Soviet bloc, thereby shattering the West's arms monopoly in the Middle East. The US canceled its aid for Nasser's Aswan Dam, and Nasser retaliated by nationalizing the Suez Canal.

More than ever, Israel was becoming frightened by Nasser's aggressiveness and his growing popularity within the Arab World. Arab nationalism, long simmering leaderless in the Arab World, was rapidly solidifying behind the profoundly charismatic Nasser. Egypt forged a mutual defense pact with Syria while pressure from Egypt had dissuaded both Jordan and Saudi Arabia from joining the Baghdad Pact. Following the attack on Gaza, moreover, Nasser had organized the heretofore irregular bands of Palestinian fighters into *fedayeen*, an organized guerrilla force trained and supplied by the Egyptian army. Their effectiveness increased apace and could not be ignored by the Israelis.

Israel was not the only country that feared the growing power of Nasser. Britain and France had been stung by Nasser's nationalization of the Suez Canal, and France was increasingly apprehensive about Nasser's support for an Algerian revolution that was threatening to engulf France itself. Negotiations between Britain, France, and Israel led to a plan for the seizure of the Canal and, presumably, the downfall of Nasser. In rough outline, Israeli forces were to march to the Canal, while the British and French intervened as neutral parties to assure that the Canal would remain safe for international shipping. Toward this end, the British and French would demand that Egypt and Israel withdraw their forces from the Canal region or face occupation by a joint Anglo-French force. Israel would accept the Anglo-French conditions, leaving Nasser in the untenable position of either engaging the British and French in a war that he could not win, or vacating Egyptian territory. The latter would cast Nasser in the role of a coward and destroy his charisma. Either way, he would lose.

The plan was executed to perfection, its only real flaw being the exclusion of the United States. The United States at the time was involved in an increasingly bitter struggle with the Soviet Union for the hearts and minds of the Third World and had determined to counter Soviet propaganda by presenting itself to the countries of Asia and Africa as the world's "first new nation" (Holland 1996). Like the Third World countries, the US had revolted against colonial oppression and therefore understood the needs and aspirations of emerging nations. To support the tripartite attack on Egypt would have placed the US in the imperialist camp and left the Soviets free to expand their influence in areas that were seething with revolution.

With its global strategy at risk, the United States pressured Israel and its allies to withdraw from Egyptian territory. Nasser emerged the victor and, as recounted in the preceding chapter, launched his campaign to unify the Arab world, perhaps the greatest nightmare of the Israeli leadership. All, however, was not lost. Israel had again demonstrated its military prowess and actively began to perpetuate the myth of its military invincibility. The more the Arabs believed in the invincibility of the Israeli Defense Forces (IDF), according to Israeli policy, the less likely they would be to initiate aggressive adventures and the more easily their troops would become demoralized. UN troops were also stationed on the Egyptian-Israeli border, thereby offering Israel security from Egyptian attack. This protection, however, was not an unmixed blessing, for it provided Nasser with time to develop his army and bring the Arab world under his sway.

The 1956 War had a profound impact on Israeli foreign policy. By choosing to ignore the United States, Israel had been denied the fruits of a dazzling military victory. The United States was too powerful and too important to Israel's survival to allow this to happen again. The interests of the United States would have to be accommodated. Even more importantly, the US would have to be convinced that a strong Israel was in its national interest. This would require the redoubled efforts of the American Jewish community, the largest in the world outside of Israel itself.

Israel had sought a formal alliance with the United States even before the 1956 War, and these efforts were now intensified. An alliance with the United States, as Sharett would write,

> would guarantee our security through a mutual pact; it would strengthen us in relation to the Arab states; it would assist peace; it would increase our worth in the eyes of the world; it would provide an incentive for capital investment; it would constitute a message to Jewry (Sharett in Rabinovich and Reinharz 1984, 96).

Ben-Gurion had returned as prime minister shortly after the 1956 War, providing the country with firm leadership. The presence of UN observers in the Sinai Peninsula increased Israel's sense of security and this, along with the growing support of the United States, facilitated the process of nation building discussed earlier. Tensions, however, remained, not the least of which was the continued gap in power and wealth that separated the Western and Eastern Jews. Also problematic was the growing debate over the role of religion in Israeli society.

The tension between the Eastern and Western Jews came to a head in 1959 when ethnic violence flared in a poor district of Haifa. As Ben-Gurion recounts, a bitter debate followed in the Knesset.

> Israel Yeshayahu Sharabi said that for many years we had been worried by the possibility of just such a flare-up of communal passions as had occurred in Haifa: "The ingathering of the exiles from all corners of the world has revealed a distressing situation, for though we are one nation in our historic awareness and our Jewish religion, we find ourselves after two thousand years of exile a people that not only has been dispersed among the nations but fragmented by sharp differences of language, food, dress, customs, concepts, ways of thinking, and other things. Nor is this the result of any conscious desire but a curse, perhaps the harshest one that has been imposed upon us by exile" (Ben-Gurion in Rabinovich and Reinharz 1984, 563).

The issue of religion would again come to the fore in 1962 with the case of "Brother Daniel." Brother Daniel, a Jew who had converted to Christianity to avoid persecution during World War II and who had played a major role in assisting other Jews to avoid persecution, now demanded Israeli citizenship under the Law of Return. His request was rejected, and the case was taken to the Israeli Supreme Court for resolution. Among other points, Brother Daniel argued "that the concept 'nationality' is not identical with the concept 'religion' and that a Jew by nationality need not be a Jew by religion" (Supreme Court Decision in Rabinovich and Reinharz 1984, 152). The case was decided in favor of Brother Daniel.

The case is significant on two counts. First, it signaled the growing role of Israel's Supreme Court in Israeli politics. Second, it asserted the state's supremacy on issues involving non-orthodox Jews who were demanding that the Israeli government recognize their marriages and conversions, matters heretofore reserved for Orthodox rabbis. Religion, as we shall see shortly, continues to be a major source of tension in Israeli politics.

It was at this point that Ben-Gurion, now in his mid-seventies, resigned amidst controversy and was replaced as prime minister by Levi Eshkol in June of 1963. Eshkol lacked Ben-Gurion's stature and was closer in temperament to Moshe Sharett. If peace could be worked out with the Arabs, he was ready to be conciliatory (Rodinson 1969, 112). Abba Eban, a gifted diplomat of similar inclination, became foreign minister and for a brief period, Israeli policy toward the Arabs softened. This softening also reflected the mood of a population that had lived in relative peace since the 1956 War and had grown weary of Ben-Gurion's siege mentality. Indeed, Eban would attack Ben-Gurion's foreign policy as "adventurist" and "bitter endist" (Rodinson 1969, 177). The United States had also eased Israel's sense of urgency by committing itself to stand "foursquare" behind Israel in case of attack. Advanced-technology US arms were also forthcoming (Peres in Rabinovich and Reinharz 1984, 176).

The Hawks chafed under Eshkol's rule, and in 1964 the ruling Mapai Party split, with its hawks forming the Rafi Party. Beyond security risks, Moshe Dayan (soon to be Minister of Defense) "warned of the danger of 'levantinization.'" Sephardic (Eastern) Jews were growing in numbers and would eventually threaten the monopoly of power long enjoyed by the Ashkenazi (Western) Jews. If Palestinians were allowed to return, Ben-Gurion argued, Israel would become little more than an ordinary Middle Eastern country. "We do not want the Israelis to turn into Arabs. We must fight against the Levantine spirit, which corrupts men and societies, and preserve the authentically Jewish values which have been developed in the Diaspora" (Rodinson 1969, 179).

The 1965 elections reflected the changing mood of the country. Eshkol was returned to office and the Rafi was repudiated. It was a choice, as Fein writes, "between Ben-Gurion and Eshkol, waning charisma and increasing petulance versus monotonous competence and dreary efficiency."

The ensuing years would see Nasser increase the stakes in his dangerous game of political brinkmanship, closing the Straits of Tiran to Israeli shipping on May 23, 1967. The Straits controlled access to the port of Eilat, the main point of entry of most of Israel's oil imports. The major powers, according to Nasser's strategy, were expected to save the situation much as they had in 1956, but they did not. The Israeli military launched a "preemptive" strike with devastating force, and the war was over virtually before it had begun. Israel was now in control of a vast swathe of Arab land stretching from the Suez Canal to the Golan Heights. The dynamics of Middle Eastern politics had undergone a dramatic shift.

The Era of Reassessment

Israel's dazzling victory in the June War of 1967 had dramatically transformed the political equation in the Middle East. Talk of driving Israel into the sea now appeared ludicrous, and the heady slogans of Arab nationalism had given way to a profound sense of mass disillusionment throughout the Arab World. If the 1948 War had been described as the catastrophe by Arab historians, the 1967 War would be referred to as the disaster.

While the Arab World entered an era of disillusionment and reassessment, the mood in Israel was one of guarded euphoria. The Jewish nation was more secure than it had been at any point in its short history, and the lands of ancient Israel had been returned. In addition to their religious significance, the occupied lands provided a buffer between Israel and its adversaries and beckoned for the settlement of an ever-larger Jewish population. Alternatively, the Occupied Territories land could also be traded for peace, thereby bringing to an end two decades of bitter confrontation.

The very magnitude of the Israeli success, however, brought new challenges. Israel had reclaimed the lands of ancient Israel, but those lands were occupied by approximately one million Palestinians. The Palestinian population, moreover, was expanding rapidly and would soon rival that of Israel itself. How was Israel to enjoy the fruits of its victory when the lands of ancient Israel remained occupied by Palestinians? The lands could be incorporated into Israel, but the absorption of a large Palestinian population represented an unacceptable security risk and threatened the Jewish character of the state. How could a Palestinian population approximately one-third that of Israel's Jewish population be allowed to vote in Israeli elections? Israel, moreover, was a welfare state with cradle-to-grave health and welfare programs that consumed a lion's share of the country's budget. The addition of a million largely destitute Palestinians to the welfare rolls would bankrupt the system. Israel's challenge, in the view of many Israelis, would be to keep the land but not its residents.

Israel also faced conflict with the United States and the Soviet Union over the disposition of the Occupied Territories. American policy dictated trading land for peace in the hope of ending a crisis that had seen the Soviets extend their influence in the Arab World. The Soviets, for their part, were under intense pressure from Arab allies to rebuild their shattered armies and to counter US support for Israel. Although the Soviets had little faith in the Arab capacity to fight, they could not deny Arab demands without losing credibility among their regional allies. The Soviets, too, were ready to trade land for peace.

The process of exchanging land for peace, however, was fraught with difficulty. A lethal blend of religiosity, nationalism, and fear had combined to threaten any Israeli government that advocated withdrawal from the Territories. The Occupied Territories, moreover, varied in their significance. The Sinai Peninsula did not constitute part of ancient Israel and, with proper guarantees for Israeli security, could conceivably be traded for peace. Jerusalem, by contrast, was the focal point of the Jewish faith and was non-negotiable. The West Bank was also fraught with religious significance, being the site of the ancient kingdoms of Judea and Samaria; the Gaza Strip and the Golan Heights, less so. While Israel could return some land, it was politically infeasible to return them all.

These problems were exacerbated by a transformation in the nature of Israeli society itself. Sephardic Jews were now a majority in the country and were beginning to assert their influence, as were a growing number of Sabra, or native-born Israelis. By and large, the Sephardic Jews and the Sabras were more religious and nationalistic than the Ashkenazi Jews and strongly opposed trading land for peace. They also had begun to question the socialist paternalism that had been the pillar of Mapai leadership and demanded a greater role for the private sector in Israel's economic affairs. The euphoria of the 1967 victory, moreover, had to some degree eased Israel's profound sense of insecurity, and the long-muted ideological divisions inherent within Israeli politics now came to the fore.

It was in this environment, then, that Israel entered an era of reassessment. Flush with victory in the June War of 1967, the newly formed Labor Alignment, an amalgamation of the Mapai and various other parties of the left including Ben-Gurion's break-away Rafi, captured 56 of the 120 seats in the 1969 Knesset elections, a near majority. The remaining seats were splintered among the religious parties and diverse parties of the political right. Golda Meir, a hard-line disciple of Ben-Gurion, was named prime minister. She remained wedded to the social policies of the past which, as noted above, were beginning to lose favor among the Israeli public.

As in the past, cabinet meetings continued to be dominated by foreign policy issues, with the new government seeking a balance between those cabinet members who wanted to trade land for peace and those who were intent on retaining the Occupied Territories for religious and security reasons. The Government had originally inclined toward returning the Territories but shifted to a wait-and-see position, a policy that led to considerable dissension within ruling circles.

As the Government vacillated, external events began to dictate the course of Israeli politics. In November of 1967, the United Nations passed UN Resolution 242 calling for Israel to withdraw from occupied territories in return for peace and secure boundaries. Israel signed the agreement, presumably under pressure from the United States, but soon lost interest in the project.

The debate was soon rendered moot as Egypt used its massive artillery strength, which had been totally rebuilt by the Soviets, to pound Israeli troops in the Canal Zone (Smith 1992, 216). Egyptian forces were not strong enough to drive the Israelis out of the Canal Zone, but they were clearly in a position to increase the costs of occupation (Heikal 1969 in Laqueur and Rubin, 414–427). In so doing, Nasser played upon the main weakness in Israel's security armor: its reluctance to accept a large number of casualties. In part, this aversion to casualties is a function of Israel's small population. The IDF is simply too small to engage in conflicts that result in massive casualties. The aversion to casualties, however, is also rooted in a deep cultural reverence for life. News in Israel travels quickly, and everyone seems to know someone who knew the victim. As a result, losses are personalized, adding to the insecurity of an already skittish population.

Israel, however, maintained its air of superiority over the Egyptians and relied on the saturation bombing of Egyptian positions to stem the assault (Shlaim and Tanter 1978). Not only would Egypt be forced to accept Israeli terms, according to Israeli strategists, but Egyptian leaders would be taught an important "psychological" lesson.

This strategy, however, assumed that the Soviets would remain passive. They did not. Rather, they joined the fray on the side of the Egyptians, manning anti-aircraft missile sites and piloting Egyptian aircraft. Israeli losses began to mount, and Israeli leaders found themselves under increasing pressure from the US to end the conflict. The last thing that the US wanted was to transform Egypt into a Soviet satellite. Israel reluctantly accepted a US-sponsored cease-fire on August 7, 1970. Once again, Israel had overplayed its hand and found itself in confrontation with the major powers (Shlaim and Tanter 1978).

Simultaneously, the situation in Jordan was rapidly disintegrating into civil war as Palestinian groups openly challenged King Hussein's throne and pressed their demands for the return of the Occupied Territories by hijacking international airliners. The logic of the campaign was devastatingly simple. The Arabs lacked the capacity to liberate the Territories occupied by Israel in the 1967 (June) War, and the Soviets refused to do so for fear of challenging the United States. They also had little faith in the capacity of the Arabs to win a war with Israel. The United States and its European allies possessed the power to force an Israeli withdrawal from the Occupied Territories, but lacked the will to do so. The hijacking of international airliners and other terrorist attacks against Western targets would force the major powers to take action to resolve the crisis. King Hussein, however, prevailed, and in 1970 the Palestinian militias fled to southern Lebanon where they transformed the Lebanese-Israeli border into the focal point of their resistance movement.

The war of attrition ground to a halt in 1970 and was followed by international efforts to reopen the Suez Canal, a process that required a partial Israeli withdrawal from the Sinai Peninsula. The cabinet divided on the issue, and negotiations broke down. Egypt had earlier accepted the international plan, and Israel's refusal to do so convinced Sadat, now the leader of Egypt, that there could be no serious negotiations with Israel until the Arabs had reestablished their credibility on the battlefield. Barring this shift of power, Israel would have little incentive to return any of the territory occupied in the 1967 War. Israeli scholars, in turn, faulted the government for not having a coherent policy. What appeared to the Arabs as intransigence, they believed, was merely the incapacity of a deeply divided government to make a decision (Shlaim and Yaniv 1980, 244).

Arab preparations for the October (Yom Kippur) War were discussed in the preceding chapter and require little elaboration at this point. Israeli intelligence had monitored the Arab buildup, and the Israeli military had begun to mobilize for war, albeit in an unobtrusive manner designed to allay Western concerns (Bartov 1981 in Rabinovich and Reinharz 1984, 240–246). Another lightning-swift victory, as Israeli analysts pointed out, would not be without its advantages. Israel would gain a breathing space of several years while the Arabs struggled to rebuild their armies, and the myth of Israeli invincibility would continue to take its toll on the Arabs and their Soviet supporters. Having been the victim of an Arab attack, moreover, Israel would be under little pressure to return the Occupied Territories.

Israeli authorities differed on the urgency of the Arab threat. How could one give credence to Arab armies that had been humiliated just five years earlier in the June War of 1967 or to an Egyptian army that had been further humiliated in the War of Attrition? Military victories were not Israel's problem. The difficulty, or so it seemed, would be in winning the political battles that followed. Sadat, moreover, had expelled the Soviets a year earlier, and it was extremely difficult to envision a sustained Egyptian attack without massive Soviet support. Sadat's domestic position had also become increasingly precarious, and his menacing gestures were easily written off as bravado designed for home consumption. Other "years of decision" had come and gone without incident. Why should this year be any different?

As a result of this vacillation, Israel was caught unprepared when Egyptian and Syrian troops launched a joint attack on October 6, 1973, the Jewish holy day of Yom Kippur. The Egyptian army displayed consummate skill in crossing the Suez Canal, and Israeli forces were forced to retreat with heavy loses. Without massive US aid and profound confusion in the relations between Egypt and Syria, the situation could have been far worse. Israel's forces eventually regrouped and by the cessation of hostilities had occupied yet more territory. The damage, however, had been done. Israel had seen its defense perimeter penetrated, and the myth of Israeli invincibility had been shattered. It was no longer certain that future wars would go as well as wars past.

The October War had also taken its toll on Israeli politics, and the 1973 elections saw Labor's position in the Knesset severely eroded. Coalitions now proved harder to form, and the Labor Party found itself increasingly hamstrung by internal bickering. Meir had resigned on the eve of the election, but more than three months would pass before Yitzhak Rabin was named to succeed her.

It was at this point that US intervention came to the fore in the person of Henry Kissinger, the US secretary of state. Kissinger was of Jewish origin and sympathetic to Israel, yet he was intensely frustrated by the immobility of Israeli politics. Israeli security, in his view, demanded peace with Egypt and the normalization of relations with the Arab world. Toward this end, and not without considerable resistance from the Israeli leadership, he used his diplomatic skills and the full weight of the US government to forge a 1974 agreement between Egypt and Israel. Under the terms of the agreement, Egypt would normalize relations with Israel while the latter would begin a gradual withdrawal from the Canal Zone and the Sinai Peninsula in return for US security guarantees and the establishment of a UN peacekeeping force in the demilitarized area.

The Israeli government lacked sufficient consensus to either resist Kissinger or to take effective action on any other issue. As described by Shlaim and Yaniv:

Yitzhak Rabin's rise to power in 1974 was attended by widely shared hopes that he would reform and revive his party.... But he has turned out to be a weak and uncharismatic leader, lacking and unable to build any real power base, presiding over a bitterly divided party and a precarious coalition government. Faced with a host of conflicting demands and an open challenge to his own position, his strategy was to play for time and avoid actions which would antagonize any significant element of his shaky coalition (Shlaim and Yaniv 1980, 251).

Rabin again headed Labor's list in the 1977 elections, but he was forced to withdraw from the election as the result of a personal financial scandal and was replaced by Shimon Peres. The Likud, a coalition of right-wing parties that had emerged a few years earlier, came to power under the leadership of Menachem Begin, a former leader of the Irgun militia in the struggle against the British. Begin, an ultra-nationalist, vowed that not an inch of ancient Israel would be returned to the Arabs. The immobility of Israeli politics had come to an abrupt end. Perhaps because of his hard-line credentials, Begin was able to pursue negotiations with Egypt that involved trading the Sinai Peninsula for peace. The Sinai Peninsula, as noted earlier, was not part of ancient Israel and possessed none of the religious overtones of Jerusalem and the West Bank. If Egypt could be neutralized, Begin argued, the main Arab army would be removed from the fray and Israel would have a free hand in dealing with its smaller Arab neighbors. His logic was impeccable.

The Camp David Accords between Egypt and Israel were duly signed on September 17, 1978, with the active participation of the United States. A formal treaty of peace between the two countries would be signed in March of 1979. The dynamics of Middle Eastern politics had undergone yet another transformation.

In summary, then, the decade that began with Israel's dazzling victory in the June War of 1967 had seemed full of promise. Israel had regained the lands of ancient Israel and her enemies were at bay. In retrospect, however, the years between 1967 and 1979 were a period of reassessment for Israel as well as for her Arab neighbors. Defense lapses in the October War of 1973 had been matched by a profound immobility in Israel's decision-making process. The firm hand of Ben-Gurion had given way to vacillation and internecine bickering within a Labor Alliance that had ruled Israel in one guise or another since the country's inception as an independent state. Perhaps reacting to a pervasive sense of malaise, the Israeli electorate turned again to a strong and decisive leader, albeit a leader of the far right that Ben-Gurion had earlier suspected of anti-democratic tendencies.

The Era of Islamic Resurgence

The treaty of peace signed between Egypt and Israel in 1979 had seen Israel trade the Sinai Peninsula for peace with its most powerful neighbor. The land would be returned in stages, thereby assuring that Egyptian authorities remained faithful to their commitment. The Peace accords also stated that Israel would provide the Palestinians with autonomy on the West Bank and the Gaza Strip within five years. A blueprint was thus forged for a final solution to the Arab-Israeli crisis. Land would be traded for peace.

There were, of course, complications. Egypt was the only Arab signatory to the agreement, and Sadat had taken it upon himself to speak for both the Palestinians and the Arab world as a whole. The Arab states rejected the agreement and severed their relations with Egypt. The damage, however, had been done. With Egypt removed from the military equation, the remaining Arab states were at Israel's mercy. This vulnerability was increased by the "special relationship" between Israel and the United States. Never, President Reagan would boast, had Israel had a better friend in the White House.

Begin had captured the 1977 elections by vowing that not one inch of historic Israel would be returned to the Arabs. Begin, moreover, was a man in a hurry. The 1981 elections were rapidly approaching, and a Labor victory, in all likelihood, would see his adversaries sacrifice the holy lands of ancient Israel for the sake of an elusive peace. The time for action was at hand.

No sooner had the peace treaty with Egypt been signed, accordingly, than Begin ignored his promise of Palestinian autonomy and called for the immediate settlement of the West Bank and Gaza by Jews. Begin acknowledged that the Accords spoke of Palestinian autonomy, but "clarified" that the autonomy provisions of the Accords applied only to the people, not the land. The Palestinians could move toward self-rule, but the land belonged to Israel. Only Jewish settlement of the Occupied Territories, in Begin's logic, could preclude a future government from trading the land for peace. Jewish settlements would create "new realities" to which the world, including his Labor opponents, would have to adjust. Perhaps encouraged by Begin's policies, radical elements in the settler community unleashed a wave of terrorism against the Palestinians. Begin seemed reluctant to control the violence, and in June of 1980 the UN condemned Israel for its settlement policy. The Palestinian Liberation Organization (PLO), for its part, had begun a long slide into civil war.

The following month would see the Knesset pass a law unifying the Old City (Jerusalem) and making it the official capital of Israel.

Begin underscored the point by moving the prime minister's office to Arab East Jerusalem. The move violated UN Resolution 242 and signaled Israel's refusal to acknowledge the status of Jerusalem as a divided city. The world's dominant powers, including the United States, also refused to recognize the change in Jerusalem's status.

Simultaneously, Begin attempted to build popular support for his aggressive Arab policy with a borrow-and-spend economic policy that provided Israelis with a false sense of economic prosperity. It also placed them deeper in debt and led to a mutiny within Begin's own ranks. Begin would narrowly survive two votes of no confidence in 1980, and the prospects for a Likud victory in the 1981 elections seemed remote.

Begin, however, remained undeterred, and three weeks before the elections ordered the bombing of an Iraqi nuclear reactor, vowing that never again would Jews be the victims of mass destruction. The Israeli left denounced the attack as an election ploy, and the bombing was duly condemned by the United Nations.

The Likud emerged from the 1981 elections with 48 seats in the Knesset, one more than the 47 seats gained by Labor. Begin, as the leader of the largest party in the Knesset, was asked to form a new Government. He did so with the support of the religious parties, beginning his second term as prime minister with a one-vote majority in the Knesset. The defection of a single vote could topple the Government.

Undeterred by the narrowness of his victory, Begin ordered the bombing of Beirut by Israeli aircraft, declaring that the PLO, now firmly entrenched in a Lebanon devastated by civil war, would not be allowed to find shelter for its activities in civilian districts (*NYT*[3], July 18, 1981). The bombing of Beirut would be followed by the formal annexation of the Golan Heights in December of 1981. A war of words erupted between Begin and Reagan, and Israel was again condemned in the United Nations. Begin was also challenged by a vote of no confidence in the Knesset, but the result was a draw and Begin remained Israel's prime minister.

On June 6, 1982, Begin ordered the invasion of Lebanon, proclaiming his intention of establishing a 25-mile security zone in southern Lebanon. With that goal accomplished, Israeli troops pushed toward Beirut, bombing the city for 11 hours on August 12 before invading its western suburbs on August 14. Reagan phoned Begin in protest, but the invasion continued. Israel's immediate concern was the curtailment of terrorist activity, but its longer-range goals were the destruc-

[3]The *New York Times*.

tion of the PLO and the transformation of Lebanon into an Israeli client
state capable of securing Israel's northern border.

Israel's desire to destroy the PLO was motivated by a variety of considerations. Israel's northern border could never be secure as long as
the PLO remained the dominant force in southern Lebanon. It would
also be impossible for Israel to establish a Christian-based client state
in Lebanon as long as the PLO controlled the southern half of the country. (A Christian state in Lebanon, the Israelis reasoned, could only
sustain itself against its Muslim adversaries by making peace with Israel. The two states would also share a mutual interest in crushing the
PLO.) In the broader scheme of things, Israel was distressed by the increasing acceptance of the PLO in international circles. Arab leaders
had recognized the PLO as the sole representative of the Palestinian
people in 1974, a move that meant the PLO would have to be involved
in formal negotiations over the final disposition of the Occupied Territories. Much to Israel's consternation, Yasser Arafat, the leader of the
PLO, had been invited to address the United Nations during the same
year, thereby implying that the PLO constituted a "state" although it
did not actually control either land or people. If this trend were to continue, the PLO's diplomatic efforts might succeed in forcing a return of
the Occupied Territories where its terrorist tactics had failed. The PLO's
diplomatic pressure continued to mount through the 1970s, and in
June of 1980, a meeting of Western European governments openly
called for direct Israeli negotiations with the PLO. Begin responded
with intense bitterness, comparing the European position to the West's
capitulation to Hitler at Munich. If Europe capitulated, could the US be
far behind? Would Israel once again win the military war only to lose
the political peace?

Israel's supporters justified the invasion of Lebanon in terms of the
objectives outlined above, but few were prepared for the horrors of
the ensuing massacre of some 800 Palestinian civilians by Israel's Christian allies in September of 1982. Sharon, Begin's Minister of Defense,
admitted that Israel had helped to plan the attack. Later investigation
also revealed that Israel had facilitated the approach of the Christian
militias and provided entry to the refugee camps (*Time*, Oct. 4, 1982).
The official commission established to investigate the massacre said
of Sharon, "We know that the consideration (of possible bloodshed)
did not concern him in the least.... The Defense Minister made a grave
mistake" (*Time*, Feb. 21, 1983). Of Begin, the commission would write,
"For two days...he showed absolutely no interest in the camps.... His
lack of involvement casts on him a certain degree of responsibility"
(*Time*, Feb. 21, 1983). Several generals were also censured. More than
100 others met privately to protest Sharon's actions. Sharon would

eventually be forced to resign as minister of defense, but remained in the cabinet. Begin, while later offering to resign as a result of the massacres, was retained as prime minister. Also tarnished was Israel's image as a nation desiring peace with its neighbors.

Two days following the massacre, Reagan vowed on national television to get the Israelis out of Lebanon and announced that he was sending US Marines to Beirut as part of an international peacekeeping force. Begin responded by saying that "Jews do not kneel but to God" (*Time*, Aug. 16, 1982). Begin resigned from office late in 1983 and would be replaced as prime minister by Yitzhak Shamir, also a former "resistance fighter" against the British. Policy would change little, and relations between Israel and the United States remained strained.

In spite of the turmoil of the preceding years, 1984 would find Israel on the verge of achieving all of its "Lebanese" goals. The PLO had agreed to evacuate Lebanon, and a friendly Christian government had been installed in Beirut. The Christian regime, moreover, had agreed to a long-term "security agreement" with Israel, thereby further isolating Syria, or so it seemed at the time. The approach of the US presidential elections also had a calming effect on Reagan's temperament and the American president now seemed more concerned with reestablishing his sagging support among the American Jewish community than pursuing a Middle Eastern foreign policy that had brought him little but grief (*NYT*, Jan. 2, 1984). Toward this end, the Reagan administration announced the signing of a new military pact between the US and Israel and seemed unmindful of Israel's accelerated settlement of the West Bank (*NYT*, Jan. 15, 1984; *NYT*, Feb. 12, 1984).

Israeli successes, however, proved more illusive than real. Lebanon had become a quagmire reminiscent of the US experience in Vietnam or the Soviet debacle in Afghanistan. Between the start of the invasion and the end of 1984, 604 Israeli soldiers were killed and nine times that many wounded. Some 141 Israeli soldiers were sent to prison for refusing to fight in Lebanon. These are astronomical figures for a small state, and they were amplified by Israel's intense aversion to the loss of Jewish life. The Palestinians had been defeated, but Israel now found itself in an unanticipated war of liberation with Shi'a militias, the dominant population group in southern Lebanon. A partial Israeli withdrawal from south Lebanon, moreover, had allowed the Syrians to reassert their influence in Beirut and had forced Lebanon's Christian government to cancel its security agreement with Israel. To add insult to injury, PLO units were beginning to return to the north of Lebanon.

Small and fleeting gains, then, had been made at great cost. To make matters worse, Israel's domestic situation was also in disarray. The occupation of Lebanon was costing over a million dollars a day, inflation was approaching 1000 percent per annum, and Israel's foreign debt had passed the $24 billion mark, giving Israeli citizens the highest debt per capita in the world. Worries over Jewish emigration from Israel were also increasing, and the intense settlement of the Occupied Territories had unleashed renewed violence by both Jewish settlers and the Palestinians.

Israelis' sense of dismay was reflect in the 1984 elections, the results of which returned Labor to power with a narrow plurality of 44 seats in the Knesset to the Likud's 41. Thirteen other parties shared the remaining 35 seats. The Likud had been repudiated, but Labor, with hardly more than a third of the seats in the Knesset, could hardly claim a popular mandate. Shimon Peres, the leader of the Labor party, sought a way out of the impasse by proposing a "national government" in which Labor and Likud would share power. Peres would serve as prime minister for the first 25 months and then relinquish power to Shamir.

Peres's two-year term as prime minister was painful. December of 1984 would find him asking the United States for an economic bailout of $4.85 billion, much of it in the form of grants (*NYT*, Dec. 20, 1984). This request was followed in January of 1985 by attempts to orchestrate a joint Israeli-Syrian withdrawal from Lebanon. When that effort failed, Israel announced its unilateral withdrawal from Lebanon with the exception of its self-proclaimed 24-mile security zone along the Israeli-Lebanese border. The security zone would be patrolled by the Christian-led South Lebanon Army with strong support from Israel. This objective was largely accomplished by the summer of 1985 (*NYT*, June 11, 1985).

The summer of 1985 would also see the United States increase its aid to Israel to $3 billion per annum. The added financial assistance, however, was accompanied by American pressure on Israel to reform its economic system, something that all previous Israeli governments had been reluctant to do for fear of losing popular support. Tensions with the United States increased further in the fall of that year when the US accused Jonathan Pollard, an American Jew employed by Naval Intelligence, of spying for Israel. Peres subsequently apologized for the incident (*NYT*, Dec. 2, 1985). Far more embarrassing was an October 1986 article in the *Sunday Times* (London) charging that Israel had been producing nuclear weapons for twenty years and possessed more than 100 atomic bombs (*JP*, Feb. 3, 2000, www). The nuclear technician who had leaked the information was subsequently arrested by Israeli police and charged with espionage. In the meantime, relations with Syria remained tense, although neither side seemed anxious for renewed conflict (*NYT*, May 19, 1986).

Such was the environment in mid-1987 when the West Bank and Gaza strip erupted in violence. Referred to as the intifada (ground rumbling), the near civil war in the Occupied Territories pitted Palestinian youth wielding stones and Molotov cocktails against fully armed Israeli soldiers. There was no question of the Palestinians defeating the Israeli army, but neither was an increasingly demoralized Israel army able to crush the intifada. Nevertheless, attempts to crush the intifada were brutal, and the world press extensively covered Israeli atrocities. US pressure for a settlement of the Palestinian problem increased apace.

The political disarray continued in the 1988 elections, with the Likud gaining a one-seat plurality over Labor. Both parties, however, had lost ground, with the Likud capturing 40 seats in the Knesset to Labor's 39. Another national unity government was formed with Shamir as prime minister, but the government remained immobilized, and policies already in place remained in force. As the popularity of the major parties decreased, the influence of the smaller parties increased apace, with the major beneficiaries being the religious parties. Israel was becoming an increasingly secular state, but its social life continued to be guided by the dictates of Orthodox rabbis.

The process of political decay intensified following the 1990 elections, with efforts to piece together a new Government bringing out the worst in Israeli politics. As described by Sprinzak and Diamond, and Brichta:

> But almost everything that took place between March and June of 1990 had happened before: coalition horse trading, political blackmail and extortion by small extremist parties; shamelessly open political bribery; blatant and obsessive partisanship by the nation's top policymakers; complete disregard for matters of national interest... (Sprinzak and Diamond 1993).

> What was special about the 1990 spring crisis was that it happened on a larger and more intense scale. The spiritual gurus of the ultra orthodox parties, anti-Zionist rabbis in their eighties and nineties, were made the ultimate judges of Israel's national interest. Hundreds of millions of government dollars were readily committed as coalition bribery to tiny parties. Top ministerial and bureaucratic positions were offered to inexperienced and corrupt MKs (members of Knesset) in exchange for their votes. Several especially unscrupulous MKs used the opportunity to split from their mother parties, instantly tripling and quadrupling their price in the political supermarket (Brichta 1998, 8 Infotrac).

The Era of the New World Order

The disintegration of the USSR in 1990 was heralded as a new dawn for Israel. Approximately three million Jews in the Soviet Union, long captive in their own country, would now be free to emigrate to Israel or other countries of their own choosing. The collapse of the Soviet Union had also weakened the military and diplomatic position of Israel's main adversaries. This was particularly true of Syria, Iraq, Libya, and the PLO, all of whom had received the strong backing of the Soviet Union in their continuing conflict with Israel. As Abba Eban, a former Israeli Foreign Minister, would write, "Israeli security was strengthened a hundredfold by the Soviet Union going from the 'anti' column to the 'pro' column. After all, it was the Soviet Union and not the Arabs that posed an existential threat to Israel in terms of life or death, to live or perish" (Eban, cited in the *Orlando Sentinel*, Jan. 23, 1994).

The demise of the Soviet Union was cause for celebration, but Israel's joy was mitigated by ongoing challenges. Israel's domestic politics, as noted above, remained stalemated as debate raged over Lebanon, the Intifada, settlements, electoral reform, and the masses' growing resentment over the dominance of Orthodox rabbis in Israel's religious life.

In January of 1991, the outbreak of the Gulf War would see Israel's worst nightmare come true as Iraqi SCUD missiles rained down on Tel Aviv and other Israeli cities. The missiles, 39 in all, did not contain chemical agents, and the damage was limited to 1 direct death, 12 indirect deaths, 200 injuries, and damage to some 4000 buildings (*JP*, Mar. 9, 1991). Reports that focused on damage control, however, totally missed the point. Israel's security perimeter had been breached, calling into question the government's ability to guarantee the security of its population. Earlier wars, moreover, had been fought by the massed and poorly disciplined armies of Israel's neighbors, armies vulnerable to the technical and organizational superiority of the IDF. The Iraqi attack, by contrast, signaled Israeli vulnerability to missile attack by countries far removed from its borders. Israel had vowed to retaliate against the Iraqi attack but was constrained by a US president fearful that Israeli involvement in the Gulf War would inflame the region. There can be little doubt that he was correct.

By the mid-summer of 1991, Shamir, under intense pressure from the Bush administration, had agreed in principle to participate in peace talks with the Palestinians that were to be held in Madrid, the major focus of which would be the return of land to the Palestinians in exchange for peace. Simultaneously, however, Shamir had assured his Likud supporters that Israel would survive this new US initiative much as it had survived those of the past. He also blasted the US for tilting toward the Arabs, with Israel's right-wing press warning of a slow sell-out by the US (*JP*, Sept. 28, 1991). Progress in the Madrid negotiations was slow at best.

Also weighing heavily on the Shamir Government was the cost of settling the influx of Soviet Jews emancipated by the collapse of the Soviet Union, most of whom required housing and a broad range of social services. Estimates placed the cost of settling the Soviet Jews at $26.5 billion, an astronomical figure for an already strained budget. Israel approached the US in search of $10 billion in loan guarantees for new housing projects, many of which would presumably be built in the Occupied Territories (*JP*, Feb. 1, 1992). President Bush agreed to the request in principle, but angered the Israeli Government by making US support conditional upon a moratorium on new settlements in the Occupied Territories and progress on the peace front. Both conditions were anathema to a Shamir intent on realizing the right-wing's vision of a Greater Israel.

It was in this environment, then, that Israelis went to the polls in the summer of 1992. Labor scored a narrow victory, and Yitzhak Rabin returned to power as prime minister. Both the US and Israel's Arab neighbors breathed a sigh of relief. Tensions between Tel Aviv and Washington eased, and the Madrid negotiations gained new momentum. The building of new Jewish settlements in the Occupied Territories was also suspended.

The Madrid negotiations dragged on into 1993 but came to an abrupt end in August of that year when the world was stunned to learn that Rabin and Arafat had been conducting secret negotiations in Oslo, Norway. Israel and the PLO signed a formal agreement for resolving their longstanding conflict on August 31, with Israel promising a negotiated withdrawal from large areas of the West Bank and Gaza in return for Palestinian recognition of Israel. Critical details remained to be worked out, but the principle of exchanging land for peace had been accepted by both parties.

The new peace accords were greeted by an upsurge in violence as extremists on both sides sought to scuttle the agreement. Violence on the Israeli side was spearheaded by the settlers and the parties of the extreme right. Palestinian violence was led by Jihad and Hamas, the leading Islamic Fundamentalist groups in the Occupied Territories. Massacres and vengeance reigned as the optimism of Oslo gave way to renewed pessimism.

Nevertheless, the end of 1993 would see Israel take the first steps in transferring control of Jericho and other minor areas of the Occupied

Territories to the Palestinian Authority (PA), the quasi-governmental body established by the Oslo Accords. The gradual transfer of territories to the PA would continue throughout 1994 and 1995, as would the accompanying violence.

Ironically, Israelis also now found themselves worrying about the effectiveness of Palestinian institutions. The Palestinians had no experience in self-government, and it was less than clear that Arafat would be able to keep order in his own ranks, let alone deal with the Fundamentalists. Such questions would come to the fore in September of 1996 when Palestinian police fired on Israeli troops in a scuffle over the opening of a tunnel under Muslim holy places (*NYT*, Sept 27, 1996, 1).

Rabin announced his intention to seek reelection in 1996, vowing to pursue the peace process to its logical conclusion. By contrast, Binyamin Netanyahu, the new leader of the Likud, promised a return to the policies of Begin and Shamir. Israeli voters now had to choose between political alternatives that would have a profound impact on the future of Israel. Adding to the tension was a new electoral system that, for the first time, would see the Israeli prime minister elected directly by the population. In prior elections, the office of prime minister had been filled by the leader of the largest party in the Knesset.

Under the new system, the prime minister and Knesset would be elected simultaneously for four-year terms. The prime minister would be elected on the basis of the popular vote, while the members of the Knesset would continue to be elected on the basis of proportional representation. If no candidate for prime minister received an absolute majority, a run-off election would be held two weeks later. This procedure assured that Israel would have a prime minister elected by a majority of the population. Presumably, this popular mandate would strengthen the hand of the prime minister and reduce the uncertainty that had plagued Israeli politics since the Ben-Gurion era.

Having provided the prime minister with a popular mandate, the Knesset hedged its bets by allowing the Knesset to remove the prime minister by a simple vote of no confidence. What it gave with one hand, it took away with the other. As described by Arian:

> The Knesset may remove the prime minister by a special vote of eighty members, on which new elections for the prime minister take place. The prime minister, with the agreement of the president, can dissolve the Knesset; such a step would also end the prime minister's tenure and would force new elections for both. The Knesset can also remove the prime minister by expressing no confidence by a majority vote (sixty-one votes) or by failing to pass the national budget, but then new elections for both prime minister and Knesset are held (Arian 1997, 179).

The new electoral system was heralded as the advent of a "Second Republic" in which the previous pattern of immobility followed by wild swings in government policy would give way to stability and majority rule. Given the power of the Knesset to remove the prime minister by a simple vote of no confidence, however, it was not certain that things had really changed much. One could also question whether a simple change in the electoral system was sufficient to compensate for deep conflicts dividing Israeli society.

It was in the midst of uncertainty concerning the new electoral system and mounting political rhetoric over the future of the Occupied Territories that Israel was shocked by the assassination of Rabin by a young and unrepentant Jewish extremist. An emotional outpouring saw Israeli public opinion surge in favor of the peace process that Rabin had been so instrumental in starting. That support, however, soon waned in the face of suicide bombings by Arab terrorists, and Netanyahu won a narrow victory in the June 1996 elections. Fear had won out over the desire for peace.

Netanyahu revived the policies of Begin and Shamir with a vengeance, demanding that the Oslo accords be renegotiated and launching a frenzied building program in the Occupied Territories. The position of the Orthodox Jews was also strengthened, and the Israeli army was told to prepare for war with Syria (*JP*, Jan. 11, 1997). The renewed settlement of the Occupied Territories ignited a new round of violence in the territories, and once again a cloud settled over US-Israeli relations. The US demanded a freeze on settlements; Netanyahu responded by expanding them. By the fall of 1997, President Clinton, Israel's best friend, had begun to snub the Israeli prime minister. As Netanyahu would quip, "He treats me like Saddam Hussein" (*IHT*[4], Nov. 20, 1997, 23).

Also problematic was the failure of Israel's new electoral system to provide the much-sought political stability. Within a year of his election, Netanyahu faced an indictment for cronyism, narrowly survived a vote of no confidence, was forced to reshuffle his cabinet, and admitted to thoughts of forming a national unity government that would include Labor. His majority in the Knesset was now down to one vote (*Economist*, Jan. 10, 1998, 35).

Beset by defections in his own ranks, scandals among his close associates, and repeated votes of no confidence—the closest of which ended in a draw—Netanyahu threw in the towel and acquiesced to a resolution dissolving the Knesset (*JP*, Jan. 5, 1999). He had been in office approximately two and a half years, well short of his four-year

[4]*International Herald Tribune.*

term. In part, his decision was a gamble that new elections would return him to office with a stronger coalition. To a greater extent, however, his decision reflected the fact that he had lost control of his coalition and doubted its ability to block a successful vote of no confidence (*NYT*, Dec. 23, 1998).

Whatever the case, the Knesset voted to dissolve itself on January 5, 1999, and new elections were scheduled for May 17 of the same year. Five candidates contested the race for prime minister, while 31 political parties vied for seats in the Knesset. A run-off election between the two leading candidates for prime ministership seemed all but inevitable.

Last-minute maneuvering, however, would see all candidates but Netanyahu and Ehud Barak, the Labor/One Israel Candidate, withdraw from the race. One or the other would become the next prime minister of Israel. The campaign was bitter, even by Israeli standards. Netanyahu questioned the courage of Barak, a former commander-in-chief of the Israeli Defense Forces and Israel's most decorated general (*IHT*, Jan. 11, 1999, www). An editorial in *Ha'aretz*, a leading Israeli newspaper, by contrast, was scathing in its condemnation of Netanyahu:

> Benjamin Netanyahu brought to the role of prime minister a style of rule, if not traits of character, extraordinary in their destructiveness....
>
> He as a prime minister was unique in the harmful influence he exerted on public life and on the country's evolution.
>
> Netanyahu was not our typical politician, making use here and there of half-truths in order to conduct affairs of state. He is a man for whom use of lies and deception is an instinctive response to ordinary pressures....
>
> He now leaves behind him a divided and feuding society, and his personal contribution to the worsening of its morbidity is incontrovertible (*Ha'aretz*, May 16, 1999, www).

For all of the campaign's bitterness, differences between the two candidates were not as great as their rhetoric suggested. Barak promised to have Israeli troops out of Lebanon within a year, while Netanyahu promised to withdraw from Lebanon without specifying a date. Both accepted the principle that some land would have to be returned to the Palestinians, but remained vague on issues of quantity. Both were firm on the need to keep Jerusalem Israeli, crush terrorism, stimulate the economy, and protect the interests of the settlers. Netanyahu advocated new settlements, while Barak was content to support and expand those that already existed.

With few ideological issues separating the two candidates, much of the debate centered on differences between their personalities. Barak was light on details, promising to guide Israel with the calm and firm hand of a former commander of the IDF. The mercurial Netanyahu, by contrast, launched a campaign of Palestinian baiting and patriotic rhetoric, both of which disrupted the peace process and deepened the rift between himself and an American president who was pro-Israeli. Both campaigns, it is interesting to note, were orchestrated by US political advisors, Barak's campaign more so than Netanyahu's (*JP*, Dec. 28, 1998, 7; Rubin 1999; Gilboa and Katz 1999).

The political right applauded Netanyahu's passionate "no concession" policy, but the majority of Israeli voters did not. Barak swept to a dazzling victory with some 56 percent of the popular vote. By all accounts, the critical element in the election had been the shift in the vote of the Russian Jews from a pro-Netanyahu position in the 1996 elections to a pro-Barak position in the 1999 elections. Both candidates had heavily courted the Russian vote, with Netanyahu making several trips to the former Soviet Union.

If the major candidates differed little on ideological issues, this was not the case among Israel's political parties, some 31 of which contested the election. As we shall see shortly, the ideological spectrum in Israel stretches from the Communists on the far left to the ultra-nationalists on the far right. Bisecting the ideological spectrum are ethnic parties (Arab, Russian, Sephardic), religious parties, environmental parties, regional parties, and even movie star parties. Of these 31 parties, 15 were able to gain seats in the Knesset, an increase of four from the recently dissolved (14th) Knesset. Barak's Labor/One Israel alliance was the largest vote getter, gaining 26 seats in the Knesset, followed by Netanyahu's Likud with 19 seats and Shas, a party representing Sephardic Jews, with 17 seats (see Figure 3.1). Interestingly enough, Israel's two largest parties, the Labor Alliance and the Likud, lost ground in the 1999 election. In terms of seats gained, the big winner was Shas, the Sephardic party.

Barak had originally hoped to form an "all Israel" Government that would include a broad spectrum of Israeli parties including the Likud (*Ha'aretz*, May 18, 1999, www). This strategy was viewed as a healing process and had the added advantage of bringing Israel's right wing into difficult negotiations over the disposition of the Occupied Territories and a probable peace treaty with Syria. The formation of such an ideal Government would not be as simple as Barak had hoped. The leaders of the Likud were divided over the offer to include them in the Government, and eventually declined. Negotiations with Shas, however, seemed promising and would have enabled Barak to form a cen-

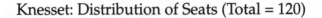

Figure 3.1
Israeli Election Results, 1999

Knesset: Distribution of Seats (Total = 120)

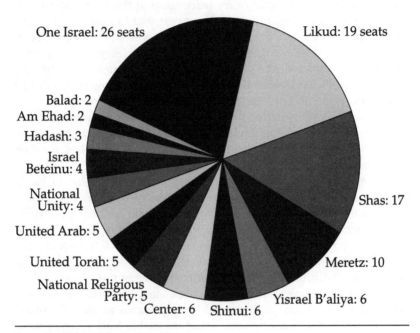

One Israel: 26 seats

Likud: 19 seats

Balad: 2
Am Ehad: 2
Hadash: 3
Israel
Beteinu: 4
National
Unity: 4

Shas: 17

United Arab: 5

United Torah: 5

Meretz: 10

National Religious
Party: 5

Yisrael B'aliya: 6

Center: 6   Shinui: 6

Source: Israeli Central Election Commission.

ter/center-right/left coalition without relying on support from extremist parties (*Ha'aretz*, May 31, 1999, www). The leader of Shas, however, had been indicted on corruption charges, and Barak refused to
include Shas in the coalition unless he resigned as party leader. This he
refused to do, citing Shas's remarkable showing in the election as vin-
dication of his claim that he had been framed. It thus seemed inevitable
that at least one of the religious parties would have to be included in the
coalition, but negotiations with the United Torah Judaism Party broke
down under the UTJ's demand that religious students continue to be exempted from service in the military, a policy that had been recently
overturned by the Israeli Supreme Court (*Ha'aretz*, June 7, 1999, www;
NYT, Dec. 10, 1998, www). Inclusion of the religious parties posed further problems by pitting the pro-settlement policy of the National Religious Party (NRP) against the anti-settlement position of Meretz, an
important component of the Israeli left (*Ha'aretz*, May 31, 1999).

It was at this point that the right-wing press began to speculate that a prime minister who had captured 56 percent of the popular vote might be unable to form a government within the allotted 45 days. In this case, a special election for the prime minister would be called. The Likud, now under the temporary leadership of the ultra-nationalist Ariel Sharon, chose this moment to suggest that the Likud might be willing to enter Barak's coalition if its terms were met. The indicted leader of Shas, however, unexpectedly resigned, clearing the way for Shas to enter the coalition. The soap opera continued until the approach of the 45-day deadline, with Netanyahu refusing to step down until a new government was formed (*JP*, June 8, 1999, www).

Despite the confusion that normally surrounds the naming of coalition governments in Israel, Ehud Barak succeeded in piecing together a coalition Government that included a broad range of parties, most of them from the center and the left.

The reign of Ehud Barak began with optimism on two fronts. First, it was hoped that the direct election of the prime minister would stabilize Israeli politics. For the first time in Israel's history, the prime minister would rule with a popular mandate. Second, there was perhaps a naïve hope that the peace process would move to a swift conclusion. This wave of optimism was reinforced by a series of negotiations with both the Palestinians and the Syrians designed to reach a definitive peace with both parties. Simultaneously, Barak announced that the Israeli withdrawal from Lebanon would take place within a few months, a step that would inevitably lead to peace with Israel's northern neighbor. The Israeli occupation of Lebanon was terminated early and was duly certified by the United Nations.

Unfortunately, the optimism of the election era was misplaced. Peace was not achieved with Lebanon, Syria, or the Palestinians. Indeed, Israel's relations with Egypt and other "friendly" Arab states deteriorated, as did its relations with France and Russia. The stress of the negotiations, in turn, exacerbated the fragmentation of Israeli society, and Barak's popular mandate gave way to partisan wrangling.

The Israeli withdrawal from Lebanon was completed in the late spring of 2000, the only area of contention being the Sheba Farms, an area of about 300 square kilometers famous for the quality of its wine production. The UN sided with Israel, saying that the farms had been under the control of the Syrian army at the time of their occupation and thus were not covered in the UN resolution calling for the Israeli withdrawal from Lebanon. Their return to Lebanon would have to await resolution of the conflict between Israel and Syria related to the return of the Israeli-occupied Golan Heights. Negotiations over the return of Syria's Golan Heights had gone well but foundered over Syria's demand that all Syrian territory occupied by the Israelis during the 1967 War be returned as a condition for peace with Israel. The Israelis, by contrast, insisted on retaining a narrow strip of land on the Syrian side of Lake Kinneret (the Sea of Galilee), a key element in Israel's dwindling water supply (*JP*, Dec. 5, 2000, www). Israel's water supply, the Israelis argued, could not be held hostage to the whims of the Syrian regime.

Hizbullah, the Shi'a Fundamentalist organization that had been the main force in driving Israel from Southern Lebanon, used the Israeli occupation of the Sheba Farms to continue its high-profile struggle against Israel. It was also Hizbullah rather than the Lebanese army that patrolled the joint border between Israel and Lebanon, as the Lebanese government refused to take control of the border areas until the Sheba Farms had been returned. In retrospect, it might have been wiser for the Israelis to return the farms to Lebanon, their eventual return to either Lebanon or Syria not being in doubt. This move would have cut the wind from Hizbullah's sails and further isolated Syria in its negotiations with Israel. This action, however, did not take place and Hizbullah captured four Israeli soldiers, causing further embarrassment to the Barak government and bringing Hizbullah rockets within range of Haifa and other major population areas. Israel had withdrawn from Lebanon but had not extricated itself from the Lebanese quagmire.

In the meantime, Ariel Sharon, the author of the Lebanese occupation and the Sabra and Chatilia massacres, had taken over the temporary leadership of the Likud Party. Strongly critical of Barak's negotiations with the Palestinians, Sharon led a delegation of Israeli legislators and the accompanying contingent of security forces on a dramatic visit to the Temple Mount, the site of al-Aqsa mosque, the third holiest site in Islam and the historical site of the First and Second Temples that play such a central role in the Jewish faith (*NYT*, Sept. 29, 2000, www). Sharon's visit was a widely publicized gesture to reclaim Israeli sovereignty over the bitterly contested Mount and thereby to derail Barak's negotiations with the Palestinians.

Sharon's visit unleashed a cycle of violence and counter-violence that would claim more than 300 lives during its first three months. The vast majority of victims of the Palestinian uprising were Palestinians, some one-third of whom were teenagers, confronting the Israeli army with stones and Molotov cocktails. As the violence escalated, the Israeli army deployed tanks and helicopter gun ships in an effort to crush the al-Aqsa intifada, as the uprising was now called, before it expanded into an uprising similar to the intifada that had rocked the Occupied Territories between 1987 and 1989, a mass uprising that had led to the

Madrid and Oslo agreements and presumed peace between Israel and the Palestinian Authority. The Palestinian Authority is a quasi-government that manages the affairs of the Palestinian population in the Occupied Territories.

The Oslo accords, however, had only sketched the broad outlines of an agreement, with all of the difficult issues to be resolved by negotiations, not the least of which was the status of Jerusalem and the building of settlements on Palestinian territory. Progress was made, but not enough. While the Israelis generally believed that Barak was making reasonable, if not generous, concessions in trading land for peace, the Palestinians despaired of ever receiving independence from Israeli occupation, a fear made even more poignant by the construction of new Israeli settlements on lands claimed by the Palestinians.

In reality, both sides were struggling to bridge a gap that was unbridgeable within the political context of their respective communities. Arafat, rapidly losing control of the Palestinian community, pleaded that he had nothing more to give. While Israel had placed some areas of the Occupied Territories under the control of the Palestinian Authority, these areas were surrounded by armed settlements and, from the Palestinian point of view, amounted to little more than reservations similar to Indian reservations in the United States. The Israelis, moreover, had remained adamant in their demand that Jerusalem be united under Israeli control, thereby bringing to an end the division of the old city that had resulted from the 1967 War. The Palestinians might have partial control over the Arab sections of the old city, but it would not be the independent capital of a sovereign Palestinian state. Indeed, the very nature of the proposed Palestinian state was open to debate. It was not to be a state that could pose a threat to Israel by maintaining a large army or harboring terrorist groups. By weakening Arafat, moreover, the Israelis were threatened with the loss of their main negotiating partner and faced the prospect that the al-Aqsa intifada would become totally dominated by Hamas, Jihad, and other Fundamentalist groups. Arafat, for his part, attempted to strengthen his grip on the Palestinian community by toting a machine gun and encouraging greater violence.

Sharon and much of the Israeli right viewed Barak's concessions as inordinately generous and launched a bitter campaign to topple the Barak Government, a movement that gained momentum over the course of Barak's reign. Indeed, approximately one year after Barak's stunning election victory, the Shas Party deserted Barak's coalition and left the Government without a majority in the Knesset. The Party continued to vote with the Government during the "emergency," as the Israelis referred to the al-Aqsa intifada, but only as a temporary measure.

The final months of 2000 thus found Barak without a majority in the Knesset, condemned abroad for the suppression of the Palestinians, and condemned by a growing number of Israelis for being too "restrained" in his treatment of the "emergency." Efforts to forge a government of national unity with Sharon and the Likud foundered on Sharon's demands that he be given veto power over any agreement with the Palestinians. Even the United States seemed to be deserting ship, with the *Jerusalem Post* complaining about the "new evenhandedness of the Clinton administration," while Israelis worried about growing strains between Tel Aviv and Washington (*JP*, Nov. 24, 2000, www). It was in this environment that a beleaguered Barak agreed to opposition demands for new elections to be held in May 2001. Ironically, public opinion polls at the time found Netanyahu to be the candidate of choice for most Israelis.

Apparently influenced by the popularity of Netanyahu in the polls and faced with the prospect of a new election a few months hence, Barak tendered his resignation to the Israeli president on December 10, 2000 (*JP*, Dec. 11, 2000, www). His resignation was a shrewd political move, for it set the stage for the direct election of the prime minister without an accompanying election of the Knesset, the term of which still had more than two years to run (*JP*, Dec. 10, 2000, www). Because Netanyahu was not a member of the Knesset, he was ineligible to run for the office of prime minister, setting up in all probability a contest between Barak and Sharon—a contest that Barak seemed likely to win.

The Labor Party duly nominated Barak as its candidate, while the Likud leadership attempted to replace Sharon, the author of Israel's disastrous invasion of Lebanon and the Sabra and Chatilia massacres, with Netanyahu, the probable victor in a showdown with Barak (*Ha'aretz*, Dec. 13, 2000, www). The Knesset passed emergency legislation enabling Netanyahu, no longer a member of the Knesset, to stand for the premiership, but he declined the Likud candidacy on the grounds that the Knesset was too hopelessly divided for any prime minister to rule effectively. He asked the Knesset to dissolve itself, thereby setting the stage for the simultaneous election of the Knesset and prime minister, but the Knesset refused.

The repercussions of the intifada, moreover, were not limited to the fall of the Barak Government. On the domestic front, the Israeli government once again found itself immobilized. The violence also had a devastating impact on the economy, with the US State Department's warning on travel to Israel resulting in a massive drop in the occupancy rate of Israeli hotels (*JP*, Oct. 20, 2000, www). Overall, Israeli economists were predicting a 2-percent drop in Israel's 2001 GNP (*JP*, Dec. 8, 2000, www). Later estimates suggested that the Palestinian uprising had cost Israel $2 billion by the spring of 2001 (*JP*, May 30, 2001, www). Although the tourism industry will revive, it is less clear that the deepening gulf between the Israelis and their Arab citizens will be bridged (*Ha'aretz*, Nov. 21, 2000, www). The al-Aqsa intifada, moreover, had spread to Israel proper, with bomb blasts rocking Jewish cities and sowing consternation among an already skittish population. Nervousness reached crisis proportions among settlers in the Occupied Territories as stone throwing gave way to armed attacks between the settlers and the Palestinians. Perhaps more threatening to the settlers were growing voices from the Israeli left suggesting that the evacuation of some settlements was a necessary price to pay for peace with the Palestinians. Indeed, the leader of the Meretz Party, a key element of Barak's coalition, declared, "We think the settlement program is the most foolish thing ever carried out by the Zionist enterprise" (*NYT*, Nov. 15, 2000, www).

On the regional and international fronts, the severity of the Israeli efforts to crush the al-Aqsa intifada forced a summit conference of Arab leaders, followed a few weeks later by a summit conference of the leaders of the Islamic world. Both summit conferences were vociferous in their condemnation of Israel but avoided taking punitive measures against the Jewish state. The conference of Arab leaders created a fund to support the intifada but sidestepped demands for a reduction in oil production. As attempts to crush the intifada became increasingly brutal, however, Morocco severed its diplomatic relations with Israel and both Egypt and Jordan withdrew their ambassadors from Jerusalem[5] and curtailed trade relations with Israel, negating strenuous and prolonged efforts to turn "enemies into partners for peace" (*JP*, Dec. 3, 2000, www). Israel also found itself confronted with demands that its treatment of the al-Aqsa intifada be investigated by an international commission, a demand vigorously opposed by Israel but ultimately supported by the United States (*JP*, Dec. 12, 2000, www). It was now the Israelis who were being portrayed by the world press as the aggressors and the Palestinians as their victims. Far worse was growing European support for an international force to separate the Israelis and the Palestinians, similar to the international force imposed upon Yugoslavia a year or so earlier (BBC, Dec. 8, 2000). Israel vehemently rejected the presence of an international force but reluctantly accepted an international fact-finding mission headed by former Senator Mitchell of the United States (*JP*, Dec. 6, 2000, www; *Ha'aretz*, Nov. 14, 2000, www). Also disconcerting was the growing transformation of the

[5]Jordan delayed the scheduled filling of an ambassadorial post that was vacant.

Arab-Israeli conflict into a Jewish-Muslim conflict and the upsurge of attacks on Jewish targets throughout the world, including attacks on Israeli diplomats in Jordan. Indeed, the Simon Wiesenthal Center reported that more than 200 attacks on international Jewish targets had occurred during the first month of the al-Aqsa intifada, commenting that the 60 attacks on synagogues represented "the largest number of attacks on synagogues since 1938, and the world has been silent" (*JP*, Oct. 20, 2000, www).

In the meantime, both Arafat and Barak vowed their support of the peace process, with Barak declaring that the Palestinian questions could only be solved politically (CNN, Dec. 8, 2000). Barak's statement was not an empty one, for without a political settlement, Israel faced the prospect of an extended guerilla war that could only compound the damage and suffering spawned by the intifada. An editorial in *Ha'aretz* echoed this view, commenting that "The policy of flexing muscles, which was shown to be a mistake in the past, may prove to be a mistake again" (*Ha'aretz*, Nov. 10, 2000). Arafat, too, was well aware of the dangers of prolonging a confrontation that had brought death and suffering to the Palestinian community, destroyed the Palestinian economy, and called into question both his authority and that of the Palestinian Authority (*JP*, Oct. 23, 2000, www). In a strange irony, the survival of both Barak and Arafat was linked to finding a way to make the peace process work.

The final weeks of the election campaign blended increasingly brutal attempts to crush an intifada that showed no signs of easing with hectic efforts to negotiate a final solution to Israel's long-standing conflict with the Palestinians. Barak offered the Palestinians their best deal to date, but the offer fell far short of meeting Palestinian demands for full control of the territories occupied by Israel in 1967, including East Jerusalem. Particularly knotty was the promised right of the Palestinians to return to Israel proper, a promise embedded in the documents ending the 1948 War. The right of return, if implemented, would allow for a massive influx of Palestinians into Israel, thereby threatening both the Jewish character of the state and its security. More practically, the former Palestinian land was now Israeli land. As such, Palestinian demands for the right to return could not be accepted by the Israeli negotiatiors, but could presumably be exchanged for full Palestinian control of the Occupied Territories. This, indeed, seemed to be the inevitable format for a final settlement, with the Palestinians receiving compensation for confiscated properties.

Barak's blend of compromise and repression played poorly among an Israeli population distraught by the violence of the intifada and dubious about the wisdom of Barak's concessions. Opinion polls during January 2001 showed Sharon building a 20-point lead over Barak amid widespread speculation that Barak would step aside for Shimon Peres, a former Labor prime minister whose popularity in the polls was roughly equal to that of Sharon. Barak, however, refused to step aside, and on February 6, 2001, Ariel Sharon swept to a 63 to 37 percent victory over the embattled Barak. The Israeli electorate had placed security before peace. No sooner had Sharon been elected, moreover, than the Knesset voted to abolish the direct election of the prime minister. The second republic, it seemed, had come to an end (*Ha'aretz*, Mar. 8, 2001, www).

Entering the Sharon Era

Sharon formed a national unity government consisting of the Likud, Labor/One Israel, and a multitude of smaller parties. Labor participation in the Government was hotly protested by many members of the Party who denounced Peres and other Party leaders for "selling their souls for a scrap of power" (*NYT*, Feb. 27, 2001, www). Peres carried the day, however, arguing that a unity government was necessary to restrain Sharon. Barak had initially agreed to join the Sharon Government as Minister of Defense, publicly supporting Sharon's assertion that he, Sharon, was not bound by the negotiations between Barak and Arafat (*JP*, Feb. 16, 2001, www). Barak withdrew following a mass outcry charging him with placing his own desire for power above the interests of the Party.

Sharon's campaign had focused almost entirely on a pledge to crush the al-Aqsa intifada, and his election to office witnessed an increase in the assassination of key Palestinian resistance leaders, the torture of Palestinians, the collective punishment of Palestinian communities, and efforts to starve the Palestinians into submission by cutting off vital supplies, measures duly condemned in the US State Department's annual report on human rights violations (*Ha'aretz*, May 30, 2001, Mar. 13, 2001, and Feb. 22, 2001, www). The death toll increased apace, with May 2001 figures recording 504 Palestinian deaths and 88 Israeli deaths (*NYT*, May 24, 2001). The efficacy of Sharon's measures was openly debated in the Israeli press; the right wing criticized Sharon's restraint while the moderate press decried the influence of Sharon's iron fist policies on world opinion and urged a political solution to the confrontation. Indeed, Peres, now foreign minister in the Sharon Government, candidly stated, "The most important lesson we have learned is that you can't put out a fire with fire" (*JP*, Mar. 7, 2001, www). Sharon countered by asserting that he would not negotiate with the Palestinians until the violence had stopped; the Palestinians vowed that the violence would not stop until they had received their independence and the expansion of the settlements had ended.

Rather than crushing the violence, Israeli tactics served only to inflame the conflict. Confrontations between Palestinian teens and Israeli troops escalated to mortar attacks on Jewish settlements and growing waves of suicide bombings within Israel itself, a move clearly designed to play upon Israeli insecurities. In one rally alone, Hamas reportedly recruited 250 suicide bombers to serve in the struggle against Israeli occupation (*JP*, May 20, 2001, www). It was the ground war that captured the world's attention, but the psychological war was equally intense.

Perhaps in desperation, Sharon launched military strikes into Palestinian-controlled areas and attacked the camps and other strongholds of the resistance with helicopter gun ships. When this measure didn't suffice, the camps were attacked by F16s provided to Israel by the United States on the promise that they would be used only for defensive purposes. The US condemned the attack, with US vice president Dick Cheney saying, "Yeah, I think they should stop; both sides should stop and think about where they are headed" (*Ha'aretz*, May 21, 2001, www).

Israel justified its actions in the name of national security, with Foreign Minister Peres stating that Israel was engaged in a "battle for its existence" (*Ha'aretz*, May 16, 2001, www). Whether or not this was the case, the Jewish settlements in the Occupied Territories were clearly at risk, as was the ability of Israel to control the nature of a future Palestinian state. The creation of a Palestinian state controlled by Hamas, Jihad, or related Fundamentalist groups would, indeed, pose a threat to the survival of the Jewish state. Arafat and the Palestinian Authority may have accepted the existence of the Jewish state, but the Fundamentalists had not.

Whatever the case, the harshness of Israeli tactics led to an outpouring of world sympathy for the Palestinian cause and brought increasingly severe condemnations of Israel from the leaders of the European community. Particularly upsetting to the Israelis was the Danish Foreign Minister's call for sanctions against Israel (*Ha'aretz*, May 20, 2001, www; *JP*, Mar. 28, 2001, www). The president of the International Red Cross added fuel to the fire by stating that Israeli settlements were "war crimes," an assertion that brought a sharp reproach from both the US and Israel (*JP*, May 20, 2001, www). Washington was muted in its criticism of Israel, but endorsed the Mitchell Report as a basis for peace between the two sides. The Mitchell Report rejected Palestinian demands for a multilateral force to separate the combatants but otherwise apportioned the blame for the violence equally between the two sides, a position that placed the Palestinians on an equal footing with the Israelis in the negotiation process. Both sides were urged to stop the violence, and the Israelis were called upon to freeze the building and expansion of settlements.

Faced with a public relations disaster, the Israeli cabinet hired an American public relations firm to handle the damage control (*JP*, Mar. 9, 2001, www). Guidelines were also sent to Israeli embassies on how best to parry the settlement issue (*JP*, May 22, 2001, www). If Israel lost the media war, international pressures to reach an unacceptable accommodation with the Palestinians could well prove insurmountable.

The Palestinians accepted the Mitchell Report, while Sharon initially responded to the Mitchell Report by approving more settlements, arguing that a freeze on settlements would be "tantamount to rewarding Palestinian violence" (*Ha'aretz*, May 10, 2001, www). Violence continued to mount on both sides but eased as Sharon declared a unilateral cease-fire and agreed to freeze building in the face of intense pressure from Washington. He did so, however, on the condition that all other terms of the report be implemented (*IHT*, May 30, 2001, www; *Ha'aretz*, June 6, 2001, www). This condition contained an implicit threat that continued Palestinian violence would justify an expansion of the settlements. Arafat called for an end to attacks within Israel proper, but Hamas showed little inclination to obey Arafat's orders (*JP*, June 6, 2001, www). Indeed, it was far from clear that Arafat had the capacity to control the violence, a topic hotly debated in the Israeli press. While Sharon blamed Arafat for the violence, high military intelligence officers openly voiced the opinion that Arafat had lost control of the situation and predicted a bitter and protracted conflict that would not run its course for several months. Other generals warned that Israel was "not far removed from full-scale war" (*Ha'aretz*, May 31, 2001, www).

Sharon also threatened to withdraw unilaterally from the Occupied Territories, building a "Great Wall of China" around Israel and the Israeli settlements, an idea that was first floated by Netanyahu and later revived by Barak (*JP*, June 5, 2001, www). The Jewish state of Zionist dreams would be secure, but dreams of Greater Israel would fall by the wayside. Sacrificed also would be Israeli control of the Jordan Valley, a security issue of primary concern (*JP*, June 5, 2001, www).

Netanyahu, in the meantime, continued to position himself for a presumed early exit of the Sharon Government by chiding Sharon for being soft on the Palestinians and placing the security of Israel at risk (*Ha'aretz*, May 31, 2001, www).

ISRAELI POLITICS TODAY AND BEYOND

In examining the evolution of Israeli politics over the past half-century, three clear conclusions emerge. First, Israel has succeeded admirably in the task of building a state that is both strong and democratic. Not only have Israeli political institutions stood the test of time, but they have enabled Israel to dominate its regional environment. Second, the Israeli political process has shifted from the firm leadership of the Ben-Gurion era to a pattern of immobilization interspersed with dramatic swings of policy. Rabin made peace, Netanyahu stalled the peace process, Barak reinitiated the peace process, and Sharon shattered it. Third, the Israeli polity has become increasingly divided into two opposing camps. One camp is largely secular in nature and is more willing to trade land for peace, while the other is religious in character and prefers a policy that will force peace without the concession of land. The Israeli electorate is also divided by a range of other issues, the nature of which will be discussed throughout the remainder of this chapter.

Israel thus finds itself in a paradoxical situation in which the effectiveness of strong political institutions is being challenged by an increasingly divided population. In the remainder of this chapter we examine the factors leading to this situation and its likely impact on Israeli politics during the coming decade. In the process, we shall have the opportunity to examine Israeli political institutions, the actors that give life to those institutions, and the broader economic, cultural, and international environments that influence the Israeli political process. All play an important role in shaping a political process that is among the most complex in the world.

Political Institutions

The structure of the Israeli political system consists of a set of "Basic Laws" that passes for a constitution, a Knesset (parliament), a prime minister elected by the population, a symbolic (but not necessarily passive) president elected by the Knesset, a Supreme Court, and a large and powerful bureaucracy. Over time, the Basic Laws are expected to evolve into a formal constitution, but that evolution will not take place until greater consensus is achieved on the question of Jewishness and other critical issues.

At the heart of the Israeli political system is the Knesset, a unicameral parliament of 120 members elected directly by the Israeli population on the basis of proportional representation. The term Knesset was adopted from the Haknesset Hagedola, the historic assembly of the fifth century BC, thereby symbolizing the link between modern and ancient Israel (*JP*, Israeli Elections Primer, 1999, www).

As is typical of parliamentary systems in general, the ruling coalition (Government) possesses the power to pass any legislation it wishes as long as it possesses a majority (61 votes) in the Knesset. There are no minority rights, and committees lack the power to alter the will of the majority. The only exception to this rule is the stipulation that "Basic Laws" can be changed only by an extraordinary majority in the Knesset.

The winner-take-all nature of the Knesset contributes to the dramatic swings in policy that have characterized Israeli politics since the mid-1970s. The winners do as they please while the losers attempt to destabilize the ruling coalition and otherwise embarrass the Government in parliamentary debates and during the question period. Opposition tactics gain wide publicity but generally do little to bring down the Government. Only one Israeli Government has succumbed to a vote of no confidence, and the average life of an Israeli government is a respectable 2.5 years (Brichta 1998). In large part, this stability results from the reluctance of party leaders to risk new elections for fear of losing their positions of power. As long as a party leader stands firm, the party's MKs (members of the Knesset) will follow suit. This sense of party discipline has had the effect of shifting power from the Knesset itself to the Government. It is not the Knesset that makes policy, but the party leaders that constitute the ruling coalition.

The vulnerability of the Knesset to dramatic swings in policy is aggravated by an electoral system that allocates seats in the Knesset on the basis of proportional representation. Any party that receives at least 1.5 percent of the vote receives seats in the Knesset in proportion with its percentage of the popular vote. This would not be a severe problem in homogeneous societies, but Israel is not a homogeneous society (Schwartz 1994). As noted in the preceding section, some 31 parties fielded candidates in the 1999 elections, with 15 diverse parties receiving seats in the Knesset.

This fragmentation, in turn, leads to the frantic process of coalition building described in the earlier discussion. It also helps to explain the pattern of immobilization interspersed by dramatic swings of policy that has characterized Israeli politics in recent decades. Relatively narrow coalitions such as those established by Begin, Shamir, and Netanyahu have tended to be relatively cohesive and have pursued their ideological objectives with a vengeance. Broad coalitions, by contrast, have had the burden of reconciling a wide range of interests and have had little choice but to pursue polices that offend the least number of coalition members. This need to reconcile diverse interests was particularly evident in the "national unity government" that saw Labor and the Likud share power between 1984 and 1990. It would be a mistake, however, to equate immobilization with a lack of policy. Rather, immobilization leads to a continuation of policies that are already in place. In the Israeli experience this has meant a continuation of settlement building and delays in formulating a coherent plan for peace.

By forcing coalition governments, Israeli election procedures also stimulate the horse trading described earlier. Religious parties impose their will on a largely secular nation, and administrative agencies are captive to key coalition partners. As described by Sharkansky:

> The rules that govern appointments in the Israeli bureaucracy are casually administered. Although they prescribe competitive procedures, there is a tradition of evading the rules to facilitate the appointment of people who are politically allied with the responsible minister. Reports prepared by the Civil Service Commission show that 20 to 40 percent of appointments are not made competitively. Appointments to positions in local authorities and in companies owned by national ministries or local authorities are not closely supervised by the Civil Service Commission and are thought to be even more open to political influence (Sharkansky 1997b, 59–60).

Finally, it should be noted that the proportional electoral system does little to force compromise among Israel's diverse factions. Israel constitutes one large voting district with each notch on the political spectrum being confident that it will receive at least a few seats in the Knesset. Parties have more to gain by "horse trading" after the election rather than they do by coming together before the election. Moving to the direct election of the prime minister in 1992 was supposed to alleviate this situation, but as we have seen in both the 1996 and the 1999 elections, it did not (Brichta 1998). The direct election of the prime minister was abolished in 2001, and the old system was reinstated.

Despite its problems, Israel's electoral system is not without some advantages. Israel is a pluralistic society, and its system of proportional representation assures that all major groups in Israeli society will find representation in the Knesset. This is an important point, for the ability of all major groups to shape policy helps to explain the legitimacy of Israel's political institutions. Conflict between groups is intense, but at least it is resolved within an established political framework.

Elites

Israel's political institutions contribute to its paradoxical position as a strong democratic state increasingly beset by periods of immobilization interspersed with dramatic swings of policy, but they are only one factor among many. Some observers attribute both aspects of Israel's political riddle to the nature of its elites (Zalmanovitch 1998; Barzilai 1999). The strength of Israeli democracy, from this perspective, lies in the democratic nature of Israeli elites. However deep their differences, the overwhelming majority of Israel's leaders have been committed to democracy, albeit with some reservations about the leaders of extremist groups. Losers have accepted defeat with relative grace, and the winners have not used their power to destroy their opponents—a rare occurrence in the Middle East. If the leaders of a country are democratic, the masses generally follow suit. This is particularly the case in Israel, a country in which leaders often attract a passionate following. In spite of the fact that the leader of Shas was convicted of corruption charges, for example, the party's vote in the 1999 elections increased dramatically.

Israeli democracy, moreover, is strengthened by the fragmentation of its elite structure. While the Israeli elite pyramid is generally headed by the prime minister and senior members of the cabinet, no single leader can speak for more than a minority of Israel's citizens. Even Ben-Gurion, the charismatic "father of the country," was forced to rule with coalition Governments. Charisma has not been a distinguishing feature of Israel's subsequent prime ministers, and all have had to share their power with the leaders of numerous competing parties. The recent change to a popularly elected prime minister has elevated the prime minister to the status of being "first among equals," but all key decisions bow to the need for solidarity within the Government. The more elites must compete with each other for popular support, the more likely they are to pay attention to the concerns of the voters.

The Israeli elite structure, moreover, is not limited to the leaders of political parties and related groups. Senior military officers exercise far more authority in Israel than would be the case in most Western democracies, a fact largely attributable to the state of tension that has long existed between Israel and it neighbors (Ben-Meir 1996). War heroes have been plentiful, and many have found their way into politics, not the least of whom are Barak and Sharon. Senior bureaucrats also have considerable latitude in shaping how government policies will be executed, controlling the expenditure of vast sums of money (Galnoor, Rosenbloom, and Yaroni 1998). Senior rabbis, including some located in New York, exercise profound influence over the social affairs of the country, just as business leaders have much to say about the direction of the Israeli economy. Labor leaders, who have long been key players in Israeli politics, remain influential but have seen their power decline in recent years (Tazbag 1995). The same pluralism that facilitates democracy, however, also facilitates immobilization. The Israeli pie is simply divided into too many pieces for any one leader to be totally dominant.

Land for Peace: Differing Perspectives

However fragmented the Israeli elite may be, the dominant voice in the policy-making process is that of the prime minister. Nowhere has this fact been more evident than in the differing attitudes of Rabin and Netanyahu toward the Occupied Territories (Shlaim 1995). Why was Rabin (and later Barak) willing to trade land for peace while Netanyahu (and later Sharon) was not?

To begin with, Rabin and Netanyahu possessed differing assessments of the Israeli national interest; the former found peace to be more important than land, while the latter held land to be sacred. The difference between the two men also included differing assessments of the role of the Territories in Israel's security. Rabin, presumably in accord with some 70 percent of Israeli's retired generals, held the opinion that the West Bank and Gaza were no longer essential for Israel's security. Netanyahu, by contrast, clung to the proposition that land was essential for security and decried the poll of former Israeli generals as being flawed and inaccurate (*JP*, Nov. 9, 1996, 7).

These differing assessments of Israel's national interests also reflected the differing values and personality styles of the two leaders. Both had begun their political careers as staunch nationalists, yet Netanyahu was an ideologue while Rabin was a pragmatist. The latter was willing to bend to the new realities of 1990s, while the former was not.

While no one had ever accused the hard-line Rabin of being soft on Arabs, he had apparently become convinced during the mid-1970s that Israel would eventually have to make peace with its Arab neighbors. Inevitably, the peace process would involve some form of settlement with the Palestinians. What, then, were the factors that convinced Rabin, the former hard-line general, that the time had come to make peace? First was the sincere willingness of most Arab states to make peace with their former enemy. Israel's peace treaty with Egypt had deprived the Arab world of their major army, and the collapse of the USSR had deprived them of cheap arms and diplomatic support. For better or for worse, peace had now become their best option.

Second, the center of gravity in the Palestinian community was shifting from the PLO to radical Islamic groups such as Jihad and Hamas.

The PLO had indicated a willingness to make peace with Israel; the latter groups, strongly supported by Iran, remained adamant in their opposition to the existence of the Jewish state (Muslih 1999).

Third, there were strong economic incentives for peace, the foremost of which was the prospect of transforming Israel into the financial and commercial center of the Middle East. Also on the economic front was the prospect of a "peace dividend." Exorbitant military budgets could be scaled back and the security zone in Lebanon could be abandoned, both items being high on Rabin's political agenda. This financial benefit was not a minor consideration, for economic crises were already forcing a cutback in military budgets. Savings from the peace dividend, moreover, could be used to cover the costs of settling Soviet Jews in those areas of the Occupied Territories retained by Israel and shoring up troubled educational and health care systems (*NYT*, Sept. 8, 1991, 42).

Fourth, Israel would be able to extricate itself from the quagmires of Lebanon and the Occupied Territories. The dual occupations had spawned terrorism, taken an increasing toll in IDF casualties, and shocked both Israelis and the world with their brutality. They had also demoralized an IDF better suited to fighting wars than pacifying hostile populations. Both occupations, moreover, were now acknowledged by many Israelis as failures (*JP*, June 17, 1996). Even the most brutal measures had been unable to quell either the intifada or the guerrilla war in the security zone.

Fifth, peace would break the garrison mentality that had gripped Israel since the country's inception. There was no question of Israel's capacity to defend itself, but the psychological stress on the Israeli population was enormous. This anxiety had been reflected in periodic surges in emigration from Israel as well as the reluctance of many former Soviet Jews to settle in Israel (*JP*, May 10, 1988; *JP*, Feb. 11, 1990).

Sixth, it was in Israel's interest to normalize its relations with its Arab and Islamic neighbors before long-range weapons of mass destruction tipped the military balance in favor of the latter (*JP*, Feb. 8, 1992, 9). The Iraqi missiles that had targeted Israel during the Gulf War had demonstrated Israel's vulnerability to external attack. Iran's purchase of advanced weapons technology from the states of the former Soviet Union and China was particularly disconcerting. Implicit, although not discussed at length, was concern over the growing sophistication of tactical weapons of mass destruction, weapons that could be deployed by extremist groups against Israel's highly concentrated population.

Seventh, Israel would be able to rid itself of responsibility for a Palestinian population that was growing at an astounding rate. As things currently stand, the Palestinian population in "greater Israel" will gain parity with Israel's Jewish population within a decade. This population shift, as Shlomo Gazit, the former head of Israel's army intelligence, writes, would leave Israel with three unfortunate choices:

1. To continue holding the entire area, imposing an apartheid regime on the Arab population;
2. To initiate the expulsion of the Arab residents;
3. To force the Jewish state as we know it to commit suicide. Any Jew who wishes to take this step is, of course, welcome to continue living as part of a minority in a Palestinian-Arab state (*JP*, Jan. 10, 1998, 12).

"Returning part of the Occupied Territories," Gazit notes, "would alleviate these odious choices by providing Palestinians with their own entity, the Palestinian Authority. Relations with that entity would continue to be on the basis of 'respect and suspect'" (*JP*, Jan. 10, 1998, 12).

Eighth, many military experts no longer viewed the Occupied Territories as essential for Israel's defense, although this picture is less clear in reference to the Golan Heights (*JP*, Nov. 9, 1996, 7).

Ninth, peace would consolidate Israel's relations with the United States and end the pervasive tension that had increasingly strained relations between the two countries. In much the same manner, peace with the Palestinians would shore up Israel's sagging relations with Jordan and Egypt.

Tenth, the risks of peace had been decreased by US security guarantees.

Why, then, was Netanyahu not persuaded by this imposing list of peace incentives? As noted earlier, part of the explanation involved deeply held values. For Netanyahu and his supporters, "tangible land" was simply more important than "intangible peace" (*JP*, Jan. 10, 1998, 12). Beyond that, the Israeli right found most of the above points to be speculative. The assertion that the West Bank was not essential for Israel's defense, for example, was hotly disputed. It was also less than clear that Arafat and the Palestinian Authority possessed the capacity to either rule effectively or to control terrorist acts perpetrated by the Fundamentalists and other radical groups. The "peace dividend," at least as represented by external investment, had been realized shortly after the Madrid talks when foreign investors, buoyed by the prospects of peace, rushed to invest in Israel (interviews with international economists, Beirut, 1999). Future peace dividends would be marginal.

The Israeli right was also more likely than the left to take a *realpolitik* view of its relations with the Arabs. The Arabs, in their view, had little choice but to make peace with Israel, regardless of its land policy. The US would continue to complain but, as always, would eventually come around to the Israeli point of view. The Palestinians, for their part, were welcome to take over Jordan, where they already constituted some 70 percent of the population. The demographic time bomb would be avoided by simply "transferring" the Palestinians from one side of the Jordan river to the other. In Israeli parlance the word "transfer" has become the code word for the forced depopulation (ethnic cleansing) of the Occupied Territories.

Fear of a shifting technological balance was more difficult for Netanyahu to dodge. Not unexpectedly, he called upon the United States to rush the development of its laser anti-missile technology. Technological superiority, from Netanyahu's perspective, would remain the foundation of Israel's security. If faced with cataclysmic circumstances, Israel could rely on its atomic weapons to deter attack by hostile neighbors.

Rabin's logic was sustained by the 1999 election of Barak, but Netanyahu's views were more than revived by Sharon's election in 2001.

THE GROUP BASIS OF ISRAELI POLITICS

In many ways, elites and groups are opposing sides of the same coin, the latter providing the power base for the former. Viewed in this light, the explanation for Israel's periods of immobilization followed by dramatic swings of policy involves the nature of Israel's political parties, pressure groups, and mass behavior.

Political Parties

Israel's political parties emerged in the colonial period as mechanisms for organizing the settlers and providing them with basic community services. By and large, they revolved around two ideological poles: a secular, socialist pole and a religious pole. Most Israelis accepted the Zionist ideology, although differences existed over its interpretation. After Israel had achieved its independence, the parties continued to provide needed services to Israel's citizens. They also strengthened the state by fostering sentiments of national awareness (Yishai 1998a).

Over time, however, Israel's political parties became increasingly focused on the narrow pursuit of specific economic, religious, and ethnic interests. In the process, Israel's larger parties have seen their numbers shrink as smaller ethnic and single-issue parties have risen to the fore. Shas, now Israel's third largest party, represents Sephardic Jews and particularly those of Moroccan origin. Yisrael Ba'aliyah, another big winner in the 1999 elections, represents Jews of Soviet origins.

Classifying Israel's political parties on a left-right continuum would be a difficult task, to say the least. Part of the problem lies in defining what is meant by "left" and "right" within the Israeli context. The left, in the Israeli context, generally refers to parties advocating socialist economic policies, welfare, and a centralized state. The left also represents a secular vision of Israeli society, stressing the cultural rather than the religious dimension of the religious state. More recently, the left has been associated with a willingness to trade land for peace and the curtailment of settlements in the Occupied Territories. Labor/One Israel, the main "all-Israel" coalition of the left, reflects all of the above concerns, but garnered only 20.2 percent of the popular vote in the 1999 elections. Labor/One Israel finds its center of gravity among the Western (Ashkenazi) Jews and, following its defeat in the 1996 elections, was criticized by one of its MKs, who described it as

> a party built around a yuppie, superior, Ashkenazi elite which doesn't grasp the sensitivities of Israeli society.... In the coming four years, Labor must develop a strategy to communicate with this new public, and build bridges to it. One way would be to open party ranks to new people, bringing in a new spirit and feeling of freshness (Shlomo Ben-Ami, cited in *JP*, June 22, 1996, 8).

Defining the Israeli right is far more problematic. The political right, at least as the term is used in Israeli parlance, variously refers to three more or less distinct themes: (1) parties advocating free-market capitalism supported by low regulation, low taxes, and low welfare; (2) parties advocating ultra-nationalism; and (3) parties advocating a religiously oriented government. Writ large, this configuration of ideological concerns has seen the political right place particular stress on maintaining Israel's control over the Occupied Territories. It has also seen the right take a hard-line stand on security issues. The Likud embodies all of the themes but tempers them with a desire to appeal to a broad spectrum of the voters on the center right, a base it requires to qualify as one of Israel's two "all Israeli" parties, i.e., parties capable of forming a Government. The Likud's ability to play this role was called into question by the 1999 Knesset elections, when the party received only 14.1 percent of the popular vote. It may have revived with the election of Sharon in 2001, but that remains to be seen.

The other parties of the right are more concerned with issues than with popularity and stress one of the three dimensions more than the others. The religious parties, for example, demand that Israel remain a

Jewish state in deed as well as name. This requires that religious law supersede secular law and that orthodox religious organizations receive favored treatment from the government. In the negotiations leading up to the formation of the Israeli state, a very secular Ben-Gurion signed a "religious status quo" agreement with the religious parties which stipulated that "the Sabbath and Kashrut (Jewish dietary law) were to be officially observed in the state, issues of marriage and divorce would be left in religious hands, and haredi circles would be allowed to maintain an independent educational system" (*JP* Israeli Elections Primer, 1999; Political Blocs and Parties, www). Shortly thereafter, coalition politics dictated that he exempt seminary students from military service. At the time, as the *Jerusalem Post* notes, "This was not a major issue for there were only a few hundred such students. Today they number in the tens of thousands" (*JP* Israeli Elections Primer, 1999; Political Blocs and Parties, www). The overwhelming focus of the religious parties is to retain and extend these benefits, and they generally side with whichever of the major parties gives them the best deal. Other right-wing parties have focused on incorporating the Occupied Territories into Israel proper, with the more extreme among them suggesting that the Arab residents be evacuated by one means or another (Sprinzak 1991).

Classification of Israeli political parties suffers from other problems as well. Most parties, for example, represent the interests of a specific group as well as a left-to-right ideology. While ideological links draw them together, group conflict pushes them apart. Shas, for example, is a religious party that also represents Sephardic Jews (Kamil 2000). As such, it often finds itself at odds with the United Torah Judaism, a religious party representing Western or Ashkenazi Jews.

Yet another difficulty in attempting to classify Israel political parties is their constantly shifting nature. Some reconstitute themselves under different names, while others shift positions on the political spectrum. The National Religious Party, for example, was a "centrist" party prior to 1967, but shifted to the right by its commitment to retaining the lands of ancient Israel acquired during the 1967 War. The One Israel Party came into existence with the 1999 elections, more or less merging with the Labor Alliance. Which of the two will survive remains to be seen.

Pressure Groups

Most of Israel's major interest groups, like its political parties, evolved during the pre-independence era. As described by Yishai,

> The Histadrut, to be sure, has always been the organization of salaried workers, but from its inception, in 1920, it did not gear its activities to

narrow trade unionist goals. Rather, its primary purpose was to help build the political and economic institutions necessary for the attainment of national sovereignty....

Israeli farmers were also harnessed to the national wagon. They were not individuals employed in agriculture but "settlers," and farming was not a vocation but a destiny and a calling.... The members of the Israeli Medical Association regarded themselves as pioneers whose primary goal was to serve the nation by providing health care services to the newcomers. Teachers were in the forefront of nation building as well (Yishai 1998a, 3, Infotrac).

In return for their service to the state, most of Israel's dominant groups were given semi-official status, participating on government boards that determined policy in their respective areas. They supported the state, and the state supported them.

Over the course of the next 50 years, Israel's interest groups—many often being indistinguishable from political parties—would be weaned from their quasi-official (neo-corporate) status and increasingly focus on the narrow pursuit of their economic, social, and political interests.

Most of Israel's larger groups have sought to enhance their political influence by forming their own political parties, a case in point being Israel's religious parties. The 1996 elections would similarly see the settler parties control seven seats in the Knesset and one cabinet position, although they represented only 2 percent of the population (*JP*, Aug. 13, 1996, 13). The settler population has continued to expand since that date and the number of settlers in the Occupied Territories now surpasses the 200,000 mark (*Ha'aretz*, Mar. 5, 2001, www).

Smaller groups, by contrast, concentrate on influencing the votes of individual MKs. With Israel possessing some 3000 registered pressure groups, this is not an issue of minor importance. Yishai quotes one frustrated MK as complaining

We have lost the intimacy of the Knesset; there are corridors that you cannot cross in less than half an hour, because they catch you on your way. You cannot have lunch without somebody hovering over your head, you cannot sit in your room as somebody will enter without first knocking on the door... (Yishai, 1998a, 5, Infotrac).

Yishai (1998a) goes on to note that efforts to regulate lobbying activities have been ineffectual and those laws that do exist are honored in the breach. More than ever, the group sacrifice of the early days of the republic has given way to the naked pursuit of special interest that has long been associated with the group process in the United States.

Some groups are also stronger than others. The power of religious groups remains strong. Histadrut, the large labor federation, exercised profound influence on Israeli politics during the early days of the republic, but has seen its power wane with the emergence of competing unions and the growing strength of business organizations (Yishai 1998a). Much the same is true of the Kibbutzim, the agricultural settlements that gave birth to many of Israel's early leaders, including Ben-Gurion. The military, as noted in earlier discussion, exercises inordinate influence on the policy-making process, with some wags suggesting that Israel is not a state with an army as much as it is an army financed by a state (Sharkansky 1997b). Nevertheless, the army's once unshakable position is being challenged by mothers' groups distraught over the loss of sons in Lebanon and the Occupied Territories. Women, while less powerful than the other groups discussed above, are represented by four major organizations and a dozen more concerned with issues of gender-related violence. Environmental groups have also proliferated, as have ethnic and religious associations. Of the ethnic associations, those representing approximately a million Jews who have immigrated to Israel since the collapse of the Soviet Union are particularly noticeable and have had a determining effect on the electoral process, swinging first to one side and then the other (*Ha'aretz*, May 9, 2000, www).

The weakest of Israel's major groups is the Israeli Arab community, some 1,000,000 strong, which constitutes approximately 20 percent of the Israeli population. This represents a dramatic increase from the some 160,000 Palestinian Arabs who became Israeli citizens at the end of the 1948 War. As Israeli citizens, Israeli Arabs seem to be concerned primarily with the attainment of equal political and economic status within the Israeli political system, rather than unification with the Palestinian state currently emerging in the Occupied Territories. Although they are treated as second-class citizens, most Israeli Arabs have a higher level of political and economic life than do most of the Palestinian Arabs living in the Occupied Territories. The goal of full equality, however, remains far from attainment because of various factors such as low skill levels, anti-Arab prejudice among the Israeli population, and lack of effective organization within the Israeli Arab community (Khalife 2001). By and large, Israeli Arabs have sought representation on the left of the Israeli political spectrum rather than using their substantial voting power to bargain between Israel's major voting blocs, a strategy that would inevitably increase their political influence. As things currently stand, the left has taken the Arab vote for granted, although the exceptionally low Arab turnout in the 2001 elections clearly contributed to the magnitude of Sharon's victory.

The sheer number of competing groups has contributed to both the democratization and the immobilization of Israeli politics. Israel is becoming more democratic in the broader sense of the word because more voices are influencing the policy-making process. The sheer number of those voices, however, has made the policy-making process increasingly complex.

Political Behavior

The growing divisiveness of Israeli society is particularly visible in election results and public opinion polls. The 1999 elections revealed a sharp divide between those who supported a continuation of Netanyahu's hard-line policies and the majority who supported Barak and a presumed rekindling of the peace process.

A more detailed portrait of the polarization of Israeli society was provided by the 1999 parliamentary elections. Of the 15 parties that received representation in the Knesset, most clustered on the political right or the political left. The right won 54 seats as opposed to 46 seats captured by the left. A prime minister from the left was thus confronted with a Knesset that inclined toward the right. The various parties of the center won only 20 seats, further reinforcing the image of a heavily polarized society. The center exists, but it is not large. Rather than driving Israeli politics, the center is significant because of its swing position between the left and the right.

It should also be noted that Israel is a very participatory society, with more than 70 percent of the population voting in the 1999 elections. While this was a decline from the 80 percent figure of early eras, it was clear that Israelis continued to take the political process very seriously (Etzioni-Halevy 1977). Be this as it may, dissatisfaction with the candidates in the 2001 election of the prime minister saw voter turnout tumble to 61 percent, with the drop being particularly severe among Arab voters (*JP*, Feb. 8, 2001, www).

Public polls paint a similar picture of fragmentation within Israeli society. A 2000 opinion poll, for example, found that "Over three-quarters of Israelis (77 percent) saw no improvement in the relationship between different sectors of the Jewish population, with nearly half predicting a deterioration in intra-Jewish relations. Only 19 percent saw Israeli Jews moving toward unity and agreement" (*JP*, May 9, 2000, www).

THE CONTEXT OF ISRAELI POLITICS

Although many political analysts attribute the complexities of Israeli politics to the nature of its institutions and political actors, others find explanations within Israel's culture, political economy, and international environment.

Political Culture

Israeli political culture has much to say about both the cohesiveness of Israeli society and its growing fragmentation. As discussed by Aronoff:

> Do Israelis share common cultural myths and visions of their destinies? Significant minorities do not identify with or actively reject the most basic symbols of the Zionist civil religion. Among those who do identi- fy with the root cultural paradigms, there are fundamental divisions over what should constitute the Jewish character and the physical boundaries of the state. There is a conspicuous lack of consensus on fun- damental values and basic public policy among Zionists. These divi- sions would appear to be linked to profound differences in a relative sense of individual and collective security, trust/distrust and amity/hos- tility toward outsiders, and temporal world views between types of Zionists. Since no hegemonic ideological interpretation of Zionism has gained dominance, what, if anything, constitutes the overarching sym- bolic framework that provides the commonality in Israeli political cul- ture? (Aronoff 1989, 141)

Aronoff answers his question by suggesting that despite all of their differences, Jews share a sense of Jewishness and its importance. "The fact that secular scholars, religious leaders, and politicians of all per- suasions engaged one another in a public debate over the consequences and implications of events that took place 2000 years ago indicates the existence of a common cultural rubric and rhetoric, which made the de- bate both possible and meaningful" (Aronoff 1989, 141).

Oz refers to the same phenomenon when he writes

> And this tribal feeling (we have barely emerged from being a tribe and not yet reached the level of being a nation) creates a perpetual intimate warmth which is sometimes necessary and comforting and sometimes sticky, irritating and disgusting. It is the feeling that 'we all depend on each other.' It is the feeling of 'family shame' that overtakes millions of people here every time some Jewish thief or embezzler is apprehended. And it is the pride (tinged with petty jealousy) that the whole tribe ex- periences on reading that some local cow or bridge-player has broken a world record... (Oz 1995, 108).

There is also ample behavioral evidence that most Jewish residents of Israel share a strongly felt Jewish identity and sense of mutual de- pendence. This shared perspective helps to explain the strength of Is- raeli political institutions as well as the phenomenal support that Israel enjoys from the world Jewish community. Whatever their conflicts, it is a rare Jew who is indifferent to the fate of the Jewish state. They may not like Israeli policy, but the survival of Israel is of vital concern to Jews throughout the world. The same sense of common identity and common destiny would seem to explain the Israeli reluctance to suffer casualties and the extreme lengths to which Israeli leaders will go in an effort to free Israeli prisoners. Jewish suffering becomes intensely personalized. In much the same manner, some authors refer to a Holocaust complex, suggesting that the past suffering of the Jews has resulted in an inordinate concern for security (Cohen 1994). Perhaps reflecting these anxieties, a recent World Health Organization survey of youth in 27 countries found Israeli youth to be the "least happy" and the "most likely to feel low" (*JP*, Feb. 17, 2000, www). On the other hand, they were more likely than their counterparts in Europe and North America to "feel close to their parents" (*JP*, May 9, 2000, www).

An abiding concern for security is matched by an intense pride in Israel's accomplishments and the invincibility of its defense forces. As Barbara Amiel writes:

> For centuries the Jews had been doing pretty much nothing but writing books, playing violins, being financiers, learned professionals, academics, pawnbrokers, tailors, shopkeepers and for this we had at various times been turned out of our homes and countries, denied the vote, driven into extermination camps, or in a more benign show of disapproval, refused admission to the better class of clubs. Now we were in tanks and fighter planes, shooting and bombing people, and the world suddenly liked us (Amiel 2000, 5, www).

Pride, however, has been qualified by a deep, pervasive sense of guilt over the means employed to assure Israel's survival, a sense of guilt, according to Amiel, that is rooted in centuries in pain and a deeply entrenched sense of justice and tolerance that pervades Jewish religious teachings.

> But suddenly…Jews woke up and found that they were faced with an entirely different set of circumstances; to create and maintain their nation state, they had to do some unpleasant, perhaps unjust and intolerant things (Amiel 2000, 5, www).

The solidifying influence of Jewish identity and mutual dependence, while a clear force in Israeli politics, is increasingly offset by deep conflicts over the key issues of land, peace, Jewishness, and security discussed throughout this chapter (Barzilai 1999; Ribak 1997; Alpher 1995). Israeli society is bitterly divided on these issues, and that division is unlikely to be healed in the near future. Indeed, Israel's political divisions seem to be growing as conservatives cling to their religious and nationalistic vision of Israel, while liberal Israelis increasingly define themselves as post-Zionists. Post-Zionism is described by Hadar as follows:

Post-Zionism is neither a political party trying to win votes in the upcoming Knesset (parliamentary) elections nor an established ideological movement with a magazine and research centers. It does not have any recognized leaders or card-carrying members. It is simply shorthand for new ideas about the future of Israel that are cropping up in newspaper columns, academic papers, think-tank discussions, the courts, theaters, and the arts.... In essence, post-Zionism is a vision of those who want Israel to become "normal," to move beyond the century-long Zionist revolution and resolve some of the contradictions that Zionism and the term "Jewish state" have introduced.... Central to the post-Zionist perspective is the goal of separating synagogue from state in order to provide Israeli Jews with the same civic and religious rights their co-religionists enjoy in North America and Western Europe—to get married or be buried in civil ceremonies and to wed non-Jews, for example.... Finally, a main post-Zionist objective is a reconciliation between Israeli Jews and Palestinian Arabs, to be accomplished by recognizing the national rights of the two peoples, as well as by transforming Israel into a truly democratic state in which all of its citizens are equal under the law (Hadar 1999).

Of particular interest on the cultural front has been the publication of three new textbooks that have rewritten Israeli history to bring it more in line with historical facts rather than with the national myths that have played such an integral part in building national solidarity (*JP*, Sept. 8, 1999, www). As reviewed by Cohen:

The book includes a section on the War of Independence which reads: "On nearly every front, and in nearly every battle, the Jewish side had the advantage over the Arabs in terms of planning, organization, operation of equipment and also on the number of trained figures who participated in the battle."

It also stresses that the Holocaust was part of and not separate from World War II, and that Zionism was one of many national movements that emerged in Europe in the late 19th century (Cohen 1999).

The Israeli right has launched a bitter attack on the new book, in some cases warning that the Jewish state is being destroyed from within (*JP*, Sept. 8, 1999, www). Adding insult to injury, Israeli archeologists have recently made unsettling discoveries:

This is what archaeologists have learned from their excavations in the Land of Israel: the Israelites were never in Egypt, did not wander in the desert, did not conquer the land in a military campaign and did not pass it on to the twelve tribes of Israel. Perhaps even harder to swallow is the fact that the united monarchy of David and Solomon, which is described by the Bible as a regional power, was at most a small tribal kingdom. And it will come as an unpleasant shock to many that the God of

Israel, Jehovah, had a female consort and that the early Israelite religion adopted monotheism only in the waning period of the monarchy and not Mount Sinai (Herzog 1999).

Whether these and similar events will alter Israel's political culture remains to be seen, but they do mark a dramatic change in Israel's concerted attempt to use myth building as the cornerstone of national solidarity.

Political Economy

While not denying the influence of culture on Israeli politics, political economists are inclined to find economic factors behind both the strength of Israel's political institutions and the growing fragmentation of Israeli society. The strength of Israel's political institutions, from an economic perspective, reflects Israel's success in providing for the basic economic and social needs of its citizens. The per capita income of Israel now hovers in the range of $18,100 per annum, a figure that brings it on par with many states of Western Europe. Ideological (cultural) legitimacy has clearly been reinforced by economic legitimacy.

The changing tenor of Israeli politics, from a political economist's point of view, mirrors Israel's transition from a largely socialist economy to an increasingly capitalistic one. Not only has this transformation strengthened the influence of capitalist groups in policy-making circles, but it has reinforced the class divisions within Israeli society, a fact played upon by Israeli politicians. As described by Smooha:

> The overall trend in Israeli society is of widening class divisions. The Gini coefficients of income inequality are around 0.33 as high as in the West. The income of the top tenth is 11 times the income of the bottom tenth. The rate of poverty is over 15%, much higher than the Western average. While the middle class keeps its large size (estimated as 45 percent of the population), the gap in the standard of living and assets between the higher and lower strata is steadily growing and strengthening (Smooha 1998, 39).

The sharp swings in policy that have characterized Israeli politics in recent decades have also been facilitated by economic factors (Bichler 1994). More often than not, regime changes have occurred during period of economic decline, a trend that continued through the 1999 and 2001 elections (*Ha'aretz*, May 26, 1999; *JP*, Nov. 26, 2000, www). In much the same vein, Sharkansky notes that Jewish emigration from Israel has generally accompanied "changes in the economic situation in Israel and overseas" (Sharkansky 1997b, 84).

Along similar lines, economic deficits—Israel's debt to GDP ratio in 2000, for example, was 105 percent—have forced the government to ease its regulation of the economy. They have spurred a reduction of defense expenditures and led to the streamlining of Israel's large governmental agencies (State of Israel 1999).

Foreign Influences on Israeli Policy

It is doubtful that any country in the world can rival Israel in the degree to which its politics are influenced by external factors. This external influence began with the formation of the World Zionist Organization, which scored its first victory with the Balfour Declaration of 1917. With a "national home for the Jews" decreed by the British, it was the Jewish agency that promoted the settlement of Jews in Palestine and that nurtured the formation of Jewish political institutions. Foreign policy has dominated the agenda of Israeli cabinets since the inception of the Jewish state, a situation that remains in place today. The pervasive influence of external pressures on the politics of Israel is too complex to be easily summarized, but several points are of particular importance in explaining the paradox of strong political institutions accompanied by chaotic policy making and an increasingly divided population.

The first point to be noted is the fact that Israel was born in war and continues to live in a condition of "no war, no peace" with key countries of the region, including Syria, Iraq, and Iran. Fear of obliteration forced a consensus on the Israeli population during the early years of statehood, just as it necessitated the development of strong political institutions. In the post-1967 era, however, Israel would emerge as the dominant military power in the region, and the need for consensus would begin to wane. Israel was still at risk, but the need for consensus eased and the inherent pluralism of Israeli society began to find expression (Ezrahi 1998; Barnett 1992).

A hostile regional environment has had other ramifications as well, including the need to divert scarce resources from development into defense. A hostile regional environment has also increased the prominence of the military in Israel's political equations, with "defense" becoming an all-compelling justification for human rights abuses in the Occupied Territories. In this regard, Barzilai (1999) argues that Israel's security dilemma has stimulated an intense sense of Israeli nationalism, if not a garrison mentality.

Second, external influence flows from the massive financial support that Israel receives from the United States and other international donors, a figure that constituted 7 percent of the Israeli budget in 1999.

It was this support, as we have seen earlier, that enabled Israel to settle massive waves of Jewish immigrants, just as it was this economic support that facilitated the ability of Israel's political institutions to meet the basic needs of the population.

In much the same manner, it was external support from the United States and other countries that facilitated Israel's victories against its Arab foes. This statement is not intended to denigrate the skill and valor of the IDF, but merely to acknowledge that Israeli military prowess has been enhanced by its ties to the US and other countries. Israel is the largest recipient of US foreign aid, receiving more than $3 billion per annum. This figure does not include special military allocations that are channeled through the budget of the US Department of Defense and are absent from normal discussions of foreign aid. Also "off budget" are special allocations designed to stimulate the Arab-Israeli peace process. The Israeli pullout from Lebanon was estimated to cost "at least several hundred million dollars, much of which was provided by the United States" (*JP*, May 9, 2000, www). A final Arab-Israeli peace agreement could cost up to $100 billion, much of which, according to diplomatic sources, would go to Israel (*JP*, May 9, 2000, www). As a senior US Congressman would comment, "We are happy to give Israel economic assistance but, for goodness sake, $100 billion so there will be an agreement to stop Israelis from killing Palestinians and Palestinians from killing Israelis?" (Callahan, cited in *JP*, Dec. 3, 1999, www). Perhaps reflecting these views, a plan is now in place to eliminate US non-military aid to Israel over 10 years.

American aid, however, has had its price, not the least of which is growing, if erratic, pressure on the Jewish state to return the Occupied Territories to the Arabs as a precondition for making peace with its Arab neighbors (Noyes 1997). The peace process has been a bone of contention between Israel and successive US governments since the end of the 1967 War, and continues to be so today with grudging US acquiescence in the establishment of an international committee to examine the al-Aqsa intifada, an event that has made Israel the focal point of international criticism. While US interests dictate trading land for a broader regional peace, many Israelis cling to the notion of a greater Israel.

The support of the World Zionist organization has also carried strings, as world Zionist leaders seem fond of second-guessing the policies of Israel's leaders. The Jewish Agency, for example, continues to pursue its support of the settlers in the Occupied Territories with little regard for Israeli policy. Indeed, the World Zionist Organization and the Jewish Agency often seem to be in competition with official settlement agencies.

A third form of external pressure on Israeli politics is to be found in the intimate links between the US Jewish community and the Jewish community of Israel, with many US Jews enjoying dual citizenship. New York, as Sharkansky notes, "competes with Jerusalem and Tel Aviv as the center of Jewish culture, religion, and politics" (Sharkansky 1997a). Some 600,000 Israeli citizens reside outside of Israel, more than half of whom vote in Israeli elections (*JP*, Feb. 8, 1997, 8). The 1999 elections saw some 6000 US Jews fly to Israel to vote, while experts anticipated that US Jews would contribute between $6 and $8 million to the campaign coffers of Israeli candidates (*Washington Post*, reprinted in *Daily Star*, May 10, 1999, 5). Senior US rabbis, moreover, often maintain a large following among Israel's Orthodox community, with a US Orthodox rabbi recently unleashing a furor by declaring that Reform and Conservative Jews were not Jews at all but members of some other religion (*IHT*, April 2, 1977, 2). Reform and Conservative Jewish organizations in the US are also intimately linked with affairs in Israel, both being vitally concerned about the dominance of Orthodox rabbis in Israel. American rabbis have also entered the fray of the land for peace debate, with more than 100 US rabbis declaring that there was no religious reason to require exclusive Jewish sovereignty over the Temple Mount, the massive stone plateau in Jerusalem, considered holy by both Jews and Muslims (*NYT*, Dec. 7, 2000). One way or another, there is little that happens in the United States Jewish community that does not have an impact on Israel.

Although tensions have always existed between Israel and the world Jewish community over the direction of Israeli policy, new concerns have been emerging over the decreasing support of that community. A US Jewish community that once contributed nearly $1 billion annually to Israel now contributes one-fifth of that amount (*Ha'aretz*, Nov. 10, 1999, www). Also disconcerting to Israeli leaders is the growing assimilation of Western Jews, with some 52 percent of US Jews choosing non-Jewish spouses (*Ha'aretz*, Nov. 10, 1999, www). Perhaps in response to these realities, new efforts are being made to unify a US Jewish community that includes some 200 local federations as well as three large umbrella associations: The United Jewish Appeal, the United Israel Appeal, and the Council of Jewish Federations (*Ha'aretz*, Nov. 10, 1999, www).

Finally, Israeli policy is influenced by its role as a guardian of all Jews, not merely Israeli citizens. This concern tempered Israeli relations with the Soviet Union during the Cold War and continues to influence Israeli relations with Russia. While Russian Jews are no longer held captive by a totalitarian regime, the chronic instability of post-Soviet Russia has seen a resurgence of anti-Semitic slogans among Russian parties of both the left and right. President Putin's opponents in the 2000 Russian presidential elections, for example, were accused of being linked to Jews, gays, and foreigners (*NYT*, Mar. 24, 2000, www). Even Israel's relations with Iran have been tempered by concerns for the security of Iran's sizable Jewish community (Sharkansky 1997b).

Israelis often complain of being manipulated by larger foreign powers, but the reality of the situation is that Israel gives as well as it gets. Rather than being a dependency of the United States, Israel has been remarkably successful in shaping the policies of its major ally (Spiegel 1985). All recent US presidents have openly proclaimed their friendship for Israel; the members of the US Congress have done likewise. The American-Israeli Political Action Committee (AIPAC) is among the strongest lobbies in Washington, and most US congressional representatives find it easier to support the Israeli cause than to oppose it. As one representative quipped, "Voting against Israel has become like voting against lumber in Washington State. Except AIPAC does it all over the country" (*Christian Science Monitor*, June 28, 1991, 3). Also to be noted in this regard is the fact that Israel is a nuclear power—as yet, the only nuclear power in the Middle East—as well as the world's fifth largest arms exporter (*JP*, Feb. 2, 2000, www).

In sum, Israel's relationship with the world is one of profound interdependence. Israeli policy making is profoundly shaped by external factors, but Israel is not a passive partner in this process.

LOOKING TOWARD THE FUTURE

Trying to predict the course of Israeli politics over the next few decades, one can see little change in the above patterns. Israeli political institutions are well established and enjoy a broad base of political legitimacy among the Israeli population. Political legitimacy is strongly reinforced by an increasingly robust economy driven by a specialization in high-tech industries. The Arabs are at bay, yet security concerns remain, not the least of which has been the threat of both Fundamentalist violence and long-range missiles. The support of the US also remains solid, as does the support of the world Jewish community. These elements of strength, however, allow even broader scope for conflict over the key issues of security, peace, land, and Jewishness. These issues are unlikely to be resolved in the near future, if ever.

4

The Politics of Syria

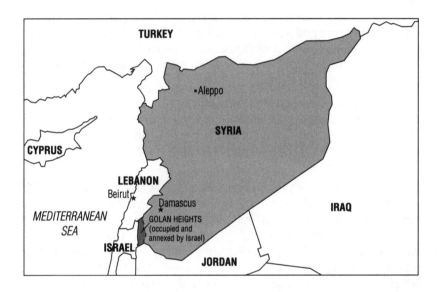

The past 30 years have seen Syria transformed from a country plagued by coups and instability into one of the most politically stable countries in the Middle East. In the process, Syria has become a major player in the affairs of the region. Syria dictates the politics of Lebanon, holds the key to any final settlement of the Arab-Israeli conflict, stands as an obstacle to Iraqi expansion in the Gulf, and serves as a conduit for Iranian influence in the Arab East. Indeed, Syria's role in the Middle East is often summed up by the adage "no war without Egypt; no peace without Syria."

Syria's transformation from a fragmented and divided country into a regional power was largely the work of a single individual: Hafez al-Asad. This was a remarkable feat, for Syria possesses a relatively small population (17,000,000) and few natural resources. The recent development of Syria's limited oil reserves has spurred a modicum of economic growth, but the country's industrial base remains largely under state control and lacks the technology to compete with the world's more developed economies on a global scale.

Al-Asad's reign has also been challenged by the military sophistication of Israel, the domineering power of Turkey, and the massive armies of Iraq, all of which share a contentious border with the Syrian state (see map). A recent treaty of military cooperation between Israel and Turkey, moreover, has placed Syria in a vise between its two more powerful neighbors.

Whatever its economic and geopolitical problems, perhaps the greatest constraint on Syria's political and economic development has been the fragmentation of its population into a plethora of religious sects, none of which care much for the others. As a traveler wrote near the end of the nineteenth century,

> They hate one another. The Sunnis excommunicate the Shias and both hate the Druze; all detest the Alawis; the Maronites do not love anybody but themselves and are duly abhorred by all; the Greek Orthodox abominate the Greek Catholics and the Latins; all despise the Jews (Kessler 1987, 7).

Although Syria is a predominantly Arab (90 percent) and Sunni (70 percent) country, it has been ruled for the past three decades by members of an Alawite minority that constitutes between 10 and 15 percent of the population, probably being closer to the former.[1] The Alawites, although Arab, adhere to an extremist branch of Shi'a Islam that accords Ali, the fourth Caliph and son-in-law of Mohammed, a religious status nearly equal to that of Mohammed himself. The term *Alawite* means followers of Ali, and a minority of the Alawites believe that the Angel Gabriel mistakenly revealed the Koran to Mohammed rather than Ali. Sunni Muslims often condemn the Alawites as heretics, and even other Shi'a treat them with suspicion. The Druze, another quasi-Shi'a sect, constitute approximately 3 percent of the population. As in the case of the Alawites, the exact nature of their religious views remains a closely guarded secret. Some 11 diverse Christian sects, many tracing their origins to the earliest days of Christianity, constitute approximately 10 percent of the population (*CIA Factbook*, 1999, www). All of the above population figures are rough estimates and vary markedly from one source to another.

Latent distrust between its diverse religious sects continues to be a fact of life in Syrian politics. Syria's leaders have traditionally filled

---

[1]The *CIA Factbook* (1999) lists the Alawites and the Druze as 16 percent of the population but does not distinguish between the two groups.

key positions in the government with family members and co-sectarians, a practice that is very much in evidence today. Alawites formed the core of President al-Asad's inner circle and dominated the command structure of the Syrian military. Of these individuals, the most influential tended to be kin of the president. Such practices, necessary for regime survival, served only to perpetuate the cycle of sectarian conflict. Whether this policy will change under the reign of Bashar al-Asad, the son of the late president, remains to be seen, but it is difficult to imagine how it could be otherwise.

Alawite domination has been facilitated by the fragmentation of the Sunni Arabs along class, family, and regional lines. The big families of Damascus have traditionally contended for power with the dominant families of Aleppo; the interests of wealthy Sunni merchants are often at odds with those of the poorer Sunni peasants; Westernized Sunni urbanites have found their domination of the Sunni community challenged by the zeal of the Sunni Fundamentalists. The Arab Sunnites may constitute the majority of the Syrian population, but it is not a cohesive majority.

Social fragmentation has also been reinforced by geographic isolation. Syria's Alawite community was traditionally concentrated in the areas surrounding the coastal city of Latakia, the Druze in the mountainous areas near the Lebanese-Israeli border (the Jebel Druze), and the Kurds near the border with Iraqi Kurdistan. The Sunni Arabs were scattered throughout the country, but dominated the larger urban areas.

Finally, group divisions have been reinforced by economic conflict. Syria is a poor country in which every group must compete with every other group for its fair share of the country's resources. Historically, the Sunnis were the winners in this struggle, and the Sunni merchant class controlled much of Syria's land and wealth. The minorities survived as best they could, but neither they nor the poorer Sunni peasants felt any warmth toward their landed masters.

Our focus in this chapter will be on the mechanisms of minority rule. We will simultaneously explore the mechanisms that kept Hafez al-Asad in power for 30 years and which will now determine the fate of his son, Bashar al-Asad. We will also examine the inherent contradictions between one-man rule and the development of sustainable political institutions.

HISTORY AND CULTURE

Historically, the region often referred to as Greater Syria stretched along the Mediterranean Sea from Egypt to Southern Turkey (Pipes

1990; Hitti 1959). As such, it encompassed the present countries of Israel, Lebanon, Syria, much of Jordan, and a small section of Turkey adjacent to the Syrian border. As with most countries of the Middle East, Greater Syria fell sway to a bewildering array of ancient civilizations including those of the Arameans, Assyrians, Babylonians, Chaldeans, Persians, Greeks, Romans, Nabateans, and Byzantines. Although each successive civilization left its imprint on Syrian culture, the most enduring legacy of the early historical era was the conversion of most of Greater Syria to Christianity. Antioch, together with Rome, Constantinople, and Alexandria, was one of the four Patriarchates of the Christian Church. Even today, some of Syria's smaller Christian sects continue to use the Biblical languages of Amharic and Syriac in their religious services.[2]

The Muslim Arabs conquered Syria in AD 636, and most of Syria's population would eventually convert to Islam. The Syrians were far more urbanized and sophisticated than Arabia's bedouin warriors— Damascus and Aleppo trace their origins to approximately 2500 BC— and soon dominated the empire's bureaucratic apparatus. Reflecting Syrian dominance, the seat of the Islamic Caliphate would shift to Damascus in 661, with the Umayyad Caliphs extending the Islamic Empire from northern India in the east to Spain in the West. Damascus's days of glory, however, were limited, and control of the Islamic Empire shifted to Iraq in 750, leaving Syria to be ruled by one or another of the contending Islamic powers until becoming part of the Ottoman Empire in 1516.

Ottoman rule lasted until the Arab Revolt of World War I, and was characterized by a pattern of governance that allowed each of Syria's myriad religious communities to be self-governing if taxes were paid and revolts were few. This policy, often referred to as the millet system, perpetuated the fragmentation of Syrian society and delayed the emergence of nationalistic feelings among the Syrian population (Gelvin 1998).

The Colonial Era

The outbreak of World War I found the Ottoman Empire, an ally of Germany, at war with Britain and France. The British, concerned with the threat of Ottoman attacks on the Suez Canal, inspired Sharif Hussein, the Arab governor of Mecca and a direct descendant of the Prophet Mohammed, to lead an Arab revolt against the Turks. Hussein's reward would be an Arab kingdom that encompassed much of

---

[2]Antioch is the current Israeli city of Akka.

what is now Saudi Arabia as well as virtually all of Greater Syria, although the details of the negotiations between the British and Hussein remain a matter of debate. British negotiations with the Arabs reflected a degree of perfidy, and in 1916 they compromised their implicit arrangement with the Arabs by agreeing with France to divide the region among themselves. The British would control Palestine and the area that is now Jordan and Iraq. The French would control the remainder of Greater Syria, including the present countries of Syria and Lebanon. This arrangement was followed in 1917 by the Balfour Declaration, a unilateral pledge by the British to make Palestine a national home for the Jews.

The Arab revolt, the details of which were recounted in the introductory chapter, led to the triumphant entrance of Prince Faisal, the son of Sharif Hussein, into Damascus in 1918 (Gelvin 1998). The triumph, however, was short-lived as Arab forces were defeated by the French in 1920. Perhaps hoping to honor something of their earlier agreements, the British made Faisal the King of Iraq while Prince Abdullah, a second son of Sharif Hussein, was subsequently named Emir (Prince) of Transjordan, the precursor to the present state of Jordan. Both princes received their royal assignments on the condition that they would rule from their respective thrones in cooperation with the British.

Consequences of the Colonial Era   The French authorities continued their dismemberment of Greater Syria by transforming Lebanon, a predominantly mountainous region inhabited largely by Christians, into an independent country. The Christians of Lebanon had long looked to France for protection from their Muslim neighbors and were far more receptive to French rule than Syria's Muslim population. France would thus acquire a secure base in the Eastern Mediterranean. To give the new mini-state greater stature, surrounding Muslim and Druze areas were added to Lebanon's Christian core, thereby assuring that the new mini-state would inherit the communal turmoil of its larger neighbor.

France continued its divide-and-rule policy by dividing Syria into more or less self-governing provinces, each dominated by a different religious group: Latakia to the Alawites; Damascus and Aleppo to the Sunnis; the Jebel Druze to the Druze; and Alexandretta to the Turks. Real power, of course, resided with the French (Khoury 1997). Alexandretta would eventually be ceded to Turkey in a move to bolster Franco-Turkish relations, a decision that continues to rankle with Syria's leaders. The French had also declared the Alawite Mountains to be a separate country, but later rescinded the declaration.

The harshness of French rule and a declining economy fueled a variety of nationalist movements, but most came to naught as a result of communal, class, and personality conflicts. Some early nationalists were supporters of Faisal and his vision of a united Arab kingdom; others sought the formation of an Arab republic that would incorporate much of the Arab east (Khoury 1997, 441–442).

The greatest stimulus of Arab nationalism, however, was not economic but the exposure of Syrian students to French culture and the seductive ideologies of nationalism, human rights, and Marxism (Dawn 1962). Those who studied at the Sorbonne or other universities dominated by French leftists were profoundly influenced by Marxist doctrine, and both Socialist and Communist parties would make their appearance in Syria during the colonial era.

In the final analysis, the main ideological doctrine to emerge from the era of French rule was not Marxism but Ba'athism. Founded by Michel Aflaq and Salah Bitar, two Syrian students studying at the Sorbonne, the Ba'ath Party represented a fusion of Marxist social and economic principles with Arab nationalism. Aflaq was an Orthodox Christian; Bitar, a Sunni Muslim. The goal of Ba'athists was the creation of a unified Arab state independent of imperial domination (Aflaq 1963). The new state would be a socialist state in which a wise government assured both economic development and the equitable distribution of the state's resources. The new state would also be a secular state in which ethnic and communal loyalties gave way to an overriding commitment to the Arab nation (Jabar 1966). The exact date of the Party's origin remains a matter of debate, but its founding congress was held in 1947 (Batatu 1999).

With its banner of "unity, freedom, and socialism," the new party soon attracted a broad base of recruits among Syria's students and junior military officers. The egalitarian and secular orientation of the Party made it particularly appealing to Syrian minorities who had long resented Sunni domination. The Ba'ath Party also found strong support among Sunni fellahin (peasants), many of whom subsisted in conditions of near servitude. Various socialist parties merged with the Ba'ath Party shortly after independence, giving the Party its formal name of the Arab Socialist Resurrection (Renaissance) Party.[3]

The French, then, could not block the emergence of Arab nationalism in Syria, but they did everything in their power to slow its progress. In the process, they deepened the fragmentation of Syrian

[3]The original party formed by Aflaq and Bitar was the Arab Resurrection Party. It merged with Hawrani's Arab Socialist Party in 1953 to form the Ba'ath Party. The Ba'ath Party also incorporated other intellectual currents and was influenced by the philosophical writings of Zaki Arsuzi, an Alawite.

society, assuring that an independent Syria would find the task of nation building to be an arduous one (Zeine 1960; Ziadeh 1957).

The Era of Revolution and Optimism

France, in the throes of World War II, agreed to Syrian independence in 1941. Elections were held in 1943, with the leaders of the National Party, an organization controlled largely by wealthy Sunnis and upper-class Christians, emerging victorious. Full independence, however, did not come until 1946 when the last of the French troops left the country under pressure from the British and Americans.

Syria's new leaders faced the challenge of forging a cohesive political community where none had existed before. They were also anxious to develop the Syrian economy, albeit in a manner that strengthened the power of Syria's landed and commercial classes. Both tasks would prove difficult (World Bank 1955). Syria's new leaders had few resources to draw upon, and none of its leaders possessed the charisma of Nasser or Ben Gurion. The country's political institutions, moreover, were untested and evinced few signs of legitimacy among the Syrian population. The National Party had assumed power with independence, but had limited support among the masses.[4] As ardent capitalists, National Party members were disinclined toward welfare programs that might have increased their popularity among the poor. The Syrian military, the ultimate guarantor of the regime, was beset by the same factionalism that divided the country as a whole and showed ominous signs of being controlled by the Alawites and other minorities. Ba'athist and Communist influences within the military were also mounting. Factionalism within the military would increase over the course of the independence era as both the Ba'athists and the Communists encouraged their younger supporters, most of whom were minorities, to enter the military college. Wealthier Sunnis, by contrast, found military service to be beneath their dignity and concentrated on commerce. The military thus served as the primary avenue of social mobility among the minorities and the poor. This trend was particularly evident among the Alawites.

The early years of independence were beset by communal tensions as well as by increasing conflict between the peasants and the large landowners. Only about one-third of Syria's peasants owned land, the remainder being sharecroppers dependent upon the good will of the landlord for their survival (Batatu 1999). Rather than meeting Syria's

---

[4]The National Party was the Damascus branch of the National Bloc, which was dissolved in 1945. The People's Party was the Aleppo Branch of the National Bloc. Both consisted of urban nobility.

social and economic problems with a firm hand, the leaders of the National Party were immobilized by internecine bickering and personality conflicts. The defeat of the Syrian army in the 1948 war with Israel further undermined popular support for the National Party and turned the army against a government that had sent it into battle ill equipped to win.

Such feelings were probably justified, for Syria had little in the way of an army at the time of independence. The National Party had entered the war buoyed by the euphoria of independence and the assumption that the Jews could not fight. The victory would be an easy one, perhaps allowing Syria to reclaim territories severed by the British and French in the aftermath of World War I. How better for the regime to shore up its sagging popularity?

The optimism that marked the beginning of the war merely added to the bitterness of defeat. A military coup d'état toppled the National Party in March of 1949, bringing to a close Syria's first experiment in democracy (Carleton 1950). The first coup gave way to a second some four months later (August), followed by another in December of the same year. The last of the three coups was executed by Lt. Col. Adib al-Shishakli and promised a return to a guided democracy. Limited welfare and land reform measures were also introduced, offering the promise of easing the tension between the landed/commercial class and the poor. Conservative opposition to the reforms led to the overthrow of al-Shishakli, followed by a counter coup by al-Shishakli in 1952. The second al-Shishakli coup brought repression rather than a return to democracy, and all political parties and unions were abolished and replaced by a regime-sponsored party. Syria's fractious groups would either work in harmony within the new party or be excluded from politics, or so the theory went.

The experiment was short-lived, for al-Shishakli was overthrown in February of 1954 and Syria returned to civilian rule. The Syrian political spectrum now ran the gamut from the old conservatives on the right to the Ba'athists and Communists on the left. They, in turn, would soon be joined by the supporters of Nasser, whose charismatic leadership had captured the imagination of the Arab world. The Nasserites espoused essentially the same goals as the Ba'ath Party (unity, socialism, and freedom), but found a broader appeal among Sunni Muslims. The Ba'ath and the Communists, by contrast, continued to find disproportionate support among minority groups. All three groups had supporters in the army. Growing Ba'athist influence in the military increased the Party's political clout but also laid the foundation for a confrontation between the civilian and military wings of the Party. The civilian leadership possessed the titles and visibility; the military officers possessed the power.

The Ba'ath Party entered the cabinet for the first time in 1949 and showed clear signs of becoming a dominant force in Syrian politics. The parties of the center and right were poorly organized affairs that had little mass support. Most revolved around key figures or families and found it difficult to work with other parties in a productive manner.

The Communists, however, had also made considerable progress. Khaled Bakdash, the head of the Syrian Communist Party, was elected to the Assembly in 1954. He was the first Communist member of parliament in the Arab world. Far more ominous, from the Ba'athist perspective, was the appointment of a Communist general as Chief of Staff of the armed forces in 1957. Nasserite power had also increased apace and surged with Nasser's political victory in the 1956 War. The Ba'athist leadership was thus threatened by fear of a communist coup on one side and the juggernaut of Nasser's popularity on the other. Adding to the Party's woes was the growing inability of its various factions to resolve their differences. Rather than presenting a united front to their adversaries, Party documents of the era spoke of "chaos" and a "breakdown of discipline" (Batatu 1999, 143).

Faced with a dilemma from which there appeared to be no exit, the Ba'ath Party proposed a merger of Egypt and Syria, thereby realizing the common dream of Arab Unity. Nasser was originally reluctant, but accepted the proposal on the condition that all political parties would be banned with the exception of his newly created Arab Socialist Union (Heikal 1962). The Ba'athist leadership accepted Nasser's conditions, probably believing that they would be free to rule Syria as they wished while Nasser contented himself with Egypt. The Syrians also believed that they were more clever than the Egyptians and that the Ba'athist organizational structure would prove superior to that of the untested Arab Socialist Union (Palmer 1960). In retrospect, they were wrong on both counts.

The Syrian Ba'ath Party disbanded itself in compliance with Nasser's wishes, although many lesser members of the party found the decision to be premature.[5] Ba'athist leaders became senior officials in the new UAR government, many moving from Damascus to Cairo. The euphoria of the moment spawned pro-unity uprisings throughout the Arab east, crowned by the overthrow of the Iraqi monarchy in July of 1958. The new Iraqi leaders vowed their loyalty to the UAR, proclaiming that full unity of the three countries was merely a matter of time.

[5]Branches of the party remained in Iraq, Jordan, and Lebanon.

Euphoria, however, soon turned to despair as the Ba'athists found that their role in governing the UAR was largely illusory. In reality, most had been exiled to Cairo to keep them out of trouble. This was particularly true of the military, for Nasser was well aware of Syria's history of instability and had no intention of risking a coup d'état. With their party disbanded and their leaders in exile, the Ba'athists watched from the sidelines as Egyptians ruled Syria with the support of Syrian Nasserites.

The more Syrians became disenchanted with the UAR, the more Egyptians asserted their authority in a futile effort to make the union work. More often than not, these efforts were clumsy and heavy-handed affairs that served only to alienate ever-larger segments of the Syrian population. Many Syrians found it ironic that an Egyptian bureaucracy that was losing the struggle to develop its own country would judge itself capable of ruling another. The final year of the union saw a misguided attempt to impose Egypt's socialist policies on Syria, a move that cost Nasser the support of a Sunni business community that had once welcomed him as a counterweight to the radical policies of the Ba'athists and the Communists.

Not all of the union's troubles, however, were of its own making. The West plotted against the union at every turn, fearing that its success would destroy Western control of the Middle East and bring the region's massive oil reserves under the sway of Nasser and his Soviet allies. The revolutionaries in Iraq had also shied away from joining the UAR, a topic discussed at greater length in Chapter 6. Even nature, it seemed, had turned against the union as Syria's largely agrarian economy suffered three successive years of drought.

The coup that brought the UAR to an end was carried out by Sunni officers on September 28, 1961. The Ba'athists and others, not wanting the coup to be interpreted as a minority putsch against a Sunni government, stood by in silent complicity. Michel Aflaq, the head of the Ba'ath Party, officially endorsed the coup after the fact.

The collapse of the UAR was welcomed by most of Syria's politicians who, now free of Nasser, returned Syria to its earlier path of confusion and instability. The Ba'athists, Nasserites, and Communists were in disarray and unable to form a government. The leaders of the People's Party, a party associated with the business community in Aleppo, formed a government but enjoyed little support from either the masses or their political adversaries.

Although the Ba'ath Party had formally dissolved itself in 1958, a small cadre of the Syrian officers posted in Cairo had formed a "military committee" to save what they could of the military wing of the Party (Seale 1988). The former civilian leaders of the Party, most of whom were now held in contempt by the military, were not informed of the Committee's activities. Hafez al-Asad, then a captain, was a junior member of the original plotters. With the breakup of the UAR, it was the Military Committee of the Ba'ath that reconstituted the Ba'ath Party. The old civilian leadership still claimed control of the "National (All-Arab) Command" but had little influence in Syria itself.

The confusion of the secessionist regime was evident in its foreign policy, the centerpiece of which was a call for reunification with Egypt, albeit on grounds more equitable to Syria. Nasser launched a vitriolic propaganda attack on the secessionist government, branding Syria's leaders as traitors to the Arab cause and lackeys of the West. Predictions of an imminent coup were so pervasive that they were openly discussed in the press.

In March 1963, a coalition of Ba'athist and Syrian Nasserites overthrew the secessionist government and immediately called for unity talks with Egypt. The preceding month had seen a parallel coalition of Ba'athists and Nasserites seize power in Iraq, and they too joined the unity negotiations. The unity discussions were short-lived, with Nasser and his allies from Syria and Iraq using the occasion to ridicule the Ba'ath Party and condemn it for the breakup of the UAR (Kerr 1971). Some flavor of the negotiations is provided in the following passage from the minutes of the negotiations, the text of which was published by Nasser as a means of embarrassing the Ba'athist leadership in Syria:

> Please excuse my frankness because this matter is absolutely basic. I have already said that the Ba'ath was responsible for secession and that it wanted a union without Nasser. Also that it aimed at destroying the U.A.R. and that its jealousy was perfectly obvious. How then, with all this legacy of bad faith, can I drag the U.A.R. into a dark future? Naturally, my remarks apply only to a Ba'athist-ruled Syria, not to the Syrian people. Union with the whole of Syria is welcome, but not with the Ba'ath Party (*Arab Political Documents* 1963, 89; United Arab Republic 1963).

Hardly had the dust settled on the unity discussions when the Syrian Nasserites attempted to overthrow their Ba'athist colleagues and reestablish the union with Egypt. The attempted coup was crushed by the military wing of the Ba'ath Party, leaving the Party in total control of the country. All, however, was not well. The Syrian government was nominally headed by Aflaq and the civilian wing of the Ba'ath Party, while real power lay with the military wing of the party and particularly the "military committee" that had rebuilt the Party in the years following the break-up of the UAR (Seale 1988). The more Aflaq attempted to assert his authority, the more tensions between the two wings of the party escalated.

While the Arabs quarreled among themselves, Israel chose the moment to divert water from the Jordan River and to extend its position in the demilitarized zone separating Israel and Syria. Syria responded to the Israeli incursions by shelling Israeli border settlements, a policy born more out of frustration than any hope of victory. Israel retaliated with air strikes, humiliating a Ba'athist regime desperately searching for a formula that would enable it to keep Israel at bay.

With few other options at its disposal, Syria played the Palestinian card. As early as 1964, Palestinian raids on Israel had been restricted by Nasser and other Arab leaders who feared that fedayeen (guerilla) activities would provoke an Arab-Israel conflict that they were ill-prepared to fight (Seale 1988). The Syrians thus formed their own Palestinian organization, Saiqa, following the Six-Day War and allowed it to attack Israeli border positions. While the Palestinians tied up the Israelis, so the plan went, the Ba'athists would have time to build a military organization capable of challenging the Israelis. Israel, however, had little interest in seeing the Arabs regrouped under the benevolent guidance of the Soviet Union, the main foreign backer of the Ba'athist regime. Guerilla attacks were met with air strikes against Syria, further demoralizing a Ba'athist leadership that was rapidly losing its grip on power.

An internal coup within the Ba'ath Party ousted the civilian wing of the Party in 1966, placing the military wing of the Party in control of Syria's affairs. More concerned with fears of a counter-coup than Israeli attack, Syria's military leaders purged the military of some 400 officers suspected of supporting the civilian leadership of the Party (Seale 1988, 113). When this figure is added to the Nasserite officers purged in 1964 and the conservative officers purged in 1963, not much remained of the Syrian officer corps. It was certainly not in a position to fight a major war.

It was in this state of internal turmoil, then, that Syria entered the 1967 War with Israel and faced certain defeat. Syrian forces were again humiliated as Israeli forces penetrated their defenses and seized the Golan Heights.

The dominant themes of Syrian politics over the course of the two decades between independence and defeat in the Six-Day War, then, were turmoil and political instability. Fleeting attempts at democracy gave way to a succession of coups and then to an abortive union with Egypt. The collapse of the union was followed by additional coups and eventual defeat at the hands of Israel in the Six-Day War. It is difficult to sort out the winners and losers in this process, for there was ample misery for all. The crowning humiliation was the loss of the Golan Heights to Israel.

The Era of Reassessment

The Arab defeat in the June War of 1967 was as devastating for Syria as it was for Egypt. The Ba'athist rhetoric of nationalism and Arab unity now rang hollow, and the Syrian military, the force behind the Ba'athist regime, had been stripped of its credibility. This was all the more the case because the long parade of generals to rule Syria since the initial coup in 1949 were of minority background and had never enjoyed a great deal of support among the majority Arab Sunnite population.

Syrian politics during the years immediately following the June War of 1967 were dominated by power struggles within the military wing of the Ba'ath Party, with each leader blaming the others for the catastrophe. The struggle ended in November of 1970 when Hafez al-Asad, then minister of defense, crushed his rivals and seized control of the government. He was named President in February of 1971. This arrogation of power rankled Sunni sensibilities, for until that date, the formal title of president had always been reserved for Sunni Arabs.

Al-Asad's goals upon seizing power reflected the complexity of his background. His most immediate goal was consolidating his power, a challenging task given the tumultuous history of Syrian politics. Al-Asad also believed in Ba'athist ideology, albeit a Ba'athist ideology tempered with pragmatism and a strong dose of Syrian nationalism. If Arab unity were to be achieved, Syria would be at its core. The wounds of the war also had to be healed, the foremost of which was the loss of the Golan Heights. All of the above goals dictated a buildup of the Syrian military. They also dictated urgent measures to revive Syria's moribund economy.

The assets available to al-Asad for achieving his goals were limited, at best. As an Alawite, al-Asad enjoyed little support among Syria's predominantly Sunni population. The Arab defeat in the 1967 War had also discredited the military and had seen nationalist fervor give way to a zealous Islamic Fundamentalism. Al-Asad, moreover, was an austere individual with few charismatic qualities. He was a gray eminence who excelled in manipulating events from behind the scenes.

For better or for worse, al-Asad's main bastion of support was the military. This, however, was not an unmixed blessing. The military was highly politicized, and even the military wing of the Ba'ath Party was divided within itself. The strongest guarantee of al-Asad's rule was not the military as such, but the Alawite core within the military.

Once in office, al-Asad moved rapidly to broaden the base of his regime. As described by R. Hrair Dekmejian, al-Asad's policies

> included a retreat from the radical socialism of earlier regimes by introducing economic liberalization to attract the support of the urban Sunni

entrepreneurial class; the ending of Syria's isolation by close cooperation with other Arab countries, particularly Egypt, Saudi Arabia, Jordan, Libya, and the Sudan; the appointment of Sunni officers and civilians to counter the minority image of the regime; and the restoration of a measure of constitutional life in which the Ba'ath and four smaller parties could play a role (Dekmejian 1991, 198).

As part of al-Asad's stabilization efforts, a new constitution was issued that allowed for an elected People's Assembly (parliament) and direct election of the president by plebiscite (only one candidate) at seven-year intervals. The members of the People's Assembly, in turn, would elect a cabinet to manage the day-to-day affairs of the state. These measures, of course, were not to be confused with democracy. The elections were "guided" and neither the cabinet nor the Assembly enjoyed any real power. It was al-Asad who made the decisions. As if to underscore this point, the Ba'ath Party was simultaneously transformed into an instrument of personal rule, a process to be elaborated upon later in the chapter.

The proposed constitution did little to quell Sunni hostility to the al-Asad regime, and Fundamentalist riots in 1973 challenged al-Asad's rule by invoking a provision of the Syrian constitution stipulating that the president of Syria was required to be a Muslim. This was a tricky proposition, for most Sunnis and many Shi'a viewed the Alawites as heretics and, ipso facto, as non-Muslims. Al-Asad skirted the issue by having the dominant Shi'ite leader in the Levant, the Imam Musa Sadr of Lebanon, issue a formal writ declaring that the Alawites were Muslims.

On the plus side, from al-Asad's perspective, the October War of 1973 had seen Syrian forces acquit themselves well before being forced back by the Israelis. Much as in Egypt, the war was considered a huge success by the Syrian population and added immeasurably to al-Asad's prestige. Syrian success in the initial stages of the October War also propelled al-Asad into the limelight of Middle Eastern politics, a position that would find him to be a strategist of consummate skill.

The end of the war, however, also brought new problems for the al-Asad regime. Egypt was moving rapidly into the American camp and showed ominous signs of signing a unilateral peace accord with Israel. Without the counterweight of the Egyptian army, Syria would be totally vulnerable to Israeli attack and could do little to force a return of the Golan Heights. Increasingly in need of foreign protection, Syria moved closer to the Soviet Union. The alliance was a natural one. Syria received economic and military aid from the Soviet Union; the Soviets, having been expelled from their bases in Egypt prior to the 1973 War, maintained a strong presence in the Mediterranean basin.

The Soviets could protect al-Asad from his external enemies, but they could do little to quell the growing tension between al-Asad and the Islamic Fundamentalists. Al-Asad's 1976 decision to aid the Christian forces in Lebanon's civil war fueled rumors that he planned to merge the Christian areas of Lebanon with the Alawite regions of Syria, thereby further fragmenting historic Syria (Seale 1988, 91; El Khazen 2000). While there was no support for such rumors, the Fundamentalists proclaimed a jihad (holy war) against the al-Asad regime.

Al-Asad's problems continued to mount throughout the remaining years of the decade as Egypt and Israel moved toward peace and attacks on the regime by the Fundamentalists became increasingly violent. Fifty military cadets, most from Alawite backgrounds, were assassinated in Aleppo in June of 1979, giving vent to speculation that the end of the al-Asad era was at hand. Merchant strikes erupted throughout the north of Syria in August of the same year, as did incidents of guerrilla warfare.

Al-Asad responded to the peace agreement between Egypt and Israel by joining Iraq in forging a unified Arab front against Egypt. Ideally, Anwar Sadat would be forced to rescind his agreement with Israel. At the very least, Egypt would be punished for breaking ranks with its sister states and a message would have been sent to Israel that the Arabs remained united. By April of 1979, even Saudi Arabia and Kuwait had severed their ties with Egypt, thereby depriving the latter of much-needed economic assistance.

Al-Asad apparently had little faith in Arab solidarity, for in October of 1980, he publicly announced his support for Iran in the Iran-Iraq War that had erupted a few days earlier. Relations between Iraq and Syria were severed, while Syria's relations with Jordan, Saudi Arabia, and Kuwait, the main supports of the Iraqi attack on Iran, turned cold. Al-Asad signed a treaty of friendship with the Soviet Union during the same month, thereby moving Syria firmly into the Soviet camp (Ramet 1990). It would be the Soviet Union, not the Arab world, that would protect Syria from Israeli attack.

On the domestic front, al-Asad responded to the Fundamentalist attacks with a blend of force and accommodation. Welfare and patronage for supporters of the regime were increased, while direct challenges to al-Asad's rule were crushed with maximum force. Falling in the latter category was al-Asad's response to the continuing buildup of Fundamentalist militias in the largely Sunni city of Hama. By early 1982, the Fundamentalists had largely taken control of Hama and had begun to expand their influence throughout the region. His regime in jeopardy, al-Asad destroyed large sections of the city, killing as many as 20,000 people, Fundamentalists as well as innocent civilians. Most sources place the figure at half that number, but by any reckoning, the loss of life was staggering.

The Hama massacre largely ended the Fundamentalist threat in Syria, with a much-divided Fundamentalist leadership fleeing to either Iraq or Jordan. Their mistake had been to shift from the hit-and-run tactics that had weakened the regime over the preceding decade to a strategy of direct confrontation with the army. Perhaps they believed that the military would revolt and join their revolution, but this was not to be. Al-Asad, always a master tactician, had selected the troops used to crush the uprising with care—they were Alawites. The Hama massacre also introduced a new brutality into Syrian politics, a brutality that would force al-Asad's adversaries to think twice before challenging the regime.

Hardly had the dust settled on the Hama massacre when Israeli troops launched a massive invasion of Lebanon, entering Beirut in September of 1982. Israel, as noted in Chapter 3, now considered Syria to be the most direct threat to its security and viewed Syrian control of its northern neighbor with concern. Israel had also become increasingly apprehensive over the alliance between Syria and the Islamic Republic of Iran, an alliance that found pro-Iranian Hizbullah guerrillas attacking Israel from bases in Lebanon. Syria made limited attempts to resist the Israeli invasion of Lebanon, losing much of its air force in the process.

Once again, it looked as though al-Asad was on the ropes. The Soviets, however, could not accept the loss of their main ally in the Mediterranean basin, and by 1983 the USSR had re-supplied the Syrian military with weapons generally superior to those that had been lost, including advanced air defense systems. The strong show of Soviet support for al-Asad blunted the Israeli-US effort to drive Syria from Lebanon while simultaneously leading to speculation that Lebanon might soon be divided between its two more powerful neighbors. This did not take place, but Israeli forces continued to maintain a large security zone in southern Lebanon.

While al-Asad had displayed an uncanny ability to surmount crisis after crisis, the strain on his health had become manifest. In late 1983, he became seriously ill, with rumors circulating that he had suffered a heart attack. Al-Asad's illness unleashed a power struggle among his major lieutenants, with each moving troops into Damascus in a bid to seize power. Dominant among these was al-Asad's younger brother Rifat, the commander of the infamous "Defense Companies" that had become the main prop of the regime. The Defense Companies were an army within an army, boasting more than 55,000 troops and their "own armour, artillery, air defense, and a fleet of troop-carrying helicopters" (Seale 1988). The showdown between al-Asad and his brother, as described by Patrick Seale in the following passage, is particularly poignant as it illustrates the role of traditional family relationships in Syrian politics:

> Repeated attempts were made to defuse the crisis through negotiations. Rifat sent his brother Jamil to intercede with Asad but the president's unforgiving answer was 'I am your elder brother to whom you owe obedience. Don't forget that I am the one who made you all.'...
>
> With Damascus divided between armed camps seemingly on the brink of war, Asad put on full military uniform and accompanied only by his eldest son Basil, drove without guards or escort through the empty streets to his brother's elaborately defended positions in and around the residential district of Mezze....
>
> At Rifat's house in Mezze the brothers came at last face to face. 'You want to overthrow the regime?' Asad asked. 'Here I am. I *am* the regime.' For an hour they stormed at each other but, in his role of elder brother and with his mother in the house, Asad could not fail to win the contest (Seale 1988, 432–433).

While al-Asad recovered from what proved to be severe exhaustion and purged those involved in the attempted putsch, the event demonstrated just how little institutional development had occurred in Syria during 17 years of al-Asad rule (Dekmejian 1991, 206). Power resided with al-Asad, and no realistic provisions had been made for a smooth transition of authority upon his passing. The power struggle, it is interesting to note, took place wholly within the ruling elite. If any other opposition to the regime existed, it remained on the sidelines.

Al-Asad addressed future questions of succession by devising an awkward three-way vice presidency that added more confusion to the issue that it was designed to resolve. Rifat was one of those named to the newly created vice presidencies, but was shortly sent into exile. Al-Asad had little interest in giving power to an heir apparent.

Syria's domestic politics stabilized with al-Asad's return to power, buoyed in part by the discovery of high-quality, if limited, oil deposits. While not comparable to those of Saudi Arabia and the Gulf states, development of the oil fields pumped much-needed money into the Syrian economy and eased al-Asad's financial dependence on his oil-rich neighbors. Al-Asad also took this opportunity to embark upon a gradual liberalization of the Syrian economy. Much as in Egypt, it was hoped that a revitalized capitalist sector would stimulate economic growth (Lawson 1996).

Tensions within Lebanon also continued to preoccupy the Syrian leader but moved toward resolution in 1989 when a Saudi-brokered peace recognized the existence of a special relationship between Syria and Lebanon. The Civil War remained in full force, but Syrian dominance in Lebanon was established. Lebanon would stabilize and revive, but the Lebanese-Israeli border remained a war zone in which Hizbullah guerrillas, supported by Iran and Syria, launched a devastating war of attrition against Israeli occupation forces. Israel would lose this war of proxy with Syria, withdrawing its forces from southern Lebanon in the summer of 2000. Syrian influence remains strong, with little happening to Lebanon that is not attributed to Syria in one way or another.

The more things seemed to improve, however, the more they fell apart. Iraq had gained the upper hand in the Iran-Iraq War and vowed retribution for al-Asad's support of Iran. Far more worrisome to al-Asad was the rise of Mikhail Gorbachev in the Soviet Union, an event that would see Syria's protector embark on a path of reconciliation with the United States and Israel. The army and the Ba'ath Party had sustained the regime internally, but it was the support of the Soviet Union that had enabled al-Asad to keep Israel at bay.

Once again it would be an external event, the Iraqi invasion of Kuwait in 1990, that would enable al-Asad to rebound from almost certain disaster. US efforts to forge an alliance against the Iraqi invasion hinged upon participation by a broad coalition of Arab countries. Barring this support, a largely US attack on Iraq would be perceived as American aggression against an Arab and Islamic country. Both nationalistic and religious emotions would be inflamed, hindering American military operations in the region and placing client governments at risk, not the least of which were Egypt and Saudi Arabia. Al-Asad's Syria, the historical center of Arab nationalism and resistance to the West, rushed to the aid of the United States, condemning Saddam Hussein as a traitor to Arab nationalism and joining the United Nations coalition against Iraq. A rogue state accused of fostering international terrorism thus became an ally of the United States. Tensions between the two countries remained, but al-Asad had gained a new lease on power by demonstrating his ability to further US policy in the region.

Syrian participation in the UN force also brought an upsurge in financial aid from Saudi Arabia and Kuwait and made Syria the partner of Egypt in protecting the interests of the oil kingdoms, neither of which could protect themselves. Syria's ties with Iran still rankled, but it seems probable that the Saudis were secretly reassured of Syrian support in case of an attack by Iran. Problems, of course, remained. The Saudis soon reconsidered their dependence on Syria and Egypt, preferring instead to strengthen their ties with the United States. Al-Asad's relations with Turkey, Israel, Jordan, Iraq, and the Palestinians remained tense.

Having parried the external threat to his regime, al-Asad also moved decisively to strengthen his position domestically. The core of his domestic program was the promulgation of Investment Law No. 10 of 1991. According to the Investment Law and related legislation, private-sector firms capable of easing Syria's unemployment crisis by creating new jobs were exempted from taxation for five years. They were also allowed to import equipment duty-free and to export their profits. Similar benefits were extended to private-sector firms that either increased exports or reduced imports (Lawson 1996, 13).

The new investment law opened the door to private-sector investment in Syria and resulted in the rapid expansion of private-sector enterprises. GDP increased by more than 7 percent over the next two years, creating a sense of optimism for the future (Melhem 1997, 3). Efforts were also made to clamp down on corruption, but most appear to have been largely symbolic. A regime that ruled by a combination of repression and corruption could hardly be expected to eliminate one of the main pillars of its authority. As Melhem noted, "Even within the still-limited private sector, 'the game is often fixed, with licenses doled out as favors to friends of the regime'" (Melhem 1997, 3).

Economic reforms were paralleled by continuing efforts to groom Basil al-Asad, Hafez al-Asad's eldest son, for succession to the presidency. Basil, a career military officer renowned for his equestrian skills, was nicknamed the "the golden knight" and reportedly enjoyed close ties with Syria's intelligence community (*The Middle East*, December 1992, no. 217: 18–20, www).

Rifat al-Asad, the president's brother, was also allowed to return to Syria in 1992, setting the stage for a power struggle between the two heirs apparent should al-Asad's reputed ill health continue to deteriorate. Rifat had retained his title of vice president (one of three), but his bases of support, including the defense companies, had long since been disbanded (*The Middle East*, March 1994, no. 232: 12).

The same era would see al-Asad begin to rein in the "regime barons," such as Ali Duba, al-Asad's security chief. Duba was "cooled out," receiving a symbolic promotion but losing much of his power (*Middle East Economic Digest*, February 19, 1993, 37(7): 30). The same year saw Basil lauded in the Syrian press for smashing smuggling operations linked to Rifat and Ali Duba, and in 1994 he began to take charge of his father's personal security (*The Middle East*, March 1994, no. 232: 12). Al-Asad, it seemed, had named his successor.

By 1994, clouds again appeared on the horizon. January of that year saw Basil al-Asad killed in an automobile accident, thereby rekindling speculation about al-Asad's likely successor. Maneuvering increased apace. Syria's large public-sector firms were also resisting privatization, and the more radical members of the Ba'ath Party decried al-Asad's shift to "guided capitalism" as a violation of the Party's socialist principles. Both feared that further cutbacks in the public sector would result in a loss of jobs and increased unemployment. Such fears were not unfounded, for Syria's government enterprises had been deliberately overstaffed in order to provide employment to as many people as possible. Welfare, not efficiency, had been their credo.

Al-Asad resolved the issue by continuing to relax restrictions on the private sector while simultaneously using the country's scarce resources to prop up a moribund public sector. Both masters had to be served: economic growth and political patronage. The compromise made no sense to Western economists who viewed capitalism as the solution to all of the world's ills, but it made a great deal of sense within the fragile mosaic of Syrian politics (Lawson 1996).

Al-Asad's effort to strike a political balance between capitalism and socialism was reflected in the results of the 1994 elections, with the ruling National Patriotic Front (an official coalition of socialist parties clustering around the Ba'ath) winning 66 percent of the 250 seats in the Assembly and independents, most drawn from Syria's business and professional communities, capturing the remainder. The results of the 1994 elections served as a clear indicator of al-Asad's shift to the right. Indeed, the Assembly had been increased from 190 to 250 members for the express purpose of providing added representation of the business and professional communities (Hamadi 1998, 20–21).

Having made a change of course on the economic level, al-Asad now found himself under intense pressure to do the same at the foreign policy level. The Oslo Accords of 1993 had resulted in a tenuous peace between Israel and the Palestinians, and by 1994 the US was increasing its pressure on al-Asad to follow suit. In typical al-Asad fashion, he bent to US pressure by joining the peace process while simultaneously supporting terrorist groups opposed to the peace process, not the least of which were Hizbullah and the Palestinian Hamas. If Israel wanted peace, it would have to pay al-Asad's price. In the meantime, al-Asad continued to maintain a military establishment roughly equivalent to that of Israel in terms of tanks, armored personnel carriers, aircraft, artillery, and warships. This was a largely defensive posture, however, for the technical capacity of the Israeli military was far superior to that of Syria and there could be no thought of a Syrian attack on Israel unsupported by Egypt. Nevertheless, the Syrian military possessed more than enough force to inflict unacceptable losses on an invading Israeli army. The military situation between the two countries thus remained a standoff.

Negotiations between Syria and the Labor government in Israel showed clear signs of progress in 1995 but were suspended in 1996 over a variety of issues including the extent of Israel's withdrawal from the Golan Heights and security measures such as the monitoring of Syrian troop movements. The two sides also quibbled over water sharing and the timing of the peace process. The critical point to be noted, however, was that all of the points under discussion were subject to resolution by negotiation assuming a degree of flexibility by both parties. Underlying these negotiations was the assumption that a peace treaty between Syria and Israel would also lead to a comprehensive peace between Israel and Lebanon. Syria would maintain its preeminent position in Lebanon and would use that position to bring an end to Hizbullah attacks on Israel. Hopes for flexibility, however, disappeared with the victory of Netanyahu in the 1996 Israeli elections.

A new round of legislative elections took place in 1998, with the balance of seats in the Assembly again being allocated in advance. The Ba'ath Party was allocated 135 seats, thereby assuring it of an absolute majority. An additional 32 seats were divided among the Nasserites, Communists, and the other five "progressive" parties amalgamated in the National Patriotic Front. The remaining seats were again captured by the pro-business independents, non-socialist parties being disallowed by the regime. Adding to the complexity of the electoral process was the constitutional provision that 51 percent of the seats in the Assembly be reserved for peasants and workers, a requirement that found wealthy businessmen posing as peasants or workers. The regime was unperturbed by such shenanigans, for as the Minister of Interior reportedly quipped, "Everyone who works in this country is a worker" (Hamadi 1998, 20–21).

US-style campaigning was also becoming evident, with candidates shaking hands with potential voters and distributing candy and posters. Criticism of the government was guarded, but it was not difficult to read between the lines. To paraphrase the comments of an independent candidate linked to the Damascus Chamber of Commerce, "The Government has progressed slowly and with great care and wisdom in pursuing economic liberalization in order to assure that the storm of economic change that produced inflation, fraud and chaos in other countries does not afflict Syria. Happily, we have avoided these problems and are now proceeding with deliberate wisdom toward this goal. We would, however, like to see faster and broader steps in this direction" (*Al-Hawadeth* 1998).

In 1998, the simmering feud between al-Asad and his brother Rifat led to the latter's "resignation" from his position as one of Syria's three vice presidents. According to Patrick Seale, al-Asad's biographer, the resignation was part of a deal between the two brothers that would see Rifat concentrate on business while his older brother took care of politics. Rifat, it should be noted, had developed a broad range of commercial enterprises, including the London-based Arab News Network, an Arabic-language satellite network that blanketed the Middle East. Rifat's other commercial activities, according to his detractors, were less visible.

Al-Asad was elected to a fifth uncontested term in office in 1999, but nature was now poised to achieve what his adversaries could not. Advanced in years and in ill health, al-Asad positioned his second son, Bashar, to succeed him as president of Syria. The grooming of Bashar for the presidency followed a well-choreographed script. Bashar's promotion to the rank of major in the Republican Guards was followed in short order by his promotion to the rank of colonel. He was also given the "Lebanese File" and followed in the footsteps of his older brother by leading the charge against corruption and smuggling (*Al-Waton Al-Arabi*, June 10, 1999). Bashar's promotion to colonel, in turn, was followed by key diplomatic assignments, including a long tête-à-tête with President Chirac of France. Rumors also circulated that Bashar would soon be elevated to the position of vice president, a position recently "vacated" by his uncle Rifat (*Al-Waton Al-Arabi*, June 10, 1999). Bashar's announcement that he had advised his father on forthcoming changes in the cabinet lent credibility to these rumors, as did widely publicized nods of approval from both King Fahd of Saudi Arabia and the recently crowned King Abdullah of Jordan.

All, however, was not well. The summer of 1999 would bring rumors of an attempted coup organized by the Sunni regime barons who had recently been purged by al-Asad as one of several steps designed to assure Bashar's succession to the presidency. Adding to the intrigue were rumors that al-Asad had been alerted to the coup attempt by the US, thereby assuring that al-Asad would remain in office during the peace negotiations. Al-Asad was a tough negotiator, but he was willing to negotiate (Mauran and Eddin 1999, 4–7).

The failed Sunni-sponsored coup was followed within weeks by an assault on Rifat's compound by Syrian security forces. As the events were reported in *Al-Waton Al-Arabi*, a leading Arabic-language news journal, Rifat's compound in Latakia had been under surveillance since January of 1999, albeit without confrontation. October 17th of that year, however, would see Rifat's compound, including his private port, surrounded by army tanks and an ultimatum for his surrender issued by the commander. When Rifat ignored the summons, the tanks opened fire, with Rifat's son and formal owner of the Arab News Network reporting extensive loss of life. The Syrian press denied these allegations, claiming that the sole purpose of the attack had been to close Rifat's illegal port. The brothers' war continued, as did the battle for succession.

In the meantime, peace negotiations with Israel resumed following the 1999 election of Ehud Barak. The negotiations proved to be a test of wills between an Israeli prime minister intent on establishing secure borders with Syria and a Syrian president committed to the return of the Golan Heights, which had been conquered by Israel in the June War of 1967. The negotiations began well but by the spring of 2000 had bogged down on the issue of a small strip of the Golan bordering on Lake Tiberius, the source of some 40 percent of Israel's water supply. Barak wanted full control of the water, while al-Asad demanded a complete return of the Golan Heights, as specified in UN Resolution 242.

Issues of succession and the return of the Golan Heights were linked. Al-Asad seemed intent on paving the way for Bashar's succession to the presidency by securing an honorable peace with Israel, a condition that required full control of the Golan Heights. With peace secure, Bashar would be free to build a base of popular support by attacking Syria's rampant corruption and leading Syria's transition to a market economy. Al-Asad's position as the "liberator" would also be secure, and he could pass from the scene with honor (*Al-Mushahid*, December 18, 1999: 10–11).

The spring of 2000 would witness a major reshuffle of the Government (prime minister and cabinet) as al-Asad continued to shift supporters of Bashar into key positions and otherwise breathe new life into a stagnant political apparatus whose prime virtue had been its loyalty to al-Asad. Of the 36 cabinet positions, 23 went to young technocrats, with only 13 positions remaining in the hands of the old guard. Those 13 positions, however, were the most powerful in the Government and included the Ministries of Defense, Interior (police), Foreign Affairs, Economy, and Finance (*Al-Hawadeth*, March 24, 2000: 30). New blood was entering the political system, but it was entering slowly.

At that time, however, Hafez al-Asad had not formally announced that Bashar would be his successor, a step that would require an amendment of the Constitution to reduce the minimum age of candidates for the presidency from 35 to 34, Bashar being 34 at the time. Plans were also made to have Bashar named a vice president of the Ba'ath Party and, presumably, to enhance his military credentials.

Steps to achieve these goals were accelerated in the late spring of 2000 as al-Asad was reported to have suffered a major stroke, but had yet to be put in place when al-Asad died of a heart attack on June 10, 2000.

Speculation about Syria's fate following the death of Hafez al-Asad ranged from imminent threats of civil war fueled by sectarian conflict and power struggles among the regime barons to a peaceful transfer of power dictated by the self-interest of the same barons, all of whom would suffer from a collapse of the regime. Bashar al-Asad would be a figurehead president while the barons ruled from behind the scenes. Between those two extremes were predictions of a lull before the storm as the major players jockeyed for position as well as suggestions that Bashar would use the transition period to continue the process of building his own power base, a process initiated under the reign of his father. The longer the son remained in power, according to this scenario, the greater would be his chances for survival.

The only one of the four hypotheses to be rejected during the initial year of Bashar's rule was the prediction that Syria would dissolve into political chaos, if not open civil war. There was no civil war, and observers of all persuasions were dazzled by the smoothness of the transition process. Indeed, the Syrian political process hardly skipped a beat during the period between Hafez al-Asad's death on June 10 and Bashar al-Asad's assumption of the reins of power on July 17. With clockwork precision, the People's Assembly amended the Syrian constitution to allow Bashar to become President of the Republic at age 34, while the Ba'ath Party duly elected him as its president, the latter being a precondition of the former. This election was preceded by Bashar's promotion to the rank of Lieutenant General and his appointment as the commander-in-chief of the armed forces.[6] The transition process was crowned by a plebiscite in which the Syrian population acclaimed Bashar as their president.

The smoothness of the transition process suggested a high level of agreement among the regime barons and other key actors less visible to the outside world, but left open the question of who ruled Syria. At least for the moment, the lieutenants of Hafez al-Asad had kept the regime intact by orchestrating Bashar's coronation as president. The period of sorting out, including Bashar's efforts to consolidate his power, had begun.

The first step in this sorting-out process was image building as Bashar's managers groomed him for the presidency. Critical to this effort was the need to convince the Syrian public that Bashar had the courage and resolve to stay the course, an issue of some doubt given his young age and lack of political experience. The only pictures of the new president that were released by the regime, accordingly, were

---

[6]These appointments were made by the interim president.

those of a stern and unsmiling Bashar, a pose that made him look older than his 34 years (*Al-Mushahid*, July 23, 2000, 18–19). Show trials of some of Syria's most corrupt officials strengthened his persona of power, as did widespread purges of the Ba'athist apparatus. Not only did Bashar demonstrate the power and resolve to "renew" the Party leadership throughout the country, or so it seemed, but the new generation of party leaders were, presumably, his people. The purges were also intensely popular, with one of Syria's more outspoken skeptics writing: "The age of unthinking dinosaurs, who have been roaming the country for 40 years, is at an end" (Moubayed 2001, 6). Also designed to convey an image of power and resolve was Bashar's firm support for the al-Aqsa intifada and his uncompromising demands for a just peace with Israel that included the complete return of the Golan Heights. In more heated moments, Bashar condemned Israel for perpetrating a "new Nazism" (*Ha'aretz*, Nov. 14, 2000, www). Relations with Iraq were also normalized in a move that demonstrated Bashar's independence from the United States, albeit an independence that was muted by Syria's strong ties with Saudi Arabia and Egypt, the pillars of US hegemony in the Arab World.

Balancing Bashar's effort to portray a persona of strength and decisiveness was a dramatic effort to build a strong base of popular support by easing the severity of his father's rule. Without criticizing his father directly, Bashar promised a new era of economic and political modernization that would bring Syria into the twenty-first century. In the economic realm, privatization and other measures designed to stimulate foreign investment in Syria were accelerated, albeit in a gradual and prudent manner that reassured workers in the public sector that their jobs would be secure. Indeed, the latter received a 25-percent salary increase, in a thinly veiled move to reaffirm Bashar's ties with Syria's large public-sector work force.

Moves in the political arena were particularly dramatic, with some 600 political prisoners being released from jail and human rights groups, most formed by old leftists of the 1960s or released prisoners, emerging in Syria's major cities (Hamedi 2001). Leftist parties associated with the National Patriotic Front also received permission to publish party newspapers and to expand their political activities on the condition that they remained free of foreign connections and kept their activities visible to the government. Syria would move in the direction of democracy, Bashar proclaimed, but not necessarily the democracy of the West. "It is necessary that we have our own special democracy that will enable us to build a strong foundation capable of withstanding shocks, whatever their difficulty and intensity. In this regard it is necessary to broaden the experiment of the National Patriotic Front and strengthen it (*Al-Hawadeth*, Aug. 21, 2000, 12; translation by M. Palmer).

Efforts were also made to humanize the presidency, with Bashar frequently praying alone in Damascus' mosques and allowing the press to discuss his private life, including his marriage to the British-educated daughter of a prominent Sunni businessman. He was also portrayed as the champion of new information technologies and education reform, issues of intense popularity among Syria's youth. All in all, then, Bashar's strategy was one of controlled economic and political liberalization blended with political stability. Things would change, but they would change gradually within the confines of Syria's social and political traditions (Hasba'ni 2000).

The strategy was well conceived and well executed, leaving observers with the eerie feeling that things had gone too smoothly—that problems lurked unseen behind a surreal façade. Indeed, no one was quite sure who was making decisions or what the balance of power was within the ruling circle (*Al-Waton Al-Arabi*, Dec. 8, 2000, 28–30). These concerns were reflected in an ambivalent Syrian response to increasingly strident calls for Syria's withdrawal from Lebanon by Lebanon's Maronite Bishop, an act that would have been most unlikely under the reign of Hafez al-Asad. Syria redeployed its troops to more remote areas, but not without threats to return to Beirut and other key areas if circumstances dictated, a statement that reflected some ambiguity within decision-making circles. It also suggested that Lebanese opponents to Syria's involvement sensed weakness in the new regime, although the Maronite initiative may have merely been a response to the new openness in Syria's relationship with its quasi-colony. Yet a third explanation of Syria's behavior was US encouragement to deploy its troops away from Lebanese areas controlled by Hizbullah, thereby avoiding a direct confrontation between Syria and Israel as a result of possible Israeli bombardment of Hizbullah strongholds (*Al-Waton Al-Arabi*, Nov. 10, 2000, 18–20).

Similar ambiguity surrounded the tribal conflict that erupted along the Syrian-Jordan border toward the end of 2000, which pitted armed Druze against armed Sunni bedouins, many of whom had infiltrated from Jordan. Was the Druze action a test of the regime prompted by signs of weakness in the government, as suggested by articles in the Arabic press, or merely a continuing pageant of tribal conflict over smuggling rights, as suggested by many of the author's colleagues at American University of Beirut? (*Al-Waton Al-Arabi*, Nov. 10, 2000, 18–20). Whatever the case, there was apparently little consensus on how to deal with the crisis, with the minister of defense urging the mobilization of three brigades to crush the Druze while Bashar adopted a negotiated approach that would "avoid another Hama"—a reference to the slaughter of the Muslim Brotherhood in Hama some 16 years earlier (*Al-Waton Al-Arabi,* Nov. 10, 2000, 18–20). Ultimately, the army intervened, but it did so with caution and with the loss of only three or four lives.

Doubts over the future, however, far exceeded concerns over an uncertain struggle for power within the Bashar regime, if such there were. Far more fundamental were questions about the ability of the new regime to transform the archaic political and economic systems inherited from Hafez al-Asad into viable instruments of rule. Far more disconcerting were doubts about Bashar's ability to gain acceptance among Syria's predominantly Sunnite population and to hold off challenges within the Alawite community, including those posed by his Uncle Rifat, who was precluded from attending Hafez al-Asad's funeral as a security threat. These questions will take years to sort out, and in the remainder of this chapter we will address the myriad problems that Bashar will face in attempting to replace the only leader that a majority of the Syrian population has ever known.

Problems also loomed on the foreign policy front with Israel bombing Syrian military positions in Lebanon in response to Hizbullah attacks on Israeli border positions. Syria, Sharon had served notice, would be held responsible for attacks on Israel emanating from its Lebanese dependency. Bashar al-Asad responded with bluster, but nothing more. Controlling Hizbullah would not be an easy task. Removing Hizbullah from the fray would also eliminate the major weapon at Syria's disposal in confronting its Israeli enemy.

SYRIAN POLITICS TODAY AND BEYOND

Hafez al-Asad's rule brought Syria three decades of unprecedented stability, but the ride was not smooth. To the contrary, the regime lurched from crisis to crisis, each accompanied by predictions of imminent doom. Some crises were regional in character, including a smoldering state of no-war/no-peace with Israel and mounting regional opposition to Syria's support of Iran. Others were domestic in nature, including the Islamic uprising of the early 1980s and the near coup precipitated by al-Asad's illness. The collapse of the Soviet Union in 1990 and the advent of the new world order again brought predictions of al-Asad's imminent collapse. How could it be otherwise? The main international protector of the regime had collapsed. Syria was surrounded by allies of the United States, with the exception of Iraq, which was also hostile to al-Asad's regime. Syrian support of Iran had curtailed financial aid from the Gulf states. Oil prices were declining, Syria's socialist economy was in a shambles, Syrian military forces seemed hopelessly bogged down in Lebanon, and domestic opposition to al-Asad's regime was building. A decade later, however, al-Asad's opponents were at bay, the Syrian economy was showing faint signs of life, and Lebanon was largely under Syrian control (Khashan and Haddad 2000). Syria, moreover, had become a "friend" of the United States and was now viewed as vital to the security of the oil monarchies.

In the remainder of this chapter, we will examine the factors that explain the remarkable longevity of Hafez al-Asad as well as the manner in which thirty years of al-Asad's rule reshaped Syria's political landscape. In so doing, we will review the major components of the Syrian political system as well as the problems that will confront Bashar al-Asad in his efforts to consolidate his power and to lead Syria into the twenty-first century.

Elites and Power in Syria: Personality and Politics

Hafez al-Asad *was* the elite in Syria. It was al-Asad who made all of the key decisions, and it was he who appointed candidates to the key positions in the security services, military, government, and the Ba'ath Party (Batatu 1999; Abdou 1999). Thus, it is difficult to explain the pattern of Syrian politics over the course of al-Asad's rule without reference to his personality.

In this regard, most observers credited al-Asad with a personality that combined intelligence and cunning with suspicion and patience. He also possessed a deep understanding of Syrian society and its intricacies. These traits enabled him to survive in a political environment that was kaleidoscopic at best. Most observers also found al-Asad to be unbending on issues of vital import, but pragmatic in his means for achieving those ends. Of these issues, two were of preeminent importance: personal survival and Syrian nationalism. Al-Asad's will to survive was written in blood and requires little elaboration. This said, the scholars and journalists who study Syria invariably paid tribute to al-Asad's commitment to Syrian nationalism. It was unthinkable, for example, that al-Asad would have accepted peace in the Middle East without the return of the Golan Heights. There could also be little doubt that he wanted Lebanon to return to the Syrian fold (Abdou 1999).

Issues unrelated to grand strategy or his personal survival were negotiable, and al-Asad displayed remarkable flexibility in adjusting to the winds of change. The same principle applied to his treatment of his subordinates. The "regime barons" ran their fiefdoms as they saw fit, fearing little rebuke from al-Asad as long as their loyalty to the regime remained above reproach (Abdou 1999). Al-Asad complained of the corruption and excesses of his subordinates, but corrective action was largely symbolic.

The dilemma that faced al-Asad throughout his 30-year reign was the essential incompatibility of his two goals. In his drive for survival, al-Asad placed loyalty to himself over all other considerations, including the sovereignty of law or the development of independent political institutions. His inherent suspicion of others (not an unreasonable trait given the nature of Syrian politics) also resulted in a dependence on relatives and members of the Alawite sect, a practice often referred to as patrimonialism. This does not mean that al-Asad trusted his relatives and co-religionists, merely that he believed that they were more likely to support him than other people were. Competence was important, but not as important as loyalty. While Alawite members of the regime prospered, there is little evidence to suggest that the Alawite community as a whole benefited disproportionately from al-Asad's rule (Batatu 1999).

As a result of al-Asad's emphasis on loyalty above all else, the development of Syria's political institutions was stunted. A massive army existed to resist Israel, yet the effectiveness of that army was lessened by the need to assure that it did not revolt. While the Israelis do not worry about the potential of a military coup, al-Asad did. Much the same applies to the Ba'ath Party, the bureaucracy, and the National Assembly. Al-Asad wanted political institutions capable of carrying out his nationalistic ambitions, but he was reluctant to give them the power to do so. Not surprisingly, the most effective institutions in Syria were the security services.

The tension between maintaining strong institutions and ensuring that those institutions would not threaten the president's position resulted in a political system that was a blend of modern organizational structures and the traditional patrimonial networks of the Middle East (Hinnebusch 1990). The organizational structure of Syrian political institutions is modern, but the process of Syrian politics is personalized and patrimonial. Herein lie the problems. By totally dominating the power structure, al-Asad reduced his subordinates to little more than ciphers. As described by a former head of the Lebanese intelligence:

> I agree wholeheartedly with those who say that one must not deliver authority to a single individual regardless of his sagacity and shrewdness...because delivery of total authority to a single individual reduces what remains of the power [structure] to an advisory apparatus devoid of independent views and virtually devoid of initiative. As a result of

this situation, administrative, economic, fiscal, security, military and even judicial authority lose their independence and become concentrated in [the hands of] the sole leader.... The remainder of the political apparatus is compelled to flattery and immortalization [of the leader] that borders on deification, and the capacity to take effective initiatives is removed from its hands (Abdou 1999, 28–29; translated by M. Palmer).

Hafez al-Asad, however, has now passed from the scene, and it is his son Bashar who must cope with a legacy of personal rule. The pre-eminent question in this regard concerns Bashar's personality. Does he possess the strength of character to dominate a political system forged by the iron will of his father? Bashar, 34 at the time of his father's passing, had been trained as an ophthalmologist and speaks both French and English fluently. He was called back from London to Syria upon the death of his brother in 1994 and, on the urging of his father, entered the Syrian military college. He subsequently passed through the ranks, becoming the commander of a tank battalion in 1994, a lieutenant colonel in 1997, a colonel in 1999, and commander-in-chief of the armed forces within days of his father's death in 2000 (*Daily Star*, June 11, 2000, 3). Missing from his credentials are the trials by fire that enabled his father to hone his political skills. Observers in Damascus quip that Bashar is far too decent to run Syria.

The Political Institutions of Syria: Form Without Power

On paper, the organizational chart of the Syrian political system is relatively straightforward. Hafez al-Asad, as president of the republic, ruled through six basic institutions: the Presidential Security Forces, the military, the Ba'ath Party, the cabinet, the parliament, and the bureaucracy. It is the leaders of these institutions, and particularly the leaders of the security services, the military, and the Ba'ath Party, who occupy the second rung in Syria's elite hierarchy. They are powerful individuals who had much to say about the execution of al-Asad's policies. Both Bashar al-Asad and his uncle Rifat al-Asad belonged to this category prior to Hafez al-Asad's death, as did the "regime barons."

The Security Forces and the Military   The Presidential Security Forces consist of at least four separate intelligence organizations, including Political Security, General Intelligence, Military Intelligence, and Air Force Intelligence (Batatu 1999). These, in turn, are followed in order of importance by the Republican Guard, an elite military force some 10,000 strong. The Republican Guard was molded by al-Asad's brother Rifat until his ouster in 1984, and was subsequently com-

SYRIA

Attendance 6/6

History (on 2/21)

manded by Hafez al-Asad's first son, Basil, until his death in 1994, after which it was placed in the hands of Basil Adnan Makhluf, a cousin-in-law from the Alawite community. The Republican Guard is supported by the Special Forces and other elite units in the military, albeit with a balanced command structure that precludes any one unit from becoming dominant (Perthes 1997). These military units, in turn, are kept in check by Party militias and intelligence organizations (Perthes 1997). Everyone is watching everyone else.

Command of the Presidential Security Forces rests firmly in the hands of the Alawites, most of whom have been drawn from al-Asad's clan. It is they, often referred to as "regime barons," who constituted the inner core of the al-Asad regime. Of the 31 highest-ranking officers in Syria at the turn of the century, 19 were Alawites. Of the 19, 12 were related to Al-Asad by either blood or marriage (Batatu 1999). Added to the list were two Sunni officers, Mustafa Talass and Farouk Shara'a, who served as the minister of defense and minister of foreign affairs, respectively. Both possess a record of loyalty to al-Asad that dates back to the origins of the Ba'ath Party. The presence of Sunni officers in the inner circle of the elite structure softened the image of Alawite dominance and strengthened alliances with the Sunni community.

Needless to say, the members of the security forces are well cared for. As described by Perthes:

> There is no doubt that the security apparatus accounts for much petty and grand corruption and other illegal business in the country. Most of the military and security bosses have become patrons of and partners in private business, or have taken commissions on contracts between the state and international suppliers. Smuggling has, to a large extent, been in the hands of the military, and has been enormously facilitated by the presence of the Syrian army in Lebanon....
>
> Even without such illicit gains, the security apparatus offers considerable privilege to its personnel. Officers and soldiers are provided with subsidized imported goods through the military's own consumer cooperative; officers can acquire cheaply comparatively high-standard family houses in what are called the Asad's suburbs, suburban settlements for military personnel. Higher-ranking officers all have their private limousines, and often more than one; lower-ranking and non-commissioned officers frequently use military vehicles for private purposes. Access to a car is a special privilege in a country where the import of automobiles has been severely restricted for more than a decade, and where even higher civil servants can hardly afford a second-hand car. Military and security personnel do not pay income tax; their pay is considerably higher than civil-service salaries and officers may make several times what a civilian state-employee earns (Perthes 1997, 149–150).

Next in the hierarchy of power comes the Syrian military itself, a formidable force which, with the inclusion of the various security services, has some 400,000 members (Perthes 1997). This figure, according to Perthes, constitutes 15 percent of the Syrian workforce and approximately 40 percent of all government employees (Perthes 1997, 147). Military training is obligatory in secondary schools and universities, and the Ba'ath Party also maintains several militias. Alawites dominate the command structure, having headed seven of Syria's nine regular army divisions during the 1990s (Batatu 1999). Sunnis, as Drysdale and Hinnebusch note, are also well represented in the officer corps, albeit in less sensitive positions:

> Nevertheless, the charge that the Syrian military is an exclusive preserve of the Alawis is false and simplistic. The regime recruited many Sunni officers with peasant or lower-class origins, and from small towns and villages, who support the Ba'ath's goals. Some of these have risen to senior positions within the armed forces, although they are mainly assigned to professional functions in noncombatant units. In addition to the defense minister and chief of staff, some 60 percent of General Staff Command officers are Sunni, as are some 45 percent of senior officers. Sunnis reportedly account for over half of the wing commanders and senior officers in the air force and command several armored or infantry brigades and divisions. Christian, and especially Circassian, officers are also disproportionately represented (Drysdale and Hinnebusch 1991, 29).

The Ba'ath Party   The Ba'ath Party probably ranks third on the power hierarchy although, as we shall see shortly, this is a matter of some debate. The Ba'ath Party (Arab Renaissance Party) as noted in the earlier discussion, emerged during the World War II era as an amalgam of diverse Marxist and Arab nationalist interests. In terms of its organizational framework, the Ba'ath Party consists of two separate organizations: the Regional (Syrian) Command and the National (Arab) Command. The National Command symbolically upholds the Ba'ath Party's status as an "all-Arab" party but enjoys little real power. By and large, it is staffed by exiles from the Ba'athist regime in Iraq.

The Regional (Syrian) Command, by contrast, was headed by Hafez al-Asad and contained senior members of the cabinet and the military, all of whom had been approved in advance by Hafez al-Asad. It is within this group that the power lies in Syria. The Regional Command crowns a broader party apparatus consisting of a Central Committee which brings together the heads of the 19 party branches that manage local affairs in Syria as well as key figures in the military wing of the party.

As the make-up of the Regional Command suggests, its members are powerful individuals who fall on the second rung of Syria's elite hierarchy. Indeed, there is a high degree of overlap between the president's inner circle and the Regional Command (politburo) of the Ba'ath Party. Lesser Ba'athist officials also control a great deal of patronage and would clearly fall on the third rung of the elite hierarchy. Most, as van Dam suggests, are also Alawites:

> The sectarian and regional backgrounds of the members of the Syrian Regional Command and the Central Committee of the Ba'ath Party installed during the Eighth Regional Congress, held in Damascus in January 1985—and still in power more than ten years later, although elections were supposed to have been held every five years—remained more or less the same as before, implying a continued extremely strong representation of Alawi officers, and of personalities from the Latakia region in particular. The new Central Committee was personally appointed by President Hafez al-Asad, and expanded from 75 to 90 members, half of whom (mostly civilians) had not been members of the previous Central Committee. As was to be expected, most of the military members retained their seats (van Dam 1996, 123).

The Ba'ath Party performed a variety of functions essential to the success of Hafez al-Asad's rule. Ba'athist ideology, for example, provided the foundation of the regime's claim to legitimacy. Al-Asad justified his policies in terms of Ba'athist doctrine and cloaked himself in Ba'athist symbols. How this played out in the hearts and minds of the Syria population is difficult to assess, but his Ba'ath affiliation was clearly a matter of great importance to al-Asad.

The Ba'ath Party also serves as the regime's link with the Syrian population and particularly its traditional base of support among the minorities, peasants, workers, bureaucrats, and soldiers. Toward this end, the party maintains cells and branches in all villages, urban residential quarters and factories. Labor unions, student groups, and professional associations are also tied to the Party, as are youth and feminist organizations. Syrian children between the ages of six and eleven are required to join the Ba'ath Party's Vanguard Organization, while older children (12 to 18 years of age) have the option of joining the Union of Revolutionary Youth. Membership in the Union of Revolutionary Youth is not compulsory but brings certain privileges. Student unions at Syria's universities are also under Party control, and faculty appointments must be cleared by Party officials. All in all, very little happens in Syria that escapes the notice of the Ba'ath Party (Hinnebusch 1980).

Most members of the Party originally came from the ranks of minorities and lower-class Sunnis and it is they, many of whom are now members of the bureaucratic middle class, who provide the bulk of the regime's popular support. While enjoying secure jobs, a modicum of power and ample opportunities for corruption, members of the Ba'ath Party have not been noted for their ideological zeal. Rather, the rank and file of the Ba'ath Party display the same opportunism and lack of zeal that characterized the membership of Nasser's Arab Socialist Union. As Hinnebusch wrote years ago:

> The typical Ba'ath party member appears to have only a passing resemblance to the tough zealous militants found in true Leninist regimes like North Vietnam or China. Many do not appear to be exceptionally alert ideologically. They talk much more than they act, and there is no evidence that they are any more disciplined or possess more drive than non-party members. In fact, culturally, they seem to reflect their society far too much to be able to radically transform it. If their detractors are right, many are more interested in privileges than in performance. Because exceptional performance is not expected of them, their privileges are naturally resented. In sum, their claim to constitute a political vanguard with a right to rule by virtue of superior political consciousness and ability seems doubtful, and, more important, it is not taken very seriously in Syria (Hinnebusch 1980, 169).

Party documents reviewed by van Dam attribute the lack of ideological zeal among party cadres to two basic causes. First, the rush to rebuild the mass base of the Party in the hectic days following the breakup of the union with Egypt resulted in the recruitment of individuals motivated more by self-interest than commitment to Party principles. Second, each faction within the Party attempted to strengthen its position by recruiting as many relatives and co-religionists as possible. Opportunism led to corruption, and religious networking to nepotism and fragmentation. There is little evidence that these problems have diminished (Quilliam 1999).

Further adding to the lack of ideological zeal was al-Asad's transformation of the Ba'ath Party from a narrow-based party that stressed the commitment of its cadres to a mass-based party that would see its membership grow from approximately 65,000 in 1971 to more than a million 20 years later. The latter figure, as Batatu notes, "constituted no less than 14.5 percent of all Syrians aged 14 and above" (Batatu 1999, 177). Of these, approximately one-fourth were females.

Whatever their shortcomings, the members of the Ba'ath Party were effusive in their support of al-Asad and have rushed to support Bashar. Meetings of the Ba'ath Party are routinely televised, and at each mention of al-Asad's name a cheering section jumped to its feet and chanted, "Asad, Asad, Asad." They now do the same for Bashar, and should he falter, they will do the same for his successor.

Far more important in the grand scheme of things is the Party's role within the regime's pervasive security apparatus. The Ba'ath Party maintains its own militias, and its local branches extend the regime's presence to the far reaches of the country. The Party also scrutinizes applications for all government jobs of any importance, a category that includes military officers, bureaucrats, teachers, journalists, and diplomats. It is difficult to find a responsible official in Syria who is not a member of the Party.

Finally, the various Ba'athist organizations are charged with indoctrinating new generations of Syrians into the catechism of Ba'athist ideology. Ba'athism is preached at youth meetings and in the schools, and it is standard fare on Syrian television. Party censors also assure that both the educational system and the mass media remain free of adverse influences. As in most areas of the Middle East, the advent of satellites has made censorship a difficult task.

The People's Assembly and the Cabinet   Below the Ba'ath Party in the power hierarchy lie the formal institutions of the Syrian state: the parliament or National Assembly, the cabinet, and the bureaucracy. The Assembly is an elected body of 250 members dominated by the Ba'ath Party, which approves all candidates for election in advance.

As a practical matter, members of the Assembly belong to one of three groups: the Ba'ath Party, other members of the Progressive National Front, or independents. The Progressive National Front (PNF) was created by the Ba'ath in 1972 and consists of the Ba'ath Party and several other leftist parties including the Syrian Communist Party, the Arab Socialist Union (the remnant of the Nasserites), and several socialist groups that had splintered from the Ba'ath. The purpose of the PNF is to reduce opposition to the regime by providing other "progressive" parties with a piece of the action. Much like the labor unions and professional organizations, PNF members have traded their political independence for security and access to patronage. The government views groups outside of this corporate arrangement with suspicion, much of which is probably justified.

While making no pretense at democracy, the People's Assembly provides key groups in Syrian society with access to government patronage. It also has played a role of growing importance in resolving conflict among competing social factions. These conflicts include both traditional communal rivalry and growing tensions between the public and private sectors.

As in most parliamentary arrangements, the People's Assembly is headed by a prime minister and cabinet who manage the day-to-day affairs of the Government. The Government (prime minister and cabinet) is dominated by the Ba'ath Party, and its senior members belong to the political elite. It is the president, however, who hand-picks the ministers, not the prime minister. This was the procedure under Hafez al-Asad and continues to be the case under Bashar al-Asad.

The cabinet also manages a sprawling bureaucracy that has traditionally been used to provide the regime's supporters with jobs and opportunities for secondary gain. Efficiency has thus been sacrificed to politics, and the bureaucracy does little to either promote economic development or build confidence in the government. The shift to capitalism has led to some restrictions on the bureaucracy, but its use as a dumping ground for the regime's supporters makes it impervious to serious reform.

Clientelism and Politics in Syria   Political power in Syria, then, is wielded through a two-stage process. Patriarchal ties (kinship, religious/ethnic loyalties, and friendship) are used to control the institutions of the state, and the political institutions of the state control the population. The key link in this process is the patron-client relationship. Hafez al-Asad was the supreme patron, and all of the major actors in the Syrian political system were his clients. They all depended upon him for their positions, and if he fell, they fell with him. This does not mean that al-Asad's supporters lacked talent. Many were extremely skilled. Loyalty to al-Asad, however, took precedence over merit. Skill is reasonably abundant in Syria; loyalty is not. It was this network that orchestrated Bashar's meteoric rise to the presidency of Syria, and it is they, at least for the moment, who are the powers behind the throne. Bashar, needless to say, is actively consolidating his own client networks, but that process remains far from complete.

Each of the patriarch's clients, in turn, serves as a patron for his own network of supporters based upon kinship, religious/ethnic, and friendship ties, a process that repeats itself throughout the diverse levels of the governmental, military, and party apparatuses.

The networks are solidified by wasta (influence or connections) and corruption. Indeed, corruption has become so much a part of the Syrian political process that people now speak of controlled corruption. As discussed by Perthes:

> Bribery is ubiquitous. Given the general feeling that both the regime elite and the business community are thoroughly corrupt and that petty state employees do not earn what they need for their living, Syria's general public does not regard petty corruption as particularly wrongful.
>
> It has been noted that Syria's political elite has indeed developed a strong tendency to "treat the state as their private property...."

Recurrent, sometimes almost permanent, anti-corruption campaigns which occasionally reach as high as a government minister cannot hide the fact that corruption is tolerated or even planned. A wide net of corruption, as noted, binds those who are involved to the regime, if only by keeping them under threat of investigation, and ensures that lower officials do not try to uncover the illicit practices of their superiors. Anti-corruption campaigns are necessary, both to make the threat of prosecution credible and thus maintain the instrumental character of planned corruption, and to avoid this instrument getting out of hand—in other words, to prevent economic damage exceeding political benefit (Perthes 1997, 186).

It is possible to move up within the Syrian political hierarchy on the basis of merit, but the higher one goes, the greater the need for support from a powerful patron. Talent is important, but it is difficult for one to go far on the basis of merit alone. This blend of patrimonial and institutional authority provided Hafez al-Asad with a monopoly of coercive force. Force was the foundation of the al-Asad regime for thirty years, and it remains so under the presidency of Bashar al-Asad, faint efforts to liberalize the regime notwithstanding.

Civil Society: The Corporatist Alternative Force was a critical element to al-Asad's regime, but it would be a mistake to believe that he ruled by force alone. Al-Asad, as noted above, attempted to link the broad base of the Syrian population to his regime by means of a variety of subservient political parties, the Workers' General Union, professional associations, women's societies, and youth groups. Most were directly incorporated into the Ba'ath Party; others were linked to the regime via the National Patriotic Front, a coalition of leftist political parties totally dominated by the Ba'ath. In a classic corporate arrangement, most groups in Syria traded their independence for a stake in the regime. They had little choice. This process is well illustrated by Hinnebusch's description of the peasants' union:

> The peasants' union exemplifies populist corporatism. Previous regimes had discouraged peasants organizing, but the Ba'ath, facing intense urban opposition, recruited leaders from the small land-owning peasantry and backed their creation of union branches in the villages. By the 1990s, much of Syria's peasantry was organized. The union's autonomy remained limited, however, and there is no record of dissident challenges to its Ba'athist leadership. Constructed from the top down rather than through struggle from below, the union today lacks the popular muscle to challenge the state.
>
> The union is not, however, a mere paper organization lacking presence in the corridors of power or the village. Its relations with the state

are based on certain shared interests. The union articulates peasant interests within the limits defined by party strategy; thus, it refrains from pressing for further land reform, since the state wishes to encourage investment in the agrarian bourgeoisie, and it has deferred to the state's interest in the compulsory marketing of "strategic" crops. In return, the union enjoys institutionalized channels of access; its leaders sit on party and state committees that make decisions affecting peasants. The union played a role in energizing the land reform process and promoting a system of cooperatives that, as channels of credit, services, and inputs, relieved peasants of dependency on landlords and merchants and protected them from renewed land concentration (Hinnebusch 1993, 247–249).

Far more tricky were al-Asad's efforts to co-opt Syria's capitalist class. Indeed, some authors now believe that the capitalists may have had greater access to the president than did the regime barons, a phenomenon that is likely to increase under Bashar. As Robinson writes:

> The rehabilitation of the entrepreneurial class in Syria began in the early 1980s, when the Damascus business community saved the regime from its Islamist opponents by not joining the anti-regime commercial strike that was in place in all other cities in Syria at the time. The new relationship was consolidated in the mid-1980s when Syria was compelled by its near-bankruptcy to adopt market reforms, further empowering the Syrian bourgeoisie. Today, political power in Syria is defined by the balancing game Asad plays between the bourgeoisie on the one hand and the Alawi military officers—the Alawi barons, as Hinnebusch calls them[7]—on the other side (Robinson 1998, 159).

Quilliam also acknowledges the growing influence of the bourgeoisie, but warns that the Syrian bourgeoisie has many parts and does not speak with a single voice.

> The state bourgeoisie refers to the select club that guides the implementation of state policies. This group has been able to use its privileged access to the state to proffer favours to selected contractors. Their ties with the children of the leaders of the regime have proved to be particularly lucrative and instrumental in forging links between the state and business classes.
>
>   The children of the leaders of the present regime are reputed to have entered business instead of following their fathers' footsteps into the military or security apparatus. They are playing a conciliatory role in binding the fortunes of the state to the interests of the indigenous business class. This shift in orientation has many consequences as the children of the regime, many of whom are Alawis, are undergoing the

---

[7]Hinnebusch, Raymond A. 1995. "Syria: The Politics of Peace and Regime Survival." *Middle East Policy* 3(4): 79.

experience of *embourgeoisement*. The transition in the social class of the new political elite from peasant, to soldier, to bourgeois, has started to cement the future of the state to the old and new bourgeoisie (Quilliam 1999, 88).

Much of Syrian politics, as the above examples illustrate, has a strong "carrot versus stick" quality. The regime has extended its hand to those willing to work with it, but it has given little quarter to its opponents. Added to this mix of coercion, control, and accommodation was a pervasive effort to transform al-Asad into an all-seeing father figure of superhuman proportions. Al-Asad, however, did not possess the charisma of either Nasser or the Ayatollah Khomeini and it is not clear whether the stern gaze of al-Asad that peered down from posters on shop and office walls was designed to inspire confidence or fear. The answer is probably both (Weeden 1998). Efforts are now underway to transform Bashar into a charismatic hero, but he seems ill-suited to the role.

The Opposition   The most visible opposition to the al-Asad regime, past and present, comes from the Muslim Brotherhood. The Brotherhood was not destroyed by the Hama massacre of 1982, but it was clearly damaged and lost much of its organizational strength. The leadership of the Brotherhood fled—one faction to Germany and Jordan, the other to Baghdad. It was also driven underground where it maintained a network of secret cells in the predominantly Sunni areas of the country. Both resident and non-resident factions continue to harass the regime, albeit without notable success.

More recently, the Jordanian branch of the Syrian Brotherhood attempted to patch up its differences with the al-Asad regime, proposing to become a member of the National Patriotic Front in return for the opportunity to retain a legal presence in Syria (Al-Qaisi 1999). This move would have placed the "moderate" branch of the Brotherhood in a strong position to dominate the Brotherhood should the opportunity present itself in the post-al-Asad era. The al-Asad regime expressed little enthusiasm for rapprochement with the Brotherhood, and Fundamentalist harassment of the regime has intensified. Indeed, close cooperation has taken place between Syria, Saudi Arabia, and Jordan to prevent the Brotherhood from developing a base of operations in Jordan or Lebanon that could be used to infiltrate men and weapons into Syria. It is not clear how successful these efforts have been (Interviews by M. Palmer, 2001).

Other traditional opponents of the Ba'ath Party have been "bought off" by the corporate arrangements discussed earlier. This list would certainly include both the leftists and a large segment of the Sunni business elite. Appearances of tranquility, however, are often deceiving. The Sunnis remain restive under Alawite rule, the National Patriotic Front is a marriage of convenience that could fall apart at the first sign of weakness, and the alliance between the regime and Syria's capitalist class remains tenuous. Even the Alawites are divided among themselves, the drama of the conflict between Bashar al-Asad and his uncle Rifat al-Asad being a case in point. All groups, including various factions within the military and the security services, have been jockeying for position in the post-al-Asad era. Tranquility born of fear and accommodation could well be the calm that precedes the storm.

THE CONTEXT OF SYRIAN POLITICS

The keys to Hafez al-Asad's longevity are also to be found within the broader cultural, economic, and international context of Syrian society. Al-Asad was remarkably successful in manipulating each to his own ends; each will test the staying power of Bashar.

Political Culture

From a cultural perspective, it was the continued strength of kinship and confessional ties that supported al-Asad's pattern of patrimonial rule. Syria continues to resemble a mosaic of confessional and kinship groups more than it does an integrated political community. Each group is jealous of the others, and distrust between groups is pervasive. This profound sense of distrust between groups enabled the regime to build its patrimonial networks and to play one group against another.

Distrust also extends to individuals, for the effectiveness of the regime's security services has made discretion a virtue. No region, institution, or sect has escaped penetration by the security services, including the security services themselves. One should not equate Syria with the totalitarianism of Stalinist Russia, but few Syrians have been willing to express their attitudes toward the regime in public, although this has begun to change, however tentatively, in the Bashar era. Even in Lebanon, a quasi-dependency of Syria known for its freedom of expression, one discusses the Syrian intelligence services in hushed tones. Anti-Syrian articles are rare and disappear from the newsstands.

Fear and distrust, in turn, have reinforced well-established tendencies to classify others into "we-they" categories. People are not neutral. They are either potential friends or potential enemies (Abdou 1999). In addition to further fragmenting Syrian society, this trend also strengthens the influence of the patron-client networks discussed earlier.

Weeden (1998) elaborates on this theme, suggesting that regimented pressures to sing al-Asad's praises created an aura of complicity. How can you trust individuals who have openly praised the regime in an effort to feather their own nest or deflect the attention of the mukhabarat (secret services)?

Beyond fear and distrust, perhaps the dominant themes of Syrian political culture have been apathy and opportunism. Revolt has become futile and, aside from the Muslim Brotherhood, one sees few overt signs of opposition to the regime. By the same token, one also sees few signs of psychological commitment to the regime. Rather, most people bend to its carrot-and-stick policies, accepting the corruption and patronage offered, but giving little in return. The most important goal is survival.

Political Economy

Political economists, as one might suspect, find Syrian politics to be a function of economics. Their argument begins with the observation that the Ba'ath Party was supported by Syria's disadvantaged classes, be they minorities or the Sunni poor. With the Ba'ath Party's assumption of power, a socialist economic system shifted wealth and power from Syria's landed and commercial classes and redistributed it to the workers and peasants. It was they who supported the regime.

Interestingly enough, the greatest beneficiaries of Ba'athist rule were Syria's landed peasants rather than the sharecroppers who lived on the margins of subsistence. As Batatu (1999) describes in great detail, it was the former who became the dominant force in the Ba'ath, and it was they, including Hafez al-Asad, who reaped the rewards of power. This Batatu (1999) attributes to the greater access of this class to educational opportunities, an advantage denied to the poorer strata of Syrian peasants. All peasants, however, have benefited from Ba'athist rule, with illiteracy being reduced to some 12 percent of the population among males and some 39 percent among females. The life of the poor, however, remains difficult. An estimated 400,000 to 500,000 Syrians work in Lebanon, most for a subsistence wage. Accurate figures, however, are difficult to come by, for many enter Lebanon by informal means.

It was the more prosperous peasants who became a new administrative middle class of bureaucrats, military officers, and Party officials, all of whom depended upon the largess of the state and the accompanying opportunities for corruption. It was also they who had a vested economic interest in keeping the regime in power.

Socialism, however, proved to be profoundly inefficient. As is true of most socialist economic systems, workers in Syria's large public corporations have displayed a profound lethargy. Wages are low, incentives few, and promotions a function of longevity—hardly a formula for a bustling economy. An average Syrian bureaucrat, for example, earns about $106 per month (*Daily Star*, May 25, 2001). Commentators speak openly of the "sickness of time" that besets the Syrian public sector and the need to liberate it from bureaucratic rigidities. Hafez al-Asad, himself, spoke of the need for Syrians at all levels to get more involved in their country and shoulder their share of responsibility (*Al-Hawadeth*, Mar. 23, 2000, 30). It was this lack of drive among public-sector workers that forced the regime to experiment with capitalist reforms.

The shift to capitalism, while far from complete, has stimulated the Syrian economy and laid the groundwork for Syria's eventual integration into the global marketplace. The regime's turn to the right, however, has not been without political costs. Socialism is enshrined in Ba'athist ideology, and the growing influence of the capitalist sector now poses a threat to the entrenched positions of both the state and Party bureaucracies. Indeed, some observers now believe that the capitalists have surpassed the Ba'athists in Syria's elite hierarchy (Robinson 1998). This transition is evidenced by the tendency of the sons of Ba'athist leaders to become capitalist businessmen. Indeed, of al-Asad's inner circle, only the sons of al-Asad and Talas, the minister of interior, have chosen military careers.

Whether or not capitalists pose a threat to the established order, the regime has maintained a careful balance between the revived capitalist class and its traditional support base within Syria's lower classes. As a result, Syria's transition from socialism to capitalism has stalled in midstream, providing some economic growth but doing little to dismantle the country's moribund public-sector firms (Robinson 1998).

As if to underscore the regime's fears that the lethargy of the Syrian economy could serve as a stimulus for mass discontent, Lawson (1996) notes that periods of economic downturn in Syria were often accompanied by regional crises as al-Asad sought to divert popular attention from the country's economic woes to external threats. Catharsis, however, provided little more than a temporary fix, and if the Bashar regime is to survive, it must revamp the Syrian economy.

It is also interesting to note that a strong tie has traditionally existed between the smaller Sunni merchants and the Muslim Brotherhood, a tie that exists throughout the region. This tie was evident in the spread of Brotherhood support in the years leading up to the 1982 massacres. Much of the financing for the Brotherhood during that era presumably came from the middle class, and Brotherhood violence was supported by merchant strikes throughout the north of Syria. Had the Damascene merchants joined the strike rather than remaining passive, its results might well have been different. They did not, illustrating the fact that regional conflict continued to fragment both religious and economic solidarity. The same link remains in evidence today, for the smaller merchants have benefited far less from the regime's shift to capitalism than have the large capitalists. The small merchants also face increased competition from the large capitalists.

Domestic Politics and the International Environment

If Syrian politics is the product of the cultural and economic factors discussed above, it also reflects Syria's tumultuous international environment. The evolution of Syrian politics outlined in the earlier section of the chapter was largely a chronicle of Syria's conflict with its regional neighbors, be they sister Arab states or Israel. Regional issues, in turn, were largely inseparable from the larger issues of the Cold War and, upon its demise, the advent of American hegemony. In many ways, it was these international pressures that forced al-Asad to pursue the policies that he did. The conflict with Israel, for example, forced the expenditure of Syria's limited resources on defense rather than economic development. It will be observed in Figure 4.1, for example, that Syria's arms expenditures mirror those of Israel but bear no relationship to the arms expenditures of Iraq, a fact indicating Syria's total preoccupation with the Jewish state. While the military developed, the Syrian economy did not. A changing world environment, in turn, forced al-Asad to enter peace negotiations with Israel under conditions that favor the latter, just as it forced liberalization of the Syrian economy.

These same international factors, however, also help to explain al-Asad's longevity in office. Al-Asad's defiance of Israel added a measure of popular support to a regime otherwise lacking in charismatic qualities. The Soviet Union provided al-Asad with both economic and military support until its collapse in 1991 (Karsh 1991). It also protected him from Israeli attack. No sooner had the Cold War ended, moreover, than Syria reaped a $3 billion windfall by siding with the United Nations in the Gulf War of 1991, much of this aid coming from Saudi Arabia and the Gulf countries (Robinson 1998). More economic aid will undoubtedly follow as an inducement for Syria to make peace with Israel, much of it provided by the West.

An unstable regional environment also enabled al-Asad to pursue a vigorous foreign policy by brokering virtually all of the major conflicts

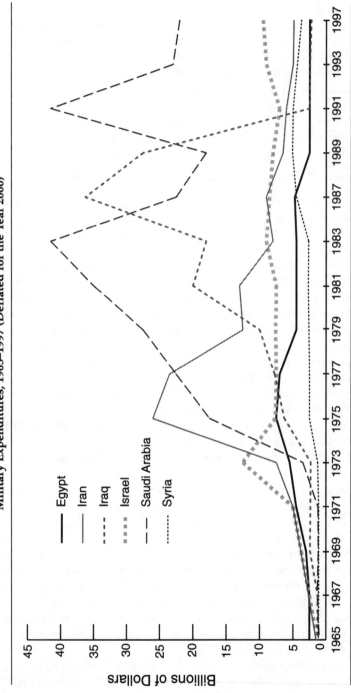

Figure 4.1
Military Expenditures, 1965–1997 (Deflated for the Year 2000)

Source: World Military Expenditures and Arms Transfers, 1965–1974, 1972–1982, and 1987–97 distributed by the US Arms Control and Disarmament Agency, Defense Program and Analysis Division, Washington, DC.

of the Middle East, including the struggle for the Occupied Territories, the Israeli occupation of Lebanon, Iraqi aspirations for dominance of the Persian Gulf, and Iranian support for Fundamentalist movements throughout the region. Al-Asad did not create these regional confrontations, but he was clearly skillful at exploiting and extending them, usually to Syria's benefit. Syria, for example, is now the primary recipient of financial aid from the oil states of the Gulf. In part, the Gulf states are anxious to strengthen Syrian resistance to Israel and Iraq; in part they are hopeful of mellowing support for the Iranians and other radical elements in the region. Bashar has vowed to maintain his father's foreign policy, but he lacks experience in this area. It also remains to be seen if he possesses his father's shrewdness.

LOOKING TOWARD THE FUTURE

The turn of the century would see Hafez al-Asad approaching his seventieth birthday. He had ruled Syria for 30 years, a remarkable record by any standard. The al-Asad era, however, was nearing its end and he died of a heart attack on June 10, 2000. His son Bashar assumed the reins of power, but the future of the Bashar regime is far from certain and remains the topic of heated debate.

This debate, and the probable success or failure of Bashar's reign, hinge on the same factors that enabled his father Hafez al-Asad to rule Syria with an iron hand for 30 years. Ironically, it may be these same factors that prove to be the undoing of his son.

Without repeating the discussion of the preceding section, suffice it to say that any analysis of Bashar al-Asad's future begins with the incontestable fact that Hafez al-Asad will be a hard act to follow. He had concentrated all power in his own hands, and he exercised that power with consummate skill. Both conditions may be difficult for Bashar to duplicate. He was kept in power by the circle of power brokers surrounding his father and, from all appearances, it is they who continue to rule. As a close Syrian friend commented, the clients of the father have now become the masters of the son. This relationship obviously could change, but that change will take time and will not be easy. The inner circle placed Bashar in power to further their own interests, and they cannot be expected to sacrifice those interests without a struggle. Much also hinges on Bashar's personality and resolve. Bashar's personality was not forged by fire nor, image-building efforts aside, does his past provide much indication of the intense desire for power that characterized his father. Whatever the case, both friends and foes are watching his performance intently.

Also adding to Bashar's woes is the questionable legitimacy of Syria's political institutions, institutions that were created by Hafez al-Asad and remained totally subservient to him. It is not clear that these institutions will be able to gain the support of the Syrian population in the post–Hafez al-Asad era. Moreover, the staffing of Syria's political institutions placed patronage, loyalty, and ethnic balance above merit and efficiency. Corruption and opportunism were part of the system, and Bashar al-Asad, for all his verbal forays against corruption, cannot alter the situation without undermining the foundations of the regime's power.

The Syrian bureaucracy, in particular, lacks the capacity to keep pace with Syria's mounting social and economic problems, not the least of which is an exploding population that has outpaced the ability of the government to provide even basic levels of service to Syrian citizens. Hafez al-Asad noted with his typical realism, "Syria has three million too many people" (Le Gac 1991). Much of this expanding population, moreover, has found its way to Damascus, Aleppo, and other major cities, thereby increasing the potential for urban violence should the resolve of the regime falter. Perhaps more threatening is the 30-percent unemployment rate among graduates of Syria's colleges and universities, a segment of the Syrian population that is both vocal and prone to political activism (Moubayed 2001).

Another consideration that should be weighed in assessing the future of the Bashar regime is the communal nature of Syrian society. Resentment of Alawite rule was never far beneath the surface, and one hears ominous warnings that the Sunni population will not tolerate an extended period of Alawite domination. The Alawites, for their part, are more divided than ever and may find it difficult to resist Sunni demands for change. This certainly was the message of the "brothers' war."

It may be dangerous, however, to overemphasize the influence of sectarianism on Syrian politics. The sociocultural and demographic context of Syrian politics has changed dramatically over the past thirty years. A country of 17 million will soon become a country of 20 million. Communal ties remain strong but have been weakened by Syria's transition from a rural to an urban society. Syria's population is also young, with approximately half under 25 years of age. As such, the younger generation has borne the full force of government socialization and has been exposed to a far broader range of experiences than were their parents and grandparents. This exposure does not necessarily translate into greater support for the Ba'ath Party, but it may mean that confessional loyalties have been diluted by a greater diversity of economic interests.

Most communal groups in Syria, moreover, are now divided between those who have prospered by cooperating with the al-Asad regime and those who continue to oppose it. Marriage alliances between the old aristocratic and business families of the pre-socialist era and the Ba'athist political elite have also become increasingly frequent, not the least of which was the marriage of Bashar al-Asad to the daughter of a wealthy Damascus businessman. The aristocrats gain access to political influence, while the political elite acquire social respectability (Seale 1988). Both have a stake in perpetuating the regime.

Bashar, for his part, is pursuing a dual strategy of placing his own people in power as rapidly as possible while simultaneously building a strong foundation of mass support based on rapid progress in the areas of political and economic liberalization. Both types of liberalization have been popular, yet both pose potential threats for the Bashar regime. The recent proliferation of civil rights groups offers the promise of movement toward a civil and more open society, but carries with it the danger that the demand for greater openness will far outstrip the permissiveness of what remains a very cautious and conservative regime that has survived by coercion and control. As Iran's Islamic regime has learned to its dismay, a little freedom can be a dangerous thing, a topic that will be discussed at length in Chapter 7. Indeed, Bashar appears far more liberal than either the military or the Ba'ath Party, both of which represent the main pillars of his regime.

Change within the economic realm is equally tricky, with Bashar attempting to pursue his father's strategy of promoting economic liberalization while simultaneously maintaining a large public sector that consumes most of the state's limited resources. Growing liberalization is expected to generate jobs and income—27,000 new jobs are required each year just to keep pace with population growth—yet the regime remains politically dependent upon the large and inefficient public-sector enterprises that provide employment and economic security for much of Syria's urban work force. In much the same manner, Syria's large state and Ba'athist bureaucracies are reluctant to relinquish their control of a Syrian economy that represents the main source of their power and secondary income. Also worrisome, at least in the short run, is the hesitancy of both foreign and domestic capitalists to invest large sums in the Syrian economy during a period of uncertain transition.

In the international arena, by contrast, the Bashar al-Asad regime would seem to be on firmer ground, with considerable evidence suggesting that the US and the European Union are very interested in seeing Bashar survive, as is Israel. All fear that chaos in Syria might lead to a resurgence of Islamic Fundamentalism, a fear shared by

Saudi Arabia, Egypt, and other conservative Arab states in the region. Syria also remains a key actor in the peace process, making US involvement in stabilizing the Bashar regime even more likely. The assumption of US omnipotence, unfortunately, is hardly supported by US performance in the region, with both its Iraqi and Iranian policies being in a shambles—a topic that will be covered at length in Chapters 6 and 7.

5

The Politics of Saudi Arabia

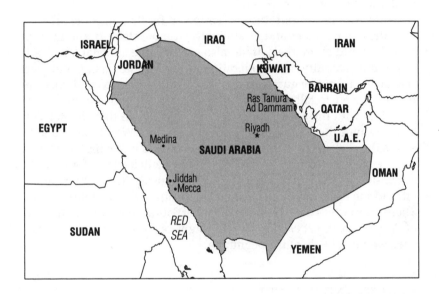

Saudi Arabia, like so many of its neighbors, is a nation of paradoxes. Great wealth has brought the veneer of modernity, yet the country remains a tribal monarchy that bears the name of its ruling family. Saudi citizens are among the most pampered in the world, yet they enjoy no political rights. The Saudi monarchy prides itself on being the protector of the Islamic faith, yet fears the Fundamentalist revival that is shaking the region. Saudi Arabia has built a dazzling network of universities to train its population, yet most of what gets done in Saudi Arabia is done by foreigners. Indeed, more than one-fourth of the Saudi population consists of foreigners. Saudi Arabia spends more on arms than any other state in the region, yet must rely on the United States for protection from its enemies.

These paradoxes suggest that Saudi Arabia may be less secure than its placid exterior would suggest. This insecurity is a matter of great concern to the United States and its First World allies, for Saudi Arabia is the world's leading producer of crude oil and possesses approximately 25 percent of the world's proven oil reserves. Deposits of natural gas are almost equally large. Saudi Arabia, moreover, is the dominant member of the Organization of Petroleum Exporting Countries (OPEC), a cartel designed to assure that its members receive the highest possible price for their oil. What happens in Saudi Arabia *does* matter to the rest of the world.

Saudi Arabia's importance is reinforced by its long-time alliance with the United States and its ability to promote stability and moderation in world oil markets. It has also used its phenomenal oil wealth to promote stability and moderation in the Middle East. Continued stability could not be guaranteed if Saudi Arabia's vast oil and financial resources were to fall under the sway of a less friendly regime.

In line with the above concerns, our objective in this chapter will be to examine the evolution of Saudi politics since World War II and to assess the challenges that the Saudi regime faces in the first decade of the twenty-first century. Toward this end, we will focus on four critical dimensions of the Saudi political equation: kinship/tribalism, religion, oil, and the royal family's special relationship with the United States. These four factors have been the pillars of Saudi stability since the end of World War II, yet each is showing signs of strain. As always, however, we must begin at the beginning.

HISTORY AND CULTURE

The defining historical event in the history of the Arabian Peninsula was the birth of Islam in AD 610. Prior to the advent of Islam, the history of the Arabian Peninsula was largely that of the Bedouin tribes that roamed its barren terrain in search of pasture and water. The struggle for survival pitted tribe against tribe, and raiding was the norm (Vassiliev 1998; Smith 1903). Nevertheless, Arabic literary culture flourished, and a few weeks each year were set aside for contests of horsemanship and poetry reading. The poets recorded historic feats of love and conquest, and spared no effort to extol the tribal virtues of independence, loyalty, courage, and personal honor. When the Saudis speak of tribal virtues, it is to these characteristics that they refer.

The days of antiquity had seen a large meteor fall in the area that is now Mecca, an event that the tribes of the region attributed to divine intervention. The meteor was eventually enshrined in a cube-shaped temple, the Kaaba, and became the focal point of annual religious pilgrimages, free passage to which was guaranteed by custom (Armajani 1970). Over time, the tribe of Quraish gained control of the region and its leaders assumed responsibility for providing pilgrims to the Kaaba with food, water, and shelter. They also constructed the city of Mecca around the Kaaba and transformed it into a major trading center linking the caravan routes from the Red Sea, Iraq, Syria, and Yemen.

The Prophet Mohammed was born into the Hashemite clan of the tribe of Quraish, and his descendants maintained the holy shrine and cared for its pilgrims until the advent of Saudi rule. The birth of Islam further enhanced the aura of the Kaaba by requiring all Muslims to make a pilgrimage to the holy shrine. The Saudi monarchy, as the latest guardian of the holy shrine, continues to provide for the needs of the pilgrims, a mammoth feat that involves caring for more than two million pilgrims during the Hajj.

The Quraish, as the tribe of the Prophet Mohammed and the protector of the holy shrines, enjoyed a special position in the eyes of Muslims. This was especially the case for the Hashemite clan, the members of which could claim direct lineage to the Prophet.

With the passing of the Prophet Mohammed and the orthodox Caliphs, the Arabian Peninsula fell under the sway of successive Islamic dynasties, beginning with the Umayyad (Syrians) and ending with the Ottomans. Aside from maintaining a presence in Mecca, few caliphs had an interest in the barren and hostile wastelands of the Arabian Peninsula and the region reverted to a life of tribal conflict. Islamic practice also became lax, and *hadiths* (sayings of the Prophet) were manufactured to justify the needs of the moment.

From the Saudi perspective, the next major event in the history of the Arabian Peninsula was the consolidation of Saudi control over the oasis of Ad-Diriyah (an oasis town near the present city of Riyadh) in the early 1700s. While most tribes of the era were nomadic, some had settled around the region's oases and had become sedentary farmers. As described by Alexei Vassiliev:

> The power of a settled emir differed materially from that of a nomadic shaikh. The ruler of an oasis did not face a tribal military-political organization. Peasants, with their weakened tribal and kinship ties, were far more dependent on the nobility than the bedouin were. It is not surprising, therefore, that the Arabian chroniclers call the oasis-dwellers *raya*, meaning 'subjects,' 'herd,' 'human livestock.' An emir (a feudal ruler) relied, on the one hand, on the oasis nobility among whom he had many relatives and, on the other hand, on his own detachments, which consisted of slaves, freedmen and mercenaries. The judicial system was usually based in the *sharia*, containing the fundamentals of

Muslim law. Justice was administered both by the ruler and by the *qadhi* (a judge who had studied jurisprudence and theology) (Vassiliev 1998, 55).

The Saudis fell in the category of oasis-dwellers, with Saud ibn Mohammed, the founder of the Saudi dynasty, having seized control of the oasis of Ad-Diriyah in 1710 (Vassiliev 1998). The Saudis soon conquered the neighboring tribes, becoming a regional power within the Najd, the central eastern region of the Arabian Peninsula. As a tribal power alone, this would, in all probability, have been the extent of their empire. In 1714, however, Saud added a religious component to his tribal authority by forging an alliance with Abd al-Wahhab, a charismatic religious leader with a broad following throughout the region.

Abd al-Wahhab's teachings condemned the laxity that had entered Islamic practice and the embellishment of its theology with mystical beliefs, not the least of which were those of the Shi'a. The practice of Islam, Abd al-Wahhab preached, must be based on the Koran and Sunna, and nothing more (de Corancez 1995). In modern parlance, Abd al-Wahhab was a "strict constructionist," with his emphasis on the "fundamentals" of Islam making him a forerunner of the Fundamentalist movement that is now shaking the Middle East (Al-Freih 1995).

Much as in Mohammed's time, tribal armies fired by the spirit of Islam and the lure of booty would conquer much of modern Saudi Arabia, including the holy cities of Mecca and Medina, a feat that was accomplished in 1803. As de Corancez writes:

> These conquests were not without reward for Abd el Aziz [the king]. If a tribe offered any resistance, its men were all massacred without discrimination, and their possessions plundered. If it surrendered willingly to Wahabi rule, Abd el Aziz, basing himself on a passage from the Koran, tithed the possessions of all his new subjects; nor was this tithe merely raised upon their households, money, livestock and beasts of burden—it also applied to men: thus out of every ten Arabs Abd el Aziz took one whom he did not pay for, whom he compelled to serve in his army. He thus found himself at the head of a large army as well as the owner of vast possessions which he amassed continuously. It is said that towards the end he became so powerful that he could at a stroke raise an army of a hundred thousand men. But in this respect we should caution against the Oriental propensity to exaggeration (de Corancez 1995, 9).

The House of Saud ruled Mecca from 1803 until 1814, when the Saudi Kingdom was crushed by Egyptian forces acting in the name of the Turkish sultan. Riyadh, now the capital of the Saudi kingdom, fell to the Egyptians in 1818, and the Turkish sultan maintained a small garrison in the city to symbolize his control of the region.

The House of Saud would reassert its control over much of the Najd, but family conflicts and the corruption of power sapped their strength and they were put to flight by the Shammar tribe in 1891 (Anscombe 1997). Granted asylum by the sheikh of Kuwait, the once-proud rulers of the Najd had become refugees dependent upon the largess of their hosts. The Turks had also sided with the Shammar in an effort to reassert their suzerainty over the Najd.

The story of modern Saudi Arabia begins in 1901 when Prince Abd al-Aziz al Saud (a direct descendant of the founder of the Saudi dynasty), generally referred to as Abd al-Aziz or ibn Saud, rallied a handful of supporters (the number ranges from 30 to 100, depending upon the source), and descended by night upon the fort guarding Riyadh. The governor was killed and the population, rebelling from the oppression of the Shammar tribe, rose in support of the Saudis. By 1902, ibn Saud was master of Riyadh and the surrounding area and, upon the resignation of his father, was proclaimed king. By 1904 the Saudis were again in control of all of the Najd and by 1913 they had extended their authority to the neighboring province of al-Hasa, now the eastern province of Saudi Arabia. Abd al-Aziz's conquests again featured an alliance with the Wahhabis, the tribal forces of the former being inspired by the religious zeal of the latter.

The real prize for both the Saudis and the Wahhabis, however, remained the Hijaz, the eastern region of the Arabian Peninsula, and thereby control of the holy cities of Mecca and Medina. For the Saudis, the conquest of the Hijaz promised unchallenged control of the Arabian Peninsula and the prestige and power that accrued to the protector of Islam's holiest shrines. For the Wahhabis, control of the holy cities offered the opportunity to extend their puritanical doctrine far beyond the sandy wastes of the Najd and to bring an end to the moral laxity of the Hijaz, a moral laxity that they attributed to the Hashemites, the traditional custodians of the shrine.

Attacking the Hijaz, however, would not be easy, for the outbreak of World War I had seen the British induce Sharif Hussein, the Hashemite governor of Mecca, to revolt against the Turks with promises of a unified Arab kingdom that included most of Greater Syria. The tribal armies of Abd al-Aziz would be no match for those of a unified Hashemite kingdom supported by the British.

The promised Arab kingdom, however, did not materialize, and in 1916 the British signed a treaty with Abd al-Aziz recognizing his control of the Najd and al-Hasa (Al-Angari 1997). While not becoming a British protectorate, the Saudis received a small stipend from the

British and agreed to respect British interests in the Persian Gulf. Britain also patched up its relations with Sharif Hussein by installing one of his sons as the king of Iraq and another as the Emir of Transjordan, a newly created mini-state designed to serve as a buffer between the British mandate of Palestine, recently proclaimed a "national home for the Jews" and its Arab neighbors. The new mini-state also had the advantage of keeping the disputed region out of the hands of the French.

Abd al-Aziz, then, had reclaimed the Saudi kingdom of old, but it was a poor kingdom with little room for expansion. Rebellion was frequent, and perpetual raiding among tribes threaten to splinter the kingdom into warring factions. Also of potential concern to the young king had been the birth of the Ikhwan (brotherhood) movement of 1912. The Ikhwan began as a group of religious zealots dedicated to reasserting the austere Wahhabi doctrine among the tribes of the Najd, the remote and migratory nature of which made religious conformity difficult. As Robert Lacy describes these Wahhabi zealots:

> The Prophet condemned personal ostentation, so the Ikhwan shunned silk, gold, jewelry and ornaments, including the gold thread traditionally woven round the dark *bhisht* or *mishlah*, the outer robe—and they also cut their robes short above the ankles. This was because the Prophet had declared clothes that brushed the ground to be an affectation, and the same went for luxuriant moustaches. So the Ikhwan clipped the hair on their upper lip to a mere shadow of stubbiness—while adopting a different rule for hair on the chin. In this case, they argued, it would be affectation to trim and shape, so beards must be left to grow as long and to straggle as far as God might will them (Lacy 1981, 142–143).

In order to better convert the Bedouin to Wahhabi doctrine, the Ikhwan began to preach the virtues of agriculture and urged their followers to settle on desert oases where they would be under the direct control of Wahhabi preachers. The first settlement was established in 1912 and soon contained more than 10,000 residents. Religious indoctrination was intense, and the warrior spirit was shifted from raiding to the glorification of Islam.

Rather than resisting the Ikhwan movement, Abd al-Aziz embraced it as a vehicle for settling the tribes and organizing their members, now fired with religious zeal, into a more-or-less standing army. As Holden and Johns write:

> In 1916 he ordered that all the bedouin tribes owing allegiance to him must also give up herding and join the Ikhwan, and their sheikhs were brought to Riyadh in relays for special religious instruction. They were to receive subsidies from the treasury and, in return, respect the King

as their Imam and swear to uphold Wahhabist orthodoxy (Holden and Johns 1981, 69).

By 1917, according to Lacy, "there were over 200 such settlements dotted all over Najd, none of them more than a day's march from another, an extraordinary military network" (Lacy 1981, 146). Although all had presumably sworn allegiance to the king, that allegiance was clearly secondary to their faith. Any conflict between the Wahhabi leaders and the king risked finding the Ikhwan on the side of the Wahhabis. Particularly troublesome was the Ikhwan's opposition to the king's growing friendship with the British, whom the Ikhwan viewed as infidels. Then, as now, the Fundamentalists viewed the Arabian Peninsula as sacred territory not to be desecrated by non-Muslims (Holden and Johns 1981, 71).

Sporadic scrimmages between the forces of Sharif Hussein and ibn Saud's Ikhwan erupted into full-scale warfare in 1919, with victory going to the latter. The British attempted to strengthen Hussein's forces but simultaneously hedged their bets by increasing ibn Saud's subsidy. One of the king's sons was also taken on a tour of England, marking the first time that any member of the royal family had ventured beyond the confines of the Arabian Peninsula. In 1922, the British worked out an amicable demarcation of much of the border between Saud's kingdom and the recently created Hashemite Kingdom of Iraq. The boundaries of Kuwait, a British protectorate, were also delineated, much to the advantage of ibn Saud who was now of growing interest to the British. The same year also saw a British firm receive the concession for the exploration of oil in Saudi Arabia's eastern province. In exchange for the concession, the king received an annual stipend of some $7000 per year. Alas, the British failed to discover oil and allowed their concession to lapse.

Although Abd al-Aziz had promised to restrain the Ikhwan from attacks on the Hijaz, relations between Abd al-Aziz and the ruler of Mecca remained tense. Abd al-Aziz made little secret of either his desire to conquer Mecca or his growing fear of attack by the Hashemite kings of Iraq and Transjordan (Kostiner 1993). The Ikhwan, for their part, were incensed by Sharif Hussein's lax enforcement of Islamic law and threatened a jihad when the ruler of Mecca barred them from making the pilgrimage to Mecca for security reasons (Lacy 1981, 82–83). The final insult came in 1924 when the Sharif of Mecca proclaimed himself to be the Caliph or successor to Mohammed, the position having been left vacant with the collapse of the Ottoman Empire.

The Ikhwan attacked, and by 1926 all of the Hijaz, including the holy cities of Mecca and Medina, was under the control of the Saudi forces. Abd al-Aziz ibn Saud was duly proclaimed the King of the Hijaz and swore to protect the holy places and provide for the pilgrims, the most profitable enterprise in the Arabian Peninsula at the time. Understanding that the residents of Hijaz were more urban than his Wahhabi Ikhwan, ibn Saud promised to provide the region with a consultative council and a constitution. The council met for a period, but the constitution was never promulgated. Nevertheless, the residents of the Hijaz were spared the full wrath of the Ikhwan, much to the consternation of the latter.

Relations between the king and the Ikhwan became increasingly tense over the course of the ensuing years and ibn Saud, fearing for his throne, recruited a new army drawn from townsfolk and loyal tribes to counter the Ikhwan. The confrontation came in 1929 when a rebellion by the Ikhwan was crushed by the king's forces. The king's authority was now absolute, but tensions between the tribal authority of the Saudis and the religious authority of the Wahhabis would remain an underlying theme of Saudi politics.

In 1932, ibn Saud unified his vast realm and named it the Kingdom of Saudi Arabia. With the Ikhwan destroyed and a new army in place, the king's rule was now secure. Indeed, the only conflict of major significance prior to the outbreak of World War II was a brief war with Yemen in 1934. The Yemenis were easily defeated, and Saud added a large section of Yemeni territory to his new kingdom.

That kingdom, however, remained desperately poor, its major sources of income being the Hajj (pilgrimage) and the meager subsidy provided by the British. This would change dramatically with the discovery of oil by a consortium of American companies in 1938 (Twitchell 1958). Profits were not immediate, but both the Arabian American Oil Company (Aramco) and the American government saw the wisdom of providing loans to a Saudi monarch perpetually in need of cash.[1] Indeed, as early as 1943 President Roosevelt had declared that Saudi Arabia was vital to America's defense, thereby paving the way for US aid to flow to the desert kingdom (Holden and Johns 1981, 128; Hart 1998). The relationship between the two countries was consolidated in 1945 when President Roosevelt hosted ibn Saud aboard an American cruiser on a return trip from the Yalta conference of wartime leaders. In the words of William Eddy, who served as an interpreter during the meeting:

> In very simple language, such as he must often have used in cementing alliances with tribal chiefs, ibn Saud then asked F.D.R. for friendship.

---

[1] Aramco was the operating company established by the consortium of US oil companies working in Saudi Arabia.

The president then gave Ibn Saud double assurance, repeated just one week before his death in his letter to ibn Saud, dated April 5, 1945: (1) He personally, as president, would never do anything which might prove hostile to the Arabs; and (2) the US Government would make no change in its basic policy in Palestine without full and prior consultation with both Jews and Arabs (Hart 1998, 39).[2]

Oil and defense, the two major pillars of the Saudi-US relationship, were now in place.

The Era of Revolution and Optimism

Other than the ascendance of the House of Saud, the most significant aspect of Saudi history in the century preceding World War II was the success of the desert kingdom in avoiding colonization by the West. Although all of its neighbors, with the exception of Yemen (North) had been exposed to varying degrees of Westernization, the Saudis had not. As a result, the Kingdom of Saudi Arabia that entered the post–World War II era differed little from the first Saudi kingdom established in the mid-eighteenth century. Ibn Saud was an absolute patriarch who ruled his vast kingdom as a tribal sheikh ruled his tribe. There were no political institutions to speak of, and the king's primary means of communicating with his subjects was the weekly *majlis* (council) at which he would meet with tribal leaders bound to him by oaths of personal loyalty. In grand patriarchal fashion, he would also hear petitions from citizens who had grievances or were in need of the king's help. This help was presented as a personal favor bestowed by a compassionate king. The majlis is a tribal institution that dates to antiquity and continues to be held by the king and the major princes as a symbol of "tribal democracy." A Council of Ministers or cabinet would not be established until 1953. Decisions were made by the king and carried out by his sons and a few trusted advisors. Religious matters, including education and morality, remained in the hands of the ulema.[3]

Oil revenues were viewed as the personal property of a king perpetually in debt, and the kingdom's financial resources were rapidly exhausted by the voracious appetites of the royal family. Little wealth trickled down to the kingdom's one million to three million inhabitants, the overwhelming majority of whom remained illiterate. Many also remained nomadic, and even those in the cities or agricultural settlements remained fiercely loyal to their tribes, far more so than to the Saudis, a sentiment particularly strong in the Hijaz.

---

[2]Eddy, *F.D.R. Meets Ibn Sa'ud.* See also *FRUS,* 1945, Vol. 17, pp. 2–3 and 7–9.
[3]Only the major trading and religious cities of the Hijaz had anything approaching an organized bureaucracy, but this was rudimentary and subject to the king's whim.

For all of their backwardness in the material sphere, the Saudis had been spared the humiliation of colonialism and remained supremely confident of their religious heritage and tribal customs. Unlike many residents of their sister states, few Saudis seemed to suffer from feelings of inferiority or the psychological anguish of being forced to choose between the spiritual virtues of Islam and the material luxury of a modern society (Holden and Johns 1981, 150). If luxury were warranted, God would provide. Saudi Arabia had also evolved from what Kostiner describes as a "loose alliance of nomads and townsmen" into a patrimonial kingdom with defined borders and a political system, however rudimentary, capable of maintaining stability in its realm (Kostiner 1993, 185).

This, then, was the political system that would guide Saudi Arabia into the era of optimism and revolution. The primary goal of the monarchy was to consolidate its hold over its vast domain. Tribal rebellions remained a threat, as did the prospect of an uprising by Hijazis chafing under the puritanical yoke of the less-sophisticated Saudis. Far more threatening were the Hashemite monarchs of Jordan and Iraq, both of whom viewed the Hijaz as their patrimony.

The king, moreover, had ruled for almost 50 years and was in ill health. It would not be the tribal warrior who guided Saudi Arabia into the post-war era, but his sons (Van der Mulen 1957). Succession was a matter of grave concern to the ailing monarch, for the Saudi kingdoms of yore, weakened by quarrels over succession, had become easy prey for their foes.

The king set the stage for an orderly succession by demanding that the contending princes, most of whom had different mothers, swear allegiance to Saud, his oldest son. Abd al-Aziz had also groomed Saud for the kingship by naming him crown prince, a position Saud used to place his own supporters in positions of authority. A Council of Ministers (cabinet) had been created just days before the king's death, and was also placed under the control of the crown prince. Saud now reigned supreme.

The situation, however, remained tricky, for Faisal, second in line for succession, possessed far greater intelligence and organizational skills than his elder half-brother. Faisal had also served as minister of foreign affairs since the 1930s and possessed far broader knowledge of the revolutionary pressures shaking the Middle East than Saud, a man who had traveled little and could speak only a few words of English.

With the passing of Abd al-Aziz in 1953, the inner circle of the royal family was forced to choose between Saud and Faisal. It was a choice between internal cohesion and competence. It was also a choice between the continuation of informal rule based on the inclinations of a single individual and efforts to provide Saudi Arabia with a formal political system capable of meeting the challenges of the future.

The crisis was settled, albeit temporarily, when Faisal embraced his brother and hailed him as king. Cohesion had carried the day. This was probably the best choice at the time, for it was doubtful that the kingdom could have survived a bitter struggle for secession between Saud and Faisal, both of whom had strong allies within the royal family. Also weighing heavily on Saudi minds was the overthrow of Egypt's King Farouk in 1952, and his prophetic quip that the world was destined to have but five kings, the king of England and the four kings in a deck of cards. The kingdom, moreover, had suffered its first labor uprising only months earlier when most of the Aramco work force had walked off the job in a quest for higher pay and better housing and benefits (Holden and Johns 1981). For the first time in Saudi history, its tribal leaders had come face to face with the consequences of modern production techniques. However rudimentary it may have been, Saudi Arabia was developing a working class susceptible to political manipulation. The golden goose had produced more than wealth.

Cohesion, however, came at high cost. Saud had gone a long way toward the consolidation of his authority and resisted the constraints urged upon him by Faisal and his other brothers. Saudi oil revenues, now in the range of $235,000,000 per annum, continued to be treated as the private domain of the king, and there were few legal restrictions on Saud's disbursement of these funds. Bribery and corruption were the order of the day, while bills went unpaid for months (Holden and Johns 1981, 180). Millions of dollars in military equipment were purchased from the United States, much of which was too sophisticated for the Saudi army to operate and remained in its crates (Holden and Johns 1981, 168, 183). Even more money was spent on palaces and yachts as well as lavish government buildings that conveyed an image of progress. In the meantime, the kingdom sank deeper in debt. Stories of corruption and mismanagement under Saud's reign are too voluminous and too bizarre for easy recounting but portray a chaotic political system unprepared to cope with either its sudden wealth or the tumultuous political environment of the Middle East. Suffice it to say that Saud's most lasting accomplishment was siring more than 50 legitimate sons and a roughly equal number of daughters (Holden and Johns 1981, 177). None would rise to prominence upon their father's passing.

In the foreign policy sphere, Saud formed an alliance with Nasser, offering the latter lavish financial support for his Arab revolution in return for Egyptian support in Saudi Arabia's "cold war" with the

Hashemite Kingdoms of Iraq and Jordan. There can be little doubt that the alliance was also a ploy to deflect Nasser's wrath from a regime that he had earlier ridiculed as being a lap dog of the West. With the explosion of Nasser's popularity following his victory in the Arab-Israeli War of 1956, Saudi aid for the Egyptian leader became little more than tribute (blackmail). Particularly dangerous was Saudi Arabia's heavy reliance on Egyptian and Palestinian workers. This was not a minor consideration, for most teachers and bureaucrats in the kingdom were either Egyptians or Palestinians, as were most oil workers. Most were fired by Nasser's rhetoric and formed a Nasserite "fifth column" within the kingdom.

As might be expected, discontent with Saud's rule was not long in surfacing. A minor military coup was put down in 1954, and in 1955 a major prince openly advocated that Saud be replaced by the austere Faisal. The suggestion was premature, but by 1957 the internal situation had become so unstable that pressure from within the royal family forced Saud to grant Faisal executive powers. A resentful Saud remained King, but Faisal was in charge. Faisal moved rapidly to constrain the profligate Saud and otherwise put the Saudi financial house in order.

The struggle between Faisal and Saud, however, had only begun. Saud had been lavish in his gifts to the tribal chiefs, a group that would increasingly form the basis of his power. The king was also much beloved by a merchant class that had enriched itself by pandering to the needs of the royal family as well by a legion of petty princes who survived on his generosity. All resented Faisal's austerity measures.

At this point, three distinct wings were beginning to emerge within the royal family. The first centered on Saud and seemed to have few concerns beyond momentary gratification. Much like Louis XV, their motto seemed to be "après moi, le déluge." A second and much smaller group of princes was caught up in the wave of Arab nationalism sweeping the Middle East and urged that Saudi Arabia transform itself into something approaching a constitutional monarchy. They were variously referred to as the "free" or "red" princes, depending upon one's point of view. Falling between these two extremes was the inner core of the royal family, whose primary concern was the long-term survival of the family and its kingdom. They were contemptuous of both Saud and the free princes: The greed of the former had placed the kingdom on the path to ruin, while the misplaced idealism of the latter threatened it with extinction. The survival of the kingdom, in their view, demanded order and discipline. That order and discipline could only be imposed by Faisal.

The struggle between Faisal and Saud was to be a torturous one. Saud remained king in name and lost no opportunity to undercut Faisal's authority. The US also harbored dreams of using Saud as a counterweight to Nasser, much as the British had rallied the Arabs around Sharif Hussein in the Arab revolution of 1916. As Eisenhower (1965) would note in his memoirs, "He [Saud] at least professed anti-Communism, and he enjoyed, on religious grounds, a high standing among all Arab nations." If anything, this policy was even more quixotic than Saud's support of Nasser and indicated just how little the United States understood either Saudi Arabia or the Middle East.

Perhaps to curry greater US support, Saud cut his ties with Nasser and endorsed the Eisenhower Doctrine, a new US program designed to contain the Soviet Union and its agents in the Middle East, a direct reference to Nasser. Saud also settled his differences with the Hashemite kings of Jordan and Iraq as tribal feuds gave way to a desperate struggle for the survival of monarchies as a political institution. If one monarch fell, the others could not be far behind. The United States, for its part, modernized the Saudi armed forces and pledged to come to the aid of the Saudi government if so requested. Yet another link had been added to the special relationship between Saudi Arabia and the United States.

The announcement of unity between Egypt and Syria in February of 1958 sent shock waves through a royal family that had begun to fear popular rebellion more than foreign attack. Consternation turned to terror a few months later when the king regent of Iraq was ousted by a military coup and his body dismembered by Iraqi mobs demanding unity with the United Arab Republic.

Further adding to the tension within the royal family were efforts by an increasingly ill and unstable Saud to move his sons into positions of power. If Saud had his way, it would be they rather than Faisal who claimed the throne upon their father's death, relegating the remainder of the royal family to secondary status.

A brief alliance had also been formed between Saud and the free princes, the latter viewing Faisal as a greater obstacle to constitutional reform than the erratic Saud. Their logic was impeccable, for a few more years of Saud's rule would have all but guaranteed the end of the monarchy. The free princes presented a draft constitution to Saud in 1960, hoping that the precariousness of his position would force him to bend to their will. Saud received the draft constitution with graciousness, using it as a ploy to build support among the more liberal elements of Saudi society. He then sent it to the kingdom's ultra-conservative ulema for evaluation and certain rejection. He was not to be disappointed, for the ulema promptly responded that the Koran was the constitution of Saudi Arabia and could not be constrained by a secular document (Holden and Johns 1981, 209–214).

The next four years would see the power struggle between Saud and Faisal intensify as Saud again granted Faisal executive powers, only to reassert his authority and undercut the latter's reforms. Saud also increased his payments to the tribal sheikhs, hoping that they would be able to turn the tide in his inevitable showdown with Faisal. The free princes weighed in by publicly freeing their slaves and concubines, a move that gained worldwide publicity and raised serious questions about the type of regime that the United States and its allies were supporting (Holden and Johns 1981, 221).

The high drama of palace intrigues, moreover, was being played out in an increasingly tense regional environment. The union between Egypt and Syria, which had lasted only three years, had fired the imagination of the Arab world and placed the Saudi monarchy in danger of attack by both Nasser and the revolutionary regime in Iraq. Fear of an Iraqi attack materialized in 1961 when the Iraqi government laid claim to both Kuwait and a large section of Saudi territory. The British stabilized the situation by sending troops to Kuwait, as did the Egyptians and the Saudis.

No sooner had the Iraqi crisis abated than the *imam* of Yemen (religious king) was overthrown by a poorly organized military coup in September of 1962, the leaders of which turned to Egypt for support. The Saudis had little love for the imam but feared the prospect of an Egyptian client state being established on their southern border. In desperation, the Saudis offered refuge to the deposed imam and began providing arms and money to the loyalist tribes. This was not a new process, for Saudi leaders had traditionally influenced Yemeni policy by bribing Yemen's tribal sheikhs, most of whom were in more or less constant revolt against the government. Direct Saudi military intervention was out of the question, for the Saudis' fear of their own military equaled their fear of Nasser. These fears were not unfounded, for the outbreak of the Yemeni Civil War had seen several Saudi pilots defect to Egypt. The Saudis also began to strengthen the National Guard as a counterweight to the regular army. The National Guard had traditionally consisted of little more than irregular tribal levies, but was now transformed into a full-fledged military organization. Tribal ties, however, continued to be a primary qualification for recruitment to the guard.

The war dragged on in Yemen for the next five years with neither side being able to claim victory. Egypt's heavily mechanized army was of little use in Yemen's impenetrable mountains, and Nasser had to content himself with control of the coastal plain and Yemen's few cities. The loyalist tribes, for their part, were no match for the heavy armor of the Egyptians and seldom ventured far from their mountain strongholds. Truces were declared but seldom held for more than a few days. The Egyptians bombed Saudi border towns, leading to fears that an increasingly frustrated Egyptian army would soon invade Saudi Arabia.

Facing disaster on both the domestic and regional fronts, the royal family forced the abdication of Saud in 1964. They had no other choice. The process was a delicate one, as procedures for succession had yet to be established. Jealousies within the family were also intense, with each matrilineal brood fearing for its future. Faisal was to be the new king, but who would follow him?

Abdication procedures began in the early months of 1964 with a procession of tribal sheikhs and senior ulema declaring their support for Faisal. This was followed by the issuance of a *fatwa* (religious judgment) by key ulema declaring Saud unfit to rule. Faisal was thus absolved of his earlier vow to accept Saud as king. This accomplished, some 60 senior princes formally announced their acceptance of the fatwa deposing Saud and indicated their support for Faisal. Only on November 2, 1964, after all of the key elements of power in Saudi Arabia—the tribal sheikhs, the ulema, and the royal family—had been brought in line, did Faisal swear on the Koran to rule Saudi Arabia according to the principles of Islam. It would be another several months before Khalid, the seventh son of Abd al-Aziz, was named crown prince. Saud, now in disgrace, would be forced to make do with an annual stipend of $43 million (Holden and Johns 1981, 239).

Faisal moved rapidly to put the Saudi financial house in order, a process aided by the ever-increasing inflow of oil revenues. Planning proceeded apace, as did efforts to rationalize the political structure. The war in Yemen remained the major preoccupation of Faisal's early years, but faded with the devastating defeat of Egyptian forces in the June War of 1967. Faisal declared a jihad (holy war) against Israel, but Saudi forces did not engage in a war that was over almost as soon as it had begun.

All in all, the dominant themes of Saudi politics during the era of revolution and optimism were confusion and internecine conflict as a tribal monarchy attempted to cope with the dual challenges of sudden wealth and modernity. Both challenges were handled poorly. Much of the country's oil wealth was squandered, and little if any progress was made in developing effective political institutions that would reach beyond the inner circle of the royal family. Indeed, the crowning success of the Saudi regime during the era was its ability to survive the onslaught of the nationalist revolution sweeping the region.

The Era of Reassessment

Although the tide of nationalist emotions had collapsed with the Arab defeat in the June War of 1967, the fate of the Saudi regime was far from certain. The process of institution building was still in its embryonic stages. Corruption was rampant, expenses outstripped revenues, and the Saudi military posed more of a threat to the monarchy than did the country's external opponents. Difficult questions also remained concerning the royal family's role in the Arab defeat. How could the regime retain its ties with the United States, many Saudis wondered, when Israel had just conquered Jerusalem, the third holiest city in Islam, with US support?

A poorly organized conspiracy to overthrow the regime was uncovered in 1969 with the presumed assistance of the CIA (Holden and Johns 1981, 277). The plot had little chance of success, but such was the regime's state of mind that it overreacted with mass arrests.

By 1970, however, Faisal had curbed the appetites of the royal family and the budget was in balance. The same year saw the death of Nasser and the beginning of an upward spiral in oil revenues. Faisal could breathe a sigh of relief on both counts. Corruption and mismanagement continued to plague the system, but the country would soon have more money than its economy could absorb. Indeed, the Arab boycott imposed during the October/Yom Kippur War of 1973 would see oil prices increase from $2.83 at the beginning of the boycott to $10.41 by 1974 (see Figure 5.1). Tensions between the United States and Saudi Arabia resulting from the boycott were a source of profound discomfort for both. The boycott also underscored the profound interdependence of the two countries. The United States needed Saudi support in maintaining world oil prices at reasonable levels, and the royal family was more dependent than ever on the US for its survival.

This mutual interdependence, heretofore based on a multitude of ad hoc arrangements and understandings, was formalized by a series of agreements signed between the two countries in 1974 and 1975. Among other things, the US agreed to modernize the Saudi National Guard and the Saudi Navy. Modern planes were also delivered. Indeed, US arms sales during the period jumped from approximately $500 million at the end of the 1973–74 fiscal year to almost four times that figure by the end of the 1974–75 fiscal year (Holden and Johns 1981, 359). Also implicit in the deal was America's continued willing-

Figure 5.1
Dubai Crude Oil Prices, 1972–1998 (US $/Billions of Barrels)

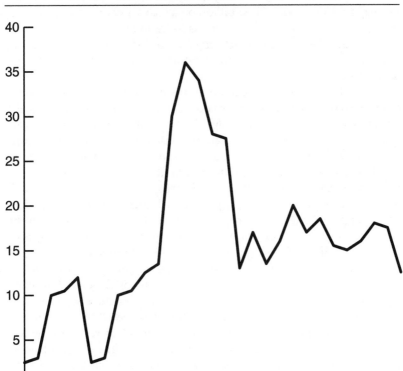

ness to ignore in Saudi Arabia human rights violations that it found objectionable in most other parts of the world. In return, Saudi Arabia stabilized world oil markets by producing more oil than her economic needs dictated. The kingdom was now awash in money.

By 1975, the firm hand of Faisal had guided the affairs of the kingdom for 11 years. Domestic stability had been restored and Saudi Arabia's special relationships with the United States and Egypt had shielded the desert kingdom from its regional adversaries. In large part, domestic stability was a function of a social contract that substituted economic security for political rights. In lieu of political rights, Saudis were encouraged to "enrich yourselves." This process had begun in an organized manner with the proclamation of the kingdom's first five-year development plan in 1970 and mushroomed with the proclamation of the second five-year plan in 1975. Whereas the first five-year plan was modest in scope, the second five-year plan called for the expenditure of some $141 billion on a vast array of projects ranging from port expansion to housing loans (seldom repaid) and everything in between. The austere desert kingdom of ibn Saud was now being transformed into a welfare state in which a pampered Saudi population wanted for little.

By and large, four main techniques were used to distribute the kingdom's vast oil wealth to the Saudi population: welfare, bureaucracy, the private sector, and corruption. Health care, education, and almost anything else that the Saudi population needed was free for the asking, as was a well-paying and minimally demanding job with the government. Those with an entrepreneurial bent were encouraged to start their own businesses, most of which prospered by contracting with the government. Anyone in a position of authority, moreover, had ample opportunities for corruption. The higher one ascended on the elite pyramid, the more abundant the opportunities for corruption. Contracts with the Saudi government required the wasta of a highly placed official, often a prince, and rare was the contract with a foreign company that did not provide a "commission" of 15 percent or more. In some cases, development proposals were designed solely for the sake of gaining a commission. Development experts thus began to distinguish between "good" corruption and "bad" corruption, the former being "commissions" that facilitated the implementation of programs that the country needed while the latter wasted money on useless projects created merely for the sake of acquiring a commission.

There were, of course, problems. Planning was made difficult by uncertain population estimates. Earlier estimates (1962) had placed the Saudi population at 3.3 million but were suppressed for being too small. The royal family had ample reason for being concerned about low population estimates, not the least of which was fear that low population estimates might stimulate attack by their larger neighbors, many of whom were desperately poor. It also seemed inadvisable to advertise the fact that foreign workers, most from other Arab countries, constituted a large share of the Saudi population. By 1973, government estimates placed the population at 5.9 million Saudis and some 700,000 foreigners. A year later, however, a British estimate placed the population at 4.3 million Saudis and 1.5 million foreigners (Holden and Johns 1981, 393). By the turn of the century, government estimates placed the Saudi population at 19.9 million, up from some 17 million in 1992, a remarkable growth rate indeed. Of the 19.9 million, approximately 25 percent were expatriate workers (*Saudi Gazette*, cited in Gulf 2000, Feb. 17, 2000, no. 9).

In addition to not knowing how many people to plan for, the early Saudi development plans were loose affairs that amounted to little more than wish lists compiled by diverse government agencies. With so much money available, spending was easier than planning. Accountability, moreover, had never been a strong point of the Saudi political system.

Faisal was assassinated in March of 1975 by a deranged prince, and Khalid, his half-brother, was proclaimed king. Henceforth, the hand on the tiller would be less firm. Khalid had minimal interest in the affairs of state, and Fahd, now proclaimed crown prince, would emerge as the power behind the throne (Holden and Johns 1981, 387). Fahd was pro-American in outlook and was anxious to strengthen the kingdom's special relationship with the United States. He was also more liberal than the royal family as a whole and far more liberal than the ulema. Also problematic was the fact that both Khalid and Fahd, the crown prince and vice chairman of the Council of Ministers (second deputy prime minister) were members of the Sudari clan, as was Sultan, the minister of defense.[4] The only obstacle to a Sudari sweep was Abdullah, the commander of the now modernized National Guard. In command of his own army, Abdullah would prove to be a powerful adversary.

Saudi policy continued along the course set by Faisal, but the change of leadership would have telling effects as corruption increased and discipline, never a strong point of the Saudi regime, declined. Also pronounced was the royal family's growing domination of the private sector. This was a relatively new development, for ibn Saud had issued a stern warning against mixing business with politics. Harmony demanded that each be supreme in its own realm. This separation was largely honored during the Faisal era, but collapsed under his successors as many of the country's dominant firms now began to acquire royal partners.

The 1970s, then, were an era of profound change for Saudi Arabia. Faisal reined in the worst excesses of the royal family and laid the foundation for a modern bureaucratic state. Once limited to a few key ministries, the Council of Ministers would expand to include a vast array of administrative agencies, most of which were dedicated to infrastructure development and social services. By necessity, Saudi commoners began to play a larger role in the day-to-day management of their country, although key positions remained in the hands of the royal family. The regime's claim to legitimacy, long based upon tribal and religious values, was now strengthened by the evolving social

[4]The king traditionally holds the title of prime minister and the crown prince that of first deputy prime minister.

contract that offered Saudi citizens economic abundance in exchange for political compliance.

The Era of Disillusionment

If the benign international environment of the 1970s had enabled the Saudi regime to consolidate its authority, the advent of the 1980s would test the resolve of the Saudi regime to a degree unknown since the era of Abdul Nasser. Sadat's peace treaty with Israel, moreover, had left the Arab states naked to Israeli attack, and Begin had thrown down the gauntlet by asserting Israel's claim to Jerusalem and the Occupied Territories, leaving the protectors of Islam to respond as they might. The US was an ally of Saudi Arabia, but it was also an ally of Israel. Far more devastating to the Saudi regime was the Ayatollah Khomeini's overthrow of the shah of Iran in 1979, an event which unleashed a wave of religious zeal that threatened to sweep all before it. Khomeini vowed to liberate the birthplace of Islam from a regime that he accused of moral laxity, cowardice, and submission to the infidels. Having long championed Islam against attacks from the left, the royal family now found its Islamic credentials challenged by an Islamic theocracy that undermined the very foundations of its legitimacy. Nor had the Saudis long to wait before the shock waves of the ayatollah's revolution reached the kingdom. In 1979, only months after the ayatollah's proclamation of an Islamic Republic in Iran, Muslim zealots seized the Holy Mosque in Mecca and demanded the creation of an Islamic Republic in Saudi Arabia. Perhaps more damning to the credibility of the royal family was its inability to dislodge the Fundamentalists without the assistance of foreign security forces. The fall of the shah also raised serious questions about the effectiveness of US security guarantees. If the United States had been unable to save the shah, perhaps its most important ally in the region, how would it be able to save the Saudi monarchy?

The 1979 seizure of the Holy Mosque in Mecca was followed in 1980 by a confrontation between police and religious fanatics in the kingdom's Eastern Province. The Eastern Province is home to Saudi Arabia's Shi'a minority, estimated to be between 300,000 and 500,000 in number, many of whom were suspected by the regime of harboring pro-Khomeini sympathies, a fear made all the more plausible by a long history of Sunni oppression of a Shi'a minority viewed as heretics by the puritanical Wahhabis (Dumas 1995; Chabry and Chabry 1987).

Tensions in the Eastern Province were even more ominous when viewed in the broader context of Khomeini's call for a Shi'a rebellion in Iraq (Abir 1993). If such a rebellion were to transpire (and many observers at the time thought that it would), the Islamic revolution would have reached the Saudi border and could well have triggered Shi'a uprisings in the heart of the Saudi oil region. Kuwait, which also possessed a large Shi'a population, would be threatened by internal turmoil as well.

Despite the overt threat posed to the kingdom by Khomeini's Islamic revolution, the king seemed unsure of how to respond. Clearly, it would be awkward for a Saudi regime that based its legitimacy on the protection of Islam to openly oppose an Islamic government which, in the view of many Muslims, had liberated Iran from decades of US domination.

The Saudis made half-hearted gestures to accommodate Khomeini, but both sides realized that accommodation could only be temporary, at best. As always, the regime attempted to bolster its popular support with lavish outlays of money. The kingdom's third five-year development plan (1980–1985) called for spending $235 billion on infrastructure development and social services, a figure that did not include defense expenditures. This represented an increase of almost $100 billion over the expenditures of the second five-year plan, which had terminated the preceding year.

Given the above fears, Iraq's 1980 invasion of Iran was greeted with enthusiasm by the royal family, public dissimulation to the contrary notwithstanding. Indeed, one of the intriguing mysteries of the era remains the role of Saudi Arabia in precipitating the war. Did the Saudis actively encourage the Iraqi attack on Iran with promises of support, a role that they had played with such success in the October War of 1973, or did they merely rush to support an Iraqi invasion that promised to crush the Ayatollah before his revolution could gain momentum (interviews in Saudi Arabia, 1983)?

The outbreak of the Iraq-Iran War in 1980 also served as the catalyst for the formation of the Gulf Cooperation Council, long a major goal of Saudi foreign policy. In reality, the GCC could offer little in the way of its own defense beyond the military capacity of Saudi Arabia, and that capacity, as discussed earlier, remained largely symbolic (An-Nafisi 1982).

Saudi problems, however, had only begun. Oil prices had begun to plummet in 1981, and by 1982 the kingdom was forced to draw upon its financial reserves to meet the expenditures promised in the new five-year plan. Saudi Arabia was also becoming the paymaster in Iraq's war with Iran, a role that further aggravated what the Saudis would refer to as a cash-flow problem.

Adding to the woes of the royal family was a lack of firm leadership. The years since Faisal's assassination in 1975 had seen a lethargic King Khalid increasingly recede into the background as Fahd became the effective ruler of the kingdom. Fahd possessed long experience in government but lacked either the shrewdness or the moral authority of the austere Faisal. His reputation for excess, moreover, was offensive to the religious community, as was his desire to strengthen Saudi Arabia's special relationship with the United States.

Khalid's death in 1982 provoked neither a crisis of succession nor a discernible break in policy, as Fahd had been the effective head of state for some time. Abdullah, the commander of the National Guard, was duly sworn in as crown prince and first deputy prime minister, pitting the conservative Abdullah against the more moderate Sudari clan. In addition to having his own army, Abdullah enjoyed stronger support than the Sudaris in the religious community.

In 1984, Saudi Arabia moved to stabilize oil prices by agreeing to become OPEC's "swing producer." If oil prices dropped, Saudi Arabia would produce less oil; if they increased, it would produce more. This would assure ample revenues for all concerned as long as all OPEC members adhered to their assigned quotas and did not cheat. The plan was a sound one, but the pressures of the Iran-Iraq War, among other things, led to massive cheating and the price of oil continued to decline, reaching a low of less than $10 a barrel in 1986.

A revenue shortfall that had been an annoyance in 1982 had now become a full-blown financial crisis that threatened to exhaust the kingdom's reserves. Urged into action by the severity of the crisis, Fahd threatened to slash expenditures in the forthcoming 1985–1990 development plan and called upon the Saudi population to work harder. The king's statements came as a shock to a Saudi population long accustomed to governmental largess, but the blow was cushioned by promises to create a National Consultative Assembly, some members of which would be drawn from partially elected provincial councils (Abir 1993). In the final analysis, neither the threatened austerity measures nor the consultative assembly were to materialize. The government continued to pamper its citizens, albeit to a lesser degree than that to which they had become accustomed, and the plans for the Assembly passed into oblivion.

Simultaneously, the king moved to strengthen his religious credentials by increasing the power of the ulema and morality police, both of whom had seen their authority eroded during the preceding decade. In much the same vein, 1986 would see the king change his title from a simple "His Majesty" to "His Majesty, the Protector (servant) of the Two Holy Shrines." Irate at the king's move, Khomeini responded to Fahd's arrogation of religious authority by provoking anti-Saudi riots at the 1987 Hajj, with more than four hundred people being killed in the melee. Ruling Saudi Arabia was not as easy as it once had been.

The Iran-Iraq War ground to a halt in 1987, but the psychological war between the royal family and the ayatollah continued. In 1988, Iran boycotted the Hajj in a move designed to embarrass the monarchy, and in 1989, two bombs rocked Mecca on the anniversary of the 1987 riots. To make matters worse, the threat of a physical attack by Iran had merely been replaced by the threat of a battle-tested Iraqi army that was now the largest in the Arab world. Would Saudi Arabia be able to control the monster that it had helped to create?

The 1980s, then, found Saudi Arabia to be in a holding pattern. The decline in oil revenues had forced a reduction in spending, but the regime avoided severe economic disruptions by drawing on its massive financial reserves. By the end of the era, however, these reserves were nearing exhaustion. Far more difficult to parry was the tide of religious zeal inspired by Khomeini's Islamic Revolution. The government responded by imposing even greater demands for piety upon the Saudi population, but made no concessions in the areas of popular representation.

The 1980s, moreover, were not a period without change. The Saudi population continued to be increasingly well educated, and thousands of students returned from the West with hopes of playing a more active role in shaping the affairs of their country. Many also found the forced piety of the kingdom to be an oppressive burden.

The Era of the New World Order

The advent of the 1990s promised the Saudi regime a reprieve from the woes of the preceding decade. The Americans now dominated the region, and the Iran-Iraq War had crippled both of the kingdom's main adversaries. Khomeini had also passed from the scene, depriving the Islamic Revolution of its charismatic leader.

All, however, was not well. The thrust of Khomeini's Islamic Revolution had been blunted, but the balance of power in the Arab world was shifting to the Fundamentalists. The latter were scoring clear gains in Jordan, Lebanon, Egypt, Algeria, and the Sudan, and Fundamentalist groups in Lebanon and the Occupied Territories had begun to dominate the struggle against Israel. Saddam Hussein, moreover, retained a massive army and was less than subtle in demanding that the Gulf states assist in rebuilding his shattered country. Iraq, Saddam Hussein proclaimed, had saved the Gulf from the scourge of Khomeini. Now the oil kingdoms could meet their moral and financial obligations or face the consequences, as yet unspecified.

The main threat to the Saudi regime, however, was internal rather than external. Barring an occasional border scrimmage, the kingdom had been spared from foreign attack by its alliance with the United States. But could the United States protect the monarchy from the enemy within? This was a difficult question to answer, for as noted above, the regime was being increasingly challenged by two contradictory forces: a Westernized middle class demanding greater participation in the affairs of the country and a Fundamentalist movement intent on imposing a Khomeini-type theocracy on the kingdom. The struggle between the House of Saud and the Ikhwan of old had resurfaced.

Also worrisome to the royal family was the growing US military presence in the kingdom. How much Western intrusion would the religious community tolerate before becoming restive? Potential threats from Iraq and Iran required a Western presence in the kingdom, yet that very presence trampled Islamic religious norms and threatened to exacerbate internal opposition.

These concerns were all the more pressing because the king was ill, remote, and had become increasingly uncertain in his decision making. Money, moreover, remained the regime's major asset, and it was in increasingly short supply.

No sooner had the New World Order begun than Saddam Hussein challenged US hegemony by asserting Iraqi sovereignty over Kuwait. The drama was closely watched by all countries in the region, for it would set the tone of regional politics for decades to come. The United States responded to Saddam's initiative with ambivalence, if not confusion. Saudi Arabia, for its part, downplayed the Iraqi threat and resisted a massive buildup of US forces in the kingdom.

Denial changed to ambivalence with the Iraqi invasion of Kuwait on the morning of August 2, 1990. Iraqi troops had overrun Kuwait in a matter of hours and immediately established fortified positions on the Saudi border. Saudi Arabia's initial reaction had been to "open negotiations with Iraq about its intentions" via a hastily constructed "hotline" (*NYT*[5], Oct. 4, 1990, A9). The Saudis also rejected an American request to close an Iraqi pipeline transversing Saudi territory for fear that the action might be construed by the Iraqis as an act of war. These concerns were justified, for Saudi sources estimated that Iraqi forces could overrun the oil-rich Eastern Province in less than 12 hours and the entire country within three days—even less time would be required if Saudi air power proved ineffective (*NYT*, Oct. 4, 1990, A9). Indeed, the Saudi regime was so ambivalent about the proper response to the Iraqi threat that its armed forces remained only partially mobilized at the time of the invasion (*NYT*, Oct. 4, 1990, A9).

[5]The *New York Times*.

Despite Saddam Hussein's assurances that he had no intention of invading Saudi Arabia, Iraqi forces made several temporary incursions into Saudi territory, the resolution of which proved increasingly difficult over the hotline. It was only at this point, according to press reports, that the king made a request for US assistance (*NYT*, Oct. 4, 1990, A9). Prince Sultan, the minister of defense, explicitly stressed that the American forces were to be purely defensive in nature and that the kingdom would not be used as a staging ground for an attack on Iraq (*NYT*, Sept. 2, 1990, 7).

Within a month, some 150,000 US troops were in Saudi Arabia, some 10 percent of whom were women (*NYT*, Sept. 24, 1990, 1). A confrontation ensued between the rights of female GIs and a Saudi regime that imposed strict restrictions on female behavior, including prohibitions on driving. These restrictions, as well as the required veiling of Saudi women and the practice of polygamy, unleashed a hailstorm of criticism against the Saudi regime in the international press. Why, Western feminists asked aloud, was the United States supporting such a regime? Compromises were worked out, with female GIs driving on military installations but refraining from doing so in civilian areas. Female soldiers were also required to wear long sleeves and otherwise do as little as possible to upset Saudi sensibilities. Neither side found the arrangement satisfactory. Presumably there were also Jewish soldiers among the US forces, but neither the Americans nor the Saudis seemed interested in discussing the matter. When European and Arab troops were added to the picture, the size of the foreign presence in the kingdom had become enormous. Unlike the earlier US presence, moreover, the Western buildup could not be confined to segregated compounds. War is a messy business.

Beyond offending religious sensibilities, the war would demonstrate just how vulnerable the Saudi regime had become to outside attack. Despite its sophisticated equipment and occasional flashes of brilliance, the Saudi military had performed poorly. There could no longer be any pretense about the kingdom's ability to protect itself from its powerful neighbors, a list that included Iraq, Iran, Syria, and Israel. The mutual defense provisions of the Gulf Cooperation Agreement had also been discredited, for none of the signatories had come to the aid of Kuwait. Perhaps more disconcerting was Yemeni, Jordanian, and Palestinian support for Saddam Hussein. In this regard, the *New York Times* quoted a senior Saudi official as saying, "What has been proven is that handouts of money do not make friends. We gave tens of millions of dollars to King Hussein and to Arafat and they turned against us" (*NYT*, Mar. 2, 1994). The same source indicated that the kingdom had "given away" some $100 billion since the early 1970s in a continuing effort to buy friends and mollify enemies. Also called into question was the loyalty of the millions of Yemenis and Palestinians working in Saudi Arabia, many of whom cheered Saddam Hussein as a liberator. Saudi dependence on foreign labor had become a threat to the kingdom's security.

Equally problematic was the apparent confusion within the royal family itself over the handling of the crisis. The king remained in Jeddah throughout the crisis, addressing the nation only to announce the arrival of the Americans. Apparently the war was managed by Sultan, the minister of defense and aviation, and his son, Khalid ibn Sultan al Saud, who had taken command of the Islamic forces.

The war drained Saudi Arabia of $55 billion, according to IMF estimates, and in spite of increased oil production, further depleted its financial reserves (Gause 1994). Indeed, the end of the war would see Western banks question the creditworthiness of the kingdom (Gause 1994).

The end of the war brought a rush of damage control. As early as November of 1990, the king promised the establishment of a Consultative Assembly, although the details of the plan remained sketchy. US troops were urged to depart with consummate haste.

The domestic repercussions of the war were not long in coming. No sooner had UN troops arrived in the kingdom than a group of Saudi feminists presented the governor of Riyadh with a petition requesting the right to drive. In addition to coming as a shock to a regime already beleaguered by the events unfolding around it, the action spoke volumes about the context of Saudi politics. The petition read as follows:

> Your Highness, we have known you as an understanding person, you have the spirit of giving to cope with this modern world, believe in the role of working women according to the Islamic teaching, thus, we appeal to you, and on behalf of the ambitious Saudi woman, who strives to serve her country under the guidance of the Custodian of the Holy Cities and his wise government, to open your fatherly heart for us and take care of our human request and that is "Driving a Car" inside Riyadh City, and this request has many justifications; the most paramount of them are as follows:
>
> 1. The existence of a foreign man in the house and the necessity of being with him in the car.
> 2. The financial costs that most families bear as a result of his existence.
> 3. The occurrence of many immoral matters within the houses as a result of the existence of the servant or a driver.
> 4. Our belief in the replacement of men by women in the time of crisis like the one our country is experiencing these days, as a result of the threat from those who harbored evil thoughts against us; these cir-

cumstances ask from men to be in the battle fronts, and from women to secure the home front.

5. Give the woman more confidence in her ability to bear the responsibilities to share in building the nation and contributing in all aspects.

Your Highness, it is only by an objective stance to our request you will notice at the end that we did not ask a right that our religion denies; on the contrary, it is a matter that our religion confirms and supported by the prophet's legacy and his orthodox califas, also to our righteous ancestors; and their dependence on woman's efforts and giving is another evidence on the competence of Islam when it gives everyone what he/she deserves (private document).

The petition was rejected (probably ignored), and a few days later some 45 women drove their cars in a prominent area of the capital city. According to the police report:

They were driving themselves, they were unveiled, many people gathered around this movement which was led by three women, repeating slogans like "Driving," "Liberty," they were raising their arms, and carrying a pamphlet they distributed and claimed that they sent it to the Governor of Riyadh. Behind them were men also supplying them with the pamphlets. People were stunned from what happened, when, the so-called Haussa Almunief got out of her car and said: I am the spokesperson on their behalf, no one touch them with any harm. Then the men of the Committee for the Propagation of Virtue and the Prevention of Vice told her: "You and whoever with you will stop"; "I will speak only with the security men," she said and drove to "Samar Hall" where she asked the security men to follow her, then said, "We want the Governor of Riyadh, we want a royal gift." Then Dr. Faten Alzamel said, "We will never get out of our cars and we will continue till we reach the Emarah (The City Hall)." And when she was asked to get in the back and let a man drive her, she answered, "Nobody but me will drive my car," "I will never belittle myself to speak with the religious men," and when the Director of the Committee of the Propogation of Virtue and the Prevention of Vice came, she ordered her friends to sit in the back of cars, and order only security men to drive, not religious men (private document).

The relevant males (fathers, husbands, brothers) of the offending females were duly chastised, but the incident served notice to the regime that Western troops meant Western reporters. Internal dissidents now played to a world audience.

No sooner had the war ended, moreover, than both liberal and religious groups presented petitions to the king demanding an end to the rampant corruption that had become the hallmark of the royal family. The liberals' petition stressed the need for greater representation in the affairs of government—democracy is too strong a word to use—while the petition of the ulema demanded an end to the moral laxity that had crept into Saudi society. Public petitions are rare events in Saudi Arabia, and both represented a challenge to the authority of the regime. The petition signed by the ulema was particularly damning, for the regime was now more dependent than ever upon the support of its religious leaders. It had also become increasingly clear that the main opposition to the regime was now coming from the religious right (Gause 1994).

In January of 1992, the king responded to the petitions with a call for moderation that included a thinly veiled threat of violence against those who lacked good judgement (Gause 1994). A few months later, he also issued three decrees designed to augment the political structure of the kingdom. Of these, the most important outlined the "Basic System" of Saudi Arabia. The Basic System could not be labeled a constitution, for that would imply the superiority of secular law to the Koran. Lest there be confusion on this matter, the Basic System specified that the Koran was the source of authority in the kingdom. The king was referred to as the ultimate executive authority in the country and also served as prime minister. No mention was made of legislative authority. The judiciary was recognized as an independent branch of government, but the king appointed all judges. All Saudis were equal before the law in conformity with Islamic practice, and both homes and private property were protected by the due process of law. Of particular interest was a provision giving the king the right to name the crown prince. This was a dramatic departure from the existing practice of consultation among the major princes in matters of succession. The very provision of a written document outlining the distribution of authority was also a new step in what had been the most informal of political systems. The other documents consisted of an enabling statute for the long-promised consultative council and a document outlining the system of government for the kingdom's 14 provinces (Gause 1994).

As described by Gause, however, the king's announcements did not quell the concerns of the ulema:

> In the summer of 1992 over one hundred members of the *ulema*, faculty at the religious universities, and other activists signed a forty-six-page "Memorandum of Advice" (*muzakkarat al nasiha*) to the king. It was unprecedented in recent Saudi history for the bluntness of its tone, its detailed critique of a wide range of government policies, and the public nature of its dissemination. Many of its general themes echoed those advanced in earlier, shorter petitions to the king: the need to curb arbitrariness in law enforcement, the need for independent oversight of government financial institutions to prevent corruption, the need for more efficient provision of government services to citizens, and the need for

independent and truthful media to report on government activities. It specifically criticized judicial practices that did not safeguard individual rights and government regulation of economic and personal status which were not sanctioned by the sharia. It was unprecedented in the specificity of its criticisms and suggestions (Gause 1994, 35).

Beyond the provisions outlined above, the petition implicitly demanded religious participation in the areas of foreign policy and economics. If granted, the provisions of the petition would come perilously close to giving the ulema powers equal to those of the royal family (Gause 1994).

The Council of High Ulema, the core of the religious establishment in Saudi Arabia, condemned the petition, but not without dissenting voices. The dissenters would subsequently resign for reasons of health (Gause 1994). The number of dissenting voices was not large, but their very presence on the Council indicated that religious opposition to the regime was not limited to a few radicals.

The 1992 petition was followed by the formation of a Committee to Defend Legitimate Rights. The Committee was founded by religious radicals, all of whom had found their activities restricted by the government. Several fled to London, where the Committee serves as a major voice of the Saudi opposition.

The aggressiveness of the ulema made a large American presence in Saudi Arabia all the more problematic for the regime. That presence, however, would be difficult to avoid, for Saddam Hussein remained in power and was poised to strike as soon as the opportunity presented itself. Much to the chagrin of the Saudis, moreover, the US now seemed intent on using the kingdom as its main base of operation in the Gulf region. Particularly unsettling was a 1992 air attack on Iraq launched from American bases in Saudi Arabia, something the king had vowed would never happen. Were US troops the guests of the regime, or had they become its masters? The monarchy attempted to save face by announcing that the attack had originated in the Gulf, without specifying the country of origin. Clouds also loomed on the economic front as Saudi financial reserves continued to decline with the decreasing price of oil.

The consultative council met for the first time in 1993, and the king announced a major reshuffle of the cabinet designed to instill greater efficiency in the operations of the Government. The king also attempted to appease the religious community by appointing a new Grand Mufti and creating a new Ministry of Islamic Affairs designed to strengthen religious teaching and proselytization (Gause 1994).[6]

[6]The position of Mufti had been vacant for some time.

Despite the king's attempts to accommodate the religious right, September of 1994 would find the Saudi authorities arresting a charismatic preacher for sedition. Between 500 and 1000 of his followers were also arrested, the number varying with the source (*IHT*[7], Sept. 22, 1994, A4; *Economist*, March 18, 1995, 25).

The situation improved little in 1995 as economic pressures continued and a terrorist bomb exploded at a National Guard base in November of that year (*IHT*, Nov. 14, 1995, 1). Five US service personnel were killed and the stability of the regime was thrown into question. To make matters worse, the king had become severely ill toward the end of 1995 and was forced to temporarily cede power to Abdullah at the beginning of 1996. Power would shift between the two men during much of that year, with lines of authority becoming blurred. A second terrorist bomb exploded at a US base in November of 1996, killing 19 service personnel and injuring scores of others. The US accused the Saudis of lax security, and would subsequently complain that the Saudi authorities were failing to cooperate with the United States in the joint investigation of the affair. Little would change during the following year, with the US continuing to accuse Saudi Arabia of failure to cooperate in the investigation of the terrorist bombings. Saudi Arabia, for its part, was becoming increasingly uneasy over the US boycott of Iraq as well as the United States' continuing support of Israel.

Nevertheless, the ensuing years would see Saudi Arabia maintaining its usually placid exterior as the kingdom moved gradually toward a reconciliation with Iran while simultaneously attempting to breathe life into a moribund Gulf Cooperation Council. The air of placidity was enhanced by a sharp rebound in oil prices, easing—at least for the moment—the Saudi "cash flow" problem. Rumors abounded concerning strains within the royal family resulting from Crown Prince Abdullah's emergence as the effective head of state, a topic that will be elaborated upon shortly. Rumors also abounded concerning the growing rift within the Wahhabi religious community, with the younger members of that community being far less sanguine about the Western presence in the kingdom than were their older brethren.

Although these rumors may have had some basis in fact, the overt manifestations of discontent that had marked the mid-1990s abated as a result of tightened internal security and the easing of the Saudi economic crisis. The kingdom also remained free of direct external threats, saber rattling by Saddam Hussein notwithstanding.

Once again, however, it was outside events that would shake the placid exterior of the House of Saud. The first of these was the al-Aqsa

[7]*International Herald Tribune.*

intifada, the Palestinian uprising that erupted in Israel during the latter months of 2000. The second was mounting US pressure on Saudi Arabia to hold escalating oil prices in check, with the US secretary of energy pointedly saying, "I urge—in the strongest terms—that all oil-producing nations recognize that the world needs more oil, not less, and needs it sooner rather than later" (Reuters, Feb. 11, 2000, www).

The royal family thus found itself on the horns of a dilemma. As the self-proclaimed protectors of Islam, the Saudi royal family was duty-bound to support a Palestinian uprising that was rapidly acquiring religious overtones. Failure to do so would fuel already strident accusations that the Saudi regime had sold out to the United States. The more radical elements in the region were also demanding that Saudi Arabia and its Gulf allies employ the oil weapon in support of the Palestinian uprising. Some suggested cutting oil exports to those Western states condoning the Israeli repression of the intifada, while others advocated imposing an intifada tax of one dollar a barrel on all exports, the proceeds of which would be used to extend the intifada.

The Americans, however, were in no mood for increases in oil prices, nor were they in a mood for further escalation of an intifada that threatened to scuttle the Arab-Israeli peace process and throw the region into turmoil. The Saudis shared the US aversion to turmoil in the region, but they were equally sensitive to the growing condemnation of their pro-US position, much of which was coming from the more radical of the Saudi Wahhabis.

The Saudis played a moderating role at the Arab Summit Conference convened in October 2000 to show Arab support for the intifada, but they brushed aside calls for employment of the oil weapon. In its place, they proposed two funds: the Fund of the Jerusalem Intifada with a capital of $200 million to support the families of the martyrs of the intifada, and the al-Aqsa Fund with a capital of $800 million designated to "help preserve the Arab and Islamic characteristics of Jerusalem, and to enable the Palestinians to liberate themselves from dependence on the Israeli economy." Saudi Arabia would contribute one-fourth of the capital for both funds, with the remainder presumably coming from the other oil-producing states (saudiembassy.net/press_release/10-22-00). The crown prince concluded with a pointed criticism of the United States, saying that:

> We view East Jerusalem as an indivisible part of the occupied Arab territories that are covered by the resolutions of the United Nations Security Council...it was expected that Israel would be deterred or at least blamed for its intransigence and practices that run counter to the principles of the Madrid conference and the agreements that it had concluded with the Palestinians. In the light of Israel's behavior and the

> international community's inability to contain or curb it, it would be normal to suspend relations and cancel any links that have grown under the peace process (saudiembassy.net/press_release/10-22-00).

In the final analysis, the Saudis had acted in accordance with the US position, but the rhetoric had changed.

SAUDI ARABIA TODAY AND BEYOND

Saudi Arabia at the dawn of the twenty-first century bears little resemblance to the desert monarchy forged by ibn Saud 100 years ago. Poverty has given way to dazzling wealth, caravan trails to super highways, nomadic Bedouins to burgeoning cities, illiteracy to state-of-the-art schools and universities, illness to world-class hospitals, and tribal warriors to one of the most technologically sophisticated armies in the world.

Invariably, the profound changes that have taken place in the physical structure of Saudi Arabia have resulted in changes in the attitudes and behavior of the Saudi population. Demands for greater "involvement" in the political system have increased, as has debate about the proper expression of religion. Saudi Arabia remains a profoundly religious society, yet "modernizers" find religion to be an essentially personal affair while conservatives press for an ever-greater involvement of the religious authorities in the lives of Saudi citizens (Yamani 1998).

If the "conservatives" and the "modernizers" argue over the proper expression of religion in Saudi society, they find common ground in condemning the excesses of the royal family, which are viewed as an affront to both Islam and modernity.

Saudi society and the Saudi economy have experienced dramatic changes over the course of the past 50 years, but the political system has not. Indeed, the Saudi political system remains much as it was during the days of ibn Saud. All power remains in the hands of the royal family, formal political institutions remain weak, if not ephemeral, and the regime bases its right to rule on its tribal origins and its role as the protector of Islam. It is this tension between an evolving society and a static political system that provides much of the dynamics of Saudi politics. Those dynamics have resulted in a political system that is profoundly cautious. It is also a political system that is often immobilized by pressures from a world that is changing far more rapidly than the regime would prefer. What passes for policy is essentially crisis management.

In the remaining pages of this chapter, we will examine the forces that underlie the extreme caution of the Saudi decision-making process. In so doing, we will have the opportunity to examine the diverse components of the Saudi political system, including the broader cultural, economic, and international environments in which it operates.

Elites and Power in Saudi Arabia: The Royal Family and Religious Leaders

The inner core of the political elite in Saudi Arabia, those individuals with a major voice in the decision-making process, are the surviving sons of ibn Saud, an outline of which appears in Figure 5.2. It is they who run the country.

The core of the Saudi elite possesses six key characteristics: It is closed, old, sick, divided, nervous and cohesive. The closed nature of the elite requires little elaboration. Entrance to the inner circle of the Saudi elite is limited to the sons of ibn Saud. Invariably, that makes them old (see Figure 5.2). Age and lifestyles have resulted in a high incidence of illness. King Fahd has suffered several strokes, while Abdullah, the crown prince and acting head of state, suffers from heart disease (Simons 1998). He has also passed his seventy-fifth birthday. Both age and illness, in turn, dictate that there will be frequent changes of monarch in the coming decades. Periods of succession create a great deal of tension within the royal family, which will add to the caution of the regime and make sustained initiatives difficult.

Intensifying the caution—nay, immobilization—of the royal family are the deep internal strains that divide it. As indicated in Figure 5.2, the major princes represent multiple matrilineal groupings within the royal family. Most are half-brothers, with the Sudaris possessing overwhelming dominance in terms of numbers. Fear of Sudari dominance is very real and threatens the power of the remaining clans. A major showdown within the family was averted when Abdullah was named crown prince following the death of Khalid, thereby assuring that a non-Sudari would be the successor to Fahd. The situation remains uncertain, however, for the sustained illness of Fahd resulted in Abdullah becoming acting king in late 1996, but not without substantial power also being given to Sultan, the Minister of Defense and a Sudari. Indeed, that period would see "rumors among Arab diplomats of an unexpected state of alert...in the Saudi military, with suggestions of mounting conflict among the princes" (Simons 1998, 306). Kinship rivalries are intensified by sharp debates over the pace of change within the kingdom. While some princes stress the need to bring Saudi Arabia in line with the dramatic changes occurring beyond its borders, others see change as a threat to both the regime and its Islamic

Figure 5.2
Major Sons and Grandsons of Abd al-Aziz bin Abd al-Rahman bin Faysal al Saud

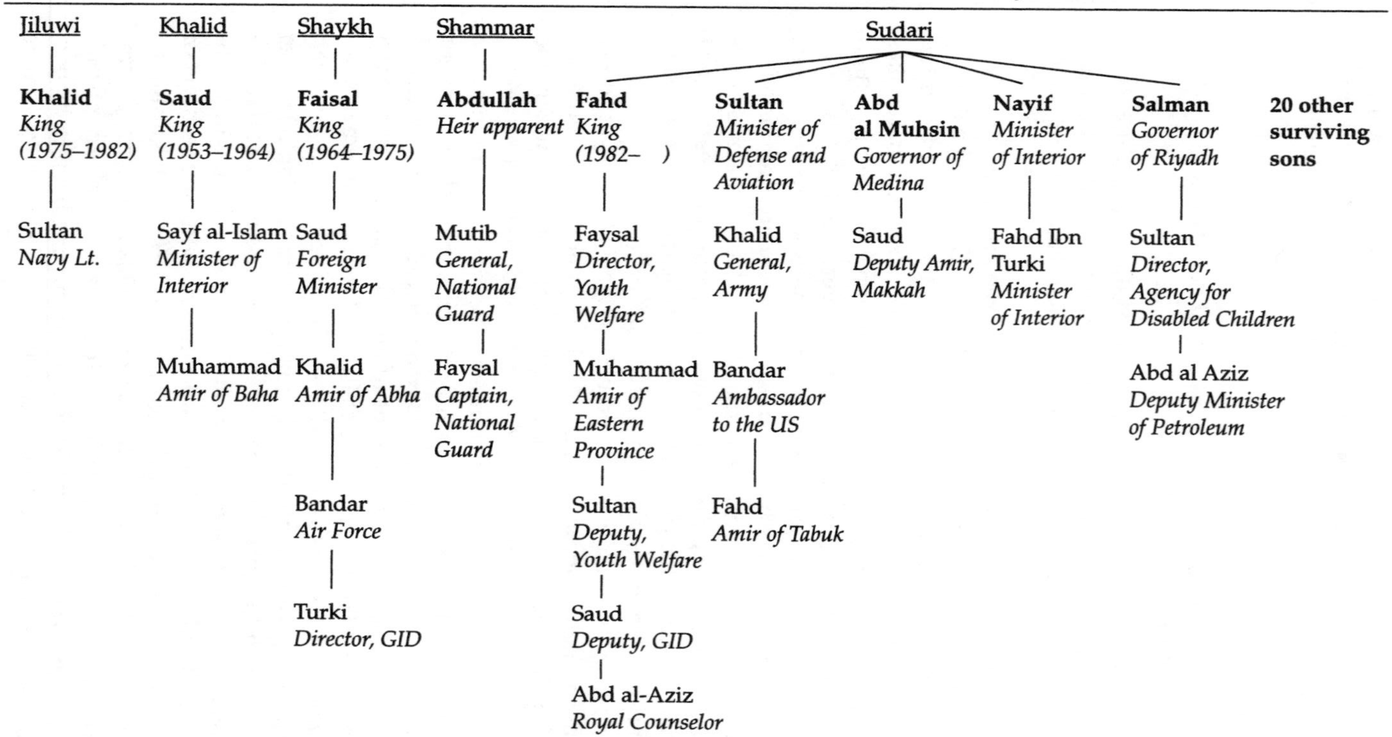

Jiluwi
- **Khalid** — King (1975–1982)
  - Sultan — Navy Lt.

Khalid
- **Saud** — King (1953–1964)
  - Sayf al-Islam — Minister of Interior
  - Muhammad — Amir of Baha

Shaykh
- **Faisal** — King (1964–1975)
  - Saud — Foreign Minister
  - Khalid — Amir of Abha
  - Bandar — Air Force
  - Turki — Director, GID

Shammar
- **Abdullah** — Heir apparent
  - Mutib — General, National Guard
  - Faysal — Captain, National Guard

Sudari
- **Fahd** — King (1982–)
  - Faysal — Director, Youth Welfare
  - Muhammad — Amir of Eastern Province
  - Sultan — Deputy, Youth Welfare
  - Saud — Deputy, GID
  - Abd al-Aziz — Royal Counselor
- **Sultan** — Minister of Defense and Aviation
  - Khalid — General, Army
  - Bandar — Ambassador to the US
  - Fahd — Amir of Tabuk
- **Abd al Muhsin** — Governor of Medina
  - Saud — Deputy Amir, Makkah
- **Nayif** — Minister of Interior
  - Fahd Ibn Turki — Minister of Interior
- **Salman** — Governor of Riyadh
  - Sultan — Director, Agency for Disabled Children
  - Abd al Aziz — Deputy Minister of Petroleum

20 other surviving sons

Sources: www.saudiroyals.com; Jerichow, Anders. 1998. *The Saudi File: People, Power, Politics.* Surrey, GB: Curzon; Lacey, Robert. 1981. *The Kingdom.* New York: Harcourt Brace; Long, David. 1997. *The Kingdom of Saudi Arabia.* Gainesville: University Press of Florida; McLoughlin, Leslie. 1993. *Ibn Saud: Founder of a Kingdom.* Houndmills Basingstoke Hampshire: Macmillan.

Note: The underlined names are matrilineal groupings within the royal family. The names in bold designate the major sons of ibn Saud.

faith. Interestingly enough, this debate tends to pit the Sudaris, who incline toward more rapid change, against their half-brothers, and particularly crown prince Abdullah, who do not. Further conflict centers on issues of foreign policy, with the Sudaris favoring closer cooperation with the United States while Abdullah and many other princes want to ease Saudi dependence on the United States and pursue a more nationalistic "Arab" policy.

The Saudi elite is also exceedingly preoccupied with security (Safran 1988). This nervousness is not difficult to understand, for as elaborated in the historical review, the regime has been a frequent target of both foreign aggression and internal subversion. Adding to Saudi worries have been the dramatic swings in oil revenues and the increase in Fundamentalist emotions. Depressed oil prices threatens the regime's support among a middle class long accustomed to handouts, while Fundamentalism challenges the regime's religious legitimacy. Whatever its origins, this pervasive sense of insecurity has made the Saudi elite reluctant to embark upon new initiatives that might upset either a major group within Saudi society or its regional neighbors. The insecurity of the Saudi elite also goes a long way toward explaining the repressiveness of the regime and its unwillingness to allow any form of mass political expression.

The cohesiveness of the royal family is, by and large, a function of their mutual insecurity. They either stand together or fall together. Be this as it may, a pervasive tension exists between the need for cohesiveness and the tendency of individual princes, all of whom are powerful individuals in their own right, to go it alone on key issues. Sons of the major princes, grandsons of ibn Saud, are rapidly consolidating their position as the elite in waiting, and now occupy key positions in the military and administration.

The Basic System recognizes grandsons of ibn Saud as being eligible for succession to the crown, and also stipulates that the king will name the crown prince. This represents a sharp deviation from the established practice, which saw the major princes select the crown prince from among themselves. Barring infirmity or lack of interest, the choice was invariably the eldest of the major princes. The new law seemingly allows the king to elevate his son (or any one of the eligible grandsons) to the position of crown prince, thereby sidelining the remainder of the royal family. Crown Prince Abdullah, for example, does not have a brother, but he does have a son. If Mutib, Abdullah's eldest son and deputy commander of the National Guard (Abdullah is the commander) is named crown prince, the line of succession could potentially follow that of Abdullah (Simons 1998). Needless to say, this prospect causes some consternation among the major princes.

Lesser positions of importance are occupied by the some 6000 princes—detractors suggest a figure of 30,000—who constitute the base of the royal family. Most are "cadet" members of the royal family, a designation that indicates that they are not in line to the throne. Many hold sensitive positions and are referred to as "His Highness" but not as "His Royal Highness" (Saudi Royals, Online Bios, 1999–2000, www). The size of the royal family adds four critical dimensions to Saudi politics. First, the family is able to occupy key positions at all levels of government in Saudi Arabia, including the bureaucracy, the military, and the local governments. Very little escapes the purview of royal family. Second, most princes of standing hold weekly sessions in which they address the problems of supplicants and grant favors. In the best of feudal traditions, this practice enables the royal family to build personal links with its subjects. It is not the state that provides, but a generous and compassionate monarchy. Third, the vast size of the royal family places it in competition with an emerging middle class for government positions and economic opportunities. It is an unequal competition that leads to considerable frustration among the Saudi middle class. Finally, a large share of the Saudi budget goes to finance the royal family and their royal lifestyle. If Saudi Arabia is experiencing a "cash flow" problem, the source of the problem is not hard to find. As Viorst writes:

> Unlike his predecessors, King Fahd is said to impose no limits on family members' spending. Some 5,000 princes and an equal number of princesses continue to receive large stipends every month for no work. The Sauds still build lavish palaces and pocket huge commissions on foreign contracts, and they pay nothing for utilities, airplane tickets, and other state services. For the first time, moreover, the king is said to condone the princes' muscling in, Mafia-style, on private businessmen. These practices are straining the patience of a class that has always been loyal to the status quo (Viorst 1996, 6).

The major princes are followed in order of importance by the senior ulema, a category that would include the Mufti, the Ministers of Waqfs and Justice, senior officials in the Ministries of Education and Higher Education, and the members of the Council of High Ulema. They may also include the members of the Supreme Council for Islamic Affairs, a new body created in 1994 to promote the influence of younger Islamic scholars whose views are more likely to parallel those of the regime than are those of the older religious elite (Joseph 1998).

It is this religious elite that certifies the religious credentials of the royal family, a position that gives them inordinate influence in the Saudi scheme of things. Indeed, it is doubtful that the regime could survive a rebellion in the ranks of the senior ulema. As described by Abir:

Travellers coming from Saudi Arabia at the beginning of January 1991 reported that King Fahd and his regime were being openly attacked in sermons in different mosques in the kingdom, the Hijaz included. The "neo-fundamentalist" theologians denounced the intention to fight for the disliked Kuwaitis and advocated that negotiations be opened with Iraq. They chastised Fahd for becoming an American tool and the Egyptian and Syrian troops for supporting him.

Opposition among the other ulema to the American presence in the kingdom (but not to the government's policies) was also on the increase, as many Saudis believed that the US would not relinquish its bases in the kingdom after the war. Yet, the great majority of the establishment ulema continued to support the regime and its policy despite their concern about foreign influences on the Saudi society. Indeed, Shaykh Muhammad bin Salih, considered the second-ranking (establishment) *'alim*[8] in the kingdom, announced that the presence of the American soldiers in the kingdom 'was the lesser of two evils' [sic] and, thus, was a sufficient justification for the invitation extended by the government to the American troops (Abir 1993).

Members of the religious establishment, as one might expect, exert a pervasive influence on Saudi politics. They control religious universities in Mecca, Medina, and Riyadh, as well as several government agencies including the Agencies for Religious Research, Legal Opinion, Propaganda and Guidance, and the Committee on Public Morality (the religious police) (Joseph 1998). The profound conservatism of the ulema also adds to the caution of the royal family, for they cannot risk a break with the religious establishment.

Despite their mutual interdependence, relations between the royal family and the religious establishment have not been free from tension. In part, this tension has centered on conflicts over the pace of modernization, with the monarchy being far less conservative than the ulema. More fundamentally, tension between the two elites represents a basic struggle for supremacy. This struggle has existed from the founding of the Saudi dynasty, with Abd al-Wahhab proclaiming himself the Pontiff, or Supreme Sheikh, and ibn Saud adopting the title of General of the Wahhabis (de Corancez 1995, 8). The battle was revived in 1926, with the Ikhwan not being fully defeated until 1930. A religious revolt is unlikely, but it is another source of worry for the royal family.

Secondary elites in Saudi Arabia fall roughly into two categories. First are the leaders of the modernizing middle class. Although commoners, they fill those senior positions in the bureaucracy, military,

[8]The word *'alim* means "scholar." It is the singular version of *ulema*.

and the private sector that have not been preempted by the royal family. Most are well educated, many with advanced degrees from universities in the West. The modernizing elite is offset by the more conservative leaders of the middle and lower class, most of whom view modernization as a threat to Islamic values. They too occupy important positions in the religious, bureaucratic, military, and business communities. Even here, however, the picture is complex, for the modernizers are not, by and large, anti-religious. Rather, they advocate a more flexible program of modernization within an Islamic context. The inherent tension between the two sets of secondary elites adds to the caution of the royal family, as does their mutual concern over the family's excesses. Important tribal chiefs also constitute part of the secondary elite, but their influence has waned in recent years.

The Political Institutions of Saudi Arabia: Their Formal and Informal Roles

The two basic political institutions of Saudi Arabia are the Koran and the kinship ties that bind the royal family. Both exert a profoundly conservative influence on Saudi politics. By acknowledging the Koran as the Constitution of Saudi Arabia, the royal family finds it difficult to expand beyond a system of politics that evolved in a far simpler time. The basic principles are valid, but the practice of politics in an era of globalization involves adaptations unforeseen by the Koran. Particularly knotty is the Koranic prohibition against payment of interest, an issue that has resulted in a strangely contorted banking system that issues depositors a share of the bank's profits rather than interest. Profits are allowed by the Koran; interest is not. The position of the Koran as the constitution of Saudi Arabia also increases the power of the senior ulema, for they are its arbiter.

The royal family, in turn, is the locus of all secular authority in Saudi Arabia, with the Basic Law stipulating that "The dynasty right shall be confined to the sons of the Founder, King Abd al-Aziz bin Abdul Rahman al Saud (ibn Saud), and the sons of the sons" (see Figure 5.2). The most eligible among them shall be invited, through the process of "bai'ah," to rule in accordance with the Book of God and the Prophet's Sunna (Article 5b, Saudi Arabian Information Resource, www). A citizen shall pledge allegiance to the king on the basis of the Book of God and the Prophet's Sunna, as well as on the principle of "hearing is obeying" both in prosperity and diversity, in situations pleasant and unpleasant (Article 6). Aside from the obligation to "rule in accordance with the Book of God and the Prophet's Sunna," there are no formal constraints on the authority of the king and the royal family.

As sovereignty resides with the royal family, Saudi political institutions have no formal legitimacy or source of power other than that granted to them by the royal family. For all practical purposes, the royal family is the state. The king serves as the prime minister of Saudi Arabia; the crown prince as the deputy prime minister. The cabinet is named by the king and serves at the pleasure of the king, as do members of the consultative council, military officers, and all other senior officials in the kingdom. All ministries considered key to the security of the regime are headed by senior princes, foremost among which are the Ministries of Defense, Interior (police) and National Guard. Less sensitive ministries are headed by technocrats, with the exception of the Ministry for Islamic Affairs, Endowments, Dawa and Guidance and Ministry of Justice, which are controlled by the ulema. The ulema also play a major role in the Ministries of Education and Higher Education.

The monarchy exercises its authority through a variety of formal institutions, the most important of which are the Council of Ministers, a massive bureaucracy guided by the Council of Ministers, the security apparatus including the military, Council of High Ulema, and the consultative council.

The Council of Ministers possesses both formal and latent functions. Its formal functions are to execute the decisions of the ruling princes and otherwise manage the kingdom's substantial bureaucracy. The latent function of the Council of Ministers is to forge a link between the regime and the secondary elite, most of which is drawn from the middle classes. Cabinet ministers supervise the spending of vast sums of money and, as such, have vast amounts of patronage at their disposal. This patronage is filtered through kinship and patron-client networks, a process that assures that key segments of the population have a stake in the system, not the least of which are the tribes, the clergy, the business community, and the bureaucrats.

The Bureaucracy   The formal role of the Saudi bureaucracy is to execute the decisions of the senior princes, as defined by the Council of Ministers. The bureaucracy is also responsible for providing the Saudi population with a reasonable level of services. Its performance in both areas has been abysmal.

The poor performance of the Saudi bureaucracy is not difficult to understand. Positions in the Saudi bureaucracy were designed to provide the Saudi middle class, now increasingly well educated, with their share of the nation's wealth. In the past, salaries were high, demands few, and performance minimal. Much of the work that got done was carried out by foreigners, especially in the technical fields. This posed minimal problems during the boom years of the 1980s, but

Saudi Arabia is now faced with a "cash flow" problem and is demanding that Saudi officials pull their weight. Indeed, one of the main goals of the Sixth Five-Year Plan (1999) is the Saudization of the bureaucracy (US Energy Information Administration, Jan. 1999, www).

Unfortunately, Saudi officials view their jobs as a right and have developed a distaste for hard work. If the government carries through with its pledge to reduce its dependence on foreigners—and it may not have a choice in the matter—the quality of services will decline dramatically. If it attempts to reform the bureaucracy by reducing excess staff, it threatens to politicize a middle class that it has bribed to be docile. Either way it loses. The same is true of Government promises to curb corruption, much of which is channeled through the bureaucracy. This, too, was a part of the regime's income distribution system. The informal influence of the bureaucracy, then, is essentially negative. It consumes vast resources, provides an obstacle to effective government, and thrives on corruption. Reform is often promised, but implementation efforts have been largely symbolic. How does one reform a bureaucracy built on patronage without threatening the regime that created it? Saudis, for their part, tend to blame the poor performance of their bureaucracy on the presence of too many foreigners, most of whom are only concerned with "ripping off" the Saudis. Needless to say, these differing explanations of Saudi Arabia's bureaucratic problems have led to tension between Saudi officials and the expatriates they supervise.

The Security Services   The same duality between formal and informal functions permeates the security services, a category that includes the regular military, the National Guard, and various intelligence services, the details of which remain sketchy. The formal function of the security services is to protect the regime from its enemies, whether foreign or domestic. Its informal function, as in the case of the bureaucracy, is to provide jobs and patronage for the regime's supporters. Patronage, however, cannot guarantee the loyalty of the military, and the royal family is ever alert to the possibility of a military coup.

Saudi efforts to preclude a military coup take a variety of forms. Sensitive leadership positions remain in the hands of the royal family, and the military is closely watched by various intelligence services. An emphasis has also been placed on hardware rather than manpower, a smaller army being easier to control than a large one. Indeed, Saudi Arabia is one of the largest importers of arms in the Third World. Fancy hardware has other uses as well. Generals like sophisticated weapons even if they are beyond the technical capacity of their troops.

Sophisticated hardware also plays well in parades, inspires the confidence of the masses, and serves as a warning to adversaries, of which the Saudis have many. As mentioned earlier, members of the National Guard are recruited from among Saudis with Bedouin backgrounds, thereby increasing the likelihood that they will share the regime's conservative tribal and religious values. Finally, the regular military and National Guard are pampered with high salaries, cars, excellent housing, and superior health care. The perks of the National Guard are the best of the best (Dahy 1988).

The price of this elaborate system of control has been high. The military consumes an inordinate share of the national budget, but does little to deter the kingdom's external enemies (see Figure 4.1). Distrust of the military adds to the caution of the regime and has increased its dependence on US protection. Even Saudi participation in the Gulf War was largely "supportive," as most of the fighting was done by UN forces.

The Consultative Council   The formation of a consultative council was proclaimed in the tense days following the Gulf War, and its first session was held in 1993. The establishment of such a council had been promised during several earlier crises but had failed to materialize.

As presently constituted, the consultative council consists of 90 members selected by the king. The council is charged with advising the king on a wide range of policy issues, but possesses no legislative authority. Indeed, the Basic Law goes out of its way to stipulate that the consultative council is an expression of administrative rather than legislative authority. By and large, the members of the consultative council are both well educated and politically colorless, a combination of attributes that fits well in the Saudi political milieu (Dekmejian 1998, 11).

Although exercising no real power, the consultative council plays three roles of importance to the monarchy. First, and much like the Council of Ministers, the consultative council provides a link between the royal family and important segments of the Saudi population including both the "Islamic traditionalists and liberal modernizers" (Dekmejian 1998, 211). As such, the council is part of the patronage system that addresses the needs of important groups. Tribes are not represented directly on the council; their affairs being handled through alternate channels (Dekmejian 1998, 214). Second, the consultative council has been particularly effective in suggesting adjustments to the kingdom's archaic commercial and legal procedures. Such adjustments are much needed, yet pose no threat to the monarchy. Third, the consultative council helps to counter criticism of the Saudi system in the West by serving as a symbol of embryonic democracy.

The danger of the consultative council to the monarchy, of course, is that it does represent an embryonic legislature, statements to the contrary notwithstanding. Kuwait and Iran both have established meaningful legislatures, and pressure is mounting on Saudi Arabia to do the same.

The Council of High Ulema   The ulema are headed by the Council of High Ulema, a body created by the king to certify that the royal family rules "in accordance with the Book of God and the Prophet's Sunna." As such, the Council of High Ulema is the monarchy's first line of defense against its religious critics. The Basic Law goes out of its way to justify the monarchy's role as the protector of religion, with Article 23 stipulating that "The State shall protect the Islamic Creed and shall cater to the application of Sharia. The State shall enjoin good and forbid evil, and shall undertake the duties of the call to Islam." In return for its support, the Council of High Ulema has been given management of Saudi Arabia's religious institutions and is allowed to censor the content of educational and cultural materials, including the mass media. It also guides the judicial process and keeps the lower ranks of the ulema in line.

The strict application of sharia (Islamic) law by the Wahhabi religious establishment—including amputations for theft and public execution for murder, drug trafficking, and rape—has led to severe criticism of the Saudi regime by human rights groups such as Amnesty International, a charge summarily rejected by Saudi Minister of Justice Abdullah al-Sheikh: "Those who raise doubts that sharia law does not guarantee human rights are the enemies of God, religion and humanity and their hearts are full of hatred." He went on to note that the critics "have misled many people with lies and fallacies which they spread through the media" (Associated Press, May 10, 2000, cited in Movement for Islamic Reform in Arabia, May 1–14, 2000).

The power of the ulema also finds expression in the presence of *mutawwatin*, or religious police, as well as in the large number of religious universities, the graduates of which have difficulty finding jobs outside of an already overstaffed religious sector. It is largely they who staff the religious police.

The king appoints the members of the Council of High Ulema, who are officials of the state, as are all members of the ulema. This gives the palace a high degree of control over the religious establishment, but that control is far from absolute, and the monarchy is facing increasing pressure from the ulema to slow the pace of modernization in the kingdom.

Summary: The Roles of Saudi Political Institutions   In sum, Saudi political institutions influence the Saudi political process in four fundamental ways. First, they give representation to important groups in Saudi society. That representation is not democratic in nature, but it does give key groups access to the regime. Second, the Saudi political institutions are a key mechanism for the distribution of wealth. In part, that distribution takes the form of salaries and benefits; in part it takes the form of regime-sanctioned corruption. Whatever the route taken, the wealth of the kingdom does trickle down to a broad segment of the Saudi population. Third, the weakness of Saudi political institutions taxes both the budget and the patience of the Saudi population. It also limits the capacity of the monarchy to implement its projects and perpetuates Saudi dependence on foreign labor. Fourth, Saudi political institutions represent a potential threat to the regime. The security services possess a monopoly of coercive force and must be kept under constant surveillance. The Council of High Ulema symbolizes the tension that has always existed between the monarchy and the ulema. The existence of a consultative council must ultimately give way to demands for a more representative parliament.

Aside from the problems outlined above, perhaps the most glaring defect of the Saudi institutional structure is that it does not provide avenues for peaceful change. There are no formal mechanisms for the resolution of conflict, nor are there formal mechanisms for the Saudi population to express discontent with the regime.

The Group Basis of Saudi Society: Politics in the Absence of Civil Society

Saudi Arabia does not possess a civil society as the term is normally used in the West. There are no elections, public opinion polls, political parties, student or labor unions, or political groups. Even random gatherings are broken up by the security apparatus. Newspapers abound but offer little more than pictures of the royal family and sporting news. Editors have little choice in the matter, for all forms of media are subject to political and religious censorship. Satellite dishes are forbidden, but exist in great profusion. The people have spoken.

Those groups that do exist are either business groups or benevolent associations sponsored by the Islamic establishment, both of which are tightly controlled by the state.[9] Business associations come closest

[9]By 1998, for example, there were some 142 charitable organizations in existence (Government of Saudi Arabia, 1998, Statement Before the Preparatory Committee for the World Summit for Social Development, www).

to resembling Western-style pressure groups and provide a link between the regime and the modernizing middle class. As described by Abir and *Al-Nashura*:

> The Council of the Saudi Chambers of Commerce and Industry, representing the upper layers of businessmen, industrialists and contractors, is located in Riyadh. It plays an essential role in consolidating middle-class support for the royal family and consequently is believed to enjoy a lot of influence over the regime. It is the only major organisation in the kingdom to elect its officers (two-thirds of its governing board are elected and a third are appointed by the minister of commerce), has its own publications and is permitted complete freedom within the scope of its interests (*Al-Nashura*, Sept. 8, 1986, 23–24).

> Still opposed to any form of professional organisations, the Saudi government in the second part of the 1980s gave its blessing to professional congresses of university professors, engineers, doctors, pharmacists, chemists, and others, whose numbers in the kingdom had grown dramatically since the 1970s. In the first congress of engineers, which took place in Jedda, some participants proposed that the congress request government permission to form a professional organisation. Although the proposal was not adopted, it was another milestone in the process of consolidating the new elites' power in Saudi Arabia. Similar demands resurfaced in the wake of the Gulf War (Abir 1993, 115).

Saudi efforts to slow the evolution of civil society are easy to understand. Most political activity is group activity, and the suppression of civil society is designed to prevent opposition groups from becoming organized. Political rallies would generate demands for greater representation, just as political groups would propose alternate candidates for the leadership of the country. It is also likely that the emergence of political parties would fragment a society struggling desperately to create a sense of national identity and national purpose. Modernizers would contend with conservatives, religious moderates with religious extremists, Hijazis with Najdis. A free mass media, in turn, would risk offending deeply entrenched religious sentiments. It is not clear that the fabric of Saudi Arabia could withstand such strains.

The suppression of civil society, however, is not without its costs. Parties, associations, public opinion polls, and a free press provide leaders with important feedback about the public mood. As a result, problems can be solved before they reach crisis proportions. The Saudi regime, however, must operate without a barometer of public sentiment, its only feedback being that provided by the secret police and periodic outbreaks of violence (Champion 1999). Lacking clear feedback on popular sentiments, the regime tends to become increasingly cautious and diffident. Better to be safe than sorry. Problems are not dealt with until they reach crisis proportions, Saudi hesitancy prior to the Gulf War being a case in point.

The absence of a civil society in Saudi Arabia does not mean an absence of group pressures in the Saudi political process. As noted in the above discussion, the ulema are a powerful group well skilled at pursuing their interests. So, too, are the military, the bureaucracy, the business community, the tribes, and the broader reaches of the royal family. Each has a paramount interest in preserving its special position in Saudi society. The modernizers and the conservatives constitute less well-defined groups, yet each represents a central current in the Saudi ideological debate (Dekmejian 1998). The debate takes place within the royal/religious framework of Saudi politics, with each side arguing how this best of all possible worlds could be made even better by greater or lesser degrees of modernization (Nehme 1994; Al-Rasheed 1996a, 1996b). The same debate permeates the military, bureaucracy, the royal family, and even the ulema. Modernization, in this regard, should not be equated with a decline in religiosity. Rather, the debate involves the expression of religion in Saudi society (Nehme 1995).

As mentioned earlier, a large middle class has evolved in Saudi Arabia, much of it educated in the West. While the middle class generally inclines toward the modernizing camp, many of its members remain conservative in outlook. The middle class also divides along Hijazi and Najdi lines (Abir 1993). The more urban Hijazis, once the backbone of the Saudi Arabian bureaucratic and technocratic class, have now seen their position in these areas challenged by an increasingly well educated Najdi middle class (Abir 1993). However fragmented, the Saudi middle class is vitally concerned about its economic and political positions. Members of the middle class want greater participation in the political system, although this does not necessarily mean Western-style elections. They also want to see the economic perks of the boom years maintained, and most are frustrated by the "royal ceiling." This frustration has become all the more evident since the era of rapid economic development has peaked. Young Saudis no longer return with Western doctorates to become deans and directors. Indeed, Saudi Arabia is now facing an unemployment problem that is particularly severe among women and graduates of its Islamic universities. As Yamani writes:

> Today, there are more girls at schools and universities in Saudi Arabia than boys, and their results are academically getting better than their male counterparts (from below 10 percent at the beginning of this century, the national literacy rate stands today at an average in excess of 65

percent, with 80 percent male and 50 percent female). The biggest challenge in the future will be finding appropriate employment for these educated women in a balanced formula that both adheres to Islamic principles and meets the heightened expectations of this important portion of the population. In view of the five million foreign workers in the Kingdom and the limited employment opportunities available at present to our educated women, the issue of replacing some of the foreigners by male and female Saudis becomes a serious economic necessity. A "Saudisation" strategy has been promoted by the government, but it is only partially successful with the private sector which logically seeks maximised profitability as an operational priority. Furthermore, Saudisation has not really addressed the sensitive issue of widespread female employment (Yamani 1998, 28).

In much the same vein, Champion cites a senior official of the Saudi Chamber of Commerce as saying that "nobody has accurate figures" on unemployment, but that estimates range from 10 to 20 percent (Champion 1999, 4).

While the regime has accommodated the groups upon which its survival depends, that has not been the case for Saudi women, the Shi'a, or the expatriate workers. Women, although increasingly well educated, continue to be secluded and can travel only in the company of a male relative, such as a husband, father, or brother (US Department of State, 1998). As the driving "incident" of 1990 illustrated, many Saudi women have become restive with the traditional ways. Increased education and the frustrations of unemployment will inevitably add to their restlessness.

Saudi women are not powerless, for much Saudi wealth is now in the hands of females. Change will continue to be slow, however, for efforts to allow females greater personal freedom must inevitably clash with ultraconservative values of the religious establishment. To date, a tenuous compromise exists between the two forces. Women are educated in segregated schools and view televised lectures of male professors. Few women enter the work force, and those who do have jobs are required to work in "secure" environments in which they are adequately segregated from their male counterparts. It is not clear, however, how long this compromise can last, for education is a poor recipe for docility.

The Shi'a of the Eastern Province are also among the dispossessed, a topic discussed earlier. Totally lacking in rights and influence are Saudi Arabia's approximately five million foreign workers, many of whom were sympathetic to Iraq during the Gulf War. Had the war not been one of the briefest in history, their activities could well have destabilized the regime. Workers of questionable loyalty were forced to leave the country following the war, with many being replaced by workers from Sri Lanka, the Philippines, and other Asian countries. Not only are East Asians politically docile, but they also work for lower wages.

The most threatening opposition to the Saudi regime, as stressed throughout the discussion, comes from the religious extremists. Although little is known of the size or structure of extremist groups, the possibility of terrorism by religious extremists remains a threat to the regime, as do their ties to foreign powers (Iran) and their moral condemnations of the regime (Fandy 1999; Al-Rasheed 1996c; Dekmejian 1994).

THE CONTEXT OF SAUDI POLITICS

Having examined the basic elements of the Saudi political system, we turn now to the broader cultural, economic, and international contexts that shape Saudi politics. These influences on Saudi politics are not a minor consideration, for the four pillars of the Saudi regime—tribalism/kinship, Islam, wealth, and the special relationship with the United States—all belong to this category.

Political Culture

The political culture of Saudi Arabia possesses several dimensions, all of which have a direct influence on the behavior of the Saudi regime. Most help to explain its conservatism and extreme caution. The first point to be noted is that kinship ties continue to provide the foundation of Saudi society, a fact amply demonstrated by the power of the royal family (Long 1997). Saudis are intensely close to their families, and most find their clans and tribes to be a vital support group. A survey of student attitudes during the late 1980s, by way of illustration, found that Saudi students would choose a moderate-paying job close to their families over a higher-paying job in a different city (Al-Nimir and Palmer 1982).

The regime goes out of its way to strengthen traditional family values, with the Basic Law stating that "The family is the nucleus of Saudi society. Its members shall be brought up imbued with the Islamic creed which calls for obedience to God" (Article 9), and "The State shall take great pains to strengthen the bonds which hold the family together and to preserve Arab Islamic values" (Article 10). This is not idle verbiage, for as noted in earlier discussion, the National Guard goes out of its way to recruit individuals from tribal backgrounds because of their greater attachment to the kinship and religious values upon which the regime bases its legitimacy.

The regime's stress on kinship also has its drawbacks. Ties to the tribe are probably stronger than ties to the nation, and as the earlier military example illustrates, the regime is particularly anxious to recruit members of "friendly" tribes. Efforts are also made to maintain a balance between tribes, thereby precluding any one tribe from becoming predominant. It is also interesting to note that a recent study sponsored by the Saudi government found that 56 percent of all marriages in Saudi Arabia are "between first and second cousins or more distant relatives" (*Washington Post*, Jan. 16, 2000, A10).

There can be little doubt that most Saudis take pride in Saudi Arabia's position as the heartland of Islam. Arabs, in general, believe that they occupy a special place in Islam, a view that is particularly strong among the residents of the Arabian Peninsula. Such views have been reinforced by the country's oil wealth, which many Saudis believe to be a sign of God's blessing. The regime is actively pursuing efforts to strengthen this sense of Saudi identity, but like so much in Saudi Arabia, data on the topic is scant (Nehme 1994).

Pride in their Islamic heritage is but one manifestation of a Saudi society that is profoundly religious. Religion pervades all dimensions of Saudi life and, as discussed throughout this chapter, is indivisible from politics. Islamic topics constitute about one-third of the curriculum of elementary schools, and approximately the same proportion of Saudi university students major in Islamic studies (Joseph 1998, 2). The monarchy presumably gains legitimacy from its role as the protector and propagator of Islam, but it is also constrained by the very intensity with which its citizens adhere to their religious values (Joseph 1998).

Saudi political culture is also characterized by a profound sense of apathy, a phenomenon that could be attributed to a variety of causes. Some observers see the Saudi population as having been bought off by a social contract that trades wealth for political docility, while others find the docility of the Saudi population to be a realistic response to a security apparatus that is as brutal as it is pervasive. A variation of this theme suggests that many Saudis possess a profound respect for power and will obey any regime that possesses the strength to impose its will. The regime's greatest mistake, from this Hobbesian perspective, would be to show signs of weakness, including bowing to demands for greater democracy. Yet another explanation for the docility of the Saudi population is the heavy dose of fatalism contained in some Islamic texts. God is omnipotent, and the will of individuals counts for little. If God wanted change, there would be change. Islam also stresses innovation and creativity, but these dimensions of Islam have received minimal attention by the religious establishment. There is insufficient data to sort out the above explanations of political docility in Saudi Arabia, but each would seem to explain part of the riddle.

Two other dimensions of Saudi culture also pose a problem for the regime, both of which focus on economic behavior. First, Saudi Arabia has become a consumer society par excellence (Yamani 1998; Krimly 1999). Saudis have developed a taste for the finest in luxury goods, all of which must be imported from abroad. This posed little problem during the boom years but now places a strain on government currency reserves (Yamani 1998; Krimly 1999). Government calls for moderation have gone unheeded, the royal family being no exception.

More problematic has been the reluctance of Saudis to engage in mundane labor. As a World Bank study commented in the mid-1980s, "The Saudis of tomorrow will be definitely more mobile, more educated, and more responsive to labor market opportunities than today. Possibly they will also develop a more flexible attitude toward acquiring and accepting middle-level skills and jobs" (Sirageldin, Sherbini, and Serageldin 1984, 183). Yamani leaves little doubt that this lack of interest in work continues to be the case today:

> In present Saudi life, we remark that the new generations are much less motivated than is necessary for our future success as a society that wishes to prosper and develop. They have very high expectations and they have been spoiled in having all their wishes met without effort or delay. The plentiful and cheap services, the subsidized existence, these have all contributed to soften our youth. When the human being gets everything material without much effort, he has very little to motivate him and he usually becomes frustrated with his existence. This situation worsens dramatically if the expected cushy job is no more available, if income is diminished, and if the stabilizing factors of family values and religion are weakened by materialism. If the individual looks around him and perceives that he cannot improve his existence, his frustration will multiply. He will feel trapped, imagine social and political injustice, reject traditional cures, and he will be pushed towards any escape from what he perceives to be his unhappy existence. This is perhaps a very simplified explanation for the problems of drugs, terrorism, and general extremism, but it is nevertheless accurate (Yamani 1998, 135).

In part, the aloofness of Saudi citizens from greater involvement in their own economy reflects traditional tribal disdain for menial labor. In larger part, however, it has been the product of sudden wealth and Government efforts to build political support by pampering the population. Attitudes toward work are changing, but they are changing very slowly (Dahy 1988).

Political Economy

Economic factors represent such an integral part of the Saudi political equation that their impact on Saudi politics is difficult to estimate. Most fundamentally, the legitimacy and stability of the Saudi regime are buoyed by the implicit social contract that trades wealth for docility. The state provides, and the population consumes. There are no taxes other than the 2.5 percent religious tax, *zakat*, imposed by the Koran. This tax is collected by the Government (Yamani 1998). Few Saudis seem inclined to jeopardize a system that has made them among the most pampered people on earth, and they note with some justification that political conditions are equally repressive throughout the region. Why should Saudis risk giving up an abundant lifestyle for a political revolution that could well plunge their country into the chaos of Algeria, Iraq, or Iran?

The link between prosperity and political stability is a more or less universal phenomenon. What is unique about the Saudi Arabian case is that its prosperity is derived almost entirely from the export of a single product, oil. In 1998, by way of illustration, oil-related revenues made up more than 90 percent of Saudi export earnings (US Energy Information Administration, Jan. 1999, www). Among other things, Saudi dependence on oil renders the regime hostage to fluctuations in the oil market. At current rates of production, to put the problem in focus, a drop of $1 per barrel in the price of oil costs the Saudi government approximately $2.5 billion per year (US Energy Information Administration, Jan. 1999, www).

As we have seen throughout the discussion, the precipitous decline in the price of oil during the 1980s and 1990s frayed the Saudi social contract that traded wealth for docility. It could not be otherwise, for the regime's revenues dropped from $101 billion in 1981 to $13.5 billion in 1986, and remained depressed until the turn of the century (US Energy Information Administration, Jan. 1999, www). Political scientists, moreover, have long argued that violence is most likely to occur during periods of sharp economic decline. Not unmindful of this fact, the Saudi Government has been very reluctant to scale back the perks to which its citizens have become accustomed. Rather, it has borrowed money and delayed payments to creditors, often for several months. The price of oil rebounded sharply at the turn of the century, providing the Saudi regime with a respite. More volatility, however, appears on the horizon. To put things in perspective, the per-capita income of Saudi Arabia in 1981 was approximately $15,000, a figure that had fallen to approximately $7000 by the year 2000. This vulnerability to fluctuations in the international oil market is increased by additional factors.

First, Saudi Arabia is often described as a rentier state—a country that lives off the proceeds or "rents" of its natural resources. The oil was discovered, developed, refined, and marketed by US firms (Al-nasrawi 1991; Aburish 1994). Aramco, the US operating consortium, was nationalized in the period between 1974 and 1980, but US operatives continue to play dominant roles in all stages of the production and marketing process. Saudi Arabia now possesses a vigorous industry based upon the production and marketing of oil-based products, but these industries are largely staffed by foreign technicians. Saudis, by and large, have little involvement in their own economy, including the production of their most vital resource. As noted in the discussion of culture, they have become consumers rather than producers. This is an important consideration, for it burdens Saudi Arabia with the salaries of a massive number of foreign technicians performing tasks that could be performed by Saudi nationals, many of whom are already on the payroll.

Second, much of the Saudi economy remains under government control and is minimally productive. Rather than creating wealth, public-sector firms, the dominant force in the Saudi economy, tend to consume wealth. As if to underscore the inefficiency of its public sector, the Saudi government has now allowed foreign firms to prospect for oil in the kingdom, a practice that had earlier been discontinued by the state. Government jobs are part of the social contract and are viewed by Saudis as a right rather than a privilege. This problem is further aggravated by the fact that the private sector employs few Saudi nationals—less than 10 percent by some estimates (Gulfwire, Nov. 13, 2000, 13, www).

Third, management of the Saudi economy remains corrupt and lacks transparency. Foreign contracts invariably include a large commission for the official who helped to arrange them, often 15 percent or more. Such practices originated as a means of distributing the nation's oil wealth to key individuals, but soon became so blatant that the government passed a law making it illegal for the same individual to serve as an intermediary for more than one contract. Whatever their merits as a strategy of distributing income, such exorbitant commissions raise the cost of doing business in Saudi Arabia and place a further strain on the Saudi budget. It is interesting to note that Prince Abdullah has eliminated such practices in procurement contracts for the National Guard.

Fourth, much of Saudi Arabia's physical infrastructure was built during the 1970s and early 1980s and is now in need of repair, an expensive proposition by any estimate. Problems of an eroding infrastructure have been further aggravated by ever-increasing demands for housing, education, and employment. About half of Saudi Arabian citizens are younger than 25, and the population is growing at a rate of 3.5 percent per annum (*Movement for Islamic Reform in Arabia*, Jan. 5, 2000). Unemployment is already a problem in Saudi Arabia, and the government may have little choice but to continue its expensive policy of finding jobs for new graduates in an already bloated bureaucracy.

In addition to its role in domestic politics, oil wealth also serves as the basic instrument of Saudi foreign policy. During the last five years of the twentieth century, the kingdom attempted to buy its way out of regional crises in much the same way that it had used its wealth to promote domestic stability. Saudi Arabia also cemented its ties with the United States and other Western powers by means of massive arms purchases, many well beyond the needs or capacity of the Saudi military. Such purchases require a great deal of money, perhaps more than even the Saudis can manage.

For the moment, however, oil prices have rebounded and optimism has returned to the Saudi population. Wealthier Saudis, as the Movement for Islamic Reform in Saudi Arabia notes, have between $450 billion and $750 billion in foreign banks and securities, "enough to pay off Britain's entire national debt" (MIRA, Jan. 5, 2000, 12, www).

The International Context of Saudi Politics

The influence of external events on Saudi politics can be discussed in terms of three general categories: external pressures for change, external threats, and external protection. The modernization of Saudi Arabia's neighbors stimulated demands for reform within the kingdom, while covetous neighbors ranging from Nasser to the Ayatollah Khomeini have threatened to overthrow the monarchy by force. Both of these factors in turn, have forced a greater reliance on protection from the United States and other Western powers.

The Kingdom of Saudi Arabia was born in an era of simplicity. Rule by kings was the norm, educational opportunities limited, urbanization minimal, and communications rudimentary. Even the Middle Eastern republics of the era were ruled by aristocratic families with minimal interest in modernizing their societies. The years following World War II, however, unleashed a torrent of revolution and change, much of it centering on the ascendence of Abdul Nasser. The nationalist rhetoric of the Nasser era found a broad following among Saudi intellectuals and pushed the regime to introduce educational and social reforms far more rapidly than would have otherwise been the case. The process of "modernization" became a rush under Faisal as the very survival of the regime was called into question by a surge of nationalism sweeping the region.

External pressures would abate with the Arab humiliation of 1967, only to be replaced by more subtle forms of foreign pressure. The oil boom of the 1970s found Saudi Arabia awash with foreign workers, many with values far different from those of the Saudis. Revenues from the oil boom also dramatically increased the number of Saudis studying abroad and transformed Saudi Arabia into a consumer society intensely aware of world fashions and fads. Saudis also became avid tourists, with the more prosperous members of the middle class maintaining homes in Europe. Traditional behavior was maintained within the kingdom, but Saudis were no longer illiterate Bedouins. Indeed, most were rapidly becoming well-educated urbanites. Pressures for democracy were slight, but pressures for wealth became intense. Wealth, after all, was the basis of their social contract with the government.

Far more subtle were pressures for change emanating from Kuwait's gradual transition to a more democratic political system. If Kuwait, a desert monarchy with origins similar to those of Saudi Arabia, could experiment with an elected legislature, why couldn't Saudi Arabia do the same? This question became all the more pertinent when Qatar and Bahrain, other tribal kingdoms, also began moving in the direction of greater democracy.

If the above pressures had coaxed the kingdom along the road to modernity, Iran's Islamic Revolution of 1979 emboldened the opponents of modernization and forced the monarchy to back away from earlier policies that had gradually eroded the influence of the ulema. The more the ulema asserted their influence, the more the regime found itself immobilized as it attempted to strike a balance between the opposing forces of modernity and change. This task was made all the more difficult by the growing US presence in the region as well as by Israel's continuing transformation of Jerusalem into a Jewish preserve. The Saudis were the self-proclaimed protectors of the holy places, and Jerusalem was the third holiest site in Islam. King Fahd vowed that there would be no peace without the return of Jerusalem, a vow that his successors would find difficult to fulfill (*Al-Waton Al-Arabi*, Dec. 4, 1989, 24–25).

All of the above pressures, whether internal or external, have created a security consciousness among the Saudi elite that is all-pervasive. This consciousness has been heightened by the regime's awareness of its own vulnerability, as evidenced by its cautious attitude toward its own military. The combination of threat and vulnerability has resulted in a steady increase in Saudi dependence on the United States and other Western powers, the watershed coming with the Gulf War. US troops had long been stationed in Saudi Arabia on a "rotating" basis that allowed the Saudi regime to claim that the US presence was not permanent, but the US presence had become very permanent, with the turn of the century finding the US secretary of defense heatedly denying any plans to alter the situation (Gulfwire, Apr. 10, 2000, www).

LOOKING TOWARD THE FUTURE

Barring a revolution, there is little to suggest that the pattern of Saudi politics will change dramatically in the foreseeable future. Opposition to the monarchy, while substantial, is poorly organized and would seem to pose little immediate threat to the regime. Most Saudis, moreover, may be reluctant to exchange the laxity of the present regime for the zeal of religious fanatics. This attitude would certainly seem to apply to the Westernized middle class. Much, of course, will depend on the kingdom's economic circumstances. Serious belt-tightening could well precipitate a crisis in the kingdom, but a recent upswing in the price of oil has provided the regime with at least a temporary reprieve. Much will also depend on the regional and international climates, but these, too, appear to be increasingly benign. Saddam Hussein is absorbed with the survival of his own regime and poses little immediate threat to Saudi Arabia, while the Iranians are moving, however tenuously, toward a rapprochement with both the Saudis and the United States. Peace on the Arab-Israeli front also appears to be in the offing, although that process may take far longer than the optimists predict.

In the long run, of course, the regime either must bend to a changing world or see its power eroded. It is difficult to predict which course it will choose.

6

The Politics of Iraq

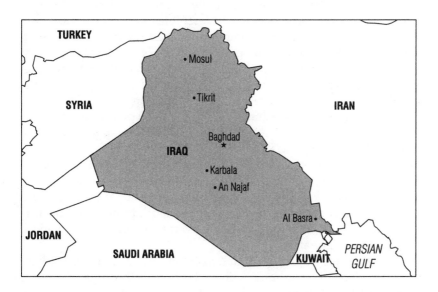

Regional politics in the Arab world have traditionally been dominated by three countries: Egypt, Syria, and Iraq. Iraq is the dominant Arab military power in the Arab Persian Gulf, and its leaders have long aspired to regional dominance. These aspirations have often found Iraq in conflict with its neighbors, but never more so than during the reign of Saddam Hussein. In 1980, Hussein embarked upon an eight-year war with Iran that would leave both countries devastated. This conflict was followed in 1990 by an Iraqi invasion of Kuwait that led to Iraq's subsequent defeat by a coalition of United Nations forces spearheaded by the United States. Undeterred, Saddam Hussein continued to pursue the development of nuclear, biological, and chemical weapons, a policy that would result in the economic boycott of Iraq by the world community. Iraq would also be divided into northern and southern "no-fly" zones, entrance to which was off limits to Iraqi aircraft. Despite these and related efforts to destabilize the regime of Saddam Hussein, the Iraqi leader has remained in power.

The survival of Saddam Hussein is all the more remarkable because of the intense internal opposition to his regime. In part, this opposition is a reaction to the devastation wrought by more than two decades of war. Rare, indeed, is the Iraqi family that has not suffered horrendous personal and economic loss in Iraq's successive confrontations with Iran and the United Nations.

Opposition to Saddam Hussein, however, runs far deeper than economic adversity. Iraq more closely resembles a mosaic of mutually hostile ethnic and religious communities than it does an integrated nation-state. Arabs constitute some 75 percent of the Iraqi population but find cooperation difficult because of sectarian differences. The Sunni Arabs, while constituting only 20 percent of the population, have dominated Iraqi politics since Iraq's inception as an independent country. The Shi'a Arabs constitute approximately 60 percent of the Iraqi population but, despite their majority status, have largely been excluded from power. The Kurds, although Sunni Muslims, are a non-Arab ethno-linguistic group that has long aspired to independence. Indeed, the Kurds have been in more or less constant rebellion against Baghdad since the inception of Iraq as an independent country. Each ethno-religious group, in turn, is fragmented into mutually hostile tribal/kinship alliances, and these are overlaid by intense ideological and personality rivalries.

The ethno-religious fragmentation of Iraq has been reinforced by considerations of geography, with each of Iraq's three major groups occupying a well-defined portion of the country: the Kurds the largely mountainous north, the Shi'a the fertile south, and the Arab Sunnis a triangle of less fertile land stretching to the north and east of Baghdad. Each of the three major groups has also received support from neighboring countries: the Kurds from Turkish and Iranian Kurds, the Shi'a from Iran (the Middle East's largest Shi'a power), and the Sunni Arabs from the predominantly Sunni countries of Syria, Saudi Arabia, and Jordan.

The profound chasm of distrust that separates Iraq's three major communal groups has reduced the prospect of national unity to a vague dream. Foreign powers manipulate minority groups to the detriment of the central government, ideological conflicts explode into violence born of historical hatreds, and flagrant disregard for human rights is justified in the name of holding the state together.

Despite its present agony, Iraq possesses all of the physical ingredients for rapid economic growth: fertile land, abundant water, and virtually unlimited oil deposits. Indeed, Iraq's oil deposits are second only to those of Saudi Arabia within the region. Iraq is also a relatively underpopulated country that does not share the population pressures of Iran, Egypt, or Syria. At least in theory, then, Iraq possesses the potential to become the most developed country in the Arab world. Politics, however, keep getting in the way.

Reflecting the above discussion, in the present chapter we will focus on the politics of religion and ethnicity. In common with our discussion of Syrian politics, we will also explore the ability of a minority regime to sustain its power in the face of both foreign and domestic opposition.

HISTORY AND CULTURE

The splendors of ancient Mesopotamia, the classical name for Iraq, rival those of Egypt. Much like the Nile valley, the fertile plains of the Tigris and Euphrates Rivers gave birth to some of the world's earliest civilizations: the Sumerians (2900–2500 BC), the Akkadians (2530–2159 BC), and the Babylonians (1894–1594 BC). The era had also seen the emergence of complex religious beliefs including references to a great flood similar to the great flood mentioned in the Bible (Cressey 1960, 48). The Babylonians created the hanging gardens of Babylon and other engineering works of incredible complexity. While these ancient civilizations have little relevance to the politics of modern Iraq, they play a central role in governmental efforts to instill within Iraq's citizens a sense of national pride. Saddam Hussein, for example, often delivers particularly emotional speeches from the site of historic Babylon.

The Arabs invaded Mesopotamia in AD 633 and converted most of the region's inhabitants to Islam. The Islam of Iraq, however, was tempered by a Persian culture rich in religious mysticism and was far less austere than that of the Arabian Peninsula. With the passing of the Prophet and his immediate successors, the battle for control of the Islamic empire centered on two rival claimants: Ali, the son-in-law and cousin of Mohammed, and Mu'awiya, the governor of Damascus. Ali centered his power in Iraq while his rival, Mu'awiya, strengthened his base in Syria. Ali was assassinated before the conflict was resolved and his second son, Hussein, was murdered in an attempt to rally the Iraqis against the Syrians. In a curious blend of politics and Persian mysticism, Ali and his sons, Hassan and Hussein, were canonized by their followers, giving birth to a fundamental and abiding split between the Shi'a, the partisans of Ali, and the Sunni or orthodox Muslims. The sites of the famous battles became Shi'a holy cities and are considered by many Shi'a to be only slightly less important than Mecca. Each year the famous battle is relived in the celebration of the camel, giving vent to a profound outpouring of emotions and grief among the Shi'a community.

Iraq would wrest power from Syria in AD 750, and the Abbasids, ruling from their newly created capital of Baghdad, extended the Islamic empire. Baghdad became the world's center of science and philosophy, and its splendors were recounted in the fables of the Arabian Nights. Iraq's days of glory, however, were fleeting and a long period of decline was capped by the Mongol destruction of Baghdad in 1258. Iraq would never recover the glories of its past.

Iraq became part of the Ottoman Empire in the sixteenth century and remained under Turkish control until it was occupied by the British in the prelude to World War I.[1] Several aspects of Ottoman rule were to shape the political character of its former province. Under a system of administration referred to as the millet system, the Ottomans allowed the members of each religious sect to manage their own affairs as long as they paid their taxes and accepted the suzerainty of the Sultan. No effort was made to integrate the Shi'a and Sunni communities, each remaining a world unto itself as, for the most part, did the Kurds. This treatment, however, did not mean that the Turks were impartial. To the contrary, the country was largely administered by Arab Sunnis, the co-religionists of the Ottomans. The Sunnis also had better access to education than the Shi'a, and only Sunnis were allowed to become officers in the Ottoman military (Batatu 1978). Indeed, a large segment of the Iraqi elite during the monarchy consisted of former officers of the Turkish army.

Also of relevance to the future of Iraqi politics was the Ottoman Land Code of 1858 (Haj 1997; Warriner 1957). Seeking to bring order to a system based on communal ownership of land, the new code registered tribal lands in the name of the tribal sheikh, thereby transforming them into his personal property. This process was extended under the Iraqi monarchy by a 1933 law outlining the rights and duties of peasants. Among other things, the new law specified that peasants (fellahin) could not leave the land if they were indebted to the landowner who, in many cases, was now a tribal sheikh residing in the more comfortable environs of the city. A foreman was left behind to supervise the peasants and collect the owner's share of the produce which, in some cases, was as much as two-thirds of the crop. As Warriner summed up the situation, "The sheikhs have now become legal owners of the dirah

---

[1]By 1914 Turkey had divided Iraq into three vilayets (provinces): Basra, Baghdad, and Mosul, with Baghdad being paramount (Dann 1969, 7).

[tribal lands], the sirkals [foremen] have become the managers and agents; and the tribesmen have become share-cropping fellahin, with no rights or status" (Warriner 1957, 136). The situation was less severe in the Sunni and Kurdish north where the land was less fertile and did not lend itself as easily to plantation or hacienda agriculture. The burden of the new feudalism, accordingly, fell largely on the Shi'a.

Britain had developed strong commercial and strategic interests in Iraq and the Arab Persian Gulf in the decades prior to World War I, most of which had to do with the region's strategic location along the route to India, the crown jewel of the British Empire. While the British would turn most of the Gulf's sheikhdoms into British protectorates, Turkey had been a traditional ally of Britain and the British saw little need for direct intervention in Iraq. This laissez-faire attitude would change in the early 1900s when control of the Ottoman Empire was seized by the Young Turks, a group of reform-minded officers with strong leanings toward imperial Germany. Plans for the construction of a Berlin-to-Baghdad railroad threatened to give the Germans a stranglehold on Britain's communications with India, and in 1915 the British responded by occupying the three Turkish provinces that now constitute Iraq, a task that took most of World War I (Elliot 1996). At the war's end, the final boundaries of Iraq were determined by a series of international conferences in which the victors in World War I divided up the colonial territories of the Axis powers. The San Remo Conference of 1920 awarded Britain control of Palestine, Jordan, and Iraq, while France was given control of Syria and Lebanon. The British staged a plebiscite in which a majority of those voting approved Iraq's status as a British mandate. The Shi'a resisted British occupation as an affront to Islam, and the British, following the path of least resistance, relied on the Sunni elite that was already in place to conduct the affairs of state. The Shi'a majority remained among Iraq's dispossessed.

A provisional council was established to select a "constitutional monarch" for Iraq who would be mutually acceptable to both the British and the Iraqis. The logical choice was Faisal Ibn al-Hussein, the son of the sharif of Mecca and, for several months, the king of Syria before being expelled by the French. Although not an Iraqi, Faisal possessed strong nationalist credentials and a lineage to the Prophet Mohammed which made him acceptable to many Iraqis. The British, in turn, were reasonably confident of Faisal's pro-British leanings and were happy to smooth British relations with his father, the sharif of Mecca. Unable to rule Iraq directly, the British would now rule it indirectly. Most of Iraq's upper-level civil servants were British, and Britain "advised" Iraq on matters of finance and foreign policy (Longrigg 1953). As Elliott explains:

This placed the regime in a dilemma: how to satisfy the populace, who expected and demanded independence, as well as the foreign power, which required collaboration. Being unable to afford giving serious offence to either, Faisal and his followers made occasional shows of nationalist resistance, but backed down when the British refused to budge. In reality they worked with the British and gained ground through the gradual application of pressure and the mandatory's own desire gradually to yield to it. Meanwhile, British authority in many respects overlapped with or overshadowed that of the government, particularly in the area of internal security (Elliot 1996, 7).

The period of British rule, although brief, would have a profound influence on Iraqi politics. First and most importantly, the British had condemned Iraq to a future of violence by piecing together a country composed of three mutually hostile communities: the Sunnis, the Shi'a, and the Kurds (Lukitz 1995). To make matters worse, the Kurds had been promised an independent Kurdish state a few years earlier, a promise briefly kept only to be rescinded at the San Remo conference. Second, Shi'a hostility to British rule led naturally to increased reliance on the Sunni elite. This reliance was strengthened by the fact that Faisal was a Sunni and most of his entourage consisted of former Sunni Arab officers in the Ottoman army (Mufti 1996).[2] Third, British colonial policy exacerbated communal conflict in Iraq by playing one group against another. Rather than laying a foundation for national unity, the British helped to destroy it.

Iraq was granted its formal independence in 1932 and was duly admitted to the League of Nations. The British, however, retained their military bases in Iraq and both trained and equipped the Iraqi army. The monarchy was also pro-British, as was General Nuri as-Said, the emerging "strong man" of Iraqi politics. The king died unexpectedly in 1933 and was replaced by his son Gazi, an inexperienced youth of 21 who lacked the ability to impose his will on Iraq's scheming politicians. Gazi was killed in an automobile accident in 1939, and power shifted to Abd al-Illah, the crown prince, who ruled in the name of Gazi's infant son.

Abd al-Illah's subservience to Britain was resented by a broad cross-section of Iraqi society, and by the mid-1930s, a variety of opposition parties had begun to emerge among Iraq's students, intellectuals, and army officers. Some were Iraqi nationalists, while others (particularly those of Sunni origin) called for the creation of a unified Arab state that would include Iraq, Syria, and Palestine. The precursors to the Iraqi Communist Party also emerged during this era, and soon devel-

---

[2]A large number of Sunni officers had defected to Faisal during the Arab Revolt, and subsequently fought with Faisal against the French in Syria.

oped a broad base of support among the urban Shi'a community. Growing political dissent erupted in periodic riots, with at least six coups and attempted coups occurring between 1936 and 1941 (Khadduri 1960). The latter year would also see nationalist army officers with strong ties to Nazi Germany seize power for a brief period before being crushed by British troops. The monarchy was restored, but Iraq remained under virtual British occupation for the remainder of the Second World War (Silverfarb 1994).

The Era of Revolution and Optimism

The years following the end of World War II found Iraq to be an island of relative tranquility in a region beset by turmoil and revolution. Abd al-Illah, the regent, continued to rule in the name of the young king, but real power resided with Nuri as-Said, Iraq's perennial prime minister and power behind the throne.

Iraq's tranquility, however, was more apparent than real. Both the monarchy and Nuri as-Said were throwbacks to an earlier era in which Iraqi politics was the preserve of ex-Ottoman officers, tribal sheikhs, and feudal landowners, the sheikhs and the landowners often being one and the same. The ex-Ottoman officers had also used their influence to acquire large landholdings and resisted mass efforts for land reform. All effective power remained in the hands of the Sunnis, but Shi'a sheikhs and landowners were allowed to prosper in return for supporting the regime. So repressive was the Iraqi regime that 1943 would find the British ambassador complaining that the monarchy was rapidly losing touch with reality (Cornwallis, cited in Elliot 1996).

In all, 61 percent of Iraq's arable land was in the hands of its large-scale landowners, with another 15 percent or so in the hands of medium-scale landowners. Landed peasants, located largely in the less fertile regions of the country, owned the remainder. The sharecroppers on the large latifundia (plantations) suffered from ignorance and disease and were considered by the courts, most of which were controlled by the families of the landowners, to be little more than chattel.

While the regime clung to the past, radical political parties flourished, the most prominent of which were the Arab Nationalists, the Communists, and the Ba'athists. The Arab Nationalists enjoyed strong support in the army and had orchestrated the attempted coups of 1936 and 1941. The Iraqi Communist Party was founded in 1934 and by 1944 controlled 12 of some 16 Iraqi labor unions, 1944 being the first year that trade unions were recognized in Iraq[3] (Smokylake.com./

---

[3]Dates of party formation differ from source to source.

Christy/history, Iraq.nd). The Ba'ath Party was of more recent vintage, being officially recognized in 1952. The Communists found their greatest support among the Kurds in the north and the Shi'a in the slums of Baghdad. The Ba'ath Party found support among both Shi'a and Sunni intellectuals and, more importantly, was able to establish a strong presence within the predominantly Sunni officer corps. Other parties existed, but these were largely symbolic affairs that revolved around dominant figures such as Nuri as-Said. The Shi'a clergy were also growing increasingly restive with the direction of Iraqi politics.

Faced with an opposition that demanded land reform, democracy, and the severance of Iraq's ties with the West, Nuri as-Said responded by strengthening his ties with the feudalists and leading Iraq into the US-sponsored Baghdad Pact, an alliance of Western and Middle Eastern nations designed to contain Soviet expansionism and stabilize the pro-Western regimes of the region. Iraq was the only Arab country to join the organization, Nasser's opposition to the Pact having scared off such staunch Western supporters as Jordan and Saudi Arabia. Opponents of the regime were brutally suppressed, and domestic economic policies were so repressive that even the British ambassador urged greater movement toward reform (Gallman 1964).

There was little, however, that the West could do to salvage the monarchy. Egypt's political victory in the 1956 War had electrified the Arab World, and the merger of Egypt and Syria in 1958 had created a wave of nationalistic emotion that threatened to sweep all before it. Iraq and Jordan, the two Hashemite Kingdoms of the Middle East, attempted to parry the nationalist threat by federating their two countries, and Iraq mobilized two military divisions for service in Jordan. Both units were fully armed and provided with ammunition—a rarity in Iraq, as General Nuri was reluctant to provide Iraqi troops with live ammunition unless they were actively engaged in combat (Gallman 1964, 203).

Arming the military units, in retrospect, was a mistake. The units scheduled for Jordan overthrew the Iraqi monarchy on July 14, 1958, as mobs dragged the bodies of Abd al-Illah and Nuri as-Said through the streets of Baghdad (Fernea and Louis 1991). Ironically, Nuri as-Said had earlier assured the US ambassador that there was little risk in sending Iraqi troops to Jordan, saying that "potential trouble-makers were limited to a few hundred students and lawyers," and that "these could be kept under surveillance." When the US ambassador inquired about the loyalty of the army, he was assured "that the army could be relied upon to support the Crown and the government" (Gallman 1964, 201).

The coup had been carried out by a tightly knit group of free officers, many of whom were ardent Arab nationalists. Despite the pervasiveness of Arab nationalist sentiments, neither the originators of the coup nor their supporters were of one mind about Iraq's role in a unified Arab state (Kienle 1990). Abdul Karim Kassem, the leader of the coup, seemed inclined toward a loose federation in keeping with Iraq's multicultural traditions. Perhaps he was also fearful of having his own power eclipsed by that of Nasser. Other officers, while nationalist in sentiment, worried about the socialist complexion of Nasser's domestic policies. Being an Arab nationalist did not necessarily make one a socialist. Countering this hesitation was a hard core of officers led by Abdel Salam Aref, the deputy leader of the coup. For Aref and his supporters, the whole purpose of the coup had been unification with the United Arab Republic. With Iraq's adherence to the UAR, the three power centers of the Arab world would be unified and the dream of a unified Arab world stretching from the Persian Gulf to the Atlantic would be at hand.

Conflict between Kassem and Aref over the question of unity with Egypt and Syria led to the ouster of the latter within a few months of the coup. Fearing an Arab nationalist backlash, Kassem turned for support to the Iraqi Communist Party, the leaders of which were only too happy to oblige (Lukitz 1995). Nasser had crushed Egypt's communists upon seizing power in 1952, and with the formation of the United Arab Republic (UAR, the union of Egypt and Syria) had lost little time in putting Syria's communists to flight. In all probability, Iraq's affiliation with the UAR would spell the end of its Communist Party. Beyond tactical political considerations, communist opposition to Nasser was also rooted in the ethnic and religious divisions that fragmented Iraqi society. The communists attracted their largest following among the urban Shi'a and the Kurds, both of whom feared that Iraq's incorporation in the UAR would render them small minorities in a Sunni Arab universe (Wiley 1992).

It was communist support among the Shi'a and the Kurds, moreover, that provided the Communist Party with its best chance of seizing power in Iraq. The Kurds, although largely tribal, had established strong ties with Moscow and were primed for revolt against Baghdad. The communists' support among the Shi'a, in turn, was heavily concentrated in the squalid slums of Baghdad. This was a matter of vital importance, for Baghdad was the nerve center of Iraqi politics. To control the capital would be to control the government. The Communist Party could now claim some 25,000 members, including a broad following among students, teachers, lawyers, and other intellectuals. These, in turn, were supported by legions of sympathizers attracted by the Party's "Shi'a Program" and promises of land grants and social welfare (Dann 1969, 118; Ibrahim, F. 1996). Both loyalists and sympathizers were organized into Popular Resistance Forces, an armed militia that provided the Communist Party with a counterweight to the military. The Party also mobilized its sympathizers in a variety of mass organizations such as the Partisans of Peace, the Federation of Democratic Youth, and the League for the Defense of Women's Rights.

For the moment, however, the communists needed Kassem as a shield while they consolidated their power. Amassing power involved efforts to infiltrate both the government and the military. It also involved intimidating the Arab nationalists and their supporters, a group that now focused largely on the Ba'ath Party. This intimidation was done by staging huge rallies throughout the country, the most provocative of which was a Partisan of Peace rally held in the predominantly Sunni city of Mosul on March 6, 1959. Some 250,000 people, many of them armed, attended the rally, overwhelming the city's residents and sparking a revolt by the leader of the local garrison, a staunch Arab Nationalist. The coup attempt also reflected the perilous nature of Iraqi politics during the era, for while the leader of the coup was an Arab Nationalist, most of the troops were Kurds who did not share his nationalist sentiments (Dann 1969). The coup was easily crushed by units loyal to Kassem, as had been an earlier coup attempt sponsored by the Arab Nationalists. Kassem's claim that Nasser had supported both coup attempts seems plausible.

The Mosul rebellion unleashed a reign of terror against the Arab Nationalists, much of it led by the Popular Resistance Force and other communist organizations. Arab Nationalists were hunted as spies and purged from both the military and the government. Many died, and thousands more were imprisoned. Brutality, much fueled by religious and ethnic hatred, became the norm.

Having achieved dominance in the streets, the communists began to press Kassem for greater participation in the government and the military, steps that would pave the way for an eventual communist takeover. They also demanded Iraq's immediate withdrawal from the Baghdad Pact. Kassem withdrew from the Baghdad Pact, which had become little more than a formality, but resisted giving more power to the communists (Haj 1997).

To safeguard his power, Kassem turned on his former allies and forged a new alliance with anticommunist officers in the security forces. The Public Resistance Force (PRF) was disarmed, and Ba'athists and Arab Nationalists were released from prison (Dann 1969, 184; Mufti 1996; Haj 1997). Formerly the perpetrators of terrorism, the communists now became its victims (Dann 1969, 289).

The remainder of Kassem's reign was preoccupied with the task of survival as he played one group against another. He also attempted to boost his popular support by launching a bold program of social and economic reform. Foremost among the social reforms was a new personal statutes law that prohibited polygamy, increased female inheritance rights, and offered women at least some protection against arbitrary divorce (Dann 1969, 246). Given the conservative nature of Iraqi society, these measures did more to undermine the regime than to support it (Ibrahim, F. 1996). Land reforms enacted shortly after the 1958 revolution were also strengthened, but many peasants had already taken matters into their own hands. As described by Dann:

> In a spontaneous movement, which appears to have sprung up without organization or known leaders, the peasants stormed, looted and burned down the residences of the big landlords. Accounts and rent-rolls were destroyed; the agents and overseers chased away. The erstwhile sharecroppers took over the machinery and settled down as owners (Dann 1969, 60).

The Kurds revolted in the spring of 1961, further sapping the power of a regime that was now adrift. In desperation, Kassem sought to regain the initiative by asserting Iraqi jurisdiction over Kuwait (June 1961), an oil-rich mini-state that had recently been granted independence by the British. Both Nasser and the British rushed to the aid of Kuwait, leaving Kassem with little choice but to back down.

Now devoid of support, Kassem was overthrown on February 8, 1963, by a coalition of Nasserite and Ba'athist officers. Aref, a Nasserite, was named the President of Iraq, but real power lay with Ahmad Hasan al-Bakr, the dominant Ba'athist officer. The institutions of state, such as they were, consisted of the invariable Revolutionary Command Council (RCC) abetted by a Council of Ministers charged with managing the day-to-day affairs of the Government. The Ba'ath Party dominated both groups (Ismael and Ismael 1991).

The year that followed was chaotic, even by Iraqi standards. Aref was to have been a figurehead president, but he rejected his symbolic role and pushed for immediate union with Egypt. Tripartite unity talks between Egypt, Syria, and Iraq were convened in the spring of 1963, but ended in acrimony as each party blamed the other for the breakup of the UAR. The Iraqi Arab Nationalists sided with Nasser against their Ba'athist colleagues and were duly purged from Iraq's Revolutionary Command Council. The Ba'athists now held total control of the country.

The Iraqi Ba'ath Party, however, was a house divided. The military section of the Ba'ath Party was dominated by Sunni officers who had joined the Party to counter Kassem's shift to the communists. The Party's civilian wing, by contrast, continued to be dominated by Shi'a

(Ibrahim, F. 1996). The gap between the two factions was unbridgeable. Still smarting from the earlier purges of Sunni officers, the military wing of the Ba'ath Party launched a reign of terror against suspected communists in the Government. Between February and November of 1963, an estimated 10,000 communists were arrested, most from Shi'a backgrounds. Hundreds were killed (Ibrahim, F. 1996).

A glimpse of the situation is provided by the following appeal issued by a leftist-dominated Iraqi foreign student organization shortly after the fall of Kassem:

> Appeal (87)
> To All Student Organizations Throughout the World
>
> In the name of human rights and dignity, and on behalf of 4,000 Iraqi students studying in 15 countries, we appeal to you, our brother students, to protest most strongly against the inhuman actions and barbarous atrocities which are being committed by the gangs of the new regime which took power with a coup d'etat on February 8th, 1963.
> Already about 10,000 of the best sons and daughters of our people, including many hundred of students, have been murdered by the fascist "National Guards," an S.S. type of secret police.
> We appeal to you, our brother students, to send protests to the Baghdad government, denouncing the mass murders and the atrocities which are being committed against your brothers, the students in Iraq.
> Your solidarity and support with the Iraqi students and people is mostly urgently needed.
>
> Secretariat of the General Union of Iraqi Students Abroad
> 16th February 1963 (Personal Document)

The largely civilian wing of the Party had not been consulted in the purges, and when its leaders protested, they were accused of pro-communist sympathies. The situation became even more complicated when extremists in the Party argued for a continuation of the Government's largely futile war against the Kurds and pushed for the complete nationalization of the Iraqi economy. They also demanded a hard line against Egypt. The moderates in the Ba'ath Party opposed all of these initiatives and proceeded to purge the extremists from the RCC. Fighting erupted in Baghdad among partisans of the two sides, giving rise to fears of civil war, if not the dissolution of the country.

Faced with the impending destruction of the Ba'athist Party in Iraq, Michel Aflaq, the Party's founder and recently restored president of Syria, came to Baghdad to adjudicate the dispute. Indeed, for a period of a few weeks it was Aflaq and other members of the National (international) Command of the Ba'ath Party that seemed to be governing Iraq. The experiment in multinational rule failed to restore unity to the

Iraqi Ba'ath Party, but remains a unique event in recent Arab history. It also illustrates the appeal of the Ba'ath Party as a truly Arab party.

Perhaps mercifully, Aref and a coalition of Arab Nationalist officers seized power on November 18, 1963. The first Iraqi experiment in Ba'athist rule had lasted only nine months and had been, by any standard, a total disaster. As we shall see in later discussion, Saddam Hussein would learn from the mistakes of his predecessors.

Aref consolidated his position by placing Arab Nationalist officers, many from his own tribe, in key positions. The latter were particularly influential in the intelligence services and secret police. Virtually all were Sunni.

Now in control of Iraq, Aref proposed immediate unification with Egypt. Nasser, however, was still smarting from the break-up of the UAR and suggested that the unification of the country be postponed until Iraq could bring its political and economic infrastructures in line with those of Egypt. Egypt, by this time, had been transformed into a socialist economy, with most political affairs being managed by the Arab Socialist Union, a government-sponsored political party. All other political movements were banned.

More pragmatic than ideological, Aref followed suit, nationalizing Iraq's banks and larger industries. An Iraq version of the Arab Socialist Union was also established and in July of 1964, Aref would proclaim that Iraq was on the "threshold of the building an Arab nation under socialism" (Mufti 1996).

Unity, however, was not to be achieved. Like its predecessors, the Nationalist regime became paralyzed by internal dissension. Aref fell victim to an auto accident in 1966 and was replaced in office by his brother Mohammed, a compromise candidate, but to no avail. The Arab Nationalist regime was beyond salvation.

The most pronounced image conveyed by Iraqi politics during the era of optimism and revolution, then, was that of a country so divided within itself that effective government was impossible. Not only had the country suffered through two decades of coups and counter coups, but each attempted to undo the policies of its predecessors. As a result, Iraqi politics was constantly being turned on its head. Each new set of elites, moreover, was wedded to an extremist position that alienated most of Iraq's already fragmented society. This was certainly true of Nuri as-Said, the Nasserites, and the Ba'athists. Kassem's flirtation with the communists sent fear through the Ba'athist and Nationalist communities, not to mention a Shi'a clergy vying with the communists for control of the Shi'a masses. Indeed, the Shi'a religious leaders went so far as to excommunicate Shi'a members of the communist party (Ibrahim, F. 1996). Each new regime, in turn, attempted to batten down the hatches by crushing the opposition. When the dam finally broke, retribution was awesome.

Under these circumstances, institution building was impossible. Iraq constitutions (each regime issued its own) were meaningless, for all effective power rested with the military. Even the army was divided against itself, and both the communists and the Ba'athists developed party militias as a counterweight to the military, hardly a move designed to build confidence among the latter.

Much the same was true in the area of administrative development as each new regime purged the bureaucracy of its opponents, replacing them with its supporters. Those not purged became immobilized with fear, for even the simplest decision might be interpreted as treason following the next coup. This danger was particularly acute if one attempted to enforce the law against the relative of a dignitary who was yet unknown.

The Era of Reassessment

By 1967, the Nasserite regime that had been in place in Iraq since 1963 was so beset by internal conflict that it had begun to crumble under its own weight. The humiliating Arab defeat in the June (Six-Day) War merely hastened its collapse. Sensing the inevitable, the Nasserites offered to form a coalition government with the Ba'ath Party. The latter, however, now sensed victory and bided its time.

The Ba'athist coup took place in July of 1968. It was the tenth coup or attempted coup in a decade (Khalil 1989). Following the customary pattern, a communiqué was broadcast over Iraqi radio announcing that the Army had seized power in the name of the people and that a new Revolutionary Command Council had been formed (Kienle 1990). The customary purges also took place within the army and the bureaucracy. Given Iraq's history of political turmoil, it was logical to assume that the Ba'athist coup would soon go the way of its predecessors and that Iraq's game of political musical chairs would continue well into the future. This, however, was not to happen. There would be no more successful coups in Iraq.

The new Revolutionary Command Council (RCC) was headed by Ahmad Hasan al-Bakr, a Sunni Arab officer who had been active in the coup of 1963. He was supported by Saddam Hussein, his protegee and relative. Saddam Hussein was an important member of the civilian wing of the Ba'ath Party who would soon be elevated to membership in the RCC and become its vice chairman (Karsh and Rautsi 1991). Both Bakr and Hussein were from the region of Takrit, as were several other officers in the RCC. During the early years of the monarchy, a senior officer from Takrit had helped the region's more ambitious youth to gain entry into the military college, and it was now this group who controlled both the RCC and the civilian apparatus of the Ba'ath Party. While the Takrit region did not constitute a tribe per se, many Takrites were interrelated in one way or another by marriage. This situation was not unusual, for marriage among cousins is a common practice in Iraq.

The preeminent goal of the new regime was to consolidate its power by stemming the chaos that had characterized Iraqi politics during the preceding two decades. The broader Ba'athist goals of unity and socialism would have to await the regime's consolidation of power.

Foremost on the minds of the new leaders was the need to remedy the mistakes of the Ba'ath Party's first encounter with power in 1963. One of the Party's biggest problems in 1963, according to Party documents, had been competition between rival blocs within the Party, a topic discussed above. To avoid a repeat of this scenario, power would be concentrated in the hands of a narrow leadership council. Debate would be encouraged, but once decisions had been taken, they would be binding on all members of the Party. Dissident currents, by necessity, would be crushed.

The Party also acknowledged that its reign of terror in 1963 had kept it from establishing a strong base of support among the masses, and toward that end created an array of women's, youth, peasant, labor, and other mass-based organizations. Membership in these organizations was voluntary, but membership had its privileges.

The Party vowed to reach an accommodation with the Kurds by acknowledging them as co-partners in a unified Iraqi state. There were also hints that the Kurds would be granted some form of autonomous status over time, although the details remained vague (Gunter 1992). The Party had little interest in greater Kurdish autonomy, but could not allow itself to be weakened by a prolonged civil war. No mention was made of Shi'a aspirations for greater autonomy, for the Ba'ath Party refused to recognize religious differences among its Arab citizens.

The Ba'ath Party began its reign by ousting two senior generals from the RCC, both of whom, while not members of the Ba'ath Party, had been instrumental in the overthrow of Aref. The ousted generals launched a counter-coup in January of 1970, presumably with the support of Syria. The counter-coup was crushed, and the Iraqi Ba'athists accused their Syrian counterparts of sponsoring the coup by smuggling "huge quantities of arms" into the country.

Having dealt successfully with their first challenge, the Ba'athist leaders tendered an olive branch to the Shi'a religious establishment.

The religious establishment had been largely apolitical up to this point and posed little threat to the regime, but its blessing would be useful in legitimizing the Ba'athist rule among Iraq's Shi'a majority. Negotiations could not overcome the legacy of distrust that separated the two sides (Ibrahim, F. 1996). The regime responded with violence but succeeded only in politicizing a growing number of Shi'a clergy. Henceforth, it would be they who organized Shi'a resistance to the regime.

The Ba'athist regime launched its social revolution in 1969 with the promulgation of a new agrarian reform law. The agrarian reforms, like those initiated by the Kassem regime, were designed to destroy the remaining power of the old landowning class, members of which continued to enjoy support among the military. Landowners were no longer entitled to compensation for lands confiscated, and much of the land was distributed free to the peasants. In the process, Iraq was transformed into a country of small and medium landowners, most of whom, the Ba'ath Party hoped, would be supportive of their benefactors.

The Ba'athist reforms were more thorough than those of the Kassem era, and the regime would soon be able to claim that "Apart from in the north, feudalism retains no real political influence in the country." Reference to the north, in this context, was a veiled admission that Ba'athist influence in Kurdistan remained weak.

Agrarian reform was followed in 1970 with the promulgation of a new constitution. The new constitution acknowledged the Kurds as partners in building a unified Iraq. This acknowledgment reflected an agreement worked out with the Kurds a few months earlier, although neither side had much faith in the other. As the Ba'athists would acknowledge:

> It must be said that in deciding to collaborate with the Kurdish Democratic Party...the Ba'ath Party leadership by no means ignored the mistaken policies pursued by some KDP factions, their suspect connections with imperialism and reaction, or their isolationist tendencies.

> As in the case of the Shi'a, Ba'athist efforts at accommodation came to naught and 1971 would see the government force 40,000 Shi'a Kurds to flee into Iran (Ibrahim, F. 1996).

In 1972, the Ba'athist regime gained broad popular approval by nationalizing the Iraqi Oil Company (IOC). Foreign ownership of Iraq's oil resources had been the last vestige of colonial domination, and the nationalization of the IOC enabled the regime to pose as the champion of Iraqi nationalism. It also provided the regime with countless new opportunities for patronage and payoffs.

The same year saw Iraq sign a 15-year Treaty of Friendship with the Soviet Union. This step followed a series of earlier technical agreements and altered Iraqi politics in three important ways. First, the USSR became Iraq's main supplier of arms and credit, and Iraq was sheltered from US pressure by the Soviet security umbrella (Shemesh 1992). Second, Iraq's accord with the USSR placed the Ba'athist regime at odds with Turkey and Iran, both of whom were members of the Baghdad Pact. Tensions with its neighboring countries would increase accordingly. Third, the Soviet Union stopped supporting the Kurds, with whom it had enjoyed a warm relationship. It would now be easier for the Ba'athist regime to rein in one of the remaining challenges to its authority.

Despite progress in suppressing its opponents, the Ba'athist regime continued to be plagued by internal divisions. These divisions surfaced in June of 1973 when the Director of National Security, an avowed foe of Saddam Hussein, attempted to overthrow the regime. The attempted coup was foiled, and Saddam Hussein seized the opportunity to purge other opponents from positions of power. Saddam also used the occasion to create a special intelligence unit of which he was the head. Whether or not Saddam Hussein was the power behind the throne at the beginning of the Ba'athist reign, he had now taken a major step in that direction.

With the immediate crisis resolved, the Ba'athist leadership continued its efforts to achieve a reconciliation with its adversaries by offering to form a "National Front" with the Communist Party. The communists were not admitted to the RCC or the Regional Command of the Ba'ath Party, but they were given symbolic positions in the Council of Ministers and the patronage inherent therein. The communists' decision to accept the offer was undoubtedly motivated by the fate of the Shi'a and the Kurds, not to mention the 1963 massacres. The creation of the National Front enabled the Ba'ath to bring a largely Shi'a organization into the government's fold and further isolated the influence of the Shi'a religious establishment. The formation of the National Front also appeased the Ba'ath's Soviet allies and enabled the regime to claim that a major step had been taken toward true democracy.

The major event shaping the future of Iraqi politics during 1973, however, was not internal but external. The outbreak of war between the Arabs and Israel in October of 1973 quadrupled the price of crude oil and transformed Iraq into one of the richest countries in the world. The Ba'athist regime now had an economic "carrot" to add to the military "stick" that had kept it in power since 1968. Those who chose to join the Party or participate in its affiliated organizations found easy access to lucrative positions in the rapidly expanding public sector.

Iraq's newfound oil wealth would also transform the country's physical infrastructure as roads, bridges, dams, airports and other public works projects mushroomed. The management of this new edifice, in turn, created a huge "petrol" middle class, most members of which owed their good fortune to the Ba'ath Party.

Shi'a increasingly joined the Ba'ath Party and its affiliate organizations, for such was the price of a government job. Even before the oil boom, however, the Party's egalitarian ideology had provided it with a reasonable following among Iraqi Shi'a. A major rift thus developed within the Shi'a community between those who supported the regime for economic or ideological reasons and those who opposed it for reasons of religious oppression (Ibrahim, F. 1996).

Lavish outlays of oil wealth also enabled Saddam Hussein to strengthen the civilian wing of the Party, of which he was the leader. Conflict between the military and civilian wings of the Ba'ath Party had almost destroyed the Party during its 1963 quest for power, and Saddam Hussein, a civilian, would not be able to attain his goal of total dominance until the principle of civilian superiority to the army had been firmly established. Bakr, fearing plots among his fellow officers, supported the shift to civilian rule (Karsh and Rautsi 1991). The army officers on the RCC formally agreed to this principle at the Eighth Regional Congress of the Ba'ath Party held in January of 1974, although it is not clear that they viewed it as more than a symbolic gesture.

Lavish outlays of oil wealth, however, were not able to quell growing agitation among the Kurds. By 1974, the Government was convinced that the Kurds were transforming northern Iraq, the center of much of Iraq's oil wealth, into a state within a state. The Government sought a negotiated solution, but the gap between the two sides was largely unbridgeable. With the collapse of negotiations, the government unleashed a full-scale military assault against the Kurds in the hope of beating them into submission. Iran, however, seized the opportunity to furnish the Kurds with "artillery, sophisticated anti-tank weapons, and ammunition" (Ahmad 1984, 208). Covert aid was also provided by the US and Israel. Iran's aid to the Kurds was motivated by Iraq's slide into the Soviet camp and lingering resentment over Iraqi control of the Shatt al-Arab. Iraqi support for the Ayatollah Khomeini, the Iranian religious leader who was directing his revolution against the shah from the Shi'a holy cities in Southern Iraq, also rankled. Not only did the Iraqis shelter the ayatollah, but they provided his movement with funds, weapons, military training, and media facilities that it required to undermine the Iranian monarchy.

Iranian aid precluded the Iraqi army from crushing the Kurdish rebellion, and by 1975 the two sides, now exhausted, had fought to a standstill. Two points, however, had become patently clear. First, the Ba'ath Party could not control Iraq without suppressing the Kurds. Second, the Ba'ath Party could not suppress the Kurds without the cooperation of Iran.

These realities set the stage for the Algiers Agreement of March 1975. Placing domestic consideration over foreign policy, Iraq agreed to provide Iran with equal rights to the Shatt al-Arab in return for Iran's agreement to stop arming the Kurds (Mostyn 1991; Biger 1989).

With the Kurds cut off from Iran and Russia, their two main bases of support, the Ba'athist Government moved rapidly to create a "Kurdish free security zone" along its borders with Iran and Turkey. While the numbers are vague, it is broadly acknowledged that tens of thousands of Kurds were forcibly resettled and their villages destroyed (Ismael and Ismael 1991, 182). Exhausted by the war and the flight of their main leaders, the Kurds could offer little resistance to the Iraqi army.

The Kurds, however, were not the only challenge to the Ba'athist regime. In February of 1977, the Shi'a south erupted in violence, heralding what radical Shi'a would later describe as "the first Islamic revolution" (Baram 1989, 454). While this is an overstatement, there can be little doubt that the Shi'a religious establishment had become increasingly politicized as a result of the regime's repression of its activities.

The regime responded with its customary carrot-and-stick tactics, repressing the religious opposition while simultaneously providing the Shi'a with representation on the RCC, the highest political body in the land. The revolution, if such it was, fizzled as a result of deep and abiding splits within the Shi'a religious establishment itself. The senior Shi'a religious leaders remained apolitical, choosing to confront the Iraqi regime with piety and prayer, a policy that deprived the radical clerical opposition of much of its support among the masses.

Ironically, the Ayatollah Khomeini, then guiding the Iranian revolution from his base in Najaf, remained aloof from events in Iraq. This did not mean that he approved of the Ba'athist regime or its policies, but merely that he was unwilling to allow events in Iraq to distract him from the revolution in Iran. There would be ample time to deal with Saddam Hussein once the Shah had been disposed of.

Having subdued both the Kurds and the Shi'a religious opposition, the Ba'athists turned their attention to the one remaining source of opposition, the communists. The communists retained a strong following among both the Kurds and the Shi'a and shared little love for the Ba'athists. The 1973 National Front agreement had been used by both the communists and the Ba'athists to buy time, but both well understood that the alliance was a marriage of convenience. In 1978, accordingly, the regime moved against the communists, many of whom were executed for "conducting political activities in the army" (Ahmad 1984, 196).

The end of the era, then, found the Ba'athists firmly in control of Iraq and Saddam Hussein firmly in control of the Ba'ath Party. All pretense of collective leadership was gone, and political influence was based upon personal contacts with Saddam Hussein and his relatives. Portraits of Saddam Hussein became ubiquitous, and his praises were offered in song and verse. While it was doubtful that Saddam Hussein believed that he was so beloved, creating the impression of omnipotence was an important tool in deterring popular unrest. There could be no doubt in the popular mind—and those of his enemies—that Hussein was in charge.

The Era of Islamic Resurgence

The Camp David Accords and the victory of the Islamic revolution in Iran had transformed Middle Eastern politics, posing a serious challenge to the Ba'athist regime in Iraq. While Saddam Hussein viewed Israel with concern, the Ayatollah Khomeini's vow to extend his Islamic revolution to Iraq was far more pressing. An Iranian attempt to seize power in Iraq seemed inevitable, for the two countries shared a common border and a majority of the Iraqi population were members of the Shi'a sect. The Shi'a uprising of 1977 had been crushed but left little doubt that the Fundamentalists had become a major political force in the Shi'a community.

On the plus side, the Camp David Accords prompted a new and rare solidarity between Iraq and its Arab neighbors, and improved relations with Syria offered a renewed promise of Ba'athist unity. Khomeini's Islamic Revolution, moreover, had pushed Saudi Arabia and the Gulf states into the Iraqi camp. For better or worse, Saddam Hussein, long viewed by the Gulf Arabs with suspicion, was now their first line of defense against the onslaught of the ayatollah. The United States increasingly held the same view and, in spite of the absence of diplomatic relations between the two countries, viewed the Iraqi regime with a somewhat kinder eye.

No sooner had Saddam Hussein pushed al Bakr from office in 1979 and been proclaimed president than he announced that Syria had been conspiring with members of the Iraqi leadership group to overthrow the regime (Kienle 1990). The accused were executed, shattering the temporary rapprochement between Iraq and Syria and bringing to an end any hopes of further Ba'athist unity. Once again, inter-Arab squabbles had precluded a united stand against Israel and Iran.

Saddam Hussein was thus left to face the growing threat of the ayatollah's Islamic Revolution without the support of either Syria or Egypt, the latter having been ostracized from the Arab community for making peace with Israel. The threat from Iran was both military and subversive. The military threat was of minimal concern, for the once vaunted Iranian army was in disarray following the collapse of the shah and the purging of its officer corps. Indeed, much of the Iranian army had simply melted away as recruits returned to their villages.

The subversive threat, however, was very real. The Shi'a uprising of 1977 had been orchestrated by clerics sympathetic to Iran, and Fundamentalist emotions among the Iraqi Shi'a had increased dramatically in the wake of Khomeini's victory. The loyalty of Iraq's Shi'a population, accordingly, remained an open question. Would feelings of Arabism and Iraqi nationalism bind them to the Ba'athist regime, or would the bonds of religion lead to a surge of support for Iran? This question remained unanswered, but there could be little doubt that at least part of Iraq's Shi'a community was sympathetic to the newly proclaimed Islamic republic. The attitudes of the Kurds submitted to no such ambiguity. Revolt would be imminent upon the first sign of government weakness.

In an effort to neutralize the Iranian threat, Saddam Hussein made a number of gestures to Iraq's Shi'a community, including the generous allocation of funds for mosques and Shi'a religious shrines. He also visited even the remotest Shi'a areas "where he made lavish promises of development, such as running water, electricity, the construction of roads and free allocations of television sets and refrigerators" (*Middle East Contemporary Survey*, 1978–79, 571). Similar promises were made to the residents of Baghdad's slums. Hussein also made overtures to the ayatollah suggesting that there was no reason the two countries could not live in peace as long as each respected the other's sovereignty. Iraq would not attempt to undermine Iran's Islamic Government if the ayatollah agreed not to foment revolution among Iraqi Shi'a.

The ayatollah brushed aside Hussein's overtures, calling upon all Iraqi citizens to rise up against the Ba'athist regime. There was only one nation, the ayatollah proclaimed, and that was the nation of believers. Supporters of his revolution were not supporters of Iran, but supporters of God. This was a clever ploy, for it countered Saddam's efforts to brand Shi'a activists as agents of Iran.

Shi'a religious activists responded to Khomeini's call for revolution toward the end of 1979; Saddam Hussein countered with waves of arrests and executions. The members of the Dawa Party, the leading secret Fundamentalist organization, were sentenced to death as a group. Most fled to Iran, as did members of various other Fundamentalist organizations.

Relations between the two countries continued to deteriorate over the ensuing months, and in April of 1980 Iraq and Iran placed their respective armies on full alert. In September of the same year, Saddam Hussein taunted the ayatollah by unilaterally abrogating the 1975 Algiers agreement that had given Iran equal control of the Shatt-al-Arab. Five days later, Iraqi forces launched a full-scale invasion of Iran, initiating a war that would drag on for eight years. Saddam Hussein also chose 1980 to announce the formation of a People's Assembly or Parliament. The Ba'ath Party was not seriously contested in Iraq's first parliamentary elections since 1958, but the reopening of parliament was heralded as a first step toward true democracy. Full democracy would come, Saddam Hussein promised, after the Iranians had been defeated.

Saddam Hussein justified his invasion of Iran as a legitimate response to Iranian interference in the internal affairs of Iraq. It is more probable that the invasion was intended as a preemptive strike against a Khomeini regime intent on revolutionizing southern Iraq. The regime was uncertain of the loyalty of Iraq's long-suppressed Shi'a population and saw little benefit to be gained by giving Khomeini time to consolidate his authority. A victory over Iran, moreover, would boost Saddam Hussein's popularity, erase the blemish of Iraq's 1975 capitulation to Iran over the control of the Shatt-al-Arab, and make Iraq the dominant power in the Gulf region. In this regard, there can be little doubt that Saddam Hussein, having consolidated his power in Iraq, now aspired for regional leadership (Joyner 1990).

It is also probable that the Saudis and Kuwaitis encouraged the Iraqi invasion of Iran with promises of financial support (Nonneman 1986). The Saudis were still reeling from the 1979 seizure of the Holy Mosque in Mecca by Islamic groups and could only guess at the ayatollah's next move. Kuwait, for its part, possessed a large Shi'a population and, along with Iraq, was a logical candidate for the extension of the ayatollah's revolution. While the exact role of the oil kingdoms in the initiation of the war is difficult to sort out with certainty, there can be no doubt that both provided massive financial support to the Iraqi war effort. The United States, now smarting from the Iranian seizure of American hostages, also seemed friendly to the venture. They, too, would bolster the Iraqi war effort, a topic to be discussed shortly.

The Iraqi invasion was also prompted by the assumption that victory over Iran would be swift and certain. Indeed, some sources suggest that Saddam Hussein believed that he could be in Tehran within a week (Seale 1988). As noted above, this assumption was reasonable. Iran was wracked by revolution and its army in disarray.

Saddam Hussein, then, had everything to gain and nothing to lose, or so it seemed at the time. Underlying this logic, of course, was an assumption of Iranian weakness. If this assumption were flawed, the results would be disastrous for both Iraq and the Gulf states that had rushed to its side. It would be the Islamic Revolution, not Saddam Hussein, who dominated the oil-rich Gulf.

Whatever Saddam Hussein's motivations, the war went poorly from the beginning. Iraqi forces penetrated deeply into the oil-rich province of Khusistan, but soon found that the pace of their advance had outstripped their capacity for follow-through. They had also expected the largely Arabic-speaking residents of Khusistan to rally to their cause, but the Iranians had foreseen this possibility and had forcibly evacuated the province's Arab residents. Also contrary to expectations was the unexpectedly stiff resistance of Iran's military units, many staffed by religious zealots welded into hastily mobilized revolutionary militias.

Hopes of Arab solidarity also faded as Syria announced its support for Iran shortly after the outbreak of hostilities. Libya's Colonel Qaddafi, a self-proclaimed rival of Saddam Hussein for Arab leadership, followed suit.[4] Much the same was true on the international front as promised shipments of Soviet arms were slow in arriving (Smolansky and Smolansky 1991). The Soviets had hoped to forestall a pro-American counter-coup in Iran by giving Syria and Libya permission to export Soviet weapons to Iran. By 1981 both countries were doing so in great numbers.

Iran, in contrast to Iraq, had little trouble procuring arms, the US ban on arms sales to Iran notwithstanding. Israel, with its typical disdain for US Middle East policy, shipped American weapons to Iran immediately upon the outbreak of the war. Washington protested the Israeli action but soon initiated its own arms shipments to Iran in an effort to extricate the US hostages. Having made a mockery of its own arms embargo, the US turned a blind eye as Israeli shipments of American arms to Iran mushroomed (Seale 1988). Perhaps encouraged by the new tolerance of the White House, Israel chose July of 1981 to bomb an Iraqi nuclear reactor being constructed by the French.

The situation worsened in 1982 as a Kurdish revolt forced Saddam Hussein to shift troops from the Iranian front to northern Iraq. Iranian forces had become increasingly well organized and by the end of 1982 had largely driven Iraqi troops from Iranian territory. Bowing to real-

---

[4]For more on Colonel Qadaffi's role, read M. Arab (1988).

ity, Saddam Hussein made overtures of peace to the ayatollah. The latter, now believing that Iraq was on the verge of defeat, rejected the peace offer out of hand. With Iraq conquered, his Islamic revolution would be unstoppable. The ayatollah was troubled by the fact that the Iraqi Shi'a had not revolted, but believed that they would surely do so once the Ba'athist regime had begun to crumble.

The onset of 1983, then, witnessed a reversal of roles. It was now Saddam Hussein who was on the defensive. Hundreds of thousands of civilians, Shi'a as well as Sunni, were forced to join the people's militia and sent to the front. While hardly being a spirited force, Hussein's elite units were ordered to shoot those who chose not to fight. Some Shi'a troops defected to Iran and fought against their Iraqi comrades, but their numbers do not appear to have been large. A cease-fire was also signed with the Kurds in 1983, but it failed to hold. Saddam Hussein responded by gassing the Kurds into submission. Before the war was over, a former Iraqi minister claimed that some 50,000 Kurds had been killed by poison gas while tens of thousands of others fled to Turkey and Iran (Ismael and Ismael 1991, 183). While such figures may be inflated, the number of Kurdish casualties was staggering. The regime also continued to target Shi'a activists, some 600 of whom were reported by diplomatic sources to have been killed during the first three years of the war (*NYT*[5], April 3, 1984).

Stung by his reverses, Saddam Hussein sought to bolster his sagging image with renewed pledges of democracy. Presidential elections were held in 1984, and while Saddam Hussein was the only candidate, true multi-party democracy was promised once the war had come to an end. Extraordinary efforts were also made to legitimize the regime's policies by placing them within the context of the Iraqi constitution and the charter of the Ba'ath Party. Far less publicized was a secret war of terror against the regime's opponents, real and suspected (Ibrahim, F. 1996, 248). It is difficult to judge what benefit was to be gained by Saddam Hussein's legalistic pretenses other than to ease the consciences of his apologists, a group that now included a United States reeling from the very real prospect of an Iranian victory in the Iran-Iraq war.

Saddam Hussein also moved to counter Iranian assertions that his regime was anti-Islamic by ordering members of the Ba'ath Party, now more than a million and half strong, to display signs of Islamic piety. Men were ordered to grow beards; women to wear head scarves and prudent clothing. This directive proved to be a mistake as Party members carried out Hussein's orders with such unaccustomed vigor that

[5]The *New York Times*.

their true loyalties were called into question (Ibrahim, F. 1996). The surge of piety also conveyed the image that the Fundamentalists enjoyed greater popular support than may have actually been the case, and the program was soon abandoned.

The ongoing rapprochement between the United States and Iraq was formally ratified by their renewal of diplomatic relations in 1984. The United States was now firmly committed to preventing an Iranian victory in the Gulf War and supported Iraq accordingly. Iraq continued to receive some support from the Soviets, although the latter also went out of their way to maintain good relations with Iran.

The course of the war over the ensuing years found Iranian forces attempting to overrun Iraqi positions in the largely Shi'a south. The Iraqis countered with high-altitude aerial bombings of Iranian oil facilities, cities, and military bases. The Iranians responded in kind, unleashing a "war of the cities," but were less well equipped for aerial bombardment than the Iraqis. The United States had also facilitated the Iraqi strategy by providing satellite data on the effectiveness of their air strikes (Karsh and Rautsi 1991). Still unable to stop the Iranians, the Iraqis resorted to the use of poison gas.

Iran launched a final assault on Iraq's Fao Peninsula in the spring of 1988, the sounds of battle being clearly audible in neighboring Kuwait. Much to the relief of the United States, the offensive collapsed and both sides accepted a UN-sponsored cease-fire that went into effect on July 19, 1988. Both sides had been devastated, leading to mutual speculation that the war had been an American plot all along.

The costs of the war for Iraq were enormous. Once boasting a capital surplus of some $30 billion, Iraq left the war with an international debt of well over $60 billion, although some estimates place the figure as high as $80 billion. Whether or not the debt would be repaid was a matter of conjecture, for much of the money had been provided by Kuwait and Saudi Arabia. In total, then, the war cost Iraq some $90 billion, not to mention the incalculable loss of life, property, and investment opportunities. If the latter are added to the equation, the total figure for Iraqi losses could reach as high as $452.6 billion. The corresponding figure for Iran would be in the nature of $644.5 billion (Alnasrawi 1994). Rare was the family that had not suffered the loss or maiming of a loved one.

The cease-fire found Baghdad rife with rumors of an impending coup, not by the Shi'a clerics, but by the Sunni elite. Hussein responded by increasing the size of the Presidential Guard, his personal army, which, according to press reports of the era, now constituted several divisions. Three key generals perished in helicopter crashes, although these events could have been coincidental. On the popular front, Saddam Hussein promised a swift transition to multi-party democracy and presented small cars and other gifts to the families of the war dead. It was later clarified that multi-party democracy did not encompass opposition groups that had sided with Iran during the war. Saddam also moved rapidly to gain the support of the business community by expanding the role of the private sector in the Iraqi economy (Ibrahim, F. 1996). This was not a minor consideration, for enormous profits were to be made from the rebuilding of Iraq's devastated infrastructure. These moves in place, Saddam Hussein turned the full force of the Iraqi military on the Kurdish opposition, the diverse factions of which had formed the Kurdistan Front earlier in the year (Ibrahim, F. 1996, 440).

In summary, the war with Iran dominated Iraqi politics during the era of Islamic resurgence. Saddam Hussein's motivations for invading Iraq, while persuasive, rested on the assumption that Iran was too weak to fight. In retrospect, the assumption of Iranian weakness was only partially flawed. Iraq was forced to relinquish its dreams of regional dominance, but Iran too had been exhausted by the Iraqi bombardments and was unable to press its advantage. In the final analysis, the big winners were the US, Israel, and the Gulf states, all of whom saw their interests advanced by the mutual destruction of Iran and Iraq.

The Era of the New World Order

The collapse of the Soviet Union and the advent of US hegemony in the Middle East did not appear to be matters of undue concern for Saddam Hussein and his Ba'athist regime. A strong relationship had evolved between Hussein and Washington during Iraq's war with Iran and, for better or for worse, he remained Washington's best hope of checking Iranian dominance of the Gulf (Smolansky and Smolansky 1991). The passing of Khomeini had also deprived the Islamic revolution of its spiritual guide and held out the hope of better relations between Iraq and its former adversary. At the very least, Iran had also been devastated by the war and would not pose a serious military threat to Iraq for some time. Admittedly, Saddam Hussein and his Ba'athist regime were not popular, but the opposition had been devastated during the war and found itself unprepared to revolt. The regime was also supported by more than a million battle-tested troops, although the army itself was reported to be restive.

Saddam Hussein opened the era of the new world order by warning Israel that a nuclear attack on Iraq would be countered by gas attacks on the Jewish state. The threat, while perhaps bluster to deflect the frustration of Iraq's long war with Iran, was soon followed up by the construction of missile launchers targeted at Tel Aviv (*NYT*, Mar. 30, 1990). Western concerns were allayed by Iraqi assurances that its weapons development program was purely defensive. Saddam Hussein's rhetoric played well in an Arab world long frustrated by Israel's monopoly of nuclear weapons and was supported by a May 1990 meeting of Arab foreign ministers that affirmed the right of Iraq and all Arab states to develop weapons of mass destruction for defensive purposes. The US had managed to soften the language of the communiqué, but the statement was a propaganda victory for Saddam Hussein, who continued to pursue his claim to Arab leadership (*NYT*, May 28, 1990).

Hussein's threats to Israel were matched by efforts to put his regional house in order. Diplomatic relations with Iran were reestablished in 1990 and Iraq's ties with Jordan, Egypt, and North Yemen, Iraq's partners in the 1988 Arab Cooperation Council, were strengthened. Iraq's ties with Turkey, a major Iraqi trading partner and Iraqi ally in the containment of the Kurds, were also strengthened. All, moreover, were close allies of the United States, adding credibility to the view that Saddam Hussein was a force for stability in the region. Relations with Syria remained tense, but al-Asad was absorbed with the Israeli threat and presented little threat to the Iraqi regime.

Aside from Hussein's bluster against Israel, the lone discordant note in Iraqi behavior was its verbal harassment of Kuwait, a minuscule country which Iraqi leaders had traditionally claimed as Iraq's nineteenth province. Iraqi harassment of Kuwait dated back to the early days of the monarchy and was easily explained away by apologists wanting to believe that Saddam Hussein was on the side of the angels. Among other provocations, Kuwait had stationed troops in a disputed border region and appeared to be pumping oil from the Iraqi side of their mutual border. Kuwait had also demanded repayment of the massive loans that it had made to Iraq during the Iran-Iraq War, loans which Iraq considered to be little more than Kuwait's contribution to keeping the ayatollah at bay. Indeed, Iraq felt that it was entitled to even greater support from the Gulf states. It was Iraq, after all, that had saved them from the Mullahs (Musallam 1996; Baram and Rubin 1993).

In retrospect, it seems that the US could have prevented the Gulf War by sending troops to Kuwait in July of 1990. The US, however, was intent on seeking an accommodation with Iraq, a strategy bolstered by assurances from both Egypt and Saudi Arabia that Saddam Hussein would not attack Kuwait. Saudi Arabia and the Gulf states were also adamant in their desire to keep US troops out of the region (*NYT*, Sept. 23, 1990, 12). April Glaspie, the US Ambassador to Iraq, met with Saddam Hussein on July 25 and reiterated the official line that the US wanted improved relations with Iraq. While the contents of the discussion remain a matter of dispute, Ambassador Glaspie is quoted in the *New York Times* as saying, "We have no opinion of the Arab-Arab conflicts, like your border disagreement with Kuwait" (*NYT*, Sept. 23, 1990, 12, 13).

Whatever the case, Iraqi forces did invade Kuwait on August 1, 1990, unleashing a wave of destruction on the pampered sheikhdom. A variety of factors undoubtedly contributed to Hussein's decision to invade, not the least of which was a compelling desire to erase the blot of his war with Iran. Beyond providing Saddam Hussein with the victory that had eluded him in Iran, control of Kuwait would propel him into regional leadership, bolster his popularity in an army reputedly primed for revolt, and provide the money needed to rebuild his war-shattered nation. It also appears that Saddam Hussein felt that he was being squeezed by the United States. Iran had been crippled, and it was now Iraq and its massive army that posed the greatest threat to US interests in the region. The pressure on Iraq was intensified by growing US opposition to Iraq's efforts to develop weapons of mass destruction, the magnitude of which had been publicized in the months leading up to the war. The US, moreover, had suddenly begun to criticize Iraq for the use of poison gas and other human rights abuses—actions that it had conveniently overlooked during the Iran-Iraq War. If a showdown with the US were to come, Saddam Hussein may have reasoned, Iraq's bargaining position would be strengthened by its control of Kuwaiti oil fields, not to mention the proximity of Iraqi troops to the major oil fields of Saudi Arabia. Would the US really risk a war under these circumstances?

Faced with the Iraqi occupation of Kuwait, the West responded with every means in its power short of all-out war. An economic boycott deprived Iraq of its oil income and an international armada was assembled to intimidate Saddam Hussein into submission. Only a madman, so the logic went, would attempt to resist the combined forces of the world community. The Kurds and the Shi'a were also encouraged to revolt, and Iraq was systematically cut off from all of its neighbors with the exception of Jordan. Saddam Hussein, however, stood pat.

In spite of the escalating tension, neither side seemed anxious to fight. Saddam Hussein had presented the West with a fait accompli and hoped that a policy of bluff and bluster would deter a Western attack. This was not an unreasonable proposition, for the US military was urging caution upon the American president. Indeed, President Bush was wavering on the issue of war until being bucked up by Margaret Thatcher, the British prime minister (Gordon and Trainor 1994).

General Colin Powell, the commander of US forces, also doubted that the US public would be willing to sustain massive US casualties for the sake of propping up a desert sheikhdom (Gordon and Trainor 1994). Indeed, news reports at the time suggested that a war with Iraq could result in as many as 30,000 United States casualties.

Neither side wanted to fight, but neither was willing to risk a loss of face, a particularly important concern for a Saddam Hussein still reeling from his war with Iran. The longer the stalemate dragged on, the stronger Hussein's position in the region seemed to become. Saddam Hussein portrayed himself as an Islamic David facing a Western Goliath intent on imposing Judeo-Christian rule on the Arab/Islamic world. This scenario played well in the Arab world, with Egypt, Jordan, and Morocco, the core of US support in the Arab world, all experiencing pro-Iraqi demonstrations. If the tensions were to drag on until the Muslim holy month of Ramadan, some two months away, an eruption of popular emotions could well have toppled the pro-Western regimes of the region, none of which enjoyed a strong base of popular support. The UN coalition was also showing signs of tension, and it was not clear how long the United States would be able to hold it together.

The coalition attack finally materialized on January 17, 1991, almost six months after the Iraqi invasion of Kuwait. The war had two basic objectives. First, Kuwait was to be liberated. Second, the Iraqi army was to be destroyed and with it, Saddam Hussein's capacity to threaten Iraq's neighbors. Presumably, Hussein would also fall by the wayside, the Iraqi people being unwilling to support the author of two disasters within the course of a single decade. Aside from the objectives outlined above, not much thought was given to the end game. This lack of foresight was unfortunate, for the ground war lasted only 100 hours, a figure that US policy makers thought had a nice ring to it (Gordon and Trainor 1994; McCausland 1993).

In retrospect, it appears that Saddam Hussein had not expected a war. Two factors support this supposition. First, the allied bombing assault found Baghdad and its airport fully illuminated, hardly a likely strategy for a regime expecting war. Second, Iraq's elite troops avoided combat with the UN forces and immediately retreated to Baghdad. By so doing, they avoided destruction, with the CIA estimating that 365 of the Republican Guard's 786 most advanced tanks remained in position to defend the regime (Gordon and Trainor 1994).

With the war at an end, the coalition forces found themselves in a quandary over what to do with an enemy that had been forced from Kuwait but not destroyed (Cockburn and Cockburn 1999). In large part, this confusion resulted from the contradictory concerns of the

United States as it attempted to reshape the Middle East in the aftermath of the war. As variously expressed by US officials, at least five concerns were preeminent:

1. Saddam Hussein was to be removed from power.
2. Iraq was to be precluded from threatening its neighbors and Israel. This goal was to be achieved by eliminating Iraq's capacity to use weapons of mass destruction.
3. Iraq was to retain sufficient strength to serve as a counterweight to Iran should the latter again emerge as a threat to Western interests.
4. The United States was to extend its presence in the Gulf region short of occupying Iraq. Western occupation of an Arab/Islamic country would serve only to inflame regional emotions and involve the United States and its allies in a Vietnam-style guerilla war.
5. Iraq was to remain a unified country. The United States feared that an independent Shi'a state in southern Iraq would ally itself with Iran, thereby breathing new life into the Islamic revolution that was threatening the region. Turkey and other regional powers were also adamant in rejecting the creation of a Kurdish state in northern Iraq, arguing that it would extend the Kurdish uprising in Turkey and otherwise destabilize the region.

How, then, was the United States to get rid of Saddam Hussein and preclude Iraq from threatening its neighbors without either occupying the country or allowing its dismemberment?

The de facto strategy that emerged, and one that continues to dictate the course of Iraqi politics today, was to starve Iraq into compliance with UN demands. No oil would be exported, and no goods, with the possible exception of medicine, were to be imported. Ideally, from the US perspective, these new realities would force the Ba'athist regime to sacrifice Saddam Hussein and his weapons of mass destruction while simultaneously retaining sufficient power to keep the Shi'a, the Kurds, and the Iranians in check (Cockburn and Cockburn 1999). The United States would retain a deterrent force in Kuwait and other friendly states including Saudi Arabia, thereby leaving no ambiguity about America's resolve to maintain its dominance in the region.

As might have been expected given its internal contradictions, the US plan was doomed from the start. No sooner had the war ended than both the Shi'a and the Kurds erupted in rebellion. Unwilling to either occupy Iraq or accept its dismemberment, the UN forces stood by while Saddam Hussein's Republican Guards crushed both rebellions. Only when the carnage reached epic proportions did an embarrassed US create a safe haven in Iraqi Kurdistan. A second no-fly zone was imposed on the south in August of 1992 to prevent Iraqi aircraft from strafing Shi'a villages.

Having allowed the rebellions to be crushed, the US attempted to regain lost ground by welding the Iraqi opposition into an anti-Hussein alliance. This task, however, proved to be a daunting one. The opposition, in addition to being skeptical of American resolve, was fragmented into some 90 groups beset by religious, ethnic, ideological, and personality conflicts, a topic to be elaborated upon shortly. Once Hussein was gone, or so the scenario went, the alliance would provide the basis for a pluralistic but unified Iraq.

Saddam Hussein countered US strategy by strengthening his personal security forces, most headed by relatives. He also played a cat-and-mouse game with United Nations inspectors sent to dismantle his weapons of mass destruction, allowing them partial access to suspected weapons facilities when the prospect of attack seemed imminent, and then closing the door once the threat had passed. It was also about this time that Hussein began to cast himself as the guardian of the faithful by imposing a strict regime of Islamic piety upon the Iraqi population.

Neither the US nor the Iraqi strategy was particularly successful. Saddam Hussein remained in power and continued to play his game of cat and mouse with the UN arms inspectors, but the rocket launchers and chemical plants that the UN could identify were destroyed and the UN blockade was taking its toll. The rationing system imposed at the start of the crisis was beginning to show signs of strain, and crime and corruption had become rampant. The oil-based middle class, beneficiaries of Hussein's rule, saw its wealth vanish as soaring inflation destroyed the value of its savings. Three years after the imposition of the boycott, an Iraqi dinar that had been worth three dollars at the beginning of the crisis was worth less than a penny, and black-market profiteering had become the order of the day (*NYT*, Oct. 25, 1994, 1).

Saddam Hussein responded to the rampant profiteering with severity, amputating the hands of thieves and executing some 43 merchants for price gouging (*NYT*, Oct. 25, 1994, 1). He then turned his attention to the Shi'a and the Kurds. In 1993, Hussein began draining Iraq's southern marshes, an impenetrable region that had traditionally provided a refuge to Shi'a dissidents (*NYT*, Nov. 12, 1994, 1). In so doing, he destroyed the lifestyle of the marsh Arabs, a community whose roots stretched to antiquity (Fulanain 1928). The same year saw Iraqi troops mass on the border of the Kurdish "safe haven," threatening to

bring an end to a de facto Kurdish government that had been established with the tacit support of the United States (*NYT*, May 24, 1993).
The Iraqis had already cut off all food supplies to the Kurdish region,
and international aid workers reported that existing stores were exhausted (Ofteringer and Backer 1994). Repression, in typical Hussein
fashion, was matched by concessions, especially to the Shi'a clergy.
Race tracks were closed, as were other licentious diversions offensive
to the clergy, and Saddam Hussein announced that he would soon
build the world's largest mosque (*NYT*, Oct. 25, 1994, 1).

The US, for its part, was facing world condemnation over its starvation of innocent Iraqis. Rare was the day in which the news media
failed to cover the horrors of starvation in Iraq and Kurdistan. Couldn't
food and medicine be allowed for humanitarian reasons? Such questions became particularly pressing in the Middle East.

Perhaps more pressing were leaks in the boycott. Turkey, Iraq's
largest trading partner, was experiencing severe economic hardships as
a result of the blockade and was far less concerned about Iraq's
weapons of mass destruction than it was about the evolution of a de
facto Kurdish state in northern Iraq. Japan and Western Europe were
also in the midst of economic recession, and trade with Iraq offered a
much-needed economic stimulus. Few of America's allies, moreover,
had any confidence that the boycott would attain its objectives.

The situation became even more muddled in the fall of 1994, when
Saddam Hussein again began to send troops to the Kuwaiti border in
what could only be interpreted as a direct challenge to the United
States. The Clinton administration rushed American troops to Kuwait,
drawing a line in the sand and daring Saddam Hussein to cross it. At
the very least, the Clinton regime had avoided the ambiguity of its
predecessor (*NYT*, Oct. 8, 1994, 1).

The crisis passed, but it was followed by speculation about Saddam
Hussein's motives in challenging the United States at the very time
that a partial lifting of the blockade seemed imminent. Perhaps it was
an act of bravado designed to demonstrate his courage, or it may have
been little more than a means of diverting the attention of the Iraqi
people from their suffering. Other explanations at the time suggested
that the maneuver was designed to put pressure on the United States
by reviving nationalistic emotions within the Arab world. Still others
suggested that the troop movements were a probing exercise designed
to gauge the willingness of the coalition forces to fight, or, if not that,
then the only remaining explanation was madness. Whatever Hussein's motivations, the incident left little doubt that Saddam Hussein
remained in command of a powerful army. His action represented a
message to his neighbors. It was also a message to the Iraqi people.

The two years following Iraq's 1994 challenge to Kuwait witnessed a continued standoff between Saddam Hussein and the United States, neither of which seemed particularly concerned about the suffering of the Iraqi people. Saddam Hussein appeared to have gotten the upper hand in the contest, as 1996 would see the United Nations agree to his terms for providing humanitarian food aid. Limited amounts of Iraqi oil would be allowed on the market, the proceeds from which would be used to buy food and medicine for the Iraqi people. The proposed oil-for-food deal had earlier been rejected by Iraq over UN demands that the UN distribute the food and medicine provided by the oil sales. This was a critical point, for control of food and medicine would indicate who controlled Iraq—Saddam Hussein or the UN. It would also determine who got the supplies—the average person or the supporters of Saddam Hussein. By capitulating to Saddam Hussein's demands for a role in the distribution process, the UN strengthened his position.

The same year saw Hussein's troops overrun the headquarters of the Iraqi National Congress (INC), an organization of opposition leaders headquartered in the Kurdish safe haven established by the United States. Particularly disconcerting for the West was the fact that the invasion had been made at the invitation of a Kurdish faction that had switched its allegiance from the United States to Saddam Hussein. Mutual hatreds within the Kurdish community, or so it seemed, were greater than hatred of Saddam Hussein. The Turks had earlier launched a devastating attack on Kurdish areas in Iraq in the hope of cutting off aid to the Kurdish uprising in Turkey. While ostensibly protecting the Kurds from Saddam Hussein, the Clinton White House contented itself with urging that "the scope and duration of the operation be as limited as possible" (*Christian Science Monitor*, Mar. 24, 1995). US allies followed events in Iraq with dismay, with most coalition partners now distancing themselves from US efforts to starve Saddam Hussein out of office. Saudi Arabia and many of the Gulf states also began to find a crippled Saddam Hussein a useful restraint to an Iranian government which, while showing signs of moderation, had sharply increased its naval power in the Gulf. The standoff, moreover, was keeping most Iraqi oil off the market.

Saddam Hussein was also having his troubles, most related to conflict within his family. The Iran-Iraq War, as noted earlier, had seen Saddam Hussein increasingly concentrate power in the hands of individuals from his home town of Takrit, most of whom were interrelated by marriage to one degree or another. Kinship ties did not necessarily imply a high level of trust, but blood, as the adage goes, is thicker than water. Three individuals, in this regard, were of particular importance: General Khairallah, Hussein's brother-in-law by his first wife and minister of defense during the latter years of the Iran-Iraq War; Lieutenant General Hussein Kamel Hassan, Saddam Hussein's son-in-law and distant cousin, who oversaw the buildup of the Republican Guards and headed Iraq's efforts to acquire weapons of mass destruction; and Barzan Takriti, one-time head of the intelligence services (*IHT*[6], Aug. 16, 1995, 2). Each, at one time or another, had been viewed as the second in command within the regime and the probable successor to Saddam Hussein. This honor was not without its dangers, for Khairallah, reportedly popular in the officer corps, died in a helicopter crash in 1989, an uncommonly frequent occurrence among potential contenders for power (*IHT*, Aug. 16, 1995, 2).

Tensions also existed between Barzan Takriti and Kamel Hassan, Takriti having earlier opposed Hassan's marriage to Saddam Hussein's daughter on the grounds that Iraqi custom dictated that the marriage should have been arranged between Hussein's daughter and Takriti's son. Hassan, however, married the daughter and, although a high school dropout, soon rose to the position of lieutenant general. This rapid ascent was made all the more remarkable by the fact that he had never attended military school (*IHT*, Aug. 16, 1995, 2; interviews).

Far more fundamental were the growing tensions between the established members of the inner circle and Hussein's two sons Uday and Qusai, both of whom had begun to move into positions of power. Uday, an inveterate playboy with a reputation for drunken orgies and abduction, had bludgeoned his father's food taster to death in 1988. When a young woman had protested her abduction, he reportedly had her dipped in honey and thrown to a pack of hungry dogs (*IHT*, Feb. 11, 1997, 1). In 1992 he engaged in a public fistfight with Kamel Hassan, and a few years later he shot Takriti, his uncle, seven times in the leg (*IHT*, Feb. 11, 1997, 1). On the official plane, Uday established a media empire and took over the country's (smuggled) oil sales, previously the preserve of Kamel Hassan. Qusai, of a more serious nature, had assumed control of the security services and was now responsible for Saddam Hussein's personal safety, replacing yet another son-in-law of Saddam Hussein and the brother of Kamel Hassan. Uday and Qusai, by all appearances, had now become numbers two and three respectively.

In August of 1995, Kamal Hassan and his brother, having been replaced by Saddam's sons, fled to Jordan with their wives, the daughters of Saddam Hussein. In addition to being a source of severe

[6]*International Herald Tribune.*

embarrassment to Saddam Hussein, the defections revealed the intensity of conflict within the regime and led to the discovery of weapons materials heretofore undetected by the UN inspectors. Also worrisome was information suggesting that Iraqi progress in developing weapons of mass destruction was more substantial than had been originally suspected (*IHT*, Feb. 21, 1996, 2). The two brothers and their wives returned to Iraq approximately six months after their defection, apparently finding little support for the planned overthrow of Saddam Hussein. One would presume that they had been pardoned by Saddam, but within a few days of their return they were killed by "irate relatives" disgraced by their defection.

February of 1996 would see clashes between forces loyal to Saddam Hussein and relatives of the defectors, many of whom had strong personal networks within the military. They had little to lose, for all faced retribution by Uday and Qusai. The uprising was swiftly crushed, but the following year Uday barely escaped an assassination attempt, being wounded several times and reportedly paralyzed. He would eventually recover. The attempted assassination was followed by "hundreds of executions and thousands of arrests," including the house arrest of Hussein's first wife who felt betrayed by the assassination of her sons-in-law (*IHT*, Feb. 11, 1997, 1). Nevertheless, the attempted assassination served notice that even the most stringent security measures, including the use of body doubles and false (empty) convoys, could not deter assassination attempts from dissidents with access to classified information.

The cat-and-mouse game between Saddam Hussein and the Clinton administration continued unabated throughout 1997 and 1998, with Saddam Hussein obstructing the activities of UNSCOM (United Nations Special Committee), only to back down when reprisals seemed imminent (Butler 2000a and 2000b; Graham-Brown 1999). Hussein's attempts to restrict the activities of UNSCOM suggest that the organization was at least partially effective in blocking Iraqi efforts to develop weapons of mass destruction (WMD). As Gause writes:

> What progress there has been in degrading Iraq's unconventional weapons capabilities, moreover, has come through UNSCOM and not the sanctions. President Clinton has famously and correctly said that UNSCOM destroyed more Iraqi WMD resources than did the Gulf War air campaigns. Since 1991, UNSCOM has demolished 48 Scud missiles, 30 chemical and biological missile warheads, 60 missile launch pads, nearly 40,000 chemical bombs and shells in various stages of production, 690 tons of chemical weapons agent, 3 million tons of chemical weapons precursor materials, and the entire al-Hakam biological weapons production facility. Furthermore, UNSCOM's very presence

diverted Iraqi resources from developing more WMD to hiding what
they already have (Gause 1999, 1).

Beyond resenting the effectiveness of UNSCOM in crippling his
weapons program, Saddam Hussein had also become convinced that
UNSCOM was being used by the CIA to monitor his movements.
Much to the embarrassment of both the United Nations and the United States, Hussein's suspicions proved to be correct, and UNSCOM
was ordered out of Iraq (Hersh 1999).

December 17, 1998, saw the hurried departure of the UN inspection
team, followed in short order by a massive US/UK air attack on Baghdad and its environs. The targets of the attack, code named Desert Fox,
appear to have been selected on the basis of information gathered by
the CIA via UNSCOM. In addition to bombs and guided missiles, Allied planes also dropped leaflets urging Shi'a in southern Iraq to rise up
against the regime (*Times of London*, Dec. 19, 1998).

Baghdad was heavily damaged by the four-day bombardment, but
Desert Fox failed to ignite either a mass uprising or a coup from within the ruling elite. Neither economic sanctions nor air strikes had been
able to dislodge the Iraqi leader. The victims of the cat-and-mouse
game were the Iraqi people. Hussein's elite troops were fed and sheltered; the masses were not. Denis Halliday, the coordinator of the Oil-
for-Food program, resigned in protest over the devastation wrought
upon Iraqi children, some 500,000 of whom were believed to have died
as a result of hunger or illnesses related to the US embargo. The Iraqi
educational system was also shattered, assuring that the impact of the
embargo would continue well into the twenty-first century (*Le Monde*,
Oct. 10, 1998).

With the end of Desert Fox, the Clinton administration attempted to
make resumption of the Oil-for-Food program conditional on a return
of UNSCOM, but it was not to be. Despite Iraq's refusal to allow the return of UNSCOM, the United Nations continued to extend the Oil-for
Food program for short intervals.

The standoff would continue throughout the turn of the century
(and beyond) as the US attempted to overthrow Saddam Hussein with
a combination of air strikes, boycotts, futile efforts to stimulate a military coup from within the ranks of Saddam's generals, and equally futile efforts to weld Iraq's opposition into a cohesive force. The
Arabic-language news journals reported at least two attempted coups
in the post–Desert Fox era, but neither was successful (*Al Kaisi*, Aug. 6,
1999). Hussein, for his part, developed a doomsday defense against
an anticipated invasion by the United States.

The spring of 2000 saw an eerie standoff between Saddam Hussein and his adversaries, with Hussein attempting to boost the morale of Iraq's citizens by predicting that the embargo would soon be lifted, a claim supported by growing dissension between the United States and its allies (*Salem*, Apr. 14, 2000).

As always during times of crisis, Saddam Hussein announced that there would be a return to parliamentary democracy after the imperialists had been defeated. As a first step in this direction, elections were held toward the end of March 2000 and, to no one's surprise, resulted in an overwhelming victory for the Ba'ath Party. Some 512 candidates contested the 220 seats in the Assembly, of whom a scant 160 were members of the Ba'ath Party. The remainder were independents who had been carefully screened by the regime. All of the Ba'athist candidates were victorious, providing the Party with a sizable majority in the Assembly (*Ousbou Al-Arabi*, April 10, 2000; *Al-Katib*, Apr. 3, 2000).

Even fraudulent elections, however, have their points of interest. Perhaps the greatest surprise of the Iraqi elections was the fact that Uday, the eldest son of Saddam Hussein, had stood for election, a feat he accomplished with 99.99 percent of the vote. Uday's entry into the Assembly led to speculation that he was attempting to use the Assembly as a base of support in a presumed power struggle with his younger brother Qusai over the order of succession to their father. Were this the case, parliamentary politics in Iraq would be vested with unanticipated interest (*Al-Katib*, Apr. 3, 2000).

A second point of interest was the fact that most members of the new Assembly were young and had been elected to the parliament for the first time. This fact led to speculation that the regime was attempting to build bridges with the younger members of the Party. It also seems probable that both Uday and Qusai were attempting to move their supporters into positions of power (*Al-Ousbou Al-Arabi*, Apr. 2000).

The Arabic press also speculated that the election of a new parliament was a face-saving device by Saddam Hussein to pave the way for a compromise with the US over the issue of arms inspections. He could not back down in the face of US pressure, but he could put on a democratic face and bow to the will of the Assembly.

Uday's election was followed by reports of a secret meeting of members of the "clan" in which Saddam Hussein reportedly proclaimed Qusai his heir apparent, a move presumably designed to preempt an escalation of tension between his two sons (*Salem* 2000). This action, in turn, led to speculation that the US had signaled its acceptance of Qusai as a replacement for Saddam Hussein. Both sides would have saved face and, assuming compliance on the part of Qusai, US policy goals would have been met. Dealing in speculation is risky, but it is the stuff of politics when reliable information is not available (*Salem* 2000).

The years 2000 and 2001 continued to see the cat-and-mouse game between Saddam Hussein and the US shift in the former's favor as the US watched its boycott of Iraq crumble (*NYT*, May 17, 2001, www). Russia, Japan, and France all announced plans to reestablish normal relations with Baghdad, as did Jordan, Egypt, and Turkey, the core of US support in the Islamic world. Indeed, the world at large had lost its stomach for starving innocent Iraqis (Gresh 2000). Hussein also appeared to be winning his covert war with the Kurds, some 23 percent of whom were now displaced despite the protection of the no-fly zone imposed by the US and Britain (*NYT*, Dec. 11, 2000).

Saddam Hussein also appeared to be successful in rebuilding his weapons plants, although this was hard to document, for he was equally successful in denying access to his country by UN arms inspectors. Internal attacks had also decreased during the preceding years, with Saddam Hussein now showing increased signs of confidence in his dealings with the US (Baram 2000). The US countered in 2001 by allocating money to the Iraqi opposition for covert operations within Iraq, a quixotic policy it had terminated some six years earlier (*Sunday Times of London*, Oct. 1, 2000; *NYT*, Jan. 2, 2001). Perhaps reflecting Hussein's greater confidence, Iraq renewed its verbal threats on Saudi Arabia and Kuwait, with Saddam's son, Uday, urging that new maps of Iraq include Kuwait as its nineteenth province.

Nature, however, appeared to be siding with the US as the world media reported that Saddam Hussein had suffered a major stroke (*Jerusalem Post*, Jan. 3, 2001, www). As in earlier reports of his demise, however, Saddam resurfaced, haggard but apparently in reasonable health (Iraqi television, Jan. 1–30, 2001). He celebrated his sixty-fourth birthday April 9, 2001, an event marked by massive celebrations throughout the country.

IRAQI POLITICS TODAY AND BEYOND

Much as in Syria, the Ba'athist regime in Iraq was able to consolidate its authority and bring an end to three decades of profound instability. The similarities between the two regimes provide an instructive lesson in the politics of multi-ethnic states. Both Ba'athist regimes were brought to power by military coups. Both were dominated by members of a minority group that had gained social and economic mobility by entering the officer corps: the Alawites in Syria and the Sunni Arabs in

Iraq. Both drew most of their inner circle from a narrow geographic region: the Latakia hinterland in the case of the Syrians, the region of Takrit in the case of the Iraqis. Both would increasingly place relatives in key security positions, and both would adopt a carrot-and-stick policy toward their country's major ethnic and religious groups, rewarding factions that chose to cooperate and brutally crushing those that did not. Both were increasingly dominated by leaders who were consumed with ambition and suspicion. (One would be tempted to describe this suspicion as paranoia, but paranoia is an irrational fear, whereas this attitude was grounded in reality.) The two regimes established virtually identical political structures, including a "National Command" of the Ba'ath Party that paid tribute to the fiction of Party unity. Both established socialist economic systems and became allies of the Soviet Union, policies that would erode in the mid-1980s as both sought closer ties with the United States and began, however hesitantly, to liberalize their economies. Both would see their sons primed to follow the father in office. Perhaps the major difference between the two regimes was Saddam Hussein's ability to establish the dominance of the civilian wing of the Ba'ath Party, while Syria remained under the control of its military wing.

In the remainder of the chapter we will outline the major components of the Iraqi political system and examine their roles in shaping the course of Iraqi politics today. In so doing, we will examine the factors that have enabled Saddam Hussein to remain in power for more than two decades. Finally, we shall examine the problems that these factors will pose for any post-Saddam regime.

Elites and Institutions

The Ba'athist regime that seized power in 1968 was a relatively collegial group that included the members of the Revolutionary Command Council (RCC) and the Regional Leadership (RL) of the Ba'ath Party. The membership of the two bodies overlapped, and at times they merged. Both the civilian and military wings of the Party were represented on the leadership councils, as were a variety of ideological perspectives, albeit perspectives expressed within the Ba'athist framework. The RCC and the RL were dominated by Sunnis, but diverse segments of the Shi'a community also found representation (Baram 1989). Saddam Hussein was a rising star, but his opponents were many and discussion was frank.

Saddam Hussein used the decade of the Bakr presidency (1968–1979) to consolidate his power. Each crisis—and there were many—saw his opponents fall by the wayside. The remainder were purged following an unsuccessful attempt to block Saddam Hussein from replacing Bakr. As Baram writes:

> By September 1979, only 16 of the previous 22 RCC members and only 15 of the 21 RL members remained…. But as before, the most important positions (the presidency and related duties: deputy chairman of the RCC and the first deputy of the prime minister, defense, etc.) continued to be held by Sunni Arabs (Baram 1989).

Now reigning supreme, Saddam Hussein began to remold the elite hierarchy. Civilians replaced generals, and members of Hussein's clan moved into the "commanding heights" of power. By 1986, according to Baram, "the president and his cousins alone formed 22.2 percent of the RCC and 17.6 percent of the RL" (Baram 1989, 45). It was they who controlled the security services upon which the regime depended for its survival.

By the advent of the twenty-first century, several key family members had fallen by the wayside as the inner circle of Iraqi politics narrowed from Saddam Hussein's broad extended family to Saddam Hussein and his two sons. Uday, 36[7], heads a family financial empire reputed to be worth billions, while Qusai, age 34, heads the national security apparatus. It is Qusai who is responsible for the security of his father and the regime. With the promotion of both sons, other members of Hussein's more or less immediate family (half-brothers, uncles, sons-in-law, etc.) were either purged or moved outside the inner circle. Saddam Hussein and his sons make the critical decisions in Iraq, followed by the security chiefs, the members of the Revolutionary Command Council, the Regional Leadership of the Ba'ath Party, the cabinet, and the parliament. In 2001, Saddam Hussein appeared to indicate that Qusai would be his successor by nominating him for election to the leadership of the ruling Ba'ath Party (*Ha'aretz*, May 20, 2001).

The Security Apparatus

A leading Arabic-language news magazine recently outlined eight major Iraqi security organizations:

1. The Special Army headed by Qusai (The Special Army is simultaneously an intelligence apparatus, rapid response force, and counter-intelligence unit.)
2. The Special Security Force
3. The Emergency Force

---

[7]As of 2001.

4. The Fedayeen Saddam militia
5. The Presidential Security Apparatus
6. The Special Guards
7. The Special Revolutionary Guards
8. The Presidential Air Force, a unit attached to the Republican Guards

Sumaida (1991) offers a somewhat different schematic of the Iraqi security apparatus. Whatever its configuration, Iraqi's security apparatus is both formidable and effective. It is also under the direct control of Saddam Hussein's son, Qusai.

The security services, in turn, give way to a military apparatus headed by the Republican Guards and they to the regular army. Shakeups in the security services and military are frequent, with Al-Iyash (1998a) reporting eight major changes in the military/security leadership between 1993 and 1998. These shakeups were designed to prevent a coup, but also reflect the growing influence of Qusai in the power structure. It is his people who are becoming dominant. Many security chiefs also find representation on either the RCC or the RL, the composition of which has been fluid.

The members of the RCC and the RL serve as advisors to Saddam Hussein and give representation to key segments of the Iraqi community including the Shi'a and, to a lesser extent, the Kurds. Neither the RCC nor the RL is in a position to countermand the orders of Saddam Hussein or his sons. Nevertheless, the members of the RCC and the RL are very important people. They are directly responsible for seeing that Hussein's orders are carried out, and the way in which they carry out those orders affects the lives of millions of Iraqis. They also dispense huge amounts of patronage. The Shi'a members of the RCC and RL, for example, have much to say about the allocation of scarce resources in the predominantly Shi'a south. Among other things, this involves countering the influence of the Shi'a clergy and building support networks capable of sustaining the regime.

Following the members of the RCC and the RL in the elite hierarchy are members of the cabinet, most of whom head Iraq's large administrative agencies. They, too, dispense massive amounts of patronage and provide links to their respective communities. Iraqi Shi'a receive representation on the cabinet more or less in proportion to their numbers.

The bottom rung of the elite hierarchy is occupied by the members of parliament. The parliament is designed to give the impression of national unity, and its members, although powerless, represent another patronage link between Iraq's diverse communities and the regime.

Whatever the structure of the elite hierarchy, all decisions of importance must be approved by Saddam Hussein. Much attention, accordingly, has been given to the analysis of Saddam Hussein's personality, and particularly the influence of an incredibly difficult childhood on his subsequent behavior. As recounted by Musallam:

> A number of outside observers, on the other hand, see Saddam as a man driven by an inferiority complex created by the trauma of his childhood experiences, the bitterness of which has haunted him ever since. Saddam Hussein had a fatherless childhood; some reports claim that his father died before his son was born, while others allege that the father simply abandoned his wife and child. In either case, Saddam's sense of rejection cannot have been lessened when his mother remarried. Her new husband was the already-married Ibrahim al-Hassan, a crude, brutal and illiterate peasant who resented Saddam and abused him both physically and psychologically. For example, to show his contempt for the boy, al-Hassan reportedly used to send his own son to school while demanding that Saddam work in the fields. In addition, contrary to Arab custom, the young Saddam was raised in the house, a humble mud-brick affair, that his mother shared with her new husband. Because of the stepfather's reputation (he was known locally as 'Hassan the liar') and the unusual situation at home, the boy is said by Bulloch and Morris to have been considered an outcast by other children. He got into fights rather frequently, and when neighbours complained about him, al-Hassan's response was to blame Saddam's mother. "He is the son of a cur" he would tell her. "Send him away" (Musallam 1996, 35).

In addition to the adverse effects of his childhood, other observers find Saddam's behavior to be a reflection of his role models: Stalin and Don Corleone, the Mafia leader in *The Godfather* (Miller and Mylroie 1990).

The Ba'ath Party

The organizational structure of the Ba'ath Party is essentially the same as that described in the discussion of Syrian politics, with a Regional Leadership or Politburo heading a political bureaucracy designed to keep tabs on the Iraqi population. The Regional Leadership is paralleled at the provincial and local levels, with Party cells penetrating offices, factories, and neighborhoods. Congresses are held from time to time to ratify changes of policy and personnel announced by Saddam Hussein, who serves as president of the Regional Ba'ath. Much as in the Syrian case, a symbolic "National Command" pays lip service to the "all-Arab" nature of the Ba'ath Party, most of its members being

Syrian exiles and opponents of former Syrian President Hafez al-Asad.

The Party also controls all civilian organizations in Iraq, including labor unions, professional associations, and various organizations for youth, women, and peasants. Popular organizations outside the Ba'athist framework are disallowed, with the exception of religious groups, many of which are also disallowed. All in all, little escapes the eye of a Ba'ath Party that is very much part of Saddam Hussein's security apparatus. The Ba'ath Party also maintains its own militia and intelligence networks, many of which were designed by Saddam Hussein during the decade of Bakr rule (Khalil 1989).

According to Iraqi colleagues, the approval of the Ba'ath Party, if not actual Party affiliation, is required for appointment to positions of any importance in the military and bureaucracy as well as for entrance to the universities. Such policies are designed to reward the supporters of the regime while precluding its opponents from attacking the system from within. Inevitably, this practice has resulted in rampant opportunism as Iraqi citizens join the Party for personal gain rather than ideological commitment. Indeed, one can question how much of Ba'athist ideology remains in Saddam's Iraq.

Such questions are pertinent, for the foundation of Hussein's rule is military and tribal rather than ideological. An interesting variation on this theme has been Saddam Hussein's courtship of Iraq's tribal leaders, a group long condemned by the Ba'athist leadership as archaic remnants of Iraq's feudal past. As Baram writes:

> First, rather than eliminating the tribal shaykh as a sociopolitical power, as dictated by party doctrine, he endeavored...to turn them into docile tools in the service of the regime. Second, and a far sharper departure from party tradition, he turned the tribal shaykhs into legitimate partners for power-sharing; he tribalized the regime's Praetorian Guard; and he worked to reawaken long-suppressed and often forgotten tribal affinities in that part of Iraqi society which is no longer tribal and to graft onto it tribal values, or what he considered to be such values. Furthermore, he even took some steps to tribalize the party itself, and tribal customs, real or imagined, permeated the state's legal system. Kinship was legitimized as a principle guiding the selection of party leaders, and leaders' tribal roots were played up... (Baram, 1997, 1).

As noted earlier, the regime also relies on the support of the Sunni community and particularly Sunnis from the region of Takrit. The closer one is to Saddam Hussein, the greater one's role in sustaining the regime. Sunnis would be the big losers should power shift to the Shi'a majority, and they are well aware of the desire of the Shi'a and the Kurds for vengeance.

Opponents of the Regime

Arrayed against Saddam Hussein's formidable security apparatus are the same groups that have always opposed Iraq's central government: the Kurds, large parts of the Shi'a community, and those elements of the Sunni community that find themselves at odds with Hussein's Takriti-dominated regime. Saddam Hussein is not fond of dissent, and least of all dissent from rival clans within the Takriti community itself. To the religious and ethnic bases of the Iraqi opposition must be added the proponents of democracy as well as the communists and the Arab nationalists (Hazelton 1994). Baram also notes that the Ba'athist regime now finds its center of gravity in the lower classes, thereby suggesting tension between Saddam Hussein and the Sunni upper and middle classes that once dominated Iraqi politics (Baram 1989).

The core of the opposition, however, rests with the Kurds and the Shi'a, communities that together constitute some 80 percent of the Iraqi population. Each has a vested interest in reversing the Sunni domination of Iraq, yet each is hopelessly divided within itself. Cooperation between the two communities also has been lacking.

The Kurds   The Kurds constitute an ethnic community of at least 20,000,000 people occupying a contiguous region that incorporates portions of Turkey, Iraq, Iran, Syria, and Russia. Turkey is home to the largest number of Kurds (10,800,000), followed in turn by Iran (5,500,000), Iraq (4,100,000), Syria (1,000,000) and Russia (5,000,000)[8] (Graham-Brown and Sackur 1995). The Kurds have pressed for an independent Kurdish state since the collapse of the Ottoman Empire, but to no avail (Khashan 1995; Khashan and Nehme 1996).

Although most Kurds are Sunni Muslims, the Kurdish community also contains significant Shi'a and Alevis minorities.[9] The Kurds share a common language, albeit a language fragmented into extreme dialects. As a sixteenth-century traveler would write, "And the Kurdish nation divides into four branches, each with its own different tongue and customs. First is the Kurmanj, second the Lur, third the Klahur, fourth the Guran" (Prince Sharafaddin Bitlisi. 1597. *The Sharafnama*, Prologue, 7–9; www.Humanrights.de).

Most Kurds today speak one of two main dialects. Sorani is the dominant Kurdish dialect in Iraq and Iran, while Kurmanji is spoken in Turkey and the Turkish border regions in Iraq. Kurmanji is also spoken in the Kurdish areas of the former Soviet Union. The Sorani and Kur-

---

[8]Numbers vary with the source.
[9]Alevis represent a separate religious sect and should not be confused with Alawites.

manji dialects are minimally compatible, making communication within the Kurdish community difficult. Linguistic and regional differences are overlaid by tribal and ideological conflicts, not to mention abiding personal rivalries within the Kurdish leadership.

As might be anticipated, the conflicted nature of Kurdish society has made sustained opposition to the Iraqi regime difficult (Barth 1953). This fact is well illustrated by the pervasive tension that exists between Iraq's two main Kurdish parties: the Kurdish Democratic Party (KDP), headed by Masoud Barzani, and the Patriotic Union of Kurdistan (PUK), headed by Jalal Talabani. Barzani and Talabani have made no secret of their antipathy toward each other. In addition to the mutual aversion of the two leaders, the KDP finds much of its support in the tribal countryside, while the PUK is favored by the urban intellectuals. The KDP also draws its support disproportionately from Kurmanji-speaking areas of Iraqi Kurdistan, while the PUK is stronger among the Sorani-speaking Kurds.

Saddam Hussein's brutal assault on the Kurds in 1987–1988 resulted in the formation of a United Front that included the PUK and the KDP as well as a number of minor political parties.[10] Despite efforts to achieve greater unity, there was little that the United Front could accomplish in the face of the government's superior force. These circumstances would change with Iraq's defeat in the Gulf War of 1991. Fired by both American calls for revolt and the Shi'a uprising in the south, the Kurdish provinces of northern Iraq erupted in revolt. The long-sought goal of Kurdish independence was at hand, or so it seemed at the time.

Optimism concerning the establishment of a Kurdish state, however, vanished as suddenly as it had appeared. Pressured by the Turks to prevent the emergence of a Kurdish state and fearful that the breakup of Iraq would find the Shi'a south aligned with Iran, the United States stood by as Saddam Hussein crushed both the Shi'a and the Kurdish revolts. The loss of life was devastating, and some sources suggested that as many as 1,500,000 Kurds, approximately one-third of Iraq's Kurdish population, were forced to flee to either Turkey or Iran (Graham-Brown and Sackur 1995, 8).

Stunned by the magnitude of the calamity it had helped to create, the United States imposed a no-fly zone on northern Iraq (see Figure 6.1). Inadvertently, and to the dismay of the Turks, the Kurdish region of northern Iraq was transformed into a quasi-independent state. Both the Iraqi and the Turkish governments rejected the new entity, with the Iraqi government slapping a complete economic and administra-

[10]The PKK, the Kurdish party in rebellion against Turkey, had little influence in Iraq.

Figure 6.1
Iraq's No-Fly Zones

tive boycott on the breakaway region. The Kurds thus found themselves suffering from two economic boycotts: one imposed by the Iraqi
government on Kurdistan and the other by the United States on Iraq
including the breakaway provinces. While the United States had made
a quasi-independent Kurdish state possible, it had no intention of sustaining it with military or economic aid. Non-governmental organizations such as the United Nations helped to fill the void, but the
economic situation remained grim.

Despite overwhelming odds against the establishment of a Kurdish
government, elections for this purpose were held in 1992. A Kurdish
university was also created to train personnel for government service
and to allow Kurdish students from the breakaway provinces, now
barred from Iraqi universities, to continue their educations.[11]

The elections demonstrated the fragility of the United Front, with
the PUK and the KDP each acquiring 50 seats in the 105-seat Kurdish
National Assembly. Neither could rule. To further complicate matters,
each party dominated the regions of its traditional strength. Rather
than having no government, Iraqi Kurdistan was now on the verge of
having two: one dominated by the KDP, the other by the PUK. As described by Graham-Brown and Sackur:

[11]Based on interviews with the president of the Kurdish University.

Since the elections of May 1992, the power-sharing system of government in the Iraqi Kurdish entity—referred to as "fifty-fifty"—has reinforced networks of patronage operated by each of the two main parties. The system of dual patronage filters all the way down to the appointment of teachers in local primary schools and the number of policemen on patrol. If one administrator, policeman or school principal is a PUK supporter, then he must be balanced by a nearby KDP member of equivalent rank (Graham-Brown and Sackur 1995, 12).

Fighting between the PUK and the KDP erupted again in 1994 and 1995, with the ephemeral Kurdish quasi-state struggling to exist as best it could. Turkey, for its part, invaded Northern Iraq in pursuit of Turkish Kurds in rebellion against Ankara. Ironically, the Kurdish quasi-government in Iraq offered little support to members of the PKK, the Kurdish group leading the rebellion against Turkey, perhaps fearing further reprisals from Ankara. Unsure of how to proceed, the United States did nothing.

The Shi'a   Iraq's Shi'a community constitutes approximately 60 percent of the Iraqi population and is concentrated largely in the southern provinces of the country (see Figure 6.1). Migration from the south has also resulted in Baghdad becoming a largely Shi'a city, with much of the Shi'a population crammed into massive slums such as Revolutionary City, an area of more than a million residents. Southern Iraq is also the site of the Shi'a holy cities, the most important of which are Karbala and Najaf, the former being the burial site of Ali's son Hussein and the latter possessing the Shrine (tomb) of Ali.

Shi'a resentment of Sunni dominance is intense and reflects the substantial differences in doctrine that separate the two sects as well as decades of Sunni oppression. Sectarian differences have also been reinforced by profound economic inequalities, with Iraqi Shi'a, on average, being far poorer than their Sunni counterparts.

Shi'a activism from the 1940s through the early 1960s was largely an urban affair organized by the Communist Party. With the crushing of the communists in 1963, the political leadership of the Shi'a community shifted to the Shi'a clergy, a group that had been largely apolitical since the anti-British uprisings of the 1920s (Batatu 1981). The stimulus for political action among the Shi'a ulema appears to have been twofold. First, the Shi'a religious elite was becoming increasingly marginalized by the growing secularism of Iraqi society, a process introduced by the British occupation and reinforced by the radical regimes of the post-revolutionary era. For the younger generations of Shi'a, technology rather than religious science had become the order of the day. Wiley, for example, notes that the number of religious scholars in the holy city of

Najaf declined from 12,000 prior to the British occupation to 600 in 1977 (Wiley 1992, 79).

Second, and more pressing, were Ba'athist efforts to bring the Shi'a clergy under Party control (Batatu 1981). The summer of 1969 would see the closing of a major Shi'a university in Kufa, the city in which Ali was mortally wounded, as well as the expulsion of Iranian students in Karbala and Najaf. Iranians represented a sizable portion of the student population in the Iraqi seminaries and were viewed as a threat by the Iraqi regime. Iraqi seminary students, for their part, were conscripted into the military, an order later rescinded in the name of national unity (Ibrahim, F. 1996). Adding insult to injury, the Shi'a religious establishments in the holy cities of Karbala and Najaf were placed under the supervision of the Sunni-controlled Ministry of Waqfs (religious endowments), a deep affront to the Shi'a clergy. Simultaneously, pressure was placed on *bazaaris* (merchants) to curtail their contributions to the Shi'a spiritual leaders. This was not a matter of minor concern, for the financial position of the Shi'a clergy had long been in decline. As if to underscore the regime's determination to destroy the financial base of the Shi'a clerics, some 3245 merchants of Iranian nationality were deported to Iran. Many of those deported were actually of Iraqi origin, but their forefathers had claimed Iranian citizenship during the Ottoman years as a means of avoiding military service (Ibrahim, F. 1996; Kelidar 1983). When economic pressures failed to achieve the desired results, prominent Shi'a clerics were assassinated, as were Shi'a merchants known for their generous contributions to the religious community, a process that intensified following the Shi'a uprisings of 1977.

Efforts to counter governmental repression took concrete form with the suppression of the Dawah Party. The Dawah, which had been founded about a decade earlier, was accused of inciting Shi'a demonstrations in both 1974 and 1977, the latter posing a direct challenge to the authority of the Ba'athist regime. Khomeini's 1979 victory in Iran further radicalized the Shi'a clergy, with both the Dawah and a newly formed Mujahedin, a smaller but more radical group, urging open revolt against the regime. By 1980, the Ba'athist regime was under siege as Baghdad witnessed guerilla warfare similar to that which had toppled the shah in Iran.

Saddam Hussein responded with maximum force. Key leaders of the Dawah Party were executed in response to the 1974 and 1977 disturbances, and 1980 would see the assassination of Sayyid Mohammed Baqir al-Sadr, the spiritual guide of the Dawah movement and a figure that opposition radio stations referred to as "the Khomeini of Iraq" (Batatu 1981, 590). Indeed, the Iraqi opposition of the era claimed that some 500 of their leaders and supporters were put to death between 1974 and 1980 (Batatu 1981). The same period also saw the continued expulsion of Iranian residents from Iraq, many with Iraqi roots that extended for centuries.

Many observers—including the Ayatollah Khomeini—expected, accordingly, that the Shi'a would rise up *en masse* during the Iraq-Iran War. They did not. A Shi'a uprising occurred after the Gulf War of 1991, but it was easily suppressed. Hussein's control of the Shi'a south remains intact despite the US-imposed no-fly zone. Why, then, has Saddam Hussein been able to impose his rule on a disadvantaged Shi'a majority that constitutes some 60 percent of the Iraqi population?

The answer to this question, while elusive and inconclusive, illustrates the complexity of Iraqi politics and particularly the politics of the Shi'a community. The first point to be noted is that the leadership of the Shi'a community was traditionally divided between three groups: secular parties such as the Communists and the Ba'athists, the Shi'a religious clergy, and the tribal sheikhs. In recent decades, the secular leadership of the Shi'a community has either been co-opted by the Ba'athist regime or crushed, as were the Shi'a tribal leaders (Ibrahim, F. 1996; Baram 1997). Shi'a opposition, accordingly, is largely restricted to the clergy. Secular Shi'a do not necessarily welcome the prospect of a religious state, and what remains of the secular Shi'a leadership finds it difficult to cooperate with their clerical counterparts in the Shi'a community (Ibrahim, F. 1996).

To make matters worse, the Shi'a religious leadership is divided among itself. Some religious leaders advocate political activism while others favor concentrating on prayer and good works. Salvation, according to the latter view, is more important in the grand scheme of things than the momentary gains of political activism. This view was long the norm among the Shi'a clergy. Equally divisive has been the bitter competition between the dominant ayatollahs for control of the Iraqi religious community and its holy cities. The above tensions, in turn, are fueled by the struggle for dominance between the clergy of Iranian origin and those of Iraqi/Arab origin. The conflict within the clergy can be traced to competition between the Iraqi city of Najaf and the Iranian city of Qum for preeminence in Shi'a affairs. Finally, even the main Fundamentalist organizations have found it difficult to agree on a common program. The Iranian-sponsored High Council for the Revolution advocates the formation of an Islamic government in Iraq while the Dawah Party and the Organization for Islamic Action advocate a pluralist democracy that reflects Iraqi circumstances (Ibrahim, F. 1996). The Fundamentalist dispute has led to violence among Iraqi exiles in Iran's holy city of Qum as well as within Iraq itself. The Organization for Islamic Action is funded by the Gulf states and claims to be more independent of Iran than either the Dawah Party or the High Council for the Revolution (Wiley 1992).

In order to clarify the above points, it may be useful to briefly summarize the ranks within the Shi'a ulema. By the nineteenth century, the practice evolved of selecting a paramount ayatollah (great sign of God) or marja'-i-taqlid-i-uzma, literally translated as "highest source of imitation" to serve as the representative of the Hidden Imam. As a representative of the Hidden Imam, a paramount ayatollah possessed the power of interpreting religious texts (ijtihad) in a manner compatible with the wishes of the Hidden Imam, a powerful position that far transcended the realm of the profane. All paramount ayatollahs were regarded with awe by the masses. Paramount ayatollahs (marji) were selected by their peers on the basis of their writings and piety, and their views were usually binding with regard to religious issues. Usually there was only one paramount ayatollah, but each region of the Twelver[12] world would generally select its own paramount ayatollah.

The paramount ayatollah or grand marja was followed in the hierarchy of religious elites by a variety of ayatollahs and they by less-established hujjat al-Islam.[13] All of the above possessed the power to issue binding legal opinions on matters of religion (ijtihad) but generally deferred to the views of their superiors within the religious hierarchy. All were selected by their peers on the basis of their scholarship and piety and each generally headed a circle of learning consisting of sheikhs or imitators. Of the latter, some were students while others managed mosques or schools. Sheikhs, in turn, were supported by the ordinary men of religion who taught children the Koran, led prayers, and performed similar religious duties. To a large extent, the influence of the ayatollahs was proportional to the size of their following among the sheikhs, the pious, and the population at large. The above hierarchy was loose, with each layer "imitating" the layer above it on a more or less voluntary basis. It was also non-political, with the ayatollahs devoting themselves to religious rather than secular issues (Batatu 1981).

This pattern would change with the ascendancy of the Ayatollah Khomeini, the leader of Iran's Islamic revolution. Under Khomeini, the power to interpret the wishes of the Hidden Imam became mani-

---

[12]Dominant branch of Shi'a Islam, of which southern Iraq and Iran are a part.
[13]Parallel ranks existed between the traditional Shi'a practice of marji'yyah (supreme authority) and the Ayatollah Khomeini's subsequent concept of the ayatollah. Authority in the former tradition was pluralistic and admitted to a variety of interpretations. Khomeini's system, by contrast, was more rigid and less tolerant of diverse opinions.

festly political and, as we will see in Chapter 7, provided Khomeini with a weapon of mass mobilization far more powerful than the guns of the shah.

The last Grand Ayatollah in Iraq was Abu al Qasim al Khoui, a profound religious scholar who eschewed political activity in favor of piety and prayer, a position that dampened the effectiveness of the more politicized ayatollahs who were attempting to stimulate Shi'a opposition to the Ba'athist regime. Needless to say, the ascetic position of Khoui was much appreciated by Saddam Hussein.

Upon the death of Khoui in 1992, the Iraqi community was left without a grand ayatollah, an event that influenced Iraqi politics in three ways. First, the religious authority of the Iranian ayatollahs increased, a situation much feared by the Iraqi regime. Second, Iraq's politicized ayatollahs, now free of Khoui's asceticism, were given greater scope for political action. Third, intense competition developed among the ayatollahs of Iraq for the leadership of Iraq's Shi'a community. Who, if any, was to become the new grand ayatollah (exalted marja)? This issue also had ethnic overtones, for many of the contenders for the position were of Iranian origin.

Saddam Hussein was vitally interested in assuring that the successor to Khoui, if such there was to be, would be both ascetic (nonpolitical) and of Arab and Iraqi origin. The first condition would dampen the influence of Iraq's politicized clergy, while the second would establish an Arab alternative to Iranian leadership of the Shi'a community (Hidar 1999).[14] By playing one religious leader against another, moreover, Hussein would be able to reduce the effectiveness of the clergy as a whole.

To further this end, Saddam Hussein identified Mohammed Sadiq as-Sadr, an ayatollah from a long line of Iraqi religious leaders, as the most suitable candidate for the leadership of Iraq's Shi'a community[15] (Nakash 1994). In addition to being an Iraqi Arab, as-Sadr shared the ascetic, non-political orientation of the deceased Khoui. Rumors abounded about a deal between Hussein and as-Sadr, with as-Sadr's opponents referring to him as the "regime marja" (*al-Katib*, Mar. 1999). Whether or not this was the case, Saddam Hussein lost little time in paving the way for as-Sadr's ascendence. As-Sadr's sermons were broadcast over Iraqi radio and television, and he was allowed a freedom of movement denied to his competitors. As-Sadr was also given

---

[14]The desire for an Arab alternative to Iranian religious leadership has also found support in Lebanon, where the Grand Ayatollah Fadlallah has established a religious circle (hauza) in competition with that of Qum (interview with Dr. Nizar Hamzeh, American University of Beirut, 2000).

[15]Mohammed Sadiq as-Sadr was a cousin of Mohammed Bakr as-Sadr, one of the dominant leaders of the Shi'a opposition to Saddam Hussein during the late 1970s. The latter had been executed in 1980.

control of foreign students studying in Najaf and allowed to open offices in Iraq's predominantly Shi'a cities, a privilege also denied to his competitors (*al-Katib*, Mar. 1999; Hidar 1999). Indeed, as-Sadr's competitors found themselves increasingly harassed by the regime, with rumors circulating that Saddam Hussein had ordered the assassination of non-Iraqi ayatollahs.

Once again, however, the regime's strategy backfired. As-Sadr's sermons struck a responsive chord among Iraqi Shi'a and, wittingly or unwittingly, he emerged as a potential competitor of Saddam Hussein. This danger would become manifest in the early months of 1998 as sermons on peace and piety increasingly gave way to criticisms of the regime. He also urged his followers to attend the Friday prayers in person rather than watching them on television (*al-Katib*, Mar. 1, 1999). Attendance at Friday prayers increased dramatically, with as-Sadr's Friday prayers reportedly attracting more than 100,000 worshipers crowded into the Grand Mosque of Najaf and its surrounding courtyards—a terrifying number for the embattled dictator (Hidar 1999). Saddam Hussein reportedly sent emissaries to as-Sadr urging that his sermons return to questions of faith and liturgy. This action was followed by the closing of as-Sadr's offices and the arrest of his lieutenants, but to no avail. As-Sadr responded by predicting that he would be assassinated, suggesting that "if Mohammed Sadr dies, [the matter] will be transferred to others" (Hidar 1999).

His prediction came true on February 18, 1999, when he and his two sons were murdered by unknown assailants. Saddam Hussein was accused of the assassinations, but Hussein was not the only party with a motive for eliminating as-Sadr. Elevation to the position of exalted marja is a function of support within the clergy, and as-Sadr's rise to preeminence posed a direct threat to the aspirations of other reigning ayatollahs. As-Sadr's competitors also blamed him for government harassment and were further incensed when as-Sadr ordered Shi'a to pay their religious contributions directly to the poor and needy rather than going through the marja and their agents. Religious contributions (zakat, the kums, and cash gifts) are normally administered by the clergy and provide the main source of their income. As-Sadr's fatwa, accordingly, attacked the economic viability of his competitors.

Iran's displeasure with as-Sadr was also intense. As-Sadr's implicit support of Saddam Hussein had dampened Iranian influence among Iraqi Shi'a and otherwise fragmented the Shi'a community. Iran also had little desire to see the emergence of a grand ayatollah among the Iraqi Arabs, nor was it anxious to see the resurgence of Najaf as a competitor to Qum as the spiritual center of Shi'a faith. Again, these were not minor issues, for Iranian dominance of the Shi'a communities in

Iraq and Lebanon had become a cardinal principle of Iranian foreign policy. To paraphrase al-Qisi in reference to the four marjas who were assassinated during 1998, "It is possible to make two lists of the assassinated marjas: those assassinated by Saddam Hussein and those assassinated by Iran and its agents" (*al-Qisi*, Mar. 5, 1999, 20).

Although it will probably never be known who killed as-Sadr, a variety of other factors also contributed to Saddam Hussein's ability to control Iraq's Shi'a majority. Iraq, for example, has long suffered from a shortage of religious clergy, a fact that has hampered the political mobilization of the Shi'a community (Batatu 1981). This shortage has grown increasingly more severe with Saddam Hussein's crippling of religious education and his expulsion of Iranian nationals.

Many of the activists in the Dawah Party and most other opposition groups fled to Iran during the war. Not only did this exodus reduce the effectiveness of the opposition, but it also led to charges that the members of the Shi'a opposition were traitors to the Arab cause.

In addition to conflict within the Shi'a clergy, political activism among the Iraqi Shi'a was also dampened by a "profound fear" of retribution by the Ba'athist regime (Ibrahim, F. 1996, 398–399). Such fears could only have been increased by the United States' refusal to support religious groups that inclined toward Iran, a topic to be discussed shortly.

The Iraqi Opposition: An Assessment   The Kurds and the Shi'a clergy form the pillars of the Iraqi opposition. They, in turn, are joined by the remnants of the Arab Nationalists and the communists, both of which had their roots in the era of the monarchy. To this list must be added dissident Ba'athists as well as Iraq's smaller minority groups such as the Assyrians, Turkomen, and Iranians.

Aside from a desire to overthrow Saddam Hussein, the diverse elements of the Iraqi opposition have little in common. As we have seen in the above discussion, neither the Kurds nor the Shi'a can speak with a single voice. No group within the opposition, moreover, is strong enough to impose its views on the others. All pay lip service to the goals of democracy and a unified Iraq, yet there is little in the behavior of the dominant groups to suggest that a coalition government of opposition parties could achieve either objective (Dabrowska 1994).

This fragmentation has been highlighted by US efforts to cobble together an effective coalition of opposition groups, all of which have ended in disillusionment. A Joint Action Committee emerged in 1991 but was undermined by internal divisions and the lack of US support for the uprisings of that year. Also problematic was the existence of between 70 and 90 opposition groups, only 17 of which were represented on the Joint Action Committee. The Joint Action Committee gave way to an Iraqi National Congress that continues to meet in the Kurdish quasi-state in northern Iraq. Like its predecessors, it has been immobilized by the same fragmentation and personality conflicts that beset Iraqi politics as a whole.

A far more serious threat, from Saddam Hussein's perspective, is the specter of treason within his own ranks. Hussein's very existence now threatens the entire Ba'athist regime, and he is well aware that many of his former loyalists are willing to sacrifice him for the sake of saving their own skins. Hussein would go, but they would stay. In spite of its attempts to weld a divided opposition into a viable alternative to Saddam Hussein, the United States also views an internal coup as the most likely means of toppling Saddam Hussein and is doing everything in its power to further that end (Shihab 1999). Hussein would be gone, but the Balkanization of Iraq would be precluded by a continuation of the Ba'athist regime. The US would also be rescued from a boycott that was as futile as it was embarrassing.

THE CONTEXT OF IRAQI POLITICS

Iraqi politics, of course, encompasses far more than the simple interactions of its actors and institutions. Those interactions, while critical to understanding Iraqi politics and Saddam Hussein's grip on power, are profoundly influenced by a variety of cultural, economic, and international factors. In many ways, it is these factors that determine the limits to Hussein's power.

Political Culture

The patterns of Iraqi politics, as we have seen in previous sections of this chapter, have been profoundly influenced by cultural factors, the foremost of which are religious and ethnic identities. For better or for worse, Iraq remains a collection of mutually hostile communities, loyalty to which is far stronger than loyalty to the state. Ethnic and religious conflicts, in turn, have resulted in a high level of distrust between both individuals and groups, as has Iraq's tribal past. Also reflective of Iraq's tribal past is the patriarchal style of rule that has characterized all of Iraq's leaders, not to mention their reliance on relatives to fill key positions within their respective regimes. Even within clans, interpersonal distrust remains intense. Blood is thicker than water, but it cannot guarantee loyalty.

Iraq, moreover, remains a society in transition. Secular ideologies such as Ba'athism and communism compete with deeply held religious attachments. The latter, in turn, have found Iraq's Shi'a population torn between loyalty to their Arabic roots and a Shi'a faith championed by the Islamic Republic of Iran.

Saddam Hussein has used the tensions within Iraq's ethnic and religious communities to fragment opposition to his regime. By the same token, the cultural tensions that have enabled Saddam Hussein to divide his opponents have kept him from transforming Iraq into a political community with shared values and a common political identity. A nation divided against itself cannot long survive.

Iraqi political culture also manifests profound feelings of alienation. Iraqis cannot overthrow the regime, but they do little to support it. The regime's dictates are enforced by coercion rather than feelings of legitimacy, and when the coercion stops, so does the cooperation of the populace. Even the members of the Ba'ath Party are motivated more by a sense of opportunism and survivalism than dedication to the Party's lofty goals. Lacking an emotional base of support, the regime has little option but to rely on force and economic payoffs to keep itself in power.

The course of past events would also suggest that Iraq possesses an authoritarian political culture with few inclinations toward democracy, the pronouncements of the Iraqi opposition notwithstanding. Iraqis have had little experience with democracy, and their traditions do not incline in that direction. The depth of hostility between Iraq's ethnic and religious communities renders democracy that much more difficult, a fact evidenced by the disarray of the Iraqi opposition.

Political Economy

Economic factors are equally important in explaining Iraqi politics. The origins of much of the conflict between the Iraqi Shi'a and the Sunni communities, for example, are economic in nature. An equitable distribution of Iraqi wealth would not bring religious tensions to an end, but it might go a long way in that direction. Evidence to support this contention is to be found in the apparent support that the Ba'athist regime enjoyed during the boom years of the 1970s. An explosion of oil prices during that period had resulted in massive development programs that benefited most groups in Iraq. It also produced a sense of economic optimism, a clear plus in efforts to rule this most conflicted of countries. This is not to suggest that Shi'a and Kurdish opposition to the Ba'athist regime are a simple matter of economics. That clearly is not the case, but it is unlikely that any regime, Ba'athist or otherwise, will succeed in welding Iraq into a unified political community until all of its major groups possess an economic stake in the system.

The Iran-Iraq War, as discussed earlier, was not without its economic motivations. Annexation of the oil-rich provinces of Iran would have made Iraq nearly as rich as Saudi Arabia. The devastation of the war, however, eroded the economic optimism of the boom years, transforming Saddam Hussein from hero to culprit.

The 1990 invasion of Kuwait had far stronger economic motivations. Kuwaiti wealth would have enabled Saddam Hussein to recoup the losses of the Iran-Iraq War and rebuild his base of mass support by launching a new round of development programs. Hussein's desired outcome, however, was not achieved. Defeat in the Gulf War and the ensuing boycott forced an even more severe concentration of available wealth in the hands of his supporters. Arab Sunnis, while suffering economic hardships, have fared far better that either the Shi'a or the Kurds. The anti-regime activities of both of the latter groups increased apace.

International and Regional Constraints

The influence of regional and international pressures on Iraqi politics rivals that of the domestic factors reviewed above. The no-fly zones imposed by the United States have crippled Hussein's control of both northern and southern Iraq, and US pressures to remove Hussein from office have forced the Iraqi leader into a "survival" posture. Indeed, Iraqi politics is largely dominated by two themes: Saddam Hussein's struggle for survival and his continuing efforts to develop a credible arsenal of weapons of mass destruction (Hamza and Albright 1998). The two themes are intimately linked, for a credible Iraqi threat to unleash weapons of mass destruction on its neighbors, including Saudi Arabia and Israel, could well force a change in Western strategy.

While Saddam Hussein appears convinced of Washington's desire to overthrow him, the behavior of the United States remains strangely ambivalent. The US Congress has earmarked some $97 million for the overthrow of the Iraqi leader, but the Administration has seemed unsure of how to proceed (*Sunday Times of London*, Oct. 1, 2000, www). If the United States possesses the military intelligence and sophistication that it is reputed to enjoy, why does Saddam Hussein remain in power? Perhaps the US is not as sophisticated as its reputation would dictate, a supposition supported by a remarkable number of glitches in its Iraqi policy, including April Glaspie's ambivalent tête-à-tête with Saddam Hussein during the early days of the Gulf crisis. Other examples of US confusion also abound, including the UN's lack of an endgame in the Gulf War, the decision not to support the Shi'a and Kurdish uprisings of 1991, and the botched CIA attempt to infiltrate UNSCOM. Indeed, some observers have suggested that US policy could serve as a primer for how *not* to overthrow a dictator.

An alternate explanation of US hesitation is that the US is willing to overthrow Saddam Hussein only if he can be replaced by a stable regime that is capable of holding Iraq together. The United States does not want to see the fragmentation of Iraq, nor does it want to become involved in an occupation of Iraq that could only result in high casualties and a loss of support in the Arab and Islamic worlds. Lacking clear policy options, the US seems intent on pursuing a contradictory policy: attempting to cripple Saddam Hussein while simultaneously leaving him with sufficient power to maintain the territorial integrity of Iraq. US economic sanctions are designed to force the Iraqi people, and preferably the Ba'athist elite, to overthrow Saddam Hussein regardless of the suffering that those sanctions impose upon the Iraqi people (Baram 2000a). The United States cannot have it both ways. American relations with the Iraqi opposition have been equally confused, with the United States urging revolt while simultaneously being reluctant to arm an opposition that it cannot control (*Al-Ousbou Al-Arabi*, June 7, 1999, 25–26).

Whatever its source, US ambivalence has given Saddam Hussein ample room to maneuver. The Iraqi leader has also benefited from international concerns over the suffering produced by US sanctions as well as the desire of many European and Asian countries to reestablish economic ties with Iraq. Even Britain, America's long-time ally, has jumped ship on the sanctions issue.

Iraqi politics also reflect tensions within the Middle East itself. Turkey is intent on weakening the Iraqi Kurds and has put intense pressure on the United States to prevent the Iraqi Kurds from creating an independent mini-state. Iran is part and parcel of the power struggle within Iraq's Shi'a community, and Saudi Arabia assists elements in the Iraqi opposition that share its conservative views. All in all, little happens in Iraq that doesn't bear the stamp of international and regional pressures.

THE PROCESS OF IRAQI POLITICS: HOW SADDAM HUSSEIN HAS REMAINED IN POWER

Much as in the case of Hafez al-Asad, the explanation for Saddam Hussein's ability to remain in power has been a riddle with many parts. Hussein has proven to be as cunning as he has been brutal. The very knowledge that he will sacrifice the Iraqi people for the sake of his personal survival has deterred both domestic and external opponents. Lest there be any doubt on this issue, recent reports of Saddam Hussein's plans to repel an American-led invasion call for a doomsday defense that will destroy Baghdad should that prove necessary.

According to the Arabic-language news journal *Al-Waton Al-Arabi*, Saddam Hussein has divided Iraq into three lines of defense. The first extends into the no-fly zones and will be manned by regular army troops supported by air defense systems, neither of which have performed effectively to date. The second line of defense has been dubbed the "war of the cities" and is designed to quell popular uprisings in Iraq's major provincial cities with the maximum use of force. The US and its allies, according to this logic, will be forced to liberate Iraq city by city without domestic support. Casualties will be high, as will regional opposition to the US assault. The third line of defense includes Baghdad itself and has been termed the "hornet's nest." Baghdad will be protected by the elite Republican Guards and other special forces units supported by "urban warfare" units. Booby traps activated by remote control, including high-impact nail bombs, will deter allied forces attempting to fight their way into Saddam Hussein's lair. Bombing will serve only to kill civilians without impairing Hussein's forces, the units of which will be divided into autonomous sections, each with its own supply and communication networks. A hornet's nest, indeed. The US has encouraged the Iraqi opposition, but it has been equally reluctant to arm an opposition that it cannot control (*Al-Ousbou Al-Arabi*, June 7, 1999, 25–26).

The secondary elite also has blood on its hands and fears vicious reprisals if it falls from grace. This secondary elite certainly includes the security forces as well as the Ba'athist and bureaucratic hierarchy. Attempted revolts have been numerous, but Saddam Hussein's security apparatus has proven remarkably effective in keeping potential traitors at bay. The same fears of retribution haunt the broader reaches of the Sunni community and particularly the Takritis. They also haunt the regime's collaborators among the Kurds and the Shi'a. All have been the beneficiaries of Hussein's rule, and there can be little doubt that all will pay the price if the regime falls. That, at least, has been the message of Iraqi history.

The masses, for their part, have been controlled by a combination of fear and manipulation. They fear the government, and Hussein's policy of playing one group against another has made them fear each other. Hussein's policy of divide and rule, as noted earlier, has been made all the more effective by a group-centered political culture that views non-members with suspicion, if not apprehension. Indeed, the behavior of the opposition and its futile attempts at cooperation confirm this assessment. Saddam's use of force and cultural manipulation, in turn, have been reinforced by his deft manipulation of Iraq's economic resources. Supporters are rewarded, and even in times of adversity they receive most of Iraq's financial resources.

The ambivalence of the international community, for its part, has allowed Saddam Hussein to survive. The UN forces were in a position to destroy Hussein at the end of the Gulf War but chose not to exercise that option. Their subsequent behavior, as discussed above, has placed rhetoric above action.

LOOKING TOWARD THE FUTURE

The same factors that explain Saddam Hussein's ability to remain in power also pose some difficult questions for those attempting to predict the future. The difficulty of finding someone strong enough to hold the country together remains problematic, not to mention finding a leader who will respect the rights of the Iraqi population and make it possible for Iraq to live in peace with its neighbors. The fragmented nature of Iraqi society argues against the emergence of a democratic Iraq, as does a political culture characterized by authoritarianism, distrust, and the preeminence of parochial loyalties. Iraq does not constitute an integrated political community, and there are few indicators that a viable civil culture capable of sustaining a democratic regime will emerge in the near future. Also problematic is the weakness of Iraq's administrative and political institutions, all of which have been subverted to Hussein's rule. Ironically, the security apparatus is the most effective of Iraqi institutions, wherein lies another problem for those anxious to see the emergence of a democratic Iraq. On the bright side, Iraq's economic potential is enormous and could provide a foundation for nation building if politics would get out of the way.

A particularly critical question, of course, concerns the action of the international community. Will the United States and Iraq's neighbors tolerate a leader strong enough to hold Iraq together, or will they attempt to impose a quasi-democratic regime that serves only to keep Iraq and its people in a state of limbo?

7

The Politics of Iran

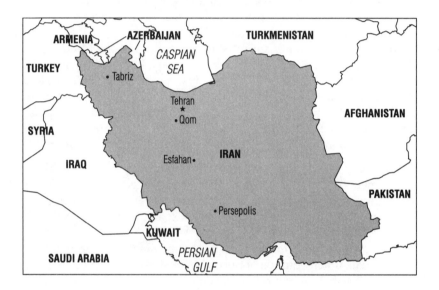

Iran is roughly the size of Western Europe and possesses a population that has surpassed the 70-million mark. This figure is double that reported by the 1976 census, and Iran's rapid population growth only recently has begun to show signs of easing.

Geographically, Iran consists of a huge central plain ringed by mountains. The Farsis or Persians constitute approximately 55 percent of Iran's population and dominate the country's vast central plateau. The remaining 45 percent of the population consists of a bewildering array of ethnic minorities, most of whom, being separated from the dominant Farsis by mountains, have retained a strong sense of ethnic identity, if not nationalism. Of these groups, the largest are the Kurds, the Azaris, the Arabs, and the Baluch.

Persians rule the country and occupy most of the important positions in the government and economy. By and large, they are either urban or farm the more fertile regions of the central plain. Iran's minorities resent Persian domination and would probably revolt if the opportunity presented itself. Revolt is all the more likely because Iran's largest minorities are part of larger ethnic communities that span two or more national borders. Iranian Azaris, for example, now share a common border with Azerbaijan, an independent Azari state created by the collapse of the Soviet Union in 1990. Iran's four million Kurds similarly view themselves as part of a larger Kurdish nation that encompasses a contiguous territory spanning northwestern Iran, northern Iraq, and southeastern Turkey.

Iran has been a dominant force in the politics of the Middle East since the days of antiquity. It remains so today. Iran is also one of the dominant powers of Central Asia, a cluster of some 14 independent states created by the breakup of the Soviet Union in 1990. Most are predominantly Muslim in character, and many possess ethnic populations that overlap with those of Iran.

Iran's influence in the region can be attributed to three sources:

1. Iran's military is more powerful than the military establishments of its immediate neighbors, with the possible exception of Iraq. Iran is also expected to possess nuclear weapons by 2010, an event that would further increase its dominance in the region.
2. Iran is the main exporter of the Islamic Revolution. Iran did not create that revolution nor does Iran control it, but the overthrow of the shah of Iran by the Ayatollah Khomeini in 1979 signaled that no government, however strongly tied to the United States, was beyond the Fundamentalists' reach. Export of the Islamic Revolution continues to be a central theme of Iranian foreign policy, albeit a theme that is being pursued with less vigor than it was during the days of the Ayatollah Khomeini. Nevertheless, most Fundamentalist groups in the region are assumed to receive Iranian support.
3. Iran is a major oil producer and has much to say about the pricing of OPEC oil, albeit far less than Saudi Arabia. Oil revenues also make Iran a major importer of Western products, a fact that has led Japan and the European Union to look kindly upon the Islamic Republic.

The Iranian government, as presently constituted, represents a fusion between traditional religious beliefs and modern (Western) political institutions. This curious fusion, once viewed as an attempt to merge two contradictory forces, may prove to be a useful experiment in creating political institutions that are more in line with the culture of the Middle East than those imported from the West. Indeed, the World Bank is attempting to find a solution to the endemic political problems of Sub-Saharan Africa by seeking ways to fuse modern institutional formats with the traditional culture of the region (Dia 1996). Such a fusion, it is hoped, will enhance both the legitimacy and the effectiveness of African political systems. The same could well be the case in Iran, but only time will tell.

HISTORY AND CULTURE

Two facets of Iranian society distinguish Iran from its Arab neighbors. First, Iranians (Persians) are not Arabs. Rather, they represent a distinct ethno-linguistic configuration whose origins are lost in the far reaches of history. Iranians write in the Arabic script much as most European languages utilize a common Latin script, but the Farsi language differs markedly from Arabic.[1] In conjunction with Turkey and Israel, Iran constitutes part of the non-Arab periphery that forms a powerful vise around the region's much-divided Arab core. Much like other members of the periphery, Iran has found security in the disunity of the Arabs and would be very reluctant to see the emergence of a unified Arab state.

Second, the citizens of Iran are overwhelmingly members of the "Twelver" branch of Shi'a Islam. All Shi'a, as noted in the introductory chapter, believe that Ali, Mohammed's son-in-law and cousin, should have succeeded to the Caliphate upon the Prophet's death. As such, they reject the Orthodox line of succession accepted by the Sunnis and believe that spiritual succession to the Prophet was vested in the sons of Ali and through them to their sons. Following the deaths of Ali's sons Hassan and Hussein, debates over succession would gradually fracture the Shi'a community into three branches: the Zaidis (Fivers), the Isma'ilies (Seveners), and the Twelvers (Zakaria 1988, 306). The Twelvers are dominant in Iran, Southern Iraq, and the Gulf, and are by far the largest of the Shi'a branches. Their beliefs are described by Henry Munson:

> Twelver Shi'is generally believe that all but the last of their twelve imams died as martyrs—the notion of martyrdom for the cause of God being more important in Shi'ism than in Sunnism. The twelfth imam is be-

---

[1] The Turks also employed the Arabic script until it was dropped after World War I as part of Ataturk's modernization program.

lieved to have been in a state of "lesser occultation" (*al-ghayba as-sughra*) from about 874 through 940, during which period his wishes were transmitted to his followers by four deputies who were the only people who could see him. As of 940, he entered the state of the "greater occultation" (*al-ghayba al-kubra*) which will last until he returns shortly before the end of time to fill the earth "with justice and equity, just as it was filled with injustice and oppression." This last imam is variously known as "the imam of the age," "the hidden imam" and *al-mahdi*, "the rightly guided one" (Munson 1988, 26).

By the nineteenth century, the practice evolved of selecting a paramount ayatollah (marja'-i-taqlid) to serve as the representative of the Hidden Imam. As representatives of the Hidden Imam, paramount ayatollahs possessed the power of interpreting religious texts (ijtihad) in a manner compatible with the wishes of the Hidden Imam, a powerful position that far transcended the realm of the profane. All were held in awe by the masses. Paramount ayatollahs were selected by their peers on the basis of their writings and piety, and their views were usually binding on religious issues. As a general rule, there was only one paramount ayatollah in each region of the Twelver world, a world that includes Iran, Iraq, and Lebanon.

The paramount ayatollah was followed in the hierarchy of religious elites by a variety of lesser ayatollahs who also possessed the power of ijtihad but generally deferred to the views of the paramount ayatollah. They, too, were selected by their peers on the basis of their scholarship and piety, and each generally headed a circle of learning consisting of sheikhs. Some sheikhs were students, while others managed mosques or schools. Sheikhs, in turn, were supported by the ordinary men of religion who taught children the Koran, led prayers, and performed similar religious duties. To a large extent, the influence of the ayatollahs was proportional to the size of their following. The above hierarchy was loose, with each layer "imitating" the layer above it on a more or less voluntary basis. It was also non-political, with ayatollahs devoting themselves largely to religious issues.

This pattern would change with the ascendancy of the Ayatollah Khomeini, the leader of Iran's Islamic Revolution. The power to interpret the wishes of the Hidden Imam became manifestly political and, as will be explained in the subsequent discussion of the Islamic Revolution, it provided the Ayatollah Khomeini with a weapon of mass mobilization far more powerful than the guns of the shah. After the ayatollah was in power, it was the hierarchy of ayatollahs and lesser religious officials that enabled Khomeini to hold the country together during the period of institutional collapse that followed the crumbling of the shah's regime.

Sunni religious leaders, it is important to note, possess neither the mystical powers of the ayatollahs nor the organizational apparatus of their Shi'a counterparts. This raises important questions concerning the ability of Sunni clerics to rule should they seize power in either Egypt or Algeria. It is one thing to overthrow unpopular leaders; it is quite another to govern a country without the religious powers and organizational networks that have been available to Iran's religious leaders.

In light of the above discussion, in the remainder of this chapter we will explore the blend of religion and politics that characterizes the Iranian political system today.

Tribal Origins

While space does not permit a lengthy recounting of Iranian history, suffice it to say that Iranian tribes entered the area that now bears their name about 900 years BC. They spoke an Indo-European language, but aside from that, little is known of their ethnic origins (Wilber 1963, 18). Cyrus seized power in 553 BC, giving birth to a world empire that would eventually include Egypt and the ancient cities of Babylon and Athens. The Persian Empire reached its peak under Darius, who referred to himself as "the great king, king of kings, king of lands peopled by all races, for long king of this great earth, reaching even far away, son of Hystaspes, the Achaemenian, a Persian, son of a Persian, an Aryan, of Aryan descent." It was under Darius that Athens was captured in 480 BC, but the city proved difficult to hold, and the forces of Darius retreated to what is now modern Turkey.

The early Iranians, as described by Wilber, had developed a highly refined concept of monarchy and administration.

> The empire was divided into about twenty provinces or satrapies, each under a satrap or governor. The governors came from noble Persian families, and the post tended to become hereditary. The basic system of an absolute monarchy and a number of semi-independent governors which was established in this period continued in Iran until the end of the nineteenth century.
>
> The army was divided into six corps of 60,000 each, with each corps composed of six divisions of 10,000 men, the cavalry mounted on horses bred in Media and armed with the bow and javelin. The ruler's personal bodyguard was composed of 10,000 members, known as the Immortals, who were drawn from the leading families of Persia proper. The provinces were linked by roads, of which the most vital was the "Royal Road" which ran from Susa up through Mesopotamia and Asia Minor to the city of Sardis, a distance of 1,500 miles. Messengers and

travelers used a post system of relays of fresh horses stationed at the many inns along the routes. Agriculture flourished, and justice was fairly administered (Wilber 1963, 22).

Arab Armies conquered Iran in AD 640, but it was the Iranians, far more civilized than the Bedouin soldiers from the desert wastes of the Arabian Peninsula, who provided much of the administrative talent in the eastern regions of the Islamic empire.

It was in an Iraq dominated by Persian culture that Ali established the seat of his Caliphate, and it was in Iraq that his son Hussein was assassinated en route to establishing a rival Caliphate to that of the Syrian Umayyads, whom the followers of Ali viewed as usurpers. The venture collapsed, but the Iraqi cities of Karbala and Najaf, the burial places of Ali and Hussein respectively, have become profoundly emotional shrines for the Shi'a. Many Iranian Shi'a make pilgrimages to Karbala and Najaf rather than or in addition to the required pilgrimage to Mecca.

With the fall of the Umayyads in AD 749, the Caliphate shifted from Syria to Iraq where, under Abbasid rule, Persian influence in the Islamic world would reach its zenith. With the destruction of Baghdad by the Mongols in the middle of the thirteenth century, however, Iran was cut off from the mainstream of the Islamic world and would fall prey to a series of invasions, most coming from Turkish tribes who eventually adopted Persian culture. Of these, the most notable was the Safavid invasion of the early sixteenth century, an invasion that would see the Safavids rule an empire that extended from the Tigris River in Iraq to northern India.

It was also the Safavids that converted Iran to Shi'a (Twelver) doctrine, thereby broadening the cultural divide that separated Iran from its Arab and Sunni neighbors (Melville 1996). Though less well known because of its minimal influence on the Arab world, the Safavid Empire rivaled that of the Ottomans in Turkey. Indeed, Middle Eastern history between the sixteenth and eighteenth centuries is a pageant of conflict between two vast empires: the Ottomans in Istanbul and the Safavids in Tehran.

The Qajars, yet another confederation of Turkish tribes, seized power in 1794 and, much like the Safavids before them, adopted Persian culture. They would rule, at least in name, until 1924. While art and culture had flourished under the Safavids, Armajani describes the Qajar rule as "inept, unimaginative, superstitious, and selfish" (Armajani 1970, 220). The Qajars knew little of the dramatic transformation occurring in Europe and soon fell prey to the growing influence of the British and Russian empires (Bakhash 1978).

The Colonial Era

Iran was not colonized by the European powers *per se*, but European influence had become so pervasive during the latter years of the Qajar empire that each new shah was escorted to his coronation by the ambassadors of Britain and Russia. Both Britain and Russia, moreover, had extracted lucrative commercial concessions from weak, profligate shahs, the most notorious being the tobacco monopoly granted to the British in 1890 (Shuster 1912). The monopoly gave a British company control of the manufacture and distribution of tobacco in Iran, and initiated a dramatic rise in the price of this most necessary of products. Mass protests forced cancellation of the monopoly and laid the groundwork for the revolt of 1905. The revolt, in turn, resulted in the proclamation of Iran's first constitution. As in subsequent cases, mass opposition to the shah was brought about by an ungainly alliance of the Islamic ulema (clergy), the merchants, and an emerging class of Westernized intellectuals. The clergy resented the infusion of Western values in its religious preserve; the bazaaris (merchants) feared the competition of Western firms; and the intellectuals longed to rid Iran of the humiliation heaped upon it by the Western powers (Upton 1960, 25).

It was this era, then, that saw the crystallization of Iranian nationalism. As in the case of Arab nationalism, which was taking root during the same period, Iranian nationalism was a reaction to the growing involvement of the West in the affairs of the East. Iranians already possessed a strong sense of Iranian identity based upon their language, culture, and Shi'a Muslim faith, and the flames of nationalism spread rapidly.

Proclaimed in 1906, the new constitution provided for an elected parliament that was to share power with the shah. The parliament has survived in one form or another since that time but has done little to curb the authority of Iran's autocratic leaders. That situation, however, may now be changing.

Iran was occupied by the British and the Russians during the First World War amidst fears that Iran's leaders would side with the Germans. Russia collapsed before the end of the war, tempting the British to transform Iran into a British protectorate. Failing in this, the British helped Reza Khan, the leader of Iran's Cossack brigade and the only organized military force in the country, to overthrow the remnants of the Qajar dynasty. The coup was successful, and Reza Pahlavi (renamed thus) had himself crowned shah in 1925 (Cronin 1997).

Aside from his autocratic rule, Reza Shah had little in common with his predecessors. Rather, he chose to follow the lead of Ataturk and introduced draconian measures designed to transform Iran into a modern state. The power of the ulema (clerics) was curbed and religious dress—veils for women and the fez for men—was prohibited. Western legal codes were substituted for Islamic law, and Iran's vast religious endowments were forcibly "borrowed" by the state. The former action undermined the spiritual authority of the ulema; the latter eliminated much of their income. A brief protest was curbed by force, with the main voice against the regime being that of a young cleric named Ruhollah Khomeini.

Unlike Ataturk, Reza Shah was not a populist leader committed to bettering the lives of the masses. To the contrary, he viewed modernization as a path for expanding his personal empire. By the end of his reign, the shah's personal landholdings included much of Iran's arable land.

The shah's regime, while essentially a military dictatorship, was supported by an aristocracy of large landowners, the members of which staffed the parliament. Upton describes the life of a typical aristrocrat as follows:

> The occupations regarded as appropriate for the aristocrat included hunting, gambling, conversation, participation in the endless intrigues of government, and, of course, procreation of a large progeny. An aristocrat usually spent his life surrounded by a large body of dependents, reported in the case of one grandee to have numbered 3,000, who looked to him for support and protection and who had, therefore, a direct personal interest in his fortunes.... The aristocrats in Persian society have been traditionally tribal leaders as well. They normally prided themselves on their skill in horsemanship and marksmanship which constituted the predominant elements in the tribal leader's education. The aristocrat tended to depend heavily on the support of his tribal kinsmen and when in trouble usually returned to his tribe. The tribal instincts of those who entered service at the Court or in the government tended to be glossed over by the polite and sophisticated attitudes characteristic of those circles, but they were seldom far below the surface (Upton 1960, 24–25).

Reza Shah made a poor puppet, and efforts to assert his independence from Britain led instinctively to closer relations with Germany and the Soviet Union. With the advent of World War II, the British occupied southern Iran and deposed Reza Shah in favor of his son, Mohammed Reza Pahlavi, then 22 years of age. The Soviets had simultaneously occupied northern Iran, while the US occupied a central zone. All three forces withdrew from Iran at the end of the war, although the Soviets did so only under intense pressure from the US and Britain.

Although the shah had been deposed, two decades of social reform and foreign occupation had produced profound changes in Iranian society. Of these, perhaps the most important was the emergence of a technical elite that embraced Western concepts of democracy, nationalism, and social equality. The more democratically oriented members of this Westernized elite formed the Nationalist Party while the leftists, with support from the Soviet Union, founded the Tudeh or Communist Party. Particularly upsetting to both parties, the nationalists and the communists, was the Darcy oil concession. This concession, like the tobacco monopoly of old, gave Britain the right to exploit Iran's oil reserves in exchange for a paltry royalty, most of which went to the shah (Elm 1992).

The Era of Revolution and Optimism

Mohammed Reza Shah remained the symbolic leader of Iran during the Allied occupation of World War II, and he assumed full control of the Iranian government with the withdrawal of the allied forces, albeit as a constitutional monarch. Just what that meant in the Iranian context remained to be seen.

Reasonable evidence suggests that the young shah was sincerely interested in pursuing a course of modernization that would improve the lot of the Iranian people (Zonis 1991). The shah was also aware that economic and social reforms were necessary to counter the growing popularity of the nationalists and the communists (Zabih 1986). This was a daunting task, for as Mackey writes, Muhammad Reza Shah's grip on power was tenuous at best.

> The shah moved gingerly from year to year carrying his burden of negatives; his wartime cooperation with the Allied occupation; the legacy of his father's autocratic rule; a dismantled army unable to defend his throne; the hostile *ulema*, still scalded by Reza Shah's secular policies, refusing to sanction his rule; and the splintered Majlis, where each of a multitude of new parties grabbed for its own power. If this were not enough, the already politically frail shah possessed neither the charisma of a Persian king nor the air of Shi'a piety beneficial to secular authority (Mackey 1996, 190).

No sooner had the last Allied troops withdrawn from Iran than Iranian nationalists headed by Mohammed Mosaddeq demanded that Iran nationalize the Anglo-Iranian Oil Company, the British operating company that managed Iran's oil production (Elm 1992; Bill and Louis, 1988). The Anglo-Iranian Oil Company now reigned as the premier symbol of foreign exploitation in Iran, and Mosaddeq's attacks on the company unleashed a wave of anti-Western emotions that propelled him into the premiership (Diba 1986). Indeed, so great had Mosaddeq's popularity become that the shah was forced to flee the country and Mosaddeq seized power supported by a coalition of nationalists and other parties of the left including the Tudeh (Communist) Party.

The moment was a glorious if chaotic one, but the glory was soon subverted by a combination of clerical hostility and foreign (CIA) intervention. The Americans were still reeling from leftist revolutions in China, Egypt, and Cuba, and could ill afford the loss of the shah.

Returned to power in 1953, the shah ceased all pretense of being a constitutional monarch and began the relentless process of transforming himself into the shah-in-shah, or king of kings (Yazdi 1990). His new persona, however, did little to increase his decisiveness. As described by Upton:

> The emergence of the Shah as the dominant political figure has been accompanied by a progressive weakening of the institutions of civil government, such as the Cabinet, Senate, and Majlis. No real expression of preference has been permitted in the elections since 1953, those candidates being "elected" by procedures similar to those which prevailed in Reza Shah's day. To the traditional frustrations which confront the members of these institutions are now added those which stem from the Shah's habitual indecision and failure to follow through when he has reached a decision (Upton 1960, 105).

The shah joined the Baghdad Pact, a US-sponsored alliance of Middle Eastern states designed to contain Soviet expansion in the region, in 1955. Other members of the alliance were Turkey, Iraq, Pakistan, and Britain, the dominant foreign power in the Gulf region. In part, Iranian affiliation with the Baghdad Pact reflected the shah's subservience to the United States following his reinstatement by the CIA. The shah, however, also had his own motives for joining the alliance, not the least of which was a desire to counter Soviet pressure on Iran and to gain a steady supply of American arms. The latter benefit was of key importance to a shah who had developed an obsession with foreign policy and military power (Zonis 1991; Upton 1960). The Baghdad Pact also provided the US with a convenient pretext for stabilizing the shah's regime should circumstances require—a matter of utmost concern to both parties following the Mosaddeq affair.

The toppling of Mosaddeq, however, had depended more on luck than the reputed sagacity of the CIA, and both the shah and his American protectors well understood that business could not continue as usual (CIA/*NYT Index* 2000). For the monarchy to survive, the shah would have to confront the economic and political problems facing his country by initiating his own revolution.

The reform process began in 1957 with the introduction of a forced two-party political system. One party would be the government party, while the other would be "His Majesty's loyal opposition." Both parties were controlled by close friends of the shah and offered little real choice to Iran's voters. Indeed, the new system enjoyed so little support that elections scheduled for 1960 had to be delayed because of popular unrest. When the elections were finally held in 1961, dissatisfaction with the results led to crippling strikes and mounting political violence, much of it organized by supporters of banned political movements such as the National Front. The shah's democratic initiative having proved fruitless, he proceeded to concentrate absolute power in his own hands (Saikal 1980).

Political reforms were followed during the early 1960s by sweeping economic reforms dubbed the "White Revolution," a term implying that a wise and caring monarch could do more to promote the welfare of his people than the bloody communist (Red) revolutions that had devastated Russia and China. The White Revolution embodied a variety of economic and social initiatives including land reform, public ownership of industries, voting rights for women, profit sharing for workers, and a literacy corps to implement compulsory education in the rural areas (Moghadam 1996; Hooglund 1982).

The White Revolution was opposed by the landowners and the clergy, both of whom feared that its reforms would undermine their power—the landowners by the destruction of the main source of their wealth and the clergy by the spread of secular education and the propagation of anti-Islamic values (Moghadam 1996). Riots organized by the Ayatollah Khomeini erupted in 1963 and were brutally crushed by the shah. Khomeini was exiled to the holy city of Najaf in Iraq, from which he continued to attack the shah's policies via sermons and pamphlets smuggled into Iran via the bazaari (merchant) network. Khomeini resided in Najaf for 13 years before being forced to flee to Paris by Saddam Hussein under pressure from the shah.

However forward-looking the shah's reforms may have been, the tensions produced by the White Revolution convinced both the shah and his American advisors that the process of transforming the shah into a popular monarch would take time (Zonis 1991). Until that goal had been accomplished, the security forces would be the ultimate guarantor of the shah's regime. Both the military and SAVAK, the shah's main intelligence organization, were strengthened and purged of suspected leftists. Iran had become a police state.

With the opposition suppressed, it was easy for the American leadership to conclude that Iran was well on its way to becoming an island of stability and development in an otherwise chaotic region (Bill 1988). Hopes of democracy had fallen by the wayside, but development theorists of the era largely agreed that such was the price of economic development (Palmer 1997). Democracy and human rights would come as soon as economic development had been achieved.

There were, of course, disquieting signs for those who chose to penetrate beneath the surface. The brutality of the SAVAK and other intelligence agencies generated alienation as well as fear (Bill 1988; Delannoy 1990). The bureaucracy was hopelessly corrupt, and mass hostility to the growing Western presence in Iran was mounting.

Having dispensed with any pretense of democracy, the shah now ruled Iran with an iron fist. With absolute power came delusions of grandeur and an obsession with transforming Iran into a world power. A vivid sign of the shah's obsession with grandeur came in the fall of 1967 when he dispensed with the constitutional monarchy and had himself officially crowned shah-in-shah, the position having been vacated by the abdication of his father some 26 years earlier. Planes deluged Tehran with roses—one for every day of his life—and the Tehran symphony "premiered the coronation hymn, 'You Are the Shadow of God'" (Mackey 1996, 230).

Increasingly confident of his power, the shah dazzled the world in 1971 with an extravagant celebration of the 2500th anniversary of the Iranian monarchy. Held at Persepolis, the ancient throne of Iranian emperors, the fête was a staggering display of excess in the midst of poverty. Many world leaders were too embarrassed to attend.

The explosion in oil prices that accompanied the Arab-Israeli War of 1973 quadrupled Iran's oil revenues and pushed the shah's obsession with grandeur to new heights. Basking in his newfound wealth, the shah vowed to transform his agrarian nation into a major industrial power. As described by Marvin Zonis, "Turning away from the emphasis on agricultural reform and rural development that had dominated economic policy since the White Revolution of 1962–63, the new oil-wealth-based goal of the shah was captured in the slogan 'Sweden by the year 2000.' Iran was to leave the Third World behind and become an industrially developed state providing a full range of welfare benefits to its citizens" (Zonis and Mokri 1991, 129).

Far from building a base of popular support for the shah, the White Revolution and the subsequent era of forced industrialization unleashed a backlash of mass hostility. The mid-1970s witnessed a dramatic increase in the activities of urban guerrilla groups, among the most active of which were the Fadaiyan i-Khalq, a group with links to the old National Front, and the Mujahedin i' Khalq, a group that blended Islamic morality with socialist economics. The supporters of the Ayatollah Khomeini had also become increasingly active and now posed a direct threat to the regime.

The shah responded to the escalating violence by announcing that henceforth Iran would be governed by a single political party, the Resurrection Party. All other political parties and movements were banned, and Iranians unwilling to work within the confines of the new party were urged to leave the country (Zonis and Mokri 1991).

The shah's quest for grandeur continued unabated throughout the era, and in 1976, approximately five years after Persepolis, he stunned the religious community by announcing that the traditional Islamic calendar based on the Prophet Mohammed's flight from Mecca to Medina would be replaced by an Iranian imperial calendar based upon the date of Cyrus the Great's ascension to the Iranian throne (Zonis and Mokri 1991). It seemed that the shah was unaware of the Islamic revival that was swirling around him.

In 1977, the shah again changed tactics by declaring that all constraints on popular expression would be lifted other than those directed at the shah himself. He was to remain inviolable (Zonis 1991). The presumed logic of this move was the vain hope that the masses would turn their hostility on Iran's politicians and bureaucrats rather than the shah himself.

In retrospect, the shah's desperate shifts of policy were an admission that he was losing control of the country (Green 1982). The beginning of the end came in January of 1978 when students and teachers in the holy city of Qum staged a strike protesting publication of a government-sponsored article attacking the Ayatollah Khomeini, who was now orchestrating the Islamic Revolution from his exile in Paris. Police fired on the crowd, unleashing a cycle of violence from which the regime could not recover. The final blow came in October of 1978 when a strike by oil workers cut Iran's oil production by more than 80 percent. The shah departed for an extended vacation in January of 1979. His relatives and supporters had preceded him, taking much of Iran's wealth with them. The Ayatollah Khomeini returned to Iran in triumph the following month.

An era that began with delusions of grandeur, then, collapsed without a murmur in the face of the Islamic Revolution. With it collapsed the naive assumption that the United States could control the affairs of its client states. The Saudis, in particular, began to question the efficacy of United States security guarantees. If the US could not protect a vital ally in its struggle against the Soviet Union, could it protect anyone?

Why did a regime as powerful as the shah's, possessing the full backing of the United States, simply dissolve? A large part of the answer to this question lies in the personality of the shah. Increasingly obsessed with dreams of empire that bordered on megalomania, the shah had simply lost touch with reality. The result was policies that squandered the country's oil wealth and ruptured the fabric of Iranian society (Zonis 1991).

Iran's senior political leaders must also accept their share of the blame, for they found it more expedient to flatter than to criticize. Indeed, one of the main reasons that the shah's policies were out of touch with reality was the fact that his advisors were reluctant to be the bearers of bad news. Loyalty to the shah, unfortunately, did not translate into honesty or effective management. By and large, Iran lacked the institutional capacity to implement the staggering pace of development envisioned in the shah's modernization program. To the contrary, waste, bottlenecks, corruption, and mismanagement became the order of the day. As described by Marvin Zonis, "Power brownouts and blackouts, overwhelmed railroad and truck transport, paralyzing urban traffic jams, and choking urban pollution added to the discontent of the population. The shah, early in the development rush, took to traveling above Tehran by helicopter. He seemed to have further isolated himself from Iranian realities by never setting foot on the streets of Tehran" (Zonis and Mokri 1991, 131).

The fall of the shah can also be attributed to his inability to keep in touch with Iran's citizens. While the shah portrayed himself as the father of his country, his support among the masses was undermined by both a resurgent left and Khomeini's Fundamentalists (Green 1982). While the former found their base of support among Iran's students and intellectuals, the latter had become the champions of rural peasants and the urban poor. The shah's efforts to counter his opponents by building a single party that would bring his regime in touch with the people merely resulted in the establishment of yet another political bureaucracy staffed with opportunists seeking personal gain.

Mass discontent, in turn, was fueled by a variety of factors, not the least of which were the unrealistic expectations created by the shah's flamboyant promises of development and welfare, i.e., "Sweden by 2000." Far more tangible was the lethal mix of unemployment and inflation brought about by the shah's forced industrialization of a largely agrarian country (Bayat 1987). Driven from the land by neglect of the agrarian sector, peasants swelled the slums of Tehran and other major cites. Some found work in the new factories, but most did not. Inflation led to escalating prices, many doubling from month to month. Savings vanished, and a once prosperous middle class found itself struggling to make ends meet.

Cultural factors also contributed to popular discontent. Most Iranians remained wedded to their Shi'a traditions and viewed the shah's reforms as anti-religious, a view reinforced by the sermons of Khomeini and others. The Westernized intelligentsia, by contrast, were offended by the shah's subservience to the United States. It would have been difficult to find a group that he had not offended in one way or another.

At least in theory, the power and resources of the United States should have been adequate to keep the shah in power during the difficult period of modernization. This, at least, was the logic of analysts who viewed the US as a master chess player orchestrating the affairs of Iran and other client states to its own benefit. The shah was, after all, a vital element in the West's encirclement of the USSR, not to mention the fact that most of Iran's oil revenues were spent on the purchase of American weapons. Alas, the US turned out to be a novice in Middle Eastern affairs (Bill 1988). As the shah's regime crumbled, the US dithered, unsure of how to shore up its erstwhile ally. Far more damning, as Jim Bill recounts in great detail, the US seemed to be as out of touch with Iranian realities as the shah himself (Bill 1988). The shah's advisors assured the US that the mounting protests were the work of a small group of extremists and that the foundation of the shah's regime was sound. The US wanted to believe that all was well and allowed itself to be beguiled by conversations with the "official opponents" of the shah's regime who, while condemning the shah for human rights violations, saw little prospect of the regime's collapse.

In retrospect, then, the downfall of the shah's regime was a broad-based phenomenon. Khomeini, while demonstrating great skill in mobilizing his supporters, probably had less to do with the success of the Islamic Revolution than did the erratic policies of the shah and the mystifying behavior of his US advisors (Arjomand 1984).

The Era of Islamic Resurgence

The victory of the Ayatollah Khomeini in 1979 served notice to the West that the Islamic revival had become a major force in world politics (Esposito 1990). The shah's regime had been destroyed and the US, by implication, vanquished. The Ayatollah Khomeini returned to Iran riding on a wave of popular emotion that swept all before it. His power would soon surpass that of the shah.

The overriding goals of Khomeini were threefold:

1.   consolidating the revolution domestically;
2.   transforming Iran into a religious state in spirit as well as form;
3.   exporting the revolution to Iran's immediate neighbors, if not the Middle East as a whole.

At a more personal level, the ayatollah had also vowed revenge against the United States and Saddam Hussein, the former for sustaining the shah's regime and the latter for evicting him from his sanctuary in Iraq's holy places.

None of the above goals, however, were likely to be achieved unless the ayatollah could solve the massive domestic problems facing Iranian society. As the first Islamic Revolution of the modern era, the Islamic regime had yet to prove that it could both govern and meet the needs of Iran's population. It was expected to fail on both counts, for the ayatollahs had little experience in either area and were wedded to a religious philosophy that had more to do with life in early Arabia than it did with the modern industrial world. The country's political institutions, moreover, were in a state of collapse as virtually everyone in positions of authority either had fled the country or had been purged by the revolution. Bureaucratic services, such as they were, had ground to a halt, and much of Iran's much-vaunted military forces had simply vanished.

Much the same was true in the economic sphere, as Iran's technological and professional elite also had fled the country. The new government would thus find itself without the cadre of engineers, doctors, and other professionals required to rebuild Iran's shattered infrastructure. Iran's neighbors and the major powers, moreover, were nervous about the new regime and eager for its demise.

On the positive side, from the Iranian perspective, the ayatollah possessed a charisma that rivaled that of Abdul Nasser. In some ways the symbolic assets of the ayatollah may have been greater than those of Nasser, for they blended charisma born of revolution with a moral authority rooted in the Islamic faith of most of the region's inhabitants.

Despite Khomeini's tremendous charisma and religious aura— many Iranians now referred to him as the Imam, or successor to Mohammed (Zonis and Mokri 1991)—the initial years of the revolution were chaotic as diverse groups vied for control of the "new Iran." The situation was clarified by a national referendum on the future of Iran that resulted in an overwhelming victory for Khomeini's vision of an Islamic Republic. Elections for a Constituent Assembly charged with drafting a constitution for the Islamic Republic were also swept by Khomeini and consolidated the authority of the religious forces. The resultant constitution institutionalized the principle of rule by the Vilayat-i-faqih (rule by a supreme religious leader), a topic that will be covered shortly. Both presidential and legislative elections were held early in 1980, and again resulted in sweeping victories for Khomeini's hand-picked candidates.

Now firmly in control, Khomeini banned his opponents, suspected and real, from all political activity. This included virtually all of the shah's supporters as well as members of the leftist groups who had supported the Islamic Revolution in the naive belief that they would soon be able to wrest authority from an antiquated clergy lacking political experience. When the dust had settled, only two groups remained on the political stage: the Islamic Republican Party (IRP), a political organization composed largely of ulema, and the revolutionary committees (Daneshvar 1996). The IRP had been cobbled together by the clergy to manage the 1980 elections, while the revolutionary committees had emerged more or less spontaneously with the collapse of the shah's regime.

The revolutionary committees, most drawing their membership from the radical Islamic groups that had spearheaded the revolution, seized control of most of Iran's local governments and ruled in the name of the revolution. The committees, although not of the ayatollah's own making, received his blessing and would become a major force in enforcing the ayatollah's dictates during the early years of the revolution (Zonis and Mokri 1991).

Despite Khomeini's power, the spontaneous nature of the revolutionary committees and other groups claiming to act in the name of the revolution made them difficult to control and often resulted in independent actions that caught the central government by surprise. Of these, perhaps the most dramatic was the 1979 seizure of the US Embassy in Tehran by students demanding that the shah be returned to Iran to stand trial for past crimes. A large number of US hostages had been detained, facing an untested Khomeini regime with the threat of American retaliation. The government was divided on how best to handle the crisis, with Bani Sadr, who had been elected to the presidency in 1980, urging that the hostages be released. Khomeini, however, sided with the students. Bani Sadr, a man Khomeini had referred to as being like his son during the election campaign of 1980, was forced from office in 1982 (Zonis and Mokri 1991).

Crises also buffeted the Islamic Republic from abroad. In December of 1979, the Soviet Union invaded Afghanistan, a neighboring Islamic country, forcing the ayatollah to either support the Islamic resistance in Afghanistan or abdicate his self-proclaimed role as the leader of the Islamic world. He chose the former course, earning the enmity of his powerful neighbor to the north.

A far more immediate threat to the survival of the Islamic Revolution was Iraq's invasion of Iran in November of 1980. With the shah's once-vaunted army in disarray, the ayatollah mobilized popular militias by drawing upon his emotional authority and the organizational network provided by the revolutionary committees. As described by Mackey:

> The Basij [popular militias] operated from nine thousand mosques, enrolling boys below eighteen, men above forty-five, and women. Primarily the zealous products of poor, devout families from rural areas, they volunteered for temporary duty in God's war between school terms or in the interim dividing one season's harvest and the next season's planting. At the front, a Basij-i could be identified by his tattered leftover uniform and mismatched boots (often picked up on the battlefield), the bright red or yellow headband stretched across his brow declaring God's or Khomeini's greatness, and the large, imitation brass key, the key to paradise, that hung around his neck. The Basij-is gained fame as human minesweepers in the massive assaults that characterized the 1982–1984 phase of the war. Boys as young as twelve, shaped by the fanaticism of the revolution, walked across minefields to clear the way for the advancing Pasdaran, followed by the army (Mackey 1996, 323).

The tenacity of the Iranian resistance stunned an Iraqi military that had overextended its supply routes, and by 1982, the Iraqi forces were in full retreat. Saddam Hussein signaled his willingness to make peace, but the Ayatollah Khomeini, sensing the opportunity to seize southern Iraq, refused. In retrospect, this was a mistake. Had the ayatollah accepted peace at this time, it is possible that Iran could have bilked Saudi Arabia and Kuwait for billions of dollars in war reparations. Both countries had helped to finance the war, and now that they were faced with the prospect of a victorious Iran, had little option but to buy their way out of a venture that had gone terribly wrong. In a key choice, export of the Revolution had taken precedence over internal development.

The war with Iraq was paralleled by Khomeini's efforts to export the Islamic Revolution, the opening shot of which was a botched attempt to overthrow the government of Bahrain in 1979. Saudi Arabia was targeted as 100,000 Iranian pilgrims to the annual Haj raised pro-Khomeini posters and clashed with Saudi police. The scene was repeated in 1983, and in December of the same year a series of bomb attacks shook Kuwait, killing six people and injuring scores more (Mackey, 1996).

In 1983, the ayatollah, still intent on precipitating a regional revolution, attacked Western targets in Lebanon, a country that also possessed a large Shi'a population. April of that year saw the US embassy in Beirut bombed by the Islamic Jihad, a militia with strong ties to Iran.

Two more bombings followed in October of the same year, one killing 241 US Marines, the other 47 French soldiers. Both Western units had been sent to Lebanon to stabilize the war-torn country in the aftermath of the Israeli invasion of 1982. The bombings were followed by the kidnapping of Westerners working in Lebanon by groups reputedly supported by Iran, and Hizbullah in particular. Iran claimed innocence, but both the Islamic Jihad and Hizbullah (Party of God) had strong ties to Iran. A contingent of Revolutionary Guards from Iran had been posted in Lebanon in 1982 and presumably played an organizational role in strengthening the militias. The US remained frustrated but help-less, having little recourse but to increase its support for Iraq in the hope of destroying the Iranian regime.

Syria and Libya, by contrast, had supported Iran from the begin-ning of the Iran-Iraq War and were key to Iran's ability to avoid isola-tion in the region. Strong ties with Japan and Western Europe also lessened Iran's sense of isolation, as did growing ties with China, the latter now becoming a major source of Iranian arms. Iran had previ-ously favored US goods, and both the Europeans and the Asian states were anxious to pick up the slack, as were the Israelis. Indeed, Israel had been selling arms to Iran since the beginning of the war, in con-travention of the US boycott.

Although incomplete, the US boycott was taking its toll in the key defense and oil sectors, both heavily geared to the United States. The ayatollah was also becoming increasingly aware of the dangers of iso-lation. As noted by Ramazani:

> Khomeini himself said on October 29, 1984 that it is "inadmissible to common sense and humanity" not to have relations with other govern-ments "since it would mean defeat, annihilation and being buried right to the end" (Ramazani 1989, 212).

The domestic pressures of the war, moreover, were mounting. In-flation had reached the 35 percent level, and Iran's "human wave" strategy of countering Iraq's technical superiority had left few Iranian families without a personal loss. Riots erupted in Tehran in April of 1985 and were soon followed by uprisings in other major cities. The riots were crushed, but an undercurrent of resentment remained (Mackey 1996). The clerics themselves were unsure of the best means of coping with the domestic pressures and increasingly divided into pro-reform (moderate) and anti-reform (hard-line) factions.

In the meantime, the ayatollah's terrorist campaign had frayed US nerves and the late summer of 1985 would see the US shipping weapons to Iran via Israel as part of an "arms for hostages" exchange. Lebanese militias released a few hostages at the request of Tehran,

paving the way for a secret visit to Iran in May of 1986 by national security advisor Robert McFarlane and Lt. Colonel Oliver North of the
National Security Council (Cavender, Jurik, and Cohen 1993). The
Americans came bearing gifts, including a chocolate cake, matched
sets of chrome-plated Magnum pistols, and spare parts for Iran's
HAWK missiles. The US had violated its own boycott. "Iran-Gate," as
the affair was dubbed by the US press, was offset by continuing US
support of Iraq, leading to charges from both Iran and Iraq that the
US was encouraging their mutual destruction.

By now the Iran-Iraq War had disintegrated into a stalemate that
pitted Iran's almost three-to-one superiority in manpower against
Iraq's superiority in air power. In a stunning 1986 victory, Iran captured most of the Fao Peninsula and moved within fifty miles of Iraq's
southern port city of Basra. Had Basra fallen, southern Iraq would
have been under the control of the Ayatollah Khomeini and Iranian
forces would have reached the borders of Saudi Arabia and Kuwait.
Basra withstood Iran's human wave strategy, but not without the use
of poison gas.

By 1987, the war had begun to tilt in Iraq's favor as Iraqi planes decimated Iranian oil facilities and modified Soviet Scud missiles began to
strike Tehran and other Iranian cities in what would later be termed the
"war of the cities." Iraqi aircraft also bombed Iranian targets well beyond their normal range, leading to speculation that they had been re-
fueled in the Soviet Union (Segal 1988, 958).

Reverses in the war further increased the conflict among the clergy,
and by 1987, the Ayatollah Khomeini was forced to take direct control
of the government and abandon his preferred strategy of shifting his
support between conservatives and reformers as the needs of the moment dictated. The Islamic Republican Party was disbanded as being
ineffectual, and the Ayatollah Khomeini enhanced his powers as Vilayat-i-faqih by now claiming to rule in the name of the Hidden Imam.
This new interpretation of the powers of the vali-i-faqih, according to
Khomeini's opponents, "overrode even the Koran, a charge heatedly
denied by the Ayatollah" (Mostyn 1991, 236).

The direct assertion of Khomeini's power stabilized the regime but
could do little to stem Iran's losses in the war. With victory no longer in
sight and the Islamic Republic on the verge of collapse, Khomeini accepted Security Council Resolution 598 bringing the war to an end in
1988. He would describe the act as being more loathsome than drinking hemlock, and would die the following year (Mackey 1996, 331).
There were no victors. Iran's military and non-military costs of the
war, including lost oil revenue, were estimated at $137 billion (Mackey
1996, 332). Casualty figures approached three-quarters of a million,

and Iran's economic infrastructure had been decimated. Alnasrawi places Iran's total economic losses from the war at some $644.5 billion (Alnasrawi 1994). The Islamic Revolution had not been destroyed, but it clearly had suffered a setback. Domestic problems also eroded the regime's popular support and left the clerics hopelessly divided among themselves.

In retrospect, the decade of Khomeini could claim a number of successes. The Revolution had been consolidated, and Iran had been provided with a new set of political institutions, the nature of which will be discussed in the following section. The Islamic resurgence had spread throughout the region and, while the Iranian regime could not claim full credit for this resurgence, it was certainly part of the equation. Iran's foreign and regional enemies had also been kept at bay, although Iran remained isolated both regionally and internationally. Saddam Hussein had not been destroyed, but his survival probably had more to do with external support for Iraq than it did with Hussein's military prowess.

The price of war and revolution, as noted above, had been devastating. Not only did little economic development take place during the Khomeini regime, but much of the economic infrastructure that had been put in place under the shah was destroyed.

The Iranian population, moreover, had been exhausted by the war and was becoming increasingly weary of the regime's rigid moral codes. This disenchantment was particularly evident among the petro-middle-class that had embraced Westernization with a passion during the era of the shah. The Ayatollah's exceptional charisma had enabled him to place his revolutionary goals above internal development. His successors would find this to be a far more difficult task.

The Era of the New World Order

The death of the Ayatollah Khomeini on June 3, 1989, was paralleled by the collapse of the USSR the following year and the emergence of a new world order dominated by the United States and its allies. Ironically, the advent of a single hegemony in the international arena coincided with an upsurge in the power of Islamic groups throughout the region, thereby setting the stage for a conflict between two seemingly irreconcilable forces—one based on its control of the world's economic and political systems and the other rooted in the body politic of the Muslim world. The policies pursued by Khomeini's successors would have much to say about the outcome of this clash of world views.

The Ayatollah Khomeini bequeathed Iran a political system that was a curious fusion of religious and secular institutions, an updated analysis of which will be provided in the concluding section of the chapter. For the moment, suffice it to say that power was divided between a supreme religious guide, a parliament or majlis, an elected president, and a variety of religious councils. No one was quite sure how this seemingly ungainly political arrangement would work, for all had been subservient to Khomeini's power. Many assumed that the new arrangement would not work at all.

The two figures who bore primary responsibility for guiding Iran into the era of the new world order were Ali Akbar Hashemi Rafsanjani, the reigning president of Iran, and Hojjat al-Islam Sayeed Ali Khamanei, the newly elected Supreme Guide. Both men were compromise candidates. Rafsanjani, the speaker of the majlis, had been tapped for the presidency after the ayatollah's initial choice lost favor and withdrew his candidacy. Khamanei, in turn, was the compromise choice to replace Khomeini when the Assembly of Experts found it difficult to agree on a more prominent theologian (Banuazizi and Weiner 1986; Gieling 1997). No one, of course, could replace Khomeini in terms of either his personal charisma or his stature as the earthly manifestation of the Hidden Imam. Be this as it may, the speed with which the Assembly of Experts moved to fill the position of Supreme Guide demonstrated the resilience of the Islamic regime, surprising many who had expected it to collapse with the ayatollah's death.

Whatever their differences, the elite that succeeded Khomeini were part of the religious establishment and possessed an overriding interest in preserving Iran's theocratic political system. As Rafsanjani, then speaker of Iran's parliament, pointedly commented, "We astonished the world (by choosing a successor to the Ayatollah Khomeini) and right now all of those wrong interpretations of power struggles and radicals versus moderates are dismissed" (*Middle East*, 1994, 221).

The elite also shared a common commitment to developing the economy and exporting the revolution, although little agreement existed on how best to achieve these two objectives. In this regard, the Iranian elite was now divided into hard-line and pragmatic factions; the former were committed to the export of the revolution and the latter argued that the revolution would be best served by internal development, even if it required building bridges with Iran's former enemies.

The ayatollah's death found each of Iran's diverse factions dominating a separate branch of the government. The pragmatists, headed by Rafsanjani, controlled the presidency, while the hard-liners, headed by Khamanei, controlled the parliament and much of the religious establishment. At least initially, the pragmatists appeared to have the upper hand, as Rafsanjani attempted to address Iran's spiraling budget deficit by reducing subsidies on food, housing, and other necessities. Restrictions on the private sector were also eased in the hope of stimulating greater economic growth than had been achieved by Iran's state-run industries. The public responded to the reduced subsidies with food riots in 1990, serving notice that the masses were growing restive with the revolution.

The regional front was faring little better than the domestic front. The war with Iraq had ended in 1988, but relations between the two countries remained tense. Border flare-ups were common, and Iraq continued to occupy some 2,600 square miles of Iranian territory (Ramazani 1992, 396). Tensions were also heightened by Iraq's refusal to repatriate more than 100,000 Iranian prisoners of war as well as its continued claims to all of the Shatt-al-Arab (Ramazani 1992, 396).

It was against this background that Iranians went to the polls in 1989 to elect a new parliament. The pragmatists, led by President Rafsanjani, rallied under the banner of the Association of Combatant Clerics of Tehran and advocated a revamping of Iran's economic and foreign policies. They were opposed by the Association of the Combatant Clergy of Tehran, a far more radical group advocating a continuation of Khomeini's polices on both the foreign and domestic fronts (Sarabi 1994). As indicated by their names, both groups were deeply rooted in Iran's religious establishment and were committed to theocratic rule. As the above discussion suggests, labels such as radical and moderate are confusing in the Iranian context (Fairbanks 1998).

The moderates emerged victorious—a victory which, according to Sarabi, marked the end of the transition from Khomeini's rule.

> During his first year as president, Rafsanjani had begun reversing the order of priorities of many agendas: economic concerns over political ones, pragmatism over ideological approaches, diplomatic activism over isolationism, and regional economic cooperation over the export of revolution. The pace of reform was accelerated by the substitution of technocrats for mullahs, the privatization of government-owned companies, the acceptance of foreign loans and investments, the unification of foreign exchange rates, the relaxation of some harsh cultural aspects of Islamic rule, curbing the influence of some radical official and non-governmental groups that undertook embarrassing foreign actions, and finally, inviting exiles back to Iran to participate in the expansion of economic life (Sarabi 1994, 94–95).

No sooner were the elections over, however, than Iraq's invasion of Kuwait on August 2, 1990, threatened to transform Iraq into the dominant state of the Gulf, a situation which, if allowed to stand, would have placed the Islamic regime in jeopardy (Ramazani 1992, 404). Iran condemned the attack and called for the immediate withdrawal of

Iraqi forces. Equally problematic was Iran's fear that the US would use the Iraqi attack as a pretext for strengthening its presence in the Gulf, a presence that would pose a constant threat to the security of the Islamic Republic.

In retrospect, Iraq's invasion of Kuwait proved to be "manna from heaven" for Iran's Islamic leaders (Ramazani 1992, 397). Faced with a war that he could not win, Saddam Hussein made a frantic effort to gain Iranian support by evacuating Iranian territory under Iraqi control and releasing his Iranian prisoners. Iranian support, however, was not to be attained. Iran declared its neutrality but formally adhered to all UN economic sanctions. With Saddam Hussein's war machine destroyed, Iran would again be the dominant power in the Gulf.

Dramatic as it may have been, the electoral victory of the moderates would prove to be short-lived. Riots erupted in 1992 and 1993, and dissatisfaction with Rafsanjani's reforms was further signaled by the narrowness of his victory in the presidential elections of 1993. Despite careful orchestration, Rafsanjani's share of the vote fell from 94 percent in 1989 to 63 percent in 1993. Low voter turnout also reflected a general disillusionment with the Islamic regime. Rafsanjani's reforms may have made economic sense, but they did little to appease a population that had suffered more than a decade of sacrifice and deprivation.

By 1994 the hard-liners had strengthened their position in the parliament—often by intimidation—and were able to further undercut Rafsanjani's authority. Many of Rafsanjani's cabinet nominees were denied confirmation, and a variety of senior and administrative positions were seized by the hard-liners, not the least of which were the Ministries of Interior (police) and Information (state security) (Banu-azizi 1994).

Rafsanjani's position continued to weaken during 1995 as inflation soared to the 100 percent level while government salaries remained constant (Viorst 1995). Corruption increased apace, with bribes being demanded for even minor services (*IHT*[2], May 30, 1995, A6). Corruption was nothing new in Iran, but there had been hopes that the new regime would prove less venal than its successors.

Somewhat quixotically, President Clinton chose this moment to impose a total trade embargo on Iran, pressuring US allies to follow suit. A forlorn effort to isolate the Islamic Republic from the world community, the embargo was honored in the breach as US allies were far more concerned with trade balances than they were with dangers posed by the Islamic Revolution. Nevertheless, the military and oil

---

[2]*International Herald Tribune.*

sectors of the Iranian economy were heavily geared to that of the United States, and the American boycott increased the price of US equipment that now had to be purchased through secondary sources. Tensions between Iran and the US continued to build during 1996 as Iran asserted its position as the guardian of the Gulf and the US Congress earmarked $20 million for the covert overthrow of the Iranian regime.

With the liberals in disarray, the hard-liners seemed prepared for a sweep of the 1996 parliamentary elections. Their optimism, however, was premature, for they suddenly found themselves challenged by a hastily assembled group of technocrats fielding candidates under the label of "Servants of Construction." The Servants of Construction supported Rafsanjani's reforms and scored impressive gains in the first round of the parliamentary elections.

The hard-liners eked out a narrow victory in the second round of the elections, but the unexpected challenge to hard-line rule had introduced a new dimension—and new excitement—to Iranian politics. Voter turnout in the first-round elections had soared to a record 71 percent. The hard-liners had also been forced to rely on bullying tactics to gain their plurality in the majlis, a clear sign that support for the hard-line position had eroded (Fairbanks 1998).

The plight of the hard-liners, however, did not become fully evident until the following year when Mohammed Khatami, the reform candidate, swept to a dazzling and totally unexpected victory in the 1997 presidential elections. Khatami's 69 percent of the vote provided him with a resounding mandate for change. Equally impressive was the staggering 88 percent voter turnout, more than double that of the preceding presidential election.[3]

After a period of vacillation, the hard-liners accepted Khatami's victory, portraying it as an affirmation of popular support for Islamic rule (Fairbanks 1998). Missing from this bit of sophistry was the fact that only candidates approved by the clerics had been allowed to run for office. Be that as it may, Iran's religious theocracy was becoming the most democratic political system in the Islamic world.

Despite Khatami's dazzling victory, the presidency continued to be subordinate to the Supreme Guide, and the hard-liners remained dominant in the majlis. Nevertheless, the size of Khatami's victory added new power to the presidency, pitting the religious authority of the Supreme Guide against the popular mandate of Khatami.

While stressing his total commitment to Islamic rule, Khatami minced few words in his efforts to reorient Iranian foreign policy. "In

[3]Some sources place Khatami's margin of victory at 73 percent.

foreign relations we need an active and fresh presence based on our independence and national interests. It is important for us to defuse tensions and seek friendship and brotherhood in the international arena" (*IHT*, Aug. 20, 1997, 6). Words were supported by deeds with his appointment of the US-educated Kamal Kharrazi as foreign minister and the Ayatollah Mohajerani as minister of culture. The latter had earlier been criticized for his advocacy of dialogue with the United States (*IHT*, Aug. 13, 1997, 2).

The first test of power between Khatami and the conservatives would come with Khatami's submission of his cabinet nominees to the majlis for ratification. Most were approved, but the hard-liners retained important cabinet positions including the Ministry of Interior (police).

Khatami's resounding victory in the 1997 presidential elections was followed by an equally resounding victory for the liberals/reformists in the municipal elections of 1999. It was against this background that both sides prepared for the parliamentary elections scheduled for the spring of 2000. Yet another victory for the liberals/reformists would dispel any hard-line pretenses of continuing to enjoy the broad base of mass support that had characterized the early days of the revolution. The 2000 elections were not a matter of life or death for the hard-liners, but they could easily be interpreted as a step in that direction.

The hard-line strategy going into the 2000 election campaign blended intimidation with legalistic maneuvering designed to disqualify key reformist candidates. The campaign of intimidation began with the assassination of prominent reformist intellectuals but collapsed amidst signs of a popular backlash. Officials in the intelligence services were duly blamed for the assassinations and removed from their positions. The campaign of assassinations gave way to legalistic attempts to curb the reformist press. The liberal/reformist newspaper *Salam* was closed in the summer of 1999 and its editors arrested on charges of "spreading falsifications, disturbing public opinion and publishing classified documents," the latter referring to the publication of the contents of a repressive press bill the day before its anticipated approval by the parliament (Samii 1999, 2). The editors in question were close to student leaders at the University of Tehran, and their arrest triggered student riots that soon engulfed Tehran and 18 other cities. The student protests, in turn, led to confrontations between the students and hard-line vigilantes, with the security forces siding with the latter. Order was restored by mid-August and, as in the case of the earlier assassinations, key hard-line officials were forced to resign from their posts, not the least of whom was the Minister of Justice (Associated Press/*Daily Star*, Aug. 16, 1999, 5). He was followed in office by a cleric of moderate views, offering a measure of impartiality to a judicial system dominated by the conservatives. This appointment, however, did not stop the legal harassment of liberal journalists, including key supporters of Khatami. In the meantime, the Council of Guardians weighed in by disqualifying some 12 percent of the 6000 candidates for the 2000 parliamentary elections, with none of the disqualified candidates being hard-liners.

Khatami, for his part, responded to the challenge of the hard-liners by urging a massive turnout for the 2000 elections and by issuing press licenses to reformist groups. Every time a reformist paper was closed down, or so it seemed, a new one would appear.

The parliamentary elections were held in the spring of 2000, and Iranian voters duly selected 290 members of the Sixth Majlis from among some 6000 candidates. The voting process, as Gary Sick recounts, was chaotic.

> Voters had to select candidates from a huge list (861 in Tehran for 30 seats) and write the names in by hand. There were no private voting booths, and the polling places turned into impromptu political seminars where people compared notes on their ballots and discussed alternative names. Since party or ideological affiliations did not appear on the ballot, most voters relied on lists prepared by various factions or newspapers to sort out the mass of names. Votes were then counted by hand, which, among other things, involved interpreting the handwriting of each voter (Sick 2000, 1).

The reformers swept to their third dazzling victory in as many years, receiving three quarters of the seats in the majlis (*IHT*, May 24, 2000, A5). Turnout was in the 80 percent range, although estimates vary from source to source.

The reformist victory was significant on several accounts. First, the conservatives had lost control of the majlis for the first time since the revolution, thereby depriving them of a pillar of political control. The loss of the majlis was all the more painful as both the judiciary and the security services had earlier been compromised by the violence of the electoral campaign. Second, the reformers were now in a position to pass legislation undermining conservative authority. Particularly important in this regard was the ability of the majlis to name half of the members of the all-powerful Council of Guardians, a topic to be discussed shortly. Also rumored to be on the agenda were plans to use the parliament's constitutional powers to investigate "the affairs of the country" as a weapon for probing the Republican Guards and the Basij, the military arm of the hard-liners. Third, the reformists were now in a position to launch the vigorous pursuit of their reform agenda, a key element of which was rapprochement with the United States.

The threat to conservative dominance posed by the reformist victory spawned rumors of a planned coup by the Republican Guards which, while not materializing, added yet another element of tension to Iranian politics (Namazi 2000). What did materialize were continued hard-liner efforts to muzzle the reformist press as evidenced by a stern warning from the Supreme Guide on the dangers of opening the Iranian press to "American-style reformers" and "domestic hypocrites" (*Daily Star*, Apr. 21, 2000). The conservatives also used their control of the Council of Guardians to strip the parliament of its ability to investigate agencies under the control of the Supreme Guide, including the Republican Guards, the Basij, the large benevolent associations that control much of Iran's wealth, and the state broadcasting system (Namazi 2000).

The stage was thus set for a confrontation between the liberal/reformers and the hard-liners on all fronts: the parliament, the press, and the street. The reformers possessed an overwhelming mandate for change, but faced the very real danger that efforts to press their advantage would force the hard-liners to resort to violence.

Even Khatami's cautious reforms, however, were met with organized and usually illegal resistance by the hard-liners. So much so, in fact, that the end of 2000 would find Khatami publicly admitting,

> I declare that after three and a half years as president, I don't have sufficient powers to implement the constitution, which is my biggest responsibility.... In practice, the president is unable to stop the violations...or force implementation of the constitution (*IHT*, Nov. 27, 2000, www).

A showdown between the two sides appeared increasingly inevitable as Iran moved toward the presidential elections scheduled for the summer of 2001. Another reformist victory seemed inevitable, but to what avail? Khatami, himself, seemed dubious about the utility of another term as president and refused to announce his candidacy for a second term in office until the closing days of the nomination process.

The elections were held in relative calm, and Khatami led the reformers to another dazzling electoral victory, capturing 77.88 percent of the popular vote. The only discordant note in the victory of the reformers was a sharp drop in voter turnout from 83 percent in 1997 to 67 percent in 2001 (*Tehran Times*, June 11, 2001, www).

Supreme Guide Khamenei accepted the results with grace, citing Iran's eighth presidential election as a sterling example of Islamic democracy (*Tehran Times*, June 11, 2001, www). Whatever the Supreme Guide's generosity in congratulating Khatami on his victory, it would be naive to suggest that Khatami and his supporters will find the path to reform eased by the results of the election. The reform process had all but stalled in the final year of Khatami's first term, and the opponents of the reform process remain well entrenched in positions of power (*Tehran Times*, June 11, 2001, www).

On the international front, the first years of the new millennium were characterized by contradictory trends. Cautious steps continued in Iran's rapprochement with the United States and Saudi Arabia, but were countered by Iranian attempts to scuttle the Arab-Israeli peace process. Such, at least, were the accusations of the United States and the Israelis (US Dept. of State, Terrorism: 1999 Report, www). Not only was Iran pursuing contradictory foreign policies, but each facet of Iranian foreign policy was seemingly sponsored by a different faction of the Iranian government: rapprochement by the reformers and export of the revolution by the hard-liners.

IRANIAN POLITICS TODAY AND BEYOND

In reviewing Iran's Islamic Revolution over the course of the past two decades, one finds a growing fragmentation of power. This fragmentation of power, in turn, has produced severe stress within the religious establishment and has resulted in policies marked by vacillation and contradiction. Bold economic reforms have been introduced only to be scaled back in the face of popular opposition; Islamic scriptures have remained the law of the land, but their enforcement has lacked the zeal of the Khomeini era; the export of the revolution has continued, but only at the covert level, and has been balanced by a growing rapprochement with the Arab world and the West (Mozaffari 1993; Baktiari 1996b). In spite of its internal contradictions, the Iran of today is a far more democratic and open society than the Iran of either the shah or the Ayatollah Khomeini.

In the remainder of this chapter we will analyze the growing tension that characterizes Iranian politics as it attempts to transform itself from an emotionally charged charismatic movement under Khomeini into an institutionalized state capable of meeting the challenges of the twenty-first century. In the process, we will analyze the major components of the Iranian political system as it stands today.

Elites and Institutions

Iran entered the twenty-first century with a dual political system that divides power between its spiritual authorities and its popularly elected leaders. Spiritual authority resides in a "vali-i-faqih," or Supreme

Guide, elected by the 80 members of the Assembly of Experts, a council composed of Iran's leading religious authorities (Banuazizi 1994, 5).

The powers of the Supreme Guide are subject to a variety of interpretations, but he is generally viewed as a divinely inspired religious scholar (jurist) entrusted to speak in the name of the Hidden Imam in matters regarding the interpretation and application of religious law (Moussavi 1992). As Iran is governed by religious law, the Supreme Guide has the final say on almost everything. Be this as it may, Khamanei lacks the stature of Khomeini, and the Supreme Guide is now viewed by some scholars as being the first among equals (Mozaffari 1993).

Also falling in the realm of religious authority are the Assembly of Experts, the Council of Guardians, and the Expediency Council. The Assembly of Experts plays a vital role in assuring the continuity of the Supreme Guide, but is less involved in day-to-day politics. The Council of Guardians, by contrast, screens legislation to assure that it is in conformity with the sharia (religious law) as interpreted by the Shi'a theologians. More often than not, a form of shuttle diplomacy occurs in which draft legislation deemed offensive is returned to the majlis for modification. The Council of Guardians also screens candidates for elected office, all of whom must be acceptable to the religious establishment. As we have seen in the discussion of the 2000 elections, the Council of Guardians disqualified several hundred candidates on religious grounds, virtually all of whom inclined toward the liberal end of the clerical spectrum. By performing these roles, the Council of Guardians serves as the interface between the two halves of the Iranian political system, the religious and the secular. If a deadlock occurs between the majlis and the Council of Guardians, the issue is resolved by the Expediency Council, the members of which represent the diverse branches of the political system. Membership on the Expediency Council is determined by the Supreme Guide, who also selects its president.

Secular authority, if that is the proper word, is exercised by a president and a majlis (parliament) elected directly by the population in a quasi-democratic environment. As described by Sarabi:

> Campaigns in Iran are a mixture of Western-type electioneering and local politics. Some of the main institutions and means for effective campaigning include Friday prayer sermons; lectures in mosques, universities, and clubs; private discussions in associations and informal gatherings; mailings; appearances on television forums and news programs; editorial and newspaper advertisements; and wall posters and tracts. In principle, political groups and individual candidates are obliged to make their campaigns "positive" rather than negative. No public

debates between candidates or mass rallies are allowed, apparently because the regime fears that negative campaigning or verbal attacks could quickly turn into public demonstrations and direct criticism of the regime (Sarabi 1994, 99).

The power of the president, by contrast to that of the Supreme Guide, rests upon a popular mandate. President Khatami, it will be recalled, received almost 70 percent of the popular vote in the 1997 presidential elections, an astounding figure that stunned the conservative elements in the religious establishment (Bakhash 1998). The great divide between the Supreme Guide and the presidency, then, is the fundamental divide between power based upon divine law on one hand, and human law on the other (Abdo 1999; Fairbanks 1998).

The president and his cabinet manage the affairs of state, direct the bureaucracy, and propose legislation to the majlis. Control of the administrative apparatus adds to the power of the president but is not his prerogative alone. The Supreme Guide also controls part of the administrative hierarchy and particularly the state security apparatus.

The Iranian parliament, or majlis, resembles other parliamentary bodies, albeit with the differences noted above. While lacking the power of either the Supreme Guide or the president, the parliament is a vigorous body that has played a major role in shaping economic policy. Its influence in the areas of security and foreign policy has been less pronounced (Baktiari 1996a; Vakili-Zad 1994). After the parliament has passed a bill, it is screened by the Council of Guardians before being submitted to the Supreme Guide for his assent. Upon approval by both the president and the Supreme Guide, legislation is sent to the appropriate administrative department for execution.

In addition to performing its legislative role, the majlis ratifies presidential nominations for cabinet positions and has failed to do so on several occasions (Baktiari 1996a). The parliament, as Baktiari notes, also serves as a barometer of factional dominance:

> The Majlis has also been at the center of elite factionalism and power rivalry. Who controls the Majlis, and in what numbers, has become an important indicator of factional victory in revolutionary Iran. The victorious faction shrewdly capitalizes on this perception to consolidate its control and power in other important institutions of governing. Following the defeat of the radicals in the 1992 elections, President Rafsanjani and his supporters moved to consolidate their influence in other institutions, most notably the judiciary and the office of the supreme leader (Baktiari 1996a, 235).

The composition of Iran's elite reflects the complexity of its political system. The elite hierarchy is headed by the Supreme Guide, followed in turn by the president, the chairman of the Council of Guardians, and the speaker of the parliament (majlis).

In addition to their formal authority, the power of the senior members of the elite depends upon their broader support within the clergy and other critical elements of Iranian society, including the masses. Much of Khatami's power, for example, rests upon his landslide victory in the 1997 and 2001 presidential elections and the subsequent victory of the reformists in the 2000 parliamentary elections.

The second tier of the elite structure includes senior members of parliament, governors, mayors of Iran's largest cities, key military and security officers, senior members of the cabinet, the higher rungs of the clergy, members of the Council of Guardians, editors of major newspapers, and key economic leaders. While not sharing the decision-making powers of the core elite, this vast secondary elite is overwhelmingly dominated by the clergy and has much to say about how the policies of the regime will be executed. Indeed, the struggle to control these key positions provides the most visible dynamic of the Iranian political system, and experts attempting to predict the course of Iranian politics devote much of their attention to keeping score of who controls what.

In this regard, four main factions now compete for power in Iran: the radical right, the conservative right, the liberals, and the pragmatists (Siavoshi 1997; Rajaee 1999). Conflicts between the four factions center on three basic issues: economic policy, social (religious) policy, and foreign policy (Banuazizi 1994, 4). The radical right and the conservative right are often referred to as the conservatives or hard-liners; the liberals and the pragmatists as the moderates or reformers.

The Radicals   The radicals favor a strict application of Islamic religious law, including its moral codes and restrictions on female dress. They also favor a quasi-socialist economic system in which land ownership would be restricted, the economy regulated, major enterprises placed under state control, labor legislation strengthened to improve the rights of workers, and increased financial assistance provided to the poor and destitute (Banuazizi 1994). The quasi-socialism of the radicals is based not on Marxism but on the Koranic concerns for equality and social justice. In the foreign policy sphere, the radicals have been strong advocates of exporting the Islamic Revolution and have taken a hard line in opposing cooperation with the United States.

The radicals were particularly strong during the early years of the Islamic Revolution but have seen their power ebb during the post-Khomeini era as the emphasis of Iranian politics has shifted from ideological fervor to finding practical solutions to Iran's pressing domestic problems. Nevertheless, the strong support that the radicals enjoy among the workers, peasants, and members of the lower middle class assures that they will remain a significant force in Iranian politics.

The Conservatives   The conservatives also demand a strict application of Islamic religious law including its moral codes and restrictions on female conduct. Unlike the radicals, however, they are staunch advocates of private property and resist government intervention in economic affairs. Chambers of commerce and other commercial or bazaari associations are closely aligned with the conservatives and have established a strong position in the bureaucracy and judiciary. The conservatives also find support in the theological schools as well as many of Iran's numerous religious associations.

The Pragmatists   The pragmatists came to the fore during the election of Rafsanjani to the presidency and generally view government as a harmonious alliance between the presidency and the clergy. While the clergy focuses on moral considerations, the presidency pursues pragmatic solutions to the problems of government and the economy, with the exact direction of policy reflecting the needs of the moment. If current conditions require greater economic liberalization or cooperation with the West, so be it. The important thing is to preserve the religious character of the revolution while strengthening its political and economic foundation. Rafsanjani was precluded by law from seeking a third term as president but was subsequently named the president of the Expediency Council, thereby assuring that the pragmatists will retain a strong voice in the politics of the Islamic Republic. He was elected to the majlis in 2000, but not by a sizable majority.

The Liberals   The liberals represent the most moderate segment of the Islamic establishment and place a strong emphasis on democracy and public rights as established by the framework of Iran's Islamic constitution. The liberals also call for a softer and more flexible application of religious rule than the fire and brimstone preached by the factions of the right, and they have become outspoken advocates of rapprochement with the United States. The moderate left also favors a strong presence of the state in economic affairs.

The liberals are avid supporters of President Khatami, but it is not clear that Khatami is as liberal as his supporters might wish. It is also important to note that the reformers are far from being a unified group, with some 18 reformist factions being represented in the Sixth Majlis (Associated Press, Gulf 2000, Feb. 24, 2000, www).

Elite Fragmentation   When the popular press refers to the hard-liners, they generally have in mind the radicals and the conservatives, both of whom favor the strict application of religious law in Iranian society. In much the same manner, the popular press refers to the pragmatists and liberals as reformers. As noted above, however, one should not lose sight of the fact that both the hard-liners and the reformers are fragmented into multiple sub-factions, with personality often being as important as doctrine.

The conflict among Iran's competing religious factions has had much to do with the contradictions of Iranian politics during the post-Khomeini era. As Ali Banuazizi notes, "One of the most remarkable features of the 'rule of the ayatollahs' has been the degree to which this relatively small group of men, in spite of their many similarities in social origin and intellectual background, have disagreed on some of the most fundamental issues concerning the nature of an Islamic society and government..." (Banuazizi 1994, 2).

The more the elite has allowed itself to become embroiled in factional conflict over priorities and strategies, the more policy has become a matter of bargaining between factions. When bargaining fails, policy becomes immobilized or each faction pursues its goals independent of the others. The radicals pursue the export of the revolution while the liberals send signals of moderation and cooperation to the West.

While competition within the elite has led to contradictions in the policy-making process, it has also democratized that process by forcing the clergy's diverse factions to seek broader group and mass support for their positions. As noted in an earlier discussion, this process dominated the presidential elections of 1997 and 2001. It could be argued, of course, that the apparent contradictions within the Iranian regime are merely a facade designed to placate the West while Iran continues to pursue the aggressive export of the revolution. This view has been championed by the Israelis, who see little confusion in the Iranian policy-making process, at least as it pertains to Iran's support of terrorism. According to the *Jerusalem Post*:

> All proposals for terrorist attacks are initially endorsed and ultimately authorized by Rafsanjani himself.... Approved proposals are then passed on to the Intelligence Section in the President's Office.... Before orders are given to execute a plan, however, its feasibility is tested by the Ministry of Information and Security. If it passes this test, the plan is presented to the 15-man Supreme Security Council (SSC), headed by Rafsanjani, for final approval (*JP*, July 13, 1996, 8).

Conflicts over priorities and strategy have also been exacerbated by the fragmentation of institutional power. While the reformists dominate the presidency and the parliament, the hard-liners have found strong support from the Supreme Guide, the Republican Guards, the Council of Guardians, the Ministry of Justice, and the intelligence (security) services. Each faction, or so it seems, possesses the institutional mechanisms to check its opponents. This situation resembles the much-lauded "checks and balances" of the American political system, but it is not clear how it will play out in Iran.

THE IMPLEMENTATION OF POLICY: THE BUREAUCRACY AND THE SECURITY APPARATUS

Institutional factors have altered the course of Iranian politics in other ways as well. The clerics had promised an Islamic paradise, but in a highly bureaucratized state such as Iran, the decisions that a corrupt and sluggish bureaucracy could not or would not implement have gone largely for naught. Reflecting this fact, a sarcastic President Khatami proclaimed that "We're not getting results in proportion to the hard work our employees put in. Our enthusiastic and hard working administrators are locked in a sedate, inert, sluggish and overlapping bureaucratic system" (Reuters/*Daily Star*, Aug. 27, 1999, 5).

As the pace of development stagnated, the elite squabbled over solutions. While some argued for stricter penalties for corruption and mismanagement, others pressed for greater reliance on capitalism and the private sector to get things done. Rafsanjani attempted to clip the wings of the bureaucracy by introducing bold capitalist reforms in the early 1990s, but once again the results were muddled. As described by the *Economist*:

> Privatisation, say Iranians, was a bad joke. The few profitable bits of government enterprises that were put on offer—seldom more than a third of a company—were quickly gobbled up by friends or relations of the new elite. Other offers, potentially available to anybody, turned out to be indigestible: widely overstaffed state-owned firms that required new private owners to apply restrictive labor laws to the letter. At the end of it all, some 86% of Iran's GDP still comes from government-owned businesses. And even of the 14% apparently in the private sector, the larger part is the domain of the *bonyads* [religious holding companies] with their massive, accountable-to-nobody, mafia-run enterprises (*Economist, Survey of Iran*, 1997, 13).

Iran's bureaucratic problems, however, were not merely the result of venal officials. They also reflected a fragmented elite that was unable to formulate clear policy objectives, as unclear and confused decisions led to flawed policy implementation. Invariably, Iran's bureaucrats were reluctant to make innovative decisions, for creativity today could become treason tomorrow if power within the ruling elite should shift radically from one faction to another. Everybody, or so it seemed, was protected by one group or another in Iran's seamless network of patron-client relationships.

The security apparatus of the Islamic Republic consists of three distinct military organizations, various intelligence and covert activities agencies, and the internal security services. The primary military organizations are the regular army and the Revolutionary Guards, each of which contains army, air, and naval components. The third military organization is the Basij, a large volunteer militia (Cordesman 1999). The intelligence and covert activities agencies include, among others, the Ministry for Intelligence and Security (VEVAK), the secret intelligence services, and Khamanei's special bureau. Needless to say, Iran's leaders are mindful of security issues.

The regular military had been the pride of the shah, but was decimated by the revolution. More than 250 of the shah's top officers were executed, while many more fled into exile. All in all, the regular military lost approximately half of its officers (Cann and Danopoulos 1997). The regular army has now been rebuilt under the watchful eye of the clergy, but it is counterbalanced by the Revolutionary Guards. The Revolutionary Guards were cobbled together from religious loyalists in 1979 in order to sustain the Islamic Revolution during its early days. Almost overnight they were thrown into battle against the Iraqis, an experience which, over the course of the ensuing eight years, would transform them into a credible and disciplined force. The process of professionalization has continued in post-Khomeini years, with the Revolutionary Guards "now being closer to a regular military force" (Cordesman 1999, 37). This professionalization is less the case for the Basij, an organization known more for its zeal than its discipline. Supporting the latter are the "gangs of street thugs" known as the Ansar-e-Hizbullah (Helpers of the Party of God) who are often aligned with specific conservative members of the clergy and act as vigilantes (Cordesman 1999, 39). The internal security forces, in turn, consist of the police, Gendarmerie, and the Islamic Revolutionary Committees, the three units being merged into the Law Enforcement Forces of the Islamic Republic in 1991 (Cordesman 1999). Little is known about the various intelligence organizations other than the fact that they are both pervasive and powerful.

The security apparatus poses a serious dilemma for Iran's religious elite. By creating a security apparatus strong enough to sustain the Revolution, the clergy has created a counterweight to its own domination. In addition to their obvious ability to overthrow the regime, it is also within the capacity of the security services to adopt a neutral position during a period of domestic turmoil such as the riots of 1994 and 1999. In both instances, it is interesting to note, the regime placed greater reliance on the Basij to control the riots than it did on either the regular army or the Revolutionary Guards.

Efforts to keep the security services subservient to the political leadership have taken at least five forms. First, each of the diverse elements in the security apparatus possesses a separate and distinct command structure. Higher committees and the centralized control of the Supreme Guide offer a modicum of coordination, but competition between the various organizations is substantial (Cordesman 1999). Second, virtually all senior command positions are in hands of the clergy (Cordesman 1999). Third, the members of the security units are recruited largely from the middle and lower classes, a stratum that has traditionally supported the revolution (Cann and Danopoulos 1997). Fourth, members of the various security units are subjected to intense indoctrination. Fifth, communication between security organizations is carefully monitored by the Ideological-Political Directorate (IPD) that has penetrated all levels of the military (Cann and Danopoulos 1997). The latter two points are described by Cann and Danopoulos as follows:

> These clergymen are responsible for ideological and political education of different segments of the armed forces. They organize indoctrination meetings to encourage the military's subordination to Islam, the clerical regime, and the Islamic Republic. The clergy also enforce Islamic code and the daily prayer within the military. In addition, middle-level clergymen in the IPD are responsible for preserving security. They monitor any horizontal communication among various segments of the armed forces to prevent possible coup attempts. They also gather information about army personnel and identify dissidents and nonconformists within the armed forces. On the other hand, the IPD rewards the loyal officers by giving them rapid promotion from the lower to upper ranks, organizing an army loyal to Islamic principles (Cann and Danopoulos 1997, 4, 19).

The ramifications of this system of control are profound. First, performance and coordination have been sacrificed to security. Competence is important, but loyalty comes first. Second, factionalism also exists within the security apparatus in spite of its generally conservative orientation. The regular army, in particular, inclines toward the moderate camp, with letters from senior generals openly supporting democracy (Cann and Danopoulos 1997).

THE GROUP BASIS OF IRANIAN POLITICS

While both the contradictions within the Iranian political system and its evolution toward a more democratic society are a function of elite and institutional conflict, they are also a function of the growing complexity of Iran's group mosaic (Amirahmadi 1996). Indeed, conflicts within the elite have facilitated, if not encouraged, the proliferation of political groups as each faction seeks to bolster its base of support (Bakhash 1998).

Political Parties

While the emergence of full-fledged political parties has been discouraged, each of the four factions outlined previously occupies a clear ideological position on Iran's political spectrum and has taken on most of the functions of a political party, including the nomination of candidates.

The 1992 parliamentary elections, it will be recalled, saw the clergy split into two formal groups, the Association of Combatant Clerics of Tehran and the Combatant Clergy of Tehran, with the former advocating change while the latter advocated a continuation of Khomeini's policies. These two groups were joined in 1996 by the Servants of Construction, a secular group of technocrats who supported Khatami in the 1997 presidential elections (Fairbanks 1998). The new groups were not officially recognized as political parties, because the clergy feared that the emergence of formal political parties would pose a direct challenge to its monopoly of power (Fairbanks 1998). Iran's quasi-parties lack a membership base and are usually little more than a coalition of like-minded factions, each headed by a dominant personality jealous of his power (Sick 2000). Perhaps the closest equivalent to a true political party at the moment is the Islamic Iran Participation Party (IIPP) headed by President Khatami's brother. The IIPP was formed prior to the municipal elections of 1999 and is the dominant group in the Sixth Majlis. The situation, however, remains fluid as entities resembling parties emerge for the needs of the moment, only to disappear and re-emerge under a new format.

Pressure Groups

In much the same manner, group pressures on government policy appear to be increasing rather than decreasing. Particularly strong, in this regard, has been the growing influence of the bonyads, the bazaaris and the technocrats.

Bonyads The *bonyads* are religious charities that were established after the revolution with funds confiscated from the shah and his relatives (Mozaffari 1991). The largest of the funds, the Foundation of the Oppressed, possesses billions of dollars in assets and controls an estimated 1200 companies including five-star hotels, shipping lines and a massive amusement park in Tehran. Some sources say the bonyads control two-thirds of the goods sold in Iran. The profits of the bonyads are designed to help the poor, but some sources suggest that they have also found their way into support of Fundamentalist militias in Lebanon and elsewhere (*Christian Science Monitor*, Feb. 1, 1995, 9; *Economist*, Sept. 25, 1993, 54). The bonyads fall somewhere between the public and private sectors, depending upon the advantages to be gained, and their leaders respond directly to the Ayatollah Khamanei. Not only does this system strengthen the power of the Supreme Guide and his supporters, but it also provides them with a huge slush fund exempt from governmental controls. The bonyads, however, have also become huge bureaucracies and have been plagued with the same corruption and mismanagement as the government bureaucracy itself.

Bazaaris The term *bazaaris*, as described by Mozaffari, refers primarily to the middle and lower sectors of the Iranian business community and is

> applied only to those socio-occupational strata such as guilds (asnaf), craftsmen (pishehvaran) small shopkeepers (kasabah), wholesalers (bunak-daran), exchange agents (sarrafan), brokers (dallalan), and retail merchants (furushandehgan), as well as a certain number of large businessmen (tujjar) who remained part of the traditional Bazari system. The Bazar is an essentially urban and petit-bourgeois phenomenon (Mozaffari 1991, 378).

Mozaffari goes on to note that the bazaaris are far more than an economic middle class (Mozaffari 1991). To the contrary, the bazaaris possess an accepted code of commercial, ethical, and religious conduct that has enabled them to act as a coherent group and thereby to dominate most of the commercial activity in the country (Denoeux 1990).

The bazaaris have long enjoyed a close relationship with the ulema, with bazaari contributions formerly providing one of the ulema's main sources of income. The two groups also share a common suspicion of Westernization, and inter-marriage between the two groups has been frequent.

The link between the bazaaris and the ulema is both cultural and economic. The more the Westernization of Iran proceeded, the more dominance of commercial activity in Iran shifted from the bazaaris to a class of large merchants with close ties to the Palace. Quite logically, this resulted in conflict between the bazaaris and the monarchy and led bazaaris to support a clergy equally challenged by the monarch's pursuit of Westernization.

Cooperation between the bazaaris and the ulema was intensified by the modernization programs of Reza Shah and his son, Mohammed Reza. Adding insult to injury were an emergent "oil bourgeoisie" that acquired fabulous wealth while the bazaaris were being subjected to regulation and increased taxation (Mozaffari 1991). The bazaaris had supported earlier revolutions against royal authority, and the Islamic Revolution would be no exception.

The bazaaris now constitute one of the main pillars of Iran's Islamic regime, and they have benefited accordingly. Most domestic trade and distribution activities are firmly in the hands of the bazaaris, as is a large share of the import/export trade. They also play a major role in the "parallel economy," a term Mozaffari uses to describe black-market activities tacitly accepted by the government to allow for the circulation of goods that would otherwise be in short supply (Mozaffari 1991, 387).

The entrenched position of the bazaaris has enabled them to shape legislation that supports both their economic and cultural interests. These interests, by and large, incline them toward the conservative faction outlined above, a faction that blends capitalism with strict adherence to religious law. The bazaaris were very active in supporting conservative candidates in the 2000 legislative elections, and failing to stem the reformist tide, they staged a strike in support of Supreme Guide Ali Khamanei (*Daily Star*, Apr. 20, 2000, 5).

Clergy   The clergy consist of about 180,000 "men of religion" ranging from the Supreme Guide, the most powerful man in Iran, to the lowest of the village mullahs (*New York Times*, Jan. 30, 2000, www). Iran is a theocracy, and the clergy dominate all positions of influence surveyed in our discussion of political elites. The clerical hierarchy substitutes for a political party in the sense that it provides the organizational network that links the elites to the masses. Elite goals are explained to the masses, and mass concerns are communicated to the elite. When demonstrations of mass support are required, it is the clergy who mobilize the faithful. The clergy are also the main agents of socialization, teaching, preaching, and assuring that Islamic values permeate the educational system and the press. The eyes of the clergy are also ever-vigilant in spotting infractions of Islamic morality and threats to the regime. Many would say that they are over-zealous and that their zeal is undermining support for the regime.

The effectiveness of the clergy in sustaining the regime is based upon a common commitment to the survival of the revolution as well an organizational structure that links the Supreme Guide to the lowest of the mullahs. All, however, is not well, for the clergy is finding it difficult to keep their factional conflicts within bounds. The election of Khatami laid the foundation for a secular challenge to the priestly powers of Khamanei, a challenge reinforced by the 2000 parliamentary elections and the re-election of Khatami in the 2001 presidential elections. Adding to the tensions between the clerical factions have been efforts by hard-liners to deprive the reformists of the gains that they have made via the ballot box. Key supporters of Khatami have been assassinated and arrested, and the Council of Guardians has systematically disqualified key liberal candidates as lacking suitable religious credentials. By blocking democratic competition within the religious establishment, the hard-liners are forcing an eventual showdown between themselves and the reformers that could well find the clergy—and the population—divided against itself. This threat of fragmentation has democratized Iranian politics by drawing the masses into the fray but it has also further immobilized the regime by raising the specter of civil conflict such as the student riots that rocked Tehran in 1999.

Students Iranian students played a key role in challenging the rule of the shah, and Iran's universities were routinely closed down during periods of crisis, often several months at a time. Ironically, a new generation of students, few with recollections of the shah, are now challenging the reign of the ayatollahs (*Radio Free Europe*, Jan. 21, 2000, v.3, n.3; *Daily Star*, May 23, 2000, 5). It was students who precipitated the riots of 1999, and a variety of student organizations have taken on political overtones, most of them being overtly supportive of the reformists. Clashes between students and hard-line vigilantes have been frequent and could easily ignite broader confrontations in the future.

Women Iranian women have become increasingly organized in recent years and have forced the government to reestablish some of the rights that Khomeini had earlier abrogated as being in contravention with Islamic practice (Paidar 1995). A wife can now sue her husband for support if the "court decides that the wife has performed her wifely duty towards her husband" (Kar 1996, 37). Winning such legal battles, as Kar notes, continues to be an uphill struggle, for all the judges are men. Banuazizi finds that Iranian women have "continued to make substantial gains in literacy and educational attainment, sustained their participation in the work force, and thereby kept a significant presence in public life as teachers, journalists, managers, and factory workers"

(Banuazizi 1994, 7). This topic continues to be the subject of heated debate on Internet chat sites (see Gulf 2000, Jan.–Feb. 2001).

Much, however, remains to be done if Iranian women are to regain the rights that they had achieved under the monarchy. With the advent of Islamic rule, Homa Hoodfar writes, "arbitrary divorce, polygamy, and temporary marriage, all of which had been outlawed or restricted by the shah's regime, have made a triumphant return, turning the lives of many women upside down" (Kar 1996). Mehranguiz Kar, in turn, notes that "a woman is not permitted to legally choose her first husband! Regardless of her age, a woman must have her marriage endorsed by her father or paternal kin for it to be legal" (Kar 1996, 37).

Other groups have experienced even more difficulty in finding their voice under the rules of the Islamic Republic. Iran's workers, for example, now belong to Islamic associations in their workplaces rather than to independent labor unions (Banuazizi 1994, 6). The voice of ethnic minorities in the affairs of the Islamic Republic has also been limited, despite the fact that they represent 45 percent of the population.

Opposition Groups   Formal opposition groups are banned in the Islamic Republic, with the most visible opposition to the Islamic regime coming from the Mujahedin-e Khalq, an Iraqi-based revolutionary organization. The Mujahedin-e Khalq has become increasingly bold in recent months, targeting offices in the center of Tehran.

Aside from the Mujahedin-e Khalq, opposition currents would include remnants of the old Iranian left, much of which is now coalescing around the reformist faction of the clergy. This is a matter of some concern to Khatami, whose liberal tendencies are far more constrained than those of his supporters. Indeed, it is probable that many in the reformist camp are merely using Khatami as a wedge to achieve their secular goals.

Politics of the Masses

The fragmentation of the elite into competing factions has been reflected in the growing politicization of the Iranian public as each of several diverse factions within the Islamic establishment has been forced to take its case to the people. While all of the candidates in Iran's elections have possessed impeccable Islamic credentials, voters do have an increasingly clear choice on issues ranging from economic policy to the rigidity of Islamic rule. This was made painfully clear when Mohammed Khatami, a liberal candidate without strong support among the largely conservative clergy, gained an overwhelming 69 percent of the popular vote in the 1997 presidential elections and an even larger

78 percent in the 2001 presidential elections. Not only was this result totally unexpected, but some 88 percent of eligible voters had participated in the election, more than double the turnout for the preceding election. Not unexpectedly, Khatami did particularly well among women, intellectuals, and voters in the 18- to 25-year-old range.[4] The popular vote, however, decreased to 67 percent in the 2001 presidential elections, but it is not clear whether the non-voters were supportive of Khatami or his conservative opponents.

The influence of mass behavior on Iranian politics in the post-Khomeini era extends far beyond the realm of voting. Cynicism and psychological withdrawal have been particularly evident among the middle class, a segment of the Iranian population that must play a crucial role in governance and the economy if the revolution is to develop effective political institutions and break the cycle of economic lethargy. People perform as scripted by the regime, but they do so without enthusiasm. While the form of a theocratic society has been established—women wear Islamic dress, and displays of Islamic piety have become ubiquitous—it is not clear that the Iranian population has embraced its spirit. TV satellite dishes abound in spite of prohibitions to the contrary. Bureaucratic corruption is rampant, and middle-class women, while conforming to the letter of Islamic dress, taunt the authorities by "using the head cover as a means of personal adornment rather than concealment, thus 'turning an object of control into one of protest'" (Banuazizi 1994, 7; Paidar 1995; Friedl and Afkhami 1994). Some dating has also returned among college students, albeit in a subdued format (*IHT*, Nov. 28, 2000, www). Also present are increasing signs of a survivalist culture that views the political system as an object of fear to be avoided whenever possible and exploited for personal gain when the opportunity presents itself. These attitudes have increased as memories of Khomeini and the circumstances that brought him to power continue to fade.

These and other non-supportive attitudes are reflected in lagging production as well as in declining participation in official celebrations and other regime-sponsored activities. Even though people have been demanding more of their government, their behavior is doing little to help the government meet those demands.

THE CONTEXT OF IRANIAN POLITICS

Beyond institutions and actors, Iranian politics is also a function of the cultural, economic, and international environments in which it occurs.

[4]The voting age in Iran was recently changed from 16 to 18.

Each of these factors will have much to say about the course of the Islamic Revolution during the coming decade.

Political Culture

As Iran's dominant religion, Shi'a Islam is a core component of the country's political culture. The vast majority of Iranians are Shi'a Muslims and have been acculturated in a Shi'a environment that influences their value structure and view of the world. This does not mean that all Iranians are religious fanatics or even that most Iranians are deeply religious. It does mean, however, that a very large number of Iranians support Shi'a values. This fact was made obvious by the Ayatollah Khomeini's ability to mobilize the Iranian population against the shah as well as his subsequent ability to prosecute the war against Iraq (Dorraj 1997). Although the zeal of the masses has abated in recent years, Shi'a Islam continues to be the main source of legitimacy for the Iranian regime. This fact is not lost on the ayatollahs, and the regime's efforts to strengthen Islamic values border on obsession (Ram 1993).

In addition to its Shi'a base, Iranian political culture includes an abiding concern for social justice, Iranian nationalism, and a belief that Western exploitation in Iran must be resisted by force (Farsoun and Meshayekhi 1992). These themes are compatible with the philosophy of the clergy and had been used to bolster support for the regime. Indeed, social justice and anti-Westernism were the dominant themes of the Islamic Revolution (Bayat 1997; Zonis and Mokri 1991; Bakhash 1998).

Iranian political culture has other elements as well. Many Iranians were exposed to the West during the pre-revolutionary era and embraced the Western values of democracy and human rights. They also developed a desire for economic development and the material advantages of Western society. Resisting the exploitation of Western colonialism is not incompatible with a desire for democracy and prosperity, and it is this desire for greater democracy and prosperity that is now finding expression in the stunning electoral victories of Khatami and the reformers.

Other facets of political culture have also created problems for Iran's Islamic leaders. The first of these is the sense of alienation and psychological withdrawal discussed above. Alienation, while a product of the shah's rule, has been extended by the severity of the religious rule and economic hardships (Bayat 1997; Zonis and Mokri 1991). Adding to this alienation is the interpersonal distrust and ethnic conflicts born of Iran's traditional origins, not to mention insecurities born of centuries of arbitrary rule (Zonis 1991).

While the above characteristics of Iranian political culture are suffi-
ciently widespread to influence the politics of the Islamic Republic, it is
important to stress that Iranian political culture is far from monolithic.
The culture of the middle classes differs from that of the masses; urban
culture from that of the countryside; youth culture from that of the
parents and grandparents; and the nationalism of the Farsi majority
conflicts with the separatist tendencies of the ethnic minorities who
constitute some 45 percent of the Iranian population. The various clerical factions also have widely differing views of how much non-Islamic
content should be allowed in the political dialogue (Siavoshi 1997).

Iran's population has also increased from approximately 31 million
at the beginning of the Islamic Revolution to almost 70 million today.
This is not a minor consideration, for it indicates that approximately
one-half of the Iranian population today was born after the revolution.
Iran's population explosion is likely to continue, for the Ayatollah
Khomeini canceled birth control programs implemented during the
shah's regimes as being anti-Islamic and a Western plot to subjugate
Iran (Zonis and Mokri 1991). This policy has now been rescinded as the
post-Khomeini elite struggles to feed and employ its exploding population, but attitudes toward birth control change slowly and the shift in
policy will take time to produce results. In the meantime, the population of Iran will continue to grow.

These children of the revolution are now beginning to reach adulthood and the future of the regime could well hinge on its ability to so-
cialize them into an Islamic way of life. This may not be an easy job, for
although the regime claims that some 96 percent of its children attend
school, the effectiveness of the regime's indoctrination program remains suspect. Iranian youth, for example, voted disproportionately
for Khatami in the 1997 and 2000 elections, indicating a clear break
with the ultra-conservative doctrines of the Khomeini era. The growing
urbanization of Iranian society, now over 50 percent, also suggests that
the newer generations will be exposed to a broader range of ideological and material temptations than their rural counterparts (Sharbatoghlie 1991).

Political Economy

The vacillation of Iran's post-Khomeini leadership is also a function
of a declining economy, as is the growing restiveness of the Iranian
population. In many ways, Iran's economy is still attempting to recover from the turmoil of the early revolutionary era and eight years of
war with Iraq. The regime is now focusing on domestic development,

but the process has not been easy (Valibeigi 1993). As discussed by Karshenas and Pesaran:

> The problems go well beyond the availability of financial resources and have deep structural roots that have been nourished by years of neglect and economic mismanagement. Public enterprises and companies under the control and supervision of various foundations function largely as bureaucratic institutions, being more responsive to political than economic forces. Legal, political, and economic uncertainties that surround private-sector investment also need to be addressed. While the importance of the private sector is recognized in the plan, there are still important ambiguities concerning property rights, the extent of private-sector participation, and the role of foreign private investment in Iran (Karshenas and Pesaran, 1995, 91).

The regime's erratic economic policies, in turn, have led to high unemployment, high prices and serious inflation, all of which have eroded its popular support (Azimi 2000). Not only do many Iranians find it difficult to make a living, but the money they do earn now buys less. There is also a growing gap between the winners and losers, with the bazaaris prospering while the poor find it increasingly difficult to make ends meet. Bayat, for example, describes in great detail the continuing immigration to the cities and the reluctance of the squatters to return to the countryside despite the hardships of urban life. Shanty towns are torn down, only to be rebuilt (Bayat 1997).

Economic factors were particularly evident in recent elections, with Khatami finding strong support among the technological middle classes and the conservatives receiving strong support from the bazaaris. The same pattern was repeated in the ensuing municipal elections and the 2000 parliamentary elections.

Also in the economic realm is Iran's continued dependence on oil for some 90 percent of its foreign exchange (money required to purchase goods and services from abroad), a fact that makes the Iranian economy vulnerable to swings in the world price of oil and punitive pressures from the United States. Iran's dependency on oil also renders it vulnerable to the whims of Saudi Arabia, a country whose massive oil revenues make it the dominant force in OPEC. The Iranians are attempting to buy their way out of their economic crises by demanding that OPEC increase the prices of crude oil, but the Saudis are more inclined to try to please the United States by keeping the price of oil in the moderate range.

Despite the fact that oil production has passed pre-war levels, unemployment has reached unacceptable rates and austerity programs have generated mass disaffection. Unemployment is especially high among Iranian youth, a particularly volatile segment of the population. While some progress has been made in improving incomes of rural citizens, incomes of people living in the urban areas have decreased (Banuazizi 1994; Azimi 2000). This disparity could pose a serious problem for the regime, for politics is overwhelmingly an urban affair. Virtually all government offices, communication systems, and industrial plants are located in a handful of urban areas of which Tehran is the most important. Strikes in one of these nerve centers, and Tehran in particular, could have a devastating effect throughout the country. Perhaps reflecting this fact, initial efforts at privatization and economic reform have been slowed lest they result in a further loss of jobs in the urban areas.

International Interdependence

The influence of foreign powers on the politics of Iran has been the single dominant theme in the preceding discussion and defies easy summary. Suffice it to say that the Pahlavi dynasty was founded and sustained by the Western powers. In the process, Iran was transformed into a rentier state whose economy was dominated by the export of oil, the proceeds from which were used to buy arms and luxury products from the West. In point of fact, the monarchy, despite spending billions of dollars on arms, did not fight a single sustained war.

The Islamic Revolution was, in large part, a popular reaction to a repressive monarchy that placed the interests of the West above those of its own citizens. The Islamic Revolution, in turn, posed a direct threat to Western interests in the Middle East and was challenged by crippling boycotts and a devastating war with Iraq. The West did not start the Iran-Iraq War, but Saudi Arabia and Kuwait, both staunch allies of the United States, were deeply involved in the process.

This is not to suggest that all of Iran's problems are of external origin, for this is not the case. Foreign intervention, however, exacerbated domestic problems and made the tortuous process of development even more difficult.

Foreign influence continues to shape the politics of Iran, with perhaps one of the most vibrant debates in Iran today being the future of the Islamic Republic's relations with the United States. The prospect of bowing to pressure from the United States is repugnant to revolutionary values, but the need for economic growth, and thereby the long-term survival of the Islamic regime, may leave Iran's leaders with little choice in the matter.

It would be a mistake, however, to believe that the United States is in a position to dictate policy to Iran. The Islamic Republic has survived in spite of boycotts and the Iran-Iraq War. It also possesses a large and battle-tested army supported by medium-range missiles (SCUD B/CL and CSS-8s), and chemical weapons. Biological and nuclear weapons are being developed, although the latter are probably a decade away (defenselink.profile.1997).

Iran's potential threat to Saudi Arabia and its Gulf neighbors gives pause to the United States, as does Iran's continuing role as the bastion of Islamic Fundamentalism. The US Department of State describes Iran as "the most active sponsor of state terrorism," and believes that Tehran is using its influence with Fundamentalist groups such as Hamas and Hizbullah to derail the Arab-Israeli peace process (US Department of State 1999).

The international environment, moreover, appears to be evolving in Iran's favor. While the US continues to impose economic sanctions, largely to its own detriment, the Europeans and Japanese are anxious to do business with an Iranian regime brandishing lucrative arms and construction contracts. This point was made poignantly clear in 1997 when the European Union and Japan granted Iran $5 billion in loan guarantees. Russia is also anxious to do business with Iran, and has increasingly ignored US warnings against selling sophisticated weaponry to the Islamic Republic (*Daily Star*, Jan. 31, 2001, 5). Even many of the US's Arab allies in the region have grown reluctant to support a policy toward Iran that is increasingly interpreted by their citizens as being imperialist and anti-Islamic (Ramazani 1998). Iran will have to compromise with the United States, but the Islamic Republic will not be without a voice in that process.

LOOKING TOWARD THE FUTURE

In sum, the confusion and seeming lack of direction of Iran's leaders during the post-Khomeini era reflects the revolution's continuing effort to sort itself out. This effort has been hampered by the loss of Khomeini's profound symbolic appeal, a shattered economy, political mismanagement, and growing dissension within the ruling elite. Despite these problems, the revolution has maintained its grip on power and has fashioned a political system that blended Islamic jurisprudence with modern concepts of political democracy.

To the extent that present trends offer a guide to the future, the preceding assessment suggests that Iran will continue to lumber along during the next decade much as it has in the past. Strong policy initiatives are likely to be prevented by the continued fragmentation of the Iranian elite as well as by the weakness of the Iranian economy and the growing apathy of the Iranian masses. The strengthening of the military and other coercive agencies, however, should assure the continued domination of the regime and enable it to shape the politics of the Gulf region. As yet, however, the Iranian military seems ill-prepared to engage in an extended confrontation with neighboring states, and especially those states aligned with the West. Pressure for internal development should also force Iran to continue its dialogue with the West, although advocates of terrorism will continue to have a strong voice within policy circles.

Present trends, however, are subject to rapid change. Although Iran's factions have maintained a balance of power for the past decade, power within the elite could shift dramatically to either the right or left. Alternatively, the growing distance between factions could lead to a rupture within the Islamic establishment and set off a coup d'état. The threat of an external shock such as the Iraqi invasion of 1980 could also change the direction of Iranian politics, as unlikely as that possibility may seem at the moment.

References

Abboushi, W. F. 1985. *The Unmaking of Palestine*. Wisbech, Cambridgeshire, England: Middle East & North African Studies Press.

Abdel-Latif, Omayma. 2000 (Nov.). "Dreaming of Better Times." *Al-Ahram Weekly On-line*, Issue 509.

Abdo, Geneive. 1999. "Electoral politics in Iran." *Middle East Policy* 6(4): 128.

Abdou, Johnny. 1999. *Al Assad: Strategy, Independence* (in Arabic). Paris: S. Abdou.

Abir, Mordechai. 1993. *Saudi Arabia: Government, Society, and the Gulf Crises*. London: Routledge.

Aburish, Said. 1994. *The Rise, Corruption, and Coming Fall of the House of Saud*. London: Bloomsbury.

Aflaq, Michel. 1963. *The Struggle of the Common Destiny* (in Arabic). Damascus: Dar El-Adaab.

Ahmad, Ahmad Yousef. 1984. "The Dialectics of Domestic Environment and Role Performance: The Foreign Policy of Iraq." In *The Foreign Policies of Arab States* (147–174), ed. Bahgat Korany and Ali E. Hillal Dessouki. Boulder, CO: Westview.

Ajami, F. 1992. *The Arab Predicament*. 2nd ed. Cambridge: Cambridge University Press.

Al Ahram Survey. 1998 (June). Public Opinion Survey: Preliminary Results (in Arabic). Cairo: Al Ahram Center for Political and Strategic Studies.

Al-Angari, Haifa. 1997. *The Struggle for Power in Arabia*. Reading, UK: Ithaca Press.

Al-Fatah, Sadeq Abdo. 1990. *Nights and Caprices of Farouk* (in Arabic). Cairo: Library Madbouli.

Al-Freih, Mohammed. 1995. *The Historical Background of the Emergence of Muhammad Ibn 'Abd-al Wahhab and His Movement*. Ann Arbor, MI: UMI Dissertation Information Service.

Al-Hadidi, Salah Addin. 1984. *Witness to the Yemen War* (in Arabic). Cairo: Library Madbouli.

Al-Hawadith. 1998 (Nov. 27). "Syria on the Door of the 7th Legislative Session," 30–34.

Al-Iyash, Esam. 1998a (Nov. 20). "Desert Thunder in the Fridge and the Alternative Is Assassinations and a Military Coup" (in Arabic). *Al-Hawadeth,* 18–25.

Al-Iyash, Esam. 1998b (Nov. 27). "Qusai Guardian of the Regime and Uday Contractor of the Dollars." *Al-Hawadeth,* 18–22.

Allam, Abeer. 2000. "Less Work, More Play for State Bureaucrats." *Middle East Times,* 2 (www.metimes.com/2K/issue2000-2/eg/less_work.htm).

Allan, J. A. 1997. "'Virtual Water': A Long-Term Solution for Water-Short Middle Eastern Economies?" An Occasional Paper, London: SOAS (www.soas.ac.uk/Geography/WaterIssues/OccasionalPapers/home.html).

Allan, J. A. 1999. "Water in International Systems: A Risk/Society Analysis of Regional Problems." An Occasional Paper. London: SOAS (www.soas.ac.uk/Geography/WaterIssues/OccasionalPapers/home.html).

Allan, Tony (J. A.). 2001. *The Middle East Water Question.* London: I. B. Tauris.

Allport, Gordon W. 1954. *The Nature of Prejudice.* Cambridge, MA: Addison-Wesley.

Al-Manoufi. 1979. *The Changing Political Culture of the Egyptian Village* (in Arabic). Cairo: Al-Ahram Center for Political and Strategic Studies.

Alnasrawi, Abbas. 1991. *Arab Nationalism, Oil, and the Political Economy of Dependency.* New York: Greenwood.

Alnasrawi, Abbas. 1994. *The Economy of Iraq.* Westport, CT: Government Press.

Al-Nimir, Saud, and Monte Palmer. 1982. "Bureaucracy and Development in Saudi Arabia: A Behavioural Analysis." *Public Administration and Development* 2: 93–104.

Alpher, Joseph. 1995. "Israel: The Challenges of Peace." *Foreign Policy* 101: 130–145.

Al-Qaisi. 1999 (Aug. 13). "Has the Hour of Liquidation Come?" (in Arabic). *Al-Waton Al-Arabi,* 20–21.

Al-Rasheed, Madawi. 1996a (Jan.). "Saudi Arabia's Islamic Opposition." *Current History* 95(597): 16.

Al-Rasheed, Madawi. 1996b (July–Aug.). "Mirage in the Desert." *Index on Censorship* 25(4): 73.

Al-Rasheed, Madawi. 1996c (Summer). "God, the King and the Nation: Political Rhetoric in Saudi Arabia in the 1990s." *The Middle East Journal* 50(3): 359.

Al-Shaibi, Kamil. 1991. *Sufism and Shi'ism.* England: LAAM, Ltd.

Al-Sharbasi, Al Sayeed Al Sharbini. No Date. *Principles of Socialism in Islam.* (In Arabic.) Cairo: Selections from Radio and Television.

Amiel, Barbara. 2000 (Nov. 27). "While the World Condemns Israel, This Tragedy Will Never End." *The Jerusalem Post Internet Edition,* 1–15.

Amin, Galal. 1995. *Egypt's Economic Predicament.* Leiden, Netherlands: E. J. Brill.

Amirahmadi, Hooshang. 1996. "Emerging Civil Society in Iran." *SAIS Review* 16(2): 87–107.

An-Nafisi, Abdullah Fahd. 1982. *The Gulf Cooperation Council: The Political and Strategic Framework.* London: Ta-Ha Publishers Ltd.

Ansari, Hamied. 1985. "Mubarak's Egypt." *A World Affairs Journal: The Middle East* 84: 498.

Ansari, Hamied. 1986. *Egypt: The Stalled Society*. Cairo: The American University in Cairo Press.

Anscombe, Frederick Fallowfield. 1997. *The Ottoman Gulf*. New York: Columbia University Press.

Antonius, George. 1965. *The Arab Awakening*. New York: Capricorn Books.

Aoude, Ibrahim G. 1994. "From National Bourgeois Development to Infitah: Egypt 1952–1992." *Arab Studies Quarterly* 16(1): 1–23.

Apiku, Simon. 1999. "Interior Minister Ruffles the Feathers of Top Brass." *Middle East Times*, 38.

Arab, Mohammed K. 1988. "The Effect of the Leader's Belief System on Foreign Policy: The Case of Libya." Unpublished Dissertation, Florida State University.

Arab Political Documents. 1963. "Minutes of the Tripartite Union: Talks Held in Cairo Between the Delegations of the UAR and the Syrian and Iraqi Republics (Excerpts)." Lebanon: PSPA Department of the American University of Beirut, 75–217.

Arian, Asher. 1997. *Politics in the Israeli Second Republic*. London: Chatham House.

Arjomand, Said Amir. 1984. *The Shadow of God and the Hidden Iman*. Chicago: University of Chicago Press.

Armajani, Yahya. 1970. *Middle East: Past and Present*. Englewood Cliffs, NJ: Prentice-Hall.

Aronoff, Myron J. 1989. *Israeli Visions and Divisions: Cultural Change and Political Conflict*. New Brunswick, NH: Transaction Publishers.

Ayrout, Henry Habib. 1962. *The Egyptian Peasant*. Translated by John Williams. Boston: Beacon Press.

Ayubi, Nazih. 1980. "The Political Revival of Islam: The Case of Egypt." *International Journal of Middle East Studies* 12: 481–499.

Ayubi, Nazih. 1982 (July). "Bureaucratic Inflation and Administrative Inefficiency: The Deadlock in Egyptian Administration." *Middle Eastern Studies* 18: 242.

Azimi, Hussein. 2000. "Acute Social and Political Tussles in Iran, Reflection of Fundamental Conflicts in the Country's Economic Structure." Payame Emrouz; *Cultural, Social and Economic Magazine* 42: 41–44 (www.netiran.com).

Bahgat, Gawdat. 1991. *The Impact of External and Internal Forces on Economic Orientation: The Case of Egypt*. Ph.D. dissertation, Florida State University.

Baker, Raymond W. 1978. *Egypt's Uncertain Revolution Under Nasser and Sadat*. Cambridge, MA: Harvard University Press.

Bakhash, Shaul. 1978. *Iran: Monarchy, Bureaucracy and Reform under the Qajars: 1858–1896*. London: St. Anthony's Middle East Monographs.

Bakhash, Shaul. 1998. "Iran's Remarkable Election." *Journal of Democracy* 9(1): 80–94.

Baktiari, Bahman. 1996a. *Parliamentary Politics in Revolutionary Iran. The Institutionalization of Factional Politics*. Gainesville, FL: The University Press of Florida.

Baktiari, Bahman. 1996b. "The Governing Institutions of the Islamic Republic of Iran: The Supreme Leader, the Presidency, and the Majlis." In *Iran and the Gulf: A Search for Stability*, ed. Jamal al-Suwaidi. Abu Dhabi, UAE: The Emirates Center for Strategic Studies and Research.

Banuazizi, Ali. 1994 (Nov./Dec.). "Iran's Revolutionary Impasse: Political Factionalism and Societal Resistance." *Middle East Report* 191: 2–8.

Banuazizi, Ali, and Myron Weiner, eds. 1986. *The State, Religion and Ethnic Politics*. New York: Syracuse University Press.

Barakat, Halim. 1993. *The Arab World: Society, Culture, and State*. Berkeley, CA: University of California Press.

Barakat, Mohammed, and Mahmood Sadiq. 1998 (Nov. 17). "Has the Thought of Religious Violence in Egypt Receded?" (in Arabic). *Al-Waton Al-Arabi*, 4–8.

Baram, Amatzia. 1989. "The Ruling Political Elite in Ba'thi Iraq, 1968–1986: The Changing Features of a Collective Profile." *International Journal of Middle East Studies* 21(4): 447–493.

Baram, Amatzia. 1997. "Neo-Tribalism in Iraq: Saddam Hussein's Tribal Policies, 1991–96." *International Journal of Middle East Studies* 29: 1–31.

Baram, Amatzia. 2000a (Spring). "The Effect of Iraqi Sanctions: Statistical Pitfalls and Responsibility." *The Middle East Journal* 54 (2): 1–31, www.

Baram, Amatzia. 2000b (Dec.). "Saddam Husayn Between His Power Base and the International Community." *Middle East Review of International Affairs* 4 (4): 1–14, www.

Baram, Amatzia, and Barry M. Rubin. 1993. *Iraq's Road to War*. New York: St. Martin's Press.

Barnett, Michael N. 1992. *Confronting the Costs of War: Military Power, State, and Society in Egypt and Israel*. Princeton, NJ: Princeton University Press.

Barth, Fredrik. 1953. *Principles of Social Organization in Southern Kurdistan*. Oslo: Brodrene Jorgensen A/A Boktrykkeri.

Bartov, Hanoch. 1981. *48 Shanah Veod 20 Yom (48 Years and 20 More Days.)* Tel Aviv: Maariv Book Guild, 482–489. (Reprinted in Itamar Rabinovich and Jehuda Reinharz, eds., 1984, *Israel in the Middle East: Documents and Readings on Society, Politics and Foreign Relations, 1948–Present*, "The Turning Point in the October 1973 War." Oxford: Oxford University Press, 247–251.)

Barzilai, Gad. 1999. "War, Democracy, and Internal Conflict: Israel in a Comparative Perspective." *Comparative Politics* 31(3): 317–318.

Batatu, Hanna. 1978. *The Old Social Classes and the Revolutionary Movements of Iraq*. Princeton, NJ: Princeton University Press.

Batatu, Hanna. 1981. "Iraqi Underground Shi'a Movements: Characteristics, Causes and Prospects." *Middle East Journal* 35(4): 578–594.

Batatu, Hanna. 1999. *Syria's Peasantry, the Descendants of its Lesser Rural Notables, and Their Politics*. Princeton, NJ: Princeton University Press.

Bauer, Yehuda. 1970. *From Diplomacy to Resistance: A History of Jewish Palestine, 1939–1945*. Philadelphia: The Jewish Publication Society.

Bayat, Assef. 1987. *Workers and Revolution in Iran: A Third-World Experience of Workers' Control*. London: Zed Books Ltd.

Bayat, Asef. 1997. *Street Politics: Poor People's Movements in Iran*. New York: Columbia University Press.

Beattie, Kirk J. 1994. *Egypt During the Nasser Years*. Boulder, CO: Westview Press.

Begin, Menachem. 1951. *The Revolt: Story of the Irgun*. New York: Henry Schuman.

Behrens-Abouseif. 1990. *Islamic Architecture in Cairo: An Introduction*. Cairo: The American University in Cairo Press.

Beinin, Joel. 1998. *The Dispersion of Egyptian Jewry*. Berkeley, CA: University of California Press.

Ben-Gurion, David. 1971. *Israel: A Personal History*. New York and Tel Aviv: Funk and Wagnalls, Inc. and Sabra Books, 561–563. (Reprinted in Itamar Rabinovich and Jehuda Reinharz, eds., 1984, *Israel in the Middle East: Documents and Readings on Society, Politics and Foreign Relations, 1948–Present*, "Social and Ethnic Tensions in the Late 1950s." Oxford: Oxford University Press, 141–143.)

Ben-Meir, Alon. 1996. "The Dual Containment Strategy Is No Longer Viable." *Middle East Policy* 4(3): 58–71.

Berque, Jacques. 1967. *Egypt: Imperialism and Revolution*. New York: Praeger.

Bianchi, Robert. 1989. *Unruly Corporatism: Associational Life in Twentieth-Century Egypt*. New York: Oxford University Press.

Bichler, Shimson. 1994. "Political Power Shifts in Israel, 1977 and 1992: Unsuccessful Electoral Economics or Long-Range Realignment?" *Science and Society* 58(4): 415–439.

Biger, Gideon. 1989. "The Shatt-Al-Arab River Boundary: A Note." *Middle Eastern Studies* 25(2): 248–251.

Bill, James A. 1984 (Fall). "Resurgent Islam in the Persian Gulf." *Foreign Affairs* 63: 108–127.

Bill, James A. 1988. *The Eagle and the Lion: The Tragedy of American-Iranian Relations*. New Haven, CT: Yale University Press.

Bill, James A., and William Roger Louis, eds. 1988. *Musaddiq, Iranian Nationalism, and Oil*. Austin, TX: University of Texas Press.

Bill, James, and Robert Springborg. 1997. *Politics in the Middle East*. New York: HarperCollins.

Bonne, Alfred. 1955. *State and Economics in the Middle East*. London: Routledge & Kegan Paul, Ltd.

Brands, H. W. 1993. *Into the Labyrinth: The United States and the Middle East, 1945–1993*. New York: McGraw-Hill.

Brecher, Michael. 1974. *Decisions in Israel's Foreign Policy*. London: Oxford University Press.

Brichta, Avraham. 1998. "The New Premier-Parliamentary System in Israel (Israel in Transition)." *The Annals of the American Academy of Political and Social Science* 555: 180–192.

Brockelmann, Carl. 1960. *History of the Islamic People*. New York: Capricorn Books.

Busse, Herbert. 1997. *Islam, Judaism and Christianity: Theological and Historical Affiliations*. Princeton, NJ: Markus Wiener Pub.

Butler, Richard. 2000a. *The Greatest Threat: Iraq, Weapons of Mass Destruction, and the Crisis of Global Security*. New York: Public Affairs.

Butler, Richard. 2000b. *Saddam Defiant: The Threat of Weapons of Mass Destruction, and the Crisis of Global Security*. London: Weidenfeld & Nicolson.

Campagna, Joel. 1996 (Summer). "From Accommodation to Confrontation: The Muslim Brotherhood in the Mubarak Years." *Journal of International Affairs* 50(1): 278–304.

Cann, Rebecca, and Constantine Danapoulos. 1997. "The Military and Politics in a Theocratic State: Iran as a Case Study." *Armed Forces and Society* 24(2): 269–288.

Carleton, Alford. 1950 (Jan.). "The Syrian Coups d'État of 1949." *Middle East Journal* 4(1): 1.

Carter, B. L. 1986. *The Copts in Egyptian Politics*. London: Croom Helm.

Cavender, Gay, Nancy C. Jurik, and Albert K. Cohen. 1993. "The Baffling Case of the Smoking Gun: The Social Ecology of the Political Accounts in the Iran-Contra Affair." *Social Problems* 40(2): 152–165.

Chabry, Laurent, and Annie Chabry. 1987. *Politique et Minorites au Proche-Orient: Les Raisons d'une Explosion*. Paris: Editions Maisonneuve and Larose.

Champion, David. 1999. "The Kingdom of Saudi Arabia: Elements of Instability within Stability." *Middle East Review of International Affairs* 3(4).

Cockburn, Andrew, and Patrick Cockburn. 1999. *Out of the Ashes*. New York: HarperCollins.

Cohen, Aryeh Dean. 1999 (Sept. 14). "Sarid Defends Authors of Controversial History Book." *Jerusalem Post*.

Cohen, Raymond. 1990. *Culture and Conflict in Egyptian-Israeli Relations*. Bloomington: Indiana University Press.

Cohen, Raymond. 1994 (June). "Israel's Starry-Eyed Foreign Policy." *Middle East Quarterly* 1(2): 28–41.

Cohen, Raymond. 1994 (Sept.). "Culture Gets in the Way." *Middle East Quarterly* 1(3): 45–54.

Cole, Juan Ricardo. 1993. *Colonialism and Revolution in the Middle East*. Princeton, NJ: Princeton University Press.

Coon, Carleton S. 1961. *Caravan: The Story of the Middle East*. Rev. Edition. New York: Holt, Rinehart and Winston.

Cordesman, Anthony H. 1999. *Iraq and the War of Sanctions: Conventional Threats and Weapons of Mass Destruction*. London: Praeger.

Cressey, George B. 1960. *Crossroads: Land and Life in Southwest Asia*. Chicago: Lippincott.

Cronin, Stephanie. 1997. *The Army and the Creation of the Pahlavi State in Iran, 1910–1926*. London: Tauris.

Cuno, Kenneth M. 1992. *The Pasha's Peasants*. Cambridge, England: Cambridge University Press.

Dabrowska, Karen. 1994. "Opposition in Disarray." *The Middle East* 240: 9–10.

Dahy, Talal. 1988. *The Military Organization as an Agent for Modernization in the Third World Countries: Case Study—National Guard in Saudi Arabia*. Ph.D. dissertation, Florida State University.

Daneshvar, Parviz. 1996. *Revolution in Iran*. New York: St. Martin's Press.

Dann, Uriel. 1969. *Iraq Under Qassem: A Political History, 1958–1963*. New York: Praeger.

Darwish, Adel. 1994 (June). "Water Wars." Lecture given at the Geneva Conference on Environment and Quality of Life.

Davis, Eric. 1987. "The Concept of Revival and the Study of Islam and Politics." In *The Islamic Impulse* (37–58), ed. Barbara F. Stowasser. London: Croom Helm.

Dawn, C. Ernest. 1962 (Spring). "The Rise of Arabism in Syria." *The Middle East Journal* 16(2): 145.

De Corancez, Louis A. O. 1995. *The History of the Wahabis: From Their Origin until the End of 1809*. (Translated by Eric Tabet.) Reading, UK: Garnet Publishing.

Dekmejian, R. Hrair. 1975. *Egypt Under Nasser: A Study in Political Dynamics*. Albany, NY: State University of New York Press.

Dekmejian, R. Hrair. 1985. *Fundamentalism in the Arab World*. Syracuse, NY: Syracuse University Press.

Dekmejian, R. Hrair. 1991. "The Arab Republic of Syria." In *Politics and Government in the Middle East and North Africa* (188–208), ed. Tareq Y. Ismael and Jacqueline S. Ismael. Miami, FL: Florida International University Press.

Dekmejian, R. Hrair. 1994. "The Rise of Political Islamism in Saudi Arabia." *The Middle East Journal* 48(4): 627–643.

Dekmejian, R. Hrair. 1995. *Islam in Revolution: Fundamentalism in the Arab World*. Syracuse, NY: Syracuse University Press.

Dekmejian, R. Hrair. 1998. "Saudi Arabia's Consultative Council." *The Middle East Journal* 52(2): 204–218.

Delannoy, Christian. 1990. *Savak*. Paris: Stock.

Denoeux, Guilain Pierre. 1990. *Informal Networks, Urbanization, and Political Unrest in the Middle East: The Cases of Egypt, Iran, and Lebanon*. Ph.D. thesis.

Dia, Mamadou. 1996. *Africa's Management in the 1990s and Beyond: Reconciling Indigenous and Transplanted Institutions*. Washington, DC: World Bank.

Diba, Farhad. 1986. *Mossadegh: A Political Biography*. London: Croom Helm.

do Ceu Pinto, Maria. 1999. *Political Islam and the United States: A Study of US Policy Towards Islamic Movements in the Middle East*. Reading, UK: Garnet Publishing (also Ithaca Press).

Doran, Michael Scott. 1999. *Pan-Arabism Before Nasser*. New York: Oxford University Press.

Dorraj, Manocheht. 1997. "Symbolic and Utilitarian Political Value of a Tradition: Martyrdom in the Iranian Political Culture." *The Review of Politics* 59(3): 489–521.

Dowell, Henry. 1931. *The Founder of Modern Egypt: A Study of Muhammad Ali*. Cambridge: Cambridge University Press.

Drysdale, Alasdair, and Raymond A. Hinnebusch. 1991. *Syria and the Middle East Peace Process*. New York: Council on Foreign Relations Press.

Dumas, Marie-Lucy, ed. 1995. *Repertoire des Partis Integristes Musulmans: Tombe 1: la Mediterranee*. Paris: C.H.E.A.M.

Eickelman, Dale F., and James Piscatori. 1996. *Muslim Politics*. Princeton, NJ: Princeton University Press.

Eddy, William Alfred. 1954. *FDR Meets Ibn Sa'ud*. Kohinur series (no. 1). New York: American Friends of the Middle East.

Eisenhower, Dwight David. 1965. *Waging Peace, 1956–1961: The White House Years*. London: Heinemann.

El-Aref, Aref. 1944. *Bedouin Love, Law and Legend*. Jerusalem: Cosmos Publishing Co.

El-Din, Khaled Mohi. 1992. *Memories of a Revolution: Egypt 1952*. Cairo: American University of Cairo Press.

El Ebraash, Wa'eil, and Kemal El Shathli. 2000 (July 8–14). "The Cleansing of the National Democratic Party" (in Arabic). *Rose El Youssef*, 12–14.

El-Gamassy, Mohammed Abdel Gani. 1993. "October War: Memoirs of Field Marshal El-Gamassy of Egypt." English translation. 1981 Arabic Translation by Gillian Potter, Nadra Marcus, Roselta Frances. Cairo: American University of Cairo Press.

El Khazen. 2000. *The Breakdown of the State in Lebanon, 1967–1976*. London: Tauris.

Elliot, Matthew. 1996. *Independent Iraq: The Monarchy and British Influence, 1941–58*. London: Tauris.

Elm, Mostafa. 1992. *Oil, Power, and Principle: Iran's Oil Nationalization and Its Aftermath*. Syracuse, NY: Syracuse University Press.

Emerson, Rupert. 1960. *From Empire to Nation*. Cambridge, MA: Harvard University Press.

Esposito, John L., ed. 1990. *The Iranian Revolution: Its Global Impact*. Miami, FL: Florida International University Press.

Etzioni-Halevy, Eva. 1977. *Political Culture in Israel: Cleavage and Integration Among Israeli Jews*. New York: Praeger.

Ezrahi, Yaron. 1998. *Rubber Bullets: Power and Conscience in Modern Israel*. Berkeley, CA: University of California Press.

Fahmy, Khaled. 1997. *All the Pasha's Men*. Cambridge: Cambridge University Press.

Fairbanks, Stephen C. 1998. "Theocracy Versus Democracy: Iran Considers Political Parties." *The Middle East Journal* 52(1): 17–31.

Fandy, Mamoun. 1999. *Saudi Arabia and the Politics of Dissent*. New York: St. Martin's Press.

Farah, T. 1987. *Pan-Arabism and Arab Nationalism: The Continuing Debate*. Boulder, CO: Westview Press.

Farid, Abdel Majid. 1994. *Nasser: The Final Years*. Reading, UK: Ithaca Press.

Farsoun, Samih K., and Mehrdad Meshayekhi, eds. 1992. *Iran. Political Culture in the Islamic Republic*. London: Routledge.

Fernea, Robert A., and William Roger Louis. 1991. *The Iraqi Revolution of 1958*. London: Tauris.

Flory, Maurice, and Pierre-Satheh Agate, eds. 1989. *Le systeme regional Arabe*. Paris: Editions du Centre National de la Recherche Scientific.

Fraser, T.G. 1980. *The Middle East, 1914–1979*. London: Edward Arnold.

Friedl, Erika, and Mahnaz Afkhami, eds. 1994. *In the Eye of the Storm: Women in Post-Revolutionary Iran*. Syracuse, NY: Syracuse University Press.

Fulanain. 1928. *The Marsh Arab*. Philadelphia: Lippincott.

Gallman, Waldemar J. 1964. *Iraq Under General Nuri: My Recollections of Nuri Al-Said, 1954–1958*. Baltimore, MD: Johns Hopkins Press.

Galnoor, Itzahak, David H. Rosenbloom, and Allon Yaroni. 1998. "Creating New Public Management Reforms: Lessons from Israel." *Administration and Society* 30(4): 393–418.

Gause, F. Gregory, III. 1994. *Oil Monarchies: Domestic and Security Challenges in the Arab Gulf States*. New York: Council on Foreign Relations Press.

Gause, F. Gregory, III. 1999 (May). "Getting It Backward on Iraq." *Foreign Affairs*, 78(3): 54.

Gellner, Ernest. 1987. *The Concept of Kinship (and Other Essays on Anthropological Method and Explanation)*. Oxford: Basil Blackwell Ltd.

Gelvin, James L. 1998. *Divided Loyalties. Nationalism and Mass Politics in Syria at the Close of the Empire*. Berkeley, CA: University of California Press.

Gershoni, I., and James Jankowski. 1995. *Redefining the Egyptian Nation, 1935–1945*. Cambridge, UK: Cambridge University Press.

Gieling, Saskia. 1997. "The Marja'iya in Iran and the Nomination of Khamanei in December 1994." *Middle Eastern Studies* 33(4): 777–787.

Gilbert, Martin. 1979. *The Arab-Israeli Conflict: Its History in Maps*. 3rd ed. London: Weidenfeld and Nicolson.

Gilboa, Eytan, and Yaron Katz. 1999. "The Media Campaign: The Shift to Alternative Media." *Middle East Review of International Affairs (MERIA) Journal* 3(4).

Gillespie, Kate. 1984. *The Tripartite Relationship: Government, Foreign Investors and Local Investors During Egypt's Economic Opening*. New York: Praeger.

Gillespie, Kate, and Clement Henry. 1995. *Oil in the New World Order*. Gainesville, FL: University Press of Florida.

Gilsenan, Michael. 1978. *Saint and Sufi in Modern Egypt: An Essay in the Sociology of Religion*. Oxford: Oxford University Press.

Ginat, Rami. 1997. *Egypt's Incomplete Revolution*. London: Frank Cass.

Gluckman, Max. 1965. *Politics, Law and Ritual in Tribal Society*. New York: The New American Library.

Goldschmidt, Arthur. 1988. *Modern Egypt: The Formation of a Nation-State*. Boulder, CO: Westview Press.

Gomaa, Salwa S. 1991. "Leadership and Elections in Local Government." *Perspectives in the Center—Local Relations: Political Dynamics of the Middle East*. M.E.S. series No. 28, 34–63.

Gomaa, Salwa S. 1998. *Environmental Policy Making in Egypt*. Gainesville, FL: The University Press of Florida.

Gordon, Joel. 1992. *Nasser's Blessed Movement*. New York: Oxford University Press.

Gordon, Michael, and Bernard E. Trainor. 1994. *The Generals' War: The Inside Story of Conflict in the Gulf*. Boston: Little, Brown.

Gorst, Anthony, and Lewis Johnman. 1997. *The Suez Crisis*. London: Routledge.

Graham-Brown, Sarah. 1999. *Sanctioning Saddam*. London: Tauris.

Graham-Brown, Sarah, and Zina Sackur. 1995. "The Middle East: The Kurds—A Regional Issue." Writenet country papers (www.unhcr.ch/refworld/country/writenet/wrikurd.htm).

Green, Jerrold D. 1982. *Revolution in Iran: The Politics of Countermobilization*. New York: Praeger.

Gresh, Alain. 2000 (Nov.). "Oil for Food: The True Story." *Le Monde Diplomatique*, 1–7, www.

Gunter, Michael M. 1992. *The Kurds of Iraq: Tragedy and Hope*. New York: St. Martin's Press.

Habib, Rafiq. 1989. *Religious Protest and Class Conflict in Egypt* (in Arabic). Cairo: Sinai for Publishing.

Hadar, Leon T. 1999. "Israel in the Post-Zionist Age: Being Normal and Loving It." *World Policy Journal* 16(1). (Internet version, no page numbers.)

Ha'fiz, Yassin. 1963. *Concerning the Experience of the Baath Party in Political Thought*, Vol. I (in Arabic). Damascus: House of Damascus for Printing and Publishing.

Haj, Samira. 1997. *The Making of Iraq, 1900–1963*. Albany, NY: State University of New York Press.

Halm, Heinz. 1997. *Shi'a Islam: From Religion to Revolution*. (Translated from German by Allison Brown.) Princeton: Markus Wiener Pub.

Hamadi, Ibrahim. 1998 (Dec. 14). "Syria: Weekly Review." *Al-Wasat*, 20–21.

Hamid, Berlinti Abd. 1992. *The Marshall and I* (in Arabic). Cairo: Library Madbouli.

Hamid, Ibrahim. 2001 (Jan. 8). "Syria: Intellectuals Organize Clubs, Civil Society and Human Rights" (in Arabic). *Al-Wasat*, 18–19.

Hammond, Andrew. 2000. "Personal Status Law Not a Personal Choice." *Middle East Times*, 3, www.

Hamouda, Adel. 1990. *How the Egyptians Mock Their Leaders* (in Arabic). Cairo: House of Sphinx Publishers.

Hamza, Khidir, and David Albright. 1998. "Inside Saddam's Secret Nuclear Program." *Bulletin of the Atomic Scientists* 54(5): 26–33.

Hamzeh, Nizar. 2000. "Lebanon's Islamists and Local Politics: A New Reality." *Third World Quarterly* 21(5): 739–759.

Hamzeh, Nizar, and Hrair Dekmejian. 1996. "A Sufi Response to Political Islamism: Al-Ahbash of Lebanon." *International Journal of Middle East Studies* 28: 217–229.

Harik, Iliya. 1997. *Economic Policy Reform in Egypt*. Gainesville, FL: University of Florida Press.

Hart, Parker T. 1998. *Saudi Arabia and the United States: Birth of a Security Partnership*. Bloomington, IN: Indiana University Press.

Hasba'ni, Ahmed. 2000 (Oct. 30). "Bashar Takes Hold of Syria's Destiny and Its Development" (in Arabic). *Al-Ousbou Al-Arabie*, 20–21.

Hassan-Gordon, Tariq. 2000. "State Regrets Election 'Inconvenience' to Journalists." *Middle East Times*, www.

Hazelton, Fran, ed. 1994. *Iraq since the Gulf War: Prospects for Democracy*. London: Zed Books Ltd.

Heikal, Mohammed H. 1962. *What Happened in Syria* (in Arabic). Cairo: National Publishing House.

Heikal, Mohammed H. 1983. *Autumn of Fury: The Assassination of Sadat*. London: Andre Deutsch.

Henry, Clement M. 1996. *The Mediterranean Debt Crescent: Money and Power in Algeria, Egypt, Morocco, Tunisia, and Turkey*. Gainesville, FL: University of Florida Press.

Hermann, Margaret G., Charles F. Hermann, and Richard D. Anderson. 1992. "Explaining Self-Defeating Foreign Policy Decisions: Interpreting Soviet Arms for Egypt in 1973 Through Process or Domestic Bargaining Models?" *American Political Science Review* 86(3): 759–767.

Hersh, Seymour M. 1999 (April 5). "Annals of Espionage: Saddam's Best Friend." *The New Yorker*, 32–42.

Herzig, Edmund. 1995. *Iran and the Former Soviet South*. Washington, DC: Brookings Institution.

Herzl, Theodor. 1896. *A Jewish State*. New York: American Zionist Emergency Council. [1946].

Herzog, Ze'ev. 1999 (Oct. 29). "Deconstructing the Walls of Jericho." *Ha'areetz Magazine*, www.

Hibra, Karem. 2000 (July 29). "Rapid-Fire Judicial Decisions." *Rose El Youssef*, 20–21.

Hidar, Asaad. 1999 (March 7). "As-Sadr in the Week Before" (in Arabic). *Al-Wasat*, 13–14.

Hinnebusch, Raymond A. 1980. "Political Recruitment and Socialization in Syria: The Case of the Revolutionary Youth Federation." *International Journal of Middle East Studies* 2: 143–174.

Hinnebusch, Raymond A. 1985. *Egyptian Politics under Sadat: The Post-Populist Development of an Authoritarian Modernizing State.* Cambridge, UK: Cambridge University Press.

Hinnebusch, Raymond A. 1988. *Egyptian Politics under Sadat: The Post-Populist Development of an Authoritarian Modernizing State.* Boulder, CO: Lynne Rienner Publishers.

Hinnebusch, Raymond A. 1990. *Authoritarian Power and State Formation in Ba'athist Syria.* Boulder, CO: Westview Press.

Hinnebusch, Raymond A. 1993. "State and Civil Society in Syria." *The Middle East Journal* 42(2): 247–249.

Hitti, Philip K. 1956. *History of the Arabs from the Earliest Times to the Present.* 6th ed. London: Macmillan.

Hitti, Philip K. 1959. *Syria: A Short History.* New York: Macmillan.

Hobbes, Thomas. 1651; reprinted 1965. *Leviathan.* Chicago: Henry Regnery.

Holden, David, and Richard Johns. 1981. *The House of Saud.* London: Pan Books.

Holland, Matthew F. 1996. *America and Egypt: From Roosevelt to Eisenhower.* Westport, CT: Praeger.

Hooglund, Eric J. 1982. *Land and Revolution in Iran, 1960–1980.* Austin, TX: University of Texas Press.

Hosseinzedeh, Esmail. 1989. *Soviet Non-Capitalist Development: The Case of Nasser's Egypt.* New York: Praeger.

Hourani, Albert. 1997. *History of the Arab Peoples.* New York: Fine Communications.

Hubbel, Steve. 1992 (Sept.). "Fundamentalist Gains." *Middle East International*, 25.

Husaini, Ishak Musa. 1956. *The Moslem Brethren: The Greatest of Modern Islamic Movements.* Beirut: Khayat.

Ibrahim, Farhad. 1996. *Confessionalism and Politics in the Arab World: The Shi'a Program in Iraq* (in Arabic). (Translated from German by the Center for Cultural Studies and Translations.) Cairo: Library Madbouli.

Ibrahim, Saad Eddin. 1980. "Anatomy of Egypt's Militant Islamic Groups: Methodological Note and Preliminary Findings." *International Journal of Middle East Studies* 12(4): 423–453.

Ibrahim, Saad Eddin. 1996. *Egypt, Islam, and Democracy.* Cairo: American University of Cairo Press.

Imam, Samia. 1987. *Who Rules Egypt?* (in Arabic). Cairo: Arab Futures Publishing House.

Ismael, Tareq, and Jacqueline Ismael. 1991. "The Republic of Iraq." In *Politics and Government in the Middle East and North Africa*, ed. Tareq Y. Ismael and Jacqueline S. Ismael. Miami, FL: Florida International University Press, 151–187.

Jabar, Kamal S. 1966. *The Arab Baath Socialist Party.* Syracuse, NY: Syracuse University Press.

Jabar, Karam. 2000a (Nov. 10). "Election File: Statements of Jamal Mubarak" (in Arabic). *Rose El Youssef*, 14–16.

Jabar, Karam. 2000b. (Nov. 17). "Election File: False Tears Succeed in Deceiving Some of the Voters" (in Arabic). *Rose El Youssef*, 16–17.

Johansen, Julian. 1996. *Sufism and Islamic Reform in Egypt: The Battle for Islamic Tradition.* Oxford: Clarendon Press.

Joseph, Nevo. 1998 (July). "Religion and National Identity in Saudi Arabia." *Middle Eastern Studies,* 34.

Joyner, Christopher C. 1990. *The Persian Gulf War.* New York: Greenwood.

Kamil, Omar. 2000 (Dec.). "Rabbi Ovadia Yosef and His 'Culture War' in Israel." *Middle East Review of International Affairs* 4 (4): 1–18, www.

Kar, Mehranguiz. 1996 (Jan.). "Women and Personal Status Law in Iran: An Interview with Mehranguiz Kar." *Middle East Report,* 36–38.

Karsh, Efrain. 1991. *Soviet Policy Towards Syria since 1970.* Houndmills Basingstoke Hampshire: Macmillan.

Karsh, Efrain, and Inari Rautsi. 1991. *Saddam Hussein.* New York: Faith Press.

Karshenas, Massoud, and M. Hashem Pesaran. 1995. "Economic Reform and the Reconstruction of the Iranian Economy." *The Middle East Journal* 49(1): 89–111.

Kassem, May (May Kaddem). 2000. *In the Guise of Democracy: Governance in Contemporary Egypt.* New York: Ithaca Press.

Kelidar, Abbas. 1983. "The Shi'i Imami Community and Politics in the Arab East." *Middle Eastern Studies* 19(1): 3–16.

Kerr, Malcolm H. 1971. *The Arab Cold War: Gamal Abd Al-Nasir and His Rivals, 1958–1979.* London: Oxford University Press.

Kerr, Malcolm H. and El Sayed Yassin. 1982. *Rich and Poor States in the Middle East: Egypt and the New Arab Order.* Boulder, CO: Westview Press.

Kessler, Martha Neff. 1987. *Syria: Fragile Mosaic of Power.* Washington, DC: National Defense University Press.

Khadduri, Majid. 1955. *War and Peace in the Law of Islam.* Baltimore: Johns Hopkins Press.

Khadduri, Majid. 1960. *Independent Iraq, 1932–1958.* London: Oxford University Press.

Khalife, Osama F. 2001. "Arab Political Mobilization and Israeli Responses." *Arab Studies Quarterly.* Forthcoming.

Khalil, Ashraf. 2000 (Oct. 22). "The Empire Strikes Back." *Cairo Times,* www.

Khalil, Samir. 1989. *Republic of Fear.* Berkeley, CA: University of California Press.

Khan, Amil. 2000. "British Lord Weighs In on Elections." *Middle East Times,* www.

Khashan, Hilal. 1995. "The Labyrinth of Kurdish Self-Determination." *The International Journal of Kurdish Studies* 8(1–2): 5–31.

Khashan, Hilal. 2000a (August). *Policy Focus: Arab Attitudes Toward Israel and Peace.* Washington, DC: Washington Institute for Near East Policy.

Khashan, Hilal. 2000b. *Arabs at the Crossroads: Political Identity and Nationalism.* Gainesville, FL: University Press of Florida.

Khashan, Hilal, and Simon Haddad. 2000 (June). "The Coupling of the Syrian-Lebanese Peace Tracks: Beirut's Options." *Security Dialogue* 31: 2, 201–214.

Khashan, Hilal, and Michel Nehme. 1996. "The Making of Stalled National Movements: Evidence from Southern Sudan and Northern Iraq." *Nationalism and Ethnic Politics* 2(1): 111–138.

Khashan, Hilal, and Monte Palmer. 1998 (Dec.). "The Social and Economic Correlates of Islamic Religiosity." A paper presented at the Middle East Studies Association for North America, Chicago.

Khoury, Dina R. 1997. *State and Provincial Society in the Ottoman Empire Mosul, 1540–1834.* Cambridge, MA: Cambridge University Press.

Khoury, Philip S., and Joseph Kostiner. 1990. *Tribes and State Formation in the Middle East*. Berkeley, CA: University of California Press.

Kienle, Eberhard. 1990. *Ba'ath v. Ba'ath*. London: Tauris.

Kingseed, Christian Cole. 1995. *Eisenhower and the Suez Crisis of 1956*. Baton Rouge, LA: Louisiana State University Press.

Kornhauser, William. 1959. *The Politics of Mass Society*. New York: Free Press.

Kostiner, Joseph. 1993. *The Making of Saudi Arabia, 1916–1936*. New York: Oxford University Press.

Krimly, Rayed. 1999. "The Political Economy of Adjusted Priorities: Declining Oil Revenues and Saudi Fiscal Policies." *The Middle East Journal* 53(2): 256.

Kunz, Diane B. 1991. *The Economic Diplomacy of the Suez Crisis*. Chapel Hill, NC: University of North Carolina Press.

Lacy, Robert. 1981. *The Kingdom: Arabia and the House of Sa'ud*. New York: Harcourt, Brace and Jovanovich.

Lane, E. W. 1954. *Manners and Customs of the Modern Egyptians*. London: J. M. Dent & Sons. Ltd.

Laqueur, Walter, and Barry Rubin (eds.). 1990. *The Human Rights Reader*. New York: New American Library.

Laswell, Harold D. 1958. *Politics: Who Gets What, When, How*. New York: The World Publishing Co.

Lawson, Fred Haley. 1992. *The Social Origins of Egyptian Expansionism During the Muhammad Ali Period*. New York: Columbia University Press.

Lawson, Fred Haley. 1996. *Why Syria Goes to War*. Ithaca, NY: Cornell University Press.

Le Gac, Daniel. 1991. *La Syrie du General Assad*. Bruxelles: Editions Completes.

Lerner, Daniel. 1958. *The Passing of Traditional Society*. Glencoe, IL: The Free Press.

Lesch, Ann M., and Mark Tessler. 1989. *Israel, Egypt and the Palestinians*. Bloomington, IN: Indiana University Press.

Levy, Reuben. 1962. *The Social Structure of Islam*. Cambridge: Cambridge University Press.

Lewis, Bernard. 1958. *The Arabs in History*. New York: Harper and Brothers.

Liebman, Charles, and Bernard Susser. 1998. "Judaism and Jewishness in the Jewish State." *The Annals of the American Academy of Political and Social Science* 555: 15–25.

Lofgren, Hans. 1993. "Economic Policy in Egypt: A Breakdown in Reform Resistance?" *International Journal of Middle East Studies* 25(3): 407–421.

Long, David E. 1997. *The Kingdom of Saudi Arabia*. Gainesville, FL: University Press of Florida.

Longgood, William F. 1957. *Suez Story: Key to the Middle East*. New York: Greenberg.

Longrigg, Stephen H. 1953. *Iraq, 1900–1950: A Political, Social and Economic History*. London: Oxford University Press.

Lukitz, Liora. 1995. *Iraq*. London: F. Cass.

Mackey, Sandra. 1996. *The Iranians: Persia, Islam and the Soul of a Nation*. New York: Dutton.

Maisa, Jamal. 1993. *The Political Elite in Egypt* (in Arabic). Beirut: Center for Arab Unity Studies.

Makram-Ebeid, Mona. 1996 (March). "Egypt's 1995 Elections: One Step Forward, Two Steps Back?" *Middle East Policy* 4(3): 119–136.

Mansingh, Surit. 1986. *Foreign Relations in India: A Country Study*, ed. Richard Nyrop. Washington, DC: US Government Printing Office, 459–502.

Marriott, J.A.R. 1956. *The Eastern Question: An Historical Study in European Diplomacy*. 4th ed. London: Oxford University Press.

Marsot, Afaf Lufti Al-Sayyid. 1984. *Egypt in the Reign of Muhammad Ali*. Cambridge: Cambridge University Press.

Mauran, Hussein, and Riyadh Elm Eddin. 1999 (Aug. 30). "Details of the Attempted Coup Against al-Asad" (in Arabic). *Al-Waton Al-Arabi*, 4–7.

McCausland, Jeffrey. 1993. *The Gulf Conflict*. London: International Institute for Strategic Studies.

McDermott, Anthony. 1988. *Egypt from Nasser to Mubarak: A Flawed Revolution*. London: Croom Helm.

Melhem, Hisham. 1997 (Spring.) "Syria Between Two Transitions." *Middle East Report*, 2–7.

Melville, Charles. 1996. *Safavid Persia: The History and Politics of an Islamic Society*. London: Tauris.

Meyer, Thomas. 1988. *The Changing Past: Egyptian Historiography of the Urabi Revolt, 1882–1883*. Gainesville, FL: University Press of Florida.

Middle East Contemporary Survey. 1978–1979. The Shiloah Center for Middle Eastern and African Studies, Tel Aviv University. New York: Holmes & Meier.

Miller, Judith. 1994 (Nov.–Dec.). "Faces of Fundamentalism: Hassan al-Turabi and Muhammed Fadlallah (Sudanese and Lebanese Islamic Fundamentalist Leaders)." *Foreign Affairs* 73: 6, 123–143.

Miller, Judith, and Laurie Mylroie. 1990. *Saddam Hussein*. Paris: Presses de la Cite.

Mitchell, Richard. 1969. *The Society of Muslim Brothers*. London: Oxford University Press.

Moghadam, Fatemeh E. 1996. *From Land Reform to Revolution: The Political Economy of Agricultural Development in Iran, 1962–1979*. London: Tauris.

Mostyn, Trevor. 1991. *Major Political Events in Iran, Iraq and the Arabian Peninsula, 1945–1990*. New York: Facts on File.

Moubayed, Sami. 2001 (Jan. 18). "Bashar Brings Unexpected Political Freedom." *Daily Star*, 6.

Moussalli, Ahmad. 1999. *Moderate and Radical Islamic Fundamentalism: The Quest for Modernity, Legitimacy, and the Islamic State*. Gainesville, FL: University Press of Florida.

Moussavi, Ahmad Kazami. 1992. "A New Interpretation of the Theory of Vilayat-i Faqih." *Middle Eastern Studies* 8(1): 101–107.

Mozaffari, Mehdi. 1991. "Why the Bazaar Rebels." *Journal of Peace Research* 28(4): 377–391.

Mozaffari, Mehdi. 1993. "Changes in the Iranian Political System after Khomeini's Death." *Political Studies* XLI(4): 611–617.

Mubarak, Hosni. 1985 (Nov. 14). "Address to the Egyptian Parliament." *Al-Ahram*.

Mubarak, Hosni. 1987 (Nov. 6). "This Is My Word to the Arab Summit in Amman." *Al-Waton Al-Arabi*, 28–33.

Mubarak, Hosni. 1999. Interview. *Al-Hawadth*: 19–24.

Mufti, Malik. 1996. *Sovereign Creations*. Ithaca, NY: Cornell University Press.

Mullaney, Francis Cabrini. 1995. *The Role of Islam in the Hegemonic Strategy of Egypt's Military Rulers (1952–1990)*. Ann Arbor, MI: UMI Dissertation Information Service.

Munson, Henry Jr. 1988. *Islam and Revolution in the Middle East*. New Haven, CT: Yale University Press.

Musallam, Ali Musallam. 1996. *The Iraqi Invasion of Kuwait*. London: British Academic Press.

Muslih, Muhammad. 1999. *The Foreign Policy of Hamas*. New York: Council on Foreign Relations.

Mustafa, Hala. 1992. "Les Forces Islamiques et l'Experience Democratique en Egypte." In *Democratie et Democratizations Dans le Monde Arabe*. Le Caire: Dossiers de CEDEJ, 379–397.

Mustafa, Hala. 1995. *The Political System and the Islamic Opposition in Egypt* (in Arabic). Cairo: Markaz Al Mahrusa. (Translated title: *The State and the Opposition Islamic Movements between Truce and Confrontation in the Eras of Sadat and Mubarak.*)

Nakash, Yitzhak. 1994. *The Shi'is of Iraq*. Princeton, NJ: Princeton University Press.

Namazi, Siamak. 2000 (April 23). "The IRGC, Khamenei, and Fate of Iran's Reform Movement." *Gulf 2000 List*.

Nash, Manning. 1966. *Primitive and Peasant Economic Systems*. San Francisco, CA: Chandler Publishing Co.

Nasser, Gamal Abdul. 1955. *Egypt's Liberation: The Philosophy of the Revolution*. Washington, DC: Public Affairs Press.

Nasser, Gamal Abdul. No Date. *Speeches and Press Interviews for the Years 1954–65*. Cairo: Information Department.

Neguib, Mohammed. 1955. *Egypt's Destiny*. Garden City, NJ: Doubleday and Co.

Nehme, Michel. 1994. "Saudi Arabia 1950–80: Between Nationalism and Religion." *Middle Eastern Studies* 30(4): 930–943.

Nehme, Michel. 1995. "The Shifting Sands of Political Participation in Saudi Arabia." *ORIENT*, 45–60.

Nonneman, Gerd. 1986. *Iraq, the Gulf States, and the War*. London: Ithaca Press.

Norton, Augustus Richard, ed. 1994. *Civil Society in the Middle East*. Leiden, Netherlands: E. J. Brill.

Noyes, James H. 1997. "Does Washington Really Support Israel?" *Foreign Policy* 106: 144–160.

Nyrop, Richard. 1983. *Egypt: A Country Study. Area Handbook*. Washington, DC: US Government Printing Office.

Ofteringer, Ronald, and Ralf Backer. 1994. "A Republic of Statelessness: Three Years of Humanitarian Intervention in Iraqi Kurdistan." *Middle East Report* March–June: 40–45.

Orlinsky, Harry M. 1961. *Ancient Israel*. 2nd ed. Ithaca, NY: Cornell University Press.

Orr, Akiva. 1994. *Israel: Politics, Myths, and Identity Crises*. London: Pluto Press.

Owen, R. 1992. *State, Power and Politics in the Making of the Modern Middle East*. London: Routledge.

Oz, Amos. 1995. *Under This Blazing Light*. Cambridge: Press Syndicate of Cambridge University Press.

Paidar, Parvin. 1995. *Women and the Political Process in Twentieth-Century Iran*. (Cambridge Middle East Studies, No. 1.) Cambridge: Cambridge University Press.

Palmer, Monte. 1960. "Iraq and Arab Unity." Unpublished master's thesis, University of Wisconsin.

Palmer, Monte. 1992 (March). "Will a Decade of Foreign Aid Be Lost?" *Al-Ahram Weekly* (Cairo), 12.

Palmer, Monte. 1997. *Political Development: Dilemmas and Challenges*. Itasca, IL: F. E. Peacock.

Palmer, Monte, Ali Leila, and El Sayeed Yassin. 1988. *The Egyptian Bureaucracy*. Syracuse, NY: Syracuse University Press.

Palmer, Monte, Earl Sullivan, and Madhia Safty. 1996. "The Relationship between Economic and Religious Attitudes in Egypt." Paper presented at the 1996 Meeting of the Middle East Studies Association of North America, Providence, RI.

Perthes, Volker. 1997. *The Political Economy of Syria under Asad*. London: Tauris.

Peters, F. E. 1994. *Muhammad and the Origins of Islam*. Albany, NY: State University of New York Press.

Pipes, Daniel. 1990. *Greater Syria: The History of an Ambition*. New York: Oxford University Press.

Polk, William R., David M. Stamler, and Edmund Asfour. 1957. *Backdrop to Tragedy: The Struggle for Palestine*. Boston: Beacon Press.

Posusney, Marsha P. 1997. *Labor and the State in Egypt, 1952–1994*. New York: Columbia University Press.

Quandt, William. 1990. *The United States and Egypt*. Washington, DC: Brookings Institution.

Quilliam, Neil. 1999. *Syria and the New World Order*. Reading, UK: Ithaca.

Rabinovich, Itamar, and Jehuda Reinharz, eds. 1984. *Israel in the Middle East: Documents and Readings on Society, Politics and Foreign Relations, 1948–Present*. Oxford: Oxford University Press.

Radwan, Zeina Abdul Majid. 1982. *First Report: The Religious Dimension in the Appearance of Veiling* (in Arabic). Cairo: National Center for Social and Criminal Research.

Rajaee, Farhang. 1999. "A Thermidor of 'Islamic Yuppies'?: Conflict and Compromise in Iran's Politics." *The Middle East Journal* 53(2): 217.

Ram, Haggay. 1993. "Islamic 'Newspeak': Language and Change in Revolutionary Iran." *Middle Eastern Studies* 29(2): 198–120.

Ramazani, R. K. 1989. "Iran's Foreign Policy: Contending Orientations." *Middle East Journal* 43(2): 202–217.

Ramazani, R. K. 1992. "Iran's Foreign Policy: Both North and South." *The Middle East Journal* 46(3): 393–412.

Ramazani, R. K. 1998. "The Shifting Premise of Iran's Foreign Policy: Towards a Democratic Peace?" *The Middle East Journal* 52(2): 177–187.

Ramet, Sabrina Petra. 1990. *The Soviet-Syrian Relationship Since 1955*. Boulder, CO: Westview Press.

Ribak, Rivka. 1997. "Socialization Through Conversation: Political Discourse in Israeli Families." *Comparative Education Review* 41(1): 71–96.

Richards, Alan. 1991. "The Political Economy of Dilatory Reform: Egypt in the 1980s." *World Development*, 19(12): 1721–1730.

Richards, Alan, and John Waterbury. 1990. *A Political Economy of the Middle East: State, Class, and Economic Development*. Boulder, CO: Westview Press.

Rizk, Hamdi. 1999a (Oct. 30). "Egyptian Muslim Brotherhood" (in Arabic). *Al-Wasat*, 31.

Rizk, Hamdi. 1999b (Aug. 16). "Egyptian Parliamentary Deputies in the Dock" (in Arabic). *Al-Wasat*, 20–25.

Robinson, Glenn E. 1998. "Elite Cohesion, Regime Succession and Political Instability in Syria." *Middle East Policy* 5: 159–179.

Rodinson, Maxime. 1969. *Israel and the Arabs*. Middlesex, England: Penguin.

Rodinson, Maxime. 1973. *Israel: A Colonial-Settler State?* New York: Monad Press.

Rubin, Barry. 1999. "External Factors in Israel's 1999 Elections." *Middle East Review of International Affairs (MERIA) Journal* 3(4).

Rubin, Uri. 1995. *The Eye of the Beholder: The Life of Muhammad as Viewed by the Early Muslims*. Princeton, NJ: The Darwin Press, Inc.

Rugh, Andrea B. 1986. *Reveal and Conceal: Dress in Contemporary Egypt*. Cairo: American University in Cairo Press.

Saadeq, Mahmoud. 1999a (April 2). "For the First Time: Thoughts of a Social Islamic Party in Egypt" (in Arabic). *Al-Waton Al-Arabi*, 4–8.

Saadeq, Mahmoud. 1999b (May 28). "Wanted Dead or Alive" (in Arabic). *Al-Waton Al-Arabi*, 4–7.

Sachs, Susan. 2000 (Jan. 28). "Egypt Makes It Easier for Women to Divorce Husbands." *New York Times*.

Safran, Nadav. 1988. *Saudi Arabia: The Ceaseless Quest for Security*. New York: Cornell University Press.

Saikal, Amin. 1980. *The Rise and Fall of the Shah*. Princeton, NJ: Princeton University Press.

Saleh, Heba. 1990 (Feb.). "Undercover: Why Are More Egyptian Women Wearing Veils? Social Scientists Suggest a Variety of Reasons." *Cairo Today*, 67–69.

Sal'eh, Mohammed. 2000 (Oct. 30). "Egypt: The Elections Revive the Soul of the Brotherhood" (in Arabic). *Al-Wasat*, 22–23.

Samii, A. W. 1999. "The Contemporary Iranian News Media." *Middle East Review of International Affairs* 3(4).

Sarabi, Farzin. 1994. "The Post-Khomeini Era in Iran: The Elections of the Fourth Islamic Majlis." *The Middle East Journal* 48(1): 89–107.

Schacht, Joseph. 1964. *An Introduction to Islamic Law*. Oxford: Clarendon Press.

Schemm, Paul. 1999. "Islamist Students Arrested before Vote." *Middle East Times*, 39.

Scholch, Alexander. 1981. *Egypt for the Egyptians!* London: Published by Ithaca Press for the Middle East Center, St. Anthony's College.

Schwartz, Nancy L. 1994. "Representation and Territory: The Israeli Experience." *Political Science Quarterly* 109(4): 615–645.

Seale, Patrick. 1988. *Asad of Syria*. London: Tauris.

Segal, David. 1988. "The Iran-Iraq War: A Military Analysis." *Foreign Affairs* 66(5): 946–963.

Sharabi, Hisham. 1988. *Neopatriarchy: A Theory of Distorted Change in Arab Society*. New York: Oxford University Press.

Sharbatoghlie, Ahmad. 1991. *Urbanization and Regional Disparities in Post-Revolutionary Iran*. Boulder, CO: Westview Press.

Sharett, Moshe. 1978. *Yoman Ishi (Personal Diary)*. Tel Aviv: Maariv, 1024–1025. (Reprinted as "Israel's Foreign and Middle Eastern Policy," 95–98, in *Israel in the Middle East: Documents and Readings on Society, Politics and Foreign Relations, 1948–Present*, ed. Itamar Rabinovich and Jehuda Reinharz. Oxford: Oxford University Press.)

Sharkansky, Ira. 1991. *Ancient and Modern Israel: An Exploration of Political Parallels*. Albany, NY: State University of New York Press.

Sharkansky, Ira. 1997a. "Religion and Politics in Israel and Utah." *Journal of Church and State* 39: 523–541.

Sharkansky, Ira. 1997b. *Policy Making in Israel: Routines for Simple Problems and Coping with the Complex*. Pittsburgh: University of Pittsburgh Press, 523–541.

Sheffer, Gabriel. 1996. *Moshe Sharett: Biography of a Political Moderate*. Oxford: Clarendon Press.

Shemesh, Haim. 1992. *Soviet-Iraqi Relations, 1968–1988*. Boulder, CO: Lynne Rienner Publishers.

Shepard, William. 1987. "Islam and Ideology: Towards a Typology." *International Journal of Middle East Studies* 19: 307–336.

Shihab, Zaki. 1999 (March 21). "Iraq" (in Arabic). *Al-Wasat*, 18–19.

Shlaim, Avi. 1995. "Israeli Politics and Middle East Peacemaking." *Journal of Palestine Studies* 24(4): 20–31.

Shlaim, Avi, and Avner Yaniv. 1980. "Domestic Politics and Foreign Policy in Israel." *International Affairs* 56: 242–262.

Shlaim, Avi, and Raymond Tanter. 1978. "Decision Process, Choice, and Consequences: Israel's Deep-Penetration Bombing in Egypt, 1970." *World Politics*: 483–516.

Shoreh, Berween. 1998 (Dec. 7). "Another AUC Book Slashed by the Censor." *The Middle East Times*, 49, www.

Shukri, Ghali. 1990. *Masks of Terror: Research on the New Secularism* (in Arabic). Cairo: Dar al-Fikr.

Shuster, W. Morgan. 1912. *The Strangling of Persia*. New York: The Century Company.

Siavoshi, Sussan.1997. "Cultural Policies and the Islamic Republic: Cinema and Book Publication." *International Journal of Middle East Studies* 29(4): 509–530.

Sick, Gary. 2000 (Feb. 26). "Iran's Election: Out of Chaos, Change." *Gulf 2000 List*.

Silverfarb, Daniel. 1994. *The Twilight of British Ascendancy in the Middle East: A Case Study of Iraq, 1941–1950*. London: Macmillan.

Simons, Geoff. 1998. *Saudi Arabia: The Shape of a Client Feudalism*. Chippenham, Wiltshire, Great Britain: Anthony Rowe, Ltd.

Singerman, Diane. 1995. *Avenue of Participation: Family, Politics, and Networks in Urban Quarters of Cairo*. Princeton, NJ: Princeton University Press.

Sirageldin, Ismail A., Naiem Sherbiny, and M. Ismail Serageldin. 1984. *Saudis in Transition: The Challenges of a Changing Labor Market*. New York: Oxford University Press.

Smith, Charles D. 1992. *Palestine and the Arab-Israeli Conflict*. 2nd ed. New York: St. Martin's Press.

Smith, Robertson. 1903. *Kinship and Marriage in Early Arabia*. Boston: Beacon Press.

Smith, Wilfred Cantwell. 1957. *Islam in Modern History*. New York: The New American Library of World Literature.

Smolansky, Oles, and Bettie Smolansky. 1991. *The USSR and Iraq: The Soviet Quest for Influence*. Durham, NC: Duke University Press.

Smooha, Sammy. 1998. "The Implications of the Transition to Peace for Israeli Society." *The Annals of the American Academy of Political and Social Science* 555: 26–45.

Spiegel, Steven L. 1985. *The Other Arab-Israeli Conflict: Making America's Middle East Policy, from Truman to Reagan*. Chicago: University of Chicago Press.

Springborg, Robert. 1989. *Mubaraks's Egypt: Fragmentation of the Political Order*. Boulder, CO: Westview Press.

Sprinzak, Ehud. 1991. *The Ascendance of Israel's Radical Right*. New York: Oxford University Press.

Sprinzak, Ehud, and Larry Diamond, eds. 1993. *Israeli Democracy Under Stress*. Boulder, CO: Lynne Rienner Publishers.

State of Israel. 1999. *Budget Policy: Israeli Draft Budget for Fiscal Year 1999*. www.

Sullivan, Dennis J. 1990. "The Political Economy of Reform in Egypt." *International Journal of Middle East Studies* 22: 317–334.

Sullivan, Dennis Joseph. 1994. *Private Voluntary Organizations in Egypt*. Gainesville, FL: University Press of Florida.

Sullivan, Tim. 1986. *Women in Egyptian Public Life*. Syracuse, NY: Syracuse University Press.

Sumaida, Hussein. 1991. *Circle of Fear: A Renegade's Journey from the Mossad to the Iraqi Secret Service*. Canada: Stoddart.

Tabatabai, Muhammad Husayn. (n.d.) *Shi'a*. Qum, Iran: Ansariyan Publications.

Tessler, Mark. 1994. *A History of the Israeli-Palestinian Conflict*. Bloomington, IN: Indiana University Press.

Tibi, Bassam. 1997. *The Challenge of Fundamentalism: Political Islam and the New World Disorder*. Berkeley, CA: University of California Press.

Toledano, Ehud. 1990. *State and Society in Mid-Nineteenth-Century Egypt*. Cambridge: Cambridge University Press.

Trapp, Frank J. 1994. *Does a Repressive Counter-Terrorist Strategy Reduce Terrorism?: An Empirical Study of Israel's Iron Fist Policy for the Period 1968 to 1987*. Unpublished Ph.D. dissertation: Florida State University.

Twitchell, Karl. S. 1958. *Saudi Arabia*. Princeton, NJ: Princeton University Press.

United Arab Republic. 1963. *Minutes of the Sessions of the Unity Discussions* (in Arabic). Cairo: Kutub Quameya.

United States Embassy. 1994. "Foreign Economic Trends and Their Implications for the United States." Report for the Arab Republic of Egypt. Cairo: U.S. Embassy.

United States Government. 1998. *Country Report on Economic Policy and Trade Practices: Egypt*, www.

United States Government, Department of State. 1999. *Patterns of Global Terrorism, 1999*, www.

Upton, Joseph M. 1960. *The Modern History of Iran: An Interpretation*. Cambridge, MA: Harvard University Press.

Vakili-Zad, Cyrus. 1994. "Conflict Among the Ruling Revolutionary Elite in Iran." *Middle Eastern Studies* 30(3): 618–631.

Valibeigi, Mehrdad. 1993. "Islamic Economics and Economic Policy Formation in Post-Revolutionary Iran: A Critique." *Journal of Economic Issues* 27(1): 793–812.

van Dam, Nikolaos. 1996. *The Struggle for Power in Syria: Politics and Society under Asad and the Ba'ath Party*. London: Tauris.

Van der Mulen, F. A. 1957. *The Wells of Ibn Saud*. New York: Praeger.

Vassiliev, Aleksei Mikhailovich. 1998. *The History of Saudi Arabia*. London: Saqi Books.

Viorst, Milton. 1995. "Changing Iran: The Limits of the Revolution." *Foreign Affairs* 74(6): 63–76.

Viorst, Milton. 1996. "The Storm and the Citadel." *Foreign Affairs* 74(1): 93–107.

Wahba, Mourad Magdi. 1994. *The Role of the State in the Egyptian Economy, 1945–1981*. Reading, UK: Ithaca Press.

Warriner, Doreen. 1957. *Land Reform and Development in the Middle East: A Study of Egypt, Syria and Iraq*. London: Royal Institute of International Affairs.

Waterbury, John. 1978. *Egypt: Burdens of the Past/Options for the Future*. Bloomington, IN: Indiana University Press.

Waterbury, John. 1983. *The Egypt of Nasser and Sadat: The Political Economy of Two Regimes*. Princeton, NJ: Princeton University Press.

Weber, Max. 1947. *The Theory of Social and Economic Organization*. New York: Macmillan.

Weede, Erich. 1986. "Rent-Seeking or Dependency as Explanations of Why Poor People Stay Poor." *International Sociology* 1(4): 421–441.

Weeden, Lisa. 1998. "Acting 'As If': Symbolic Politics and Social Control in Syria." *Comparative Studies in Society and History* 40(3): 503–523.

Wilber, Donald N. 1963. *Iran: Past and Present*. Princeton, NJ: Princeton University Press.

Wiley, Joyce N. 1992. *The Islamic Movement of Iraqi Shi'as*. Boulder, CO: Lynne Rienner Publishers.

Winrow, Gareth. 1995. *Turkey in Post-Soviet Central Asia*. Washington, DC: Brookings Institution.

Wittfogel, Karl A. 1957. *Oriental Despotism: A Comparative Study of Total Power*. New Haven, CT: Yale University Press.

Woodward, Peter. 1992. *Nasser*. London: Longman.

World Bank. 1955. *The Economic Development of Syria*. Baltimore, MD: Johns Hopkins Press.

World Bank. 1992. *World Bank Report, 1992: Development and the Environment*. New York: Oxford University Press.

World Bank 1996. *World Bank Report 1996: From Scarcity to Security: Averting a Water Crisis in the Middle East and North Africa*. New York: Oxford University Press.

Yamani, Hani A. Z. 1998. *To Be a Saudi*. London: Janus Publishing Co.

Yazdi, Majid. 1990. "Patterns of Clerical Political Behavior in Post-War Iran, 1941–1953." *Middle Eastern Studies* 26(3): 281–308.

Yishai, Yael. 1998a. "Civil Society in Transition: Interest Politics in Israel." *The Annals of the American Academy of Political and Social Science* 555: 147–162.

Yishai, Yael. 1998b. "Regulation of Interest Groups in Israel." *Parliamentary Affairs* 51(4): 568.

Youssef, Hassan Pasha, Head of Royal Diwan. 1983. Interviews with author in Cairo.

Zabih, Sepehr. 1986. *The Left in Contemporary Iran: Ideology, Organization and the Soviet Connection*. London: Croom Helm.

Zahran, Gamal Ali. 1987. *Egyptian Foreign Policy, 1970–1981* (in Arabic). Cairo: Library Madbouli.

Zakaria, Rafiq. 1988. *The Struggle within Islam: The Conflict Between Religion and Politics*. London: Penguin Books.

Zalmanovitch, Yair. 1998. "Transitions in Israel's Policy Network." *The Annals of the American Academy of Political and Social Science* 555: 193–208.

Zaqzuq, Hamdi D. 1999 (Jan. 4). "Interview with the Minister of Wafqs" (in Arabic). *Al-Wasat*, 23–25.

Zein, Rania. 1996 (March 6). "Old Theory Rekindles New Debate. Kissing Cousins: Marriage among Relatives Sets New Records in the Middle East. Social Benefit or Medical Danger?" *Al-Jadid*, 9.

Zeine, Zeine N. 1958. *Arab-Turkish Relations and the Emergence of Arab Nationalism*. Beirut, Lebanon: Khayat.

Zeine, Zeine N. 1960. *The Struggle for Arab Independence*. Beirut, Lebanon: Khayat.

Ziadeh, N. A. 1957. *Syria and Lebanon*. New York: Praeger.

Zonis, Marvin. 1991. *Majestic Failure: The Fall of the Shah*. Chicago: University of Chicago Press.

Zonis, Marvin, and Cyrus Amir Mokri. 1991. "The Islamic Republic of Iran." In *Politics and Government in the Middle East and North Africa*, ed. Tareq Y. Ismael and Jacqueline S. Ismael. Miami, FL: Florida International University Press, 114–150.

Index

Abbas (Shah), 32
Abbasids, 30, 278
Abd al-Aziz Saud. *See* Ibn Saud
Abd al-Illah, 280, 282
Abduh, Mohammed, 21–22
Abdullah (Saudi Arabia), 242, 250, 253
Abdullah (Transjordan), 177
Abir, Mordechai, 256–257
Abu Bakr (Caliph), 27
Activism, Islamic, 89–90. *See also* Islamic Fundamentalism
Ad-Diriyah, Saudi Arabia and, 223
Afghani, Jamal al-Din, 21–22
Afghanistan, Soviet invasion of, 351
Aflaq, Michel, 178, 182, 286–287
Age, respect for, 11
Agrarian reform. *See* Land
Alawites (Syria), 174–175, 186, 187, 199, 205, 218
Albania, 31
Alevis, Kurds as, 318
Algeria, Fundamentalism in, 16, 44–45
Algiers Agreement (1975), 293
Ali (Caliph), 27, 28, 277, 340
Aliyah, 110
American-Israeli Political Action Committee (AIPAC), 171
American Jews, Israel and, 117, 170

Amiel, Barbara, 165
Anadalusians, 30
Anglo-Iranian Oil Company, 343–344
Anti-democratic attitudes, 25–26
Anti-Semitism
  in Russia, 170–171
  Zionism and, 109–110, 112
Aoude, Ibrahim G., 67
Al-Aqsa intifada, 143, 144, 146–147, 148, 197, 250–251
Arab(s)
  conquest of Iran by, 45
  invasion of Egypt by, 45
  in Iran, 335
  Israeli, 162
  in Mesopotamia, 277
  revolt by, 177
  in Syria, 173, 176
  unified kingdom of, 225
Arabian Peninsula, 9–10, 31. *See also* specific countries
  Saudi control and, 225
Arab-Israeli Wars
  of 1948, 49, 104, 112–113
  of 1956, 54
  June War (1967), 23, 40, 41, 55, 123
  Yom Kippur War (1973) and, 61, 126–127, 186, 291–292

conflict within, 240–241
contemporary society of, 252–274
corruption in, 238
disillusionment in, 240–243
domestic repercussions of Gulf
  War in, 246–248
economy in, 241, 242, 247, 252,
  269–272
efforts to liberalize, 246–248
Egypt and, 231–232, 235
elites and power in, 253–258, 273
under Faisal, 230–234, 235, 236,
  237, 239
and foreign presence during Gulf
  War, 245
foreign workers in, 238, 267
government of, 248–249
group basis of society in, 263–267
history and culture of, 222–229
under ibn Saud, 229
insecurities in, 221–222
Iran, oil, and, 380
Iran-Iraq War and, 296
Iraqi invasions of, 245
Israel and, 240
Khalid in, 235, 239, 241–242
Khomeini and, 241, 242
Kingdom of, 228
Mecca pilgrimages and, 223
monarch in, 13
new world order and, 243–252
political institutions of, 258–263
reassessment in, 236–240
revolution and optimism in,
  229–236
society in, 229–230
succession in, 230–231, 235,
  255–256
Syria and, 190
United States and, 222, 228–229,
  236, 244
US troops in, 245
women in, 246–247
Yemen and, 234
Saud ibn Mohammed, 224
Saul (Israel), 107
SAVAK (Iran), 345, 346
Schism, Sunni-Shi'a, 28
Schools, colonialism and, 38
Seale, Patrick, 189, 194

Sea of Galilee, 143
Secularism
  in Iranian politics, 364–366
  vs. religion in Iraq, 329
Secular Jews, in Israel, 105
Secular nationalism, 41
Security
  in Iran, 370–371
  in Iraq, 314–316
  in Israel, 116, 124, 149, 165
  in Saudi Arabia, 255, 260–261
  in Syria, 202–204, 207
Semitic peoples and languages,
  9–10, 106
Sephardic Jews, 104, 124
Settlements, in Najd, 226–227
Seveners. *See* Isma'ilies (Seveners)
Shah-in-shah. *See* Mohammed Reza
  Pahlavi
Shah of Iran. *See* Mohammed Reza
  Pahlavi; Reza Shah Pahlavi
Shamir, Yitzhak, 112, 132, 135–136
Shammar tribe, 225
Shara'a, Farouk, 203
Sharabi, Hisham, 15, 39–40
Sharett, Moseh, 115, 117
Sharia, 21, 262
Sharkansky, Ira, 153
Sharon, Ariel, 131–132, 143
  Barak concessions to Palestinians
    and, 144–145
  as Israeli prime minister, 148–150
  land for peace and, 155, 158
  Mitchell Report and, 150
Shatt-al-Arab, 296
Sheikh al Islam, 31
Sheikhs, in Iraq, 278–279
Shi'a Muslims, 6, 20. *See also* Gulf
  War; Iran-Iraq War; specific
  countries
  Abbasids, Fatimids, Egyptians,
    Spaniards, and Safavids as, 30
  division among leadership of,
    323
  Hizbullah and, 143
  in Iran, 337, 340, 349, 378–379
  in Iraq, 276, 277–278, 279,
    289–290, 295–296, 305–306
  Islamic interpretation and, 22
  Kurds as, 318